LOVE FROM NANCY

The Letters of Nancy Mitford

NANCY MITFORD was born in 1904, the eldest child of Lord Redesdale and his wife Sydney. Except for a year at Francis Holland school in London, and a short spell at finishing school in Gloucestershire, she was educated at home by a long line of governesses. In 1929 she began to write articles for *Vogue*, *Harper's Bazaar* and *The Lady*. In 1931, she published her first novel, *Highland Fling*, which was soon followed by *Christmas Pudding*, *Wigs on the Green* and *Pigeon Pie*. She married Peter Rodd in 1933 but the war and diverging interests drove them apart, and by 1945 their marriage was over. During this period she worked at Heywood Hill's bookshop in Mayfair. The huge success of her comic masterpiece, *The Pursuit of Love* (1945), gave her the financial independence to move to Paris to be near Gaston Palewski, the Free-French Colonel with whom she had fallen in love. She remained in France for the rest of her life, and wrote three further best-selling novels: *Love in a Cold Climate*, *The Blessing* and *Don't Tell Alfred*. In mid-life she turned to writing historical biography and achieved great success with *Madame de Pompadour*, *Voltaire in Love*, *The Sun King* and *Frederick the Great*. She died in 1973, after a long and painful illness.

CHARLOTTE MOSLEY is married to Nancy Mitford's nephew, Alexander. She has worked as a publisher and journalist and has edited a selection of Nancy Mitford's journalism, *A Talent to Annoy* (1986).

Also edited by Charlotte Mosley

*A Talent to Annoy: Essays, Journalism and Reviews by
Nancy Mitford 1929–1968* (1986)

Edited by Charlotte Mosley

LOVE FROM NANCY

The Letters of Nancy Mitford

SCEPTRE

First published in Great Britain in 1993 by Hodder & Stoughton
An Hachette UK company

First published in Sceptre paperback in 1994

5

A CIP catalogue record for this title is available from the British Library.

ISBN 978 0 340 59921 1

Typeset by Rowland Phototypesetting Ltd, Bury St Edmonds, Suffolk

Printed and bound by Clays Ltd, St Ives plc

Hodder & Stoughton policy is to use papers that are natural, renewable and
recyclable products and made from wood grown in sustainable forests.
The logging and manufacturing processes are expected to conform to the
environmental regulations of the country of origin.

Hodder & Stoughton Ltd
338 Euston Road
London NW1 3BH

www.hodder.co.uk

CONTENTS

PREFACE

By these effervescent, and sometimes sharp,
letters she will, if they are ever published *in
toto*, be chiefly remembered in the years to
come.

James Lees-Milne

Nancy Mitford's letters are an essential part of her artistic output. Infused with the same acute observation, wit and fantasy that she brought to her novels, they plunge the reader into a colourful world, part reality and part Nancy's own creation.

Her letters were tailored, more than most people's, to the person to whom she was writing. She set out first and foremost to make her correspondents laugh, at times she intended to provoke or to flatter, often she was trying to convince herself of the truth of the image she wanted to project. By embellishing and exaggerating the facts she contrived to conceal her real life and to present an idealised picture.

Teasing featured prominently in all Nancy's relationships. As a tease she was in a class of her own. Her jokes were generally gentle and affectionate, but she had an unerring eye for the vulnerabilities of her family and friends. She could not resist teasing Evelyn Waugh about his misanthropy and the intemperate aspects of his faith. Her darts were directed at Violet Hammersley's pessimism and miserliness. In letters to her sister Jessica, a resident of San Francisco, she maintained that living in America was one of life's greatest handicaps.

A favourite tease on her mother, who was often the victim of Nancy's most mocking jibes, was to accuse her of having under-fed her as a child. Writing to her from Paris, shortly after the end of the war, Nancy's letters were scattered with declarations about how well she was feeling, how, '*above all*', she was getting enough to eat, how food was 'a recurring delight', and how the shops were 'crammed with lovely strawberries & cherries, cheeses, foie gras & all sorts of good things'. This, in a city that was still suffering from the results of four years of occupation and where, by other more reliable accounts, food was in very short supply indeed.

Nancy died before being able to write the autobiography she was planning, so her letters are the nearest we can get to her own account of her life. One can feel hesitant about publishing someone's private letters, bashful about revealing them to the public gaze. In Nancy's case this need not be a concern as she clearly realised that hers would one day be published. She was a prolific letter-writer from early childhood, but her move to Paris in 1946 meant that letters became, more than ever, an essential means of keeping in touch with family and friends in England. She clearly understood the value of her letters, describing them to her sister Deborah as 'unique in this generation and as such there can't be too many of them'. In 1948 she was already writing to Evelyn Waugh to suggest that his daughter might one day edit their correspondence and call it 'The Lady of the Rue Monsieur'. She was, however, conscious of the problem of publishing the letters in her lifetime, warning that in each there was 'at least one major libel suit as well as one or two suicides'.

In 1957, with a mocking eye on her future editor, she wrote to Heywood Hill: 'Are you moling me a Smythsons?[1] Goodness the foot-notes this would require in our collected correspondence.' And to her sister Diana she once wrote: 'Won't the editor of my letters have a jolly time, I often think.' She has.

[1] Heywood Hill arranged for Nancy's yearly appointments diary, supplied by the Bond Street stationers Smythson, to be embossed with the Mitford family emblem: a mole.

EDITOR'S NOTE

While editing a selection of Nancy's journalism, *A Talent to Annoy*, I became aware of the huge number of her letters that had survived. Some of them, particularly the ones to her family, had been seen by her biographers, but most remained unsorted and unclassified, stuffed into brown envelopes and crammed into cardboard boxes. I thought that someone should go through these letters, identifying the cast of characters, while Nancy's family and friends were still able to help. As her sister Diana's daughter-in-law, I seemed in an ideal position.

On the understanding that the letters could not be published until the year 2000, I began the job of transcribing and annotating with Diana's help. About a year later, there was renewed interest from publishers who had been pressing for the letters ever since Nancy's death. Realising that a balance needed to be struck between publishing too soon, and thus offending many people, and leaving it too long, Nancy's sisters decided to allow the publication of the letters to go ahead on the twentieth anniversary of her death.

Over eight thousand of Nancy's letters have survived – dated between 1909 and 1973 – indicating the value put on them by their recipients. Nancy's family and friends started keeping her letters long before the publication of *The Pursuit of Love* in 1945 made her famous. The main challenge while editing this correspondence has been to choose from among this vast quantity of letters. In selecting about five hundred I have not set out to cover Nancy's life; it has already been told in her friend Harold Acton's memoir, in Selina Hastings's biography and in *The House of Mitford* by her nephew Jonathan Guinness and great-niece Catherine. I chose those letters that amused and interested me or that pointed up a particular aspect of Nancy's character and her relationship with her correspondent. The object was that each letter should earn its keep. The introductions to each section are designed to provide just enough information for the letters to be seen in their context. Biographical notes on those who figured most prominently in her correspondence are to be found in the Biographical Notes at the end of the book.

Most of Nancy's letters to the Mitford family are at Chatsworth where they have been collected by her sister and literary executrix, Deborah, Duchess of Devonshire. Many letters remain with Nancy's correspondents or with their heirs. Still others have found their way to museums and university libraries in England and in America. In all, the letters are addressed to some 125 correspondents. The largest number, and the most interesting ones, are those that make up a sustained correspondence with about twenty friends and members of her family, and it is from these letters that I have mostly drawn. Nancy kept many of the letters she received from her family and friends; these are all held at Chatsworth.

I am not aware of any major gaps, with three notable exceptions. Only one letter to Nancy's husband, Peter Rodd, has survived, the rest probably having been lost during the course of his peripatetic life. Letters to Victor Cunard were deliberately destroyed, after his death, by his brother. And the entire correspondence with her publisher, Hamish Hamilton, has vanished except for a dozen photocopies made before this mysterious disappearance.

I hesitated before rectifying Nancy's idiosyncratic spelling. She never mastered the apostrophe, rarely distinguished 'its' from 'it's', the correct spelling of 'correspondence' eluded her all her life, and after her move to France words like 'envelope' and 'develop' sprouted double l's and p's. However, in the interests of easier reading, and because Nancy deplored her own inaccuracy, her spelling in all but the very early childhood letters has been silently corrected. Misspelt names of people, places and books have been rectified.

Punctuation, as Evelyn Waugh liked to point out to Nancy, 'is clearly not your subject'. She dashed off her letters, rarely crossed out a word and never rewrote. Full stops are often omitted, question marks and quotation marks are infrequent and the use of commas erratic. To preserve the pace and flavour of the letters – intrinsic to their style – the punctuation has been left unchanged, except for the insertion of full stops when the next sentence begins with a capital letter, and the occasional comma to avoid ambiguity. Her old-fashioned use of a semi-colon at the end of an abbreviated word has also been kept.

The letters have all been transcribed from the original or from a photocopy, except for those to Randolph Churchill and Valentine Lawford which have been taken from typescripts.

No letters written entirely in French have surfaced; Nancy spoke and wrote the language well, but most of her French friends understood English. French words have been translated, unless their meaning is unmistakable. Translations of single words are shown in a square bracket in the letter itself; anything longer is consigned to a footnote.

Nancy attached great importance to the quality of her writing paper. As a child she wrote on small sheets headed with her nickname, 'Nance', printed in gold against a coloured oval. On the rare occasions when she used a plain sheet of ordinary paper she apologised to her correspondent. Most of her letters were written from home, usually in the morning sitting up in bed. In middle age she had some travelling paper embossed with the Mitford emblem, a golden mole. Her letters spread over both sides of a sheet, or over all four sides of two sheets, and occasionally more. But whatever their length, Nancy had the knack of coming to the end of what she had to say at the bottom of a page exactly. She wrote in ink, in a legible, pleasing hand. The great majority of her letters are dated, or easy to date from internal evidence. Only occasionally did she omit an address.

To include as much material as possible, I have drawn on letters that are not included in the main body of the work for use in the footnotes. Wherever feasible I have used Nancy's own descriptions of people, or have expanded a note with her own words.

Excisions in the text are indicated by three ellipsis points. Nancy hardly ever used this convention and, when she did, rarely confined herself to just three points. Most cuts have been made to avoid repetitions and to spare the reader lengthy details about her travelling plans. I have sometimes removed a passage which, in order to be comprehensible, needed a long quotation from a letter addressed to Nancy. Half a dozen potential libels have been deleted, and I agreed to the Duchess of Devonshire's request to remove as many passages again where it was felt that Nancy's spite could have been unduly hurtful to living people.

Charlotte Mosley
1993

ACKNOWLEDGEMENTS

My greatest debt of thanks is due to the Duchess of Devonshire, Nancy's literary executor, whose continual help, support and hospitality made much of the preparation of this book nothing but a pleasure; and to Lady Mosley whose remarkable memory shone light on every corner of Nancy's life and who, with unfailing patience, explained so much. I would also like to thank Pamela Jackson and Jessica Treuhaft for their help and co-operation.

Helen Marchant was of inestimable help at Chatsworth, where I also benefited from the assistance of Peter Day, Michael Pearman and Ian Fraser-Martin, who helped to photograph family documents.

I am indebted to Lady Selina Hastings who gave me generous help in locating letters and answering queries; to Alan Bell who read the manuscript, compiled the index and made many erudite suggestions and corrections; to Stuart Preston who also read the manuscript; and to Bernard Minoret whose guidance in identifying Nancy's French friends was invaluable.

I would like to thank Ion Trewin who started as my editor and Richard Cohen who took over; and Jane Birkett who gave me essential help in checking the manuscript. Anne-Pauline de Castries' typing and deciphering skills were a godsend.

I am grateful to the following for making letters available and in many cases for giving useful information: Sir Harold Acton; the late Comte Jean de Baglion; Richard Bailey; Nicholas Baring; Lady Beit; Lady Dorothy Heber-Percy for letters to Lord Berners and to Robert Heber-Percy; Jacques Brousse; Dr Henry Gillespie for letters to Dr Stephen Blaikie and Dr Powell-Brett; Lucy Butler for letters to Robert Byron; Prince Clary for letters to his father; Artemis Cooper for letters to Lady Diana Cooper; Sir Francis Dashwood for letters to his mother; Ken Davison; Lord and Lady Egremont; Kay Gaudin; Lord

14 ACKNOWLEDGEMENTS

Gladwyn; Sebastian Yorke for letters to Henry Green and Adelaide Yorke; Desmond Guinness; Lady Harrod; Sir Rupert Hart-Davis; Lord Hartwell for letters to Lady Hartwell; Alethea Hayter; Sir William Hayter; Joy Law; the late Valentine Lawford; Walter Lees; Alvilde Lees-Milne; James Lees-Milne; Prince and Princess Loewenstein; the Countess of Longford; the Dowager Viscountess Mersey; Lady Sophia Morrison; Alexander Mosley; Max Mosley; Mary Motley; Lord Moyne; George D. Painter; Burnet Pavitt; Brian Pearce; Anthony Powell; Lady Violet Powell; Peter Quennell; Desmond Shawe-Taylor; Julian Slade; Madeau Stewart; Gillian Sutro; Lady Emma Tennant; Lord Thomas.

The following institutions gave generous assistance: All Souls College, Oxford; Beinecke Rare Book and Manuscript Library, Yale University, for letters to Alan Pryce-Jones, James Lord, Rebecca West; University of Bristol; BBC Written Archives Centre; Manuscripts Department of the British Library for letters to Evelyn Waugh; British Library of Political and Economic Science for letters to Lady Beveridge; Department of Western MSS., Bodleian Library, Oxford; Mugar Memorial Library, Boston University, for letters to A. D. Peters; Christ Church, Oxford, for letters to Tom Driberg; Columbia University Library for letters to Robert Halsband; Derbyshire Record Office; School Library, Eton, for a letter to Brian Howard; Special Collections Division, Georgetown University Library, Washington, for letters to Christopher Sykes; Huntington Library, California, for letters to Graham Greene and Lord Kinross; John Rylands University Library of Manchester for letters to the *Manchester Guardian*; St John's College, Cambridge, for letters to Cecil Beaton; Lilly Library, Indiana, for letters to Heywood Hill; Lincoln College, Oxford, for letters to Sir Osbert Lancaster; Ohio State University for letters to Jessica Treuhaft; Pierpont Morgan Library, New York, for letters to Charles Harding; Princeton University, New Jersey, for letters to Raymond Mortimer; University of Reading for letters to Lady Astor; Taylor Institution Library, Oxford, for letters to Theodore Besterman; Harry Ransom Humanities Research Center, University of Texas at Austin, for letters to Cass Canfield, Princesse Dilkusha, Gerald Hamilton, Ogden Nash, Derek Patmore, A. D. Peters, Society of Authors, Leonard Russell, Lady Waverley, Edward Weeks; Department of Special Collections, McFarlin Library, University of Tulsa, for letters to Cyril Connolly; University of Victoria for a letter to Sir John Betjeman; Wadham College, Oxford.

I would also like to thank the following people, who searched for

letters or who helped in other ways to make this book possible:
Jane, Lady Abdy; Mark Amory; Constantia Arnold; Rosemary Bailey;
Rosemary Baldwin; Sally Bedell-Smith; Sybille Bedford; Antony
Beevor; Olivia Bell; the Earl of Belmore; Lesley Blanch; Cheryl
Bridge; Lee and Emily Brown; Mollie Buchanan; Manuel Burrus;
Edward Chaney; Contessa Anna-Maria Cicogna; John Cornforth;
Roderick Coupe; Caroline Dawnay of Peters, Fraser & Dunlop; the
Marchioness of Douro; Patrick Drury-Lowe; Viscountess Eccles;
Peter Elwes; Audrey Emerson; Dominique Ferbos; Daphne Fielding;
Lavinia Fleming; Caroline Forbes; Midi Gascoigne; Vincent Giroud;
James Gladstone; Yvonne Hamilton; Charles Harding; Alan Hare; the
Marquess of Hartington; Andrew Harvey; Priscilla Hastings; Richard
Hastings; Christopher Hawtree; Lady Anne Hill; Derek Hill; Philip
Hoare; Eardley Knollys; James Knox; Lady Pansy Lamb; Lady Lan-
caster; Guy Lesser; Deirdre Levi; Mary Anna Marten; Ian McKelvie;
Teddy Millington-Drake; Viscount Montgomery of Alamein; Ian
Montrose; Sheridan Morley; Ian Morling; Jean Mosley; the Earl of
Mulgrave; Nigel Nicolson; Evelyn Nightingale; Vicomte and Vicom-
tesse d'Origny; Ann Paludan; Gabriele Pantucci; Graham Payn; John
Phillips; Joan Rodzianko; Comtesse de Rosnay; Margaret Ryan; John
Saumarez Smith; the Earl of Seafield; Richard Shone; Christopher
Sinclair-Stevenson; Sir Reresby Sitwell; Lord Skidelsky; Lady
Soames; Sir Stephen Spender; Lord Stanley of Alderley; John
Stefanidis; Georgina Stonor; James and Jane Stuart; Hugo Vickers;
Joseph de Vilmorin; Iain Watson; Auberon Waugh; Elizabeth Winn;
Dr Cornelia Wohlfarth.

I am grateful to the following who have kindly given their permission
for the use of copyright materials: Sir Harold Acton for permission to
quote from *Nancy Mitford: A Memoir*; Anthony Blond for permission
to quote from *Brian Howard: Portrait of a Failure* by Marie Jaqueline
Lancaster; Art Buchwald for permission to quote from his articles in
the *New York Herald Tribune*; Jonathan Cape Ltd for permission to
quote from *Ruling Passions* by Tom Driberg; the Estate of Cyril
Connolly, and Rogers, Coleridge & White Ltd, 20 Powis Mews,
London W11 1JN, for permission to quote from *The Unquiet Grave*
and *Sunday Times* articles by Cyril Connolly; Lord Hartwell for permission to quote from Lady Hartwell's letters to Nancy Mitford;
Hodder & Stoughton for permission to quote from *The Fringes of
Power* by John Colville; James Lees-Milne for permission to quote
from *Ancestral Voices, Midway on the Waves* and *Harold Nicolson
1930–1968*; Candida Lycett-Green for permission to quote from a

letter from John Betjeman to Nancy Mitford; Diana Mosley for permission to quote from *A Life of Contrasts, Loved Ones* and from her letters to Nancy Mitford; Lord Moyne and Catherine Guinness for permission to quote from *The House of Mitford*; Rosaleen Mulji for permission to quote from *Potpourri from the Thirties* by Bryan Guinness; Curtis Brown Ltd and Little, Brown & Co. for permission to quote from 'MS. Found Under a Serviette in a Lovely Home' from *Verses From 1929 On* by Ogden Nash, © 1956 by Ogden Nash; © renewed 1984 by Frances Nash, Isabel Nash Eberstadt and Linell Nash Smith; George D. Painter for permission to quote from *Marcel Proust* and from his letters to Nancy Mitford; Peter Quennell for permission to quote from *Customs and Characters* and from his letters to Nancy Mitford; Jessica Treuhaft for permission to quote from *Hons and Rebels* and from her letters to Nancy Mitford; Auberon Waugh for permission to quote from *The Letters of Evelyn Waugh, The Diaries of Evelyn Waugh* and *Helena* by Evelyn Waugh, also for permission to quote from Evelyn Waugh's unpublished letters.

LIST OF ILLUSTRATIONS

All the illustrations are from private collections, unless otherwise stated.

With thanks to Caroline Forbes and Valmaure S.A.

CHRONOLOGICAL TABLE

1904   28 November 1904. Nancy born at 1 Graham Street (now Graham Place), Belgravia, London
1907   Pamela Mitford born
1909   Tom Mitford born
1910   Francis Holland School, London
       Diana Mitford born
       The Mitford family moves to 49 Victoria Road, Kensington
1914   Unity Mitford born
1916   Death of 1st Lord Redesdale
       The Mitford family moves to Batsford Park, Gloucestershire
1917   Jessica Mitford born
1919   The Mitford family moves to Asthall Manor, Burford
1920   Deborah Mitford born
1921   Hatherop Castle School
1922   Tour of France and Italy
1923   First London Season
1927   The Mitford family moves to Swinbrook House, Oxfordshire
       Slade School of Fine Art
1928   Meets Hamish St Clair-Erskine
1929   First articles for *Vogue* and *Harper's Bazaar*
1930   Weekly articles for *The Lady*
1931   *Highland Fling*
1932   *Christmas Pudding*
1933   Marriage to Peter Rodd and move to Strand-on-the-Green
1935   *Wigs on the Green*
1936   Moves to 12 Blomfield Road, Maida Vale
1938   *The Ladies of Alderley*
1939   *The Stanleys of Alderley*
1940   *Pigeon Pie*

1942   Assistant at Heywood Hill's bookshop, Curzon Street
        Meets Gaston Palewski
1945   Death of Tom Mitford
        The Pursuit of Love
1946   Moves to Paris
1947   Moves to 7 rue Monsieur, Paris VII
1948   Death of Unity
1949   *Love in a Cold Climate*
        Weekly article for *Sunday Times*
1950   Translates and tours with *The Little Hut*
        The Princesse de Clèves
1951   *The Blessing*
1954   *Madame de Pompadour*
1955   U and Non-U article in *Encounter*: 'The English Aristocracy'
1956   *Noblesse Oblige*
1957   *Voltaire in Love*
        Divorce
1958   Death of Nancy's father
1960   *Don't Tell Alfred*
1962   *The Water Beetle*
1963   Death of Nancy's mother
1966   *The Sun King*
1967   Moves to 4 rue d'Artois, Versailles
1968   Onset of illness
1970   *Frederick the Great*
1973   Dies on 30 June at rue d'Artois

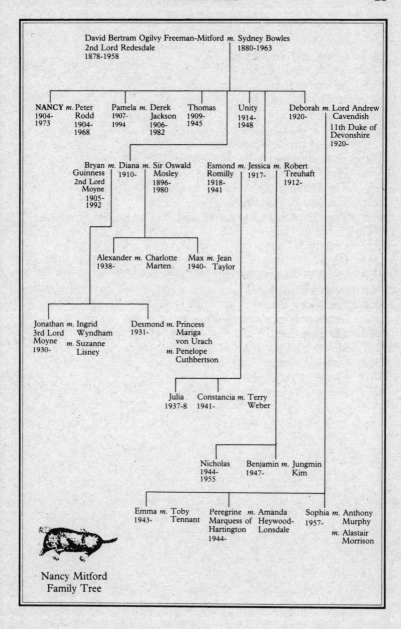

David Bertram Ogilvy Freeman-Mitford *m.* Sydney Bowles
2nd Lord Redesdale   1880-1963
1878-1958

NANCY *m.* Peter   Pamela *m.* Derek   Thomas   Unity   Deborah *m.* Lord Andrew
1904-   Rodd   1907-   Jackson   1909-   1914-   1920-   Cavendish
1973   1904-   1994   1906-   1945   1948   11th Duke of
        1968   1982   Devonshire
                                                    1920-

Bryan *m.* Diana *m.* Sir Oswald   Esmond *m.* Jessica *m.* Robert
Guinness   1910-   Mosley   Romilly   1917-   Treuhaft
2nd Lord   1896-   1918-   1912-
Moyne   1980   1941
1905-
1992

Alexander *m.* Charlotte   Max *m.* Jean
1938-   Marten   1940-   Taylor

Jonathan *m.* Ingrid   Desmond *m.* Princess
3rd Lord   Wyndham   1931-   Mariga
Moyne   *m.* Suzanne   von Urach
1930-   Lisney   *m.* Penelope
                    Cuthbertson

Julia   Constancia *m.* Terry
1937-8   1941-   Weber

Nicholas   Benjamin *m.* Jungmin
1944-   1947-   Kim
1955

Emma *m.* Toby   Peregrine *m.* Amanda   Sophia *m.* Anthony
1943-   Tennant   Marquess of   Heywood-   1957-   Murphy
            Hartington   Lonsdale   *m.* Alastair
            1944-   Morrison

Nancy Mitford
Family Tree

I thought of writing down the bald facts of my life, not for publication but as a record. But they are so very odd I wonder if people would believe. Do you think everybody's real life is quite different from what they manage to make it seem? Very likely. No dark secret, but everything different from the façade.

NM to Evelyn Waugh, 31 January 1951

Darling Muv, and Toad - ~~rather~~ catcher,

I hope you are quite well, I am teaching Violette
Music. We went to the prize giving and it
was very nice. One of the things among the
needle-work was something like what Geat
Granny does only in silk, colered. Pam
sends her love, Baby and Tom do too.
Tom has just been to see a new cow at
the farm. Miss Poole sent a box of
chocolates the other day. Yesterday we
saw an airoplain, it seemed to sway
about a lot, and aferwards we were
told that it nearly came down.

When we went to the convent
we found Hal was with us and
as he refused to leave us we put
him in the stable and forgot him.
Sargent said he would fech him
but suddenly he came home.
            Love
                Nance.

To Hon. David and Mrs Mitford, 1913

1904–1920

CHILDHOOD

> I think in my drowsy way of my memoirs and
> believe they ought to be funny, and then such
> a good idea to eliminate that tiresome child-
> hood, already *done* in the novels.
> NM to Joy Law, 11 August 1971

Nancy Mitford was born on 28 November 1904, the eldest of a family
of six girls and a boy, the children of David, the 2nd Lord Redesdale,
and his wife Sydney, daughter of Thomas Bowles. Nancy descended
from two unusual grandfathers: Bertram Mitford, the 1st Lord
Redesdale, was a diplomat, gardener, courtier and writer; during his
lifetime he published best-selling volumes of memoirs, now totally
forgotten. He also wrote interesting accounts of his long stay in Japan
as one of the first Westerners to penetrate that hermetic and mysterious society. These studies would have been even more fascinating
had he not practised Victorian autocensorship at its most prudish. He
was a friend of Houston Stewart Chamberlain and translated his book
on Kant from the German.

Thomas Gibson Bowles, Nancy's maternal grandfather, was the
natural son of Thomas Milner-Gibson, a Cabinet minister; he knew
nothing of his mother except her name, Susan Bowles, and was
brought up by his father. He made his way in Victorian society by
dint of a wayward brilliance and pugnacity. As a young journalist in
1871 he sent reports by balloon from besieged Paris to his editors in
London; he founded the magazines *Vanity Fair* and *The Lady*. In 1892
he was elected Conservative MP for the Norfolk port of King's Lynn.
Thomas Bowles was an ardent sailor and yachtsman and his children

grew up on board ship; Sydney kept a deep and abiding love of the sea all her life.

Probably as a reaction against the intellectualism and bohemianism of their respective parents, David and Sydney Mitford adopted an outwardly conventional way of life. David, once he was able to leave London, engaged in the country pursuits of farming, shooting and fishing, and Sydney devoted herself to her home and to her children, although not enough according to Nancy.

For the first three years of her life Nancy was an only child, the centre of her parents' affections but, what is more important, of her nanny's. She grew up in a milieu and in a generation where parents did not concern themselves closely with the daily lives of their young children. In Nancy's case the distance was widened by her mother's character: affectionate, but aloof and vague. In the nursery, however, Nancy became queen. She was expelled from this early Eden by the successive arrival over a period of sixteen years of six siblings: Pamela, Tom, Diana, Unity, Jessica and Deborah. When Pamela was born, Nancy's adored nanny transferred all her attention to the baby, causing such misery to Nancy that Sydney decided to sack her. Nancy's relations with her mother never fully recovered, and she harboured feelings of unresolved resentment towards her all her life.

Jealousy and disappointed love were thus acutely present in Nancy from an early age. Her chosen defence was to look on her life and on her family as a tremendous joke. This gave her a shield, while as a weapon she perfected the tease. Teasing provided a safe way of showing anger and frustration. She soon learned to hide her real feelings and continued to keep a tight check on them throughout her life. She once told her friend James Lees-Milne that her upbringing had taught her never to show to others what she felt. His reaction was that it had succeeded all too perfectly and that there was a vein of callousness in her that amounted almost to cruelty. Cyril Connolly complained to a friend about her unkindness and when the friend retorted: 'But Nancy is so *kind* underneath', Connolly replied, 'Yes, but so *unkind* on top.' The price Nancy paid for turning her life into theatre was that emotions could be apprehended only superficially. In someone as sensitive and gifted as she was this produced a complex character, full of contradictions and inconsistencies. Along with the sharpness and affectation ran a river of deep kindness, loyalty and generosity, and in a secret part of herself she suffered as much, if not more, than most.

What made up for any amount of teasing was Nancy's great and irresistible funniness, evident from a very young age. It compensated for her apparent flippancy, for the fact that she was prepared to sacrifice anything for a joke, and it made her family and friends readily forgive her mockery. Even her sister Pamela, who was closest to her in age and suffered most from Nancy's teasing, dissolves into laughter when she talks of their childhood. Nancy's loyalty and affection for her sisters was fundamental, and despite underlying resentment and envy that erupted from time to time in furious rows, she remained unusually attached to them and relied on them all her life.

Until the outbreak of the First World War the Mitfords lived in London and spent summers in a cottage in High Wycombe or at Batsford Park, Nancy's Redesdale grandparents' house. When Nancy was five she became a pupil at Francis Holland School where she stayed until 1914 when her father was called up and the family migrated to a cottage on the Batsford estate. In 1916 the 1st Lord Redesdale died and Sydney and the children moved into Batsford itself. At the end of the war Nancy's father embarked on what she described, with typical exaggeration, as his building mania: 'He would build a new house every time there was a boom, when labour was scarce and expensive. He would then live in it for a while, but as soon as there was a slump, as soon as labour became easy and cheap, he would sell what he had built at a vast loss and we would all move on to the next house whose foundation stone would be laid on the first day of a new boom.' In fact Lord Redesdale sold Batsford after the war because it was too large and expensive to keep up. He planned to build a house on some land he inherited near Swinbrook and meanwhile moved the family to nearby Asthall Manor, where they spent six years until Swinbrook House was eventually completed.

Nancy's earliest letter dates from 1909; addressed to her father, it is dictated to her mother: 'There's lots of news that I want to tell you but I'll tell you in the next letter. The news I want to tell you now is, everyone is very well. It has been raining all day.' Most surviving letters from this period are written to Sydney. Few, however, have been selected; although they are sometimes fluent and show occasional flashes of Nancy's sharp observation and love of jokes, they are primarily of interest only to a mother.

To Hon. Mrs David Mitford[1]
[1912]

TELEPHONE:
3960 WESTERN.   49, VICTORIA ROAD,

MY DEAR MOTHER. W.

I WISH YOU WOLD HAVE
THE HONRE OF DRINKING
AND EATING WITH ME.
LOVE QUEEN, NANCY

[1] Sydney Bowles (1880–1963). Nancy's mother (Muv). Married Hon. David Mitford
on 6 February 1904, just nine months before Nancy's birth on 28 November 1904. See
Biographical Notes.

To Hon. Mrs David Mitford   The Old Mill Cottage[1]
[1912]   High Wycombe
                                              Buckinghamshire

My darling Muv, it has been hot and sunny it is now cold and wet.
please tell Farve[2] –
          there was an Old farve of Victoria Rd[3] which was a
          very nice abode. four children a wife who lived a
          happy life such a jolly Old farve of Victoria RD.
     We went for a drive and saw a hawk, we saw the young swallows
peeping out on the stable roof.

          from X Coco[4]

[1] A cottage belonging to Lord Lincolnshire which the Mitfords rented for the summer.
Nancy's mother bought it at the end of the war.
[2] Hon. David Mitford (1878–1958). Nancy's father (Farve). Succeeded as 2nd Baron
Redesdale in August 1916. See Biographical Notes.
[3] In order to accommodate a growing family, the Mitfords had moved in 1910 to a
large house in Victoria Road, Kensington.
[4] Nancy was nicknamed Koko, after the character in *The Mikado*. Unlike most of her
sisters who were blonde with blue eyes, Nancy had green, triangular eyes and a mass
of curly brown hair.

TO HON. DAVID AND MRS MITFORD   49 Victoria Road
23 October 1913   London, W.

Dear Muve and farve,
    I do so licke the *Rose and the ring*.[1] We went to tea whith Miss
White[2] who gave us all presents. I am so glad that you know some
one on bord.[3] We are going to tea with Grand-mother[4] on Mundy if
tom's[5] cough is better. I hope you find the shrimp past good. Is'nt
this a GOOD phota of Farve. Is the shack nice, I *know* farve likes it.
What *do* you think, we were siting on a seat this afternoon and had
susa[6] with us and a gentelman past us and said to susa 'thats the sort
of chap that would take you by the leg before you knew it.' Was'nt
that horrid? I felt as if I'd like to put a bulit in where farve got his,[7] I
gess he would'nt survive it as Farve did do'nt you. I am sorry I did
not write last mail, but I did not know there was one untill I saw
Nanys letter stuk down whith the stamp on.

    Much love
        Coca
P.S. Excuse a overlong letter but it was to bore[?]

[1] W. M. Thackeray, *The Rose and the Ring* (1855). The last of his 'Christmas books',
which he produced and illustrated himself.
[2] A neighbour in Kensington.
[3] Nancy's parents were on their way to Canada to prospect for gold; her father had
staked a claim on a new field in Northern Ontario where he hoped to make his fortune.
Although they returned to Canada several times, spending weeks living in a primitive
wooden cabin, no gold was ever found. Nancy harboured a secret longing for her
parents never to return so that she could be left in charge of her younger brother and
sisters, just like the Radlett children who 'would rush for the newspapers every day
hoping to see that their parents' ship had gone down with all aboard; they yearned to
be total orphans.' *The Pursuit of Love* (Hamish Hamilton, 1945), p. 10.
[4] Lady Clementina Ogilvy (1854–1932). Nancy's paternal grandmother. Married 1st
Baron Redesdale in 1874. 'A merry, rosy, immensely fat old lady . . . With her many
chins, pink complexion and dimples she looked innocent and babyish. Every new baby
in our family when it first opened its blue eyes was said by Nanny to be "very like the

Dowager", though the truth was the other way about.' Diana Mosley, *A Life of Contrasts* (Hamish Hamilton, 1977), p. 3.

[5] Tom Mitford (1909–45). Nancy's only brother. See Biographical Notes.
[6] A mongrel terrier belonging to Nancy's father.
[7] David Mitford had had a lung shot away during the Boer War.

TO HON. DAVID AND MRS MITFORD
30 October 1913

Toad[1]   Muve

My dear Muve (and toad)

We have just come home from Dick and Tony[2] as it is only ten minutes past 6. Please look at farves photo and Muves. I do not care much for fractions but simply love decimals. Here is another phota of farve

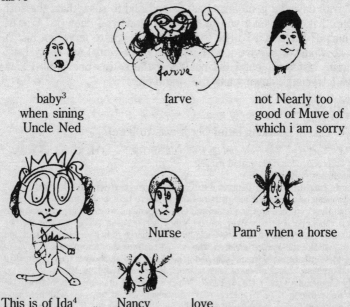

baby[3]   farve   not Nearly too
when sining   good of Muve of
Uncle Ned   which i am sorry

Nurse   Pam[5] when a horse

This is of Ida[4]   Nancy   love
                                   Nancy

[1] Nancy's nickname for her father.
[2] Richard and Anthony Bailey; Nancy's first cousins.
[3] Diana Mitford (1910–). The third Mitford daughter. See Biographical Notes.
[4] A nurserymaid.
[5] Pamela Mitford (1907–94). The second Mitford daughter. See Biographical Notes.

TO HON. DAVID MITFORD[1]   [Batsford Park[2]
[27 April 1916]   Moreton-in-Marsh]

[Nancy's father corrected and returned her first attempt at French.
His commentary is shown in italics.]

LANGUAGE TAUGHT BY CORRESPONDENCE IN
3½ MINUTES
Unsolicited testimonials from many thousands of deaf mutes
Corrected & returned 4-5-16

27 April
What year???

Mon cher Père
Chère petite Crâpeau
    Comme il fait beau ce matin!
    How should I know from here?
    Ma chèvre est très bonne, elle aime beaucoup le soleil, et elle
mange les chous que je lui donnés.
    I cannot see why she should be praised for her affection for cabbages.
    Je crois que Tom fait très bien le Français, mais Pam n'est pas très
avancée.
    A peu près comme toi?
    J'ai commencé mes leçons ce matin, et Pam et Tom aussi.
    J'aime beaucoup les leçons.
    Not as much as the chèvre likes the choux.
    Il y a un nid de rouge-gorge dans un arbre.
    This is a very common occurrence – it happens most years.
    J'ai écouté le coucou ce matin.
    Not easily avoided when they are about. Try cotton wool.

        limier
    Votre ~~chien~~ est très sage il est dans la mason
    J'aime les lapins de ma tante

De la part de votre affectionée
Nancy (*blob*)

For the next lesson the pupil, if apt and of ordinary intelligence, should find no difficulty in translating the best English poetry into French.

I

> *Unusual things have come to pass,*
> *A goat gets praise for eating grass!*
> *A robin in a tree has built!*
> *The coo coo has not changed its lilt!*
> *And I have no desire to quench*
> *My child's desire for learning French –*

II

> *Might I ask without being rude,*
> *Who pays the bill for Bonne Chèvre's food?*
> *Are cabbages for goats war diet?*
> *Or are they given to keep her quiet?*

---

[1] This is one of the few surviving letters from Nancy to her father. His insistence on correct dating has stood the editor in good stead: all but a few of Nancy's letters are fully dated.
[2] Nancy was staying with her Redesdale grandparents at Batsford Park.

To Lady Redesdale   20 Linton Road[1]
15 November 1918   Oxford

Darling Muv,

Nanny says as I'm writing, she won't, and that we are all quite well.

Foust [*sic*] was lovely, except that they missed out the scene in the Cathedral, I can't think why, as Farve says that that was one of the best. The only one that acted well was Meffy,[2] Marguerita and the others were all more hideous than it is possible to imagine, but Meffy was lovely, and not at all affected, and simply made me *shiver*!

He was dressed in black and red, and was all pointed like this:

and frightfully fat. Foust had hair like this: and was very ugly and affected, and when he tried to tremble he shook himself like a dog. Valentino wasn't bad, and sang a lot of stuff after being stabbed, which is more than I could or would do. Foust came in at the last dressed like a respectable old lady in a black blouse covered with jet, and an ordinary black skirt which I discovered afterwards to be a black cloak and leggings. He was an ass, and at first when he appeared in a dressing gown, he showed everything through it, as it kept coming open. It was in English, but it might have been in Hindoostanee for all we understood. We knew it was English, however, as twice during the performance we heard the words 'I love you', and once 'she is mad', and once 'I am dead'!

It was very creepy, and I really began to think it was happening really, until they came back and bowed. It was great fun, and Nan loved it.

> Love from
>   Cocoa

P.S. We all do our music. We are all as well as could be expected under the circumstances.

[1] Invalided out of the war, Lord Redesdale had been made Assistant Provost Marshal at Oxford, where he lived in rooms at Christ Church. Lady Redesdale took a small house nearby so that he could spend time with the family.
[2] Mephistopheles, Marguerite and Valentin: characters from Gounod's opera, based on Goethe's *Faust*.

TO LADY REDESDALE   Asthall Manor
1 April 1920   Burford
                                                   Oxfordshire

My Darling Muv,
    How exciting![1]
    Now please do send me a letter and say:
    What its name is going to be,
    If its fair or dark,
    And how much does it weigh?

Perhaps I ought not to call her 'it', but how disgusting of the poor darling to go and be a girl.[2]

Was she an 'April Fool'?

When can her future godmother see her? *Do* call her either Iris or Dorothy – besides being her aunts' names they are so pretty.

A woman has written to Steele asking for a sitting of Camps.[3] Shall I write and say 'yes', if you don't answer I will.

Much love
    Cocoa

[1] The Redesdales' sixth daughter, Deborah, was born on 31 March. See Biographical Notes.

[2] Nancy used to assure Deborah when she grew up: 'Everybody cried when you were born.' Years later she wrote to her on her birthday: 'Once again we come to the day when Fate made a Fool of Muv. How well I remember the Church bell tolling – the very cattle in the fields moaning & the horror with which one realised that the nursery was to have another furious occupant, shrieking like a cage of parrots. No, no!' (NM to Duchess of Devonshire, 1 April 1965)

[3] Nancy was referring to Khaki Campbell ducks; Steele was the Redesdales' game-keeper.

1921–1933

THE PURSUIT OF LOVE

I have come to the conclusion that I am an
entirely 2 dimensional person, do you understand what I mean. It depresses me.
            NM to Tom Mitford, 26 January 1928

The family spent only six years at Asthall Manor before moving to
Swinbrook in 1927, but it is this period above all that provided Nancy
with the raw material from which she fashioned her fictional version
of the Mitford childhood. Her mocking but affectionate portrayal of
her family, and in particular of her father as the engaging but terrifying
Uncle Matthew, made her novels classic masterpieces of comedy.

The Mitford household was by now a large one: seven children, a
governess, nanny and nurserymaid, a lady's maid, three housemaids,
a cook, two kitchenmaids and two parlourmaids. This was not an
exceptional number of servants in the days before household appli-
ances but it was a heavy financial burden: the Redesdales were always
hard up. As a child, Nancy earned pocket money by keeping goats
whose milk she sold to her mother or to the village, and all her life
she suffered from a feeling of financial insecurity (even after becoming
a famous author with books selling in millions).

The children's mornings were taken up in the schoolroom. In later
life Nancy liked to complain about her education and blamed her
mother for not having sent her away to school. When Aunt Emily, in
The Pursuit of Love, is praised for believing passionately in the education of women and taking immense pains to have Fanny properly
taught, even to the point of moving house in order to be near a good
day school, Nancy is surely describing her ideal education and directing

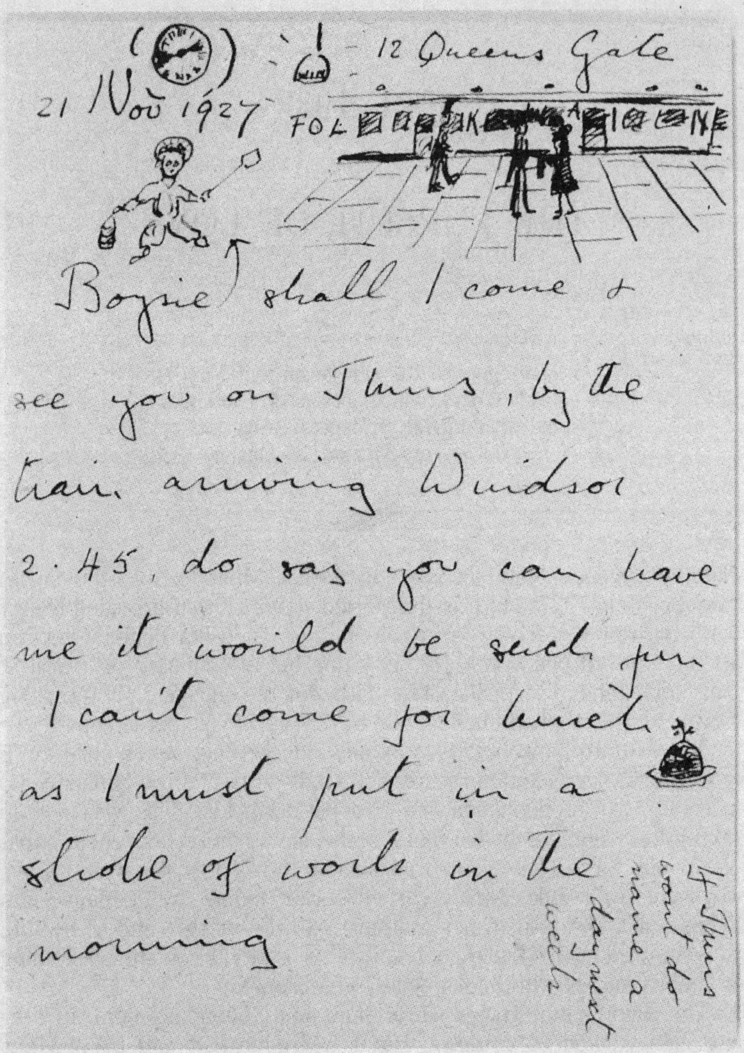

21 Nov 1927

12 Queens Gate

Boysie shall I come &
see you on Thurs, by the
train, arriving Windsor
2.45, do say you can have
me it would be such fun
I can't come for lunch
as I must put in a
stroke of work in the
morning

4 Thurs
won't do
name a
day next
week

To Tom Mitford, 21 November 1927

a barb at her mother. Whatever the shortfalls of the governesses, Nancy nevertheless grew up speaking fluent French, reading omnivorously and developing an original, spirited style of writing.

The rest of the day at Asthall was taken up with long walks, hunting, occasional children's tea parties and caring for numerous pets. As the eldest, Nancy was the first to rebel against this routine and in 1921, when she was sixteen, her parents agreed to send her as a boarder to Hatherop Castle School in Gloucestershire for a year. In 1922 she went with schoolfriends on a cultural tour of France and Italy. The letters she wrote to her mother chronicling this visit are the only ones to have survived from the period 1921–4.

Gradually Nancy's parents started to relax their supervision, strict even for the 1920s, and she began to see some of the world outside her family circle. She celebrated her eighteenth birthday with a dance at Asthall and 'came out' the following year. As a debutante she spent weekends away from home, was allowed guests to stay and went to all the balls and parties she could cope with. In 1927 she attended the Slade School of Fine Art and realised she was not a painter; she toyed with the idea of acting, learned to play the ukelele and took Italian lessons. She became a Bright Young Thing, a member of the society set whose existence was a continuation of nursery life by other means. It was a world described by Nancy as 'a life of total frivolity . . . We hardly ever saw the light of day, except at dawn; there was a costume ball every night: the White Party, the Circus Party, the Boat Party, etc. Old-timers still talk about them.'[1] Nancy poured out the tales of this round of pleasure to her brother Tom, who kept over a hundred of her letters written between 1924 and 1928. Their cumulative effect tends to be somewhat repetitious and juvenile, for which reason I have limited the selection.

Nancy's earliest attempts at journalism date from this period. She wrote an occasional article for *Vogue* and *Harper's Bazaar* and, in 1930, was taken on by *The Lady* to write a weekly article at five guineas a week: her acid wit is already apparent in her maverick reports of the debutante round. Anxious to increase her income, she started on her first novel, *Highland Fling*, a light comedy of manners with a Wodehousian flavour, which was published in 1931 and earned her £90. Encouraged by this success she began her second novel, *Christmas Pudding*, which was published a year later.

---

[1] 'My Friend Evelyn Waugh', *A Talent to Annoy*, edited by Charlotte Mosley (Hamish Hamilton, 1986), p. 77.

Above all during these years Nancy developed her exceptional talent for friendship; she formed a wide group of acquaintances, several of whom became lifelong friends. Among those who were drawn to her sharp intelligence, beauty and infectious love of life were an outstanding group of young men. These included Mark Ogilvie-Grant, who became her principal correspondent and confidant until her marriage; the writers Robert Byron, Christopher Sykes, Henry Green, Harold Acton, Patrick Balfour and Evelyn Waugh; the poets John Betjeman and Brian Howard; the painters Oliver Messel and William Acton; the film producer John Sutro, and, fatefully, Hamish St Clair-Erskine, the second son of the Earl of Rosslyn.

Nancy was twenty-four when she fell in love with Hamish. There had been no serious romance in her life until then. Her letters reveal her as emotionally immature, taking innocent delight in childish pranks such as putting the clock back several hours at a dance. It would be difficult to think of a more unsuitable object for her love than Hamish. Although he had charm and could be good company, he was vain, self-centred and dissolute, described by Robert Byron as 'not immoral but without morals'. He was also homosexual. None of this deterred Nancy from believing that she and Hamish were made for one another. She was naïve and may have imagined that his preference for men was a phase he would outgrow, just as her brother Tom, who had had an affair with Hamish at Eton, went on to have numerous affairs with women. There was an elfin, disarming side to Hamish that brought out Nancy's maternal instinct; she humoured him, indulged him and convinced herself that marriage would turn him into a good husband. No measure of appalling behaviour could make her see Hamish for what he really was. Their unsatisfactory relationship lasted on and off for four years, to the despair of both sets of parents. Although they were never officially engaged, Nancy regarded Hamish as her fiancé and at times he pretended to be serious about marriage. To begin with he was flattered by her adulation, but eventually he felt trapped by the improbable role she had cast him in and coldly broke off their relationship by pretending to be engaged to another woman. He was too cowardly to tell Nancy himself and asked her sister Diana to do it for him.

In Hamish, Nancy chose to love someone who was unable to reciprocate her love, a pattern she was to repeat throughout her life. It was also characteristic that once her mind was made up it was very hard to shake her determination to go on seeing things as she wished them to be. This capacity for viewing all her geese as swans is one that should be borne in mind when reading her letters.

To Lady Redesdale   Hotel Grande de Bretagne
[15] April 1922   Firenze

Darling Muv,

In my last letter, which I was in a hurry to get off, I never told you about the monastery at Fiesole. It is at the top of a terrible hill (terribly steep) & built of yellow stone in the middle of Cypresses & Olives.

It is old, one of the things we saw, a lovely dresser built in the wall, early 14th Century. A dear old monk showed us round. Half way Miss S.[1] asked in English what order he belonged to. He looked terribly surprised & rather amused & said he didn't quite know what she meant. So we said 'Benedictine?' Then he shrieked with laughter & said he thought she had said 'what hors d'oeuvre do you have'. He never stopped laughing all the time, he was a perfect old sweet. They turned out to be Franciscan. The others took his photograph (alas I forgot to bring my camera like an idiot). He was most flattered. Such an old pet.

I have bought 3 more reproductions, coloured, of my favourite pictures.

This morning we went to the Duomo & saw a wonderful procession, a real cardinal in a mitre & jewels under a satin & gold panoply carried the Host round the Church. It was lovely. Such a nice old man he must be.

This afternoon to the Pitti. Lovely pictures but so badly arranged. About one beauty in each room, the rest rubbish. The frames are too awful & about twice as big as the pictures. No words of mine can describe how appalling the rooms are. We saw Mme le Brun, & several other things, Raphaels especially & Titian. The Uffizi is thousands of times nicer. The truth is we are all very tired of sightseeing.

To-morrow the fireworks. If you think I ought to pay that 12/6[2] will you deduct it from the £2 you are sending me to Venice? I really think perhaps I ought.

How I love the pictures. I had no idea I was so fond of pictures before, especially Raphael, Botticelli & Lippo Lippi.

Giotto (Ruskin's adored) is disappointing, except in colouring. Most primitive, also Cimabue. . . .

Easter Sat. evening

We saw the fireworks this morning. It was well worth it. I will describe in my next as it will need a fresh mind so to do, & I am terribly tired. The heat to-day was *dreadful* & we have trudged about such a lot. We all clamour for cottons, people are bathing in the river, lucky things. I have spent almost my last L20 on a dear little coral necklace for someone (presumably Bobo[3]). I have spent a fearful lot on myself, but when you see the things I have got you will agree that it was worth it. It is rather unfair that I should be having this heat who hate it, while others who would like it are so cold. Or is it equally boiling in Inghilterre?

I must post this now or I shall procrastinate again. Easter Day to-morrow. We are going to early Service at the English church & Mass in the Duomo. Then we shall try to go to some races in the park here.

I hope the point to point was fun.

> Much love to all from
>   Nancy

Only 3 more days here, how shall I tear myself away? Thank you *so* much for sending me, I am having a perfectly *heavenly* time, I have never been so happy in my life before, in spite of such minor incidents as *fleas*!

If you knew what it is like here you would leave England for good & settle here at once. . . .

[1] A Miss Spalding was in charge of the group.
[2] '. . . about the fireworks on Easter Sat. Windows to seat 3 cost L150, & Miss S. is very anxious for them, but refuses to pay & says we must. L50 seems such a lot (12/6) & we would just as well stand in the crowd, but she hates the idea!' (NM to Lady Redesdale, 14 April 1922)
[3] Unity Mitford (1914–48). The fourth Mitford daughter. See Biographical Notes.

To Lady Redesdale   Albergo Grande de Bretagne
17 April 1922   Firenze

Darling Muv,

Thank-you for your letter of Good Friday. The races yesterday were *lovely*, most exciting & amusing. One steeplechase & the rest flat races. There was one jockey called J. Kennedy[1] who came in last each time! To-night we are going to see a film called *Dante*, which they say is quite marvellous.

Such an amusing thing happened last night. We had asparogas [*sic*], & we were talking about the story of King Edward & the old Shah of Persia. We dared Marigold to throw her stalk over her back & she actually did it! (she has gone up one in my estimation). Imagine the horrific surprise evinced in the faces of all around, especially Miss S.! There is one old man who had an awfully nice face sitting opposite us, & he did laugh! Then afterwards we were explaining to Elsa why we call her 'turnip' in the sitting-room & he came in without our seeing him & said 'has that got anything to do with asparogas?' Then we began talking to him & I found that he is also an adorer of Ruskin. He seemed very surprised that I had read most of Ruskin's books & we talked for ages. Unfortunately (disgratiatamente) he went away this morning. I called him 'my old man' ever since we came. The others said he wasn't old but he is really, quite 45. . . .

I really have learnt a lot about pictures & statues here, more than twice what I knew before. I can tell a good one from a bad now, & can tell more or less who it's by & whether it's painted in tempera or oils & a lot of other things. Such a lot of pictures have amusing stories about them. I love Raphael although it's not the fashion to now. . . .

I will finish to-morrow. While I think of it, you put too little on your last letter, I had to pay 15 c. on it.

18th April, Tuesday

Thank you for your letter of Easter Sat: I am *so* sorry you have had no letters, I am sure I wrote on Tuesday last. Perhaps you have had one by now?

Dante last night was most bloodthirsty & exciting. 11 murders close to with details, a man's hands chopped off *very* close to & *full* of detail, & [a] man dying of starvation & eating another man *very very* close to & the death of Dante with great detail helped to add a mild excitement to a film full of battles (on land & sea), molten lead, a burning city & other little everyday matters! It lasted with two intervals from 9 to 12.15! I never saw anything like it before, it was enough to make you dream for nights. There was a seedy contingent with permanently waved hair wandering about in the desert, called the prophets of Peace, they stumbled on dead bodies at every step; a most realistic scene from hell, the devils reminded one of those drawn by Bobo. Every time a person was murdered you saw him being taken down there with dire results.

People died off so fast that only one character was left alive by 12.15 & it is a huge cast. That shows you! The one who did survive had just killed his wife, so one imagines he then goes mad.

I am quite miserable at leaving here to-morrow. We get up at 6!! We have been to the Uffizi to-day, very sad, to see our favourites just once more. I do hope I shall come back some day, I couldn't bear not to. I have never had such a lovely time before, & have loved every minute of it.

Even the heat which I hate only helps to show up the colours, & the blue sky is heavenly. I *can't* like Venice as much as this. The hills around are so lovely, the highest ones have snow on them. Then the olive, orange, lemon & cypress trees are so pretty. The roses are all out, for 3d (L1) you can get a lovely bunch.

I must stop now to go & pack. Do you think I shall ever come back here? I positively *must*!

    Much love from
        Nancy

P.S. Please thank Chunkie[2] for her ill-spelt missile [*sic*].
P.P.S. Not so ill-spelt as this!
To-day we went to the Ricardo & Badia.

[1] The agent at Batsford was also called J. Kennedy.
[2] Pamela Mitford.

To Tom Mitford   Villas St Honoré d'Eylau[1]
27 November 1926   76 à 88 Avenue Victor Hugo
                                  Paris

My dearest Youngest & most Noseless Hatte –[2]

Ah poore ladd opération att wonce – no chloro? Ze agonie weel be véry grate.[3]

Are you now George Hyde's double & shall I know my favourite broz when fozér mozér seestér brozaire meet once more? Poor mite. I really am very sorry & large greasy tears are rolling down my hairy cheeks as I write. I too have been tossing on a bed of sickness but am better now.

I've been having such fun lately, Pam & I went to stay with some divine French people last week end & on Sat night they took us to dine with the Robert de Rothschilds[4] – a dinner of 40 all French. It was the greatest fun, we danced after. Baron Robert de R. knew Grandfather Redesdale very well & it is his sister, Lady Sassoon,[5] who did that bronze bust of him. The girl, Diane,[6] is so charming, I made friends with her at once & the next day we went for a long walk together. She is a really intelligent girl & v. good looking in a rather Jewish way not at all a Jewish nose though.

All the French young men were so nice & amusing so you can imagine how I enjoyed myself.

Tom, when you see my shingled hair you *are* to say – in front of the birds[7] – how you simply adore it etc even if you think it's too beastly, they've really been *nasty* to me about it & say that whereas I was plain before I'm now downright ugly etc. & Muv said the other day 'well anyhow no-one would look at you twice now'. As a matter of fact I've been much more admired since I cut it off & everyone else says they like it much better. So lovey your role in this matter has now been indicated.

Isn't *Childe Harold fascinating,* I read it on the *Arraguaya,*[8] I'm so glad it cheered your sick bed. I wavered much between that & a translation of Michael Angelo's sonnets but decided that no translation of poetry, however good, can be terribly worth reading – except possibly the greater classics, so I got the other.

I'm now soaking myself in French history, art & literature of the 17th–18th centuries which is passionnant. At the moment I'm reading Mme Campan's memories[9] & I've just finished *Marie-Antoinette et l'affaire du Collier* by Brentano & *Marie-Antoinette: Dauphine* by de Nolhac who is the greatest living authority on M.A. & the keeper of Versailles. Don't the two go well together. I *would* like to be here with you one day. The other day I was invited to go to Wiesbaden for a week but of course I wasn't allowed to.

Middy O'Neill[10] is here staying with the Crewes,[11] he is her grandfather, so the other night I dined at the Embassy & we went on & danced at the Florida which was divine fun. My drawing goes on apace but I haven't been to the studio for some days, not having been well. I think & hope the Slade may take me when I get back. I think on Sunday I'm going to Fontainebleau with Middy, I hope so as I've never been there.

> Much love, get well soon
> Nance

You say you are suffering from shock, what shall we suffer from when we see you?

[1] Nancy spent the last months of the year in Paris with her mother and sisters while Lord Redesdale supervised the building of the new house, Swinbrook.

[2] 'Hat' was one of Nancy's nicknames for Tom, who had just had his adenoids removed, hence 'noseless'. Although four years younger, Tom was an ideal correspondent; he was quick-witted and well read and, above all, he knew intimately the world and the people Nancy was describing.

[3] 'Nancy invented for herself a persona, a "Czechish lady doctor", who would express in a heavy foreign accent her longing for "Moi Czecho". The lady doctor's voice became the first of the Mitfords' private family languages.' Jonathan Guinness with Catherine Guinness, *The House of Mitford* (Hutchinson, 1984), p. 247. Nancy continued to use the voice in her speech and in correspondence with her sisters until the end of her life.

[4] Baron Robert de Rothschild (1880–1946). One of the heads of the Rothschild bank in Paris. Married Gabrielle Beer in 1907.
[5] Aline de Rothschild; married Sir Albert Edward Sassoon in 1887.
[6] Daughter of Robert de Rothschild.
[7] The 'parent birds'.
[8] The ship in which Nancy had toured the Mediterranean earlier that year.
[9] *Mémoires sur la vie de Marie-Antoinette* (1899). Madame Campan was lady-in-waiting to the Queen.
[10] Hon. Mary O'Neill (1905–91). Married Derick Gascoigne in 1934. Middy was one of Nancy's greatest friends when they were young. At the end of 1927 they boarded for two months at the London house of Middy's grandmother, Lady O'Neill. The arrangement came to an end after a party which they held became rather rowdy; Lady O'Neill accused the girls of holding an orgy and Nancy was sent home.
[11] First and last Marquess of Crewe (1858–1945). Married to Sibyl Graham 1880–87 and to Lady Margaret Primrose, daughter of the Prime Minister Lord Rosebery, in 1899. He was Ambasssador in Paris 1922–8.

To Tom Mitford   Swinbrook House[1]
[December 1926]   Burford
                                  Oxford

Darling Fatty

I'm sure you must have laughed not once but many times today into that progressive but unattractive growth on yr chin at the thought of what my journey must have been like with B![2] I must (tired tho' I am) try & tell you all about it.

First of all, hardly had you gone than he said in the tones of a tragedie queene Nancy there is something which I don't quite know how to tell you about but which you must know & turned his gaze upon the ankles of the other young man in the corner. I also looked & perceived to my astonishment that this youth had multicoloured silk tassels hanging from the top of each of his spats. We giggled about this till the train left Paris & I'm afraid the poor young man must have noticed something as he retired for a long time & returned minus tassels.

B & I had a most delightful conversation all the way to Calais & he paid for my lunch (a oouh) so here's the 30f.

But the real fun began when we arrived at Calais in a snowstorm. Brian looked out of the window & said Ah my hair will get all snowy. NM – *Brian* haven't you got a hat? B – No they are so expensive. He then drew a small Picasso out of one of his market bags, wrapped it in a pair of pyjamas (dirty) to keep it dry & thus equipped we sallied forth into the snowstorm. I did so wish all my sticky relations had been travelling by that boat!

Brian was seriously afraid that we should founder at any moment & we walked about on deck until it got really rather rough when I retired into the ladies cabin & B sat on a little seat just outside. He was so sweet & sympathetic, luckily I wasn't sick at all.

At Victoria hearing that Farve would probably meet me (happily he did) B vanished instantly into the fog. My dear I've never enjoyed a journey so much & *laugh* – well really I never stopped. B kept saying *Why* didn't we meet in Paris & I must say I wish we had as he is such amazingly good company. All the customs officials were very suspicious of his market bags & rootled like anything among the dirty linen.

Brian encouraged me *so* much to go on painting & have an exhibition which he keeps saying he could arrange for me in Paris & also imploring me to break with the family as soon as I could. I must say he is a *very* sweet person you know & probably much maligned.

I must go to sleep but couldn't before telling you about my *killing journey*. Finish tomorrow.

We *did* have fun didn't we the last few days I've never enjoyed anything more.

I'm quite decided now after my conversation with Brian to work for an exhibition in the spring, he says paint 20 or 30 rather large pictures & leave the rest to him.

I begin today, wish me luck. I've no idea what to paint, I shall just sit in front of a canvas till one comes! Just think, if I had a successful exhibition in Paris the family would have no more hold over me at all.

Best love bearded one
      N

[1] Ugly, cold and inconvenient, 'the Buildings', or 'Swine Brook' as Nancy called the new house, was disliked by all the family except Deborah, and proved a disappointment even to Lord Redesdale. To escape the cold the children took refuge in the linen cupboard, the origin of the Hons' Cupboard in *The Pursuit of Love*.
[2] Brian Howard (1905–58). Anglo-American writer and poet. Talented, exotic and outrageous, he reached a peak of brilliance at Oxford. He described Nancy as 'a delicious creature, quite pyrotechnical my dear, and sometimes even profound, and would you believe it, she's hidden among the cabbages of the Cotswolds.' Harold Acton, *Nancy Mitford: A Memoir* (Hamish Hamilton, 1979), p. 23. In later life he declined into alcoholism and depression and eventually committed suicide. After his death, Nancy wrote, 'I often think people miss wicked old creatures like Brian more than normal, satisfactory city-going, church-going ones.' (NM to Heywood Hill, 23 January 1958)

To Diana Mitford   Women's Union Society
[early 1927]   University College
                                    London WC1

Dearest Ling

Isn't this too grand?[1]

So awful, I *ought* to be drawing but the professor has been so beastly to me in a piercing voice, everyone heard & I rushed away to hide my shame in the writing room. Very soon I shall have to go back & face my brothers & sisters-in-art.

They are so awful to you, they come up & say What a *very* depressing drawing, I wonder how you manage to draw so foully, have you never had a pencil in your hand before. . . . They burble on like this for about ½ an hr & everyone else cranes to catch each word. Luckily they are the same to all. I now burst into loud sobs the moment one comes into the room, hoping to soften them.

Very soon it will be lunch time & I shall be seated between an Indian & a Fuzzy-Wuzzy degluting sausage & mash oh what a treat. I'm learning Italian here now which I enjoy. In fact I love being here altogether, it's the greatest fun.

I hope you are in rude health & enjoy your matutinal cold bath.[2]

So awful, the head of the whole university had us all up the other day & said there is a lady thief among us. I tried not to look self conscious but I'm sure they suspect me. I now leave my old fur coat about everywhere, I long for the insurance money.

I must now advance upon the sausage mash so goodbye lovey. Give my love to Geneviève[3] & delicately hint that I'm longing to stay with her when asked.

    Love
        Nance

[1] After much wrangling with her parents, Nancy had been allowed to enrol at the Slade School of Fine Art. She had little artistic talent, received small encouragement from her two teachers and left after a few months.

[2] Diana was learning French in Paris and lodging with two elderly sisters. 'There was no bath. Twice a week the maid brought a shallow round tin, the same as Degas so often painted, into my room.' Diana Mosley, *A Life of Contrasts*, p. 51.

[3] Geneviève de Neuflize; the daughter of a banker, and a friend of Diana and Nancy in Paris.

To Tom Mitford   Swinbrook House
17 July 1927   Burford, Oxford

My dear fat Thomas

Deep depression has the Mitford family in its clutches, the birds never speak save to curse or groan & the rest of us are overcome with gloom. Really this house is too hideous for words & its rather pathetic attempt at aesthetic purity makes it in my opinion worse. I mean I would rather it were frankly hideous & Victorian because then it would at least have atmosphere whereas at present it is like a barn rather badly converted into a temporary dwelling place & filled with extremely beautiful & quite inappropriate furniture.

I made an awful float at lunch because Muv said of course these pictures look awful in this sort of room, so I said why not store them until Tom has made sufficient money to have a proper house. Which is how I think this strikes one, not somehow like a house at all.

However we have much to be thankful for having a roof over our head I always have said.[1] I had a terrific fight with Muv about staying with Nina[2] & she said at last, go if you like but I'd rather you didn't which is always so unsatisfactory so I said I'd go. Do you think it was very nasty of me, after all it means a fortnight less here which is no mean consideration & also I think at 22 one is old enough to choose one's own friends don't you, specially as I'm to pay for it myself.

I went once more to the ballet before leaving London, with Edward Stanley[3] on Wed afternoon. We had Aurora's Wedding, music by Tchaichowsky (spelling?) which is one of the most heavenly of all.

Everyone I knew was there, Nina, Mark,[4] Oliver Messel,[5] Christopher,[6] Tanis Guinness[7] etc etc & all sitting quite near us which was so funny. I hope this letter hasn't bored you, you might answer as I only live for the posts, it feels so odd having nothing to do after months of hecticness.[8]

Much love
    Nance

[1] In a draft for a broadcast following publication of *The Pursuit of Love*, Nancy wrote of her childhood, 'We lived under the shadow, so to speak, of two hammers, the builder's and the auctioneer's, and fidgeted about from one house to another on different parts of my father's estate.' Quoted in Acton, *Nancy Mitford*, p. 21.
[2] 12th Countess of Seafield (1906–69). Married to Derek Studley-Herbert 1930–57. A peeress in her own right, Nina inherited a large fortune and vast estates in Scotland when her father died in 1915. Lady Redesdale mistrusted rich people on principle and

was afraid that Nina would be a bad influence on Nancy. The two girls remained fond of one another but soon outgrew their close friendship. Years later when Nina bought a flat in Paris, Nancy wrote, 'I love seeing her once a year but as a neighbour NO.' (NM to Mark Ogilvie-Grant, 25 November 1958)

[3] Hon. Edward Stanley (1907–71). Cousin of Nancy. Succeeded as 6th Baron Stanley of Alderley and 6th Baron Sheffield in 1931. Married five times. 'A good, warm-hearted man, who always liked to fall into the pose of a belligerent eighteenth-century peer, spoiling for a knock-down fight.' Peter Quennell, *Customs and Characters* (Weidenfeld & Nicolson, 1982), p. 152.

[4] Mark Ogilvie-Grant (1905–69). Cousin of Nina Seafield. A lifelong friend and confidant of Nancy's and the first of her contemporaries to become a regular correspondent. He was part of an Oxford set that included Harold Acton, Brian Howard, Robert Byron, John Sutro, Michael Rosse and Henry Yorke, all of whom became Nancy's friends. 'Mark Ogilvie-Grant is the most amusing creature I have met for ages, fearfully vulgar & talks with a comic drawl. He has got the most cherubic face & what's known as a disarming smile.' (NM to Tom Mitford, 22 March 1925) See Biographical Notes.

[5] Oliver Messel (1904–78). Became one of the most sought-after and highly-paid scenery and costume designers of his time.

[6] Christopher Sykes (1907–86). Author, scriptwriter and producer for the BBC. Biographer of Evelyn Waugh. Married Camilla Russell in 1936. 'Christopher is really wonderful . . . Perhaps the best of all our friends.' (NM to John Sutro, 10 June 1967)

[7] Tanis Guinness (1908–). Married to Hon. Drogo Montagu 1931–5, to Howard Dietz, the American librettist, 1937–58, then to Edward Phillips.

[8] Nancy had returned to Swinbrook after leaving the Slade. Much to her younger sister Jessica's disgust, she had also given up her furnished bedsitting room. ' "How *could* you! If I ever got away to a bed-sitter I'd never come back." "Oh, darling, but you should have seen it. After about a week, it was knee-deep in underclothes. I literally had to wade through them. No one to put them away." ' Jessica Mitford, *Hons and Rebels* (Gollancz, 1960), p. 35.

To Tom Mitford   Swinbrook House
25 February 1928   Burford, Oxford

My dearest Brother

The last courier who was *late*, owing to violent snow & hail storms brought me no news from you[1] but nevertheless I am not *too* much agitated as I have news of you from the hen bird.*

I am not quite alone now, having with me an *old* friend,** so *old* indeed that we have nothing *new* to say to each other but sit & *yawn* all day.[2]

However we were joined last night by Togo Watney[3] & your friend Jim Lees-Milne[4] & we should have been a very merry & contented party if an unfortunate argument about the war had not been started after dinner. I am sorry to say that our respected male parent lost his temper rather badly with poor Jim which made us all feel very akward (I vow I cannot spell that word but I feel sure that my dear

Brother will understand me as *always*). In fact that nobleman has been so rude & unkind to the unhappy youth ever since he first arrived that the feeling in this house is one of terrible strain whenever they are in the same room together.

I sometimes think that parties here are more *misery* than *pleasure*. The argument ran on the usual lines.

Lord R.   Why not show the Cavell film, a good thing if we do hurt the feelings of the Germans.

N.M.   Why is everyone so cross because the Germans shot a spy, surely we shot spies?

Lord R.   Yes *shot* them but we didn't begin by breaking their legs & shooting slowly upwards.

N.M.   I suppose Edith C stood quite still on her broken legs while they went on up. How people can believe these awful lies I can't imagine.

Jim L.M.   Anyhow talking of atrocities the worst in the whole war were committed by the Australians.

Lord R. (shouting)   BE QUIET AND DON'T TALK ABOUT WHAT YOU DON'T UNDERSTAND (loud aside) young *swine*.

General discomfiture.

Diana (loud aside)   I wish people needn't be so rude to their guests.

N.M. (loud aside)   Of course we know that your generation really enjoyed the war & what you all want more than anything is another war but as it happens we *don't want* one.

Muv (sarcastically)   Oh yes of course we *enjoyed* it enormously.

Exeunt all to bed, *trembling* with rage.[5]

I haven't been in such a ghastly temper for years & for once wasn't at all put about by Farve's furious shouting & would gladly have been *very* rude to him. Apart from the argument it makes one so giddy with rage when people are so disgusting to their guests. Really parties here are *impossible*. The truth is that the poor old man having no building left to do is in a *very bad* temper. However we all have our faults have we not.

I'm told that Spanish ladies are très séductives so pray be careful.

Write again soon I implore you & alleviate the boredom which is assailing your affectionate sister.

N

Ah Señor Mitford—!

* It is said that the Mitford children used to refer to their mother by this disrespectful epithet.
** Miss O'Neill, later the Countess Leitnitz.

[1] Tom was in Vienna, studying music and learning German.
[2] Nancy had been reading Byron's letters and for a few months she adopted their style in letters to her brother.
[3] Oliver Watney (1908–65). A member of the brewing family and a neighbour at Swinbrook. He was briefly engaged to Pamela Mitford in 1928, before marrying Christina (Kirsty) Nelson in 1936.
[4] James Lees-Milne (1908–). Architectural historian, biographer and diarist. National Trust Historic Buildings Committee Secretary 1936–51 and architectural adviser 1951–66. Married Alvilde Chaplin in 1951. A friend of Tom's since prep-school days, he had gone up to Magdalen College, Oxford, in 1927.
[5] After this row, Lord Redesdale ordered Jim out of the house. It was raining hard and his motorcycle would not start so he crept back indoors and went to bed. He rose at six the following morning with the intention of leaving Swinbrook and bumped into Lord Redesdale, who seemed to have forgotten the previous night's incident and greeted him warmly. (For discrepancies between James Lees-Milne's and Nancy's sisters' recollection of this incident, see Guinness, *The House of Mitford,* pp. 291–2.)

To Tom Mitford   Swinbrook House
18 March 1928   Burford, Oxford

Dearest & only Boyse

  Such a funny thing has happened. Decca[1] had a lot of children to tea the other day & told them (in her bedroom) a lot of things *little* children are hardly expected to know. The result is that poor Muv has had frightful letters from all their parents or guardians, and Nanny has been sent to Coventry by all the neighbouring nurses. Also no little girls are allowed to come to the house, so at Debo's birthday party there were nothing but little boys, or very unrespectable little girls. But nobody like the McCalmonts (say) will allow their children to come. I think it's too awful for poor Muv but all the same SO funny. Can't you just *see* Decca doing it!!!

I warn you that Muv is setting forth for Vienna with battle in her eye, she thinks your Austrian friends are 'getting hold of' you – don't ask me what she means by that. . . .

The poor old Dad is being had up in the courts again,[2] we think he should leave the Marlborough & join the keep-straight club instead.

I've been reading nothing but Shakespeare lately & it becomes more & more of a mystery to me why one *ever* reads anything else for pleasure! I'm going to London all next week for a lot of fun & am looking forward to it quite enormously.

The Buxtons who have bought Widford came to tea today, he is just a typical soldier rather like old Archer[3] & she is British to the Backbone, she told us in one short hour that Kipling is her favourite poet, Bridgeman her favourite politician, laurel her favourite sort of hedge et cetera. She has a curiously uncomplex sort of nature. He is Archer's uncle.

I do nothing now but have *fearful* quarrels with Archer & then make them up again. Luckily he goes abroad in May, it becomes a little wearing.

I've been doing a lot of painting & I think have improved very much.

You might depart from your usual custom & answer this, said she acidly, anyhow *swear* to write from Italy, I'm longing to know how it impresses you. We'll go to Greece together one day, or Rome. Mark simply *raves* about Greece & he says the people are *exactly* like the statues of the old Greeks.

Much love
N

---

[1] Jessica Mitford (1917–). The fifth Mitford daughter. See Biographical Notes. Jessica remembers this incident taking place on the roof at Swinbrook where she imparted 'some delightful information that had just come my way concerning the conception and birth of babies. The telling was a great success, particularly as I couldn't help making up a few embellishments as I went along.' *Hons and Rebels*, p. 11.

[2] One of Lord Redesdale's least successful money-making ventures was to design papier-mâché caskets, in the shape of Spanish galleons or Buddhas, to hide ugly wireless sets. He was taken to court for slander by a South American casket maker after accusing him of being a false marquis. Lord Redesdale won his case.

[3] Archer Clive (1903–). A young soldier whom Nancy had met the previous year and with whom she had a mild flirtation. 'Archer is being too beastly to me, he never spoke

to me yesterday except to say he'd like to bang my head on the floor & the day before he said among other acid remarks that if it weren't for my extraordinary ideas & my men friends I should be quite nice.' (NM to Tom Mitford, 14 August 1927)

To Tom Mitford   26 Rutland Gate[1]
25 May 1928   London, SW7

Dearest Boyse

It will be quite interesting to see how long you expect me to go on writing to you without an answer, I can assure you Mr Mitford that this state of things cannot last!

Nina & I & Patrick Balfour[2] went to the Pageant of Hyde Park through the ages on Tuesday.[3] Alas old B [Howard] wasn't Disraeli, he ran out at the last moment. This quite saddened us as well it might. Mark looked lovely in a white wig & knee breeches & Oliver Messel was *too* wonderful as Byron, I nearly fainted away when he came limping on to the stage, this proves that I must have been Caroline Lamb in a former incarnation. He built up his face with putty & looked the living image of Byron. Stephen Tennant[4] as Shelley was very beautiful. Lord Furneaux[5] was a modern 'young-man-about-town' & Frank Pakenham[6] in a sailor suit rode on one of those enormous bicycles.

Yesterday I went to a cocktail party in Oliver's studio which was *greatest* fun. He just had Nina, Mark, Johnny[7] & me so we had a very amusing gossip over the fire. He's got a lovely studio & oh Boysie he *can* paint. Of course I knew how *wonderful* his masks are, everyone does but I'd no idea he painted such lovely pictures. He's so amusing too & does the most killing imitations in his masks. Last night Nina, Mark & I went to *Young Woodley*,[8] which I've seen before, it *is* a good play.

We're having a dinner for the Glasgows'[9] dance (fancy dress) on 6th July, can I count on you as one of the young men? I think it will be the greatest fun, masks until 12 o'clock. This is a very bad letter as literally while writing I'm having a good gossip with Diana.

How lovely it'll be having you back again. You must meet all my more entertaining friends.

It's so awful, Patrick Balfour is going to put an article in the gossip page of the *Weekly Dispatch* about Muv rowing on the Serpentine, I know she'll think I egged him on to do it!! I must say it might be very funny.

I'm going to hint to Nina to ask you to stay in Scotland, would you if she did? Did I tell you I met Harold Acton[10] the other day, he's *fascinating* I think.

Well I must go to bed.

Do write soon.

All my best love

N

[1] A large house near Hyde Park, bought by Lord Redesdale when Asthall Manor was sold. The family lived there during the London Season.

[2] Hon. Patrick Balfour (1904–76). Traveller, writer and journalist. Succeeded as 3rd Baron Kinross in 1939. Married to Angela Culme-Seymour 1938–42. He drew on his experience as gossip columnist for the *Weekly Dispatch* and the *Daily Sketch* to write *Society Racket: A Critical Study of Modern Social Life* (1933). His best-known book is *Atatürk. The Rebirth of a Nation* (1964).

[3] Brian Howard to William Acton: 'Lady Birkenhead is getting up an enormous pageant at a London Theatre (Daly's) in May – directed by Oggie Lynn – entitled *Hyde Park Since 1765* in which I'm going to be Disraeli and Oliver (Messel) is going to be Byron. I don't know which of us will be the more ridiculous.' Marie-Jaqueline Lancaster, *Brian Howard: Portrait of a Failure* (Anthony Blond, 1968), p. 257.

[4] Hon. Stephen Tennant (1906–87). Eccentric and exquisite youngest son of 1st Baron Glenconner. 'Stephen's dottiness would fill a book. I find him in his mad way excellent company.' (NM to Diana Mosley, 20 December 1946)

[5] Viscount Furneaux (1907–75). Biographer of his father, the politician F. E. Smith (1959), of Halifax (1965) and of Walter Monckton (1969). Succeeded as 2nd Earl of Birkenhead in 1930. Married Hon. Sheila Berry in 1935.

[6] Hon. Francis Pakenham (1905–). Politician and author. Created Lord Pakenham in 1945 and succeeded his brother as 7th Earl of Longford in 1961. Married Elizabeth Harman in 1931. In 1927 he came down from Oxford with a First in Modern Greats.

[7] John Drury-Lowe (1905–60). A lieutenant in the Scots Guards, married to Nancy's friend Rosemary (Romie) Hope-Vere 1930–32.

[8] *Young Woodley* (1928). A slight but charming play by John van Druten in which a boy falls in love with his housemaster's wife.

[9] Mr and Mrs Arthur Glasgow, wealthy Americans from Richmond, Virginia. Their daughter Marjorie was a debutante.

[10] Harold Acton (1904–94). Writer. His first collection of poems, *Aquarium* (1923), was published when he was at Oxford, where he was the leading aesthete of his generation. It was followed in 1928 by *Cornelian*, a prose fable, and *Humdrum*, a novel. His best-known work, *The Bourbons of Naples*, was published in 1956. He lived in Peking 1933–9, then settled in Florence at the villa La Pietra. Knighted in 1974. A lifelong friend of Nancy, he was also her first biographer. They corresponded regularly, but not all her letters, in particular some quoted in *Nancy Mitford. A Memoir* (1975), have been made available to the editor.

To Tom Mitford   26 Rutland Gate, SW7
[June 1928]

My Dearest Brother

I hope this will find you as it leaves me.

I am having a rollicking time at present, this season is being such

fun. I saw Alex Spearman[1] the other day & he says he asked Mr
Birley[2] to dinner to find out what he thought of us (so like A.S.!) but
that Mr B wouldn't say anything except that he thought we were very
quick! And that during that game which we played I had behaved
characteristically but whether he meant with characteristic stupidity
or not I don't know. I long to see Mr Birley again. I'd really forgotten
all about him until that conversation.

It's impossible to write a coherent letter in this house as the telephone rings *quite* incessantly! Finish later.

Afterwards Alex said to me, What did you think of John[3] so I said
rather rashly that I preferred young men to be less clever but more
cultured which seemed to annoy him rather.

Apparently J.S. said to Alex that I had the Russell[4] type of brain
but even this didn't make me feel more kindly towards him. Oh what
a man, he really does need shooting or even torturing to death.
Creature!

Greenwich is more lovely than anything I've seen for ages, an
enormous Wren palace, quite heavenly.

Muv has gone to Cortachy[5] for the week end.

Tell Herr von Almasi[6] that I'm having hay fever most terribly badly,
is he? It really does wreck one's life.

I met Simon Morrison[7] the other day, he seems rather a half baked
sort of youth & too arty for me but I daresay very nice really. How
is one to find the perfect young man, either they seem to be half
witted or half baked or absolute sinks of vice or else actively dirty
like John Strachey. All *very* difficult!

Kindly write to me, this is my last letter as you'll be back in little
more than a week oh joy!

Best love
    N

[1] Alexander Spearman (1901–59). Conservative MP. Knighted 1956. Married to Diana
Doyle 1928–51 and to Diana Ward in 1951.
[2] Robert Birley (1903–82). Master at Eton where Tom made friends with him. Subsequently headmaster of Eton 1949–63. Knighted 1956.
[3] Evelyn John Strachey (1901–63). Labour MP and writer. Married to Esther Murphy
1929–33 and to Celia Simpson in 1933. His bohemian habits offended Nancy.
[4] Bertrand Russell (1872–1970). In 1928 he published *Sceptical Essays*. Nancy and
Russell were related through her paternal grandmother Lady Clementina Ogilvy, whose
mother was a sister of Russell's mother, Katherine Amberley. '. . . he has a distant
cousin who admires him more than anyone alive.' (NM to Tom Mitford, 8 June 1928)
[5] Cortachy Castle in Scotland belonged to the 6th Earl of Airlie, Lord Redesdale's first
cousin.

[6] Janos von Almasy. Tom's Hungarian host at Schloss Bernstein in Austria.
[7] Simon Morrison (1903–69). First cousin of 1st Baron Margadale.

To Tom Mitford   Leith Hall[1]
19 September 1928   Kennethmont
                                           Aberdeenshire

Beloved B

At least not really very beloved as you simply *never* write to me. You are a great fat bore.

I'm staying here with Middy, it's being very nice & peaceful, no other guests & the country round is divine. The visit to Mary[2] was fun too, she had a charming couple called Wiggin,[3] he is first secretary in Rome & she's Spanish. They are really delightful, so cultivated & he is brilliantly clever & a philosopher.

Tom! I've been reading such an entrancing book called *Civilization* by Clive Bell. It is an absolute hand book to Kr[4] you simply must read it. He says that most people today are uncivilized (which I've always felt) that the Romans were not highly civilized, that the only 3 *real* civilizations we know of were the Greeks, the Italians of the Renaissance & French 18th Century. It is a most charming book & expresses things I have always felt & sometimes tried to say. We'll start a new civilization at Kr, can't we begin soon oh dear why aren't we fearfully rich.

Can you get English books or shall I send it you, only if I do you must swear to read it. It's quite short.

I hated leaving Cullen[5] it was a perfect fortnight among highly civilized people!! Most of the people I know are frank barbarians (Muv & Farve specially) but Nina, Mark & Hamish[6] are civilized, so am I & so are you. Oh the fun I had there. Nina & I are going to Paris in the autumn. I hope you'll be there, we *should* have high jinks.

How is Baby?[7]

I hear Muv has taken herself off to those gloomy Netherlands, does she imagine she's a reincarnation of Philip II or what? Perhaps she is & Farve's Bloody Mary, I really think there is something in that idea, it would account for a lot. . . .

Do write to me soon *please*, I leave here Monday next so you'd better write to Swin.

Best love angel
    Nancy

[1] House belonging to Charles Leith-Hay, who was married to Middy O'Neill's Aunt Louise.
[2] Mary Milnes-Gaskell; married Lewis Motley in 1934. Nancy and she had become friends at Hatherop Castle School.
[3] Arthur Wiggin (1892-1935). Diplomat. Married Carmen Fernandez-Vallin Parrella in 1921.
[4] An imaginary country invented by Nancy and Tom, 'where nothing ugly will ever enter into our lives at all'. The opposite to life at Swinbrook.
[5] Cullen House, Banffshire, belonged to Nina Seafield.
[6] Hon. James Alexander (Hamish) St Clair-Erskine (1909-73). Second son of 5th Earl of Rosslyn and a friend of Tom at Eton. When Nancy met Hamish in early 1928, he was in his first year at New College, Oxford. She was drawn to his high spirits and rebellious behaviour and he, although homosexual, was flattered by her admiration and delighted to have found someone to indulge his own love of childish pranks. By the summer Nancy's initial attraction had turned to infatuation and she became unofficially engaged to Hamish.
[7] Countess Erdödy, a neighbour of von Almasy's in Austria. Tom was in love with her.

To Tom Mitford   Castle Grant[1]
[May 1929]   Grantown
                                             Strathspey, N.B.

Darling

Isn't it too sickening about Pam,[2] I'm simply furious aren't you? But Muv says she seems to be taking it all fairly calmly & anyway what a let off in the way of brother in laws. I do so wish you were here, it is being great fun really only I have to share a room with Nina & she talks in her sleep all night. There are about 18 people here some nice & some not, I expect you know more or less who they are so I won't enumerate them. People arrive by the 9.28 AM so one comes down to brek every morning to find about 6 new faces, black from the train & cross from being awake all night. I escape quite a lot & write at length to John Sutro[3] who is a marvellous correspondent because you really can say what you think to him. I believe I may make enough to get home by taking photos of the party for the *Tatler*. How are your finances, at present mine are unmentionable.

I'm probably going to stay with Evelyn Waugh[4] in Islington while the other Evelyn[5] goes away to write a book which would be great fun, can I park[6] with you too sometime?

Tom Driberg[7] sends his love, he is in the same condition as us, pecuniarily I mean, it is such a satisfaction to think that others are isn't it? His camera is in pawn so he's going half shares with mine for the *Tatler*.

Wasn't it awful Edward J's[8] mother dying after all his ribaldry in the garage that night.

Well best love ducky
      N

[1] Castle Grant was another of Nina Seafield's houses.
[2] Pamela Mitford's engagement to Oliver Watney, the Mitfords' neighbour at Swinbrook, had been broken off by mutual consent.
[3] John R. Sutro (1904–85). Film producer. Founder of the Railway Club at Oxford whose members combined gastronomy and oratory on railway excursions. Sutro's gifts as a mimic were legendary. 'So many dying parties have been revivified, so many dwindling ones swiftly re-populated, by the sleight of his tongue.' Brian Howard, *Cherwell*, 1927. Quoted in Lancaster, *Brian Howard*, p. 185. Married Gillian Hammond in 1940. Nancy valued Sutro as a correspondent when they were young; unfortunately none of her early letters to him has survived. They remained friends until her death, though meeting and corresponding increasingly rarely.
[4] Hon. Evelyn Gardner (1903–94). Married to Evelyn Waugh 1928–30, to Sir John Heygate 1930–36 and to Ronald Nightingale 1937–55. She and Nancy had been friends for several years, but after the Waughs' divorce Nancy's loyalties remained with 'He-Evelyn'.
[5] Evelyn Waugh (1903–66). *Decline and Fall* (1928) had made him a well-known writer. He was working on his second novel, *Vile Bodies* (1930), and was anxious to finish it in time for autumn publication. He spent most of the week writing in the country, coming up to London only at weekends. See Biographical Notes.
[6] Tom was reading for the Bar and living at the mews behind Rutland Gate, which he called 'the garage'.
[7] Tom Driberg (1905–76). Author, journalist, Labour MP and homosexual. Created Lord Bradwell in 1975. In January 1928, Edith Sitwell had given him an introduction to the *Daily Express*, where he began as a gossip writer for the 'Talk of London' column. In his frank autobiography he described what he wrote at the time as 'pretty frivolous stuff, though not, I venture to think, quite so vulgar and trivial as some of today's gossip, since it was often about people, such as Mitford and Waugh, who were intrinsically interesting.' *Ruling Passions* (Jonathan Cape, 1977), p. 102. In 1933 Beaverbrook made him the first 'William Hickey' on the *Express*.
[8] Edward James (1907–84). Capricious poet and collector of Surrealist paintings. Inherited an immense fortune from his father at the age of five and was not fond of his beautiful, but distant, mother, Mrs Willie James. Married the actress and dancer Tilly Losch 1931–4.

To Tom Mitford   Old Mill Cottage
5 June 1929   High Wycombe

Darling B.
I'm going to be photographed at 8 Essex Street Strand on Monday at 11.30, could I come to lunch with you after? It ought to be fairly near oughtn't it? I don't know what Evelyn will be doing, I might bring her too (of course I'll pay for the 2 of us).

The car has been very useful here, Nanny & the babies[1] do like to go in it for a change & I've been to Oxford twice. But honestly you know I think it's falling to pieces! It rattles in the most alarming way. I'll bring it back to you on Friday – or can I keep it in Islington? . . .

My address after Friday is 17A Canonbury Square, Islington,[2] will you let me know there about Monday, also whether you want the car.

John [Sutro] says he likes my article & he thinks it 'will annoy Scotchmen, always a public service'! Are you going to his party on the 12th?

Hamish *was* funny yesterday. I do wish you'd been there to wink at, he had 5 glasses of brandy & crème de menthe (on top of sherry etc) & then began to analyse himself. He said 'The best of *me* is that I can talk Homer to Maurice[3] just as well as Noel Coward to you, in fact I am clever enough to amuse everybody.'

I was faintly peeved at being put in the Noel Coward class!

I do worship that child.

Best love duckie
    Nancy

[1] Nancy's youngest sisters, Jessica and Deborah, were still in the schoolroom.
[2] Nancy occupied the spare room of the Waughs' small flat. Her stay was brief: she left after a month when the Waughs' marriage broke down.
[3] Maurice Bowra (1898–1971). Classicist and author. Warden of Wadham College 1938–70. Vice-Chancellor of Oxford University 1951–4. Knighted in 1951. Nancy met him when he was a don at Oxford and they remained friends until his death.

To Mark Ogilvie-Grant   Redesdale Cottage[1]
30 December 1929   Otterburn
                                         Northumberland

Dearest Mark

Here I am as you see banished from Hamish for 3 weeks. I thought I should die but am bearing up nicely partly because I adore this place & partly because my grandmother is such an angel. Also I'm working really hard. Had a typical St Clair-Erskine letter from Mary[2] to day – 'so tragically sad for my poor sister to have her 2nd husband die suddenly as he did this morning also so annoying for us as we couldn't go over to Poole Place[3]–––'

When all my children die in agony it will be a great consolation to feel that nobody is really minding except me won't it. Only I think

Hamish will at least pretend to mind – no he *really* will I think don't you?

He & I dined with Nina & Studeley[4] thing was there blind drunk & told me unrepeatable stories so I said to Hamish either we get rid of that thing or I go home, so I went up to where Evie was in bed the angel & borrowed £2 from her & we went to the Café de Paris leaving Lord & Lady Seafield to dreer their own Dree or whatever the expression is.

Well then we found (when we'd got there) that after paying the bill we had 7½d between us. We were panicking rather when the sallow & disapproving countenance of old Mit[5] was observed. He cut Hamish but lent me £1 & we went to the Bat. As we never pay there now we are treated as poor relations & put behind the band where we can neither see nor hear & we have the buttered eggs that the Mountbattens have spat into & left. All so homey & nice don't you think.

Still I feel we lend a certain *ton* to the place. Hamish has been an angel lately, not drinking a thing, I really think bar all the good old jokes which no one enjoys more than I do, that he has *literally* the nicest nature of anyone I know. He gets nicer every day too.

My Grandmother is divine about him although she knows & hates all his relations & forbears. A propos of his religion[6] she said 'so long as a person is devout it doesn't the least matter what his religion is, only I (no doubt wrongly) would never feel *quite* the same about a very devout Hindu or Buddhist. And of course Low Church people are very holy but they do so treat God like their first cousin.'

I must go to bed. It is dark here all day & I keep looking out for the mid day moon, haven't seen it yet.

Give my love to Robert[7] if you see him.

Have had to alter the book quite a lot as it is so like Evelyn's in little ways, *such* a bore.[8]

Best love
   Nancy

[1] Nancy was staying with her grandmother, the Dowager Lady Redesdale, who moved to Redesdale Cottage after the death of her husband.

[2] Lady Mary St Clair-Erskine (1912–93). Hamish's sister. Their half-sister was Lady Rosabelle Bingham whose first husband, David Bingham, was killed in the war and whose second husband, John Brand, died on 28 December 1929. Lady Mary was married to Sir Philip Dunn 1933–44, to Robin Campbell 1946–58, to Charles McCabe 1962–9, and again in 1969 to Sir Philip Dunn, who died in 1976.

[3] A small house at Climping, Sussex, belonging to Bryan and Diana Guinness. It was lent to Evelyn Waugh in autumn 1929 to write his travel book, *Labels. A Mediterranean Journey* (1930).

4 Derek Studley-Herbert, soon to be married to Nina Seafield. He disliked all her friends and they him.
5 Tom Mitford.
6 Hamish was a Roman Catholic.
7 Robert Byron (1905–41). Writer, traveller and expert on Byzantine art. Author of *The Station* (1928), a book about Mount Athos. Nancy admired his iconoclasm, vitriolic intolerance and peppery humour and was strongly attracted to him, although she knew him to be homosexual. Evelyn Waugh even thought that they might secretly have got married. Twenty-five years after his death at sea, Nancy wrote to Mark Ogilvie-Grant: 'The fact is it's the people one jokes with whom one misses – the loving, the good & the upright much less. Robert is still the person I mind about most.'
8 Nancy had begun her first novel, *Highland Fling* (1931). It was dedicated to Hamish who contributed to the character of its hero, Albert Memorial Gates. The novel is similar to *Vile Bodies* in that both are comedies dealing with the fashionable world of the Bright Young Things. Lady Redesdale had suggested the title *Our Vile Age*, a pun on Mary Russell Mitford's *Our Village* (1824), but this was made impossible when *Vile Bodies* appeared.

To Mark Ogilvie-Grant   Olde Mille
23 January 1930   [High Wycombe]

Dearest Mark

Can you forgive this paper,¹ I ought to be working & it's a sop to my conscience if I write on this paper! I've got a job offered me to write a weekly article² for £3 a week & I keep putting off & putting off but can't start this evening as I've just spent the day in Oxford with you know who & that always stops me working. He's going to Canada in March for ever, & we're both so unhappy about it specially me, isn't one's life perfect hell, that beastly old Harry³ has found a job for him at £120 a year with a rise of £10 every 6 months, which looks as though he'll be able to support me & our 5 children jolly soon doesn't it. However he's being such an *angel* about it that one simply must not put him off & it may be the making of him yet I suppose.

Surely the trustees ought to stop Nina from compromising herself with that young man which she is doing. All London is talking about it, it makes Hamish & me miserable but what can one do. Among others she has invited to Scotland for the wedding is Mr Hudson⁴ of the Bat, I'm to be a bridesmaid but heaven knows who else, she's not asked Marjorie [Glasgow]. One can only hope that between now & April she'll see sense, it's no good telling her is it. We laughed about your telegram.

I went to a concert with John [Sutro] & we got down to a good old gossip (not during Schnabel's playing but afterwards at the Café de

Paris). He's leading his gay bachelor Whitehall Court life & invited me to stay there with him.

I was photographed yesterday by Hamish's protégé, Peter Rose Pulham, odious youth who scarcely conceals that he thinks I'm as ugly as sin.

Evelyn had a dinner for his book, Harold [Acton], the Yorkes,[5] Rebecca West,[6] Olivia[7] & us. Very amusing, at Boulestin's. The book is selling wonderfully. He was divorced last week. Heygate[8] now writes daily articles signed A Bachelor.

You won't know Hamish again, he's a reformed character, gets up at 9.30 every morning & has quite given up drink & intends to work like a slave in Canada. I love him *much* more than ever.

Best love, do write.
        N

Poor old Peter Watson[9] has been sent down.

[1] A sheet of rough, unheaded paper.

[2] For *The Lady*, founded in 1885 by Nancy's grandfather, Thomas Bowles. Nancy contributed articles on such topics as 'The Chelsea Flower Show', 'The Fourth of June', 'The Debutante's Dance' and 'The Shooting Party'.

[3] Hamish's father, the Earl of Rosslyn.

[4] Nightclub owner.

[5] Henry Yorke (1905–66). Industrialist and highly-regarded novelist who wrote under the pseudonym Henry Green. His first novel *Blindness* (1926), begun at Eton, was published while he was at Oxford. *Living*, which drew on his experience of working in his father's engineering factory in Birmingham, appeared in 1929, the year he married Hon. Adelaide (Dig) Biddulph.

[6] Rebecca West (1892–1983). Literary critic and author. Her critique of Waugh's book in the *Fortnightly Review* ended: '*Vile Bodies* has, indeed, apart from its success in being really funny, a very considerable value as a further stage in the contemporary literature of disillusionment.' (February 1930)

[7] Olivia Plunket Greene (1907–55). Evelyn Waugh had been in love with her before his marriage.

[8] John Heygate (1903–76). Succeeded as 4th Baronet in 1940. His affair with Evelyn Waugh's wife led to him being cited as co-respondent in the Waughs' divorce; shortly afterwards he married 'She-Evelyn' (1930–36). His involvement in the divorce forced him to resign from the BBC and he took up writing. In 1932 he published *Decent Fellows. A New Novel*, about Eton.

[9] Victor William (Peter) Watson (1908–56). Rich homosexual, adored by Cecil Beaton. His father was the Maypole margarine magnate. He funded the magazine *Horizon*, of which Cyril Connolly was editor and he arts editor. Later that year Nancy wrote to Tom, who was in hospital, 'Peter Watson has bought a coral coloured Rolls Royce inlaid with gems & with *fur* seats. I love him quite a lot but it is no use – I won't go into the reason why because the matron might read this during your moments of delirium & it would be awkward for you.' (1 November 1930)

To Mark Ogilvie-Grant   Old Mill Cottage
19 February 1930   High Wycombe

Dearest Mark

Oh how I hope you'll come back in March[1] – I feel that everything
would come right if you did – can I tell my affianced that it is on the
cards, swearing him to secrecy?

I have been lately in a state of complete depression. I suppose it
comes from living here & seeing nobody & whenever I see poor
Hamish I'm quite beastly to him & go on telling him how miserable I
am & of course he can't do anything poor angel.

Then Farve is furious because I see Lady Rosslyn, & has written
to Lord R to say that it's all gone on for long enough etc.

But anyway thank *heaven* Canada is off for the moment, I really
think it would have killed me.

If you pass Gib: on your way home don't forget sweet Johnnie
[Drury-Lowe] is staying at Government House holding the rock (with
a handful of gallant men) against all comers.

I can't say any more about Nina & can't bear to think of it, nothing
has ever upset me so much.[2] Budge[3] should be crucified or done to
death in some other suitably Eastern manner.

I *loathe* Romie H[ope] V[ere] but don't tell Hamish because he adores
her & I have to pretend I do too. Will he ever grow out of liking all these
painted dolls I wonder or will our house overflow with them always?

I've just finished Maurois' *Byron*,[4] very readable. Byron is so like
Hamish in character, the other day H. said to me in tones of the
deepest satisfaction 'you haven't known a single happy moment since
we met have you'. Very true as a matter of fact; what he would really
like would be for me to die & a few others & then he'd be able to
say 'I bring death on all who love me'. It's so sad. When you're away
there's nobody I can laugh about Hamish with & he *is* such a joke
isn't he. I do sometimes with Peter Watson (to whom I've become
very attached) but Hamish can't bear that.

The grind was too horrible everybody drunk & Maggie[5] & Romie
the drunkest of all. Hamish was quite good really considering, I don't
think he does drink as much as he did. Nancy Beaton[6] is another cross
I have to bear but I expect during the season I shall have a perfect
forest of crosses if H. is in London as he now expects to be.

Did I tell you I have got a job of writing weekly articles for *The
Lady* at about £250 a year (they haven't quite settled my wages yet).
It is rather fun to do but a bit of a strain every week to think of
subjects.

My book has gone to the agents whose verdict I await in a state of palpitation. I'm afraid it won't be accepted, everyone thinks it very bad, specially Hamish.

Poor Mark what a depressing letter I'm so sorry, will write again when in a better temper.

Best love
    Nancy

[1] Mark was in Egypt, working as Secretary to the High Commissioner, Sir Percy Loraine.
[2] Nina Seafield had married Derek Studley-Herbert on 24 January.
[3] Dowager Lady Seafield's companion.
[4] André Maurois, *Byron* (1930).
[5] Maureen Guinness (1907–). Married to 4th Marquess of Dufferin and Ava 1930–45, to Major Harry Buchanan 1948–54 and to Judge John Maude in 1955.
[6] Nancy Beaton (1909–). Sister of Cecil Beaton. Married Sir Hugh Smiley in 1933.

To Mark Ogilvie-Grant   Old Mill Cottage
10 March 1930   High Wycombe

Dearest Mark

I hope you don't object to this perpetual shower of letters.

Yesterday I lunched with Helen,[1] Nina & Stubbly were there, rather sweet & very fond of each other. After lunch Nina said let's drive to Oxford so we did, Nina & Stubbly in one car & Helen, Michael Colefax[2] & me in another. Well when we got to Oxford Helen said don't we know anybody we can go & see? So I said well I know someone called Erskine & I'm not certain where he lives but I know it's New Col. So we went to New Col & I said to the porter, which is Mr Erskine's room? So he showed us & we went & of course no one was there but there was a lovely gas fire & we sat down to get warm.

Then I saw Michael Colefax & Helen's eyes light first on one photograph of me then on another, then on a telegram I'd sent the day before & then on a postcard I'd sent the day before that so I got rather embarrassed & said hadn't we better go home. Well as we were charging down the High St I suddenly saw Hamish & Christopher [Sykes] & John [Sutro] & Roy[3] walking along so we all went & had tea with Roy. So wasn't that nice. But Nina & Stubbly would go & have chocolate cake at Fullers which is so right when newly married & so unlike what Hamish would be under the circumstances.

Oh dear *how* unhappy Hamish does make me sometimes, nobody knows except I think you do because you know us both so well. I'm

so exactly the wrong person for him really that I simply can't imagine
how it all happened. It's all most peculiar. But sometimes I really wish
I were dead which is odd for me as I have a cheerful disposition by
nature. I'm sorry to grumble like this. I really do honestly think everything would be all right if we were married, it's partly living down
here that makes me so depressed & miserable.

My book has been accepted by the agents which is a cheering
thought. I don't know how much that means but I suppose they don't
take something that's absolutely unmarketable. I know they refused
Bryan's book.[4]

I like Helen rather, do you? I think she's full of good sense &
capability. You should hear Harold on the subject though, acid simply
pours out.

What do you really think of *Vile Bodies*? I was frankly very much
disappointed in it I must say but some people think it quite marvellous.

I met M Boulestin the other day such a little dear & he says he's
going to start a restaurant in Oxford. So I told John & John was *furious*
& I couldn't make out why & at last he said 'Oh & to think there was
nothing like that when I was at Oxford.' Poor sweet, I so understand
that point of view. He & Christopher are so *silly* together I couldn't
stop laughing.

There is some lovely Bach on the wireless, I must listen to it so
goodbye for the present.

Love from
    Nancy

That awful grumble doesn't mean anything except that I'm in a very
bad temper so don't take the smallest notice of it *please*.

[1] Helen Eaton (1899–1989). Married Sir John Dashwood in 1922; they lived at West
Wycombe Park in Buckinghamshire. Nancy called her Hell Bags: 'You see she's like
an old smelly dog, that nobody else can stick . . . there are lots of nastier uglier dowdier
more boring more snobbish people who for some reason everybody likes – it's a stupid
witch hunt & I *can't* join in, but she is a heavy cross to carry.' (NM to Diana Mosley,
30 August 1946)
[2] Michael Colefax (1906–88). Younger son of Sibyl Colefax, the hostess and decorator.
[3] Roy Harrod (1900–78). Economist. Knighted in 1959. At this time he was a Student
of Christ Church, lecturing in economics and modern history. Married Wilhelmine (Billa)
Cresswell in 1938.
[4] Hon. Bryan Guinness (1905–92). Poet, novelist and playwright. Succeeded as 2nd
Baron Moyne in 1944. Married to Nancy's sister Diana 1929–34. 'The more I see of
Bryan the more it surprises me that Diana should be in love with him, but I think he's
amazingly nice.' (NM to Tom Mitford, 30 October 1928) In 1936 he married Elisabeth
Nelson. His book *Desires and Discoveries* 'did not recommend itself to the literary agent

to whom I sent it, nor indeed very much to myself'. *Potpourri from the Thirties* (Cygnet Press, 1982), p. 20.

To Mark Ogilvie-Grant   4 Rutland Gate Mews
26 March 1930   London, SW7

Dearest Mark

What a fiend you are, not writing for so long & I suppose you're not coming back now either.

I'm up here for a party Lady Evelyn[1] is giving tonight, I shouldn't think I shall know a single soul as ordinarily I just scrape along by knowing you & Johnny & Robert [Byron] & Eddie[2] but as you're all abroad I foresee the wall for N.M. especially as my dress is unusually drab, Michael[3] having covered my only nice one with coffee at William's[4] last week. A curious evening, ending up for no known reason at Mme de Peña's[5] house at 5 in the morning, one of those sort of evenings. Romie was there, I like her now.

I am enjoying a period of grass-widowhood as Hamish having killed a man while drunk has left the country with Peter Watson in search I can only suppose of more & cheaper drink.[6]

Ava[7] & Maggie are apparently going to announce their engagement on Ava's 21st birthday, *lucky lucky* they are.

Diana's baby[8] is curiously unattractive & exactly like Tom but she adores it & is the picture of successful motherhood. Brian Howard says My dear it is so *modern* looking, the nurse was slightly astonished.

I'm making such a lot of money with articles – £22 since Christmas & more owing to me so I'm saving it up to be married but Evelyn says don't save it, dress better & catch a better man. Evelyn is always so full of sound common sense. The family have read *Vile Bodies* & I'm not allowed to know him, so right I think.

We shall be at 26 Rutland Gate after Monday for 2 months. Do come home or failing that write to your devoted

                Nancy

[1] Lady Evelyn Guinness (1883–1939). Diana's mother-in-law.
[2] Edward Tatham; owner of the nightclub Night Light.
[3] 6th Earl of Rosse (1906–79). Married Anne Armstrong-Jones (née Messel) in 1935.
[4] William Acton; painter. Younger brother of Harold.
[5] Madame Alfredo de Peña; American-born hostess. Said to have been responsible for introducing the cocktail party into London in 1922.
[6] A typical invention of Nancy's.

[7] The Marquess of Dufferin and Ava and Maureen Guinness were married in July 1930.
[8] Jonathan Guinness was born on 16 March 1930. Succeeded his father as 3rd Baron Moyne in 1992. His godfathers were Evelyn Waugh and Randolph Churchill.

To Mark Ogilvie-Grant   26 Rutland Gate, SW7
17 April 1930

Dearest Mark

Once more must you assume the ungrateful rôle of confidant for which I can only hope that your reward will be a heavenly crown because I fail to see how any earthly benefit can be your share.

More to-dos of course need I say in the Hamish affair. Oh Mark talk about getting to know each other or knowing one's own mind – if I had been married to Hamish for 5 painful years & borne him 6 male children I couldn't know him better & the curious thing is that I'm quite certain that I shall never be so fond of anyone again. All this as I am on the point of losing him for I don't see how he can fail to break off our engagement after what I've done.

It's a very long story so I'll tell it as shortly as I can. For the last 3 weeks Hamish has been, with Lady R & Mary,[1] at Hunger Hill[2] & for at least a fortnight Romie & a few gay sparks have been staying there. Well Hamish has telephoned & written fairly regularly & from his accounts but much more from Romie's I gathered that the party *for a fortnight* has been one long orgy – drinking, gambling & never in bed till past 3. On Tuesday last I had a perfectly heartbroken letter from Lady Rosslyn telling me all this & more & saying Hamish is going to the bad as fast as he can, can't you advise me what can be done? So in a white heat I took my pen & said 'The bottom of all this is *Oxford* – Hamish at Oxford doesn't lead one single day of ordinary normal life – these parties which are incessant will ruin him etc etc. Can't he be taken away now & given some job – if this were done I would give my word not to marry him' & so on.

Meanwhile Harry [Rosslyn] returns from Canada, this morning I get a telegram 'May I show yr letter to Harry Vumble Rumble' to which I could only say yes. However I can't & won't plot with Hamish's parents behind his back, so wrote at once & told him all. Mark, he'll *never* forgive me if this results in his leaving Oxford. Developments are evidently pending as Harry rang up this afternoon & asked where a letter would find me tomorrow – I happened to answer & it was his voice.

Then by this evening's post a screed from Hamish saying everybody nags him the whole time & that Farve has written again to Lord R complaining we see each other too much. Oh my life is too difficult between trying to manage Hamish *and* the family. And what will he say when he hears this, I can't bear to think of it – & rightly because what business is it of mine to find fault with his character, much more for him to complain of mine really considering our relationship.

But if anybody was ever worth a struggle it is Hamish because you know underneath that ghastly exterior of Rosslyn charm etc he is pure gold, at least I think so, in fact I'd bank everything on it but what chance has he – Lady R an angel but ineffective & neurotic & Lord R rotten through & through. Sometimes I think it is too much for me or anybody else. Only I really believe that I'm something quite solid in his life which is the only comforting reflexion.

So that's that – I'll let you know if anything sensational happens.

N

---

[1] Hamish's sister, Lady Mary St Clair-Erskine.
[2] Sussex home of Hamish's father, 5th Earl of Rosslyn.

To MARK OGILVIE-GRANT   4 Rutland Gate Mews, SW7
10 December 1930

Darling Mark

Oh *when* is the cover[1] coming? Thornton Butterworth is dans tous ses états[2] about the beastly thing & rings up 5 times every day. It will be a black Xmas for me if it doesn't come soon.

I've just been lunching with your mama & inadvertently gave her a letter of yours to read in which a lift boy is described as a Driberg's delight. 'What *is* a Driberg's delight? Dear Mark has such an amusing gift for describing people!' She is worried about the clothes Hamish borrowed for Basil [Dufferin]'s wedding, I don't wonder, you'll be very lucky if you see *them* again. However I've promised to do my bit (awful the way everyone treats me as Hamish's nanny isn't it). I believe he's been sent down from Oxford, at least everyone I see tells me so but perhaps it is only a merry joke. Personally I shan't mind if he is, I find Oxford very dull now.

I've got out of going to Switzerland thank *heavens*, it is a blessed relief to feel that I have escaped those snowcapped peaks. Like my hairdresser, when I said why do you hate Switzerland '*Ah* les *montagnes*' was all he could say in a sort of groan. I so agree don't you – I think natural scenery is THE END.

Foggy & cold & I must go out to tea with old Kitty Shenley. I hate tea but when up for 2 days make it a point of honour to be out to every meal with the result that I go home afterwards & sleep the clock round twice. Yesterday was very peculiar, Muv, Decca & Peter (my dog) all fainted. Peter's faint was terrifying, *much* the worst I thought he had died.

Much love & give my respects to Derek Millar.[3]
          Nancy

[1] For *Highland Fling*.
[2] In a terrible state.
[3] Frederick Hoyer Millar (1900–89). Diplomat. Second Secretary in Cairo 1930–34. Created Baron Inchyra in 1962. 'Derek Millar with whom I was in love once, I still think him a bit of a stunner, I always like pompous men so much.' (NM to Diana Guinness, 19 November 1934)

TO MARK OGILVIE-GRANT   4 Rutland Gate Mews, SW7
4 February 1931

Darling Mark

Hamish's family, behaving with their usual caddery have taken him away for ever to America. I've broken off the engagement. So there you have the situation in a nutshell.

I tried to commit suicide by gas, it is a lovely sensation just like taking anaesthetic so I shan't be sorry any more for schoolmistresses who are found dead in that way, but just in the middle I thought that Romie who I was staying with might have a miscarriage which would be disappointing for her so I got back to bed & was sick. Then next day I thought it would be silly because as we love each other so much everything will probably be all right in the end.

I went to see the publishers yesterday & after a ROYAL row with them I persuaded them to scrap their *awful* cover & use yours. But Mark, the dreadful thing is that as they have to pay for theirs they won't pay any more – do you mind? You see it was a tiny bit your fault for being so late with it. I thought that as you've done it now you'd probably rather it was used & not paid for than not used at all! Anyway you shall have the very first copy, it comes out on the 12th March.

I've made friends with a sweet & divine old tart called Madame de Peña – she rang a young man up the other day at *11 A.M.* & said 'What a dull night it's being, let's do something.' She *is* nice & has lovely parties & adores Hamish who confides in her & then she tells

Highland Fling

by

Nancy Mitford

Just Published   7s. 6d. net
Thornton Butterworth Ltd.

Mark Ogilvie-Grant's cover for *Highland Fling*

it all to me which is lucky because it is things I like hearing. But I am really very unhappy because there is no one to tell the funny things that happen to one & that is half the fun in life don't you agree?

Do write to him because he is very unhappy too, Hunger Hill will I suppose forward things.

Tom is very miserable because Tilly[1] married Edward, it's an effing world altogether.

I'm in the state in which I can't be alone but the moment I'm with other people I want to get away from them. It will be fun when my book is out.

Patrick[2] is marrying an heiress in March but doesn't intend to sleep with her. Oh gosh I hope this letter is read out in no court of law don't you, it would give me such a social uplift. Mabel's (the parlourmaid) greatest friend is dying of cancer. Why were any of us born?

How can I possibly write a funny book in the next 6 months which my publisher says I *must* do? How *can* I when I've got practically a pain from being miserable & cry in buses quite continually? I'm sorry to inflict this dreary letter on you, as a matter of fact everyone here thinks I don't mind *at all* – rather a strain but I think the only attitude don't you agree?

Best love from
    Nancy

Do you realize that your drawing for the cover is the living image of Nina? *Won't* she be pleased?

[1] Ottilie (Tilly) Losch (1904–75). Beautiful Austrian actress and dancer. Married to Edward James 1931–4 and to 6th Earl of Carnarvon 1939–47. Tom did not want to marry Tilly but thought, rightly, that she would be unhappy with Edward James. He avoided being cited in James's acrimonious divorce suit because of Diana's friendship with James, but both he and Nancy were called as witnesses.
[2] Patrick Balfour's engagement to Marion Burrell, daughter of the shipping magnate and art collector Sir William Burrell, was announced on 10 February and broken off on 17 March. In 1938 he married Angela Culme-Seymor.

TO MARK OGILVIE-GRANT   Old Mill Cottage
15 March 1931   High Wycombe

Darling Mark
    Thank you so much for your letters, they are lovely & long when they do come I must say. Those devilish publishers still haven't sent my 6 free copies so I can't get yours off. I long to know what you think of it.

Hamish has come back & it is all too frightful, we met at a party & of course it all began over again.

Heaven knows what will happen in the end, he seems at present to be busy drinking himself to death saying 'my bulwarks (that's me) have gone.' We aren't seeing each other at all. I suppose it will have to be the gas oven in the end. One can't bear more than a certain amount of unhappiness.

The book is doing well I'm glad to say, has had very good notices already specially in the *Evening News* & *Standard*[1] which really count as I don't know who writes them. Old Driberg & Patrick of course had to come up to the mark for very shame which I must say they did, nobly. The *News* & *Standard* were proper reviews, not gossip. I'm keeping a little book of cuttings. Everyone thinks your cover *too* good, a dreadful man called Geoffrey Gwyther said to me 'I must buy your book, it has such an amusing cover.' I adore the way it is signed on the man's knees.

It's too awful, I've just spilt a mass of ink on Muv's favourite carpet & am sitting with my foot on the place hoping she won't notice. She will soon of course. Oh dear.

They have been simply too odious lately, & had a fearful row the other day ending up by accusing me of drinking. I must say I do go to awful sorts of parties so I'm not surprised they are in a state, but if one can't be happy one must be amused don't you agree? Besides I always have John to chaperone me!

I must go & take the dogs for a walk.

Best love
    Nancy

The gas story is quite true, it makes Robert laugh so much.

[1] *'Highland Fling* is a pure lark . . . The naked frankness and unaggressive wilfulness of the young people is engagingly and convincingly done.' *Evening Standard*.

To Mark Ogilvie-Grant   Old Mill Cottage
28 March 1931   High Wycombe

Darling Mark

I shall probably see you in May because (if I can pass the tests etc) I have been engaged to act in a film in Kashmir, leaving London for 3 months at the end of May.[1] John thinks we could probably meet for a moment if I do & I expect I shall be longing to see a human face by then, as my co actors, the ones I've seen, are hardly exciting to say the least of it.

But it will take me away from London for 3 months & that's all I care about – obviously I shall either die of some unsavoury disease or be raped away into Mr A's harem – preferably of course the latter. For this I get £150 the day I sail, 1st class return tickets & a share in the profits, if any, of the film, besides a *good* chance of becoming the English Garbo. Anyway material for at least 3 novels. All this of course depends on whether I can pass the necessary tests which I try for at Elstree after Easter. Oh I do hope I shall.

I'm through with Hamish for good, he has the grace to appear thoroughly miserable & depressed & sits at parties (I'm told) gazing sadly into space. I meanwhile have settled down into soured spinster-hood. It is sad as we were so completely suited to each other.

What d'you think of *Highland Fling* (let me know if you don't receive the copy I sent as it was insured). It went into a second impression last week & sells a steady 30 a day which I'm told is definitely good for a first novel.

Robert & John have just been down for the day, they are all in favour of my film project & offer me Gavin[2] as an escort as they say he has nothing whatever to do & will probably end by producing the whole film. I can't tell you how much I long to go but alas I am very doubtful about the tests, I've never done any acting at all you see.

It will be quite an exciting part, riding about over rocky passes etc. Diana holds out small hopes of me ever returning alive & I think she may be right. Robert's parting present is to be a small file [*sic*] of poison for when I'm about to be tortured by enraged Tibetans, & John's of course, a pot of caviar. The family, which seems odd, don't mind at all & are rather intrigued by the idea, as for me I can hardly sit still for excitement but oh the tests are a fearful snag.

It is to be in sound *and* colour & opens with Tibetan music whatever that may be. Well, see you I hope in May.

Best love from
        Nancy

Saw your mother for a moment in the street, she wailed about yr cover – 'what an awful thing' etc, but everyone else *adores* it, it makes the book twice as attractive.

---

[1] This project, Nancy's first and only attempt at acting, came to nothing.
[2] Hon. Gavin Henderson (1902–77). Labour MP. Succeeded as 2nd Baron Faringdon

in 1934. A Bright Young Thing, he became interested in public affairs and joined the Labour Party in 1934. Married to Hon. Honor Chedworth Philipps 1927–31.

TO JAMES LEES-MILNE   Old Mill Cottage
31 March 1931   High Wycombe

My dear Jim

What a nice letter you wrote me, thank you millions of times for it, such letters are far more encouraging than reviews in newspapers.

The book is going fairly well, it went into a second impression 3 days after it came out but won't I fear be a best seller or anything like that. The publishers are pleased & surprised at the amount sold.

By the same post as yours I had a letter from an aged friend of mama's saying that the silliness of my young people is only equalled by their vulgarity & that if by writing this I intend to *devastate* & *lay waste* to such society I am undoubtedly performing a service to mankind. And a great deal more. I fear now that I shall never be mentioned in her will.

We all return to Swinbrook on Saturday so I hope we shall see you soon.

   Love from
      Nancy

TO ROBERT BYRON   Swinbrook House
18 September 1931   Burford, Oxford

My dear Robert

No I shall never be in London again – unless I walk. I can't possibly afford the train fare & have no clothes to wear even if I could, which is sad as I rather fancy the marquise hats & feel no doubt wrongly that I should look a treat in one. My allowance (already nearly non existent) is being cut down to about half as far as I can make out. Apparently while I was sunbathing on the Côte d'Azur there was a crisis in the old country. It is all too drab for words.

Chickens are cheerless birds,[1] I advise you to keep geese which can be taught to follow like dogs, one needs all the companionship one can get in these days. How do your neighbours in the Adelphi fancy the idea of a poultry yard over their heads? (The droppings don't forget make valuable manure & should be kept in the dark.)

There is *nothing* I don't know about all sorts of poultry, send a stamped addressed envelope for advice to Auntie Nancy. Muv says the only way is to start very small & gradually increase your stock, but I shouldn't think that balcony will allow for a very considerable increase so I fear you must cut your coat according to your cloth.

Let me know if you are ever in these parts.

Love from
    Nancy

[1] The Mitford children all kept chickens: 'These hens were in fact the mainspring of our personal economy. We kept dozens of them, my mother supplying their food and in turn buying the eggs from us – a sort of benevolent variation of the share-cropping system.' Jessica Mitford, *Hons and Rebels*, p. 12.

TO MARK OGILVIE-GRANT   Swinbrook House
22 January 1932   Burford, Oxford

Darling Mark

Sir Hugh[1] laid his ginger bread mansion at my feet last Monday, & incapable as ever of giving a plain answer to a plain question I said I couldn't hear of it anyhow until my book[2] is finished. So now I get letters by every post saying hurry up with the book, it is rather awful, I didn't do it from the usual feminine motives of liking rides in his car etc but believe me from sheer weakness. However it's *all* right, I shall wriggle out somehow & anyway the book can't be finished for months.

Meanwhile he intends to go into Parliament, little knowing how much I abominate politicians & all their works. But it is awful how easily one could be entrapped into matrimony with someone like that because it *would* be nice to be rich.

I'm not surprised girls do that sort of thing. Besides the old boy is really awfully nice & kind in his own way. But think of having blond & stupid children. But then one could be so *jolly well dressed* & take lovers. Romie thinks I'm mad & so do the babies who go on at me like a pair of matchmaking mothers. But it is better to retain one's self respect in decent poverty isn't it? My life is a bore, I would so much much rather be dead.

I stayed with Helen [Dashwood] last week end, she had lots of high up debutantes & I played bridge which I've got a passion for.

Hamish gave me a ring from Cartier which has been a consolation to me in these hard times.

I don't think it's caddish telling you about Sir H. because of you being so far away & also you don't know him do you, or do you? Which makes it all right I think. Besides you know all the details of my cheerless existence.

> Best love & write soon
> N

[1] Sir Hugh Smiley (1905–90). An officer in the Grenadier Guards, he was a persistent admirer of Nancy. At one point she accepted his proposal of marriage but only because 'I was so bored down here & Muv went on at me about it & said you'll die an old maid & I hadn't seen Hamish for months so I toyed with the idea for 5 minutes.' (NM to Mark Ogilvie-Grant, 19 February 1932) Married Cecil Beaton's sister Nancy in 1933.
[2] *Christmas Pudding* (1932). 'It is about a retired tart, a lady MFH, a foreign office young man – Hamish when young – & a fat, fair, slightly bald & intensely musical youth called Squibby.' (NM to Mark Ogilvie-Grant, 4 December 1931)

To DIANA GUINNESS   Swinbrook House
14 March 1932   Burford, Oxford

Darling Bodley[1]

I am so unhappy for you on account of this terrible tragedy.[2]

I can't help thinking that for her it must have been best, as she didn't do it on an impulse *when* he died it shows she must have considered it & decided that life without him was & always would be intolerable. But for you & all her friends it is a terrible loss, I am so so sorry darling. The children are miserable.

Please give my love & sympathy to Bryan.

> V. best love
> Nance

[1] As a baby, Diana's head was thought to be rather too big for her body, so she was called The Bodley Head.
[2] The Bloomsbury painter, Dora Carrington (b.1893), a friend and neighbour of Diana and Bryan, had shot herself two months after the death of Lytton Strachey, the love of her life.

To MARK OGILVIE-GRANT   31 Tite Street
20 June 1932   London, SW3

Mark my angel

Here I am, installed in the Widow's[1] house & only waiting for the front door bell to ring & you to be announced. When will that be? Can you dine on July 7th for Diana's party?

Hamish is going to America on the 2nd to seek our fortunes. This is in the well known Mitford wail. I am frightfully unhappy but slightly hopeful at the same time. After all, better that than this awful waiting about in England. Hamish's character is so much improved, we travelled from Scotland in a 3rd class sleeper with 2 commercial travellers overhead & he never murmured once! He is a *sweet* angel isn't he?!!!! I enclose a letter from Romie which will amuse you, a wonderful exposé of Castle G[rant] life, if you remember to will you send it back.

Last week end I stayed with Diana & Randolph C[2] tried to rape me, it was very funny. This is a secret.

Doris C-rosse[3] (Castlerosse I mean) was there & Alfred Beit[4] & others. Great fun.

Betjeman[5] is now engaged to Penelope Chetwode & Johnnie Churchill[6] is engaged to a girl called Halleotosis who Randolph had at one time & who is eloping to America with Hamish (but I approve of that) (faute de mieux).

So there is a general mix up. The Dumfries-es are being annulled already[7] & the Westminsters have parted company.[8] Isn't this a nice scandalous letter.

Do come home soon because I am looking young & pretty & have some pretty clothes too.

By the way Sir Hugh went from me to a woman called Holloway who got 2 emerald rings & a Rolls Royce out of him & then gave him the raspberry. I am so pleased & so are Cartiers & the R.R. Company who have done but little business of late. How I wish I was a gold digger, when I think that all I got was a coral pendant –

Now make haste & come back please.

Best love
    N

[1] Violet Hammersley (1877–1964). A great friend of Nancy's mother, she was loved by all the Mitford children. After her husband's death in 1912 she became known as 'Widow', 'Wid' or 'Mrs Ham'. Nancy's surviving letters to Violet Hammersley date from after her marriage, when 'the Widow' became one of her main correspondents. See Biographical Notes.

[2] Randolph Churchill (1911–68). Journalist, only son of Winston Churchill. Married to Hon. Pamela Digby 1939–46 and to June Osborne 1948–61. In 1932 he was taken on by Lord Rothermere to cover the elections in Germany for the *Sunday Graphic*. 'There is *nothing* to be said for Randolph but, Clementine Churchill being my cousin . . . I really love him & have never experienced, though often witnessed, the rough side. He was my brother Tom's greatest friend.' (NM to Sir Hugh Jackson, 18 February 1965)

³ Doris Delavigne (1904–42). Married to Viscount Castlerosse 1928–38. A girlfriend of Tom Mitford.
⁴ Sir Alfred Beit (1903–94). South African industrialist. Married Nancy's first cousin Clementine Mitford in 1939.
⁵ John Betjeman (1906–84). Poet Laureate. He had previously proposed to Nancy's sister Pamela, who turned him down. Married Hon. Penelope Chetwode in July 1933, clandestinely as her parents opposed the marriage. In 1931 he joined the *Architectural Review* and published *Mount Zion*, his first book of poems. Knighted in 1969.
⁶ John Spencer-Churchill (1909–92). Painter and composer. A nephew of Winston Churchill. He was unofficially engaged to Penelope Chetwode before her marriage to Betjeman. Married to Angela Culme-Seymour 1934–8.
⁷ The 5th Marquess of Bute (1907–56) married Lady Eileen Forbes on 26 April 1932 and remained married to her for life.
⁸ The 2nd Duke of Westminster was married to his third wife, Hon. Loelia Ponsonby, 1930–47; they led separate lives from 1935.

To Hamish Erskine   Biddesden House[1]
15 September 1932   Andover

Darling Hammy

I've just been over to see Robert [Byron] & he says (only don't quote this) that the Loraines[2] are moving heaven & earth to get rid tactfully of Mark & Alastair[3] because they say & I expect with truth that one competent lady secretary could get through four times the work they do. I think this is quite a funny piece of catty gossip don't you & I believe quite true because R. got it from another member of the staff.

Robert's in very good form & comes over here or we go there most days.[4]

Tomorrow Barbara H[5] & Victor R,[6] Phyllis de Janzé,[7] Mitty,[8] Randolph, George Kennedy[9] & we hope John S. are coming & on Sunday we're all going to join up with *Cecil's*[10] party.

Diana is absolutely maddened by Barbara & Victor after 3 weeks alone with them abroad, she says they are much worse & more annoying than any honeymoon couple could be. However they are going to be given the bridal chamber & left to it. (Bryan, with his usual worldly tact suggested quite seriously that as there is a shortage of rooms they should be doubled up & Victor not given a dressing room.) Aren't people extraordinary?

Would you like to write & say that my nose is interesting by the way? I really do loathe that awful *Bystander*.

Mark is going to *illeostrate*[11] my book with all the people – you, Betj etc drawn to the life.

Do let me know what happens about your job.
Later
I've just had a letter from Mark saying 'I've decided to go back to Egypt for 1 more year.' Poor Loraines!!!

When do you come South? I've got a mass of gossip from Diana with which to regale yr unwilling ears.

John Banting[12] has left. I absolutely adore him.

V. much love
        N

I hear Evelyn has definitely left Heygate. Oh dear!

[1] Nancy was staying with Bryan and Diana Guinness.
[2] Sir Percy Loraine (1880–1961). Diplomat. High Commissioner in Cairo 1926–9. Married Louise Stuart-Wortley in 1924.
[3] Alastair Graham (1904–85). Honorary Attaché in Cairo. Appears under the pseudonym 'Hamish Lennox' in Evelyn Waugh's *A Little Learning* (1964). 'Alastair announced all the people's names wrong at the luncheon party. Captain Huddleston became Captain Balfour and Captain Balfour became Captain Russell and Captain Russell's name he just admitted not knowing.' (Mark Ogilvie-Grant to NM, 28 March 1932)
[4] Nancy described Robert Byron's house in Savernake Forest as 'very amusingly furnished, on the walls there are wool pictures & a caricature of Queen Victoria, all very good, just what one always sees in cottage rooms but all of the very best'. (NM to Tom Mitford, 11 June 1928)
[5] Barbara Hutchinson (1911–89). Married to 3rd Baron Rothschild 1933–46, to Rex Warner in 1949 and to Nicholas Ghika, the Greek painter, in 1961.
[6] Nathaniel Meyer Victor Rothschild (1910–90). Succeeded as 3rd Baron Rothschild in 1937.
[7] Phyllis Boyd (1894–1943). Married Vicomte de Janzé in 1922. One of the most beautiful women of her generation, she had many lovers: at her house in Chapel Street her bedroom was what would normally have been the drawing room and she called it her office.
[8] Tom Mitford.
[9] George Kennedy; architect. Designed the swimming pool and gazebo at Biddesden.
[10] Cecil Beaton (1904–80). Photographer, designer and diarist. His country house, Ashcombe, was about thirty miles from Biddesden. 'I suppose if one saw him every day one would be in perfect happiness.' (NM to Diana Mosley, 9 November 1949)
[11] The spelling is to suggest Cecil Beaton's tremulous vowels.
[12] John Banting (1901–72). Surrealist painter.

TO HAMISH ERSKINE   Swinbrook House
24 October 1932   Burford, Oxford

Darling Hamish

    The others have all gone off to a circus but I remain here by the fire & with D. H. Lawrence's letters. Terrible to have reached an age (or a stage) when one would rather hear about a pony counting to 9 with its foot than bother to go & see it do so. Lawrence's letters are terrifying – would you read them if I sent them to you? But they must be read – *all* & carefully or no use & there is a vast quantity of them.

Your dress[1] is lovely, really divine, I hope you'll think so too. I tried it on this morning. As to hair, I now think it would be better if you had a wig, one of those small tight ones tying in the nape of the neck. But you must decide that. I hope you'll be pleased with the dress, it will be nicer if you can arrange a fitting. . . .

How is your work? Diana asked me up this week, but I can't manage it at present, no money for one thing. I shall have some soon though from the book.

I feel very happy & pleased with life at present, but I suppose that's nothing but a bad omen, always at such times one gets some knock out blow, quite unexpected.

Give my love to Mark & anybody you see, & lots to you.

> Nancy

The children are back – the pony counted to 20 AND LAUGHED OUT LOUD. Well well.

[1] For a fancy-dress party given by Diana at Biddesden.

To Diana Guinness   Swinbrook House
27 November 1932   Burford, Oxford

My darling Bodley

Thank you for the lovely week I had, I enjoyed myself to the full.

Mitty & I spent the whole of yesterday afternoon discussing your affairs[1] & are having another session in a minute! He is horrified, & says that your social position will be *nil* if you do this. Darling I do hope you are making a right decision. You are SO young to begin getting in wrong with the world, if that's what is going to happen.

However it is all your own affair & whatever happens *I* shall always be on your side as you know & so will anybody who cares for you & perhaps the rest really don't matter.

> With all my best love
> Nance

[1] Earlier in the year Diana had fallen in love with Sir Oswald Mosley (1896–1980), who launched the British Union of Fascists on 1 October 1932. Sir Oswald was married

to Lady Cynthia Curzon, he had three children and had no intention of leaving his wife. Diana, however, had decided to divorce Bryan in order to be free to meet Mosley whenever he could spare time from politics and his family.

To Diana Guinness   Swinbrook House
29 November 1932   Burford, Oxford

Darling Bodley

Oh I feel as if I were sitting on a volcano (thank you, by the way, a million times for the life saving gift of £5 THE LAST). You know, back in the sane or insane atmosphere of Swinbrook I feel convinced that you won't be allowed to take this step. I mean that Muv & Farve & Tom, Randolph, Doris [Castlerosse], Aunt Iris,[1] John [Sutro], Lord Moyne[2] & in fact everybody that you know will band together & somehow stop it. How, I don't attempt to say.

Oh dear I believe you have a much worse time in store for you than you imagine. I'm sorry to be so gloomy darling.

I *am* glad you like the book,[3] so do Robert & Niggy,[4] it is a great comfort. But so far there's not been *one* single review – is this rather sinister? I think I had quite a lot in the first week of *H. Fling*.

Mitty says £2000 a year will seem tiny to you & he will urge Farve, as your trustee, to stand out for more.

Do let me know developments, I think it better in every way that I should stay here at present but if you want me at Cheyne Walk I'll come of course. Only I think I can do more good down here. I wish I felt certain it *was* doing good though, it would be so awful later to feel that I had been, even in a tiny way, instrumental in messing up your life. I wish one had a definite table of ethics, for oneself & others like very religious people have, it would make everything easier.

   Much love always darling
       Nance

[1] Hon. Iris Mitford (1879–1966). Lord Redesdale's unmarried sister.
[2] 1st Baron Moyne (1880–1944). Diana's father-in-law.
[3] Nancy's second novel, *Christmas Pudding*, was published in November 1932. Its hero Bobby Bobbin was Hamish 'TO THE LIFE'. (NM to Mark Ogilvie-Grant, 26 October 1932)
[4] Nigel Birch (1906–81). Conservative MP. Created Lord Rhyl in 1970.

Do you remember that delightfully amusing novel

HIGHLAND FLING?

•

Well, NANCY MITFORD'S

new book

CHRISTMAS PUDDING

is even
    more *subtle*,
    more *funny*,
    more *witty*,
    more *wicked*.

*And it has
some perfect
illustrations by*
MARK OGILVIE-GRANT

7s. 6d. net.

Publicity for *Christmas Pudding*

To Hamish Erskine   Swinbrook House
24 December 1932   Burford, Oxford

Duckie

Now that Lord Moyne is back there seems – as far as I can make out – to be some slight hope of the divorce being off. He & Farve went to see M[osley] (who was dead white & armed with knuckle dusters[1]), they said to him 'are you prepared to give up Diana now?' 'No.' 'Then,' said Lord M, 'we shall put detectives on you.' 'Very well.' Lord Moyne absolutely refuses to have Bryan divorced & Diana is determined *not* to *be* divorced & isn't going to give a particle of evidence so at present things have reached a deadlock. Meanwhile

Farve, who is really an extraordinary character, goes to Lord M & says 'I suppose you know that my daughter is laying in a store of furs & diamonds[2] against the time when she is divorced.' Bobo [Unity] had apparently told Muv this, half out of mischief & half as a joke. So now Lord M is not unnaturally in a fearful rage with Diana whom he was on good terms with before.

Isn't it unbelievable of Farve though?

Bryan is going to Switzerland for 3 weeks, having forbidden Mosley the house. The truth is that Lord M has at last put some guts into Bryan.

So I think it better, for the present, if we don't talk much about it as there is now no question of an immediate divorce, in fact we can deny that there will be one.

I say – amalg anthracite[3] –! I've been hopping about with excitement.

The book is selling 75 a day regularly. Think out something for my Ashanti money please.

See you next week end.

Have a *lovely* Xmas sweetie.

Love
    N

Burn this please.
Love to Doris & Phyllis [de Janzé].

---

[1] An invention of Nancy's; not to be taken literally.
[2] The 'furs & diamonds' were in fact a pair of country shoes. 'I remember saying to one of my sisters "I hate country shoes & had better get some while I'm rich."' (Diana Mosley to the editor.)
[3] Nancy had asked Hamish to invest her book earnings and he had written to advise her to take shares in the company Amalgamated Anthracite.

TO HAMISH ERSKINE   2 Eaton Square[1]
14 June 1933   London, SW1
5 p.m.

Darling Hamish

I can't sleep without writing to say I am so sorry & miserable that I was unkind to you just now. I shan't send this straight away, perhaps never but I must write it, for my own sake.

Because I must explain to you that if you had told me you were engaged to Tanis, or Sheila Berry,[2] I could never never have made that dreadful scene.

Please believe me. I should have been unhappy for myself certainly but happy for you & as I love you better than myself I would have overcome my own feelings for your sake.

But darling you come & tell me that you are going to share your life with Kit Dunn.[3] *You*, whom I have always thought so sensible & so idealistic about marriage, you who will love your own little babies so very very much, it is a hard thing for me to bear that you should prefer *her* to me.

You see, I knew you weren't *in love* with me, but you are in love so often & for such tiny spaces of time, I thought that in your soul you loved me & that in the end we should have children & look back on life together when we are old. I thought our relationship was a valuable thing to you & that if you ever broke it you would only do so in order to replace it with another equally valuable. But that isn't so, & that is what I find intolerable.

Please understand me.

Please think of me with affection always & never blame me for what I may become without you. Don't think of me as a selfish & hysterical woman even if I appeared so tonight.

God bless you & make her be kind to you, I shall pray always for your happiness.

      Nancy

Now for Bodley's divorce[4] – isn't one's life like an obstacle race?

[1] Nancy was staying in a small house rented by Diana after her separation from Bryan Guinness.

[2] Hon. Sheila Berry; married Frederick, 2nd Earl of Birkenhead, in 1935.

[3] Kathleen Dunn; sister of Philip who was married to Hamish's sister Mary. Hamish had no intention of marrying Kit, a wild and eccentric character; the engagement was a brutal means of making a final break with Nancy.

[4] Diana and Bryan's divorce became final in 1934. In May 1933, Lady Cynthia Mosley had died suddenly of peritonitis, leaving Sir Oswald free to marry Diana.

G. HEYWOOD HILL LTD. • 17 CURZON STREET LONDON W.1 • MAYFAIR 0647-8

OLD AND NEW BOOKS

21 Dec 43

Darling could I have Nicky Mosleys address
from disconsolate feathered friend rang up &
ordered some books for him – only one of
which have I been able to get but will make
an effort after Xmas.

A girl I know was in Trafalgar Sq. that
day, trying to get to the tube. In order to do so
she was obliged to join a queue & shout in unison
Put Him Back. If you didn't shout you were
flung out of the queue & no chance of getting
to the underground! Then she had to stop twice
& sign things - also in order to keep her
place. After which she was very late for
tea. You must say –

"Poor Swan is very low" yes it is the fly
in the ointment"

I met an awfully nice dotty fascist called
Jebb at Leslie Hartleys did you know him?
He only talked about Uncle Rupert who was
his best friend it seems.

• Just had a wonderful week end at Faringdon
I hear Gerald is going to stay with you Best love
N

To Diana Mosley, 21 December 1943

1933–1944

MARRIAGE AND THE WAR

> Love is a punchy physical affair & therefore
> should not be confused with any other side
> of life or form of affection, & while it makes
> an agreeable foundation from which to begin
> a marriage the absence of physical love, *love*
> in fact, should never be allowed to interfere
> with the continuity of marriage. Marriage is
> the most important thing in life & must be
> kept going at almost any cost, it should only
> be embarked upon where there is, as well as
> physical love, a complete conformity of
> outlook.
>
> Note in NM's appointments diary for 1941

Nancy announced her engagement to Peter Rodd in July 1933. Her sister Diana believes that Peter proposed just a week after her relationship with Hamish ended. In a letter to Nancy dated 31 July Peter hints that he had suggested marriage as a joke. But Nancy was nearing thirty and had wasted four years on a sterile affair; she was longing to leave home, to have her own house and to lead her own life.

Peter was the same age as Nancy. He was good-looking and very sure of himself; he had a clever, if pedantic, mind and was a natural linguist. He was also an intolerable know-all and an excruciating bore. His friend Edward Stanley wrote, 'Whatever topic is under discussion, he will pose as an authority outstanding over anyone present: the time he claims to have spent acquiring professional knowledge would, in the sum, have occupied several full lives. To quote him: "I know, I know, I *am* a hospital nurse." "I know, I know, I *am* a war criminal." "I *am* a displaced person/painter/journalist/financier/poet/Italian

pimp." [1] His career before he met Nancy bordered on delinquency:
he was sent down from Oxford for entertaining women in his rooms
and was then dispatched to work in a bank in Brazil where he was
arrested for being destitute. His father, the diplomat Lord Rennell,
and his elder brother Francis used their influence to find him a succession of jobs, from all of which he was sooner or later sacked. But
Nancy was a romantic. She had decided to fall in love with Peter and
remained blind to his shortcomings. They were married in December
1933 and went to live in a small cottage in Strand-on-the-Green,
Chiswick, overlooking the Thames. For a few years Nancy presented
a face of happiness and seemed content to live a quiet domestic life.

The year 1936 was one of upheaval for the Mitfords. Very few
letters have survived to record the sale of Swinbrook, Diana's marriage to Sir Oswald Mosley or Pamela's marriage to Derek Jackson.
Nancy and Peter left Chiswick for a small house overlooking the
Regent's Canal. By now the cracks in Nancy's marriage were beginning to show. She was no longer able to ignore Peter's behaviour; he
was unfaithful, was drinking heavily and spending recklessly. Between
them they had an income of about £500[2] a year, made up from small
allowances from their parents, Nancy's book earnings and Peter's
salary – when he managed to hold down a job. Nancy rarely complained
to her friends: she was always publicly loyal to Peter, making light of
her difficulties and turning his behaviour into a joke. To help make
ends meet, she published four further books during this period: *Wigs
on the Green*, a satirical poke at Unity and Diana's right-wing politics;
The Ladies of Alderley and *The Stanleys of Alderley*, collections of
family letters; and *Pigeon Pie*, a novel which appeared in 1940.

The years leading up to the Second World War splintered the Mitford family. The 1930s was a decade of ideological extremes; people
felt that liberalism and democracy were failing to deal with the worsening economic situation and the increasing threat of another war in
Europe. Three of Nancy's sisters took up extreme political positions:
Diana espoused Fascism, Unity Nazism and Jessica Communism.
Nancy, who grew up partly during the frivolous twenties and partly
during the political thirties, wavered between the two poles. Having
briefly flirted with Fascism she then sent it up in *Wigs on the Green*;
she ended the decade firmly in the socialist camp, helping to find
homes for Republican refugees from the Spanish Civil War.

---

[1] Lord Stanley of Alderley, *Sea Peace* (Peter Davies, 1954), p. 82.
[2] Equivalent to £13,000 today.

Political dissension between Nancy's parents led to the eventual break-up of their marriage. They remained in touch and wrote to one another regularly, but from 1940 they lived apart. Lady Redesdale remained anti-war, even after war was declared. Lord Redesdale, who had been an admirer of Hitler, swung to being violently anti-German when Poland was invaded and believed victory should be fought for at any cost. Unity's suicide attempt in 1939 and her subsequent illness were an additional strain on their relationship. Lady Redesdale devoted herself to protecting and caring for her daughter, who was an invalid until her death in 1948. Lord Redesdale, who had always been fastidious, could not bear to be in the same house as Unity for long.

Nancy spent the 'phoney war' as an Air Raid Precautions volunteer at St Mary's Hospital, Paddington, where she wrote much of *Pigeon Pie*. Peter, with a commission in the Welsh Guards, was given his own company and fought at Dunkirk before being posted to Addis Ababa to help with refugees. For the remainder of the war they saw one another only occasionally. On Peter's rare periods of leave he preferred to stay at his London club and asked his friends not to tell Nancy of his visits. To add to her unhappiness, Nancy suffered two miscarriages, in 1938 and 1940; then, as the result of a brief affair in 1942 with a Free French officer, André Roy, she had an ectopic pregnancy which left her unable to have children. It was a cruel disappointment as she had been yearning for a family for nearly ten years. Her marriage was effectively over.

During the war years Nancy had to make do on very little money. Peter sent cheques infrequently and when they arrived they were too small to cover her living costs. She found a job with French soldiers interned after Dunkirk and later helped with Jewish evacuees from the East End who were being housed at 26 Rutland Gate, the Redesdales' London house. In March 1942 she found more congenial work at her friend Heywood Hill's bookshop in Curzon Street.

Violet Hammersley, a friend and near contemporary of Lady Redesdale, became Nancy's principal correspondent during this period. Nancy adopted her as a mother figure, someone in whom she could readily confide. She viewed her with a mixture of deep affection and comic exasperation. They shared a mordant wit, and Violet's deep pessimism was a source of great amusement to Nancy. She emerges from their letters as a tragi-comic figure. It is surprising that Nancy never portrayed her as a character in her novels; she was certainly the butt of some of her fiercest teases.

To Mark Ogilvie-Grant   Highcliffe Castle[1]
14 August 1933   Christchurch
                                                   Hants

Darling Mark

Thanks for the merry p.c.'s. I wonder if you are getting letters at all? Anyway I've nothing to do at the moment so here goes.

Well, the happiness. Oh goodness gracious I am happy. You *must* get married darling, everybody should this minute if they want a receipt for absolute bliss. Of course I know there aren't many Peters[2] going about but still I s'pose everybody has *its* Peter (if only Watson). So find yours dear the sooner the better. And remember TRUE LÒVE CAN'T BE BOUGHT. If I really thought it could I'd willingly send you £3 tomorrow.

What I want to know is why nobody told me about Peter before – I mean if I'd known I'd have gone off to Berlin after him, or anywhere else, however I've got him now which is the chief thing.

Well, through the haze of insane happiness in which I live, I noticed a coming out dance here for yr niece. Cuckoo was sweet & I was glad to see her. It all went off very well.

We are going to be married early in Oct & then live at Strand on the Green, we are taking the Jacksons'[3] house there. We're going to be damned poor you see. When are you coming back – soon I hope. I gather that Demi-Monde[4] is with you in which case give him my fond regards.

With love from
       N   xxxxxx

Please excuse these lunatic ravings.

[1] Nancy was staying with Violet Stuart-Wortley, Peter Rodd's aunt.
[2] Hon. Peter Rodd (1904–68), (Prod). Second surviving son of 1st Baron Rennell. He and Nancy had known one another slightly for some years and had many friends in common, including Hamish. When he proposed to Nancy he was working, with great reluctance, for an American bank in London. 'A brilliant youth . . . A young man who could "do anything" . . . With his pallid, handsome face, bristling fair hair & sullenly imperious look, he overshadowed all his neighbours . . . His only genuine success was having married Nancy Mitford.' Quennell, *Customs and Characters*, pp. 157–8.
[3] Lady Ankaret Howard (1900–45). Married William Jackson in 1927. She was a friend of both Peter and Nancy.
[4] Hon. Desmond Parsons (1910–37). Traveller and Sinophile, he died of Hodgkin's disease.

To Mark Ogilvie-Grant   Swinbrook House
28 August 1933   Burford, Oxford

Darling Mark

Many thanks for your letter, it does sound fun. Venice I mean. I wonder in which quarter romance has appeared for you – could it be Lord Melchett[1] or has Chips[2] fallen from his married estate already? Apart from them there only appears to be Mr Odom[3] with whom I am not acquainted.

I have no news, the happiness is unabated at present & shows no immediate signs of abating either. I have left Yvonne's[4] as she is very shortly reproducing her species & am up & down between here & London mostly. I wrote you a long letter from Highcliffe but I s'pose it got lost & I s'pose this one will as well (I hope for your sake that it doesn't fall into alien hands).

I don't expect we shall be married much before Nov: which gives you plenty of time to save up for a deevey presey *not* I hope that awful picture of the 2.

We think of living in a house called Glencoe at Chiswick.

Pray let me have more of your news only don't mention your travels [travails?] because I can't read about other people's hardships. Stick to personalities if you want to interest yours sincerely Nancy Mitford.

[1] 2nd Baron Melchett (1898–1949). MP and industrialist. Married Gwen Wilson in 1920.
[2] Henry Channon (1897–1958). An American from Chicago, universally known as 'Chips', who arrived in London in 1918 and made a rapid rise in English society and politics, becoming an MP in 1935 and PPS to Rab Butler 1938–41. *Chips*, his candid diaries, was published in 1967. Married to Lady Honor Guinness 1933–45. Knighted in 1957.
[3] William Odom; an American interior decorator who rented Palazzo Barbaro in Venice.
[4] Yvonne Marling; married to Gustaf (Taffy) Rodd, Peter's younger brother, 1932– 48. Nancy wrote of her sister-in-law: 'I think she is really rather nice only a great bore, the Rodd theory is that she is really very nasty but undeniably attractive. She bores me beyond words.' (NM to Diana Guinness, 5 August 1934)

To Diana Guinness   Swinbrook House
6 November 1933   Burford, Oxford

Darling Bodley

The Rennells[1] came for the week end & were charming. I like her awfully she is really rather gorgeous & I feel sure you or I would get on with her but obviously Yvonne & Mary Smith[2] wouldn't if you see what I mean. Mitty says he saw Yvonne at a party in almost fancy dress (medieval) & if *he* noticed that what must it have been like?

I had a long talk with Mit & he gave me his solemn word that *never* – even if Edward died & she were free tomorrow – would he marry Tilly. So that is a satisfaction. Apparently the poor little child has discovered that you don't love her & is upset.

We *can* be married in Smith Square, in fact Peter says the parson, clerk etc are awfully excited for it. He has to see the parson once more, it will be either the 4, 5 or 6 Dec, we hope the 4th.

I'm awfully pleased there has been no hitch. Also we can live in the Rennells' house, they will be away, until ours is ready.

T.P.O.L.'s[3] meeting was fascinating, but awful for him as the hall was full of Oxfordshire Conservatives who sat in hostile & phlegmatic silence – you can imagine what they were like. I think he is a *wonderful* speaker & of course I expect he is better still with a more interesting audience.

There were several fascinating fights, as he brought a few Neander-thal men along with him & they fell tooth & (literally) nail on anyone who shifted his chair or coughed. One man complained afterwards that the fascists' nails had pierced his head *to the skull.* Bobo was wonderful, cheering on we few we happy few.

Longing to see you darling. . . .

Love from
   N

[1] 1st Baron Rennell (1858–1941). Diplomat. Ambassador to Italy 1908–19. Married Lilias Guthrie in 1894. Nancy's parents-in-law.
[2] Hon. Mary Smith (1901–82). Married Lord Rennell's eldest son Francis Rodd in 1928.
[3] The Poor Old Leader, i.e. Oswald Mosley. T.P.O.M., The Poor Old Male, was a Mitford nickname for their father. T.P.O., by extension, was often used as a prefix by Nancy.

To Mark Ogilvie-Grant   Rome[1]
15 December 1933
[postcard]

This of course is *much* the prettiest thing in Rome I go & look at it every day. I am having a *really dreadful* time, dragging a badly sprained ankle round major & minor basilicas & suffering hideous indigestion from eating goats cheese. However I manage to keep up my spirits somehow.

>   NR

And all my shoes hurt.

[1] Nancy and Peter were on their honeymoon, staying in the Rennells' flat in Palazzo Giulia. Her teasing postcard shows the garish Victor Emmanuel monument.

To Mark Ogilvie-Grant   As from: Rose Cottage
20 January 1934   Strand-on-the-Green
                                       Chiswick

Poor Old Gentleman sad indeed to be fêted & courted in youth, mistrusted in middle age & neglected when an octogenarian by those few friends who have not yet passed Beyond.

I am awfully busy learning to be a rather wonderful old housewife – my marriage, contracted to the amazement of all so late in life is providing me with a variety of interests, new but not distasteful, & besides, a feeling of shelter & security hitherto untasted by me. Why not follow my example & find some nonagenarian bride to skip to the altar with? Remember 'tis better to be an old girl's sweetheart than a young girl's slave. May I suggest the Duchess?[1] Or the Widow?[2] Think this over, pray.

Do you return Tues? If so pray come down to Chiswick *at once* & view the Shelter for the Aged which has been erected there. You take tube to Gunnersbury, bus from there to Kew bridge & then ask for S on Green. You will have no difficulty once there in spotting the winning house, for one thing we have a pig & two parrots over the porch.

I'll ring you up – or else just come will you?

>   Best love from
>   A.R.W.O.L.[3]

[1] Gladys Deacon (1881–1977). Married to 9th Duke of Marlborough from 1921 until his death in June 1934; they had lived apart since 1933.
[2] Violet Hammersley.
[3] A Rather Wonderful Old Lady. In 1933 Nancy wrote an unpublished short story called 'The Old Ladies', based on herself and Diana. The two old ladies live in Eaton Square where their greatest friend and neighbour is an old gentleman who wears a 'rather terrible curly, butter coloured wig'. The Old Gentleman was Mark Ogilvie-Grant, who lived in nearby Cliveden Place.

To Diana Guinness   Rose Cottage
7 November 1934   Strand-on-the-Green

Darlingest Bodley

Oh I do miss you (Nanny's voice).[1]

Well wasn't it lovely about T.P.O.L. And £5000 will do such a lot
of good in the party not to speak of the publicity etc.[2] Peter said 'I
expect Diana will get a lovely diamond bracelet' so I thought oh no it
wouldn't be *nearly* enough for a bracelet – if it had been £50 000 she
might have had a hope! . . .

Oh darling I lost £36 in that gamble & have had to pawn everything
I possess to raise it. Serve me right anyway. Farve put some money
on Togo's horse to stop it winning[3] & gave me £3 share which came
in handy. Poor old cliperon[4] & all my rings have gone, except my
weddinger.

Basil Murray[5] may be standing as Labour MP for Putney against a
Tory & independent Randolph. Funny?

Peter says I can't put a movement like Fascism into a work of
fiction[6] *by name* so I am calling it the Union Jack movement, the
members wear Union Jackshirts & their Lead is called Colonel Jack.
But I shall give it to you to edit before publication because although
it is very pro-Fascism there are one or two jokes & you could tell
better than I whether they would be Leaderteases. They are set off
by the fact that (a) the only nice character is a Feedjist,[7] & (b) the
only Conservative is a lunatic peer. But I don't want to Leadertease
as the poor man could hardly have me up for libel under the circumstances!

Yvonne's sister is fearfully ill, probably dying, so everyone is very
upset & I am suffering remudse.[8]

Peter went to a cocktail party at the Lancasters[9] & says Osbert
was making his wife miserable by making a terrific pass at – NANCY
QUENNELL!![10] Well well.

Oh the royal wedding[11] – I *know* I shan't make it. Must ring up Dig.[12]

Much love darling
    NR

---

[1] Ethel Higgs, nanny to Winston Churchill's children and then to Diana Mitford's boys,
began every sentence with 'Ooh'.
[2] Oswald Mosley had brought a libel case against *The Star* and was awarded damages.
The newspaper had reported that he was planning to take over the Government by
violent means.
[3] Lord Redesdale was always supposed to be unlucky.

[4] A brooch.

[5] Basil Murray (1907–37). Son of Professor Gilbert Murray. Married Pauline Newton in 1927. 'Do you remember books I wrote about a character called "Basil Seal" – a mixture of Basil Murray & Peter Rodd.' *The Letters of Evelyn Waugh*, edited by Mark Amory (Weidenfeld & Nicolson, 1980), p. 593.

[6] Nancy was writing *Wigs on the Green* (1935), a satirical novel about Fascism in which the heroine, Eugenia Malmains, was based on Unity. On a visit to Germany in 1933 Unity had fallen under the spell of Nazism and spent most of her time in Munich.

[7] 'Fascist' in Boudledidge, a language invented by Unity and Jessica.

[8] Boudledidge for 'remorse'.

[9] Osbert Lancaster (1908–86). Cartoonist on the *Daily Express* for forty years, author and theatre designer. Knighted in 1975. Illustrated *Noblesse Oblige* (1956), to which Nancy contributed, and her book of journalistic writings, *The Water Beetle* (1962). Married to Karen Harris 1933–64 and to Anne Scott-James in 1967.

[10] Nancy Quennell was married to Peter Quennell (1905–93), the writer and critic; editor of *Cornhill Magazine* 1944–51 and of *History Today* 1951–79, and author of *Byron* (1934), *Alexander Pope: The Education of a Genius* (1968) and many other works.

[11] The Duke of Kent married Princess Marina of Greece on 29 November 1934.

[12] Hon. Adelaide (Dig) Biddulph (1901–85). Married the novelist Henry Green in 1929. A friend of Nancy since childhood.

To DIANA GUINNESS   Rose Cottage
29 November 1934   Strand-on-the-Green

Darling Nardie

Thank you for the wonderful present, you are *much too* kind.

The wedding was very pretty & exciting, Decca & I saw wonderfully as we were just opposite the Abbey. I think Prince Paul[1] looks too attractive but Pete tells me he's a bumble.[2]

I lunched today with the Rennells & there was an obscure M.P. sitting next to me who said he was interested in Fascism but thought it would be better if they had Lord Burghley[3] instead of the Lead.

. . . It was an awful lunch, most of the guests had to be carried upstairs on account of senile debility & there were 5 courses. So now I feel ill & liverish & cross. How silly to have a savoury at lunch don't you agree. However everybody else ate bang through it.

> *Much* love, come back soon[4]
> Nance

[1] Prince Paul of Yugoslavia (1893–1976). Regent for the young King Peter whose father was assassinated on 9 October 1934. Married to Princess Olga, sister of Princess Marina of Kent.

[2] Homosexual.

³ Lord Burghley (1905–81). Succeeded as 6th Marquess of Exeter 1956. Olympic athlete and MP, known for his right-wing opinions.
⁴ Diana was spending six weeks in Munich, learning German and sharing a flat with Unity.

TO DIANA GUINNESS   Rose Cottage
25 April 1935   Strand-on-the-Green

Darling Bodley

Please excuse this vile note paper – I have run out of the other.

I hear you are in retreat with the Father Superior.¹ I am awfully glad, & hope you will derive much spiritual & other benefit from the proximity of that gentle soul.

Well, I have a lot of things to pick over. My week end at Biddesden has been waiting its turn for some time but is almost too painful for the written word – it can however be summed up – the coldest week end of the spring, no central heating, only one fire (none in the hall, drawing room etc), cold bath water the whole week end & dinner at 7. Poor May² wore a spencer *over* her cotton dress by way of protest, however Bryan said he thought it very pretty!! Her gusty sighs added to the other piercing draughts produced a really painful atmosphere.

On Sunday morning an ancient house-maid collapsed from the cold & nearly died.

But darling, dinner at 7 –! How that poor civilized house must regret your reign.

I am horrified by Garrett's³ engagement. The girl is an ex mistress of Eric Siepmann's⁴ & nasty at that. I call it all very sad. We met her once with Eric & I hated her so much that I insisted on going home instead of to Quaglino's – it was after some first night. She's not even pretty, what does it all mean!

I saw the Betjemans a lot over Easter & dined twice with Gerald⁵ who had Maimie⁶ & Hubert⁷ staying with him. The B's took me to see Ashdown & Coles Hill. They had the Connollys⁸ who made themselves very agreeable but looked strange in rural surroundings.

Woman⁹ has got a wonderfully snob new car, you will laugh when you see it. Peter didn't enjoy his cruise much as they had such bad weather. Evelyn appears to have behaved very well.

The clear-out at Swinbrook has been terrific, trying to make up one's mind to throw away childhood's treasures, however I was very sensible & threw nearly everything. Fancy dresses are such a problem aren't they.

Best love darling & love to the F.S.
Nance

[1] Oswald Mosley.
[2] May Amende was Lady Evelyn Guinness's parlourmaid before going to work for Bryan and Diana in 1929.
[3] Viscount Moore (1910–89). Managing director of the *Financial Times* 1945–70, chairman of Royal Opera House, Covent Garden, 1958–74. Succeeded as 11th Earl of Drogheda in 1937. Married Joan Carr in 1935.
[4] Eric Siepmann; journalist and author of *Confessions of a Nihilist* (1955), an autobiography.
[5] 14th Baron Berners (1883–1950). Musician, painter and writer. Portrayed as the delightful Lord Merlin in *The Pursuit of Love*. Nancy met him through Diana who later wrote of him: 'Clever, talented, witty, original and private-spirited, he was the best companion as well as the most loyal friend anyone could be lucky enough to have.' Diana Mosley, *Loved Ones* (Sidgwick & Jackson, 1985), p. 131.
[6] Lady Mary (Maimie) Lygon (1910–82). Married to Prince Vsevolode Joannovitch of Russia 1939–56.
[7] Hubert Duggan (1904–43). MP and younger brother of the writer Alfred Duggan.
[8] Cyril Connolly (1903–74). Author and critic. Co-founder and editor of *Horizon* magazine 1939–50. Married to Jean Bakewell 1930–45, to Barbara Skelton 1950–54 and to Deirdre Craig in 1959. *Enemies of Promise* was published in 1938. Nancy and he enjoyed an uneasy friendship and corresponded occasionally. 'I must say I *love* his company in spite of his terrible unscrupulousness – he is such a clever man.' (NM to Violet Hammersley, 29 November 1948)
[9] Pamela Mitford.

To Unity Mitford   Amberley Castle
7 May 1935   Amberley
                                                    Sussex

Darling Stone-Heart Bone-Head –

I am very glad to hear that you are returning anon.[1] Do leave all your rubber truncheons behind & pump some warm palpitating blood into that stony heart for the occasion. I have taken out all reference to the F.[2] (not the P.O.F.,[3] the other F.) in my book, & as it cost me about 4/6 a time to do so, you ought to feel quite kindly towards me now.

The Jubilee[4] was wonderful – specially the King's procession. I cried. Then we came down here for the bonfire, which was on such a high hill that we could see 23 other bonfires. We had a torchlight procession onto the downs which looked too pretty. It was rather nice to be out of hot stuffy London, though I expect the high jinks there must have been lovely fun too.

Nardie [Diana] is off to Rome so you'll miss her which is sad.

Lottie is away being married – oh how sweet. I long for the puppies – her husband is an angelic dog.

Just as well about Nardie – now you won't be able to hot each other up about me.

Head of Bone
Heart of Stone
Sister-hater
Mother-baiter
I will finish this poem later

Love from your (undoubtedly) Genius Sister
    NR

[1] Unity's enthusiasm for Nazism and her admiration for Hitler were undiminished. On 9 February she had been introduced to Hitler and considered herself 'the luckiest girl in the world'. Over the next four years she saw him frequently but, contrary to many rumours at the time, they were rarely alone together and were never lovers.
[2] The Führer.
[3] Poor Old Führer, i.e. Oswald Mosley.
[4] George V's Silver Jubilee.

To Diana Guinness   Rose Cottage
13 May 1935   Strand-on-the-Green

Darling Bodley

When did you leave?[1] I heard you had rung up, but we were in such a state of fatigue after the jube that we retired to Evelyn's.[2] I must say I was glad that we did because she had a wonderful bonfire on the downs, 40 feet high & made chiefly of motor tyres which burn like fury, & from there we could see 23 other bonfires, all over Sussex, which was really exciting.

Well, the jube itself. One piece of news which may please (specially Gerald) is that Duncan Grant,[3] who was in the courtyard of Buck Pal itself, told me that the King was *tremendously* made up. Every eyelash stuck together just like any debutante. I must say they both looked wonderful, & they & the Yorks got all the cheering. Kents & Wales nowhere. Marina looked exactly like a mannequin, she will learn in time I suppose, to dress with a more royal distinction on these occasions!

I saw a copy of the *Worker* next day. It said the King & Queen drove through empty streets & were booed by a few workers in Trafalgar Square – otherwise nobody took any notice of them at all. Rather pathetic really.

My father in law was at St James's Palace when the Colonies presented their addresses & he said the Queen was crying all the time & at last the King said 'Well Mary, when you have stopped crying we'll go home.'

I must say I feel floods of loyalty for them don't you?

It's awfully lucky, my mother in law is going to the June ball so she is lending me a tiara & a diamond necklace tomorrow. I am longing for it.

Garrett [Moore]'s young woman has been married twice before – once to a violinist in some 3rd rate hotel & once to a rich old man. I found all this out from Eric [Siepmann]. She is about 35. It does seem awfully sad. However he says she is a really good musician. I don't see why he has to *marry* her quite. Eric got the sack about 6 months ago, he supposes on account of G.

Our libel suit[4] is now 70 down the list. I saw Richard Elwes[5] who says Birkett[6] has taken a quite special interest in it. Meanwhile 3 other people are suing the *Bystander* for libel, & that particular page has stopped – apparently this will be a point in our favour, also a *great* point is that my engagement to Ham was once announced in a paper & denied by Farve the following week.

Richard seems very confident that we shall win. I would give anything to stop it now, but Peter insists on carrying on, backed up by Richard & Motford. I'm afraid the P's[7] will mind awfully, however I couldn't be in worse favour with them than I am already.

Well, give my love to Gerald & Pete [Watson] & Gladwyn Jebb[8] if you see him.

Much love
Nance

[1] Diana was staying with Lord Berners in Rome.
[2] Hon. Evelyn Rodd (1899–1980). Nancy's sister-in-law. In 1923 she married Thomas Emmet (d.1934); created Baroness Emmet of Amberley 1964.
[3] Duncan Grant (1885–1978). Bloomsbury painter.
[4] Nancy and Peter brought a case against an illustrated gossip magazine for publishing the following passage: 'A Lady dining with her ex-husband's cousin; an ex-husband in earnest confab with his divorced wife; and Mr Hamish Erskine whirling round the room with Mrs Peter Rodd – ye gods, what an evening! We, too, are all in favour of reviving the good old days.' *The Bystander*, 11 December 1934.
[5] Richard Elwes (1901–68). Barrister. Married Freya Sykes in 1926. Knighted in 1958.

[6] Norman Birkett (1883–1962). One of the most prominent advocates of his day, High Court judge from 1941. Knighted in 1951 and created a peer in 1958.
[7] Nancy's parents.
[8] Gladwyn Jebb (1900–). Entered the Diplomatic Service in 1924. In 1935 he was serving in the Embassy in Rome. Ambassador to France 1954–60. Created Baron Gladwyn in 1960. Married Cynthia Noble in 1929.

To Diana Guinness   Highfure
18 June 1935   Billinghurst
                                                       Sussex

Darling Bodley

My book[1] comes out on the 25th inst:, & in view of our conversation at the Ritz ages ago I feel I must make a few observations to you.

When I got home that day I read it all through & found that it would be impossible to eliminate the bits that you & the Leader objected to. As you know our finances are such that I really couldn't afford to scrap the book then. I did however hold it up for about a month (thus missing the Spring list) in order to take out everything which directly related to Captain Jack, amounting to nearly 3 chapters & a lot of paragraphs. There are now, I think, about 4 references to him & he never appears in the book as a character at all.

In spite of this I am very much worried at the idea of publishing a book which you may object to. It completely blights all the pleasure which one ordinarily feels in a forthcoming book.

And yet, consider. A book of this kind *can't* do your movement any harm. Honestly, if I thought it could set the Leader back by so much as half an hour I would have scrapped it, or indeed never written it in the first place.

The 2 or 3 thousand people who read my books, are, to begin with, just the kind of people the Leader admittedly doesn't want in his movement. Furthermore it would be absurd to suppose that anyone who was intellectually or emotionally convinced of the truths of Fascism could be influenced against the movement by such a book.

I still maintain that it is far more in favour of Fascism than otherwise. Far the nicest character in the book is a Fascist, the others all become much nicer as soon as they have joined up.

But I also know your point of view, that Fascism is something too serious to be dealt with in a funny book at all. Surely that is a little unreasonable? Fascism is now such a notable feature of modern life all over the world that it must be possible to consider it in any context, when attempting to give a picture of life as it is lived today.

Personally I believe that when you have read the book, if you do, you will find that all objections to it except perhaps the last (that my particular style is an unsuitable medium) will have disappeared.

Oh darling I do hope so!

Always much love from
NR

[1] The publication of *Wigs on the Green* attracted little attention, but it seriously strained relations between Nancy and Diana. Oswald Mosley refused to have Nancy to stay at Wootton Lodge in Staffordshire where the Mosleys lived for four years after their marriage in 1936. Although Diana and Nancy continued to meet and correspond occasionally, they made up their differences only after the war. Nancy refused to allow the novel to be reissued at a later date: 'Too much has happened for jokes about Nazis to be regarded as funny or as anything but the worst of taste.' (NM to Evelyn Waugh, 8 November 1951)

To Unity Mitford   Rose Cottage
21 June 1935   Strand-on-the-Green

Darling Head of Bone & Heart of Stone
Oh dear oh dear the book comes out on Tuesday. Oh dear, I won't let Rodd give a party for it, or John Sutro either, who wanted to. Oh dear I wish I had never been born into such a family of fanatics. Oh dear.

Oh dear, this is probably the last letter you'll ever get from me because it's no use writing to Stone-Hearts.

> Miss Stony Heart
> What shall I do
> Oh how I wish I was
> Stone hearted like you

Please don't read the book if it's going to stone you up against me. Anyway Eugenia is the only nice character in it except for Lady Marjorie who becomes nice after joining up with the Union Jack Shirts. *Do* remember that.

Oh dear *do* write me a kind & non-stony-heart letter to say you don't mind it *nearly* as much as you expected, in fact you *like* it, in fact, after *I Face the Stars*[1] it is your favourite book even more favourite than mine comf.[2]

I wonder what Mr Wessel[3] will think of it? Are you yachting with him by the way?

Oh dear, I am going to Oxford with Nardie tomorrow, our last day together I suppose before the clouds of her displeasure burst over

me. She doesn't know yet that it's coming out on Tuesday. Oh dear
I have spent days trying to write her diplomatic letters about it. Oh
dear I wish I had called it mine un comf now because uncomf is what
I feel when ever I think about it. Oh dear.

So now don't get together with Nardie & ban me forever or I shall
die. Could you forgive me quite soon? Otherwise Xmas & other feasts
at home will be *so* uncomf.

So now write quite soon & say you forgive me. I did take out some
absolutely wonderful jokes you know & all the bits about the Captain.
OH! DEAR!

O H D E A R

Love from
    N R

---

[1] Geoffrey Moss, *I Face the Stars* (1933). A novel set in 1923 in defeated Germany.
It charts the fate of a Rhineland family and is dedicated to 'Those who have stood for
the Polish corridor and for the war guilt clause in the treaty of Versailles and to the
sons of the readers of this book who in consequence will lose their lives in the next
war.'
[2] *Mein Kampf.*
[3] Hitler.

TO MARK OGILVIE-GRANT   Rose Cottage
9 November 1935   Strand-on-the-Green

Dear Old Gentleman

I suppose you are either dead or insane by this time. In case not I
thought you might like to know that I am writing a book about a demon
decorator called Matthew Mcpherson Gray who takes an insane pleasure in RUINING the houses of the rich & arty but mends the roofs
of the poor for nearly nothing like Robin Hood. When I add that he
is a curious, crabbed little bewigged old man you might be able to
guess, if I gave you 3 guesses who it is MEANT TO BE.

I hear that Bobo & Diana are going to stand outside the Polls next
polling day & twist people's arms to prevent their voting, so I have
invented (& patented at Gamages) a sham arm which can be screwed
on & which makes a noise like Hitler making a speech when twisted
so that, mesmerised they will drop it & automatically spring to salute.
I expect to make quite a lot of money out of this, hope you will get
one & advise your friends to do the same – I saw Diana at a lunch of
Syrie's[1] 2 days ago, she was cold but contained & I escaped with my
full complement of teeth, eyes etc.

By the way I have discovered that we had a Jewish great grand-mother called Miriam Schiff – a dear old lady with 14 brothers all rabbis. Decca & Debo were called after 2 of their wives. Don't forget to tell anyone who might feel interested – I am writing off to Hitler as I think he SHOULD KNOW. . . .

Pete & me never go out in the evening now as he is working very hard & gets too tired so I never see anyone.

Could we meet in London – say Wednesday or Friday after lunch & see some pictures together – I'm lunching in town both those days & could meet you anywhere after. It would be awfully jolly. Of course you are always welcome at Rose Cottage but I know the difficulties.

Now do arrange something I am bored with never seeing ye.

NR

[1] Syrie Barnardo (1879–1955). Daughter of the orphanage founder. Fashionable interior decorator. Married W. Somerset Maugham in 1916. 'I would like to write up & say how terribly kind Willy always was to me from my earliest and dullest days – so was Syrie.' (NM to Heywood Hill, 22 May 1966)

TO SIMON ELWES[1]   12 Blomfield Road[2]
14 November 1936   London, W9

Darling Simmie

(I would put darling Golly & Simmie only I like to think 'Mrs P. Rodd corresponded with many of the most famous *men* of her time' & corresponding with one's brother & sister in law isn't quite like that somehow – see.) . . .

Dear you should see this house. You see everybody's houses are so pretty nowadays so I set out to try & make this as ugly as I could for a change & my goodness me I've succeeded. But it is really a fine idea because everyone that sees it can say to themselves well anyway my house is twice as pretty as that (& whoever they are they'll be about right) & that will set them up for weeks. See the idea?

I hope you are minting money. The house I wanted you to buy in Essex is being bought by the Channons,[3] it makes me *sick*.

The house next door has been bought by a godlike young architect & his wife & they are like the ants to our grasshopper – that is they arrive at 7.30 in the morning & do WITH THEIR OWN HANDS things that we pay people sums like £50 to do. It is very discouraging. However, the boom. That's all Rodd says when I point out what a jolly set of new bailiffs we are acquiring. Because I find that making a house really ugly is much more expensive than making it pretty but still it's worth it I think. And it's lovely being *in* London because now Rodd can go out with his girl friend[4] who has a spoon face & dresses at Gorringes & I can go to bed & this is fine for everybody's temper. Also I can go out with people like Raymond Mortimer[5] & Willie Maugham[6] who like the sound of their own voices punctuated with my giggle, but who hate being told about the origin of toll-gates by Rodd.[7] And all these things were more difficult at Rose Cottage. . . .

Lottie has 2 beautiful puppies which are a great help with the new carpets of course. Rodd plans to show them both on the principle that as they are quite different in every respect *one* is certain to win a prize.

There is a cousin of mine called Pamela Stanley[8] acting in New York. I wonder if she is any good.

Well goodbye & a lot of kisses, everyone is suffering from broken hearts here except me & I'm in love with Gladwyn [Jebb], otherwise I should be too.

> Nancy

broken ♡s on yr account of course I mean.

[1] Simon Elwes (1902–75). Painter. Married Nancy's sister-in-law, Gloria (Golly) Rodd, in 1926. 'Adored by most women & greatly liked by some men.' (NM to Viscountess Mersey, 11 March 1970)

[2] Nancy and Peter had moved to a small house overlooking the Regent's Canal.

[3] Chips Channon bought Kelvedon, near Ongar, in May 1937.

[4] Peter was having an affair with Mary Sewell, daughter of the architect Sir Edwin Lutyens.

[5] Raymond Mortimer (1895–1980). Critic and editor. Literary editor of the *New Statesman & Nation* 1935–47. He became a close friend of Nancy in Paris after the war and was, with Evelyn Waugh, her chief literary mentor. 'Raymond who is a sort of saint of literature in helping young writers . . . the last truly scholarly critic we have got.' (NM to Duchess of Devonshire, 11 April 1973)

[6] W. Somerset Maugham (1874–1965). Novelist and playwright. Married to Syrie Barnardo in 1916. In 1930 he had published *Cakes and Ale*.

[7] One of Peter's most recondite areas of knowledge was the toll-gate system of Great Britain.

[8] Hon. Pamela Stanley (1909–91). Daughter of 5th Baron Stanley of Alderley. Married Sir David Cunynghame in 1941. She was in New York playing in *Hamlet* with Leslie Howard.

To Jessica Mitford   12 Blomfield Road, W9
14 March 1937

Darling Sue[1]

I got back to find such a *mass* of things to do that I haven't time for a long letter.

I saw the family yesterday & they are miserable. Susan it isn't very respectable what you are doing[2] & I see their point of view I must say.

Oh dear you *were* stupid on the platform, those men were quite bamboozled until you got back on the train – battering on my door & asking if you were there. *Why* didn't you stop in the cabinet?[3]

Here is a letter from Rodd. I am inclined to agree with it – after all one has to live in this world *as it is* & society (I don't mean duchesses) can make things pretty beastly to those who disobey its rules.

Susan do come back. No Susan. Well Susan if anything happens don't forget there is a spare room here (£4.10. bed).

Love from
　　Sue

[1] Nancy and Jessica always wrote to one another as 'Susan'.
[2] Jessica had run away to Spain with her cousin Esmond Romilly who had joined the International Brigade. Nancy and Peter were sent by the Redesdales to try to persuade Jessica to return. They met up in France on 11 March, but Jessica refused to leave. Despite her parents' opposition and a pompous letter from Peter Rodd, which made the curious point that 'it is only in the Faubourg that you can get away with sexual irregularities', Jessica and Esmond were married in Bayonne on 18 May 1937.
[3] Nancy had tried to persuade Jessica to avoid reporters by hiding in the train lavatory.

To JESSICA MITFORD　　　　12 Blomfield Road, W9
20 July 1937

Darling Sooze
　　It seems to be rather a business to send even a narst diamond ring to France[1] so I thought I would wait perhaps until Mr (or Il Marchese) Dyer is going over to tell you some more dilishwish things we have said & give it to him to take, eh what?

Susan I am just off to Naples so do come along any time, let me know to Villa Trentaremi Posillipo Napoli[2] anyway write to your poor Susan there.

I must just tell you about the week end. Well our host took us to tea with the Minister for Overseas Trade & he begged Rodd to behave & so Rodd was very good & the MFOT was very pompously telling us about some Japanese delegates who had been staying with him & how one of them was ill & he then said to me rather difficult to know what to do with a sick Japanese & I hadn't been attending very much

THE HON. JESSICA MITFORD
IN SPAIN—*Exclusive Picture*

Daily Express picture of the Hon. Jessica Freeman - Mitford, Lord Redesdale's daughter, at Bermeo, near Bilbao. It was reported that she had gone to Spain to marry her cousin, Mr. Esmond Romilly. It is now understood that she is returning to England.

Daily Express, 9 March 1937

Sunday Pictorial, 11 December 1938. Lady Redesdale once commented rather sadly: 'Whenever I see the words "Peer's daughter" in a headline, I know it's going to be something about one of you children.'

so I said Oh *I* should send for the vet & oh Susan, Rodd & Edward Stanley simply rolled on the ground & nobody else laughed at all.

Sooze the aeroplane awaits you.

    your
        Susan

. . .

[1] Nancy wanted to send a wedding present to Jessica in Bayonne, where Esmond had found work with Reuters. 'I know it is nice to have things of popping value even if only for a few pounds.' (NM to Jessica Mitford, 14 July 1937)
[2] The summer retreat of Nancy's parents-in-law, Lord and Lady Rennell. 'According to Gerald [Berners], he and Gerry Wellesley and some others at the embassy in Rome twenty years before had held a competition for designing the most hideous house imaginable, and the winning drawing had been stuck on the wall of the Chancellery. Lady Rodd happened to see it. "My dream house!" she exclaimed, and asked if she might borrow the drawing. She used it for the Posillipo villa, a crazy jumble of styles.' Diana Mosley, *A Life of Contrasts*, p. 132.

To ROBERT BYRON   Alderley Park
20 December 1937   Chelford
                                                   Cheshire

Dearest Bert

I thought you might like to know my search has been almost *too* successful.[1] 10 000 letters all quite legible. However, as a start I have abstracted about 1000, from Maria Josepha S of A to her d in law Henrietta Maria S of A 1840–1850. Simply fascinating I think. I have been working 9 & 10 hours a day & am the Wonder of Cheshire, & have enjoyed every minute of it. Now the real work will begin.

They are *so* funny & at the same time disclose a character of such real goodness that I feel they must be of interest to the public although they only deal with family affairs. Really Maria Josepha's own jokes are only equalled by N Mitford's, her *gr gr gr* granddaughter, who will not, in this case, be obliged to invent ONE WORD.

Do tell Mr Young[2] if you see him I am really as much excited as if I had struck oil (& maybe I have).

How is Our Boy? Perhaps Mumsie will be the next gold medallist in the family – she fancies herself as a serious literary lady more than a little. Thank goodness I came here, none too soon as the papers were getting very mildewy in the loft to which your hero consigned them (you know he blew up his ancestral home,[3] some 54 rooms & now lives in a stable the low fellow).

Well, happy Chrissie boysie dear from
    Mum

(Now that is the kind of thing that drives the wretched reader of 100 years hence *nearly mad*. It took me a whole day to discover that the singing bird was really a gentleman called Dr Nightingale, & some of the jokes are too esoteric to be unravelled at all.)

---

[1] Nancy was editing the letters of her ancestress Maria Josepha, Lady Stanley of Alderley, and Maria Josepha's daughter-in-law, Henrietta Maria Stanley. These were published as *The Ladies of Alderley* (1938) and *The Stanleys of Alderley* (1939).
[2] G. M. Young (1883–1959). Historian, essayist, and friend of Robert Byron.
[3] Edward Stanley had demolished part of Alderley Park.

To ROBERT BYRON   West Wycombe Park[1]
13 August 1938   Bucks

Dear Bert

I think I ought to put you au fait of one or two munching teases which I tried out to good effect on the Girouards[2] last week end. First of all when they ask for the car to go to church one just says mium mium, licking (& smacking) the lips. This enrages them. Then, at bridge, one is heard to insinuate that those of Romish persuasion are not always perfectly straight as they need so desperately to win money for their indulgences. When they have made a rubber of 5 one asks politely how many years off that will be? If they say in superior tones that Protestant Churches are often locked up in the day time one observes that R. Catholic ones are always barred & bolted at night while nuns & their babies are being walled in. Which also accounts for loud & continuous music during the day & of course incense.

If they are sufficiently ill-advised as to leave a prayer book lying about one hands it to them, politely murmuring 'the menu I believe.'

I really quite *reduced* the Girouards by these tactics.

I am in the family way isn't it nice.[3] But only just so don't tell anybody as I don't want the Rodds to find out, they are such demons of gynaecological enthusiasm. Besides it may all come to nothing. I am awfully excited though.

I wonder what you are up to. Bobo is ill with pneumonia & pleurisy but not seriously, she has Hitler's dr[4] breathing down her neck also mama & next week papa & I shall be at Swinbrook looking after Debo. I put off going to the Hudsons[5] because of the journey & being careful but I believe Pete has gone. He has been in camp & I have heard absolutely nothing of him for days.

Diana is in the family way did you know[6] & I believe Nina.[7] I do hope that's true but have only heard it rumoured.

Well goodbye

Love from
      NR

What a nursery letter. But I have no other news. I do hope that war won't break out.

[1] Nancy was staying with Helen Dashwood ('Hell Bags').
[2] Richard Girouard was married to Lady Blanche de la Poer Beresford 1927–40.
[3] Nancy had been trying to have a baby for several years; when she had failed to conceive her gynaecologist recommended curettage. She became pregnant at the beginning of the summer but miscarried in September. Characteristically, the loss of her baby is not mentioned in any of her letters.
[4] Dr Theodore Morell.
[5] Viscount Hudson (1886–1957). Diplomat and politician. Minister of Agriculture for most of the war. Married Hannah Randolph in 1918.
[6] Alexander Mosley was born on 26 November 1938.
[7] Lord Reidhaven, later 13th Earl of Seafield, was born on 20 March 1939.

To Billa Harrod[1]   West Wycombe Park
29 October 1938   Bucks

Dearest Billa

I *was* disappointed at the result[2] – but on 2nd thoughts if pro Chamberlains are only 5–4 it only requires some further enormity on the part of the Govt: to swing the doubters, especially when the glorious memory of Godesberg[3] – an old man on his first flight – Mrs C on her knees in the Abbey – when I was a little boy etc etc has somewhat faded. I must say I do wish the socialist party or better still liberal party had one or two more solid figureheads.

The young prospective candidate (Cons: of course) for here dined last night. He said he was a pacifist, that England was always manufacturing quarrels & this must end, that he was glad of the Nazis as they will prevent, by their menace, the young of England from becoming decadent. Even Helen got a bit restive. I think ordinary people are at last getting sufficiently interested in politics to prevent all these ½ witted young public schoolers from being returned so easily in future don't you. I'm afraid Mr Lindsay was not a good candidate, why doesn't Roy stand next time? . . .

I so enjoyed our evening it was fun I wished there had been more time to chat. I will come & stay though & that will be better still. I'll suggest a date if I may next week – I'm going to Hannah Hudson & am not sure how long she expects me. It is rather nice there as Rob [Hudson] is in the govt & one hears things which sound impressive, also she is entirely on our side which is such a comfort & I suppose why Rob doesn't get into the Cab:

Much love from
    Nancy

[1] Wilhelmine (Billa) Cresswell (1911–). Married the economist Roy Harrod in January 1938. They lived in Oxford where he was University Lecturer in Economics. Nancy's friendship with Billa Harrod began in the early 1930s; when Nancy moved to Paris, Billa was one of the first visitors at rue Monsieur. She contributed to the character of Fanny in Nancy's novels, the sensible, down-to-earth narrator whose happy, long-lasting marriage and delight in her children contrasts with the fate of the heroine, Linda, and indeed with that of Nancy herself.
[2] In an Oxford by-election the pro-Chamberlain Quintin Hogg, later Lord Hailsham, had beaten the anti-Munich, Independent candidate, A. D. Lindsay. The Munich Conference which made Germany the dominant power in Europe took place on 29 September.
[3] Neville Chamberlain flew to Godesberg to meet Hitler on 27 September, to try to reach an agreement over Czechoslovakia.

To Billa Harrod   Shillinglee Park[1]
7 January 1939   Chiddingfold

Darling Billa
Clever punctual girl, many *heartfelt* congratulations I am awfully jealous. Give my love to Roy who I am sure is delighted with a boy.[2]

It is very nice here, I work all day & am tormented at meals by Eddie (Winterton) saying 'My dear Nancy I wish I could read you such an extraordinary despatch I have just had about Hitler – or Mus – or Carol – unfortunately it is confidential.' He regards Peter as a red agitator in the pay of Russia & Monica said would I like to stay here as a refugee, she thinks I look sufficiently Jewish, 'but I won't have Peter.'

I did simply love my visit to you, so comfy & such fun. Of course I know who *didn't* enjoy having *fussy old* Mrs Rodd there & I don't blame her I must say.

I hope you are feeling very well. I see Roy tried to carry a coffin into Downing Street the beastly red & was quite rightly thwarted by the noble constabulary.

Best love to all
      Nancy

[1] Nancy was staying with the 6th Earl Winterton (1883–1962). Irish peer and MP. Chancellor of the Duchy of Lancaster with a seat in the Cabinet 1938–9. Married Hon. Monica Wilson in 1924.
[2] Henry Harrod was born on 6 January 1939.

To Lady Redesdale   Tivoli-Hotel[1]
16 May 1939   Boulevard Clemenceau
                                     Perpignan

Darling Muv

(I have had a row with this hotel & we are leaving today.)

You can't imagine what it's like here, I never saw anybody work the way these people do, I haven't had a single word with Peter although I've been here 2 days. They are getting a boat off to Mexico next week with 600 families on board & you can suppose this is a job, reuniting these families.

The men are in camps, the women are living in a sort of gymnasium in the town & the children scattered all over France. Peter said yesterday one woman was really too greedy, she already has 4 children & she wants 3 more. I thought of you! These people will all meet on the quayside for the first time since the retreat.

Peter sees to everything, even down to how many S[anitary] T[owel]s are to be allowed! I believe he will be here for life, refugees are still pouring out of Spain where it seems the situation is impossible for ex-Government supporters & their families. Over 100 a day come out –

There is the original General Murgatroyd[2] here, called Molesworth oh goodness he is funny. He has been sent by the govt to help with the embarkation, speaks no French or Spanish but bursts into fluent Hindoostanee at the sight of a foreigner & wastes poor Peter's time in every possible way. All the same he is a nice old fellow & very pro refugee. Indeed no one who sees them could fail to be that, they are simply so wonderful. I haven't yet been to one of the awful camps, just the women's one in the town & to a hostel which Peter started at Narbonne where people who are got out of camps can be cleaned up & rested before they go off to their destination. There are about 70 there & it is very nice indeed, with a garden which they have planted with vegetables. It is run by an English girl entirely on her own there, most of the present occupants are going in this ship to Mexico.

Peter has 2 helpers, one called Donald Darling[3] is a young man who owned a travel agency in Barcelona & is now of course ruined. He only thinks of the refugees although his own future is in as much of a mess as theirs. The other is Humphrey Hare,[4] a writer who lives in the S. of France, came over to see the camps & stayed on. They both, like Pete, work 14 hours a day for no pay, & all three look absolutely done up. It is a most curious situation apparently the préfet here said 'supposing there were refugee camps for Norwegians in England & 3 young Frenchmen went over & began telling the English how they should be run' –

Actually however they have got the French quite fairly docile I can't imagine how! The French here are not very nice – I mean in the hotels & shops, apparently this is famous for being the nastiest part of France both as regards climate (there is a perpetual gale which never stops even in summer), people, food & scenery. Very unattractive. I must go & pack.

Love from
    NR

[1] Nancy had joined Peter in France where he was working as a volunteer among the thousands of refugees who had fled the Spanish Civil War.
[2] Character in *Highland Fling* based on Nancy's father. Adumbration of Uncle Matthew in *The Pursuit of Love*.
[3] Portrayed as Robert Parker in *The Pursuit of Love*.
[4] Humphrey Hare (d. 1965). 'Randolph Pine, a young writer who, having led a more or less playboy existence in the South of France, had gone to fight in Spain, and was now working in Perpignan from a certain feeling of responsibility towards those who had once been fellow soldiers.' *The Pursuit of Love*, p. 117.

To Lady Redesdale   Hotel de France
25 May 1939   Quai Sadi-Carnot
                                     Perpignan

Darling Muv

If you could have a look, as I have, at some of the less agreeable results of fascism in a country I think you would be less anxious for the swastika to become a flag on which the sun never sets. And, whatever may be the *good* produced by that régime, that the first result is always a horde of unhappy refugees cannot be denied.

Personally I would join hands with the devil himself to stop any further extension of the disease. As for encirclement, if a person goes mad he is encircled, *not out of any hatred* for the person but for the safety of his neighbours & the same applies to countries. Furthermore, I consider that if the Russian alliance[1] does not go through we shall be at war in a fortnight, & as I have a husband of fighting age I am not particularly anxious for that eventuality.

You began this argument so don't be cross if I say what I think!

Well we got our ship off. There was a fearful hurricane – she couldn't get into Port-Vendres so all the arrangements had to be altered & she was sent to Sète (150 miles away from P.V.) & at 3 hours' notice special trains had to be changed etc etc the result was Peter was up for 2 *whole* nights, never went to bed at all. However he is none the worse; I was up all yesterday night as the embarkation went on until 6 A.M. & the people on the quay had to be fed & the babies given their bottles. There were 200 babies under 2 & 12 women are to have babies on board. One poor shell-shocked man went mad & had to be given an anaesthetic & taken off, but apart from that all went smoothly if slowly. The women were on the quayside first & then the men arrived. None of them had seen each other since the retreat & I believe thought really that they wouldn't find each other then, & when they did you never saw such scenes of hugging. The boat sailed at 12 yesterday, the pathetic little band on board played first God Save the King, for us, then the Marseillaise & then the Spanish National Anthem. Then the poor things gave 3 Vivas for Espana which they will never see again. I don't think there was a single person not crying – I have never cried so much in my life. They had all learnt to say Goodbye & thank you & they crowded round us so that we could hardly get off the ship. Many of them are great friends of Peter & I know a lot of them too by now as some have been working in our office, & it was really sad to see them go – to what? If all Mexicans are as great horrors as the delegate here they will have a thin time I am afraid. Franco's radio has announced that the ship will not be allowed to reach her destination & we shall all feel anxious until she has safely left Madeira.

And now there still remain over 300 000 poor things to be dealt with, 500 000 counting the women, & more arriving all the time.

The Red X are not much help, they issue shorts which Spaniards abominate, having a sense of dignity, & refuse to help with special diet for the many cases of colitis in the camps.

Milly[2] had quads, it seems she is not quite well which worries me.

I expect I shall come home soon as we can't really afford for me to be here & keep B. Road going.

Much love fr
  NR

[1] In April the USSR had proposed a defensive alliance with Britain.
[2] Nancy's French bulldog.

To LADY REDESDALE   12 Blomfield Road, W9
4 September 1939

Darling Muv

Thank you very much for the heavenly time at Inch K,[1] I really did love it.

I am driving an ARP car every night from 8–8.[2] So far have had only one go of it & feel more or less O.K. (it is mostly waiting about of course). Soon I hope they will have more drivers. There is only one other woman & she & the men in my lot (about 30) have had no sleep for 4 nights & have to work in the day, they are all in & all going on again tonight.

When I went to fetch my car from the garage which is lending it, I immediately & in full view of the owners crashed it into another car, wasn't it awful. It is a large Ford. However I have it under control now but driving in the dark is too devilish. All the other people of course are charming, they think I'm rather a joke, so obviously incompetent. I have signed on for a year.

I wonder if you have nice children & are nice to them. The girl who deputized for me on Sat said the country people were too dreadful & the London ones too wonderful.

I must now go to sleep.

Love from
  NR

Peter is working day & night at a 1st aid post in Chelsea – our Mabel is really wonderful, quite unmoved when we cower in the shelter & has suddenly become an excellent cook!
I suppose Debo is being receptionist to torpedoed Americans.

[1] Inchkenneth, a small island in the Inner Hebrides. Lord and Lady Redesdale visited it on impulse in 1938 and bought it with the proceeds from the sale of Swinbrook. Lord Redesdale gave the island to Tom but lived there himself during much of the war. Lady Redesdale moved to Inchkenneth in 1944 and spent every summer there until the end

of her life. Nancy dreaded her visits: 'There is a perpetual howling wind, shrieking gulls, driving rain, water water wherever you look, streaming mountains with waterfalls every few yards, squelch squelch if you put a foot out of doors (which of course I don't). The only colour in the landscape is provided by dead bracken & seaweed which exactly matches it. No heather, black rocks shiny like coal with wet, & a little colourless grass clinging to them.' (NM to Diana Mosley, 28 September 1946)

[2] Nancy was working as an Air Raid Precautions volunteer driver at the First Aid Post, St Mary's Hospital, Paddington.

To Violet Hammersley[1]   S.M.H. 1st Aid Post
15 September 1939   Praed Street
                                                          London, W2

Darling Mrs H.

Thank you for your letter. I can't remember if I was here when I last wrote, this is my 9th day & feels like 7 years (which I am told the war will last). Anyway in case I didn't I must tell you about the foreheads. Well my job is writing on the foreheads of dead & dying in indelible pencil. *What* I write I haven't yet discovered. What happens when a coloured man presents *his* forehead I also ignore. I was just about to ask all these little details when the Queen arrived to see over (in fawn) so I have never found out. Isn't it awful.

Meanwhile I sit twiddling my indelible pencil & *aching* for a forehead to write on. I think I shall write Mrs Hammersley 31 Tite Street & see what happens, it might produce interesting complications in a case of loss of memory.

I simply can't remember what I told you so you must forgive me if I repeat myself. Sitting in this hateful cellar (gas & therefore air proof, electric light all day & cold as the grave) my brain has become like the inside of a bad walnut. 11 A.M.–7 P.M. are my hours.

Well the family. Muv has gone finally off her head. She seems to regard Adolf[2] as her favourite son in law (the kind of which people say he has been like a *son* to me) & when one says Peter has joined up she replies I expect he will be shot soon which is so encouraging. Poor thing I suppose she is quite wretched so one must make allowances. Bobo we hear on fairly good authority is in a concentration camp for Czech women which much as I deplore it has a sort of poetic justice.[3] Peter is going to make the Aostas[4] get her out in a month or two when she has had a sufficient dose to wish to go. This seems a sound plan. Farve has publicly recanted like Latimer, in the *Daily Mirror*, & said he was mistaken all along (& how). What have THEY done now any different to before, I ask myself.

Decca. I believe it would be of no use for them to return[5] as I am *told* the army won't take anybody who fought in Spain. Haven't heard since the war began.

Tom is stationed near us & comes to dinner most days. He is tired but cheerful.

Robert [Byron] is coming next week as P.G. I hope to have 2 P.G.s when Peter goes as it is gloomy living alone, but he won't be leaving it seems for 3 weeks.

I saw the Scallywags[6] at Patrick Kinross' (Balfour), they were full of pep. He of course is looking for a job in London of *non military* character.

I really see nobody, impossible to lunch out & in the evening I am too tired & it is too dark & frightening to go out.

Darling I am *so* pleased you are better, that is a ray of good news, better than the Poles holding Wooch [Lódź] or whatever it's called.

I find I can only read old dry books like Carlyle's *Life of Sterling* & Macaulay's *Essays*, isn't it funny. Luckily & thank goodness the London Library is still with us.

The war has had an extraordinary effect on our new maid – from being unable to boil an egg she has suddenly become a cordon bleu. What can this mean?

I must now go to a gas lecture, my one relaxation. Do write again I long for letters – one is more isolated here than ordinarily living in the country.

Much love
NR

[1] This is among the first letters of Nancy to Violet Hammersley to have survived, although their correspondence probably started much earlier. In 1960, four years before she died, Violet Hammersley returned more than three hundred of Nancy's letters. With eventual publication in mind, Nancy began to annotate them, adding surnames and a few short explanations or comments. But she was realistic: 'I admit they are rather amusing, but nothing can be done with them for many years . . . Shall we ask Debo if they can go into the Chatsworth archive? In 100 years' time somebody (some dear old Chink) will like to read them.' (NM to Violet Hammersley, 5 September 1960)
[2] Lady Redesdale first met Hitler in 1935, while staying with Unity in Munich, and was unimpressed by him. In 1938 she attended the Nuremberg rally and was invited to a party given by Hitler for foreign guests. From then on she came to admire Nazism and believed that England should not go to war with Germany.
[3] Unity attempted suicide on 3 September by shooting herself with a pistol. The bullet lodged in her brain but did not kill her. She was taken to hospital in Munich where she remained unconscious for two months. The Germans made the matter a state secret which allowed all kinds of wild rumours to circulate, including the one about a concentration camp. News of her illness eventually reached her family at the beginning of

October but it was not until Christmas that she was well enough to travel home.
[4] The Duke of Aosta, head of the Italian army in North Africa during the war, was a cousin of the King of Italy and a neighbour of the Rennells in Italy.
[5] Disillusioned with life in England, Jessica and Esmond Romilly had moved to America in February 1939.
[6] Cyril and Jean Connolly.

To Violet Hammersley   S.M.H. 1st Aid Post
10 October 1939   Praed Street, W2

Darling

At risk of crossing letters I *must* write & tell you of the Great White's Scandal. Well, about ten days ago Ed Stanley played backgammon with your charming neighbour (grandson, as I believe he designates himself, of the Bloody Bard) Lord Tennyson,[1] & lost £800. In these days of capital depreciation you can imagine how inconvenient poor Eddy found it to sell out enough shares to pay in full. He did so however in 2 days. A week ago last Monday they played again & Edward won £3700, & at the end of the last game, which alone had doubled up to about £2000, Lord Tennyson said that Ed was a cheat & that he refused to pay. The cheque for £800 meanwhile had been cashed. The following day Peter was sent for by Edward to White's where, he says, the spectacle of the 2 lords at the bar* surrounded each by his own adherents & both busily canvassing the committee was a very moving one. It was enhanced by the fact that Edward had just come from Randolph's wedding & was in the full fig of his *grandfather's* GREY FROCK coat with a giant chrysanthemum in his button hole & a grey top hat still firmly planted on the back of his head.

You can imagine how all London hummed with the Great White's Scandal, how a new Tranby Croft case was envisaged, how the war was forgotten & *even Randolph's wedding* (of which more presently) faded into the background of men's minds. However nearly everybody was finally on Edward's side; Lord Rosebery said to Ld T in Peter's hearing 'you know Lionel this is not the first time this has happened – I remember very well a case of a chemmy game at the Ritz where you lost £800 & refused to pay, saying there had been cheating.' 'I did pay however' says Ld T. 'Well' says Ld R 'Clare's trustees paid if that's what you mean.' In the end, after a great deal of delightful chi-chi it was settled by the committee of White's that Ld T should disgorge the original £800, apologize to Ed & resign from White's.[2]

Apparently it was clear that he really couldn't pay so much as £5 & nobody wanted a first class scandal. So I hope you enjoyed all that.

Randolph's Wedding

Again we are indebted to that entirely admirable character Lord Stanley of Alderley for the following narrative. It seems that his lordship was taking a cordial with Lady Diana Cooper[3] when in came Randolph with Miss Digby[4] whom he had met that day for the first time. Edward knew Miss D already, a pretty, luscious little piece, & so he asked her out to dinner but she said she was already going out with Randolph. Next morning at 8 Edward was rung up by Miss D who sounded rather distracted & said he must go round to see her at once. Curiosity of course prised him out of his bed & round he went, & found Miss D in quite a stew saying she had promised to marry Randolph. What! You only met him yesterday. Yes & he says he is not in love with me but I look healthy & he wishes to perpetuate the name of Churchill before he is killed. Edward then spent 2 hours giving the girl fatherly advice, punctuated no doubt with chaste kisses, but all, as you know, in vain. It seems that she was the 8th girl Randolph had proposed to since the war began, his best effort being 3 in one evening.

Tom is now staying with me, ill. *His* leisure hours are beguiled by a belle from Watford.

Well darling where is that letter?

Much love
    NR

* You can guess to what sort of bar I refer – not that of the H of C for instance, nor that to which the Bloody Bard himself referred when he said Let there be no moaning at the bar when I put out to sea.

[1] 3rd Baron Tennyson (1889–1951). Married to Hon. Clarissa (Clare) Tennant 1918–28 and to Carroll Donner in 1934.

[2] He did not resign.

[3] Lady Diana Manners (1892–1986). Reigning beauty of her age. Married Alfred Duff Cooper in 1919. Nancy and Lady Diana knew one another only slightly at this stage; they became friends after the war in Paris when Duff Cooper was Ambassador.

[4] Hon. Pamela Digby (1920–). Married to Randolph Churchill 1939–46, to the American producer Leland Hayward 1960–71, and to the American statesman W. Averell Harriman in 1971. Latterly a legendary Washington hostess and leading light of the Democratic Party.

To Violet Hammersley   S.M.H. 1st Aid Post
14 October 1939   Praed Street, W2

Darling Mrs Hammersley

Your letter duly popped into a shagreen cigarette box, hope Rodd doesn't smoke it. How awful for you having Polish friends, thank goodness I don't know any.

There isn't a pin to put between Nazis & Bolshies – if one is a Jew one prefers one & if an aristocrat the other, that's all as far as I can see. *Fiends.*

Oh dear the *Royal Oak*[1] I believe Dick Bailey[2] is on board. It has just come through on the radio, I do feel worried for poor Aunt Weenie[3] (perhaps I am wrong however let's hope so).

Peter is all dressed up in his uniform looking very pretty – he goes to Essex for training on Sat: next. Tom has been staying with me. Now mind you come & stay soon for ages, London I am sure is the only endurable place in these days. I'm simply as happy as a bird, I adore my work here (chiefly because I have nothing whatever to do which I adore doing. I read Macaulay's *Hist of Eng* all day) & in my spare time I dig for victory with the oddest looking results.

The family leave their fastness next week for High Wycombe. What *will* they do there? I really think it rather queer that out of 7 able-bodied Mitfords only Tom and I are attempting any sort of war work.

Is Hitler hedging from conscience or nerves I would love to know. I think quite likely the former – he can't want all these millions of Germans to be killed & surely at least he loves his own people.

I am hoarding, in a very small way, shoes & olive oil. I so dread not having enough fat for cooking. I have also bought a length of tweed for making up next year, & 12 pkts of you know what, which I'm told are already nearly unobtainable! That's all!

Now come & stay very soon & we will have some lovely bridge at the new WAR STAKES (based on the theory of money now being valueless & anyway we shall all be dead soon).

Much love
    NR

[1] HMS *Royal Oak* had been reported sunk at Scapa Flow that day.
[2] Richard Bailey, Nancy's first cousin, survived the war.
[3] Dorothy (Weenie) Bowles (1885-1971). Lady Redesdale's younger sister, married to Percy Bailey.

To Jessica Romilly   S.M.H. 1st Aid Post
25 October 1939   Praed Street, W2

Really Susan you Americans. Of course it's worse to have Hitler & Stalin than Eddie [Winterton] & Rob [Hudson]. The proof of the pudding is in the eating. I mean if I saw Eddie or Rob in Harrods I should say hullo duckie but if I saw Hit or Stal I should say I think I had better trot, & trot upstairs to the loo & lock myself in for hours. See?

Anyway Eddie is in Washington so I expect you have met up with him at parties etc & I hope you were nice to him. I am dining with Monica [Winterton] tonight.

I shan't know what to do with your friend[1] but I'll try, but Americans seem so queer. I mean in books they are always wallowing in blood & insides etc but in real life they are so terrified of war & air raids it all seems different.

Hon Henderson[2] has just arrived from the island & lunched with me here. She is amazed by London, all the sand bags & paper on the windows & balloons etc. It must really look queer when you see it for the first time, it has all happened round me so to speak. The black out is heaven when there is a moon, so pretty, & of course it is lovely having nearly no traffic.

Peter looks divine in his uniform – masses of gold on his hat & a *wonderful* coat lined with scarlet satin which cost £25. Certainly it is nice to be in the Guards for the above mentioned reasons. He has got about 6 of his best friends in too so they will all go off together & that is nice too.

Poor Bowd *do* write to her it must be lonely, & the *D. Express* say that she is ill with attempted suicide which might I feel be true.[3]
Next day
I fetched your letter[4] from Blomfield so as to answer the questions.

1. No, Eddie & Rob don't note that they are as bad as Hit & Stal for above mentioned reasons (& nor do I).

2. I gather the Fem[5] is engaged upon an acrimonious correspondence with her MP about how wicked it is to attack dear little Hittle. Last war she would have found herself in jail – now however:

3. Pacifists are allowed to bleat as much as they like & Mosley & the C.P. hold meetings daily & drop pamphlets on everybody. There is a Communist meeting every day at 4 in Star St (near here) & I often go as it is really funny. But all our Cudm[6] friends seem to have gone poum[7] & I think most of the French ones have too.

4. No, spy hunting, chivalry to enemy aliens & nice kisses for conchies are a feature of the war.

5. I think most people do hope for Winston but old Chamberpot says he feels years younger & better than ever, so – as there won't be any elections – I doubt if they'll get him out.

Giles[8] is still on the *D.E.* He & Rodd have had a fearful row & Rodd lost his temper & was most awfully rude (quite like Farve, & I have never seen it happen before, I was quite shaken up) so I don't suppose we shall see him again. I am sorry really as I like him.

Well they say there'll be air raids soon so perhaps there'll be something to do in this place after all. At present I write letters & knit & read & write a novel for 7 hours in the freezing cold. The other people are *heaven* luckily.

Oh Susan, Milly. Well I hardly like to say it but she had her puppies (they are called the Wings, right wing & left wing) in your armchair when nobody was looking. So we had to have a new seat put on it. Otherwise your furniture is O.K. & Mark (brains for breakfast)[9] has your bed – I evacuated it as Kew is supposed to be safe.*

Do write again soon. I will note the war graphs[10] for you as they occur.

Love from
   NR

* Also all yr eggs are not now in 1 basket for incendiary bombs.

---

[1] Jessica had injudiciously given an American acquaintance, Joan White, an introduction to Nancy.

[2] Deborah Mitford. 'Hon Henderson comes from a Honnish poem based on two sources: John Anderson my Jo John (Burns) hence Hon Henderson my Ho Hon; and Lars Porsena of Clusium. Hence Hon Henderson my Ho Hon / By the nine Gods she swore / That the great House of Henderson / Should suffer wrong no more.' (Jessica Treuhaft to the editor.)

[3] '. . . Unity made up her mind that if it [war] came she herself would disappear from the scene. Her love of Germany was deep, but it was equalled by her love of England. Rather than see these two countries tear each other to pieces she preferred to die.' Diana Mosley, *A Life of Contrasts*, p. 155.

[4] Jessica's letter has not survived.

[5] Lady Redesdale.

[6] 'Communist' in Boudledidge.

[7] POUM, the Marxist party during the Spanish Civil War.

[8] Giles Romilly, Esmond's elder brother, was a journalist on the *Daily Express*.

[9] Mark Ogilvie-Grant. ' "Brains for breakfast, Mark!" Farve roared genially at one of his capriciously chosen favourites, who, to maintain status, had staggered uncertainly into the dining-room, looking haggard and drooping, on the dot of eight.' Jessica Mitford, *Hons and Rebels*, p. 32.

[10] 'N & I were travelling . . . and I picked up the *D. Telegraph* & said "I must just note the graph". For some reason N. thought that very funny so it was used for ever – for example, "I long to note your graph" meant "I long to see you".' (Jessica Treuhaft to the editor.)

To Violet Hammersley   S.M.H. 1st Aid Post
30 October 1939   Praed Street, W2

Darling

Oh I have such a dreadful cold *and* the cold in this place – I think I am one of those unsuspected heroines.

Poor Bobo, of course we have no news. They say it is attempted suicide. I remember so well, some 5 years ago Peter wrote an immense letter to Farve begging him to remove her from a situation which *must* lead to tragedy. The family were very pooh pooh-ey & thought it all great impertinence. Fools.

Can't think of anything jolly to tell you. I am writing a novel.[1] As I write it here with enormous va et vient, radio etc I should think it will read very queerly. It is about me married to Francis Rodd[2] & Peter is my lover & Mary Rodd is Francis's mistress. Hope you've got there.

Your lover Edward [Stanley] has lent me his house so I shall make a clear profit on my let except for those 7/6 in the poundses. I lunched with him yesterday he was very outrageous – looking very pretty in sailors uniform though not so pretty as Pete.

I have chummed up with 2 heavenly French colonels who are over here on a mission. They intersperse gallantry with dissertations on the cultural bounds of the Roman Empire which I very much like. They are coming to dinner on Wed. They also say we shall win the war & they say it so much as if it were a matter of course that one feels quite jollied up.

I *dote* on your letters how could you doubt it?

Dined with mama last night she is *impossible*. Hopes we shall lose the war & makes no bones about it. Debo is having a wild time with young cannon fodders at the Ritz etc. Apparently Muv said to her '*never* discuss politics, not even for 5 minutes, with Nancy.' Rather as some devout RC mama might shield her little one from a fearful atheist!

Oh my headache.

Much love
    NR

[1] *Pigeon Pie* (1940). 'Published on 6th May 1940 it was an early and unimportant casualty of the real war which was then beginning.' (NM in the introduction to the second edition of the novel, 1951.)
[2] Hon. Francis Rodd (1895-1978). Peter Rodd's eldest brother, succeeded as 2nd Baron Rennell in 1941. Married Hon. Mary Smith in 1928.

To MARK OGILVIE-GRANT   12 Blomfield Road, W9
13 November 1939

Must tell you how the book is developing. Well you are called Mr Ivor King the King of Song & your wigless head[1] horribly battered is found on the Pagoda (headless wig, favourite, on Green) so you are presumed dead & there is a Catholic, because you are one, mem: service at which Yvonne [Rodd] appears as a Fr. widow. Well as you were about to open a great world campaign of Song Propaganda for the BBC, SABOTAGE is suspected –
   UNTIL
   your *dreadful* old voice is heard in Germany doing anti-British propaganda & singing songs like 'Land of Dope you're Gory'.
   Well both the English speaking and Catholic worlds are appalled & yr wife the Papal Duchess, the only woman to be buried inside the Vatican grounds is quickly dug up & removed to the Via della Propaganda. Pope diplomatically explains this by saying that owing to petrol shortage some of the *younger* Cardinals are learning to bycycle (*can't* spell it) & unseemly for them to continually fall over the P.D.'s grave.
   Well of course in the end you have been a gallant old spy all along & you are made an English Bart & Papal Duke & covered with praise from all.
   So –
   Darling our lovely lunch & heavenly flowers. I must see you soon for COPY.

        NR

Think of some wonderful old songs for me.[2]

[1] The main character in *Pigeon Pie* is recognisably Mark Ogilvie-Grant. In Nancy's unpublished story 'The Old Ladies', the Old Gentleman wears a wig, 'apparently less from motives of deceit than as a jolly ornament, for he would often take it off in order to scratch his head, or even to wave it at the ducks in the park.'
[2] Mark had a good voice and used to enjoy singing around the piano at Swinbrook.

To Jessica Romilly   S.M.H. 1st Aid Post
23 November 1939   Praed Street, W2

Darling Soo

Oh Miss White. Thinking of another & oh how different Miss W.[1] I asked her to stay & she stayed a week & would be there now only I let the house. Susan how could you? All I can say is she's the first American I have ever met & if they are all like that you must be *mad* to stay there & like all mad people convinced you are sane. I would rather have bombs I would rather be killed I would rather see Hitler & Stalin in Harrods every day – in other words Susan I do *not* like Miss W. Enough of this painful topic.*

I have let the house & been *lent* another which you must say is clever.

I am also writing a funny book about spies it is very funny indeed (*I* think!)[2]

London is really very jolly although I believe we shall soon all be starving, the jokes are good & the parties incessant.

Susan really about Miss W – do tell the put [point]. She says she gave you all her summer clothes so I suppose in a way . . . But I can't tell you what she is like as a guest – & she never wrote to thank or telephoned or anything after a *whole week* which you must say is queer (& never gave me any winter clothes either so I suppose my luck was out). Next time you send somebody let them be nicer Susan because of course I took her completely on trust after your letter although Edward Stanley who knows her did warn me about her.

However she has given me a mass of ideas for my book in which the chief spies are 2 Americans called Heatherley Egg (Heth to his friends) & his girl friend Florence. But do write & tell about her & was it just a tease or what? I mean it *was* a tease but was it meant to be?

Cord[3] is having another baby in March. I hardly see the family at all except for Swine [Deborah] occasionally.

I think I shall be leaving here soon as the wives of officers have masses of odd jobs to do for the regiment & I think that would be more interesting in its way. Fancy all the men are Welsh so Rodd is learning it like mad he says they are terribly nice, & he adores the whole thing & you shld *just see* the prettiness of his clothes. Also I can travel 1st class for nothing which wld be heaven except that, working here every day I never leave London, & I can't take taxis for nothing though I feel that would be only fair.

Now Soo don't think I am beastly about Miss White but tell – Miss

Wilde was HORRIFIED. Poor Miss Wilde she is very ill but very cheerful & sends you her best love & so do I.

>   love from.
>   Susan

* Miss W's young man thinks as I do & is refusing to marry her.

[1] Dorothy (Dolly) Wilde; the attractive and witty lesbian daughter of Oscar Wilde's brother Willie. Well-known in Paris in the circle of Natalie Barney. She died of an overdose in 1941.
[2] *Pigeon Pie* was to have been called *The Secret Weapon: A Wartime Receipt.*
[3] Diana Mosley. Her son Max was born on 13 April 1940.

To Violet Hammersley   Old Mill Cottage
7 January 1940   High Wycombe

Darling I hasten to write a word (I am struggling as you know to finish a book).

The whole thing is most poignant.[1] She is like a child in many ways & has very much lost her memory (a mercy I expect) does not know why she was ill but seems to think the doctor made a hole in her head. The bullet is still there & must be removed presently.

She shot herself in a sort of public garden, was seen to do so. They fetched a nurse to the hospital saying 'you can go on your holiday tomorrow, she cannot live the night.'

She is very happy to be back, keeps on saying 'I thought you all hated me but I don't remember why.' She said to me You are not one of those who would be cruel to somebody are you? So I said I was very much against that.

She saw Mr X[2] continually, the last time 2 days before she left. Don't tell this. She was unconscious for 2 months.

I think that is all of interest, such a scribble but you do understand. They were literally hunted by the press who, it is thought, caused their ambulance to break down so that they could get a picture. Of course M & F were *not* clever –!

Much love darling.

I am staying here for the present to help a little with her.

>   NR

[1] Nancy had been to a nursing home in Oxford to see Unity following her return from Germany on 3 January. When Unity was well enough to travel, Hitler had arranged for her to be sent from Munich to a clinic in Berne where Lady Redesdale and Deborah went to bring her home.
[2] Hitler.

Unity Mitford Back In
England To-day

Special Ambulance Train Supplied By Hitler : Father's Long Vigil

MISS UNITY MITFORD, the 25-year-old daughter of Lord Redesdale and the former friend of Hitler, is arriving back in England to-day.

She is travelling in an ambulance train supplied by Hitler. Her mother and sister are with her.

Miss Mitford has been in Munich since the war began. According to reports received in this country she now has a bullet wound in the head.

Father Waits

Wrapped in a muffler and heavy overcoat, Lord Redesdale waited all yesterday at Folkestone, pacing anxiously up and down, for the arrival of the cross-Channel boat.

As the train sped from Germany Miss Mitford lay on a stretcher talking to her mother and her younger sister Deborah.

It was thought probable that if conditions were favourable the stretcher, on which Miss Mitford lies, could be placed in an aeroplane to-day and the rest of the journey to England made by air.

In London

It was a day or so before Christmas that Lord Redesdale and his family learned that his daughter was out of Germany.

Directly Miss Mitford reaches this country arrangements have been made to take her direct to London, possibly to a nursing home.

Miss Unity Mitford

Evening News, 2 January 1940. Four months after her attempted suicide in Munich, Unity was well enough to return home to England

Daily Mail, 7 January 1940

To Violet Hammersley   Old Mill Cottage
27 January 1940   High Wycombe

Darling

Now you mustn't feel low, that is playing into Hitler's (and Muv's) hands. I say what a new horror, have you seen – the Nazis are employing pigmy spies so small that they can hide in drawers. I just *daren't* open mine now to look for a hanky.

You see I don't mind the atrocities quite so much now Peter & Christopher[1] are in uniform & marching off to the rescue. When it tortured me was when your friend Chamberlain was offering that gout-twisted hand to the chief perpetrators. Did I tell you I sat next to the Polish Ambassador at lunch & he said the Nazi atrocities were 100% worse than the Russian ones. He was very much surprised (because I imagine Poles hate the Russians far more really than Germans) at how decently the Russians were behaving, to all except the gentry who they shoot, as he says, without tortures & indignities first. The rest of the people are allowed to live in peace, & this is not so in the German part.

I got *Why Britain*[2] – oh too excellent & so funny. I have bought several copies & sent them to various people – feel it can't be too widely read. How funny he is about Chamberlain, very friends Romans countrymen sort of praise!

Such a disgusting day & I am off to a smart luncheon party – how to arrive with clean stockings.

Nothing from Oxford, where Bobo is. When Muv rings up it is always from her room so she can't say much, perhaps she does it on purpose.

28 January

Well I went out to lunch & stayed to dinner it was really very nice.

When I told about the midget spies Eddie [Winterton] said he had seen in *The Times* that Mrs (Gouty) Chamberlain now gives midget sandwiches at her teas what can this portend?

On my way I saw in the bus a lecture advertised in the Cinema here

Mad Europe Gallops to Destruction
Does God hold the reins?

I must go & find out.

Lady Colefax[3] is very nice isn't she really. She says she is a cousin of my mother in law & I see points of resemblance especially in looks – she has a sort of negroid type I think. Also that great energy.

Milly's baby is too angelic & I am in full swing of puppy life, which as you know I can't have too much of. She is a week old today & soon her eyes will open.

Isn't this a good long letter quite a Ladies of Wilmington effort.[4]
Much love

They say *everyone* in the army is ill with 'flu & terrible after effects of going about with temperatures – young Ednam[5] has meningitis at Windsor from this. Don't tell Monica.[6] I do hope her husband is better now & will get his commission soon.

NR

[1] Christopher Hammersley; Violet's eldest son.

[2] Harold Nicolson, *Why Britain is at War*, published as a Penguin Special in November 1939.

[3] Sibyl Halsey (1874–1950). Married Sir Arthur Colefax in 1901. Hostess in literary and political London, famous for her wartime luncheons at the Dorchester. In 1938 she went into partnership with John Fowler and established the interior decorating company Colefax & Fowler.

[4] Violet Hammersley lived at a house called Wilmington on the Isle of Wight. An indirect reference to *The Ladies of Alderley*, the selection of her ancestors' letters which Nancy edited in 1938.

[5] Viscount Ednam (1920–). Eldest son of 3rd Earl of Dudley. Married to Stella Carcano 1946–61 and to Maureen Swanson in 1961.

[6] Violet Hammersley's daughter, married to David Stokes, an architect.

To Violet Hammersley   Old Mill Cottage
10 February 1940   High Wycombe

Darling

The Oxford doctor seems to have told Muv she will get quite all right but to have spoken very differently to Farve. I think, for her sake, one should cling to the former don't you?[1]

Things are terrible – Muv & Farve absolutely at loggerheads. Muv goes so far as to say now *'When* the Germans have won you'll see, everything will be wonderful & they'll treat us very differently to those wretched beastly Poles'. It drives poor Farve absolutely dotty & can you wonder.

I had a wildly gay week in London staying with ma-in-law. Edward [Stanley] has been on leave – he knocked Ld Castlerosse down for saying he was an embusqué[2] & was sent for by 4 admirals & nearly dismissed the service. However it has all ended for the best as he has his wish & will go to sea. So he gave a grand huge party at the Ritz & will soon be off. Thank heaven Pete was not with him say I or there would no doubt have been the same séance with 4 generals.

Peter's course at Cambridge – prepare to laugh. It seems he is to do German local government with a view to becoming a gauleiter when the war is over. I think it's a wonderfully foreseeing idea actually & would never have credited our Gov with so much gumption.

I dined with the Jessels[3] – Dick says we have confiscated £4,000,000 worth of contraband from the American *mails*, no wonder they want a peace move. Dear little treasures.

Then my ma-in-law had a tea for Mrs Gouty,[4] pure heaven. During the course of it I overheard:

'Do tell me Lady Rennell, is that a Pintoricchio?'

'No! It's ME.'

. . . Robert is arriving for the day so I must go.

Goodbye & much love from
    NR

---

[1] Lady Redesdale consistently tried to play down the gravity of Unity's condition; a belief in her eventual recovery made the difficult task of looking after her a little easier to bear. But Unity had suffered severe brain damage and was left with the mental age of a young child. 'She had blasted away the pains, as well as the faculties, of her adult self, and henceforth her smaller miseries were no more than her diminished abilities could cope with. In a sense, therefore, her suicide attempt had been successful.' Jonathan Guinness, *The House of Mitford*, p. 438.

[2] A shirker from enlistment for active service.

[3] Richard Hugh Jessel (1896–1979). Financier. Worked at Ministry of Economic Warfare 1939–41. Married to Margaret (Peggy) Lewis in 1923.
[4] Mrs Neville Chamberlain.

To JESSICA ROMILLY   12 Blomfield Road, W9
1 March 1940

Darling Sooze

I haven't written for ages but it is so difficult to think of things to say when I haven't seen you for so long.

Dear Miss White rushes from job to job it seems in Gloucestershire. Anyway she's off my conscience now I know she's not your B.F. Simon [Elwes] says she cried on his shoulder until his suit was wet like a sponge & that the wet patch dried with a white edge (salt, Susan).

My book, *Pigeon Pie*, will be out in another month. You are in it, called Mary Pencill, & Eddie Winterton & Co are called Ned & Fred. The chief character is Muck (brains for breakfast). I will send you a copy, or can't one? Anyway R. Savage[1] is trying to get it published in America but I don't imagine it would tickle them much, myself.

Bowd is so wonderfully much better, I expect you have heard from Fem of her really remarkable recovery. When first I saw her I had to go out of the room to cry, but now she is her old self again. Of course very ill still, but the same person, not a *quite* different one. I have been there a lot.

Milly has an illegitimate child called Abbey (because conceived in Westminster A.). Although only 6 weeks old she is a *terror* & also rules the entire household more than even my dogs usually do. She is like a very evil teddy bear.

Well Sooze I don't know how you can stick America though I expect *Gone with the Wind* is nice & they say we shan't have it here until after the war so p'raps you were right.

    Much love
      NR

[1] Raymond Savage; Nancy's literary agent at the time.

To MARK OGILVIE-GRANT   Weston Manor[1]
24 May 1940   Olney
                                Buckinghamshire

Dear Old Creature

Knowing what an old skin wig you are I had planned to send you a copy but when I got home I found that Rodd had bagged all my comp: copies to give to his brother officers. So now I am trying to get one back but it looks to me as if the Germans will get it first.

I went to Essex to see Rodd. He now has a company (don't expect you know what that is) & is very busy. It is fantastic down there, all roads barricaded after 8 p.m. & so on.

I am thankful Sir Oswald Quisling has been jugged[2] aren't you but think it quite useless if Lady Q is still at large. . . .

Well no more news.

Love from
    NR

P.S. *Pigeon Pie* is *well worth* 7/6.
Not at all pessimistic now, I consider we have a wonderful Gov[t] which was the only thing we lacked before to back up all you brave fellows with.

[1] Nancy was staying with Lady Diana Duncombe (1905–43), daughter of the 2nd Earl of Feversham, married to William Greville Worthington in 1927. He was accidentally shot by a British patrol in 1942 and she drowned herself in the River Ouse.
[2] Oswald Mosley had been arrested under Defence Regulation 18B, which gave the Government special powers to detain people without trial, and was imprisoned in Brixton.

To Violet Hammersley   12 Blomfield Road, W9
20 June 1940

Darling

Oh it is too heartbreaking – all our poor refugees too who have had such a terrible year & now no doubt will be handed over for Franco to shoot them.[1] Then everybody says there will be famine in Europe such as the world has never before known, & of course the people who will suffer least are the Germans.

Poor Zella[2] whom I saw says she wishes she could have died before this moment – I however wish to *live* & see vengeance.

Peter is back for a few days – before joining the 1st battalion.

I have just been round to see Gladwyn[3] at his request to tell what I know (very little actually) of Diana's visits to Germany.[4] I advised him to examine her passport to see how often she went. I also said I regard her as an extremely dangerous person. Not very sisterly behaviour but in such times I think it one's duty?[5]

I am just off to dine with Farve, will finish later.

Farve in great spirits just back from the secret session[6] where I gather, not from him tho', that Chamberlain & Co got a proper beating up. BEASTS.

Edward [Stanley] has turned up & I've just (5 p.m.) come away from lunching with him at the Ritz. He was at Dunkirk on his ship. Oh the stories from the chaps who were there are incredible, exactly like something out of the *Boys Own*. Richard Elwes apparently says (I haven't seen him) the Green Howards, armed only with spades & the officers with canes were put on to hold the Germans at bay so when they had beaten a few of them to death with the spades they very naturally got a bit scattered & Richard found himself quite alone in a huge, very luxurious château so he seized the opportunity to RETIRE (the loo Mrs Ham) & when well tee'd up he suddenly heard beroomph beroomph & this was German tanks coming up the drive. He was so frightened he couldn't move & remained on the loo & after about 5 mins they beroomphed off down the drive again & away.

Simon [Elwes] is back & has joined the Welsh Gds so will be vastly junior to Pete which is nice.

How wonderfully Tim's[7] regiment fought, it must be a consolation. Oh *poor* things.

Mr Maugham[8] I hear is missing among others.

Highcliffe[9] had tremendous fireworks I gather 2 nights ago, just as well to be in Glos, probably one of the quietest counties at present. I go back to H. for a week or two, to keep Aunt Vi company while Louise [Loraine] comes up to see a doctor. Then am quite vague again but would like a job on the land. True I am very soft at present but I could get fit no doubt & it would be nice to feel one was growing things. Talking of which we are living here on rich vegetables grown in the garden don't you call that good?

Much love & love to Aunt Weenie.[10]
    NR

Golly [Elwes] & Adelaide Lubbock[11] are sending their children away by the next boat.

[1] On 14 June the Germans entered Paris. Of the 260,000 Spanish refugees who fled to France in 1939, 12,000 are estimated to have been rounded up by the Nazis and sent to Mauthausen concentration camp in Austria, where 80 per cent died; the remainder were used as forced labour for French and German enterprises in France under conditions of near-slavery. Those who were able to escape played an active role in the

Resistance. In all, some 25,000 Spanish refugees lost their lives in the struggle against Germany.

[2] Vanda Séréza (Mrs Stern); the Mitfords' French governess.

[3] Gladwyn Jebb was seconded to the Ministry of Economic Warfare 1940–42.

[4] In 1937 Diana had made several visits to Germany to try to obtain a concession for a commercial radio station, similar to 'Radio Normandy', a successful concern set up by the MP Captain Leonard Plugge. Diana was negotiating with the German Minister of Posts on behalf of W. E. D. Allen, chairman of an advertising firm, and his associate, Oswald Mosley.

[5] Nancy really did denounce Diana – this was not one of her teases.

[6] Secret sessions on questions of home defence had been held in both Houses of Parliament.

[7] Timothy Bailey, Nancy's first cousin, had been taken prisoner of war. Anthony and Christopher, his two older brothers, were killed.

[8] Somerset Maugham had been evacuated from the Riviera on a coal barge which took twenty days to reach England.

[9] Highcliffe Castle, the home of Violet Stuart-Wortley.

[10] Violet Hammersley spent part of the war at the Baileys' house, Maugersbury, near Stow-on-the-Wold in Gloucestershire.

[11] Hon. Adelaide Stanley (1906–81). A cousin of Nancy. Married Hon. Maurice Lubbock in 1926. She later became a girlfriend of Peter Rodd.

To Lady Redesdale   Highcliffe Castle[1]
8 July 1940   Hants

Darling Muv

Many thanks for the cheque – most welcome.

Yes I think the Dame of Sark very stout – she is a great friend of Lady Dunn who had a letter from her announcing that she would stay with her 600 people[2] but begging Lady D to send her a doctor as their only one had fled. But the letter arrived too late.

Perhaps she will get one from France – apparently it would have been quite easy to find one here who had been struck off the register, but by the time the letter arrived the Germans were there.

Peter is near London – his regiment was in the end much less cut up than at first feared – about half lost at Boulogne & less than half in Flanders where they were holding the rear guard all the time & did magnificently. The casualties in Flanders seem to have been amazingly small – the soldiers who are here never lost a man all through & keep saying what *fun* it all was.

Did you see a letter in *The Times* about consuls & giving a tribute to Mr Whitfield that man at St Jean de Luz who was so kind over Decca. No I haven't heard for months from them.

I saw poor Lady Dunmore[3] in London in the street we talked for ages. She looks really *ravaged* with grief poor thing & about 70.

I would offer to come & be with Bobo[4] for a bit, but literally they do seem to think we are very likely to be invaded here & to regard it as a dangerous area & I simply can't leave Aunt Vi & Louise, who can hardly walk & is really ill. And once I leave this area it seems I can't return. But perhaps the situation will become a little less obscure presently. How extraordinary it all seems. Mrs Gould the parson's wife has hidden her jewels in the potting shed! Fortunately this house has formidable cellars which might have been built for just such a contingency.

Percy Loraine is here also Monty Abingdon,[5] for a day or 2 both full of exquisite bits of inside information some of it very funny I must say.

Monty tried his best to make Aunt Vi leave but she is perfectly determined not to I am glad to say.

I am working really hard, 5 hours a day but not on end. The children are very satisfactory, they no longer cry for tinned salmon but wolf the fresh vegetables etc. I think most are going to Canada soon so that side may shut down. Don't you think it a good idea – they need more settlers overseas & some will probably stay & the others come back very tough & healthy. I'm all for it.

What *can* Holloway be like really?[6] What lives we do lead.

Much love
    NR

[1] Nancy was staying with Violet Stuart-Wortley, initially recuperating from a second miscarriage and later helping with an early consignment of evacuees.
[2] The channel island of Sark was invaded on 1 July 1940 and remained under German occupation during the war.
[3] Lady Dunmore's son, Lord Fincastle, had been killed in action.
[4] Lady Redesdale had taken Unity to convalesce at a cottage in Swinbrook where they spent most of the rest of the war. Looking after her was a demanding task as Unity was unpredictable, often incontinent, and given to sudden rages.
[5] 8th Earl of Lindsey and Abingdon (1887–1963). Married Elizabeth (Bettine) Stuart-Wortley in 1928.
[6] On 29 June Diana too was arrested under Defence Regulation 18B and imprisoned in Holloway. She left behind her four children, including Max who was just eleven weeks old; they spent the war with various relations. Diana remained in prison until November 1943 when, because of Mosley's ill health, she and her husband were released under house arrest.

To Violet Hammersley   31 Grove End Road[1]
9 August 1940   London, NW8

Darling

Many thanks for yr letter – I have (very rare) the morning off so hasten to reply. I never knew what hard work was before, only hope I can stand up to it. I am getting rather horrid swollen glands & losing weight, but am perfectly happy & simply love the frogs more & more.

. . .

I got the Cardinal to go to the W[hite] C[ity]. Sounds rather odd so they kissed his toe or whatever it is & enjoyed themselves v. much. Their only priest has foutu le camp[2] (excuse me) & only comes back, holding his nose, for ½ an hour on Sunday to give Mass. Mrs Huxley is very don't careish about religion. I am a horrid pagan but believe in people having what they like & if they like Cardinals tant mieux pour eux[3] if I can buy them one. Mrs H is nice all right but but. I wish to pick her over with you one time.

Everybody here most kind but trying to induce me to leave my (I must say wretch of a) husband which I find odd in Catholics. As it is only a question of £. s. d. & the said hubby having a hole apparently in his pocket like a bottomless pit, I shall struggle on in matrimony despite them. How people do long to break up ménages I have often remarked on this in life. 'Somehow one had hoped' is a profound observation really.[4]

I must go.

Much love
   NR

Poor things about Tim [Bailey]. But one hears everywhere that prisoners are well treated.

[1] Nancy was staying with Julian Huxley, the biologist, and his Swiss wife Juliette. Nancy and Juliette were working in a canteen at the White City where French soldiers repatriated from Dunkirk were interned.
[2] Buggered off.
[3] So much the better for them.
[4] Violet Hammersley relished bad news. When told that the marriage of a Mitford friend to a rich and clever young man was going well, she said in her hollow voice: 'Somehow one had *hoped* they'd be *so* unhappy.' The words passed into the Mitford language.

To Violet Hammersley   12 Blomfield Road, W9
9 September 1940

Darling the nights![1] Nobody who hasn't been in it can have the smallest idea of the horror one is going through. I never don't feel sick, can't eat anything & although dropping with tiredness can't sleep either. No doubt one will get used to it soon – last night I shall never forget as long as I live. I emerged this morning confident that, apart from 12 Blomfield, not one stone in the neighbourhood could possibly be left upon another. Actually, search as I might, I could see no damage of any kind! However there has been a good deal actually & very near, in streets behind the house. To add slightly to my misery Gladys[2] was caught in Hyde Park where the poor thing spent the night in a trench. Ten hours is *too* long, you know of concentrated noise & terror, in a house alone. Thank heaven for Milly (dog) who is a rock. So is Gladys – really a heroine. She arrived back at 6 this morning all smiles & was ready with my breakfast punctually at 8, & when I announced rather hysterically that I intended to spend tonight in my trench in the garden she cheerfully said she would come too. Peter however assures me that this is too silly & the ground floor quite as safe.

Oh the whistling bombs oh goodness.

Can't think of any jokes for you. I do wish I was brave it is terrible to be such a coward & everybody else seems *so* wonderful only very tired of course. I suppose here they are aiming at Padd: I hear they have got Vic & Waterloo – also the Natural Hist Mus, Mad: Tussauds, Harrods (only some broken windows, & no casualties) Putney Bridge & evidently some gas mains as our gas is off. The winter will be delightful won't it. Also, burglars are abroad – 15 in Belgravia on Sat night alone, Robert [Byron's] house twice, Phyllis de Janzé etc. I sleep with a gun to hand.

Oh *darling* when shall we meet again?

Love to all there
     NR

P.S. Oh the *happy* times before the war shall we ever see them again?

[1] The London Blitz had begun.
[2] Nancy's maid.

To Violet Hammersley   12 Blomfield Road, W9
12 September 1940

Darling

I nearly sent Aunt W[eenie] such a funny taxi load –

Peter, on Tuesday, turned up with the 2 babies (5 & 3) of one of
his soldiers. They and their mother had had their house in Brixton
collapse on them & the mother had a ghastly miscarriage & was dying.
The poor man couldn't even be given 4 hrs leave to arrange things –
they are Welsh & have no relations here so Peter went to Brixton,
where they were sitting in the street, fetched them away & we put
them to bed where we were both (me & the maid) sleeping by then,
the kitchen. All night we had a fearful bombardment & at 2 AM a
Molotoff bread basket descended on the next door house which caught
fire. Having sent for the fire brigade I took the babies in a taxi up to
Zella [Stern], at Hampstead. Darling it was like leaving Sodom &
Gomorrah – great fires the whole way & fearful explosions. Put the
children to bed & returned here, shot at on the way by a Home Guard
because the taxi didn't stop. Had a *fearful* pasting here all the rest of
the night – 5 large houses in the next street just vanished into thin
air, you never saw such a crater.

Next day (Wed) decided I couldn't keep the children here & at
9 AM got a very sporting taxi driver to say he would go to the country
so put Gladys, Milly, the babies, my fur coat & all my linen into the
taxi & despatched them to Diana Worthington.

The angelic Zella invited me to go to her & there I am for the
present (Highlands, Redington Road, Hampstead) under the nose of
a big gun. This part (Mai Vale) has got it worse than almost anywhere
(except the East End of course) as they are trying for Padd. On
Sunday night & again Tues: they never let up for 10 hours. Too
long you know. There is a *lot* of damage. Last night again they tried
apparently & people are leaving this neighbourhood for other parts of
London – our pretty canal is an excellent guide it seems.

Well, when cogitating where to send them I thought of A.W. but
she was spared on acc/ of being so far away. They were such darling
children & so good.

I find my nerves are standing up to the thing better now – I don't
tremble quite all the time as I did.

Gladys was too wonderful & furious at leaving, I had to explain it
was her war work to take the children. Actually I think every living
thing that can be got out of this hell should be – NOBODY can have

the slightest idea of what it is like until they've experienced it. As for the screaming bombs they simply make your flesh creep but the whole thing is so fearful that they are actually only a slight added horror. The great fires everywhere the awful din which never stops & the wave after wave after wave of aeroplanes, ambulances tearing up the street & the horrible unnatural blaze of light from searchlights all has to be experienced to be understood. Then in the morning the damage – people ring up to tell one how their houses are completely non existent, & in nearly every street you can see a sinister little piece roped off with red lights round it, or roofs blown off or suddenly every window out of a house, & lorries full of rubble & broken furniture pass incessantly. Of course the number of deaths is absolutely tiny but everybody now sleeps in the shelters, at about 7 one sees them queuing up with thermos flasks & blankets for the night. People are beyond praise, everyone is red eyed and exhausted but you never hear a word of complaint or down heartedness it is most reassuring.

I am trying to get some work in the East End – am temporarily rather cross with the Frogs who really are behaving like spoilt children, complaining they are kept awake at night & one today started a long histoire about how he hadn't been taken to the theatre at all. Ça je trouve *un peu* exagéré quand même.[1]

Oh dear there are the sirens again what a horrid life.

Well, I can't tell you much news because one never sees anybody – no vie sociale you understand & when one does the talk is always on craters, shelters & what happened to so & so's mother or aunt. Winston was *admirable* wasn't he, so inspiring. I know the army are on their toes let's hope this time all will be well.

Love darling from
    NR

[1] Well, I do find that *a little* exaggerated.

To Violet Hammersley   26 Rutland Gate, SW7[1]
1 October 1940

Darling –

As I wrote that word a bomb appeared to drop in this very room but here we are. It must have been jolly near though.

Oh I can so imagine all that – let's have lunch – so much more interesting, how it would donne sur les nerfs,[2] I hadn't quite pictured it before. Like when [indecipherable] who, when I arrived from London, crying because the BEF was lost, greeted me with '*Now* I consider we have won the war'.[3]

Don't believe too much of what you hear is down – it generally proves an exaggeration – one bomb can't, except perhaps a land mine – destroy a house like Holland House.

Poor Peggy Jessel has lost her pretty house, was dug out of the cellar & is very gallantly I think staying in London. As for losing one's house & belongings I don't think anybody in London cares much any more – also to comfort *you* one can nearly always save a good deal, except from an absolutely direct hit. Generally one or 2 rooms, not by any means always the upstairs ones, go entirely but the rest are more or less intact, specially the case with a solidly built house like yours.

Do come up for a day & I will devote anyhow most of it to you. I am awfully busy but expect to be less so later (but I have expected that for days now & it doesn't quite work out).

I think the Jews, rich & poor, are being awfully good, as for my sweet refugees no kind of person could possibly in any way be nicer – I shall always love Jews for their sake. Most of my rich gentile friends have found some reason for leaving London, but as it happens none of the Jews I know have done so. The Readings I have made friends with & as they live next door they are a great stand by. So *sensible* & nice. The Sutros, Zella's old husband, & other obscure ones I happen to know have all refused to leave & really seem to mind less than one does – as for Peggy, I never knew anybody make so little fuss & you know she loved her pretty things. When I said how horrible for you she said my dear how can one *think* of chairs & tables nowadays – very true but I think I should shed a tear or so.

Poor Muv – I daresay you heard they had a land mine at Swinbrook it must have bounced them. She isn't a bit frightened or wasn't when she spent a night here but I have noticed deaf people mind far less. . . .

I have got Milly back which is bliss – I evacuated her at the beginning but couldn't bear it any more so got her back again. Such a comfort.

I meant to tell you in my last letter – Farve the 2nd day the Jews were here got up at 5.30 to light the boiler for them & charming Mr Sockolovsky, who helped him said to me 'I did not think the Lord would have risen so early'. Wasn't it biblical. I am never away from Rabbis they are *heaven* & we are having 2 services in the drawing room this week – shades of Muv.

Much love & XXX do pray I shan't be hit,* I feel you have a pull. Talking of which how is Miss Freeman?[4]

NR

* Do so fearfully want to see what happens next in the serial story.

[1] Nancy had moved from Blomfield Road which, being on the Regent's Canal, was an easy target for German bombers aiming for Paddington Station. She was living at the family home in Rutland Gate which was requisitioned to provide temporary accommodation for Polish Jews evacuated from Whitechapel.
[2] Get on your nerves.
[3] This paragraph has been scored through and underneath Nancy has written: 'Mrs H crossed this out.' Violet Hammersley was staying with the Baileys at Maugersbury and had complained that they refused to discuss the war. Because of her gloomy outlook, Colonel Bailey put up a notice which read: 'In this house we are not interested in talk of defeat.'
[4] Agnes Freeman; Violet Hammersley's unmarried sister.

TO VIOLET HAMMERSLEY   26 Rutland Gate, SW7
11 November 1940

Darling

You can't have any conception of how busy I am here – I honestly couldn't do anything like going to Tite Street.[1]

Every day I wake up wondering how I can get through all the things there are on my list. After all I do, not only the housekeeping for 50 people, but quantities of other things as well, like going to the East End to see about their furniture, finding out educational facilities for the young etc etc, & now the raids begin at 6.30 the day is far too short as it is. I am awfully sorry but there you are – *really not* possible.

Have very little news. Robert [Byron] came to luncheon & said the Greeks are all the more wonderful because we had told them we didn't intend to help at all, & that the Min: of Inf: had written them off from the beginning. Let's hope it won't be another Finland.

There is a little colony of chums at the Athenaeum Court – Cyril Connolly, Brian Howard, Peter Watson. Then William [Acton] is ARP warden at Tite St & Harold entertains the Chinese at Eaton Place. I can't often see people as I can't lunch out much, must see it served here or there are troubles (it is an hour late, or the bread hasn't arrived) & in the evening I am really too tired, also from 6.30–8 is a very busy time as those who work can only see me then. Robert says Cyril is happier than at any previous time in his life – I think that is true of quite a lot of people actually. Busy & interested where before they were neither – & I suppose the bombs do add a kind of excitement – the nights when there are no raids seem quite flat now you know.

Zella went to see Diana – says she seems on top of the world & tremendously well.[2] But oh I would *die* of the lights out at 5.30 rule wouldn't you? I suppose she sits & thinks of Adolf.

What of Anna Wolkoff[3] do you remember she was Pam's greatest friend.

I don't thank for the Polish book as it has not yet arrived – not lack of gratitude.

The Huxleys go to their shelter as the sirens sound – as for the Dorchesterites[4] a friend of mine paced out the shelter & found it is under that little pond & there are only a few inches of tarmac between them & certain death. As they are all convinced there are 7 storeys of ferro concrete it comes to the same! The Gros House rats it seems will all be drowned by a bursting sewer. There is of course great snobbery between those who do & do not sleep in shelters but I always think it must be very souring for those who do to see their beds unscathed in the morning. I couldn't bear it personally. It's like those who fall flat in the street when you hear a bomb coming, they get up so muddy & sheepish, I never can bring myself to dirty my clothes.

I wouldn't empty Tite. I firmly believe there will soon be an enormous demand for furnished houses, there will be so few available & it may give one the opportunity for a spot of profiteering. And then with William as yr warden what *could* happen to it?

Darling do come to London soon, it would cheer you up. Do you want to hear of a few more ruins? Well that pretty Naval & Military in Piccadilly, also the little church (St James's) there. About 6 new ones in the Row which bounced us rather & 2 in Prince's Gate. One very near the Oratory in the B. road. Dolphin Square (several). All these in the last week except the church. Green St is a fearful mess, Gt Cumberland Place utterly wiped out also those houses, Connaught Place I think it was called facing the Park, very pretty. Bryanston Sq will have to come down & I believe Montagu. The Channon house in Belgrave Sq, Lady Cunard's[5] in Gros & 'the Mutilated House' is mutilated now in very deed. I *should* enjoy showing you the sights so do come soon.

Much love from
    NR

[1] Violet Hammersley's London home was in Tite Street, Chelsea.
[2] This was wishful thinking; in her autobiography Diana Mosley wrote, 'I read Carlyle's *French Revolution* at this time. I thought if, like the prisoners he describes, I had to stay many months in gaol, I would prefer to die.' *A Life of Contrasts*, p. 186.
[3] Anna Wolkoff (d. 1969). A Russian refugee and high-class dressmaker who had made clothes for Pamela. She was convicted of spying and sentenced to ten years' imprisonment.
[4] The Dorchester Hotel's reinforced concrete construction was considered to offer protection from bombs and was much favoured by the fugitive rich.
[5] Maud Burke (1872–1948). Married Sir Bache Cunard in 1895. Known as 'Emerald' from 1926. An American from San Francisco, she became one of London's leading hostesses between the wars. Her house at 7 Grosvenor Square was the setting for some of the most lavish parties of the time.

To VIOLET HAMMERSLEY   26 Rutland Gate, SW7
20 December 1940

Darling

I have been too busy to write almost too busy to think in fact I really have hardly even enjoyed Libya[1] to the full.

In addition to buying presents for all my Jews (they keep Xmas did you know it is the Feast of Queen Esther – I was terrified they wouldn't but all is well) I am arranging a ball for nearly 100 – Yids & Welsh Guardsmen mixed, with W.G. band.

Then Peter & I have moved from the Mews in to 26 where I have put my nicest furniture from 12 B[lomfield] R[oad] into Muv's bedroom so we live there in state with Peter's soldier servant Thomas. All this took some arranging. Peter you see is now here every evening so time for letter writing hardly exists. Also Debo has been here – very exigeante little creature & dreadfully selfish like all the very young, & now Farve has turned up roaring like a bull because everything is not just as he always has it. And so on.

Muv has been here most weeks, very embittered about the alleged ill treatment of Diana. But it can't be serious as Zella who went to see her says she has never looked more blooming.

Darling I will write again after Queen Esther's feast, this is just to indicate that I am still with you.

    Much love
      NR

[1] General Wavell had opened the offensive in North Africa on 9 December and on 16 December the Italians were driven across the Libyan border.

To Violet Hammersley   26 Rutland Gate, SW7
26 December 1940

Darling

   Queen Esther's feast (at least the shopping part of it) being over I
can turn my thoughts towards Maugersbury without any inward feeling
of guilt. The tea party, complete with Lord Mayor's tree, was a big
success & I had presents for so nearly everybody that I did not hastily
have to wrap up my own favourite ones as a last minute resort. Our
ball is on Sunday next I am longing for it.

   Oh dear a little creature here aged 16 is in the family way. I advised
her, in the words of Lady Stanley, a tremendous walk a hot bath &
a great dose but will this have any effect on a tough little Jewess? Or
shall I be obliged to wield a knitting needle & go down to fame as
Mrs Rodd the abortionist? (I might join Diana which would be rather
nice.) Really, talk about big families I feel like the mother of 10 here
or old Mummy Hubbard.

   You can't imagine how beastly Muv is being – she now regards me
as a Jewess I believe & is so horrid both to & about me. Also says
if she had all the money in the world she would not ever live in the
house again after the Jews have had it. Exaggerated?

   Did you cut your arm with broken glass after Winston's speech?[1] I
was quite alone but could not forbear to cheer. I hope the Royal Family
(wop) was listening, nobody else understands English unfortunately &
Peter says the translation lost all its fire and energy. He Pete is going
to broadcast to Italy next week I believe.

   Francis has reappeared. The great Francis, his job is liaison officer
to de Gaulle in W Africa rather a come down I feel?[2]

   Isn't *Sacred & Profane Love*[3] a curiosity. I am enjoying it but what
a funny fellow he is to be sure.

   We had a great bounce here on the 23rd – Rutland Court, Trevor
Square & the top of Sloane St all in one great wallop. And such a
huge bomb fell on Ebury Bridge that it broke one of our windows.
These ton bombs are Hitty's new joke & quite a good one the effect
is that of an earthquake & besides you hear them screaming down
for ages, they come from a huge height & sound like a train so one
has great fun guessing where they will land. Ha ha ha *such* a little
comedian.

   By the way do ask Aunt Weenie something. When I last stayed
with her she was very great on country people being superior to
townspeople. Does she admit that the bombing has proved the former

ABOVE LEFT: Nancy, aged eleven.
ABOVE RIGHT: The Mitford family in
1912: *left to right*, Nancy, David, Tom,
Diana, Sydney, Pamela

Swinbrook House, built by Nancy's
father in 1926

Tom Mitford in 1926, the year before
he left Eton

LEFT: In the grounds of Christ Church, Oxford, 1931: *in tree from left to right*, Dig Yorke, Nancy, Roy Harrod, Johnny Drury-Lowe; *on the ground from left to right*, Ronnie Drury-Lowe, Henry Yorke, Alan Lennox-Boyd. ABOVE: Diana and Nancy, early 1930s

BELOW RIGHT: Left to right, Roy Harrod, Deborah Mitford, Diana Guinness, Harold Acton at Biddesden House, 1931

Drawn by Cecil

Nancy by Cecil Beaton, *c.*1930

Nancy and Robert Byron at a
Roman party given by John
Sutro at the Savoy, 1932

Mark Ogilvie-Grant at the
Café de Paris, Leicester
Square, *c*.1928

Hamish St. Clair-Erskine,
early 1930s

Nancy's wedding to Peter Rodd, 4 December 1933

Nancy, Edward Stanley, John Sutro, 1935

Nancy and Peter on their honeymoon

Swinbrook, 1934: *left to right*, Lady
Redesdale; Nancy, Diana, Tom, Pamela,
Lord Redesdale; in front, Unity, Jessica,
Deborah

ABOVE: Unity with Hitler, Bayreuth, *c.*1936

RIGHT: Nancy at the beginning of her
marriage

Diana and Sir Oswald Mosley with their son Alexander, 21 May 1940, the day before Sir Oswald's arrest

Esmond and Jessica Romilly

Lord Redesdale, Unity, Lady Redesdale at the Mill Cottage, Swinbrook, 1942

Tom Mitford, Palestine, 1944

The Mitford
sisters drawn
by William
Acton, 1937–8

Nancy

Pamela

Diana

Unity

Jessica

Deborah

Violet Hammersley in the garden at Wilmington, Isle of Wight

LEFT: Evelyn Waugh; RIGHT: Heywood Hill in 1939, three years after he first opened his bookshop in Curzon Street

to be ghastly cowards & the latter wonderful heroes? I hear nothing but stories of yokels lying on the floor & taking aspirins every time there is – not a raid but a mere warning, & when I was staying with Diana Worthington I was really shocked by the cowardice of the villagers, who have never had a bomb nearer than 2 miles but who faint (literally one woman does) every time there is a warning. One of the men came to Diana & said 'These raids are getting the women down', & one day I went for a walk & heard 4 bombs in the extreme distance – 10 minutes later came upon a hearty young yokel cowering in a ditch & saying 'Did you hear the bombs – I can bear *anything* but that.' As though he had anything else to bear anyway! What does it all mean? *Do* tease her for me. I have always preferred cockneys to yokels anyway & now think I am perfectly right –

Pam & Derek[4] came to London for a few days & talked such Fascism that the whole town is speculating on how they manage to remain OUT.

Cyril, Hog Watson[5] & many another lefty are avoiding military service by dint of being editors of a magazine (*Horizon*) which is a reserved occupation isn't it brilliant. Jeannie [Connolly] has fled to California but C has managed to nab her 1200 a year & lives with a glamorous houri[6] on the proceeds at the Athenaeum Court. How *can* they I mean the houris. Jeannie too has a lover – hope for all I feel.

What a long letter do write one soon.

Love from
    NR

[1] In a broadcast on 23 December, Winston Churchill urged the Italians to turn against Mussolini. Nancy enjoyed teasing Violet Hammersley about her alleged political sympathies.
[2] Francis Rodd was the Rennells' favourite son, as reliable and satisfactory as Peter was rebellious and unsatisfactory.
[3] Sacheverell Sitwell, *Sacred and Profane Love* (1940). A book of reflections on art and travel.
[4] Professor Derek Jackson (1906–82). Distinguished physicist, amateur jockey and much-married heir to the *News of the World* fortune. Married to Nancy's sister Pamela 1936–51. In 1940 he joined the RAF, winning the Distinguished Flying Cross in 1941. In 1942 he transferred to Fighter Command and was decorated with the Air Force Cross.
[5] Peter Watson once telephoned Swinbrook and Lord Redesdale answered. 'That hog Watson wants to speak to you,' he shouted. To the family he was Hog Watson thereafter.
[6] Lys Dunlap (1917–). One-time fashion model, married in 1938 to Ian Lubbock, a struggling actor and teacher. In 1941 she left him to live with Cyril Connolly; she

changed her name by deed poll to Connolly in 1945 and stayed with him until 1950, but they never married.

To Diana Mosley   26 Rutland Gate, SW7
7 January 1941
[passed by prison censor 9/1/41]

Darling Diana

I had no idea I was allowed to write – as I now hasten to do – & thank you for your kind present.[1] I have bought myself some much needed facial condiments with it & am most grateful – actually managed to find a Guerlain lipstick in an obscure chemist's shop which must have given me the same sensation a bibliophile would have on coming across a 1st folio of Shakespeare.

I sent the Wid[ow] a box of soap called Modestes Violettes & she wrote back 'Coming downstairs in a rather specially sad mood . . .'

No wonder she is rather specially sad, freezing at Maugersbury & Aunt W *won't* pick the war over with her – 'I said I hear that Holland House has quite gone & she said come on let's have luncheon, *much* more interesting.' Can't you see it.[2]

Harold [Acton] longs to go & visit you, he is living in Annette's[3] house with all the little treasures gone & only bare necessities left, & entertains extensively for the Chinese Embassy. William is still in Chelsea, learning I believe to be an air raid warden.

I saw your little Alexander the other day he *is* a darling how I wish they were living with me – I had almost forgotten what heaven Nanny is.

   Much love from Nance

[1] Diana was able to send money to her mother from her bank in order to buy presents for the family.
[2] Violet Hammersley spread such gloom and despondency at Maugersbury that eventually the Baileys turned her out.
[3] Anne Messel (1902–92). Married to Ronald Armstrong-Jones in 1925 and to 6th Earl of Rosse in 1935. She appears in Nancy's story 'The Old Ladies' as the Pretty Young Lady.

To Violet Hammersley   4 Rutland Gate Mews, SW7
3 March 1941

Darling

I have been reading Ethyl Smyth's book on Maurice Baring[1] – have you read it – do you agree with her estimate of his work & who is

Vernon Lee?[2] I asked Victor Cunard[3] the last question & he was very snooty, said I might as well ask who George Eliot was which got me but little further. I could only think of Mrs Vernon Castle[4] but I gather it's not the same pair of shoes.

Do you think a book on Victorian marriage largely culled from letters & memoirs (I mean with extensive quotations) would be amusing? I have asked my publisher if he likes the idea. One could have the Intellectual Marriage (Carlyles), the Society Marriage, Childless Marriage (Lady Canning), Political Marriage (Disraeli) & so on. Or one could do it like this, chapter headings – Coming Out, Engagement, Wedding, Honeymoon & so on. Do say what you think. Letters on that subject are always fascinating.

Have you read *Family Homespun*?[5] We are all very pleased about Debo[6] – he is a dear little fellow & I am sure she will be happy. Also it will be easier for Muv as she & Bobo get on so badly.

I simply so long to leave here, now I have decided to, I can't take the same interest in the house, & long to begin a book (not a novel).

I had a luncheon party today to do honour to a piece of beef I have been nursing in a marinade for a week at least. It was a great success.

A friend of mine at the War Office (M.I.) begs me (this is a secret) to worm my way into the Free Frog Officers' Club in any capacity & try to find out something about them. They are all here under assumed names, all splashing mysteriously large sums of money about & our people can't find out a thing about them & are getting very worried. I'm afraid it's no good for me as I have never moved in Frog society & wouldn't know who was who anyway. I feel it is *your* duty! I do see that it's very difficult for our people. For example I met a horrible couple called Sellier – they admit it's not their real name – who have taken a 10 gn flat near here. They told me they both work at the Quartier Général. I met another officer calling himself Violet (why not Pansée) who says he works there & has never heard of anybody called Sellier. He swears he knows every soul at the Q.G. This *kind* of thing happens every time one sees a frog. It is known they are riddled with spies e.g. Dakar.[7] Isn't it tricky. Seriously I don't see what I could do & it would bore me to death to work in an officers' club anyway.

When do you take the veil?[8]

Much love
    NR

[1] Ethel Smyth (1858–1944). Composer, writer and suffragette. Author of *Maurice*

Baring (1938), an admiring appreciation of the life and work of the prolific author of *Cat's Cradle* (1925), *Daphne Adeane* (1926) and *The Coat without Seam* (1929).
[2] Vernon Lee, pseudonym for Violet Paget (1856–1935). Writer of some thirty books, principally on Italian culture. Of Maurice Baring she wrote: 'One loves him all the more because there are little things to forgive: a nervous laugh, a tendency to lie on the carpet and suck his boot, etcetera.' *Maurice Baring* (Heinemann, 1938), p. 5.
[3] Victor Cunard (1898–1960). *Times* correspondent 1922–33. Settled in Venice for most of his life except during the war when he was attached to the Political Intelligence Department of the Foreign Office. A homosexual, and lifelong friend of Nancy. 'His extra-dry humour appealed to Nancy's, though it was fraught with infectious malice.' Acton, *Nancy Mitford*, p. 116.
[4] A famous Edwardian ballroom dancer.
[5] Blanche Dugdale, *Family Homespun* (1940). Memoirs of the granddaughter of the 8th Duke of Argyll.
[6] Deborah was engaged to Lord Andrew Cavendish (1920–), second son of 10th Duke of Devonshire; they were married on 19 April 1941.
[7] The plans for a raid on Dakar in West Africa, headed by General de Gaulle, were leaked to the Vichy Government and the attempt ended in failure.
[8] Violet Hammersley was invariably swathed in scarves, shawls and veils.

To Jessica Romilly   12 Blomfield Road, W9
9 July 1941

Darling Sooze

I found a delicious piece of Hotel Montalembert[1] notepaper but didn't dare write on it for fear fitz censor[2] shld object so I wrote to a glamorous Free Frog[3] I know instead & I expect he'll think it a poor-taste joke.

Also before fitzy he was a very rich & important frog so I suppose the Hotel Montalembert will seem to him about what the Rembrandt Hotel[4] would to us, also he will be surprised at why I stole the note paper (not being acquainted with old Rodd).

Oh dear I minded very much about Miss [Dolly] Wilde. So many of my best friends are now dead – still it will make heaven more matey in a way. Miss Wilde did not exactly commit it – she was terribly ill & the dr said if she went on taking some drug it would kill her in the end so she did & it did. But that's not *quite* the same as holding one's head under the tap is it. Victor C. says she was quite jolly & herself to the end.

Susan, about wants. We don't *need* anything here so don't pay any attention to those who say we do. Food is frightfully dull but there is masses of it. As for lav paper, I laid in a small store & Woman has enough for 10 years. Actually you can still get it & if not the [*Tele*]-*graph* would be useless, you should just *note* the *graph* that's all it is much smaller than a short letter & needed, every bit of it, for lighting one's boiler. I found an old pre war *graph* the other day & couldn't believe my eyes. Whatever did they find to say in all those pages?

I saw Rud[5] at a fête at D. Worthington's. She looked beautiful but so sad – I fear Riccy is dying He was there, a terrible sight. Poor Rud I believe she knows it without realizing it which is perhaps just as well.

I think Constancia[6] a heavenly name & I am going to make a will & leave her all my things if Rodd & I are both killed – if only me I can't leave her much as poor old Rodd will have to be able to boil himself an egg but I have a diamond brooch & £20 in war savings (& Susan no blowing on c-tail ptys before of age is come by Constancia).

I have 6 hens & grow all my own veges so wasn't it lucky I took a house with a large garden.

There is a system of sending telegrams to soldiers by numbers (1. means 'got yr letter' & so on) so I sent one to Rodd with all the things like was run over yesterday. I do hope he'll see the joke.

Everybody in London is giving the clenched fist salute, it would remind you of the old days in Spain – it brings back to me that summer in Perpignan & the Duchess of Atholl[7] doing it. Aren't the Reds wonderful such a tease on the Germans after they showed such poor form in Finland.

I live in a slight world of frogs now, always the nicest & funniest. You can't imagine how wonderful they have been, the free ones I mean, & what good ideas General de Gaulle has about post war settlements.

Actually I do believe that this war is going to bring about incredible reforms, quite unlike the other, *unless* there is slaughter on a ghastly scale leaving everyone too shattered & exhausted.

Did you hear about Id's[8] marriage to the son of the Mayoress of Westminster? He looks old enough to be the Mayor & I hear has several wives but she is very happy.

Much love Sue you can't say this isn't a long letter from
    Susan Rodd

[1] An hotel in Paris on the Left Bank.

[2] A prefix derived from a friend of the Mitfords called Mary Fitzgerald.

[3] Roy André Desplats-Pilter (1904–45). Nom de guerre André Roy. He had come to London in 1940 to join de Gaulle's Free French Forces. He and Nancy met in 1941 when he was working as liaison officer at the Quartier Général. Nancy was lonely and unhappy and they entered into a light-hearted love-affair which lasted throughout the summer. Roy died of tuberculosis at the end of the war.

[4] An unfashionable hotel in Kensington.
[5] Joan Farrer, Nancy's first cousin, married to Riccy de Udy.
[6] Constancia Romilly (Dinkie), Jessica's daughter, was born on 9 February 1941.
[7] Wife of 8th Duke of Atholl; although a Conservative MP, she supported the Republican cause during the Civil War and was known as the Red Duchess.
[8] Ann Farrer; sister of Joan, married David Horne, an actor.

To Violet Hammersley   12 Blomfield Road, W9
12 July 1941

Darling

Fancy you having dashed off to Totland,[1] how did you manage the journey? I was so anxious about you & on the point of writing to Bath for news when I got yr letter.

I am now in a slight whirl of free froggery, very agreeable the way the French chaps look at one, kiss one's hand etc without being rendered gaga with love first like the English ones, if you see what I mean. I am fire watching,[2] one of the dreariest occupations of war time life, it is 1 A.M. & I am nearly dropping after a particularly hard day's work. How lovely the island must be in this weather, you are lucky.

The chap who is fire watching with me was in Dachau. He seems to bear no grudge against the Germans, says that everywhere you will find a few brutes & proceeds to tell such ghastly horrors of *our* treatment of refugees that I feel quite cast down. His wife is a doctor in Merthyr Tidville [*sic*] & he writes her 14 pages every day – is hard at it now.

Up the Reds! Aren't they heaven quite my favourite allies. I lunched today with Rob & Hannah [Hudson], the Minister in his shirt sleeves very gloomy 'Oh they'll betray us.' N.R. 'Who cares so long as they kill a million Germans first.'

I really do work so hard[3] – so far have sent away 160 people which, when you remember I do everything from interviewing them to looking up the trains is not so bad! They write such charming grateful letters or come back to see one & say how lovely it has been in nearly all cases. But we need masses more hospitality it is heartbreaking how many we have to send away.

I doubt if I could ever get to Bath, as I work Sat morning & must be there 9.30 Monday & I am so tired at weekends I only long to sit about. Actually this Sunday I am making an effort for the Entente &

taking the glamorous Capitaine Roy to West Wycombe for the day. Praiseworthy?

  Much love & let me have a word from time to time
    NR

[1] Violet Hammersley's house Wilmington was in Totland Bay, Isle of Wight.
[2] Nancy was asked to broadcast some talks on fire-fighting which were discontinued after a short while. When she inquired why, Nancy was told, 'Well you see, it's your voice. We've had several complaints; someone even wrote in and said they wanted to put you on the fire.'
[3] Nancy was earning £3 a week helping to find homes in the country for London evacuees. 'A man rang me up yesterday & said he could never remember having such a holiday in his life . . . That is the sort of thing that makes the work so nice – the hair raising part is that they seem incapable of catching trains, getting off buses where told etc etc! And then the "hostesses" get absolutely rabid very naturally & we suffer!' (NM to Lady Redesdale, 22 June 1941)

To DIANA MOSLEY   University College Hospital
22 November 1941   London, WC
[passed by prison censor 28/11/41]

Darling Diana
  Thank you so much for the wonderful grapes, you are really an angel & grapes are so good for me. I have had a horrible time, so depressing because they had to take out both my tubes & therefore I can never now have a child.[1] I can't say I suffered great agony but quite enough discomfort – but darling when I think of you & the 18 stitches in your face[2] it is absolutely nothing.
  The Rodds have been wonderfully true to form – my mother in law was told by the surgeon I shld be in danger for 3 days, & not one of them even rang up to enquire let alone sending a bloom or anything. I long to know if they bothered to look under R in the deaths column, very much doubt it however.
  I never hear from Peter or he from me it is too depressing like the grave. Also he never gets his pay.
  Muv was wonderful, she swam in a haze of bewilderment between me & Debo. When my symptoms were explained to her she said 'ovaries – I thought one had 700 like caviar'. Then I said how I couldn't bear the idea of a great scar on my tum to which she replied 'But darling who's ever going to see it?'
  Poor Debo it must be wretched the worst thing in the world I should think[3] – except losing a manuscript of a book which I always think must be *the* worst.

Have you read *Mémoires d'outre tombe*[4] it is so wonderful. I've had a heavenly time reading my books in peace, such a change from rushing off to the office at 8.30.

I've left my address book at home so must send this to Muv.

Nigel [Birch] has just been to see me rather optimistic in mood which is entirely new for him, I nearly fell out of bed.

I saw John [Sutro] & his new wife the other day, she is like a glamorous Pussette.[5] Then I took a very belated wedding present round to Hall Road & found Mr Sutro, aged 83, living there all alone. Poor old man he was like a dog let off a lead at seeing me – he kept saying an old fellow like me ought to be dead not using up rations. Oh dear it must be dreadful to be so old & alone – she died about a year ago I think. The house just the same, it did bring back the happy old days to me. I asked about Charles[6] & he said Charles has a new wife so now he has 2 but one is the mother of his children & the other not.

I spent the week end before I got ill (in considerable pain most of the time) with Roy & Billa. They have an ideal child called Hen[ry] – I think the prettiest, most amusing little boy I ever saw.

Oxford society is very pleasant I think, everybody so amiable & nice, most unlike what one would imagine such a small highly cultivated world to be. Gerald [Berners] has taken up his residence there. Apparently he has a mania for tea shop life & Billa says it is a kind of task, undertaken in turns to face Gerald across rather grubby check tablecloths at mealtimes.

It would amuse you, in the office where I work the girls are 2 actresses, one ex hat shop assistant & one wholesale agent. Well I suppose they are *New Statesman* fans or something but anyway I soon found they revered me for knowing Eddy Sackville-West,[7] Gerald, Peter Quennell, Cyril Connolly & others I shld have thought utterly (outside their own circle) obscure. But it seems they are household words to the middle classes. I hope they never find out, wild horses wouldn't make me tell them!

   Much love darling & many more thanks for the grapes
      Nancy

[1] Nancy's affair with André Roy had resulted in an ectopic pregnancy.
[2] Diana was badly injured in a motor accident in 1935.
[3] Deborah's first child was stillborn.
[4] François René de Chateaubriand's autobiography (1849–50).
[5] Clementine Kearsey; first cousin of Nancy.
[6] Brother of John Sutro.

7 Hon. Edward Sackville-West (1901–65). Novelist and music critic. Succeeded as 5th
Baron Sackville in 1962. The inspiration for the eccentric Uncle Davey in Nancy's
novels. After her operation, Nancy and he were fellow guests of Helen Dashwood at
West Wycombe. Years later she described Eddy to Evelyn Waugh: 'The tiny black
suede shoes, the shivering, in a cape it used to be then with heavy silver buckles.
Before breakfast, the array of pills before his plate. Well, all described in *The Pursuit
of Love* really . . . I'm glad you love him, so do I.' (27 May 1950)

To Billa Harrod   12 Blomfield Road, W9
13 June 1942

Darling Billa

I was so pleased to have your long letter oh I never heard anything
so ghastly[1] no wonder you can't think of it. Awful for any mother but
when one has a *treasure* like Hen – I never knew of it at all which
shows how the war has slowed up even gossip.

How lovely having Roy back & not to think of him risking life &
limb in those WVS cars every day.

I hope the pictures in the book aren't frightening I think them very
fascinating but perhaps a little macabre, but I believe modern children
aren't frightened.

Oh I did laugh. A very modern mother (Mrs Mass Observation
Tom Harrisson)[2] came into the shop[3] & said she had just sacked her
nanny because she had found her in bed with an airman. So I said I
thought nowadays people liked that to happen because then the nanny
doesn't prey on the affections of the children (or some rot, I said it
to tease of course). She replied in very governessy tones 'Not at all,
quite wrong for the censor figure to be found in bed with an airman.'
So you see perhaps our poor old grandmothers had the right ideas
after all!

I don't know if I ever told you, I have a French friend called Captain
Roy who went to see Roy & said after what a world of difference
there is between an intelligent person like that et ces politiciens de
carrière.[4] He rang up to ask him to dine but was told he was in Oxford.
He is a great charmer with very good ideas on all subjects.

I really can't alas manage week ends, shop hours are very strict &
there's a lot of work in the garden every minute I can spare.

Oh dear Gladys may have to go I am too miserable. She got 3
months extension for me to find somebody else & of course I can't
even look because it makes her so wretched. I suppose I shall get
some ghastly German spy in the end. What does make me rather
cross is if I had still been in the Red X they would have let her off,

though what I'm doing now is quite as useful twice as hard work &
no more pay. Also the unfairness of Helen [Dashwood] who has never
done a stroke having still 3 in kitchen & one housemaid all of call up
age because she has put being a bart's wife over her local labour
exchange.

Isn't it funny how unfairness gets one down very childish really.

Never mind, I am on the causeless wave of optimism about the war
which is an agreeable state of mind.

I say what about Baedeker raids, have you got a reasonable shelter
to go to? I should pile into the car & get away if I were you – I mean
when it begins you'd be down that road in a minute & out of it all.
Can't be much fun, a bad raid on a small town. I hoped you had gone
away for the summer & what about the bottling?

I've been in bed with food poisoning very prevalent & very horrid
– better now.

   Much love to all
      NR

Oh do come to the shop. Hen would love it, so many musical boxes.

[1] The Harrod children had been very ill.
[2] Tom Harrisson (1911–76). Married to Betha Clayton 1941–54; they had one son.
Founder in 1938, with Charles Madge, of Mass-Observation, which set out to record
what people were doing, thinking and saying in Britain. The validity of the surveys was
such that the Ministry of Information used them for studies on civilian morale during
the war.
[3] In March Nancy had started work as an assistant at Heywood Hill's bookshop in
Curzon Street. '. . . the one centre of old world gossip.' Waugh, *Letters*, p. 182.
[4] And these career politicians.

To DIANA MOSLEY   12 Blomfield Road, W9
24 August 1942
[passed by prison censor 26/8/42]

Darling Diana

They[1] are bliss, so awfully nice & thoughtful & tidy, the easiest
guests I ever had. Jonathan is so funny too. It was awful, on Sun:
evening we couldn't get into any cinema, I suppose my idiocy for not
getting seats but as I literally never go I had no idea they'd be so full.
Anyway they were simply sweet about it & it must have been so
disappointing.

How nice Elisabeth Guinness[2] is, I'd never seen her before, she
really seems to be a kind of angel. Desmond lost his coat (my fault

really) & she never even flicked an eyelid, just said how wonderful of you to keep the bigger coat. Now the only other person I know who would have been so good natured is you – I really was impressed.

Desmond's *eyes* lured Vic O[3] from the stage. I daresay they told you. *Darling*, Vic O – how could Sarah. I suppose he is a change from the pin stripe young men she was brought up with. (Never seen him before.)

In the shop J. made a beeline for a book called *The Miracle of the Human Body* – the nearest thing we have to pornog: – here he was riveted to the *Peerage*. So make what you like of that –

Will send Scott as soon as may be.

> Much love
> > NR

[1] Desmond and Jonathan Guinness, aged ten and twelve, had come up from the country to stay with Nancy in order to visit their mother in prison.
[2] Elisabeth Nelson became Bryan Guinness's second wife in 1936.
[3] Vic Oliver; stage and wireless entertainer, married to Winston Churchill's daughter Sarah 1936–45.

To DIANA MOSLEY   12 Blomfield Road, W9
28 November 1942
[passed by prison censor 1/12/42]

Darling Diana

How *could* you be so wonderful it brings tears to the eyes. You can't imagine the horror of the stocking situation in a book shop where one is forever on one's knees & I spend my week ends darning. Anne Hill[1] wears black & white check wool ones but I somehow can't –

Bobo enjoyed my party. She brought a ghastly old dress full of moth holes so I crammed her into my only good black one which we left undone all the way down the back & she kept on a coat so all was well but it was rather an awful moment when I saw what she did propose to wear. Then she refused to make up her face but the adored Capitaine Roy took her upstairs & did it for her. So in the end she looked awfully pretty.

There is an extraordinary wave of Ritz arrivals – Doris, Emerald & Mrs Corrigan.[2] As Cecil [Beaton] puts it 'so wizened-up you wouldn't know them.' What can it portend?

Osbert S.[3] on top of the world as he has been left £10 000 by Mrs Greville.[4] I told him it will kill the Wid. Sachie[5] whom I saw rather sour 'Ten pounds would have been so welcome but she left 1000 to Reresby.' Lord Dundonald[6] was asked by Bettine [Abingdon] if he got anything 'No – no nothing. I got my fee of course £5000, but she didn't leave me anything.' As Bettine says fee for putting on a top hat & going to the funeral –!

Cecil came into the shop 'such an oasis' & roared with laughter for an hour. The shop is really very gay now, full of people all day, & I am installed *in* the gas fire so manage to keep fairly warm.

Fancy favourite aunt how blissful. I can't think why as I am completely tongue tied by children, even yours, & at a loss how to behave. I long for a niece can't you provide one. . . .

It would be fun to see you with Dig & Henry [Yorke] as I hear you suggest though *slight* waste not to see you alone.

Goodness I feel old, going grey & bald & look terrible. I've been doing far too much & need a week in bed.

Much love
  NR

[1] Lady Anne Gathorne-Hardy (1911–). Married (George) Heywood Hill in 1938 and worked as his assistant in the bookshop. 'She is truly one of the world's worth-while women, so intelligent, male-minded, and deliciously humorous. She is "a dark mare" and worth a million more than the glittering women . . .' James Lees-Milne, *Ancestral Voices* (Chatto. & Windus, 1975), p. 161.
[2] Laura Whitlock (1879–1948). Lumberjack's daughter from Wisconsin, married steel magnate James Corrigan in 1916. Indefatigable hostess in London between the wars.
[3] Osbert Sitwell (1892–1969). Writer. Succeeded as 5th Baronet in 1943. Earlier in the year he had completed *The Cruel Month*, the first part of his five-volume autobiography, 'Left Hand! Right Hand!' (1945).
[4] Margaret McEwan. Acerbic daughter of a millionaire from Scotland. Married Hon. Ronald Greville in 1891. Died in 1942, leaving an estate of some £2 million; her jewels were bequeathed to the Queen, and to Osbert Sitwell she did indeed leave £10,000.
[5] Sacheverell Sitwell (1897–1988). Writer. Married Georgia Doble in 1925. In 1942 he published *The Homing of the Winds* and *Splendours and Miseries*. Succeeded his brother Osbert as baronet in 1969 and was succeeded by his son Reresby.
[6] 14th Earl of Dundonald (1918–86).

To Diana Mosley[1]
29 November 1943

> G. Heywood Hill, Ltd., *Booksellers*, 17 Curzon Street, W.1.
>
> *for* DIANA   Mayfair 0647-8   29 Nov 43
>
> Hasten to acquaint you that there is a brand new book called Endocrine disorders in Childhood ILLUSTRATED
>
> 15/- shall I write for it ? !!!

> Put MOSLEY back in GAOL!   Stamp
>
> Don't you think its rather poor taste of people to stick this on letters to me! Didn't you adore Osbert's cartoon this morning –

Osbert Lancaster
Daily Express,
29 November 1943

[1] Diana was under house arrest and had asked Nancy to keep Jonathan Guinness supplied with books at Eton. As a tease, Nancy sent him a highly unsuitable medical manual. 'He was very nearly sacked for it, the dame found it, pure porn, *illustrated*. And I was of course blamed as there was a card.' (Diana Mosley to the editor.)

To Lady Redesdale   12 Blomfield Road, W9
26 February 1944

Darling Muv

. . . You never saw anything like the burning – I pack a suit case
every night & always dress which I *never* did before, but the raids
are very short, exactly one hour, so that's no great hardship only
chilly. Also we have a very good fire party here so I have great
hopes that we could get anything under control. Still you never can
be certain.

I spent the morning looking at clothes – the most utter horrors
(dresses) you ever saw for £23, cheap & dreadful looking, what is
one to do? Then I tried to get a suspender belt – they have wooden
suspenders. So the squander bug went hungry away. It makes the
burning even more of a bore doesn't it.

The last straw is Harrods won't stamp one's note paper any more.
On which note of despair I will close!

    Best love
        NR

To Jessica Treuhaft[1]   The Rookery
11 March 1944   Ashford
                                                Derby

Darling Sooze

For the 1st time for 6 months I am having 3 days off & have a
moment in which to write.

I do long for news of you – sometimes get it from Muv – but I
know how one can't write to people abroad, I am always paralysed
when I try to do so. Poor Brains for Breakfast in prison in Germany
I try & try to think of things to say & even the old tollgater, who has
now been away 3 years is quite a problem & I always end up by
writing an endless grumble about his mother or brother Francis (the
horror!)

I am here with Debo & the completely round Emma[2] which makes
me die more than ever for Constancia.

If you can ever bear to write do say if you would like me sometimes
to send you books or don't you have much time to read? I am still
entirely running the bookshop & like it though I get rather tired &
discouraged sometimes. Also I have at home various children's books
of yours – would Constancia like me to send them?

Our Villa at Naples is entirely destroyed & (isn't life queer) Prod finds himself living near the ruin, looked after by our old servants & burning my ma in law's frightful furniture for fire wood. He goes to the beach head every day & says it is hell on earth.

Do send me a photograph of Constancia – I hear they are so good but as I hardly ever see any of the family I haven't seen one.

Much love Soo
    NR

[1] Esmond Romilly was killed in action in November 1941. Jessica stayed in America and in 1943 married Robert Treuhaft, an American attorney.
[2] Emma Cavendish was one year old.

20 Rue Bonaparte VI

10 Oct 45

Darling My life has resolved itself
into a mole-like struggle not to
leave this spot (Paris I mean) Miss
Chetwynd, owner of the flat, wrote &
said when M. de Seyres arrives you
must instantly go as he is very sad,
has lost his wife, & must be alone.
I'm ashamed to say I haven't gone &
am leaving here, for an hotel, only on
Sunday, a week after I got her letter
I blush at my awful behaviour. But
the col mched off to Brussels & I
hardly saw him between Rhine land
& that & must stay & say goodbye.
So I made his secretary find me a
room, but there wasn't one until Sunday
anywhere in Paris. Now I hope to stay
until after the elections wh has always
been my real aim! The weather is
boiling like June, really too divine &
the trees are all yellow - just the time
for Paris.
Little Marie de Beauvau turned up
& took me round the night clubs

To Violet Hammersley, 10 October 1945

1944–1947

THE COLONEL

She was waiting, unconsciously, for that revolution which often comes in the life of a
woman no longer young and directs the future
course of her existence.

Nancy Mitford, *Voltaire in Love*

Nancy's affair with Gaston Palewski, the 'Colonel' as she always called
him, after his rank in the French Air Force, began in September 1942.
He had been one of the first Frenchmen to rally to General de Gaulle
in support of his crusade to wrest legitimacy from the collaborationist
Vichy regime. When Nancy met him he was head of de Gaulle's *cabinet*
which was quartered in Carlton Gardens, off The Mall. He had
recently returned from Ethiopia where he commanded the Free
French Forces. In Addis Ababa he had seen Peter Rodd, and on
arrival in London he got in touch with Nancy to give her his
news.

To those who were impervious to the Colonel's charm it was difficult
to understand the transformation that he brought about in Nancy. His
physical appearance was unprepossessing: he was a short, squat man,
his skin was scarred by acne and his features suggested Mr Punch.
His main weaknesses were vanity, social ambition and, in political life,
a desire to have a finger in every pie. But he possessed irrepressible
vitality and an infectious joviality, and unabashedly enjoyed the company of women. He had great taste, loved art, and took sensuous
pleasure in collecting beautiful objects. He spoke good English, having
spent a year at Oxford preparing a thesis on the Victorian novel, and
he was witty, civilised, kind and loyal. During the eight months that

he was in London Nancy provided a welcome distraction from his long and difficult hours at work. Like Scheherazade, she used all her powers to keep him entertained with gossip and stories of her family. His delight in her childhood recollections made Nancy realise their full potential as source material for her novels.

For Gaston, Nancy represented an enchanting interlude. Her adoration flattered him, he was genuinely fond of her and valued her friendship, but he was not, nor did he ever pretend to be, in love. For Nancy, Gaston became the very centre of her existence and after meeting him she never looked at another man. This asymmetry was summed up by Nancy in a letter to Diana Cooper: 'I say to him, "d'you know what Colonel – I love you" & he replies, "that's awfully kind of you."' There were, however, aspects of this arm's-length relationship that suited her very well; it allowed her to sustain her romantic illusion and to keep fantasy and reality apart. At a distance Gaston could provide inspiration for her books. Many of her hero figures, from the Duke of Sauveterre in *The Pursuit of Love* to Louis XIV in *The Sun King*, are modelled on her idealised image of Gaston.

When war ended, Nancy was determined to live in Paris to be near the Colonel. He did his best to discourage her – his letters are formal, courteous, dull and resolutely uncompromising. He used his political position as an excuse not to get involved: General de Gaulle had old-fashioned views and an affair with a married Englishwoman could have been injurious to his career. But Nancy was undeterred, and spent the last three months of 1945 in Paris, ostensibly buying books for Heywood Hill when in reality living for the moments that the Colonel could spare from his political and social activities – and innumerable love affairs. Some of her friends thought it would have been kinder if he had refused to see her altogether since he could never satisfy the fanatical depth of passion he had aroused, and could only, in the end, make her unhappy. While the rational side of Nancy knew that she could never be Gaston's wife, she continued to nurture a secret hope.

The instant success of *The Pursuit of Love*, published in December 1945, allowed Nancy to return to Paris the following spring. She moved between cheap hotels and rented flats while looking for a permanent home, and never went back to live in England again. For the first time in her life she was free from her family, her husband – Peter had become a shadowy presence, an occasional annoying visitor – and her background. Her love for Gaston and, through him, her love of France and the French, became Nancy's cause, in the same way that her sisters had espoused political causes through their love of a man.

Nancy set out to enjoy herself in a city where people were determined to forget wartime austerity. Whenever she could afford to, she would buy clothes from Dior or his followers: the ample skirt and well-fitted tops of the 'New Look' was a fashion that suited Nancy's tiny waist and tall, slender figure perfectly. Despite remaining unmistakably English, she became truly elegant. She started to make friends among French intellectuals and among the less stuffy aristocrats and soon became a regular addition to the cosmopolitan, and sometimes raffish, entourage of the Duff Coopers at the British Embassy.

Nancy's move to Paris was obviously important for her letter-writing. Although she had – in a sense – turned her back on England, her English friends were irreplaceable and she hungered after their news. They in turn looked forward to the regular treat of receiving her letters. Two friendships in particular began to develop on paper, with Evelyn Waugh and Heywood Hill, who were both good sources of London literary and social gossip. Curiously, Heywood's extremely amusing letters to Nancy did not provoke her best letters in return. For this reason few, relative to the number she wrote, have been included. Much of what she said to Heywood she also wrote to Evelyn, and it was for him that she reserved her most sparkling accounts. She continued to send a weekly letter to her mother, finding it easier to communicate in writing than in conversation. Her sister Diana also became a favoured correspondent during this period. Nancy was eager to overcome their wartime coolness and, of all her sisters, she envied Diana the most, but probably also loved her the most.

To Gaston Palewski[1]   12 Blomfield Road, W9
24 June 1944

Harper's Bazaar (an American fashion paper) asked me to do an article
on the Face of London, so as they pay very well I went round to see
the editress. She showed me a cable from New Y. saying please
immediately send an article bringing in the Carcanos.[2] Really, at this
stage of the war! So I bowed myself out. We are evidently having a
silly season, as *Lilliput* then asked if I would do one on slimming. So,
fortified by sur le ventre, I am embarking on that. (No doubt *they* will
say I must bring in the Carcanos before I get my money.)

I lunched with Tony G.[3] en tête à tête today. He said 'I am very
fond of Carmen[4] but sometimes she reminds me of her mother & *of
course that is very disagreeable.*' So different to a father in a novel 'she
reminds me more every day of her dear dear mother.'

Colonel I have begun to miss you most dreadfully again you wicked
Col. Do you get my letters? Please please say.
25 June
Now where am I sitting? In Mr Luxmoore's garden,[5] waiting for Jonathan to finish his Sunday lesson. Two boys have just wandered by &
I thought I heard one of them say 'Oh, Eddy DO let's.' It all reminds
me of *20 years ago* when I used to visit Tom – toi que voilà qu'as tu
fait de ta jeunesse?[6] Is one's failure in life always absolutely one's own
fault – I believe it is. Everything really happens inside one's head
doesn't it & Verlaine couldn't have felt more enclosed in a prison cell
than I do.

I went yesterday to see a news reel of the Gen[eral] & got one
glimpse of my dear Col looking very happy – Oh Col I hope soon
you'll look like that all the time.

A telegram from dotty Marc[7] has just arrived saying no news. How
could there be as he has never divulged his address. He is in Alabama
– surrounded no doubt by designing blondes. I wrote him a long letter
which I now see is all about you – I seem to make the worst of every
world – but then as I'm always trying to explain to a doubtful Colonel
I really am not cut out for *this sort of thing* at all.

Osbert Lancaster said at luncheon on Fri: that Aly F[8] told him you
were so frightened in that raid on Thurs: that you kept ringing him
up – I said furiously that is a total lie I was with Palewski *all night.*
Sibyl Colefax: *all night*? N.R. Well, you know what I mean.

[1] Gaston Palewski (1901–84). In May 1943, eight months after his first meeting with
Nancy, Palewski left London for Algiers where he remained until the beginning of June

1944. His letters to Nancy over this period are punctuated with 'écrivez, écrivez' and indicate that she wrote to him frequently with news and gossip of London. Palewski joked that he would publish her letters under the title 'La revanche de Madame du Deffand'. Unfortunately none of these letters has survived; they would have given a unique picture of wartime London and shed light on Nancy's early relations with Palewski. When he came back to London on 5 June to assist de Gaulle during a week of talks with Churchill and Eisenhower, Nancy's happiness was like Linda's in *The Pursuit of Love* when Fabrice returns for a day and 'all was light and warmth'. Then, on 14 June, he left to take up the post of de Gaulle's Directeur de Cabinet. See Biographical Notes.
[2] Dr Don Miguel Carcano; Argentine Ambassador in London 1942–6. His two daughters married Englishmen: Ana Inez, the Hon. John Astor 1944–72, and Stella, Viscount Ednam 1946–61.
[3] Don Antonio de Gandarillas (d.1970). Opium-smoking Chilean diplomat. Portrayed as Baroness von Bülop in Cecil Beaton's spoof memoirs *My Royal Past* (1939). 'For many years, if a person more of social ornament than utility, he was attached to the Chilean Embassy in London. But his true vocation lay in his friendship and more particularly, he had artists and musicians for close friends.' Sacheverell Sitwell, *The Times*, 27 January 1970.
[4] Daughter of the above.
[5] A garden at Eton, bequeathed to the school by a master.
[6] '. . . Dis, qu'as tu fait, toi que voilà / De ta jeunesse? . . .' Paul Verlaine, *Sagesse* (1881).
[7] Prince de Beauvau Craon (1921–82). Member of the Free French Forces. A friend of Palewski and thus welcome company for Nancy.
[8] Alastair Forbes (1918–). Journalist. 'I really love Ali Forbes, & so does the Col, I think he is the only clever young man I know with a heart.' (NM to Diana Mosley, 29 October 1947)

To Lady Redesdale   12 Blomfield Road, W9
8 July 1944

Darling Muv

Thank you so much, you *are* so kind. I must say life is very expensive, or perhaps I am extravagant. I had to get a pair of sheets so thought I would swallow the bitter pill of cotton ones, but was laughed at – it seems they don't exist, & nor do linen ones & finally I found a pair of linen ones not at all nice – £20. After all we can't sleep between blankets but it did go to my heart. However I've at last found someone who will mend my linen so shall be able to struggle on now I suppose!

About Tom – of course he is living in a garçonnière in Curzon St. Seriously, people always turn up a month after they say, I've never known it otherwise, so don't expect him till you see him.

Nobody minds the bombs any more (I never did) but they are doing a fearful amount of damage to houses. One going over here knocked panes of glass out of my neighbour's top window simply from the vibration of the engine, which is unbelievable unless you have heard the thing. One going off on the Wycombe grammar school broke a lot of Helen's windows 3 miles away. Why do they always go for the hospitals & crèches – I am terrified as we have a day nursery in this street & I can't feel it will escape. I've put off my holiday – it is all a dreadful bore. But how can the Germans be so stupid as to get everybody into a temper now, just as they must see they have lost, it is really too idiotic of them & seriously I think minimizes the chance of a decent peace – quite civilized people like for instance Sigrid[1] are simply mad with fury, much more so than in the big raids funnily enough. I can't say it has that effect on me but I do dread losing the house because oh *where* would one live?

There is at last a wonderful book I can recommend – *Memories of Happy Days* by Julien Green. It is in dreadfully short supply so be sure & get it from the library in good time. I think it the *best thing* there has been since I was in the shop! His first written in English.

Much love
    NR

[1] Nancy's Norwegian maid.

To Lady Redesdale   12 Blomfield Road, W9
24 September 1944

Darling Muv

Many thanks to Farve for the rabbits – most welcome indeed.

I am in bed with laryngitis – have had a relaxed throat for a fortnight now & have now lost my voice & feel v. sorry for myself.

The fact is I must have a holiday but in order to have what I really need which is a month I should have to leave the shop altogether as it would be quite out of the question for Mollie[1] alone to do more than a week without me. Neither Hill has been near it since the bombs began & they say they won't come back to London until an *armistice* has been *signed*. (He of course is in the army but even when he has leave he doesn't come to London!!)

If I didn't like the work so much nothing could induce me to go on with such people, specially as I am so underpaid,[2] & I have a very good mind to chuck it & write a book. But then I couldn't afford to live here & should have to let this, & that means breaking up my present life & Gladys etc & I *can't* make up my mind!

Are you ever going back to the Cottage? I so long for a few days of country air, & to see you and Song [Unity].

Poor little Debo seems quite distracted – she was in London meeting Kick[3] – all these deaths must terrify her for Andrew, though Peter says there aren't many casualties in Italy now & the worst there is over.

I am angling like mad for a job in Paris, but all rather nebulous at present, tho' I think it may come off. If so I should insist on a month's holiday first, as really I am not wèll, & so thin again. I got a lot of books from there last week by a wangle, the only bookseller who has. They are like water in a drought & I sold £20 worth the first day! all quite cheap things, novels & reproductions of pictures etc. Their book production has advanced as much as ours has gone back so they were most refreshing to look at apart from the excitement of the 1944 Valéry[4] & Simenon.[5]

Oh to live in Paris, I'd give anything.

I swapped my diamond clip for a pair of diamond daisies, awfully pretty, *and* £40. Don't you call that good – considering it cost £50 in the 1st place & the daisies were £30. And considering what cheats jewellers are.

All the chaps who come back from Paris (English) say the fashions are hideous but I bet we shouldn't think so. It's just as you said, the women are a *different shape*. Skirts above the knee & huge & hats twice as high as their wearers.

I rather shudder for my 2 new suits, but suits are always classic really aren't they?

Ad [Lubbock] & her children went to the cottage & simply adored it.

Do say when you are coming back.

Oh dear I'm so *bored*, dumb, in bed!

My mother in law announced she was dying. I forced Peter with great difficulty to go & see her & he found her hoeing in the garden.

He expects to be posted somewhere next week but he would rather like to leave the army & join UNRRA[6] which he really ought to do.

Best love
    NR

[1] Mollie Friese-Greene helped with the accounts at Heywood Hill. In 1949 she married

Handasyde Buchanan, who also worked for the bookshop and who later became a partner.
[2] James Lees-Milne interceded on Nancy's behalf and asked Anne Hill if her wages could be raised: 'She did not resent my interference but explained laughingly that whereas Nancy got paid £3.10s.0d she only got £2.10s.0d; that the shop barely paid its way.' *Ancestral Voices*, p. 161.
[3] Kathleen Kennedy (1920–48). President Kennedy's sister. Married the Marquess of Hartington, Deborah's brother-in-law, on 6 May 1944; he was killed in Belgium four months later. She died in a flying accident in 1948.
[4] Paul Valéry (1871–1945). Considered one of the greatest French writers of his generation. His collection of poems *Variétés V* was published in 1944.
[5] Georges Simenon (1903–89). In 1944 he published *Signé Picpus*, *Le Rapport du gendarme* and *Les Nouvelles enquêtes de Maigret*.
[6] United Nations Relief and Rehabilitation Administration.

To HEYWOOD HILL[1]   12 Blomfield Road, W9
28 October 1944

My dear Heywood

Thank you so much for your kind letter. Now do let's really find out how the shop *is* doing, can we? You know I have its good at heart & don't want to push it under by being a super cargo at all. So let's wait until we really do know, & if it seems OK you can pay me the extra back to this date. About partnership – could we wait until the end of the war & then think? I could get capital from my Ma in Law who offers me £5000 to start a shop every time I see her, but you know I don't think I do much want to play at bookshops all the rest of my life, though I may have to. Also I believe we might find it difficult to work together, both having been bosses, though probably that's just imagination. Anyway thank you very very much for suggesting it & for all the kind things you say.

I've just come back from Eton with that Eton headache I remember so well of old. Did some really splendid buying at Mrs Brown's, sets of Shakespeare, Milton, Eliot, M. Edgeworth & a mass of useful oddments & *so* cheap, I am simply delighted (all so pretty). I fairly skimmed the cream, thought she didn't seem absolutely delighted, tho' quite cordial really. *She* has been in a bookshop 50 years – oh help!

I say I've just seen a *rocket*![2] It's like the most frightening dream you ever had, exactly like a setting November sun hurtling out of the sky. I can't get over it.

Love from
    Nancy

[1] (George) Heywood Hill (1907–86). Spent seven years with the antiquarian bookseller Charles Sawyer before opening his own bookshop, on a shoestring, in August 1936. Married Lady Anne Gathorne-Hardy in 1938. He was called up in December 1942, by which time Nancy had joined the shop which had become a favoured meeting-place for writers and book-lovers alike. Nancy and Heywood exchanged over four hundred letters; he preserved all hers and she most of his. 'Yes I keep all Heywood's letters, worth £1 a word.' (NM to Robin McDouall, 10 July 1972)
[2] The V-2, German long-range rocket which carried a ton of explosives.

To CYRIL CONNOLLY   12 Blomfield Road, W9
29 November 1944

My dear Cyril

I am most extremely touched & gratified at being sent the Grave[1] & have been gobbling about in it the whole evening & can't wait to begin again – in fact I see it is going to be a *great great* pleasure to one. It is really very much like talking to you, always a major pleasure.

Are you sending one to Evelyn or Harold? Let me know, sometime. I have had a fearfully funny letter from Evelyn – Randolph is driving him quite mad it seems.[2]

Oh the lemurs,[3] I so *long* for one now, more than ever.

With love from
      Nancy

[1] Palinurus [Cyril Connolly], *The Unquiet Grave*, first published in *Horizon* magazine in 1944.
[2] Waugh was in Croatia, as part of a British military mission accredited to Marshal Tito, and was living at close quarters with Randolph Churchill and Frederick, 2nd Earl of Birkenhead.
[3] Connolly's book includes a lament for his pet lemurs: 'black and grey bundles of vitality, eocene ancestors from whom we are all descended'. *The Unquiet Grave* (Hamish Hamilton, 1945), p. 84.

To DIANA MOSLEY[1]   12 Blomfield Road, W9
29 November 1944

Darling your present – popular indeed & with all. Oh you can't think what it is like this year, shopping, there *is no food*. Funny but it's the worst, in London, since the war. A bit of boiling bacon therefore is indeed a treat.

Whom did I lunch with today? You'd never guess. Back from America &, as they all are, clean looking & *unlined* (I suppose it's the food) Syrie [Maugham]! I was really most delighted to see her – I never can help it. People run away & live in luxury & come back looking 20 but I can't really blame them much. There is I believe some feeling over her (specially Sibyl!)

I had a party (dinner) last night & Pete got me 3 bottles of champagne, it was a great success. Alvilde[2] & Anthony Chaplin, Ed Sackville-West, Peter Derwent,[3] Adelaide [Lubbock], Tuggie.[4] Haven't embarked on such a thing for years.

Much love & 1000 thanks again
    NR

[1] The Mosleys had been released from prison in November 1943 and were living under house arrest at Crux Easton in Berkshire.
[2] Alvilde Bridges (1909–94). An expert on gardens and garden design. Married to Viscount Chaplin 1933–50 and to James Lees-Milne in 1951.
[3] 3rd Baron Derwent (1899–1949).
[4] Anne, Countess of Rosse.

To Diana Mosley   12 Blomfield Road, W9
4 December 1944

Darling Diana

I did say to Jonathan that I would go again this ½ – but now Bryan is back what do you think? I imagine he goes a good deal? When do they break up?

Fancy I met Scott's widow.[1] I said I am keen on Captain Scott she said So am I & we talked for an hour. She was fascinated at me knowing so much. I asked if she thinks there might be another expedition & she says certainly after the war, & a woman might go as far as The HUT but not on a serious journey. *Oh dear.* She was dressed (Ritz) from head to foot in pale blue hand woven but I thought her heaven. She said Marie Stopes[2] very nearly went on THE journey & Scott had to exercise his full will power to stop her!

Lunched with Syrie who is back from America, cut by many & hit by Sibyl but I was pleased to see her. We talked of *nothing* but Liza's[3] health. She offers Tilly as a wife for Tom I said no thanks.

I see the French Ambassadress[4] a lot & am *kept awake at night* by her clothes – haven't wanted new clothes at all until now, but oh! She is a nice person, full of energy & good intentions.

Evelyn writes (boxed up with Randolph & Freddie B at Tito's) that he & Freddie, hoping to keep R quiet have bet him £20 he won't read the Bible in a fortnight but it hasn't had the hoped-for result. 'He has never read the book before, is hideously excited, keeps slapping his thigh & saying God isn't God a shit.'

> Best love
> NR

[1] Kathleen Bruce (1878–1947). Married to the Antarctic explorer Captain Robert Falcon Scott 1908–12 and to 1st Baron Kennet in 1922. The story of the tragic expedition to the South Pole had left an indelible impression on Nancy as a child and Scott remained one of her heroes.
[2] Marie Stopes (1880–1958). Botanist, geologist and early proponent of family planning. Her research into fossil fuels had made her eager to investigate the coal seams in Antarctica.
[3] Elizabeth Maugham (1915–). Syrie and Somerset Maugham's daughter. Married to Vincent Paravicini 1937–48 and to Lord John Hope in 1948.
[4] Odette Massigli, married to René Massigli, the French Ambassador in London 1944–55.

To Evelyn Waugh   12 Blomfield Road, W9
22 December 1944

Darling Evelyn

Brideshead[1] has come, beautiful in orig. boards, a triumph of book production. And a great English classic in my humble opinion. Oh how I shld like to chat about it – there are one or 2 things I long to know. Are you, or not, on Lady Marchmain's side? I couldn't make out. I suppose Charles ends by being more in love than ever before with Cordelia – so true to life being in love with a whole family (it has happened in mine tho' not lately). *Oh* Johnjohn & Caroline & that awful wife are simply perfect. Sebastian reminded me of Henry Weymouth[2] & a little of Andrew Cav[endish]: so glad you're nice about Brian[3] this time too. One dreadful error. Diamond clips were only invented about 1930, you wore a diamond *arrow* in your cloche. It's the only one, which I call good – the only one I spotted at least. I think Charles might have had a little more glamour – I can't explain why but he seemed to me a tiny bit dim & that is the *only* criticism I have to make because I am literally dazzled with admiration. I must read it again as I *had* to skip sometimes to get on with the story & I read it all night till one with increasing eye strain & very tired. (Xmas rush.) I told Osbert [Sitwell] today how wonderful it is & he said I am jealous of all writers except Evelyn whom I regard as being on our side.

Mr Trumper died this week. He cut off Driberg's ear & died.[4] The shop (Trumpers) shut for a day & Mollie & I wished it had been

Dearest [Heywood Hill] so that we could shut for a day too. It's like hounds not meeting, isn't it, a new point of etiquette to me.

I must tell about Alan Lennox-Boyd.[5] Well he went to get his annual injection against colds, got a whopper & went to the House where he was on a committee. He felt queer, rather in a coma, when he heard a man opposite him say to the Chairman 'I think I must be going mad because Alan L.B. seems to have swollen in the last few minutes to twice his usual size.' 'My God' said the chairman 'he has.' And he had. And the dr had given him elephantiasis by mistake.[6]

Well, it took 2 ambulances to get him away & he now lies on 4 beds with his trunk hanging out of the window. Let nobody say that war time London lacks fantasy. Gerald [Berners] has wired that I am to let him know if Chips turns into any sort of animal as that would be worth coming up for.

Love from
    NR

[1] Evelyn Waugh, *Brideshead Revisited* (1945). Nancy had been sent an advance copy.
[2] Viscount Weymouth (1905–92). Succeeded as 6th Marquess of Bath in 1946. Married to Hon. Daphne Vivian 1927–53 and to Virginia Parsons in 1953.
[3] Brian Howard contributed a few characteristics to Anthony Blanche in *Brideshead Revisited*.
[4] Geo F. Trumper, gentleman's hairdresser in Curzon Street, was established in 1875. Mr Lenard, who joined the firm in 1946, does not recall hearing of this incident but confirms that it is not unknown for a hairdresser occasionally to nick his customers' ears. Tom Driberg's injury was probably no more than a small cut.
[5] Alan Lennox-Boyd (1904–83). Conservative MP for mid-Bedfordshire. Created 1st Viscount Boyd in 1960. Married Lady Patricia Guinness in 1938.
[6] Alan Lennox-Boyd was a large man even before being given the wrong injection.

To Diana Mosley   12 Blomfield Road, W9
10 January 1945

Darling
   . . . I've thought of you so much this week – endless parties for *sweet* Poulenc[1] & Bernac,[2] all the old dreary buddies have blossomed & become incredibly gay. Tony Gandarillas on Sunday, last night the French Embassy which was very brilliant & the greatest fun. They have taken Lowndes House you know, do you remember Muv had it once. Alvilde also had a dinner for them which I went to & today the Clarks[3] which I had to refuse as really I can't every night. Haven't been so gay – really – since the war. The fly in the ointment is Mme Massigli's clothes which make one feel *Cinderella in the cinders*.

Luckily all the other English are in the same boat – or really perhaps unluckily as they all look too incredibly moth eaten for words & almost spoil everything.

How I've been wishing you were here[4] to enjoy it all too – really the monde is great fun when in modified doses which is all one gets nowadays. But oh how old everyone is. Poulenc is fearfully thin & worried looking & looks old but I suppose (is he about 40?) he & I were the youngest there last night except for Alvilde & some old young men like Garrett [Moore] who, as they are all as bald as coots I never can remember are younger than me! Oggie,[5] Emerald, Juliet,[6] Violet Trefusis[7] – you know! The Massiglis for the moment have fallen into that world & I shall be fascinated to see if they remain there or if she hasn't at heart other, more pompous ideas. Anyhow long may it last as it will be a most agreeable addition to one's life while it does.

Evelyn's book not yet out. Not as good as *Work Suspended* but more important I suppose – anyhow highly enjoyable.

Yes Cyril *is* a brilliant person. His conversation now is almost unbelievably accomplished – the most in London I should say. He went off to Paris today lucky him. He says he no longer suffers these agonies & that the tortured bits like the ferret[8] (I so well remember that happening) were written 10 years ago. I don't know, perhaps he flatters himself, I think people can suffer at any age. Emerald continually talks of suicide & Princess Winnie[9] died, in a way, of a broken heart at 78! When he falls in love again I expect it will recommence.

Much love
    NR

P.S. I've just seen a photo of the 'regent'[10] wh reminds me of a story that made me shriek. A few months ago a Greek bishop with a great beard like that went to Buck Pal: & the Queen whose great gambit is always where do you come from said

'I suppose you come from Athens?'

'No Madam I am a Lesbian.'

The regent is the image of grandmother isn't he.

The other story I adore about the Q is a Polish airman describing his deeds for wh he was decorated.

'I shot down one Fokker & there were 2 more on my tail but I managed to shoot them down as well.'

'Oh – were they Messerschmitts?'

I thought where Cyril said Marriage is a perpetual conversation was so good. Poor C how he hankers after that awful Jeannie who is drinking herself to death in America. He is living with a dear pretty little thing called Lys Lubbock but never throws her one kind word in the whole book tho' she cooks & sews & slaves for him.

So like life!

[1] Francis Poulenc (1899–1963). French composer, one of 'les Six'; wrote airs for many poems and adapted Guillaume Apollinaire's *Les Mamelles de Tirésias* and Jean Cocteau's *La Voix humaine* as operas.

[2] Pierre Bernac; singer and interpreter of Poulenc's songs.

[3] Kenneth Clark (1903–83). Art historian. Director of the National Gallery 1934–45. Created life peer in 1969. Married to Elizabeth Martin (Jane) 1928–76, and to Nolwen de Janzé in 1977. Presenter of the television series *Civilization* (1969).

[4] Diana was still under house arrest.

[5] Olga Lynn (1882–1961). Diminutive concert singer and teacher whose company was greatly sought after by those in search of amusement.

[6] Lady Juliet Lowther (1881–1965). Married to Sir Robert Duff 1903–14 and to Major Keith Trevor 1919–26; thereafter resumed her former name of Duff.

[7] Violet Keppel (1894–1972). Minor novelist. Married Denys Trefusis in 1919. Eloped several times with Vita Sackville-West. Nancy and Violet maintained an uneasy truce. 'I must say I think she's dangerously dotty – she's like Matilda who told such dreadful lies it made one gasp & stretch one's eyes . . . a terrible trouble maker. She goes back to France next week (in a way I shall miss her because one can't help being fond of her in spite of all).' (NM to Gaston Palewski, 3 March 1946)

[8] Connolly's pet ferret 'strayed from the garden and entered a cottage kitchen where she sat up to beg as she had been taught, until ignorant peasants kicked her to death, and brought back to us her limp body'. *The Unquiet Grave*, p. 82.

[9] Winnaretta Singer (1865–1943). Sewing-machine heiress and learned patron of the arts. Married Prince Edmond de Polignac (1834–1901) in 1893; a marriage of reason: she loved women and he preferred men.

[10] Damaskinos; the Archbishop of Athens.

To Evelyn Waugh   12 Blomfield Road, W9
17 January 1945

Dearest Evelyn

I have a great deal to say – 2 air letters (1/-, agony) if necessary & the whole evening before me. So long as my pen behaves (it has been more of a fountain than a pen lately) & so long as V[-2] leaves me alone (& all London *prays* for it to get me as I am the only person who doesn't mind, so it's an ill wind) we are all set for an immense tome.

I am answering your letter about *Brideshead*. I quite see how the person who tells is dim but then would Julia *and* her brother *and* her sister all be in love with him if he was? Well love is like that & one never can tell. What I can't understand is about God.[1] Now I believe in God & I talk to him a very great deal & often tell him jokes but the God I believe in simply *hates* fools more than anything & he also likes people to be happy & people who love each other to live together – so long as nobody else's life is upset (& then he's not sure). Now I see that I am absolutely un religious. I also see this because what is a red rag to a bull to several people about your book is the *subtle clever* Catholic propaganda & I hardly noticed there was any which shows I am immune from it.

Now about what people think:

Raymond [Mortimer]: Great English classic.

Cyril: Brilliant where the narrative is straightforward. Doesn't care for the 'purple passages' i.e. death bed of Lord M. Thinks you go too much to White's. But found it impossible to put down (no wonder).

Osbert: Jealous, doesn't like talking about it. 'I'm devoted to Evelyn – are you?'

Maurice [Bowra]: Showing off to Cyril about how you don't always hit the right word or some nonsense but obviously much impressed & thinks the Oxford part perfect.

SW7 (European royal quarter): Heaven, darling.

Diane Abdy:[2] Like me & Raymond, no fault to find.

Lady Chetwode:[3] Terribly dangerous propaganda. Brilliant.

General View: It is the Lygon family.[4] Too much Catholic stuff.

I am writing a book,[5] also in the 1st person. (Only now has it occurred to me everybody will say what a copy cat – never mind that won't hurt you only me.) It's about my family, a very different cup of tea, not grand & far madder. Did I begin it before reading *B.head* or after – I can't remember. I've done about 10 000 words & asked Dearest for a 3 month holiday to write it which I believe I shall get. I'm awfully excited my fingers itch for a pen.

[1] Evelyn Waugh had replied to Nancy's letter of 22 December 1944 with: 'Lady March-main, no I am not on her side; but God is, who suffers fools gladly; and the book is about God. Does that answer it?' *Letters*, p. 196.

[2] Lady Diana Bridgeman (1907–67). Married to Sir Robert Abdy 1930–62.

[3] Alice Cotton (1871–1946). Married Field Marshal Chetwode in 1899. Mother of Penelope Betjeman.

[4] The two sons and three daughters of 7th Earl of Beauchamp were great friends of Waugh. 'The family situation of the Flyte family was unquestionably taken from that of the Lygon family in the early 1930s.' Christopher Sykes, *Evelyn Waugh* (Collins, 1975), p. 252.

[5] *The Pursuit of Love*, completed between January and March 1945. Never again would Nancy find a book so quick and easy to write.

To Diana Mosley   12 Blomfield Road, W9
4 March 1945

Darling Diana

I really meant to say middle of April – I go to Debo 15 this month
& then am supposed to go to Gerald[1] I think for about 10 days (he
says that absolutely impossible thing do stay as long as you like). But
if it's better after the holidays, then I could come in May, my holiday
goes on till June.

I simply *can't believe* I haven't got to struggle up tomorrow morning
at 9 with my sore throat which now seems quite chronic – oh the
heaven!

I do not like hard regular work – I've had it for 4 years & am quite
certain I don't. However many people, it seems, *do* which is lucky.

I went to a farce last night with Emerald. It was roaringly funny, I
laughed till I choked. E. sat very seriously as tho' at Shakespeare or
Ibsen, looking at the actors through opera glasses.

Gerald's latest fantasy is he has to wear dark glasses because he
has such kind eyes that beggars etc swarm round him asking favours.
He *is* a fool.

Much love
    NR

[1] Lord Berners's house, Faringdon, near Oxford, was the inspiration for Merlinford in
The Pursuit of Love.

To Jessica Treuhaft   12 Blomfield Road, W9
13 April 1945

Darling Sooze

I thought you would like a line to say Muv & Farve are being simply
wonderful & much much better than we had feared at first. But it is
almost unbearable oh *Tud*[1] if you knew how sweet & nice & gay he
has been of late & on his last leave. That is a comfort, it shows he
was happy & I know he enjoyed the journey out very much. But I
shall miss him dreadfully, I'd seen a lot of him during the war.

Old Rodd often thinks of you. The other day his mother said to him
if I leave you some money who will you leave it to & he said Decca's
children so now of course she won't as she wants it for her own
grandchildren! But I was so surprised & really touched & thought
you would be. Dear old thing, I'm thankful to say he's in England for
the moment.

I'm writing a book about us when we were little, it's not a farce this time but serious – a novel, don't be nervous!

More photographs please. Oh Susan I shall never see you again & I would so like to.

Much love from
    Sooze

[1] Tom Mitford died of wounds in Burma on 30 March 1945; he was thirty-six.

To LADY REDESDALE   12 Blomfield Road, W9
27 April 1945

Darling Muv

You will be glad to hear that Mark is back.[1] He looks like a horror-photograph, his knees are enormous lumps & his arms like sticks, but alive & well & *immensely* cheerful. He says in prison they dreamed of nothing but food & *his* dream was – do you remember that layer-cake with jam you used to have? Well that! Isn't it too funny, I'd quite forgotten it but of course it used to be a feature of our lives. He has been in 13 prisons.

The dinner party was a great success & luckily he got back the day before so could come, his first outing. Peter has been turned back as he was about to embark & put on to a job here with German prisoners, very important priority work but what he doesn't yet know. I must say I'm thankful he doesn't have to go to Germany.

Gerald has just rung up with an account of his visit to Diana wh. he very much enjoyed. I go to him tomorrow.

Most of my book has been taken off to be typed by Phil[2] who suddenly appeared out of the blue & spent a day here. She seems *very* happy, I'm so glad. Her boy Richard, suddenly decided not to join the Merchant Navy but the army & without saying a word he sold the £80 worth of equipment she had got him for £5. Aren't boys dreadful!

Much love
    NR

I hope you got a boatman?[3]

[1] Mark Ogilvie-Grant had been a prisoner of war.
[2] Phyllis Bowles (d.1968). Nancy's first cousin and great childhood friend. She married Michael Prynne who had a unique reputation amongst naturalists as a repairer of wild birds' egg shells. Author of *Egg Shells* (1963).

[3] Lady Redesdale's only means of getting from Inchkenneth to the nearest island, Mull, was by rowing boat or a small motor boat, the *Puffin*.

To Lady Redesdale   12 Blomfield Road, W9
24 May 1945

Darling Muv

Kingsley Martin[1] has just rung up & given a very good account of Decca & her husband whom he saw in S Francisco.

The husband he says is a pleasant quiet little chap,[2] he liked him very much. I asked if he seemed to be a recent refugee & K said he saw no indication of that, that he was a lawyer before the war & appeared absolutely American.

Decca asked him to tell us all that the reason she doesn't often write is she lives in such an utterly different world it's difficult to know what to tell, which I can believe. He says she sees nobody but proletarians & CP members & that it is indeed a strange & different world to any over here, but he says very fascinating.

The thing is he really was most reassuring about Treuhaft – he says he's difficult to describe but he made a very definite impression & an agreeable one. He says she is as pretty as a picture – which certainly must mean she is happy I think. He was to have seen their children, but in the end he couldn't. He had evidently taken a lot of trouble & had written down a series of notes which he read me. I think I've told all he said, if you want to ask any questions I'm sure he would answer to the best of his knowledge.

I'm sending you a present from Farve, on Monday. You must unpack it carefully Mollie says, as there are bits of it done up separately. The shop is very short handed as the grand duchess[3] suddenly went mad (oh the histoires) & we have nobody to pack. I return, most unwillingly, on Monday for 2 months.

Debo comes up on Tues: & I am going to make her get a proper hat, she must be weaned from Rita[4] whatever happens. She says will the parsons' wives shriek? But as the hats are all à la Queen Mary they should be delighted. I've just fetched mine it is ravishing. The woman there is a keen fan of the family & says she never saw such beauties, beginning with Lady Beit.[5] Wait till she sees Debo, as I told her. Can we get Woman away from Henry Heath?[6] Ay there's the rub.

Peter has rushed off to Transport House to see about a constituency egged on by me, as candidates get 90 coupons! I fear it will be no good though, married to a Mitford. They say Andrew hasn't a hope either![7]

I had tea with Farve – yes he seems very well & quite cheerful.

Much love
    NR

---

[1] Kingsley Martin (1897–1969). Editor of the *New Statesman & Nation* 1931–60.
[2] Robert Treuhaft (1912–). New York-born Jewish lawyer; he was working in the Office of Price Administration when he met Jessica.
[3] Mrs Kentall, who packed and delivered books and was never seen by the customers.
[4] A hat shop. 'So we went to Madame Rita, and I tried on all the hats in the shop . . . and wondered why it was that hats never seemed to suit me, something to do with my heather-like hair perhaps.' Fanny in *Love in a Cold Climate*, p. 104.
[5] Clementine Mitford (1915–). First cousin of Nancy. Married Sir Alfred Beit in 1939.
[6] A maker of sporting hats, specialising in ladies' plain felt headgear.
[7] Peter was never given a constituency; the Marquess of Hartington unsuccessfully contested Chesterfield, Derbyshire, in 1945 and 1950.

To LADY REDESDALE   G. Heywood Hill Ltd
[June 1945]   10 Curzon Street
                                     London W1

Dear Muv

. . . Farve is really all right, rather weak of course, but up all night making tea wh is a good sign! I'm going home again tonight as they all seem to think I can.

What *do* you think I did? I decided not to come here Sat: morning as I was really tired, & forgot to lock the door on Friday, so the shop was full of wandering people trying to buy books from each other. Wasn't it a *nightmare*. By the mercy of Providence Heywood was passing through London & happened to look in. HE WASN'T BEST PLEASED. And I don't blame him. The fact is I'm too tired but it's no excuse for such dottiness.

Best love
    NR

To LADY REDESDALE   G. Heywood Hill Ltd
8 June 1945   10 Curzon Street, W1

Darling Muv

You'll be glad to hear Hamish Hamilton[1] is enthusiastic over my book (the word brilliant has been used) & is giving me a £250 advance which I call enormous. I've never had more than £100 before.

Just got your post card re Waugh too late alas. I've been lunching with him (12.30) & Gerald (1.30) & feel fit to jump over the moon – all my trouble is under nourishment I've often remarked.

Much love, must go, I wanted to tell you about the book.

NR

P.S. If I can't get a Waugh for you will lend you mine.

[1] Hamish Hamilton (1900–88). Founded his publishing company in 1931. Changed his name by deed poll to 'Jamie'. Married to the actress Jean Forbes-Robertson in 1929 and to Countess Yvonne Pallavicino in 1940. Hamilton had seen promise in Nancy's first three books and published her fourth novel, *Pigeon Pie*. His faith in her was fully rewarded: *The Pursuit of Love* was an instant success when it appeared in December 1945 and sold over 200,000 copies during the first year. Nancy retained Hamilton as her publisher until the end of her life. Unfortunately, all but a few letters from their extensive correspondence have disappeared from the publisher's archives.

To Lady Redesdale   12 Blomfield Road, W9
19 July 1945

Darling Muv

Thank you very much for these[1] – so sad but it is best to know what really happened. When people are very ill they don't in the least want friends or dear ones, just nurses – I know that from when I was. That he didn't suffer is everything – but again I believe very ill and dying people usually don't, what a comfort. Evelyn Waugh, on fire from head to foot never felt anything. Randolph called loudly for morphia, E. said to him Randolph are you in pain? to which he replied no, but one ought to have morphia on these occasions! I've seen him all day, quite an hour in the shop & then at tea with Emerald, he is in a most exuberant state!

Went to Drummonds[2] about my passport wearing my new hat,[3] the typists & clerks got such terrible giggles they were paralysed & couldn't attend to anything, it must have made their day. Did I tell you a woman on a bus said, if she could see herself as others see her! Have new hats always aroused such passions, I don't remember.

Hateful wind here all the time all the summer, so dirty & dusty.

Much love
    NR

[1] Letters about Tom Mitford's death.
[2] Drummonds Bank. Exchange control was in force.
[3] It cost fourteen guineas and was 'straw coloured with huge velvet bows'.

TO LADY REDESDALE   G. Heywood Hill Ltd
29 July 1945   17 Curzon Street, W1[1]

Darling Muv
  I'll try for *Tom Brown*.
  Has Farve told you I think of using the money he gave me to become a partner? It seems sensible. Anyhow I'm going to go on working for the present part time, until I go to Paris which will be as soon as I've got all my papers (I hope in 10 days or so but you never can tell).
  Fearfully pleased about the election[2] as you can imagine. I went to the Rothermeres'[3] party for the results where such intense crossness prevailed that I went back to my shop. Osbert [Sitwell] came in, in tremendous spirits, seized my bag & rushed off with it saying 'Labour has begun.' A furious old lady came in & said 'Do you really think Attlee can cope with Stalin?' to which Osbert replied 'Well he has coped with Churchill, hasn't he?' Evelyn then put on my hat in which he looked just like Mary Kingsley[4] & the old lady retired discomforted.
  Did you roar when they sang 'Jerusalem', I thought you would.
  Just off to see Gerald. His heart is too high & they are lowering it in a nursing home, so they come in every 5 minutes & say things like 'Lady Juliet Duff is outside' to make it sink, or so we suppose.
  Saw the Woman – highly disgusted – & Diana for a moment only though.

    Much love
      NR

[1] The bookshop had moved from no. 17 to no. 10 Curzon Street in 1942. Nancy was using old writing paper.
[2] Labour won a landslide victory in the general election on 26 July.
[3] 2nd Viscount Rothermere (1898–1978). An unwavering Conservative. Proprietor of the Associated Newspaper Group, which includes the *Daily Mail* and many other papers. Married to Margaret Redhead 1920–38, to Ann O'Neill 1945–52 and to Mary Ohrstrom in 1966.
[4] Mary Kingsley (1862–1900). Intrepid Victorian spinster who travelled extensively in Africa.

To Lady Redesdale   Hotel Pont Royal
17 September 1945   Paris VII

Darling Muv

 I have found a flat & found a char & move in tomorrow – do write,
I long for letters, 20 rue Bonaparte VI.

 Absolute ruin *and* starvation because I don't like to ask for a ration
card & one can't even get bread without (even at meals, in a restaurant) but I am so completely happy here it is worth it. I must come
& live here as soon as I can, I feel a totally different person as if I
had come out of a coal mine into daylight. Meanwhile I shall stay until
the cold weather – at present it is hot like Venice, one sheet at night
& cotton dresses, oh the heaven. It seems silly when I struggled for
a year to get here not to stay as long as possible.

 Diana Cooper is being too angelic. I am captivated completely by
her beauty & charm, she is simply perfect at her job & in those
surroundings she makes, as they say, a picture. She gave a literary
cocktail party for me & John Lehmann[1] & we met all the nobs, you
must say it was kind. And she really persuaded me to stay on here,
I couldn't quite make up my mind & was leaving on Friday. She said
stay, yesterday at Chantilly where they have a house, & today the
weather persuaded me & I fixed the whole thing up. The flat belongs
to Betty Chetwynd[2] do you remember her? So I sent a telegram to
see if I could have it & she's delighted. The angelic concierge (how
helpful the French are) got into the Métro at rush hour for me, went
all the way to Montmartre & returned with the prettiest femme de
ménage you ever saw, all like magic. Imagine a London porter, all
grumbles & groans & puttings off & certainly no lovely girl at the end
of it!

 Oh my passion for the French. I see all through rose coloured
spectacles! There was a tremendous row in this street this afternoon,
two men roaring at each other & ending up et vous – et vous – &
this refrain was taken up by a hundred heads out of windows, chanting
et vous – et vous. It was like a scene in a film.

 I'll write again from my flat – you must say it's dashing, to have a
flat in the rue Bonaparte!

     Much love
     NR

[1] John Lehmann (1907–87). Author, publisher and editor of *New Writing* and of the
London Magazine 1951–61. Godson of Violet Hammersley.
[2] Elizabeth Chetwynd (d.1961). An English bluestocking who reviewed books on

French literature for *The Times Literary Supplement*. Her flat was handy for Nancy as Palewski lived at 1 rue Bonaparte.

To Lady Redesdale   20 rue Bonaparte
25 September 1945   Paris VI

Darling Muv

Thank you *so* much for the butter which arrived safely. Don't send any more as I have nothing to eat it on, I gave it to Palewski & was glad to do so as he has been more than angelic to me in every way – it was very well received.

Yesterday I went to Lelong. Why is it the clothes at these places always dangle well out of one's reach? The pre-war price of about £40 I could now afford (anyway London things are all that) but £100 really is out of the question. Oh I had to make an effort though. The devil whispers get it – you'll never see anything pretty again for years & years, & you'll wear it for 10 years, & that's only £10 a year. If the franc goes to 400 while I'm here the devil might win, but even he can't make me spend twice what a thing is really worth (he did over the hat to be sure).

I went on Sunday to the Fould Springers[1] at Royaumont – perhaps the most beautiful house I've ever seen. 10 years ago Decca lunched there, taken by Paulette Helleu[2] – at luncheon somebody said & what are your politics? At which a clenched fist flew over the table. It has never been forgotten. Palewski enchanted – 'La famille Mitford fait ma joie.'

Paulette has been all the war in Lisbon, comes back next week, so I may see her.

I'm doing business in rather a desultory way – writing one or 2 articles for French papers which pay frightfully well, selling & buying books etc but really I'm having an absolute rest & the result is I feel so wonderful I don't know it's me. Enough to eat twice a day, always a glass of wine & staying in bed most of the morning have made a new woman of me.

I don't know when I shall return, but suspect the cold will soon drive me back. This flat is an ice box, never a ray of sun, when the weather gets chilly I shan't be able to stand it.

You would roar if you could see the women at the collections. Their enormous bare hairy scaly legs sprawl about quite unconcernedly – they seem to have given them up as a bad job & forgotten about them – they tug their skirts up above their hideous knees & leave it at that. Down to the knee they are smartness itself! I must say the really

elegant aren't like this but you know what the collections are, always
half full of tricoteuses. They are so funny too – you say to the vendeuse how much is this – out comes her pencil, price of dress, tax,
PRICE OF COUPONS, all added up without a tremor. Debo would like
that, being such a coupon purveyor!

When do you come South I wonder. I long for you to be there on
my return.

Tell Song [Unity] I met a painter called Oberlé who says he would
like to marry her – I promised I would pass on the proposal. He is
very nice, about 40, lame, speaks English.

> Much love
>   NR

[1] Baron Eugène Fould-Springer, a rich industrialist, bought a Palladian abbot's palace,
Royaumont, at the beginning of the century. The house was built by Marie-Antoinette's
friend l'Abbé de Balivière and lies fifty miles north of Paris. The baron's son, Max
Fould-Springer (1906–), inherited the house on the death of his father.
[2] Paulette Helleu (1906–). Daughter of the painter Paul César Helleu, who was a friend
of Nancy's parents. Married Rear-Admiral Clarence Howard-Johnston in 1955.

TO EVELYN WAUGH   20 rue Bonaparte, VI
29 September 1945

Darling Evelyn

I couldn't write to Randolph for £2 what I write to you for nothing,[1]
I don't believe it would work. I'm writing articles for French papers
like mad & getting £10 for 500 words (thank heaven for paper shortage) which you must say not bad. You would roar – any subject from
feminism to LITERATURE & as I know the eye of no mocking buddy
will ever fall upon them I race ahead with perfect serenity.

I found this empty flat & moved in a fortnight ago. Today, like
R. Crusoe, going to the kitchen to hot up a pannikin of washing water,
I found an EGG which certainly hadn't been there before. I awaited
the next development with some trepidation & presently in came a
fat bald little Frenchman & said he lives here too & do I mind? No,
so long as he doesn't turn me out, & indeed I haven't seen him since
& suspect he just lays his head here & that's all. But next week a
Swiss lady returns from her holiday who seems to be the terror of
the whole neighbourhood & then I feel I may have to go. Fabrice[2]
says shall he have her stopped at the frontier but I thought that was
going too far all the same! Oh how I don't want to leave this happy

life, the lovely food, the always champagne even for luncheon & all the fun & gaiety. . . .

I can't begin again on Linda[3] so I am a journalist. Besides I meant Xian to be like that even if Communism isn't. Fabrice made *many* of the same criticisms as you but he seems gratified that the book is dedicated to him on the whole tho' he rather dreads the Communists here getting on to it (fatal name of Mitford). They have got a tremendous anti-Fabrice campaign going on at present & all their papers are nothing but caricatures of him – some very funny. He thinks if they get in they'll pop him straight into prison.

I've bought a lot of nice books, & sold a lot too for the shop. But nobody in London takes the slightest interest in my activities, Dearest doesn't answer my letters & Mollie just says it makes more work for her – I see her point vividly but it's all rather discouraging I must say. What I've done in fact is to establish a branch of H.H. here wh will take up to any amount of books from us @ 30% more than we pay for them which must be quite a cop, specially as the ones they want happen to be ones it's quite easy to get. Among the books I've bought is a history of RHG[4] with very pretty coloured plates – never seen it before.

I had a wonderful description from a French friend of Smarty-boots[5] meeting Valéry. The French don't think SB knows the language at all & they said they could see it was dreadful torture to him to be in the same room with the master & not be able to understand one word he said. SB turned first one ear then the other but all in vain.

You see – Hamilton advertises Linda as one long scream. I knew it. But Fabrice says he thinks in many ways it's more serious than your book but perhaps that's just sucking up. He's greatly tickled by the portrait of himself but says it makes an unlifelike figure as Fr dukes are not at all like that – he then introduced me to one to show & indeed he could hardly have been more like the late Hartington[6] & less like Fabrice. Still – fiction.

Somebody asked F what he thinks about the atom bomb to which he replied 'Comme amateur de porcelaine –'

I'm glad you're back in your house except I suppose one will never see you now.

I'll try Randolph & see what happens but feel doubtful really.

Love from
　　NR

P.S. Just been to the kitchen for my pannikin – shockingly late – find a note saying do have some coffee or an egg & anything you like.

Well you must call that kind – I haven't had any breakfast for a month as have no ration card.

Fabrice not awfully pleased at hearing a male voice when he rang up – not too easy to explain with M[ale]V[oice] in the next room either! Bedroom farce situation develops apace.

I've written to Randolph, don't know if it's what he wants, we can but see. Social gossip not my strong point specially not here where I see nobody.

[1] Evelyn Waugh had told Nancy that Randolph Churchill, at the time correspondent for an American newspaper, wanted her to send him 'gossip about Paris'.

[2] Palewski was the model for Fabrice, Duc de Sauveterre, hero of *The Pursuit of Love*.

[3] Waugh had criticised *The Pursuit of Love*: 'I am sorry you have not been able to rewrite the unsatisfactory section of your book in time for the first edition . . . There is a very good theme in the Spanish refugees camp and it was vicious to falsify the facts to make them fit . . . [The] husband [Christian Talbot] with his zeal to re-equip the militant workers for the class struggle in Mexico could be excellent. It would give point to her bewilderment that the Spanish gentry did nothing to help. You could make a dramatic climax in the sailing of the evacuation ship with the communists taking off the distressed families in order to pack it with international thugs.' *Letters*, pp. 212–13.

[4] Royal Horse Guards, Evelyn Waugh's regiment.

[5] Virginia Woolf's nickname for Cyril Connolly.

[6] Marquess of Hartington (1917–44), who was killed in action on 10 September.

To RANDOLPH CHURCHILL   20 rue Bonaparte, VI
30 September 1945

Dearest Randolph

I am not sure I make out just what you want but here goes.

I arrived about a month ago and lived at first in an hotel which was exactly like camping out – no food, no bath and no service and where I paid £3 a day. Then most luckily I found this empty flat and moved into it – the luck was great because there is an even more acute shortage of accommodation here than in London – my French friends give peacock shrieks of envy when they hear of it and nearly always suggest that I might also like to accommodate their cousin from Egypt, their brother from America, who are arriving next week. However, I remain firm. The flat is in an 18th-century house and is built round a courtyard so that from my bed I can see across into my dining room window. The courtyard is full all day and all night with loud French noises – like Italians the French never sleep it seems and the concierge is as ready to conduct a furious argument at 4 a.m. as she is at

4 p.m. (I say like Italians because I am very much struck, after all these years away from it, by the fact that Paris is much more like a Mediterranean than like a northern town.)

The elections are of course the great topic. Everywhere you come across groups of people saying 'Moi Oui-non' 'et moi Oui-Oui' and on all the walls is chalked up the Oui-Non of the Communists. Only real old Faubourg fogies will vote Non Oui. What strikes me very much, and I read all the papers, you never see direct attack on General de Gaulle. All the attacks, and they are many and venomous, are directed against Palewski, who is presented as a sinister Eminence Grise l'ennemi du peuple. G.P.R.F. (Government Provisoire de la République Française) which is on all their motor cars etc, is said to stand for Gaston Palewski Regent de France.

Food and fuel situation not yet good for the very poor, is admitted to be greatly improved. The bread is excellent and there is plenty of it, next month it will be off the ration. I have my meals in a restaurant where I pay between 5/- and 10/- for an absolute blow-out, makes Ritz or Dorchester look silly. Typical menu – potage, tomato salad, omelette (real eggs), pâté maison, brie or pont l'évêque and a verre de vin. Never more than 100 francs, which for French people is only 5/- as the exchange is greatly against us. So you see people of moderate means should be all right, the very poor I believe are having a tough time. I gave some coffee and sugar to a maid in the hotel and she burst into tears.

Is this the kind of thing – if so send a word and I'll repeat next week. I think I am going to Laval's[1] trial.

Having a heavenly time.

Love from
    N

P.S. Should add the coal allowance is laughable but gas and electricity are working tho' rationed so everybody can cook something hot and wash in hot water. Haven't had a bath since I arrived, but I'm used to it now.

[1] Pierre Laval (1883–1945). French politician. Led the Vichy Government under Pétain. He was tried and executed for treason in October 1945.

To Diana Mosley   Hotel Pont Royal, VII
25 October 1945

Darling

Positively – you won't believe it I know – I am coming back on
Tues. I go to the country on Fri: till then. So I wondered if I could
get to you for the weekend to cheer myself up or perhaps you can't
have people yet in which case you wouldn't come to me for a night
or 2? Let me know, to Blom. (I dread Gladys's crossness almost
more than leaving the Col.) . . .

The Col says we must get Debo over here & open her eyes. I say
there is no need at all to go opening a lot of new eyes when there
are all those old ones longing to be kept open. He says one thing is
a great relief to him – that I have killed Fabrice! Oh dear you would
so love him, he is the funniest man in the world.

Do you realize it is exactly 20 years since we were in the Av:
V. Hugo? I went to Versailles on Sunday, it is looking just like Helleu's
bad oil paintings with the fountains full of leaves. Apart from love or
anything I must come & live here, & if one makes up one's mind
things generally happen don't you think. And now I must go & get
my ticket – OH.

    Much love darling
        NR

I've mislaid Crowood[1] address, how idiotic.

---

[1] With the end of the war, Regulation 18B was lifted and, released from house arrest,
the Mosleys moved to Crowood House, Wiltshire, in September 1945.

To Randolph Churchill   [Le Mé Chaplin,
4 November 1945   Jouy en Josas
                                           Seine et Oise]

Dearest Randolph,

I am staying here with Alvilde Chaplin in the little house which
Princess de Polignac left her and she has undergone two occupations
– one very correct by the Germans who left everything in apple pie
order, and one very incorrect by the Americans who did the oddest
things like cutting a great square piece out of the Aubusson carpet
and smashing the lavatories.

The American black market in the village is fascinating. We asked,
as we have no facilities here for cooking, if we could déjeuner in the

local pub. They said no they had no food. We looked sad and they said wait and rang up the local aerodrome. In a few minutes an American arrived in a jeep, sold them some army rations which were immediately converted into a delicious meal. This happens now every day and couldn't be done more openly. When the Germans were here they had a great trick of swapping furniture from one house to another 'You've got 2 pianos, we'll trade one of them for a bed and a cooking stove' and so on, so there is now a fearful sorting out going on, with a vast furniture dump in Versailles where people go and claim their things.

Went to a music party at the Comtesse Jean de Polignac,[1] who is the great musical hostess here, for Benjamin Britten.[2] Some new songs of his, settings for the religious poems of Donne, were sung for the first time. The French are really impressed by Britten.

Great relief over the elections[3] among all classes as far as I can see. The people undoubtedly love de Gaulle very much – among the upper reaches of political thought the line seems to be 'We don't want him, but he can't go'. Nobody would prophesy the result of the elections but I believe the Government expected 160 Communist seats. The problem now is to marry Blum and Schumann. They are said to be in love but there are religious differences, one is a converted Jew and the other is not.

Montherlant,[4] the writer, who collaborated, is hiding in Paris but nobody bothers to look for him. Rather humiliating, like when one hides for sardines and nobody comes!

Everybody very much intrigued by the return of Bergery[5] and why he did it. Some say he is such a megalomaniac he thinks he will win his case by cleverness in court, some that he was broke and couldn't live abroad any more, and some that he was so dying of homesickness that he thought it would be worth 2 years of travaux forcés to be able to live in France again. Everybody very sorry for his wife who is much loved.

The food situation in Paris is enormously improved even since I have been here. You now see quantities of meat, bread is off the ration, cheese and butter exist once more. Fuel situation is serious but not desperate like last year. There is gas and electricity so that people can at least cook, and everybody has a tiny allowance of coal. Out here in the country there is wood for all and even though this is really a suburb of Paris, plenty of black and white market food. Goods trains ply to and fro on this little line all day and all night, and there is a great feeling of bustle and recovery and optimism in the air.

I'm coming back on Tuesday so this is my last letter. In floods of tears, I do so love it here.

Love from
Nancy

[1] Marie-Blanche di Pietro (1897–1958). Pretty daughter of the dressmaker Jeanne Lanvin. Married to Dr René Jacquemaire, son of Georges Clemenceau, in 1920, and to Count Jean de Polignac in 1924. She held a famous musical salon frequented by all the great French and foreign musicians, from Francis Poulenc and Erik Satie to Vladimir Horowitz and Artur Rubinstein.

[2] Benjamin Britten (1913–76). His opera *Peter Grimes* had its premiere at Sadler's Wells Theatre on 7 June 1945.

[3] The election for the new French Constituent Assembly had resulted in the Mouvement Républicain Populaire (MRP), led by Maurice Schumann, and the Socialists under Léon Blum, being returned in equal strength. De Gaulle became head of government.

[4] Henry de Montherlant (1896–1972). Controversial novelist and playwright. Affected a haughty nobility of spirit which deserted him during the German occupation. Committed suicide when he began to lose his sight.

[5] Gaston Bergery (1892–1974). Former left-wing politician who saw in the defeat of France the possibility of bringing about social revolution and became Vichy Ambassador to Russia and Turkey. He returned to France voluntarily, was tried for collaboration and acquitted. He married, as his third wife, an elegant American, Bettina Jones, who worked for Schiaparelli and shared his taste for the international smart set.

To John Betjeman   12 Blomfield Road, W9
28 December 1945

My dear John

Praise from you is praise indeed[1] – I am infinitely gratified, & you say all the things I would have liked somebody (whose judgement I respected) most to say. In fact I am happily purring.

I was at Eastbourne for Christmas it is made for you, perhaps you know it. All were snatching *New Bats*[2] from each other but oh where is phone for the fish knives Norman?[3] I am bitterly disappointed. Never mind – Miss J H-D.[4] And I like the dedication very much.[5]

How nice & clever we all are.

Uncle Matthew sat with his nose in the book & grunted out various corrections: 'Never got the stock whips in Canada, a bloke from Australia gave them to me' & so on. He was delighted with it but cried at the end & said he read a sad book once before called *Tess of the D'Urbervilles* & had hoped never to read another.

Thank you *so* much for writing – have a happy New Year.

Love from
    Nancy

[1] 'Cold from the G[reat] W[estern] R[ailway] in which I have just been finishing *The Pursuit of Love* I write to tell you on this lovely *writing paper* how v. greatly I enjoyed it. You have produced something that really is a monument to our friends.' (John Betjeman to NM, 19 December 1945)
[2] *New Bats in Old Belfries* (1945). A collection of poems by Betjeman.
[3] First line of the poem 'How to Get On in Society'.
[4] Miss Joan Hunter Dunn, heroine of the poem 'A Subaltern's Love-song'.
[5] Presumably Betjeman's handwritten dedication in Nancy's copy of the book, which has disappeared. The printed dedication reads: 'To the Warden in memory of Nicholas and Dorothy Wadham.'

To RUPERT HART-DAVIS[1]   12 Blomfield Road, W9
9 January 1946

My dear Rupert

Oh how kind you are to write such a lovely long letter about Linda, which, coming from you, has set me up for the day.

A Hon (H as in Home) shld say chimney piece – a mantel piece is one of those Victorian objects with pigeon holes for ornaments – & is a word never used hitherto in literature.

Evelyn W. found this out, either in *Fowler* or *Ox Dic* I forget which.

Uncle Matthew is my father & all the early part is absolutely auto-biographical, which is probably why it rings more true. I wld have made it longer but as a bookseller can't but be aware how much the ordinary reader *loathes* childhood & didn't want to inflict more than was necessary on him. Now I wish I had, as everybody seems to like that part.

Thank-you again *so* much for writing.

Yrs ever
    Nancy

[1] Rupert Hart-Davis (1907–). Publisher, editor and author. Knighted in 1967. Nephew of Duff Cooper.

To GASTON PALEWSKI   12 Blomfield Road, W9
13 January 1946

I have had an entirely French week dear Col which I always very much enjoy – Massiglis, Rochés,[1] Violet [Trefusis] & Tony [Gandarillas]. London is full of the French of course. . . .

Odette M. is mad about my book & says she is going to translate it herself – both she & the Ambassador spoke of you with great affection. . . .

Debo said 'I've had *such* a letter from the Colonel, I'm sticking it into my photograph book.' *Colonel, enough now.*

Col come to UNO – it is full of pretty women, Mrs Roosevelt & so on, made for you. Truly, the papers are full of ravishing señoritas who seem to be taking part with luminous eyes & carefully crimped hair no worse than many members of that list –

I do hope you had a good holiday & feel better darling Colonel, but what you need is a month at least. Everybody has suddenly got a great down on Alvilde – I must say she isn't very nice to her friends, & Violet turned on her at the Rochés' party & said 'If Nancy were nasty like you she would be dangerous, but you are merely pathetic' which made a lot of good feeling all round.

Did I tell you I went to tea with Marc's mother[2] – goodness what a stupid woman. The step father is perfect hell & looked slightly dazed by Emerald, Tony & all the galère! I'm afraid I wasn't very nice to poor Marc but he has a proprietary attitude as if he had been my lover for 25 years which I find impossible to bear. I sent him to have tea with Debo – that was all right as she likes Princes (did I tell you I had a book in the shop called *Maquis* & she thought this was French for Marquis & bought it, but very soon brought it back again).

Somebody asked that wicked Violet who Marc was & she replied 'don't you know, he's the child of Gaston & Nancy.'

Really, one's friends –!

There was a party for the re-opening of the Tower of London & Violet said 'When I got to the Traitors Gate I heard 2 well known voices & it was Emerald & Daisy.'[3]

She is a funny woman – & she simply *loves* you Colonel – but then who doesn't?

Really the description of Charlus doing Jupien in that shop – I'd forgotten how fearfully indecent Proust can be. . . .

[incomplete]

[1] Louis Roché was First Counsellor at the French Embassy in London.

[2] Mary (Minnie) Gregorini Bingham (1896–1970). Married to Prince Charles-Louis de Beauvau Craon in 1920 and to Lieutenant-General Sir Humfrey Myddelton-Gale in 1945. She was a girlfriend of Palewski.

[3] Marguerite (Daisy) Decazes (1890–1962). Daughter of a French duke and an American heiress. Married to Prince Jean de Broglie 1910–18, and to Hon. Reginald Fellowes

in 1919. Often described as the best-dressed woman in the world, and famous for her malicious remarks.

To Evelyn Waugh   12 Blomfield Road, W9
17 January 1946

Just had a letter beginning 'I've only twice before written to an Author – once to a very old American who wrote a book about a white mule & the other was to Evelyn Waugh about *Put Out More Flags* but I never posted that one –'

Randolph has just telephoned, very governessy 'please make a note of my new number.' I forgot until I'd accepted to go & see him that I'm not on speakers with him because of his behaviour to Fabrice[1] – but it's no good not being on speakers with R.dolph because many have tried it before & not succeeded.

I must now confess that *The Tablet*[2] got lost – *entirely* my fault, it was given to me, but I simply must have mislaid it. But I can read it in a day or 2 as Gerald will lend me his/Penelope [Betjeman]'s copy. *Don't* be cross, it was the s. fever[3] day & I was disrupted.

Xopher [Sykes] tells me the Bloomsbury Home Guard are gunning for me – he says Smarty's friends think my book utterly indecent on acc/ of not being about cabmen's shelters & Hons' Cupboard makes them vomit & they are all the more annoyed because they think it's quite well written.

I've just had this month's Smarty's Own Mag[4] & of course the great joke is one does write better than all of them (not SB himself) because even when they quite *want* to be understood they can't be. As Tonks[5] used to say 'Why don't they stick to cooking?'

Diana [Mosley] has been in her flat & somebody has written shit & things on the door & D said 'Of course they think the busy little housewife will clean it off, but really darling I *can't* be bothered.'

Fabrice has invited Debo & Andrew for a week in Paris, they are thrilled & so is he, & will no doubt give them a wonderful time.

In spite of your counter-honish thoughts I never got the fever you see.

Picasso is a Hon – I've now got 3 lovely books about him in the shop so I gloat all day. . . .

Prod is off to Spain[6] he hopes for the revolution – I might go with him as far as Perpignan, I hear it's very gay, & the hotel we used to stay in is now the Roussillon Ladies Socialist Club – made for me!

I am warmly & happily in bed & can't switch on the wireless until after Northern Music Hall is over which is why you are getting this screed.

Goodness Proust is smutty – I'd forgotten. I wonder if the Scotchman[7] really puts it all in?

Love

NR

P.S. Xopher is writing about Robert[8] – have you any letters?

[1] Randolph had written 'an absolutely hateful' article about Palewski for a French left-wing newspaper: 'probably the most hated man in France today. Hated in the same way that Madame de Pompadour once was, and that Harry Hopkins was during the time of President Roosevelt. But, as one of his numerous adversaries pointed out unkindly, Mr Palewski has neither the beauty of Mme de Pompadour nor the charm of Harry Hopkins.' *Libération*, 12 December 1945.
[2] The first three chapters of Waugh's novel *Helena* were published in an abridged form in the Catholic weekly, *The Tablet*, 22 December 1945.
[3] Nancy had been in quarantine for scarlet fever.
[4] *Horizon*. 'I said to Duff "ought I to keep my *Horizons* etc for the English hospitals?" He replied furiously "I really don't see why you should *add* to their sufferings like that." ' (NM to Diana Mosley, 22 February 1949)
[5] Professor Henry Tonks (1862–1937). Painter, and head of the Slade School of Fine Art when Nancy was a student there in 1927.
[6] As a reporter for *Picture Post*.
[7] C. K. Scott Moncrieff, translator of *A la recherche du temps perdu*.
[8] Robert Byron is the subject of an essay in *Four Studies in Loyalty* (1946) by Christopher Sykes.

To GASTON PALEWSKI   12 Blomfield Road, W9
17 January 1946

Your darling voice & your darling handwriting within an hour of each other is almost *too* much happiness. And I suppose the next best thing to having one's sentiments returned is to have them appréciés.

Colonel if you come to London I *beg* not the Connaught.[1]

Now about the American edition – must I alter a great deal of Fabrice? Surely the harm, if any, has been done now?[2] But I will do *just as you say*. Anyhow all the French has to come out (be translated I mean) as it seems the dear Americans don't know any French. (A very rich neighbour of Debo's who is a wild fan of mine told her that he had sent the book to a translator as he didn't understand the French words. He must have been surprised at the result.) . . .

Everybody seems to think every word literally of the book is true. Nancy Cunard[3] is here & Victor said to me 'she gives a much more gloomy account of Paris than you do, but then of course nobody took a flat for *her* or gave *her* all those fur coats –'

Goodbye dear dearest Colonial I've got to rush off to my work now. NR

You are *not* to tease me about Marc, Colonel, because I mind very much – & really Col . . . *think* of the list. Oh *Colonel* –
P.S. The Hat won't be ready for another 10 days.[4]

[1] A reference to an incident when a receptionist at the Connaught Hotel had prevented Nancy from going up to Palewski's room with him after dinner.
[2] Palewski, although flattered by the portrait of himself as Fabrice in *The Pursuit of Love*, was concerned that the Communists would make the association between Nancy and Unity.
[3] Nancy Cunard (1896–1965). Rebellious only child of Emerald; a first cousin of Victor Cunard. The model for Lucy Tantamount in Aldous Huxley's *Point Counterpoint* (1928).
[4] Nancy had painted a picture of a straw boater for Palewski.

To GASTON PALEWSKI   12 Blomfield Road, W9
20 January 1946

Colonel I am distracted by this terrible cold – I can think of nothing but how bad it is for you, already not strong & overtired.

And those *beastly* deputies.[1] But I believe you rather enjoy struggles so perhaps that is all right & ever since you went to Algiers it has always really been like this.

I've just written you a long sad letter which I've torn up – I don't think you like being invited to regard me as a serious character, & anyhow you have enough sadness in your own life – perhaps everybody has.

Gerald says Diana says you are cross with me about the boring Lamballe woman.[2] Don't be cross, I can't bear that. As for the B.L.W. herself, tell her to write a book about *me* – I am very vulnerable. I hate her – hateful Lamballe who deserted you when you were a lonely exile & ran off with her own soul. It was a mean & shabby trick. All the same I will take anything you tell me out of the American edition, if you think it worth while, now.

This is my Sunday letter – I've been writing to you for hours because the letter I tore up as well as being *very* sad was also *very* long. What will happen to me on Sunday mornings when I have to stop writing to you? Oh darling Colonel.

Debo is so excited for her visit – it is nice because little things of that age have had no fun, only the war in their lives. She's written to you, Andrew can have a week's leave in April.

Come soon to London dearest Col – don't be cross – (you must be rather pleased with Fabrice really he is such a heavenly character & everyone is in love with him!)

I've just been reading Millar's wonderful new book[3] about the French Resistance (he is the one who wrote *Maquis*, which so disappointed Debo). The French must be all right, they must be made to be, & the Gen will make them. In the bedroom of a woman resister he describes 'a heavy twin photograph frame with Gen de G looking coldly at Fifine' – made me so laugh.

Colonel if Debo meets the Gen I will NEVER NEVER speak to you again.

    NR

P.S. I've sent you an electric hot water bottle to warm your hands.

[1] Hostility towards de Gaulle from the Socialists and the Communists had been steadily mounting since he took office.
[2] Nancy had used the name of one of Palewski's girlfriends in *The Pursuit of Love*.
[3] George Millar, *Horned Pigeon* (1946). An account of the author's escape from Germany in 1943.

To GASTON PALEWSKI   12 Blomfield Road, W9
23 January 1946

Colonel I know of nothing worse than when somebody one loves is far away & unhappy & one is quite quite incapable of helping them.

Not only do I love you very much but also the Gen – & the hateful way in which he has been treated[1] wounds me to the heart.

Darling Colonel come to London. I am very rich. I can lend you masses of money a thousand pounds if you like.

Please remember that.

I can't settle to anything or sleep – it makes me feel ill & wretched the whole thing.

  I *beg* for a word from you.
    NR

[1] General de Gaulle had resigned as head of government on 20 January.

To Gaston Palewski   Faringdon House
27 January 1946   Berkshire

You were a love to telephone dear Colonel because I was so worried
about you[1] (though I had already rehearsed in my own mind 'Colonel
are you sad?' 'Not at all') but the sound of your voice reassured me.
Now you will have a holiday & be able to devote more time to the
pursuit of love. Oh dear.

Talking about the *P of L* I have had various offers for French
translations & what I shall do is, they must send the typescript to
you & you can alter it as you like. And soon Colonel you must tell
me what you want done for the American edition?

In March Peter is going to Spain then *please* come & stay with me
– he wouldn't mind. I said to him, about my will, would it hurt your
feelings if I left some money to the Colonel? Peter said hasn't he got
any money? NR: No. PR: Then I think it is a good idea, he ought to
have some. But the trouble is I'm not dead.

I saw Edwina d'Erlanger[2] yesterday she sends you her love & says
her husband loves you very much too.

Such a relief you have a nice flat to go to – but I liked you being
where I knew the set-up. When I felt sad I used to go past those
men at the gate, past those men at the table, up the stairs, past that
little squinting man & into the room where my darling Colonel was
working & working, & I felt well there he is, I know. Now it is all in
a mist – & then there are those hateful nieces. Don't laugh & don't
say I know. Can I come to Paris – you are the door-keeper of Calais
to me.

There will be a long long silence now, no petite chose noire, seulement l'épingle d'Alger[3] – & I don't like long Colonial silences.

Prince Peter[4] said something about Morocco?

My friend Brunier (the bookseller with the beautiful wife, no need
for *you* to know him) says he can get me a room at Claridges any
time I like & I'm sure the Massiglis (fancy I call her Odette now) will
give me a visa. But you are the door-keeper.

Gladys has gone. She left on Sunday 20th Jan after a holiday. I am
really delighted, it is like a sack of coals off my chest she had become
so disagreeable. Now I must get somebody really nice.

Oh dear the little hat is cleaned & varnished & now I can't send it.
When you come you will fetch it? . . .

Goodbye darling Col
    NR

You won't like the Métro very much I fear.

[1] Following de Gaulle's departure, Palewski had also resigned from his post.
[2] Edwina Louise Pru; married to Leo d'Erlanger in 1930.
[3] Palewski's handwriting was so difficult to read that Nancy pretended he used a rusty pin; she begged him to use instead 'a little black thing', i.e. a typewriter.
[4] Prince Peter of Greece.

To GASTON PALEWSKI   12 Blomfield Road, W9
3 February 1946

A ball,[1] my dearest Colonel. The talk for weeks has been of nothing else & I must say it was great great fun. I haven't been to a ball for 6 years – one or two were given in the war but I never would go, it seemed unnatural. But last night I rigged myself up in white satin & dined with Violet & went off to it. I must say I felt like a drowning man, the whole of my past life was there.

Chips said to Emerald, surveying the scene 'This is what we have been fighting for' to which clever old Emerald replied 'Why, are they all Poles?'[2]

I sat next to M. Massigli at dinner who suddenly became very matey – I've always found him difficult before. As for Odette, I am getting very fond of her.

Prince Peter invited us to dinner in a kind of Chinese swimming bath (I do think foreign royalties are extraordinary). There were two horrible little Greek insect-women, one called Mrs Sitwell (I told Osbert & he said 'Oh yes, those are the Jigga-Jigga Sitwells').

Prince P has a Norwegian girl friend who seems to wait faithfully for him & sees him once every 6 years, exactly like me. I felt for her. He, I must say, is a great love & can be very funny.

Colonel, a simply maddening thing has happened. When I sold the book[3] to America I made an absolute condition I was to see the proofs – now in the most casual way they announce that the book will come out next month & there's no time to send proofs. When I made a fuss they said 'Oh nothing will affect the sales over here, it is certain to go well' as though sales were the only thing that matters in the world. Apart from alterations you might have wanted, it is maddening for me as, it seems, they have translated all the French. Oh the brutes. About the French edition I wrote yesterday to my agent, & kept a copy, saying I insist on seeing the typescript before they begin to print, & won't sell on any other terms at all.

I've already had one offer, from Heinemann & Zolnay but have turned it down as they have a rotten translator. Perhaps you would like the dedication[4] taken out of the Fr: edition? And perhaps you would be an angel & look over the typescript for me? If you have time.

I hope you are rested and better, Col. Darling Colonel. Come to London, your fans await you (as an Eton boy said in a letter yesterday to me).

Did you get the little Mme de Gaulle[5] book – isn't it amusing?

The on dit here is that you have refused an embassy. I'm very glad you telephoned as everybody says hopefully 'I suppose the Colonel is very low?' & I am able to reply '*bursting* with happiness, joy, high spirits & so on' & they look very disappointed you know how people love other people to be got down.

A Marquise de Brissac is here. She gives a very poor account of some other members of her family – ?

A friend of mine called Lady Pat Russell[6] writes from Austria that she was raped by 6 Cossacks. (Hard cheese as she is a Lesbian.) Very topical & in the swim of her isn't it. I wrote back & told her what the Americans were like here to cheer her up.

Can't get the *Canard*,[7] perhaps it has struck?

Dear Col I shall ring you up in a week or 2, lucky I'm so rich isn't it?

This letter is very long – oh how I *hate* getting long letters, I never finish them.

I saw Penelope at the BALL – she is going back to Paris lucky her. You would have loved the ball & oh the pretty young women back from running away to the country now the war is over – come to London darling Colonel *do* & I promise you can *see* them (mustn't touch).

Love from
    NR

P.S. I hear your brother is *absolute heaven*, Colonel you are a beast the way you keep him to yourself. I hear he simply is you (in a blond wig) en mieux.

[1] Given by Sir Michael Duff (1907–80).
[2] NM to Evelyn Waugh: 'Chips said to Emerald "*This* is what we have been fighting for" (we?)' (3 February 1946) In his diary Chips Channon records this remark as having been made at the reception for Viscount Ednam's marriage to Stella Carcano on 10 January 1946.
[3] *The Pursuit of Love* was published in America by Random House.
[4] The novel was dedicated 'To Gaston Palewski'.

[5] Probably Joséphine de Gaulle, General de Gaulle's grandmother; an extraordinarily prolific writer whose bibliography takes up eight pages in the Bibliothèque Nationale catalogue.
[6] Lady Patricia Blackwood (1902–83). Married to Henry Russell in 1926.
[7] *Le Canard enchaîné*, the satirical weekly.

To Mark Ogilvie-Grant   12 Blomfield Road, W9
8 February 1946

Dear old fiend
I got a PC to send you of some thoughtful sheep in deevey Perthshire scenery but suppose I must answer yr letter now. Glad you liked the book, it is doing well – I've *already* made £1250 here & £100 in America so I have suddenly become la tante à héritage & lazy Daze (i.e. Desmond Guinness . . .) has been most deferential of late. I'm hoping for big things in the States & film folk are nibbling. . . .

I spent yesterday at Brighton buying jet jewellery & PCs & once more the voice was heard, while an antique yellow wig could almost be seen whisking round the next corner. (By the way I really can't dedicate *all* my books to you, you know.)

I'm off to Paris again I hope in about a month. . . .

Prod went to see his mother & she began telling him about the allowances she gives the others. 'I give Taffy £2000 a year & Gloria £4000 a year & so on (she gives us O) so Prod, goaded, at last said 'Well what about me?' 'Oh *you always* manage to keep alive somehow.' Isn't she bliss. She said 'Sir Stafford Cripps[1] likes Nancy's book but he doesn't like the *subject* & I don't like the *subject* either.' Did it remind you of Swinbrook days? Brains.

Your letter took 3 days to get here which seems phenomenal.[2]

Pretty Joan[3] has turned up, everybody very pleased to see her. You must have rather fun together as everybody there sounds nice I must say. But oh how UNO long to get you out.

Well even dried eggs are off here & starvation is on.

Love
        NR

Got a prison letter from you yesterday all crossed out by the censor except dear O.L.

Joan Eyres Monsell (1912–). Married to William Rayner 1939–47 and to Patrick Leigh Fermor in 1968.

To Gaston Palewski   12 Blomfield Road, W9
10 February 1946

Cruel heartless fickle faithless Colonial I see you have given me up for Debo. You have vanished into a mist & I long to hear from you & as I presume you still have une petite chose noire (since Debo would certainly be incapable of reading the product of l'épingle Algérienne) I *order* you to make use of her on my behalf.

Colonel come & stay with me in March. Peter is going to Spain at the end of this month – he wouldn't mind even if he knew. Nobody need know because you can say you are staying with M. Dressé du Crab who has no telephone – many people are in that position now so it would astonish nobody.

As for money I've got plenty. I've already made £1400[1] out of the book so you see I am rolling. So Colonel *do* there's a dear Col.

Oh how I adored the Cincinnatus picture, it is the best caricature of you I've ever seen.[2] You must get a hat like that. . . .

Cincinnatus

I can't think of anything more to say. You are in a mist for me now & don't seem real. Come out of it Colonel. Come to London in March.

NR

P.S. A letter from Snake Cecil [Beaton] saying 'I *do* hope Gaston will soon be back in that gilded wagon-lit.'
P.P.S. Did you know Winston got £12 000 for his secret session speeches from the American paper *Life*? Pretty low isn't it.

[1] Approximately £26,000 today.
[2] The cartoon, which appeared in *Le Canard enchaîné*, shows de Gaulle sowing a field with crosses of Lorraine. Palewski, at his side, is spraying the crosses with lavender water, an allusion to his reputation as a ladies' man.

To Gaston Palewski   12 Blomfield Road, W9
20 February 1946

Colonel I must love you very much. Not only do I get restless & miserable if too many weeks go by without a word from you, but also I am thrown into an extraordinary state of agitation when I see somebody who has recently met you. I saw Venetia[1] yesterday who spoke of you as happy, gay, & much fêted by your friends.

I then lunched alone with Ava[2] who said 'But aren't you terrified by the idea of all these tea parties (Wigs[3] used to say "Palewski lives on cake").' I said not really terrified – but of course I *am*, & Ava doesn't know you are looking for a fat girl to marry.

I am *very* very sorry dear Col about the book – I blame myself for not letting you see the original typescript – I know you won't believe me but when I was writing it Jacqueline was never meant to be Mme X who was really the dead Louise. (Equally everybody now says Tony is Alf Beit, & I see he is, but he was *never* intended for him.) However if it annoys that hateful Mme X I am all for it – only I don't like having annoyed you. If you will help a little with the translation I shld be *more* than grateful.

It has I believe been accepted by Plon & when things are a little more advanced I want to go to Paris & see the translator – I must go sometime to get some books & some clothes.

Tomorrow I dine with the Rothermeres – I will ask about a column for you, but anonymous – that might be a difficulty.

Good joke the Americans selling the atom to Russia – really jokes get better & better.

No news from France in the English papers & the only French

paper I see, the *Canard*, has become utterly boring without the eau de lavande. Venetia most uninformative & seems to know nothing, not even what the Spring hats are like.

A woman said to me 'I suppose Fabrice is your dream man' to which I replied 'oh no, just a Frenchman I know.' She looked rather surprised I must say.

Colonel this is just to thank you for your letter. I will write again when there is any news.

> NR

P.S. . . . Did the Gen know about Mme de Gaulle – is she his grand-mother?
Ava & I looked up le Comte de Noue in the *Bottin*[4] – she said he can't be very grand because here is a Mlle de Noue, & as you know, Nancy, French women of good family either marry or they become nuns – never never are they allowed to remain spinsters & have their names in the *Bottin mondain*, only tarts do that –

[1] Hon. Venetia Stanley (1887–1948). Married Hon. Edwin Montagu in 1915. Asquith's confidante during the First World War.
[2] Ava Bodley (1896–1974). Married to Ralph Wigram 1925–36, and to Sir John Anderson in 1941 who was created 1st Viscount Waverley in 1951.
[3] First husband of the above.
[4] *Bottin mondain*, French equivalent of *Who's Who*.

To EVELYN WAUGH   G. Heywood Hill Ltd
21 February 1946   10 Curzon Street,
                                     W1

Darling Evelyn

You know how Eddie Devonshire[1] persecutes me by saying 1st he is Uncle Matthew, & 2nd Linda is Debo & how dare I give him an immoral d in law. Well, the Macmillan girl went to stay with the old Duch of Dev:[2] lent her *Brideshead* smelt burning rushed downstairs found D of D *trying* (viz library at Alexandria) to burn *B.head* & saying 'how *dare* he write about my family like this.' So it must be a family mania to think all books are about them.

Have you heard about the Mouse @ Bay?[3] Some other women were saying how the virility of men is in relation to the size of their noses & the M at B jumped out of her chair & said 'It is quite untrue, Cyril has a *very* small nose.' Also about Brownell[4] being raped by Heygate[5] & telling somebody how dreadful it had been & how he has

S[yphilis] & G[onorrhoea] & ending up '& the worst of it is he doesn't seem to realize what Cyril stands for'. Perhaps you knew all this how dull for you if so, but if not, rather enjoyable.

Are you coming to London soon? I've got a lot to tell you – a long story about Prod & the Duchess of Kent.[6]

Love
    NR

[1] 10th Duke of Devonshire (1895–1950). Married Lady Mary Gascoyne Cecil in 1917.
[2] Wife of the 9th Duke; her daughter Dorothy married the statesman Harold Macmillan.
[3] Lys Lubbock, who was working as a general assistant at *Horizon*.
[4] Sonia Brownell (1918–80). Also an assistant at *Horizon*. Inspiration for Julia in George Orwell's *Nineteen Eighty-four* (1949). Married the dying Orwell in 1949. After his death she became a Left-Bank bluestocking in Paris, where her name was linked to many avant-garde writers.
[5] After his divorce from Evelyn Gardner, Sir John Heygate was married to Gwyneth Lloyd 1936–47 and to Dora Gillespie in 1951.
[6] No record of this meeting has survived, but Nancy's apprehension is evident in an earlier letter to Evelyn Waugh: 'I've offered Prod 2/6 not to embarrass me, as I used to do with my sisters when young men were coming to stay but I fear Prod is less venal & I dread his views on monarchy being aired.' (10 February 1946)

To DIANA MOSLEY   Hotel de Bourgogne
12 April 1946   7 rue de Bourgogne
                                         Paris VII

Oh Honks[1] the bliss. It's far more fun than last time because A. I am so rich & B. the Col is no longer governing France, so instead of always waiting about to be rung up & then hurrying round for ½ an hour I can see him for hours every day. He is now back in his old flat, with furniture lent by Rothschilds, but the only worry is he has no money. So when he isn't asked out he eats things in tins which have been sent him from time to time by American friends & luckily conserved by his faithful Pierre – high grade pork etc. Yesterday morning he rang up & said 'franchement ma chère j'en ai assez du High Grade.'[2] Isn't it dreadful. Of course I've begged & implored him to have some of my millions but it simply makes him cross so I've had to desist.

Yesterday I gave a luncheon party for 6 people – 2 bottles of champagne & 2 of red wine – lovely snails, chicken & port salut (don't cry) which with tip came to £9. You must say that's pretty cheap if one thinks of London. I had Maurice Bowra, Col, Marie-Louise Bousquet,[3] Paz Subercaseaux[4] (Gerald's enemy) & Marc de Chimay,[5] adored by the Col but who seems utterly pointless in every way to others. Why do all men have these curious friendships, I've never known one who didn't.

Maurice is wonderful here, he launches unashamed into the most extraordinary French, never draws breath, & the frogs utterly love him. He so adores the tuck & swig, & owned to me that after one luncheon party he went to sleep & only woke up at 5 the next morning.

Darling I've ordered *the dress*. As I never get asked to grand evening parties I shall always wear it at Crowood, hope you don't mind. It takes up a whole suitcase to itself so in every way is a highly practical INVESTMENT. This is an extraordinary town – at least 3 people have already said to me I hear you have ordered the black velvet dress. They take such an interest in everything which is so attractive.

Dined at the Embassy last night [Julian] Huxley, Steve Spender,[6] the famous Lulu,[7] who I must say is a fascinator & Raimund von H.[8] John Julius[9] as host. I take very much to him, he has that clever dissipated look of Ld Birkenhead.

Diana [Cooper] had confided to Steve that she thinks Huxley is common – I believe she's quite right too. They are both staying there.

Sold my book for £100 which I get here & now in francs, to éditions Charlot which is a new firm & appears to be good.[10]

I must go. The day is far too short for all I have to do – it is the one bother because it takes such hours to get to places, I am always running, always late often in tears!

Lunched with Marie-Laure[11] who asked much after you, I like her better this time. She had one of the padded dresses (I believe I've told you all this though).

Much love
NR

[1] Diana's nickname from childhood. It was later adopted by Evelyn Waugh and applied to Lady Diana Cooper. For clarity, 'Cooper' has been added in square brackets when Nancy is referring to Lady Diana.

[2] 'Frankly, my dear, I've had enough of High Grade.'

[3] Vivacious Parisian hostess, described by Cecil Beaton as 'the marionette of *La Fée Carabosse*'; married to the satirical writer Jacques Bousquet. After her husband's death she worked for *Harper's Bazaar*. The academic and literary gatherings which she had held every Wednesday became a Thursday salon where 'one saw less and less of Paul Valéry and more and more of Cecil Beaton'. Jean-Louis de Faucigny-Lucinge, *Un Gentilhomme Cosmopolite* (Perrin, 1990), p. 92.

[4] Madame Léon Subercaseaux. 'A well-educated, cultivated, rather earnest Chilean.' James Lees-Milne, *Midway on the Waves* (Faber and Faber, 1985), p. 143.

5 Prince de Caraman Chimay; nephew of the poet Anna de Noailles.
6 Stephen Spender (1909–). Poet and critic. Co-editor of *Horizon* 1939–41 and editor of *Encounter* 1953–67. Knighted 1983.
7 Louise de Vilmorin (1902–69). Author of several slight novels, including *Madame de . . .* (1951), and volumes of minor poetry. Married to an American, Henry Leigh Hunt, 1925–37, and to Count François-de-Paule Palffy 1938–43. A seductive, witty member of Lady Diana Cooper's *petite bande*, and a mistress of Duff. She lived at Verrières, a beautiful house outside Paris.
8 Raimund von Hofmannsthal (1906–74). Married Diana Cooper's niece, Lady Elizabeth Paget, in 1939.
9 John Julius Cooper (1929–). Only child of Duff and Lady Diana Cooper.
10 Editions Plon had turned down *The Pursuit of Love*.
11 Marie-Laure Bischoffsheim (1902–70). Poet, novelist, collector, and friend of the Surrealists. Eccentric both in her looks and behaviour. Married Vicomte Charles de Noailles in 1923. She and her husband backed Buñuel's famous film *l'Age d'Or* (1930); they also financed and performed in Cocteau's film *Le Sang d'un poète* (1930), but later edited themselves out because they considered their scene blasphemous. 'Marie-Laure is such a feature of one's life here, she must be seen once! What Kek [Cecil Beaton] calls "that living Daumier." ' (NM to Diana Mosley, 30 November 1946)

To Diana Mosley   Hotel de Bourgogne, VII
25 May 1946

Darling

What with my film & writing Randolph's articles for him I haven't had a moment to write for days. The film is too easy, & immensely long. I'm getting bored with it. Nearly finished however. I should think it will be a terrible film but I suppose one can't really tell.[1]

Last night there was a 'gala' at a picture gallery. It was said that the ladies had all 'fait folies' to have new clothes for it so I hopefully went in mine. Dined at La Rue with Vi Tre[fusis]: (do tell Gerald this). I was sitting waiting for her (one hour late) with Duff[2] & darling Jacques Février[3] when suddenly Jacques seized my arm & I thought would break it & I saw the following apparition: Violet practically naked to the waist & *smothered* in birds of paradise. Oh *could* you all have seen. She had also hired a regalia of jewels from Cartier. Well we dined & afterwards went on & there was a terrifying crowd in the street, we all got separated & breathlessly packed in a sort of surging tide of flesh, Violet's feathers like some brave little bark [*sic*] occasionally to be seen breasting a wave. I was *really* frightened, when the Col (who hadn't dined with us) appeared from nowhere, extricated me & we went for an hour to the Embassy, after which we got in quite easily & it was great fun & lovely lovely pictures. My dress a sensation that's all. Daphne[4] who is here says at Diana [Cooper]'s

levee this morning D. said 'now we will talk about Nancy's waist.'
Daphne says did my waist burn? I must say it *is* a wonderful dress,
& much much the prettiest there, in spite of the folies – Of course
one comes into one's own, with a small waist & huge hips, for the
1st time in 20 years.

Darling I shall have to come back – I'm simply eating up money
here. The boring thing is not knowing a bit what one will be liable for
in the way of taxes, but I suppose they will take most of the glamorous
thousands.

Randolph is a dotty boy, he said I'll give the Col £50 for a few little
details of how the Gen spends his time at Marly. The Col of course
hardly even saw the funny side he was so cross. Last night in the
crowd I said what will you pay me not to shout 'Palewski – au pouvoir.'
He always half thinks one might do these things & got awfully ratty
& nervous.

Odette Massigli who is such a dream figure in London is here &
hardly seems smart at all – while Jacqueline Roché[5] is definitely dowdy
here. Isn't it funny. As for the Ritz, it is full of English girls in navy
blue with white touches, can't you see them (Oh Mr Nissen[6]) & one
hears O but English on that side of the river. I keep away like mad.
Romie, Joan Moore & little blondes one had forgotten the existence
of.

Don't forget to tell Gerald about Vi's get-up. I can't write it all again
but he would enjoy. And give him my love.

　All love darling
　　　NR

The Col has a confidential report on results of the atom bomb which
makes awfully jolly reading.

What price Decca's behaviour –![7]

Got yr ribbon –!

[1] Nancy was translating the script for a film of Turgenev's *Torrents of Spring*, to be
produced by John Sutro and directed by Claude Renoir. The film was never completed:
the backers pulled out and the project eventually collapsed.
[2] Alfred Duff Cooper (1890–1954). Politician, diplomat and writer. Married Lady Diana
Manners in 1919. Ambassador in Paris 1944–7. Created Viscount Norwich in 1952. 'I
loved Duff, & he was one of the few people in the world I was rather frightened of,
so unusual with me & so salutary.' (NM to Diana Cooper, 2 January 1954.)
[3] Jacques Février (1900–79). Worldly concert pianist.
[4] Hon. Daphne Vivian (1904–). Beautiful wife of Viscount Weymouth (6th Marquess
of Bath) 1927–53, and of Major Alexander Fielding 1953–78. Biographer of Emerald
and Nancy Cunard.

⁵ Wife of the First Counsellor at the French Embassy in London.
⁶ A London tailor.
⁷ Jessica was insisting that her share of Inchkenneth, which the Mitford sisters had inherited from Tom, should be given to the Communist Party. 'One way to look at it is that my share will go to undo some of the harm our family has done, particularly the Mosleys and Farve when he was in the House of Lords.' (Jessica Treuhaft to Lady Redesdale, 21 May 1946)

To Diana Mosley   Hotel de Bourgogne, VII
2 June 1946

Darling

At last I've finished the film, except for correcting the type script, which, since Renoir's secretary neither knows English nor can read my writing, is a terrible job! Now I await John-en [Sutro] whose wife is to have a large part in it (*Torrents of Spring*).

Chips & Petticoats[1] are here. The pansy world has been in a ferment for this event, half longing to see Petti whose fame has preceded him & half terrified that the particular loved one will be bewitched by him! However I don't think there have been any terrible dramas – Chips has devoted himself entirely to Princesses of Bourbon-Parme & the like, while Petti, looking curiously English & correct beside Bébé,[2] Boris[3] & Co has been rather inclined to attach himself to such as me.

I dined at the Embassy for Mr, Mrs & Miss Hynd[4] (Duchy of L) & they were so like the famille Choops[5] that if any of you had been there I'd have burst. They looked utterly furious to begin with but mellowed up, & Diana [Cooper] gave the hideous Miss a hat from Reboux, & when they left they were quite human.

Awful old Bernstein[6] was there – he said would I go dancing with him so I made the Scarletts[7] take me home & as we left I saw Bernstein looking extremely cross sallying to the night clubs with Chips & P!!

Daphne was here – oh what a bitch she is. She made a terrific pass at the Col & her tactics were absolutely all in, for getting me out of the way. However the Col roared with laughter & (I believe) resisted. Do you suppose Debo can really like her or is it policy? Evelyn thinks D looks very miserable but I can't say I do, she always seems the soul of cheerfulness.

I found the Hulten–Jones murder[8] trial on the quais & read it with utter fascination – there are wonderful descriptions of the death cell, though not so vivid as yours. Oh Jones, the horror of her – I've also been reading Laval – do you want it by the way – completely absorbing like all trials.

Randolph has produced rather a pathetic little thing the ex-wife of Rex Harrison whom he is living with at the Ritz, having fallen in turns & always without success on all the presentable French women here. She's called Colette[9] & is a regular mouse at bay –! Everybody much relieved that his sexual instincts are now canalized –! . . .

All love darling
    NR

[1] Peter Coats (1910–90). An intimate friend of Chips Channon since 1939. ADC to Field Marshal Wavell during the war and latterly an expert on gardening. Author of an autobiography, *Of Generals and Gardens* (1976).

[2] Christian (Bébé) Bérard (1902–49). Belonged, with Pavel Tchelitchew and Eugène Berman, to the Neo-Humanist group of painters. Launched by Cocteau, he became France's leading stage designer.

[3] Boris Kochno (1904–90). Ballet historian and choreographer, one-time secretary to Serge Diaghilev. Christian Bérard's companion.

[4] Henry Hynd was PPS to the Minister of Defence.

[5] Mr and Mrs Hooper were groom and laundrymaid to the Redesdales.

[6] Henry Bernstein (1876–1953). Larger-than-life author whose plays were wildly popular with the Parisian bourgeois public, who saw their lives reflected in his dense and powerful dramas.

[7] Peter Scarlett was First Secretary at the British Embassy.

[8] Karl Hulten, an American paratrooper, and Elizabeth Jones were sentenced to death for the murder, in 1944, of a London taxi-driver. Hulten was hanged and Jones's sentence was commuted to life imprisonment.

[9] Colette Thomas married the actor Rex Harrison in 1934.

To Diana Mosley   Hotel de Bourgogne, VII
8 June 1946

Darling

I can't think why you always pretend you're not a writer – your letters are *models*. . . .

The Bourbon-Parme ball. Well, the Colonel took one look round the room, said 'neither an English person nor a French officer can stay here' & removed me under the nose of the Princess. It seems it was full of the most scandalous collaborators, & Paris has been humming ever since – even people like old Marie-Louise, who doesn't really take sides, were horrified by the company.[1]

Luckily the first part of the evening was great fun, a cocktail & dinner party of Bébé & as you know I'm not much of a one for balls. Only I was terrified that Dolly Radziwill,[2] who had asked for me to go, would be offended – but it seems she just feels furious with B.P.

The General has removed himself to his country seat 5 hours from Paris & the Col has to keep going there – it is a great bore & so tiring for him & I can see will happen weekly now. I'm planning to come home in about a month & try to make proper arrangements about Blomfield & so on so that I can come & live here.

It's too silly going on like this, week by week, & terribly extravagant.

Basil Murray's little girl,[3] aged 18, is here. I've taken greatly to her, she is *so* like we were & it's fun showing her round. She's in a family & of course in perfect bliss. Not pretty but all there.

I've just lunched with Syrie-bags, how I love her (in spite of having Liza [Paravicini]'s 2 accouchements for the 100th time). She is a dear good friend. It seems Lady Mendl[4] has arrived. Having had 2 heart attacks in the aeroplane she leapt out crying I've *made* it I've *made* it!

All my clothes have come except your stuff which will be ready next week. That is, 3 day dresses, one evening, one coat, one printed suit, & out of the lot only one failure which is a sort of washing dress. Not bad I think do you – I always find choosing so difficult. I tried on yours & really think it will be the best of the lot. If you simply love it you must have it for yourself. Two hats haven't succeeded but one I managed to sell to B. Dawson.[5] One is bound to have failures, don't you agree, but of course they do rather weigh on one at present prices. Bébé says my black velvet dress is the prettiest he ever saw, & I really think so too.

The weather has begun to boil, & I've found a place on the roof where I can lie nude, with my head hanging over into the Place, gazing on one hand into Mme de Chambrun's[6] windows, on the other into Marie-Louise's & with a view of all Paris up to Montmartre. It is utter bliss & I can hardly tear myself away.

Later

Just been with Syrie to the British Embassy garden party for Peace. It was exactly like a Church Bazaar, & made more so by the sudden & perfectly drenching rain which soon began to descend. The utter ghastly drear of the Embassy wives must be seen to be believed – they *all still* dress at Debenhams, after years here. Isn't it strange – And, in some mysterious way, get their thin hair done in London – do they fly over once a week to some little man in the Cromwell Road? Well, the Colonel says I look more English every time he sees me so I suppose it is a rubber stamp for life.

Horrid old Hoffman's Tale[7] is here with Liz. Not a man I like at all.

Poor Umberto,[8] having to leave beautiful Italy. That must be the worst part of it I should think. . . .

Much love darling
      NR

[1] Evelyn Waugh, to whom Nancy had also described the ball, replied: 'Collaborationists my foot. Does it not occur to you, poor innocent, that that continental colonel went back to the aristocratic ball – that while you lay sleepless with your fountain pen, he was in the arms of some well born gestapo moll?' (11 [June] 1946)

[2] (Dolly) Princess Dolores Radziwill (1886–1966). Nancy's greatest friend in Paris. She had the dark, thin looks of a Goya Infanta and a very sharp tongue. Born a Radziwill, she was twice married to Radziwills, then to Mogens Tvede, a Danish architect, in 1932, 'but rather naturally goes on being Radziwill. I love her beyond words.' (NM to Evelyn Waugh, 31 July 1949)

[3] Ann Murray (1928–). Married to John Powell-Jones in 1949 and to James Paludan in 1969.

[4] Elsie de Wolfe (1865–1950). American actress who made a fortune as an interior decorator after her retirement from the stage. Married in 1926 to Sir Charles Mendl, Press Attaché to the British Embassy 1926–40.

[5] Beatrice 'Bumble' Dawson (1908–76). Costume designer and a neighbour of Nancy in London.

[6] Countess René de Chambrun (1911–91). Daughter of Pierre Laval and passionately devoted to his memory. She lived on the Place du Palais Bourbon opposite the National Assembly.

[7] Raimund von Hofmannsthal.

[8] Umberto II of Italy (1904–83). Succeeded his father on 9 May 1946. Left Italy on 13 June following a referendum which gave a majority in favour of a republic.

To DIANA MOSLEY   Hotel de Bourgogne, VII
15 June 1946

Darling

Peter's idea for the island, which I have forwarded to Muv, & seems excellent to me, is that there should be a sale, advertised as little as possible, that Muv should buy it if it goes for something within reason, & *only* pay Decca but owe the rest to us to be paid sometime, or out of her estate when she dies. It seems foolproof to me. If you think a good idea do suggest it to the others. Like that the CP will probably get *much* less than £1500 & Muv can afford to have it comfortably.[1]

What a love she is to give us £500, so agreeable, just when everyone must be dying for new clothes too! . . .

Tomorrow is an exciting day for us here – & soon I think Good Time Charley as Randolph calls him will be firmly installed again. If only he could get the people *fed*, I keep telling the Col this but he can't seem to be interested in that small detail. As far as I can see all they need do is take off controls & rationing & let the thing find its own level. Half the time the rations aren't honoured as it is.

Off to the country – I'll finish later –

16 June '46

At last I've fixed something quite definite. I've taken a furnished flat (the one I had before) for the winter from October. So I'll come back next month, let Blomfield, see you all, & come back here & then, without having burnt any boats, really see if I like living here best. It's got 3 bed & 3 sitting rooms so if allowed I could have some Woodley[2] life in the Xmas hols. This is all a great relief to me as I couldn't see my way after next month. But in life the path often becomes clear as one goes on I find.

Peter writes that Bertie[3] has definitely packed up on Diane. He & Joan Moore are here (who isn't?) Will they marry I wonder? *Poor* Joan.

Rain in June means all's in tune[4] made me simply so shriek, & also Eddy [Sackville-] West whom I told it to – I thought he'd have a seizure.

There's a wonderful exhibition of Rothschild pictures & the Col went to it alone saying he couldn't take me because of the shrieks he knew there would be. Isn't he hateful. He says I shall be seen sunbathing on the roof here & the papers will start a thing about La Folle du Palais Bourbon – & then there'll be the great day when they discover that La Folle is La Soeur d'Unity Mitford.

The Colonel is at Bayeux – I can't wait to hear how it went off – I thought the speech was lovely stuff I must say.

I asked Papy[5] yesterday what's the truth about food here. He says the truth is about 15 million people are fearfully hungry & the others eat as much as they want – that is, everyone in the country & the wage-earners in the towns. I expect he's just about right. Of course country people are coming into their own all over the world aren't they. Are people upset by the bread rationing at home? Is it a fairly big ration?

I've utterly run out of money, a most uncomfortable feeling. I can borrow from the Colonel so it's not desperate, actually.

Best love darling from

    NR

P.S. I saw the Windsors[6] – he a *balloon*, she like the skeleton of some tiny bird, hopping in her hobble skirt. (Oh the tight skirts – oh the misery. I still think they won't really take on here & that they are purely American, but I suppose after 6 years of the others there's

bound to be a change.) They both look ravaged with misery – & said to the Col 'you ought to marry, look at us.'
17th Your birthday – many happy returns. Present to go back with Mollie [Friese-Greene].

[1] In the event, the Communist Party turned down Jessica's offer of her sixth share of Inchkenneth.
[2] 'Woodley' refers to any young boy, usually friends of Diana's sons, after John van Druten's play, *Young Woodley*.
[3] Sir Robert Abdy (1896–1976). Married to Lady Diana Bridgeman 1930–62.
[4] 'About the time of the [V Day] procession I saw Baker [the gamekeeper at Crowood] & said terribly wet, Baker. Yes he replied, his mind on farming, but they do say Rain in June keeps all in tune.' (Diana Mosley to NM, 10 June 1946)
[5] Jacques Papy; a friend of Nancy's whose wife Janine made an attempt at the French translation of *The Pursuit of Love*. Nancy was unhappy with the result and it was eventually translated by Daria Olivier.
[6] The Duke and Duchess of Windsor had returned to live in France after spending the war in the Bahamas where he had been Governor.

To Lady Redesdale   Hotel de Bourgogne, VII
1 July 1946

Darling Muv
    . . . Peter has a wonderful job, making 2 documentary films for Rank, in Ethiopia & Czecho Slovakia, 20 gns a week & all expenses. So now we *must* be domiciled abroad, otherwise, out of the odd £7000 I have already made this year & his pay *and* his allowances we should only net under £1000. So Blomfield & the flat must go. I shall come home end of this month & decide what to sell & what to store & see you all & then come back here for good. *Oh the heaven.* Peter comes next week to talk it over.
    We think of getting a legal separation so as not to pay taxes together, as we have no children I can't see that it would matter, & if ever he became Lord Rennell I should be spared that name of, to me, unpleasant associations!! (Of course no opening of Parliament but I suppose one could bear to forgo that!)
    What I long for, & can easily find, is some little house ½ an hour from Paris with a bit of land, goats, hens etc. I've already heard of two, they cost about £2000.
    My book is out in America & has had glittering reviews. Not one bad one & not one 'but' even in the good ones. I don't know if they're always like that there.
    Including the cheap edition not yet ready I shall have sold 200,000

(two hundred thousand) in England this year! I enclose one or two American reviews, they are all much the same.

It is intensely hot here. Mollie is wilting a little but of course it makes a new woman of me & I lie out on the roof for hours until the leads become too hot even through layers of blanket!

I'm getting really quite fat, you won't know me. The idea of ever again living in a country where there is no black market *utterly appals me* (don't tell Aunt Iris I said so!)

Lovely butter came with Mollie, so kind of you. Don't send any more, I've even found where I can get that (£1 a kilo, but well worth it). The only thing one can't get at all is milk & as you know I don't care a bit. . . .

Much love
    NR

Love to Song, I will write soon to her.

To Diana Mosley   Hotel de Bourgogne, VII
29 July 1946

Darling

Aunt Weenie [Bailey] has soon turned out, like the Connollys, to be *not as nice as she looks*. I took great pains, took her to a very expensive place & gave her & Tim a delicious luncheon & arranged for her to buy olive oil & cheese & took her to my hat shop. My reward was a great pi jaw on not rallying round Muv who she says is utterly utterly wretched, in fact *suicidal*.

Well I said she is surrounded by adoring daughters. A sniff. Well *one* (I didn't make out which one, Debo I think). Then the jam came 'Of course this affair of Bobo & Mosley must be the very last straw for her.' So I said 'You don't tell me anybody believes that old story?' 'Of course we all believe it.' 'Who?' 'Well, Madeleine,[1] Margaret,[2] well I may as well tell you I believe anything of him.' So I said 'Yes I'd believe anything of anybody except that an extremely attractive man who has had all the prettiest women in London society could bring himself to lay a finger on such a pathetic wreck. Have you *seen* Bobo?' I said. I think this shook her a bit. 'I hadn't thought of that.' Funny how people who know nothing about sex never do think of that sort of thing – I mean people like Uncle Tommy[3] if they meet a bugger always expect to be fallen upon tooth & nail.

So then I laid it on & said Madeleine & Aunt Margaret must be without any knowledge of life at all if they could conceive of such a thing & how really it made laughing stock of them. Then I told her that Gerald & I, bursting with laughter, had told you ages ago & that Kit[4] first thought it a terrific joke but then got rather cross & had given Bowd a great lecture – etc – making a joke of it all & laying on about how some people really are *too* naïf poor old things, which she didn't much like. I think I really have convinced *her*. But of course if poor Muv really believes it, that is a shame & must be fixed – have you had it out with her ever? Really I *hate* Bowleses & wish I hadn't a drop of that acidulated blood in my veins (except darling Muv & even she can be, or could in the past, exceedingly disagreeable). I promise you the whole afternoon there was hardly a word without its sting, the general implication being what a bad, wicked daughter you are. Actually what I'm hoping is Muv will come for a nice long stay in Oct: which I believe will do her good – as you know I regard being here as a panacea for all ills!! But if I were at Blomfield as good as gold I should see her about once a month – you know – anyway I don't have to excuse myself to *you*. If I have become what I suppose they all regard as wicked, *that is* Muv's fault because if I had had a family[5] there would have been no Col & that's quite certain. But I can't say that. And if Peter doesn't complain it's nobody else's business that I can see.

Goodness I'm in a temper. What has made my day is I've found Garth[6] in French, in a paper called *l'Etoile*. I've sent him to Jonathan, will try & get one to enclose in this. Of course he *is* Randolph, & R. would be well advised to adopt that maternity robe –

I don't know if I ought to have bothered you with all this Weenie hatefulness except I can't keep it bottled up & also think you must now, if you haven't already, have it out with Muv & perhaps also with Bowd's doctor – I think it's *too* much all these old harpies gloating about it.

Oh bugger the sun as Alexander would say.[7]

Much love darling
    NR

P.S. What about a word with Tello[8] – she always seems a sensible old thing.
Greatly soothed by a long walk by the Seine on a boiling night with new moon. It really would be impossible to be happier than I am here. . . . Fascinating how they all *want* to believe the worst about all of us, isn't it? Imagine if it were something to do with Emma [Cavendish],

one of us forcing itself to believe horrors, so queer. They must simply
hate us & it's a funny way of showing their great affection for Muv –

[1] Madeleine Tobin; married to Lady Redesdale's eldest brother, George.
[2] Dowager Lady Stanley of Alderley; mother of Edward Stanley and a first cousin of
Nancy's mother.
[3] Hon. Bertram (Tommy) Mitford (1880–1962). Succeeded as 3rd Baron Redesdale
on the death of Nancy's father in 1958.
[4] Mosley was known to his pre-war friends as Tom, and as Kit after his marriage to
Diana.
[5] According to Nancy, the doctor who performed her hysterectomy during the war
asked if she had ever been in contact with syphilis. When she mentioned this to her
mother, Lady Redesdale said, rather vaguely, that Nancy's nurserymaid had been
infected with it. Although Nancy showed no symptoms of having the disease, she
thereafter blamed her mother for her inability to have children.
[6] Muscle-bound hero of a *Daily Mirror* strip cartoon. 'I'm Garth on the mountains of
the moon,' shouts seven-year-old Sigi in *The Blessing*, to which his father replies: 'Oh,
do be Napoleon crossing the Alps. This Garth is really too dull.' (Hamish Hamilton,
1951), p. 40.
[7] Said, in fact, by Max Mosley aged five, when the sun shone in his eyes.
[8] Rita (Tello) Shell had been governess to Lady Redesdale and her brothers and sister.
When their mother died in 1887, she became their father's mistress and had three
children by him. She called herself Mrs Stewart and edited *The Lady* which was founded
by Thomas Gibson Bowles.

To Evelyn Waugh   Hotel de Bourgogne, VII
9 August 1946

Darling Evelyn

Oh how glad I am you feel this about Lulu[1] – I can't sit in a room
with her she makes me so nervous. And vicious – why she even
shocked Romie with her suggestions for a happy evening once. She
is much more like a middle European than a French woman & the proof
is that before, & some say during, the war she lived for preference in
Berlin.

I will tell you now about the French, after 4 months of study I have
come to certain conclusions. The French upper classes are very dull
indeed or else very vicious. I don't see one person I should like to
be great friends with. The dull ones are worse than Pont St & the
vicious ones think such as me a standoffish prig. In any case none of
them count in the life of the country they are a sort of side line.
But the middle class intellectuals are absolutely delightful & have no
equivalent that I can see in England. I mean all the people on the
fringes of literature, booksellers, translators, publishers & so on – I
don't know any of the important writers – but I have great friends

now among the ones I describe & absolutely *love* their company & have the greatest regard for them as human beings. Then servants, shop people etc etc are far nicer to one than in England, so friendly & anxious to please, & say hullo if you see them in the street as though it was a village. In fact all those relationships are more like those of the English countryside when I was a child & before it became full of deck chairs. A waitress from a restaurant I go to stopped me in the street & said 'you never come now – & where is the fat gentleman (Randy).' Imagine in London –! Another thing. English servants, if you lie on your bed all day reading a book, or just lying, give great furious sniffs & clearly regard you as a disgusting rotter. The French, even the maids in an hotel, regard reading & thinking as highly honourable occupations.

I know now I couldn't bear to live anywhere else. The country bores me you see, & London is a factory more than a town, & so so ugly & I live a great deal by my eyes. Also I like to be warm. But there's no doubt I shall find that friends like you & Gerald are irreplaceable, for the reasons I have mentioned. So you must sometimes come & stay – it's not as though one had retired to the South Pole.

I adored your renewed Boots-bait.[2] Mr Cockburn,[3] who is in this hotel, is also delighted as he says it all spurs on idle old Boots to be keener on the Party.

Are you a Garth addict? (*Daily Mirror*) If so tell me as I've found Garth in French & will send, it's utter bliss.

Have you read *La Princesse de Clèves*?[4] She might take the taste of Lulu out of your mouth. . . .

[incomplete]

[1] Evelyn Waugh had described Louise de Vilmorin as 'a Hungarian countess who pretended to be a French poet. An egocentric maniac with the eyes of a witch . . . She is the Spirit of France. How I hate the French.' *Letters*, p. 232.
[2] Waugh's scathing review of *The Unquiet Grave*, 'Palinurus in Never-Never Land', was published in *The Tablet*, 27 July 1946.
[3] Claud Cockburn (1904–81). Author, journalist, editor of the Communist newspaper *The Week*, 1933–46, and contributor to *Private Eye*.
[4] By Mme de La Fayette (1678). Translated by Nancy in 1950. 'I like fact better than fiction and I like almost anything that makes me laugh. But my favourite book falls into neither of these categories: it is *La Princesse de Clèves*.' 'A Taste of Honey', *The Times*, 20 November 1961.

To Gaston Palewski   Edensor House
23 September 1946   Bakewell
                                                      Derbyshire

You dear Colonel I am leading a very family existence. I found my
mother aged & depressed I thought & am motoring to Scotland with
her, shall spend a few weeks on her island as otherwise she would
have been quite alone there. We've been at Debo's the last 2 nights,
off again today to the Lake District which I've never seen & rather
wanted to.

I suppose Colonel Mitford[1] knows it well? But oh I suppose now he
is Colonel Bath as I hear La Marquise is never away from Paris. Alas.

Yesterday we made an expedition to see Osbert's house.[2]

Colonel you would have laughed, there is one room with a lace
wallpaper, all pink & white as for a bride – the man who showed us
over (Osbert is in London) said 'Mr Horner's[3] room.' Don't repeat
Colonel dear please because Osbert is a great friend & it is so cattish,
for your ear alone. I thought of you. I thought of you too as Debo &
I gave a chorus of mimiery[4] 'Oh! oh! ah! ee!' It is a very fascinating
house, a sort of genuine Groussay[5] if you see what I mean.

I'm reading a new life of O Wilde[6] – very good. He did make such
wonderful jokes, better than anybody. When he was arrested he said
'The lower classes are behind me, to the last boy.' How I wish I'd
known him.

Dear darling hateful Col don't forget me I'm having a sad time. I
guess you are pretty busy too & not only with La Marquise.

With love you dear Colonel.
          NR

I said to Debo's little boy[7] 'Can you talk?' He replied 'Not yet'. . . .

---

[1] 'Violet Trefusis says the Colonel is getting so English he ought to be called Colonel
Mitford while I get more foreign every day & should be La Palewska.' (NM to Deborah,
Marchioness of Hartington, 23 August 1946)

[2] Renishaw Hall in Derbyshire.

[3] David Horner; Osbert Sitwell's 'orchidaceous' inamorato.

[4] A Mitford word for exaggerated admiration.

[5] An early 19th-century house which had been transformed into a neo-Palladian mansion
by Carlos (Charlie) Beistegui (1895–1970), the son of the Mexican Ambassador in
Madrid. Very rich and very fond of women, Nancy described him as 'a sort of born old
maid, fussy & pernickety & difficult beyond words'. (NM to Raymond Mortimer, 20
August 1955)

[6] Hesketh Pearson, *The Life of Oscar Wilde* (1946).

[7] The Earl of Burlington was two and a half years old.

To GERALD BERNERS   20 rue Bonaparte, VI
11 November 1946

Dearest Gerald
  At last I am installed in a cosy little home of my own, in great
comfort with a really wonderful cook even by French standards, & a
very hot stove which has now been discovered by the English visitors
here. In theory they don't come to Paris to see boring old English
friends, in practice, as the chill of the evening creeps over their partially heated hotels they can't resist the lure of the stove. I keep the
key under the mat, which worked nicely until the Serge[1] appeared &
with trans-Atlantic tactlessness double locked me in with a Major (the
friend of a friend) after which no power on earth would move the lock
in any direction. At last, supper time approaching, I said 'I can see I
shall have to eat this Major' which gave him, the Major, a sort of
supernatural strength & he undid the door. The Serge has brought
no money but a blue overcoat which he hopes to sell – I believe he
expects me to wheel it round on a barrow for him. So all my (rather
feeble I must say) expectations of rich meals, soirées de gala à l'opéra,
etc, have fallen rather flat – nor has he brought so much as a mouthful
of Ness café or any other comestible.
  Roddy Henderson[2] is here, he is *so* funny, did you know? A great
pleasure in one's life I find. Unfortunately he is off again almost at
once.
  Violet has finally chucked her Prince[3] because she says all his friends
are dentists – she has now taken up with a chap called M. de Grand
Guignol,[4] with whom she gave a cocktail party of great brilliance.
Goodness I do love her.
  Michael[5] sent me his book, but what can one say? *Heaven*, I wrote
to him – non committal I thought!

    Much love & to Robert[6]
        Nancy

Anyway, parasol is one of *the words*, isn't it,[7] I'm surprised he didn't
know.

[1] Stuart Preston (1915–). Art historian who served in the US Army. 'The American
sergeant so famous in the war that the King once said to somebody who was late
"never mind I expect you've been to St George's Hospital to see the Sergeant." ' (NM
to Jessica Treuhaft, 17 December 1963)
[2] Hon. Roderic Henderson (1909–). Younger brother of Lord Faringdon.
[3] Prince Rodolphe de Faucigny-Lucinge (1898–1985). He escaped from the clutches

of Violet Trefusis only to sell himself, at the end of his life, to a rich widow.
[4] Count Jean de Gaigneron (1890–1976). Gossip and painter. Portrayed unkindly as
the Marquis de Chaumont in Harold Nicolson's *Some People* (1927).
[5] Michael Duff, *The Power of a Parasol* (1948). A novel in which Lord Berners's
companion, Robert Heber-Percy, appears under the name Robert Oddman.
[6] Robert Heber-Percy (1911–87). Known as 'The Mad Boy'. Married to Jennifer Fry
1942–7 and to Lady Dorothy Lygon in 1985. Inherited Faringdon from Lord Berners.
'His high spirits, elegant appearance and uninhibited behaviour enchanted Gerald . . .'
Diana Mosley, *Loved Ones*, p. 104.
[7] Nancy considered 'parasol' Non-U and preferred 'sunshade'.

To Evelyn Waugh   20 rue Bonaparte, VI
26 November 1946

Dearest Evelyn
    I hope Miss Harriet[1] will shortly receive a muff, from me. May she
please be allowed to wear it, as it is intended to keep her hands warm,
delicate & white, & *not* to be stuffed away in a drawer.
    I am in great despair – I *can't write a line*. I try & try, make
beginnings which get no way at all & simply nothing happens. Isn't it
awful – meanwhile the thousands on which I foresee I shall have, in
the end, to pay 19/6 in the £ (because this thing about living abroad
is most tricky unless you lived there before the war) are flying out of
the window in a truly hateful way. And oh oh I missed the big prize
in the lottery (8 000 000 fr:) by one figure last week, you must say
almost unbearable.
    Maurice [Bowra] came, he *was* nice. He gave the Colonel & me a
truly wonderful blow out at the grandest & prettiest of all the restaurants here (it was shut when you were here last) called the Véfour.
    Fancy, I've been reading a book by Mr Maugham & it says Mr
Waugh despises people who write in the 1st person.[2] Do, or did you?
    What did you think of Xopher [Sykes] on Robert[3] – I enjoyed it but
it didn't make the Colonel like Robert so then I felt it can't be quite
right all the same. He thought R sounded violent & silly. I don't know,
can't say, I loved Robert too much to read it objectively I daresay.
Wonder what Mrs Byron[4] thinks. . . .
    Everybody here says Queen Mary stole the Windsor jewels[5] – is
that the view at home?
    When do you come? Soon I hope – perhaps when Jonathan is here
that would be very nice.
    I've made a great new friend called Madame Auric you wouldn't

like her. She has painted, & sold me, a truly wonderful picture of the Colonel it makes my life.[6]

Much love & come soon
    Nancy

[1] Harriet Waugh (1944–). Nancy's goddaughter. Author and book reviewer. Married the art critic Richard Dorment in 1985.
[2] In *Cakes and Ale* (1930) Somerset Maugham quotes Evelyn Waugh on the 'contemptible practice' of first-person narration.
[3] Evelyn Waugh: 'Christopher Sykes has written an exquisite life of his great-uncle and a lot of balls about the late Robert Byron.' *Letters*, p. 241.
[4] Robert Byron's mother.
[5] Many of the Duchess of Windsor's jewels had been stolen while she was staying with Lord and Lady Dudley at their house near Sunningdale. There was a rumour that among them were uncut emeralds, said to have belonged to Queen Alexandra.
[6] Nora Auric (d.1982). Austrian-born society painter. Married the composer Georges Auric in 1930. In order to make the portrait, entitled 'l'Homme au gant', fit an oval frame, Nancy cut off the bottom thus removing the glove of the title and the artist's signature. To add insult to injury she copied the signature, wrongly spelt.

To Evelyn Waugh   20 rue Bonaparte, VI
16 December 1946

Darling Evelyn
    So glad she liked the muff, it's such fun getting things for a little girl, nearly all my relations of that age are boys except Emma [Cavendish] who has too many adorers & doesn't even glance at a present if you give her one.
    I feel very worried about your operation – the only thing is I believe it is always a guaranteed cure for ever. I've never had piles, understand they are past a joke – not that I ever regard physical pain as a joke myself.
    Stephen Tennant is here, he makes my life. You know you're not allowed to take jewels out of England, so as he can't be parted from his he went to the Board of Trade & asked what to do, so they put them under a B of T seal, in a parcel, & he brought them like that, but 'not a tiny *trinket* for the train.' The Colonel is perfectly fascinated by him – at the same time likes him. You really can't help it, there's something very sweet about him.
    The French hatred of UNESCO is very funny! I expect you don't know what it is, well a lot of Americans headed by Prof: [Julian] Huxley have come here to educate the French. The first thing they want to do is to shut the museums – of course a roar as of a wounded

bull has gone up – you know how the French love their musées. What can be the idea? These hateful beasts live like millionaires on the Black Market in well heated rooms & wish to take their only pleasure from people who can do neither. In return they recite poems by Steve Spender to music on the wireless, cold comfort indeed. I feel you will be on my side over all this.

Are you coming? Oh *please* do. Diana Cooper is now so dazzled by Lulu [de Vilmorin] that she has no time for anybody else, & when people go there at 6 they are shown straight into Lulu's bedroom where Ran[1] lies weeping across the foot of her bed. Couldn't you do a little debunking? Nobody else could. (Don't repeat all this it is for your private ear – you know how much I love & revere Diana.)

Sorry about Gormanston.[2] Even I couldn't stand Butlin quite so near though of course I'm glad to know that it exists. I thought Lady G was a young wife who, supposing her husband to have died in the war, married again & had some trouble when he returned in explaining away the pram in the hall & the Teddy Bear on the sofa. Is this all what Romie calls a pigment of my imagination? I showed the photograph to my mother who has been here & she said 'Suitable for religious bodies – *very* suitable then for Mr Waugh.' My mother dined with the Colonel, picked all the truffles out of her omelette & left them. The Col delighted – '*Most* people pick out the truffles & leave the rest, very patrician of her.'

Have a Happy Xmas, love to Laura[3] & you from
        Nancy

[1] 13th Earl of Antrim (1911–77). Married Angela Sykes in 1934.
[2] 'The Irish trip was enjoyable but unsuccessful. Gormanston Castle was vast & grim & haunted & I had decided to buy it when just in time the announcement appeared that Mr Butlin has purchased a site within a mile of it for a Holiday Camp.' (Evelyn Waugh to NM, 12 December 1946)
[3] Laura Herbert (1916–73). Married Evelyn Waugh in 1937.

To Christopher Sykes   20 rue Bonaparte, VI
30 January 1947

My dear Christopher
    I hear you are back – must write you a word about *Loyalties*.
    I think you did wonders over Robert, whom I should have found an almost impossible person to write about just as I find it almost impossible to convey to people who didn't know him what absolute

heaven he was. I've never known anybody so complex – even his physical appearance was entirely unlike his character.

Oh goodness I do miss him, more & more.

Need I say how I gloated over the other C[hristopher] S[ykes] – the coffin,[1] dear how dreadful. I remember my grandmother speaking of him in tones of horrified awe, no wonder.

I'm so glad, for Mrs Byron specially, you did write that, & also I hear G.M. [Young] did a broadcast. I think it must all be a little comfort to her.

Have you read Rémy *Mémoires d'un Agent Secret?*[2] It is made for you. I'm trying to find out if it's being translated as I think most important it should be – do you happen to know? It's far & away better than Bénouville.[3]

Shall you come over at all? If so pray let me know, I would love to see you.

Politics very queer. The papers just print pictures of Ramadan[4] (or Ramasse-miettes) with spots on his nose & leave it at that.

A maker of Church Furnishings has murdered his mistress & Algerians with hatchets continue to wipe out whole families in the Midi. Also they pretend that an English wife has beaten her pederastic husband to death with a toy boat but of course *this can't* be true, it's just because of the Ruhr coal I expect.

> Give my love to Camilla & you from
> Nancy

[1] The coffin of Sykes's great-uncle was too long fit his grave.
[2] Colonel Gilbert Rémy, *Mémoires d'un agent secret de la France libre* (1946).
[3] General Guillain de Bénouville, *Le Sacrifice du matin* (1946). An account of the French Resistance.
[4] Paul Ramadier (1888–1961). Elected head of government on 21 January. He had previously been Minister for Food, hence the sobriquets Ramasse-miettes ('crumb sweeper') and Ramadiet.

To DIANA MOSLEY   20 rue Bonaparte, VI
19 February 1947

Darling

A heavy blow has fallen which I must say I've been expecting for some time – a hateful weekly paper here has come out with enormous headlines 'Hitler's mistress's sister dedicates daring book to M. Palewski'.

I haven't seen it & the Col won't let me because it is apparently

too revolting – but of course he is in a great do about it & really I
think I shall have to go away from here for a bit. You see he is such
an ambitious man & you know how the one thing that can't be forgiven
is getting in their way politically –!

Of course it was madness, the dedication, & what I can't tease him
with now it was *entirely* his own doing. I said shall I put To the Colonel
– To G.P. & so on & he absolutely insisted on having his whole name.
At the time I suppose he was powerful enough for it not to matter,
now with everything in the balance the Communists have pounced.
He says the General will be furious. Luckily in a way Peter is back
& wants very much to spend the summer in Rome which I suppose
I shall have to do – haven't seen the Colonel yet, he sounds very low
& though chaps always mind less than ONE does about these things
I suppose he will miss me very much too.

To cheer myself up I went & ordered a suit at Dior. The skirt has
sort of stays at which one tugs until giddiness intervenes – the basque
of the coat stuck out with whale-bone . . . Terribly pretty. I shall
have the coat copied in white linen so that I can wear it the whole
summer except in really boiling (!!) weather.

Got some wood by a miracle this morning, just as I was completely
without one stick, & that also cheers me up.

I'll write & say what happens. All this is *only* due to love of publicity
– first, Bobo's which we have always agreed to have been fatal, &
second, one must say it, to the Colonel's –! But very few human
beings are without it & in the end it always leads to bother, if not
worse, & yet seems irresistible. I'll write again when I've seen the
Col but I fear this is all really very serious.

Much love darling
NR

You see apart from anything else the Gen is such a dreadful old puritan
– gone are those cheerful days when Fr politicians expected to die in
the arms of their mistresses –

To DIANA MOSLEY   20 rue Bonaparte VI
21 February 1947

Darling

There've now been 2 more dreadful articles & it's quite clear I shall
have to scoot, so you will probably be seeing me next week.

The Colonel thinks I'd better go away for a couple of months by which time it should all have blown over. He is very giggly about it & not reproachful thank goodness, he keeps saying it is like *Brief Encounter*[1] (every French person's favourite film).

. Fortunately in a way I have had an enormous film offer, doing dialogue,[2] & think I should have been obliged really to come over & see about that, & it makes an excellent excuse.

If only the weather was warmer, also I'm worried about leaving the flat empty – fortunately we never seem to have burglaries in Paris it's a purely English pass time.

See you very likely.

All love
    NR

Next day

I'm really *in* despair, not so much as I keep telling him, at leaving the Col as the horror of moving all my things again – what to leave & what to take –! The impossibility of purchasing anything at home adds to one's difficulties – oh do be sorry for me!
Thawing hard thank goodness.

[1] The 1945 film based on Noel Coward's play *Still Life*, about two people in love, each married to someone else.
[2] Nancy had been asked to revise the script for *Kind Hearts and Coronets* (1949), an Ealing comedy directed by Robert Hamer, starring Alec Guinness and Dennis Price. Several reviews mentioned particularly the excellence of the script: 'Yes, it is the words that are most memorable here; a rare quality in a film.' *Punch*, 6 July 1949. 'Urbane, satirical, witty, sophisticated, altogether adult.' *Spectator*, 24 June 1949.

To GASTON PALEWSKI   707 Hood (Cagoulard) House[1]
18 March 1947   Dolphin Square
                           London, SW1

You dear Colonel I haven't written because no good writing wails & whenever I took up my pen I found myself wailing. Now I feel a little calmer, the snow has gone for one thing, & a letter from you always makes me happy.

I'm coming over on the 25th, next Tuesday, by Air France because I no longer mind being carbonisée [burnt] now I see how dreadful one's life can suddenly become at a moment's notice. Gerald says God has given up & GONE AWAY & left as his deputies Evelyn Waugh & Mr Shinwell[2] & we must pray to them now.

Peter is completely set on buying the Drian[3] house. I think it's a

sensible thing to do, from every point of view, & I expect we shall.
It won't be heaven, like living in the rue Bonaparte, but neither will
it be so compromising for you.

One thing about having come over here, I've got the most lovely
birthday present for you so do be excited.

I did wish you could have seen the King's pictures (over now) –
the Canalettos beat any I have ever seen in my life, & a whole room
full of them.

We go to Spain for a month on the 30th & Bridget[4] is coming. . . .

I had letters from Violet & Alvilde by the same post – *both all* about
a bidet – the poor girls seem to be going native.

Dined with a friend of mine who has been for years in India, he
knows the Black List very well, & says she, & indeed all the Rajahs
are utterly delighted we are leaving India because now they will be
able to fulfil their highest ambition which is to live at Suvretta House,
St Moritz.

See you soon dear Col

[1] Nancy was staying at the Mosleys' flat. The Cagoulards (which means 'hood') were
an extreme French right-wing party.
[2] Emmanuel Shinwell (1884–1986). Labour MP. Created a life peer in 1970. Minister
of Fuel and Power in 1947.
[3] Adrien Etienne; portrait and landscape painter who signed his work 'Drian' from the
early 1920s. Peter never did buy his house, Moulin de la Tuilerie, an old mill twenty-five
miles west of Paris; it was bought in 1952 by the Duke of Windsor.
[4] Lady Bridget Parsons (d.1972).

To Gaston Palewski   707 Hood House
20 March 1947   Dolphin Square, SW1

Oh you dear Colonel that naughty Mme Champion[1] uses some method
of postage by which I have only today received a letter you wrote on
the 5th. I expect, like many English people, she can't believe that
those dear little blue boxes in the walls of cafés are really meant for
letters – I must tell her.

How I wish you were pleased about the Treaty[2] – bother (as
Princess Elizabeth said). I can't help feeling it's nicer for me to reside
in the country of an ally.

There was a party at the House for the Supreme Soviets & one of
the S.S. said to Gladwyn, looking round at the wives of the Labour
M.P.s, 'In Russia we are told that English women are tall & beautiful:
I see this is not the case.'

My wicked father has decided, in spite of all our wails, to sell everything. He says he must eat. (He admits that his income is £10 000 a year – 5 million francs.) However he will give me some linen thank heavens & perhaps a bed or 2.

My book in Swedish would make you die of laughing. It says on the back 'the beautiful & eccentric Mitford sisters are known to the round-the-world-folk of London Paris Rome & Berlin (!) & play equally happily with Lords & Revolutionaries.' No dédicace, thank goodness.

I saw somebody who has read Lulu's letters to Ran – she said never, in fact or fiction, has she read such burning love letters.

Ran, it seems, talks quite openly (over the cradle of his week-old son) of the day when she will settle down with him among the bogs of Old Ireland.

Did you hear Rosamond Lehmann's[3] terrible gaffe? Lulu (introduced as Css Palffy) said 'I used to see you with Mme de Polignac.' Rosamond: 'Ah! Those days! Do you remember the beautiful Louise de Vilmorin?'

Only 5 more days here & then heavenly Paris. I rather long to go back to the flat, as I've paid for it to 10th April, but I see your papers have at last appeared, & don't want to undo all the good which this hateful going away may have done, so have ordered a room at Bourgogne. Off to Spain on the 30th – oh dear.

I've lunched & dined out literally every day since I've been here, quite up to your standards – la Palewska de Londres. Dined with the Swiss Min: – she in a great do as she had 3 chucks between tea & dinner, a misfortune she attributed entirely (she is Italian) to the malocchio of the poor Q of Spain who had been to see her in the afternoon. 'Must be kind to the Queen of Spain' my mother in law keeps saying. 'She has no money poor woman.'

Goodbye dear dear Colonel

. . .

[1] Palewski's secretary.
[2] The Anglo-French Treaty of Dunkirk.
[3] Rosamond Lehmann (1901–90). Novelist. Married to Hon. Wogan Philipps 1928–44. Her books include *The Ballad and the Source* (1944), *The Echoing Grove* (1953) and *The Swan in the Evening* (1967).

To Lady Redesdale   Hotel Madison
9 May 1947   Bd St Germain
                                                 Paris VII

Many many happies. I can't afford to telegraph as I'm in my usual
state of having no francs – just enough for meals *with* care & *without*
wine – & isn't it strange how when these crises are on ghastly BLOWS
fall? I had to get a document witnessed at US Embassy 720 francs!!!
Luckily I've been asked out a lot, so I eat & stuff in utter silence till
I feel I must burst & then am *more* hungry than ever.

Awful Peter went & lost £50 worth of francs (stolen) it's his fault
& not my lack of foresight. . . .

Still don't know about London – if I do I shall see you which is
wonderful.

Meanwhile I've got a job here, English adviser & translation super-
visor to a new publisher – £400 a year *and* (even more precious because
it means I can't be forced back into the tunnel) a carte d'identité de
travailleur. Now I must find a flat. Ritz here is £6 a day for room alone
so is not exactly the answer to every problem, otherwise I agree!!

Boiling hot & having meals out on the pavement, so heavenly. I'm
beginning to wonder if I was mad not to buy the Moulin – it will
continue to tease me, in fine weather! The garden, the cows, & all
for less than a really very mediocre flat here would be – they charge
£1000 a room now.

Very funny letter from Evelyn back from Hollywood where he
seems to have spent his whole time in the cemetery. It's called South
Lawn,[1] organ music peals from the flower beds & the loved ones (as
they call the corpses) are frozen & kept in drawers. The children's
section is called Slumber Land. The keeper of it said to Evelyn 'We
have *great* trouble keeping pince nez on the loved ones' noses.'

Lots of buddies here for Winston Day including dreadful but always
endearing Randolph. Duff & Diana are back but Duff looks terribly ill
& not himself at all – I dined there yesterday & really felt worried
about him. Alex Clifford[2] back from Russia & Jenny (his wife) from
America – *both* terrified & both definitely on the side of Russia if
choice must be made. What a mix up it will be – I shan't take sides
at all, just wait for my eyes to be liquefied & enjoy myself till then.

I must know my plans today or tomorrow & will write, so don't
answer for a few days. . . .

All love and to Bowd.
       NR

[1] South Lawn was actually the name of the old house pulled down by Nancy's father when he built Swinbrook; the cemetery in *The Loved One* is, of course, Forest Lawn.
[2] Alexander Clifford (d. 1952). War correspondent for the *Daily Mail*. Married to Jenny Nicholson, daughter of the poet Robert Graves.

To DIANA MOSLEY   Hotel Madison
11 May 1947   Bd St Germain, VII

Darling

I've run out of paper. How go the passports?[1] . . .

I went again to the Moulin – a lovely hot day, it looked twice as fascinating as before. If it weren't for the Col I shouldn't hesitate a moment, it really is a dream in summer at any rate, with the waterfall & the little walled gardens.

Just had such an evening. Col & I dined with Momo[2] & Randolph – dinner wasn't ordered, in a crowded restaurant, before Randolph began bawling insults about General de Gaulle & this continued until coffee. Everybody listening with fascination.

The Col tried to laugh it off, then became angry – couldn't get up & go because hemmed in by the table & Momo & because it would have made more of a thing – you know. I'm *exhausted*. Colonel says when we got into the street (we left as soon as we had swallowed our coffee) he said Ma chère Nancy! to which I replied Ma chère Colonel! Indeed I was almost in tears. Never never again. Odious little creature – spitting, sweating, shrieking, oh the horror of him.

Well darling, à très bientôt – my only consolation.

All love
NR

[1] After the war, the Labour Government refused to issue passports to the Mosleys until 1949.
[2] Maud (Momo) Kahn (d. 1960). Daughter of the wealthy American banker, Otto Kahn. Married General Sir John Marriott in 1920. She was having an affair with Randolph Churchill whom she called 'The Problem Child'. 'She fills a great gap in my life here of best friend & gossip.' (NM to Lady Pamela Berry, 11 February 1952)

To GASTON PALEWSKI   [Hotel Madison
17 May 1947   Bd St Germain, VII]

You dear darling Colonel this is to say goodmorning on Monday morning. Do miss me. Do miss saying 'I've got a heavy political day LET ME SEE – can you come at 2 minutes to 6?' . . .

Colonel dear, Mlle Marguerite (waitress chez Georges) has signalé a flat, a whole floor 'en plein midi dans l'hotel particulier du Duc de Sauveterre – 50 000 francs.' In the Marais, 10 Rue du Parc Royal. I've asked kind Miss Chetwynd to investigate.

I am very drunk as Jacques found me crying at Georges & fed me on marc. Like those Canadians the first time I left who gave me gin all night.

> Darling Colonel good bye
>   NR

I know one's not allowed to say it but I love you.

To Gaston Palewski   71 Kew Green[1]
20 May 1947   Kew
                                                Surrey

You dearest darling Colonel

It is terrible, do be sorry for me. It is really only terrible because of you not being there ('I know'). Otherwise it's a pretty good joke. My day is like this:

I go to the Studios. They say Mr Hogsbottom isn't awake yet. I say all right I'll go away. They say no no he must see you at once, they put me in a large car & off I go to Mr H's house. Mr H appears & says his headache is terrible he must have a rest. However thank goodness I came because he needed me badly. Now I must go at once & see Mr Pigswhistle.

Another car, another immense drive. Mr P is in a great hurry & is off to see the censor but thank goodness I came as he needed me badly. Will I go home & read this book & say what I think of it. I go home & sadly begin to wade through some awful twaddle when the telephone bell rings & Mr H & Mr P say will I come *at once* they need me badly. I dash off & when I arrive Mr H & Mr P say thank goodness it's me & now they have to go, but see me tomorrow.

That's my day, & each of these days I am earning about £10 so *that's* all right!

I am living in such a pretty place with charming servants & a charming host & shall see Diana [Mosley] at the week end. It's only that I hanker after you.

I will write soon more amusingly – I'm really very tired just wanted to say where I am. But there will be no social news as I can't go to

London, I have to hang about here waiting for H. & P. to ring me up.

Goodbye you dearest Col

In great despair as I left your photograph at the Madison. *Please* keep another for me in case they don't.

[1] Nancy was staying with Mark Ogilvie-Grant while she worked on *Kind Hearts and Coronets*.

To Mark Ogilvie-Grant   20 rue Bonaparte, VI
4 July 1947

You dear old gent I can't get a word out of hateful Ealing but have written to say it wld suit me (much they care) better to go back in Sept.
    If they accept that idea you might feel ready for a 2nd dose.
    Very hot & delicious here, absolute Mediterranean weather which always makes me blissful. The kind owners of this flat are putting up me *and* Prod so we are in perfect comfort – we go to an hotel next week & back again here for August when they go away. But letters here will always find us.
    I am in full house hunting campaign & trudge the streets following up clues sometimes with terrifying results as this morning when I had to go & see a lunatic & ask if he would unbrick a room of a prospective flat (what can he keep there – Prod thinks a nun). I had to go alone as all was said to depend on charm & an English accent which he is said to love. However he took one look at me & said he didn't want any tappage [prostitution]. I said, hissing my SSes like L'Honorable Mrs Pemberton in *Lakmé* that I wasn't a tappeuse. He softened rather & may consider me –! But it's always the same & always leads nowhere, so discouraging!
    Huge Gaullist meeting of 40 000 people the other day. I went, feeling awfully like my sisters. It was a wild success. . . .

    All love
        NR

Post enclosed for me & save 6d – thanks *so* much.
Moans[1] is very well he had a lovely party & I wore my new dress.

[1] Mogens Tvede (1897–1977). Danish architect and painter. Married Dolly Radziwill in 1932.

To Diana Mosley   20 rue Bonaparte, VI
15 August 1947

Darling

I very much deprecate the silence which has descended on N.W.
Britain – not a word from any of you. I only hope it means baking
weather, lovely sun baths & swimming in warm water –!

I nearly cried yesterday. Duff said 'aren't you jealous, the new
military attaché got a flat in one week.' 'Don't tell me – *how* did he?'
'It seems it belongs to Hugh Sherwood[1] who has been longing to let
it for ages –' I really see no hope – French people are unable to find
anything for themselves & these black market ones always fall
through. I can't face the winter here without a *Bécuwe*[2] so it looks as
if I shall have to go to Rome which really I could scarce endure. Poor
Mrs Millard (at the Embassy) says her marriage is breaking up on
account of hotel life month after month & I can easily imagine it.

Pam Berry[3] is here in great beauty. What an example she is of how
it pays to spoil children – look at her & poor Eleanor.[4] Randolph has
been here & left us all morally (& Pam says) physically bruised. Duff
said 'I heard a scuffle last night.' 'Yes' she said sadly 'that was Randolph
& me.' Thank *heaven* he has now gone to Japan. You see he rings
up, sounding like a rusty old bicycle going up a hill, & is very disarming
– then one goes to see him & is subjected to an hour's bellowing
roaring unpleasantness. I always say never again & always succumb.

Diana [Cooper] has found, at the Marché aux Puces, a Louis XVI
settee made entirely of arrows & bows – I never saw such a beautiful
object – for £12. I'm beginning to be corroded with jealousy, my new
vice.

Haven't been to see any clothes yet, the weather is too wonderful
to sit in a stuffy shop, but I hear they are literally to the ankle now.
Think of the bliss in winter – a long coat over one's poor old legs.

The concierge has been making a scène de jalousie now for 4 hours
without a break, *yelling* at her husband. She's quite a nice woman but
really it's beginning to wear me down – why doesn't he go off to the
pub? He's rather handsome & she's so dirty I feel on his side.

. . . I leave here on 30th & don't even know where I'm going –
Madison has become too expensive.

    Much love to all
        NR

It seems I am known in Paris as Mrs Perch on account of Rod &

Pole. Although the kind of joke I deprecate I can't but think it rather funny –!

¹ 1st Baron Sherwood (1898–1970). Liberal MP 1923–4 and 1935–41. Married to Hon. Patricia Berry 1942–8. Lover of Daisy Fellowes who called him H.L. (Hated Lover).

² A wood stove.

³ Lady Pamela Smith (1914–82). Celebrated political hostess. Daughter of 1st Earl of Birkenhead. Married in 1936 to Hon. Michael Berry (created Baron Hartwell 1968), proprietor of the *Daily Telegraph*. She and Nancy shared the same mischievous – at times malicious – wit and a delight in gossip. 'I love her all right.' (NM to Evelyn Waugh, 21 January 1954)

⁴ Lady Eleanor Smith (d.1945). Novelist and elder sister of the above.

To LADY REDESDALE   Hotel Jacob et d'Angleterre (!)
3 September 1947   Rue Jacob
                                     Paris VI

Darling Muv

This is the kind of hotel O Wilde died in – *aucun confort*, no bathroom, or loo except dans le couloir,¹ dry bread & water for breakfast etc. You see utter parsimony has set in, I'm rigid with terror lest I shall run out of money & be forced home. (However love has walked in & the housemaid *gave* me a pound of Normandy butter for my breakfast (worth 15/-) you must say touching, she fled from the room when I began to say I must pay.)

So I eat in workmen's restaurants mostly little bits of cat I think, & feel alternately very hungry & very sick. Like this I can live on £1 a day for everything – rather wonderful. I suppose when the weather gets cold I shall die, like a geranium.

Meanwhile I'm negotiating for a flat so large & grand that Doris Duke² thinks it would be too expensive for her & has rejected it! It consists of 3 vast painted state rooms & nothing else so I shall have to pitch a tent in one of them & empty my pot out of the window from time to time. For water, the Seine.

Duff came back full of horrid news. It seems if one goes to England one won't be allowed out again – he's not even going to be allowed to have John Julius out for the holidays. So I've told my film people I can't possibly come back, dreadful though it is to break a contract. They say a huge underground shuttle-service, as in the war, will be the next thing.

Meanwhile the town is full of English eking out their last few francs before going back to prison.

Went to Dior yesterday – the winter coats to the ankle are the prettiest I ever saw, I think I shall sell my fur coat & get one. *Think* how warm too. You can't imagine the yards & yards of stuff they manage to cram in! Who d'you think I saw there, looking like 2 disapproving old nannies, the sisters Rita (hat shop do you remember?)

Do you live on whale steak? I hear of O else from the English they say it is dark blue. It must be delicious – I have a feeling the laws of your race[3] would forbid.

Do you think the name of this pub the funniest thing you ever heard?

All love
    NR

A long, very pompous letter from Pat[4] advising me to emigrate to Rhodesia. How I shrieked –!

[1] In the passage.
[2] Doris Duke (1912–93). Much-married American tobacco heiress.
[3] Lady Redesdale adhered to the dietary laws of Moses.
[4] Patrick Cameron was Nancy's friend and stockbroker.

To Gaston Palewski   Andorra[1]
19 September 1947

You dear dear darling Colonel life without you is so terrible ('it must be') that I don't see how I can endure spending the winter in Rome. But perhaps it won't happen – though if I can't find a flat it will. What a pity I don't know that nice Polish gentleman who lives at 1 rue Bonaparte – they say he can find flats for all his friends.

That other nice Polish gentleman's[2] flat is so expensive, but in the end perhaps I'll take that & let it every summer to rich American lady friends of the Bonaparte P.G.'s.

I'll be back next Wednesday I think ('– allo – allo'). No news you dear Col because I don't suppose you are one to appreciate landscape letters & les femmes du monde do not abound in these mountains – even the European bear is becoming scarce, the shepherds will kill him, what would they do to femmes du monde I wonder – Lolly – Dolly – Marie-Blanche – Marie-Laure – old uncle Tom Cobbley & all, old uncle Tom Cobbley & all.

A tremendous hug you darling from
    NR

[1] Nancy was on a motor tour with her husband and Humphrey Hare. One of Peter's schemes was to try to obtain Andorran domicile.
[2] Nancy had visited Count Zamoyski's flat in the 17th-century Hôtel Lambert, on the tip of the Ile St Louis, which was for rent at £250 a year.

To EVELYN WAUGH   Andorra
19 September 1947

Darling Evelyn

May I ask your help – it's about my next novel.[1] I've got a story for it & the story is roughly this: Ld & Lady Mondor, infinitely grand & rich, he an ex Viceroy, absolutely top Englishman, she a vulgarian not unlike my ma in law. They have one daughter Leopoldina no heir. This is not much of a sorrow to them as they love their daughter so much, but they do rather imagine that she will marry, if not the Prince of Wales, then some terrific Duke. Rather disturbed when she reaches the age of 23 unmarried. (She is beautiful but dumb.) Lord Mondor has a sister married to a Mr X who is a great deal at their house & fetches & carries for Lady M & probably is her lover as well. Lady Patricia X very delicate, stays at home a good deal. She dies. Picture the situation when, a week after the funeral, Leopoldina announces that she is going to marry X (allowed by law since 19?).

She does so & is extremely happy, though persecuted in every possible way by her mother (I may say the mother is the central character in the book). Then Lady Mondor dies. Leopoldina prostrated with grief takes a wild hatred for her husband, X. X is an odious character but he suffers. He suffers intensely & after a bit he has a stroke. (Must bring in Simon [Elwes]'s stroke.) Leopoldina does not behave nicely – she wishes he were dead & says so. He dies & she settles down to an extremely conventional country life, beloved by all her neighbours (not sure of the end, hope I shall get ideas as I go).

Now I need the impact of the Radlett family upon the Mondors – contrast between Aunt Sadie & Lady M, the 2 (neighbouring) households & the Radlett children's comments on the whole affair. Lady M sends Leopoldina there hoping she will be talked out of the engagement. I've got over them not having met in the *P of L* by the Mondors being in India – Leopoldina is younger than Linda & Linda has been married a year or 2 when all this happens. What I want to ask you is can Fanny tell the story again? I find it *so much* the easiest formula, but I know people did object & said I cheated by Fanny describing things she didn't see. Do be kind & advise me.[2] I'll be back in Paris next week, 20 rue Bonaparte VI will find me. If Fanny doesn't tell it I think it will be a struggle to write it because of how much to leave out – for instance I would rather leave it a mystery how far things had gone by the death of the aunt, & whether in fact X was Lady M's lover or only a tame poodle. Leopoldina's character, a mystery to her friends in many ways, is explained by her extreme but hidden sexiness which exists under an exterior of the utmost conventionality. Lord & Lady Mondor are going to be excellent characters I hope – he, grand & noble & taking everybody in, but *silly*, she tough vulgar snobbish dreadful &, like her daughter, very sexy. I'm in a great do about it because of not knowing quite how to tackle it, but I've got a great many of the situations in my head & ought soon to begin.

I'm here with Prod – oh it is a funny place. No rules of any kind – result, a great boom going on in a tiny mediaeval village – every form of contraband for sale in every cottage & 1 Andorran in 3 is said to have a motor car. Prod busy egging them on to send a wedding present to Princess E. We leave tomorrow, motoring slowly back to Paris.

I do apologize for bothering you, but you are always so kind. The fact is I've begun to be appalled by the difficulties of technique, a thing which has hitherto never worried me at all –

    Best love
       Nancy

[1] *Love in a Cold Climate* (1949). The idea for the plot had come from Christopher Sykes.
[2] 'I am sure you should stick to first person. It suits you perfectly . . .' Waugh, *Letters*, p. 260.

To Gerald Berners   19 quai Malaquais[1]
3 November 1947   Paris VI

Dearest Gerald

. . . I've just spent a week end with Alvilde & the young Stravinskys were there. He says his father always says that you are the only English composer worth anything at all. Alvilde is greatly improved since Princess Winnie [de Polignac]'s day, much nicer, I think you would like her now. She told me she suffers dreadful remorse over having been horrid to the Princess – I never thought it was quite her fault, they were thoroughly on each other's nerves.

Funny you've been reading Tolstoy – I re-read *Anna Karenina*. I see it is quite different from what I remembered – Anna so hateful, Karenin such a charming man, Vronsky such a bore. Far the best drawn character is Dolly – his own wife I suppose. It's nothing like so good as *War & Peace* is it – which did he write first? . . .

Did I tell you that on my 1st night in this utterly luxurious flat I was woken up by a vast RAT sitting on my tummy? So like Paris somehow. It jumped off (when I spoke to it) with exactly the same amount of noise & impact as a great dane would have made & galloped away over the parquet like a cart horse.

I'm having a dreadful time with my new book, tortured with problems of technique. The story I think promising but then again the *New Statesman* will tease because it is a Vie de Château book. The story is, adored only daughter of very grand earl (ex Viceroy etc) marries her uncle. Earl & wife half-dead with misery out of duty, send for the heir, who is Stephen [Tennant] + Brian [Howard] + Derek Hill[2] & they immediately love him *far* more than they ever loved her. He gets had up (or killed in the war?) mother dies of a stroke, daughter comes back & keeps house for her father, leaving poor old uncle who also dies of a stroke. (Not quite sure about all this part yet.)

Do hope you are feeling better – I am much, it's such a blissful feeling when one has been really ill. I must rush out so won't begin a new page.

---

[1] Nancy had been lent a flat by Audrey Pleydell-Bouverie (d.1968), sister of Edward James. She was married to Dudley Coats 1922–7, to Marshall Field 1930–35 and to Hon. Peter Pleydell-Bouverie 1938–46.

[2] Derek Hill (1916–). Portraitist and Irish landscape painter.

To Lady Redesdale   19 quai Malaquais, VI
14 November 1947

Darling Muv

Thank you so much for the cheque & stamps which as you see I am making use of at once. It is a great save otherwise I find I spend a fortune on writing letters.

Yes the book is in progress & I want some renseignements [information] please. It takes place in the 1930s.

In 1930 was Aunt Mabell a lady in waiting & was she called Mabell Countess of A[irlie] or Dowager? (Don't be alarmed, it's only to quote the Court Circular – Lady Elizabeth Motion has succeeded – as l-in-w etc but must get it *right*.)

At a ball one never wore rings outside one's gloves (horrors) but what about bracelets?

Try & remember when the law about people being allowed to marry their uncles was passed –? Evelyn says they've always been able to, but I'm certain I remember a law & Winnie Crook benefiting? All I must know was if it was before 1930 or after & if so when after. Perhaps Farve would know, he must have passed it.[1] . . .

Audrey brought some milk in a gin bottle & I must say it is a treat in one's coffee. Betty says the French simply don't care whether they have it or not & she must be right because if there were a demand it would be on the black market whereas you never see a drop anywhere.

My social barometer must be rising – Lady Kemsley[2] kissed me. Also my book has been taken off the list of indecent books not allowed in Eire – so I was informed by somebody who takes in the *Irish Times*! Just had such a blow out at the Ritz that I spent 2 hours lying like a cobra on my bed, too full even to go to sleep. *Pure* pleasure! I don't believe you adore eating & having overeaten as much as I do, I'm really beginning to live for it, sign of middle age I suppose – how awful Heaven will be if there isn't anything (or were banquets mentioned I believe they were).

Very much fascinated by Audrey [Pleydell-Bouverie] who is a personality – very rare. Not specially clever but with such energy vitality & force of character as one rarely sees. And of a niceness & generosity impossible to describe – I like her very much. She *goes* for the French like a wild tigress – of course the proper way with them & far more effective than my soppy pleading (Madame est la gentillesse même,[3] but nothing ever gets done).

V. best love
    NR

A man at a ball would wear the garter ribbon over his boiled shirt? (Knee breeches I know.) The book is about an older & grander & more eccentric Helen [Dashwood]. I don't think she'll realize –
Just got yr letter of family news & more stamps – thank you very much. Also one from Gerald giving me £50 in francs for Xmas I am so excited.

[1] Under the Marriage Act of 1931, restrictions on marriage with a father's deceased sister's widower were lifted. Winnie Crook kept the post office at Swinbrook, and may have married her uncle.

[2] Edith du Plessis; married to 1st Viscount Kemsley, the newspaper proprietor, in 1931.
[3] Madame is kindness itself.

To Humphrey Hare[1]   19 quai Malaquais, VI
23 November 1947

My dear Humph

I've talked to various people about Swinburne – the great trouble is that all the publishers here are en faillite [bankrupt], and also there was such a demand for translations after the war that every sort of rubbish was hurriedly done & brought out & now the attitude is save us from English books.

I thought your article[2] simply excellent & die for the whole thing. I suggest we should wait until the book itself appears & then, armed with it & a sheaf of laudatory reviews, I will make a determined assault upon any publisher who may still be on his feet then.

Aren't novels the devil. Mine is so dull I can hardly bring myself to write it – never mind, people love dull novels I keep saying, the longer & duller the better.

This millionaire's flat I've been lent is so unlike me in every way, but I have happily settled down in it & shall miss all the comfort when the time comes to leave again. Though huge it is easy to heat which is the great thing – now, with the temperature at 64 & blazing sun one hardly realizes the cold weather can't be very far off. I sit for hours every day in the garden.

Poor Pss E seems to have looked even more terrible than one had feared[3] – did you go & loyally stand? I'm having my portrait done & the chap[4] arrived with a wireless so we had it all – the Frog commentator translating the wedding service was a yell. Anyway it must have been a nice outing for all those decayed old royals – the poor little Yugoslavs were thrilled & spent happy weeks having their jewels re-set. *I'm* in love with King Mike,[5] he looks a wonderful cad doesn't he.

The great thrill here is M. Lecomte[6] who, with a curtain of golden hair to the shoulders, has ordered Balmain's shell pink & coral ball dress & 6 other dresses, & looks, so we are told, a dream in them. Everyone is trying to get to know him & be asked to the soirées when he wears his toilettes.

When does Swinburne appear? Awfully exciting.

Love from
     Nancy

1 Humphrey Hare was the author of *Swinburne: A Biographical Approach* (1949).
2 'Swinburne and "le vice Anglais" ', *Horizon*, 1947.
3 Princess Elizabeth and the Duke of Edinburgh were married on 20 November.
4 Mogens Tvede; his portrait shows Nancy sitting primly, her back ramrod straight, on the edge of an 18th-century *bergère*.
5 King Michael of Romania (1921–). Reigned from July 1927 to June 1930, and again from September 1940 to 30 December 1947.
6 'I saw Dolly Radziwill just now and she told me the following story. Her *vendeuse* at Balmain had a new client, a M. Lecomte, who chose about six dresses and said, "My wife is not well, will you bring them round for her to see." So round she goes – luxury flat, exquisite creature appears with a curtain of gold hair, darling little waist, long elegant legs and so on and they begin trying on the dresses. Suddenly the *vendeuse* becomes aware that the pretty little bosoms are *not quite real* – looks again at the face – horrors! M. Lecomte himself!!' Quoted in Acton, *Nancy Mitford*, p. 71.

To Lady Redesdale   19 quai Malaquais, VI
27 November 1947

Darling Muv

The posts are rather uncertain so Audrey will post this. The great shriek here are the English papers – don't believe *one word* you see in them. The trains they say are on strike – Duff has just arrived comfortably by Arrow. All P.O.s open just as usual, bread as usual (nasty as ever). Telephone (said to be striking) never quiet for a moment. Buses & Métros more than ever. Gas blazing away – electricity ditto. I've just had my hair done by M. Antoine, dryer as usual. So you do see?

I went to the Halles this morning & never saw so much meat in my life, even Mrs Ham wld have been satisfied.[1]

Diana very busy with the ball[2] which is the great excitement & we all try on our own & each other's dresses all day. I've had my black velvet altered & it's a dream I must say.

Audrey's description of the wedding – specially 'Edwina'[3] who she says looked exactly like Gandhi & bowed to her public more than the Queen & had 2 huge feathers which Ld Louis spent the whole service taking out of his mouth!!

The great feature of the ball it seems were the mutton pies, she says nobody talked of anything else for days!

I think I'll come home for Xmas if I see a reasonable prospect of getting back here all right. What are everybody's plans? Audrey thinks of bringing her 2 boys here for a spree so I shld have to move out & thought I'd go home then instead of Feb perhaps.

Rather cold, how is it with you?

Just off to see Diana. Last night I dined with Capt Molyneux,[4] he's a great charmer I've only just got to know him, & such pictures you never saw (very famous, but even better than one could have hoped).

V best love
NR

[1] 'When the Wid wakes up in the morning her first thought is how does she feel (herself) how did she sleep & her second thought *will she get any MEAT*? So she skips off to the butcher's shop where she performs the dance of the 7 veils & comes back with a bleeding lump like J. the Baptist's head on a charger . . . She longs for meat so terribly that she can't look at the sheep on the downs, she *craves* their *legs.*' (NM to Lady Redesdale, 3 March 1953)

[2] The Coopers gave a farewell ball before leaving the Embassy in December. 'As with most, the preparations before & the potins [gossip] after were the best part of it.' (NM to Heywood Hill, 12 December 1947)

[3] Hon. Edwina Ashley (1901–60). Married Earl Mountbatten of Burma in 1922. He was Viceroy of India 1947 and Governor-General of the New Dominion of India 1947–8.

[4] Edward Molyneux (1891–1974). The couturier and collector of Impressionist paintings.

To Lady Redesdale   19 quai Malaquais, VI
2 December 1947

Darling Muv

The air mail (only) has begun to arrive & I got yr letters & hanky & stamps thank you *very* much. A rather unreliable poster (I suspect) took a letter for you yesterday but I had to stop in the middle of writing it. Thank you a million times for sending flour, I do so hope it will come & please don't do it again if it deprives you in the very least.

Do you remember my dog Milly was called Lady Effie Millington-Drake[1] & once when she was going to be 'married' Monica Winterton bought an awful little wedding cake & sent it to Lady E M D at Blomfield, & the shop most officiously sent it instead to her real address with Mon's card saying 'Best wishes for your future from us both' & poor Mon *never* got over the shame of it!! Eddie [Winterton] was simply furious with her too.

I think & hope I've found a flat I can have for a year when I leave this in Feb. I simply hate the maid here now & she is a most awful cook into the bargain, so shan't be sorry to go. I've given up the idea of coming home, half the time the planes don't go & when they do they often circle London & come back. Peter is v. much against me flying in this weather & it does seem rather silly when there is no *real* need to – also those ghastly journeys at home. Better come in the Spring don't you think? Perhaps between this flat & the next one. Oh *how* I hate moving!! . . .

Dragged Prod to see the wedding but it's nothing but photos of Corgis *exactly* the same shape as the plucky little Queen. I did see Lady Louis à la Gandhi, I roared. From what I can make out it all caused more pain than pleasure – the poor little Yugoslavs dished themselves up for the party & were just leaving Claridge's when they found they weren't expected but only the following night, & I keep hearing that people were either furious at not being asked or furious at being put behind a tomb in the dark.

Diana [Cooper] saw absolutely nothing *and* lost her car. However she heard a policeman saying Mr Eden's[2] car will not be wanted so she gate crashed that, 'a miserable hireling, like our own.' She has had 600 acceptances for the ball in spite of the fact that no letters have been delivered for a week.

I'm dining with the Benderns[3] – do you remember Pat Douglas, once a flirt of Tom's? She is as pretty as ever, quite a star of the English colony here.

The Coopers are staying here for ever thank goodness[4] & have been accorded full diplomatic privileges by the French govt.

I rather pity the Harveys[5] I'm bound to say except they are *so* drear there won't really be much competition.

Love to Debo when she gets back do tell her to write (*don't* tell I said about the corgis!)

Much love
    NR

[1] Lady Effie Mackay (1895–1984). Married the diplomat Sir Eugen Millington-Drake in 1920.
[2] Anthony Eden (1897–1977). Statesman. Created Earl of Avon in 1961. Deputy Leader of the Opposition 1945–51, Prime Minister 1955–7.
[3] Count John de Bendern was Private Secretary to Duff Cooper 1946–7. Married to Lady Patricia Douglas 1938–50.
[4] The Coopers moved to the Château de St Firmin in Chantilly. Lady Diana's feud with her successor, Lady Harvey, soon became the talk of Paris.
[5] Sir Oliver Harvey (1893–1968). Succeeded Duff Cooper as Ambassador in Paris 1948–54. Married Maud Williams-Wynn in 1920. Unlike the Coopers, who gradually fell in Nancy's estimation, Nancy's feelings about the Harveys improved over time. Before their arrival they were: 'typical F.O. Bores' (NM to Lady Redesdale, 28 October 1947). Then she found Sir Oliver *odious*, but Maudie a very nice person' (NM to Lady Pamela Berry, 15 January 1950). Soon she was writing, 'I've greatly taken to the

Harveys, can't tell you what an interesting man he is when he has got over being shy – he understands the French backwards, sees the whole thing crystal clear & loves what he sees. Just like me!' (NM to Lady Pamela Berry, 26 June 1950)

To EDWARD SACKVILLE-WEST   19 quai Malaquais, VI
6 December 1947

Dearest Eddy
. . . How are you & why don't you ever come? I can't read the Naggers[1] any more now all you Brontës[2] have given it up so now there is nothing to read of a Saturday except *Samedi Soir* which is always full of crimes moyenageux [medieval], & types who castrate a chap with whom they had hitherto lived on terms of bon voisinage [good neighbourliness] & who, when asked *why*, simply burst into shrieks of insane laughter just like ONE would. Well low brow as I may be I do sometimes like a faintly more literary approach.

Charles Ritchie[3] has had arsenic poisoning & the itch unto death & lay in the Hertford Hospital nude with blue & green spots. He's all right again & off to wed a lovely Miss Smelly.

No news except Diana's ball we are all *ill* with excitement, more & more English stream in for it & the Embassy is like a country house on the eve of a hunt ball, only when one was 17 & magnified a thousand times. But oh the horror of them going. People say they hear the Harveys are very nice & Lady H. likes artists but it's no good because *they have been seen* (by me, at an Ordinary[4]). It's the dark night of the soul & no mistake.

I'm writing a *very* dull novel. Davey is in again with some blissful treatments, it only comes to life at all when he appears. My great consolation is that people do *love* dull novels don't they?

I've at last got a wonderful wonderful flat, an 18 Cent pavilion (ground floor) garden, furniture from Petit Trianon & all for nearly nothing. For at least 18 months – I hope to move in before Xmas but it depends if Audrey can find a substitute for me here. Perhaps you'll come & stay.

Have you heard about the New Look? You pad your hips & squeeze your waist & skirts are to the ankle it is bliss. So then you feel romantic like Mme Greffulhe & people shout ordures at you from vans because for some reason it creates class feeling in a way no sables could.

The Communists are being awfully cowardly as you will have noticed & now Leclerc's[5] boys are pouring in, it is like a mobilization, very exciting if only the Communists were a bit braver. The mere sight of a truncheon & off they scoot.

Give my love to all the dear ones I do so die for them.

Love from
    NR

This counts as your Xmas card.

¹ *New Statesman & Nation.*
² In 1945, Eddy Sackville-West moved to Long Crichel House, Dorset, which he shared with Eardley Knollys, a painter, and Desmond Shawe-Taylor, music critic for the *New Statesman & Nation.* They were joined a few years later by Raymond Mortimer. Like the Brontë family, they formed a close-knit literary and artistic group and – like most of the Brontës – they were unmarried.
³ Charles Ritchie (1906–). Canadian diplomat. Married Sylvia Smellie in 1948. In 1949, when he was Counsellor at the Embassy, he complained wistfully to Diana Cooper that he felt neglected. Diana, with the help of Nancy, organised a 'Ritchie Week', to be funded by means of a 'Ritchie stamp, à la Général de Gaulle'. Nancy painted five hundred balloons with 'Remember Ritchie' which were released in the Embassy courtyard with an attached postcard asking the recipients to return them to Ritchie with their good wishes.
⁴ The name given by Sibyl Colefax to her luncheons at the Dorchester during the war.
⁵ Marshal Leclerc (1902–47). Commander of the Free French Forces. His troops were being brought into Paris to break strikes.

1947–1949

RUE MONSIEUR

I feel almost too much on top of the world –
how nice it is to be happy in middle age after
a wretched youth instead of the other way
around.
                    NM to Diana Mosley, 31 March 1949

At the end of December 1947, Nancy moved to 7 rue Monsieur. The flat suited her perfectly. On one side it had windows that gave on to a courtyard leading to the street and on the other overlooked a typically Parisian garden, enclosing a parterre of ivy. Nancy was eventually able to extend her initial two-year lease; she stayed at rue Monsieur for the next twenty years.

The Colonel lived not far away and frequently visited. The pattern of their relationship soon became established: he would lunch or dine with her but would never spend the night. For him, Nancy's charm consisted above all in her company and jokes; she wrote to her sister Diana, 'The Col persecutes me with racontez [tell] & I have to take all your letters to read to him to try to keep him amused – he's an utter slave driver.' Whenever Peter made his unwelcome appearances Nancy would instead make brief visits to the Colonel's flat in rue Bonaparte. Gaston was always as discreet as possible and obliged Nancy to be equally so; they were never regarded as a couple by the Parisians and many of his friends, especially his women friends, were unaware of their relationship.

Though her moments with Gaston continued to provide the frame-work – albeit a precarious one – of Nancy's daily existence she filled in the gaps by enjoying herself to the full. Her flat, according to Harold

7 Rue Monsieur 7

29 Dec 47   Suzrène 7665

Darling Muv

These long aeroplane journeys are desperately
tiring, you wld simply have to stay more than 2 days.
I hope you won't make any definite plans until you've
seen me. I'll come over end of this month (Jan)
sometime, according to what is the best time for
everybody. I'm in torments already over the journey.
Golden knows the most comy: but going back you
have to leave at 9 A.M. The Ferry boat is liked by
some but 3 hours on the sea. If you fly you risk
hours & hours circling London & then being brought
back. Oh you can't think —!!

No parcel from Harrods yet but I expect it will
turn up — I've never lost one so far. 60 lbs of butter
& lbs of sugar have come from America — old Marie
who has always taken goodness been with careful
people can't believe her eyes — still doesn't pour
enough butter on to food for my taste though no
doubt she'll soon learn.

I've never liked any house I've lived in as much as
this one or even known even among your servants
such a treasure as Marie. She simply literally
never thinks of herself at all, never wants any
time — let alone a whole day — yy. She is an
excellent & reliable without being wonderful cook.
The flour is a great thing as we are able to have

To Lady Redesdale, 29 December 1947

Acton, became a 'cultural annexe of the British Embassy, a congenial rendezvous of French and English letters'. She could now afford to indulge her passion for expensive clothes ('a matter of health') and, advised by Gaston, decorated her flat with fine pictures and antiques.

Through Violet Hammersley, Nancy met Countess Costa de Beauregard, who was to be the model for the Marquise de Valhubert in *The Blessing*. Nancy was a frequent visitor at her house, Fontaines-les-Nonnes, thirty miles north of Paris. She also left Paris at times to visit the Duff Coopers at their house in Chantilly and she sometimes stayed with Dolly Radziwill and her husband Mogens Tvede at their cottage near Marseilles, but never for too long – a few weeks were the most she could manage without the 'Magnetic Colonel'.

Love in a Cold Climate, published in 1949, was another great success, becoming the first novel ever to be chosen simultaneously as Book of the Month by the Book Society, the *Daily Mail* and the *Evening Standard*. At the end of 1949 Nancy was taken on as a contributor to the *Sunday Times* and continued with a regular column for four years.

The courtyard at 7 rue Monsieur, by Vivien Hislop

To Billa Harrod   7 rue Monsieur
29 December 1947   Paris, VII

Darling Billa

What is your news? Are you coming here at all? Oh *do*. I can put you up in my bed-dining room so long as you promise not to tell H. Dashwood who is rampaging *just* the other side of the Channel waiting for any flag to drop.

You know I finally spent months in Heath's hotel[1] (Jacob et d'Angleterre) & bliss it is. I used to see poor Heath waiting at the window –

Now I've got this heavenly flat, with a garden, for 2 years so I'm in perfect happiness. I think of going home end of Jan for a few weeks – come back with me then?

I want to pump you like mad about Oxford life. I'm writing a book, told once more by Fanny, with a good deal more about Fanny herself & long to know any details about early days in Oxford, first dinners with other dons' wives & so forth. I imagine I can really use the duller members of the Embassy here as copy – charades, imitations of Eastern dances, parlour tricks & so on? I must go to England really for other copy – there is a character a cross between Brian [Howard] & Stephen [Tennant] qu'il faut étudier. The pansies here are all so pompous in comparison with our darling English ones. Brian came here with a terrible creature called Sam, I thought I would hurt myself with laughing. Brian *must* have been a gov:[2] in a former life.

How are you all? I suppose you had a lovely Norfolk Xmas & good gorge. Here everybody offers one turkey & plum pud on account of being English & I don't terribly like them.

Do you still go to London for dancing lessons once a week? I *must* see you.

Prod has gone off to the Sahara & left a huge tin of medicaments against prickly heat by mistake here. Think how he must be prickling by now & goodness knows it's useless to me.

V best love, do write
        Nancy

---

[1] Neville Heath, the sadistic murderer executed the previous year, had killed his victim, Mrs Margery Gardner, in a seedy guesthouse in Notting Hill Gate.

[2] Short for 'governess', Nancy's name for Americans. Her anti-Americanism was fierce and deep-seated; she feared the cultural homogenisation that she saw America imposing upon Europe. 'To us in Europe there's no difference *whatever* between Russia & America just two huge countries where there are no servants & everything is machine

made'. (NM to Lady Redesdale, 9 August 1957) She easily made exceptions, however, for her many American friends.

To Gaston Palewski   4 Rutland Gate Mews, SW7
15 January 1948

You dear dear Colonel I miss you dreadfully on account of being UNDER your THUMB. Make Madame C[hampion] write one line, respectueusement, *here*, just to say how you are. Next week I go to see my old dad, nearly 70, at Redesdale – back to Paris 28th.

Somebody said to me, speaking of le beau frère [brother-in-law], 'it's really very odd, he was over 40 when he met Diana & had led a rip-snorting life till then, but now he has simply turned into a Mitford – talks in their voice & behaves *just* like them in every way.' Are you shrieking Colonel?

I read my Grandfather's mémoires while with my aunt & it's full of all your stories 'C'est vous le nègre – continuez –'[1] & so on, I was fascinated.

Goodbye faithful (sic) Colonel, do be good & rest a little & leave the pretty ladies to their own devices.

        NR

[1] In *Memories* (1915), Lord Redesdale quotes a famous remark made by Marshal MacMahon at a distribution of prizes at a school in Paris. 'As boy after boy was brought up, he said, "Continuez, jeune homme! Premier prix de mathématiques, très bien. Continuez jeune homme." At last a Haitian boy was brought up to him. "Ah, c'est vous le nègre. Continuez, jeune homme, continuez." ' (vol. I, p. 75)

To Evelyn Waugh   7 rue Monsieur, VII
9 February 1948

Darling Evelyn

The *heaven* of *The Loved One*[1] oh you are kind to dedicate it to me, thank you thank you for it. I've been utterly shrieking ever since it arrived, luckily was lunching alone. I must say I couldn't quite do it & the foie de veau together (just coincided with the massaging) but combined it happily with a banana, & am now in despair at having finished it. Can't wait to give it to the Colonel.[2]

I had too much of a rush after I saw you to be very enjoyable & was only in London 3 days. I dined with Smarty & thought him sad, but perhaps I bored him. I went to Gerald [Berners] & he only longed to get rid of me, I could see I bored *him*.

I was glad to be back – now my English money is blocked so I can never come again anyway, rather a comfort. One evening I enjoyed very much, & I was pleased to see Mark unchanged but everybody else seemed depressed & rather cross. Not Diana. Debo I missed. . . .

I go pegging on at my book but without much conviction.

Did you read the Ruskin one?[3] I felt so much on his side, such rot to talk of martyrdom, when there must be millions of women whose husbands hardly ever go to bed with them which after all comes to the same thing as never, for practical purposes.

I do so hope you'll come here before very long – I can offer you my bed dining room & a gentil acceuil.[4]

Much love
        Nancy

Dined with a young American last night & told him your book was to be called *The Loved One*. 'What a beautiful name' he said. Poor him.

[1] Evelyn Waugh's novel *The Loved One* was published as a whole issue of *Horizon* in February 1948. Waugh dedicated the book to Nancy, 'as the hardest hearted well no toughest is the word girl I know'. (Evelyn Waugh to NM, [March 1948])
[2] 'The Colonel says it's wonderful how you have brought out the best in American civilization.' (NM to Evelyn Waugh, 11 February 1948)
[3] Sir W. M. James, *The Order of Release. The Story of J. Ruskin, Effie Gray and John Everett Millais* (1947).
[4] Warm welcome.

To Cyril Connolly   7 rue Monsieur, VII
9 February 1948

My dear Cyril

Thank you *so very much* for sending *The Loved One* – I've been shrieking happily away for an hour. I must say it's rather STRONG MEAT & I long to know how the public will take it – I rather foresee complaints from some quarters. But I suppose so much modern literature is about torturing & beatings up of people still alive that what happens to the dead is quite immaterial – it ought to be anyhow. It will be fascinating to see what is said.

I think as a work of art it is simply perfect – oh dear it makes everything I've written lately look so dusty and redundant. But one must go on pegging away I suppose.

I thought you seemed rather sad Cyril – which doesn't mean that I didn't immensely enjoy our evening, I did. If you would put up with my bed dining room I'd so love you to come & stay & I don't think you'd be uncomfortable. Raymond [Mortimer] is coming so he can report on what it's like! I can never go to England again as my English money is now blocked (new rule) but I don't very much mind, I felt tired & out of sorts the whole time I was there & sank back gratefully into my little life here. The Wallace Collection was a great treat but alas it has made me unable to look at all the dirty ormolu here in the musées. Of course in private houses it glitters, but it is a great work to keep it clean & the musées are said to be so poor. I should have thought all those dreary old guardians who hang about could do a bit of unscrewing – I do wish France could be rich again, it is so important that she should be.

Do think of coming, I would so love it & would really try & see that you don't suffer!

Love from
　　　Nancy

To Diana Mosley　　　　　　　　　　　　　　7 rue Monsieur, VII
10 March 1948

Darling

I've just had the affreuse bergère[1] to stay, but he proved to be a *terrible* Sat afternoon.[2] I believe it is really that I can no longer stand sissies – also a little bit that this flat is not made for visitors, & after Billa's visit I'm going to supprimer[3] the spare room.

Except of course for Jonathan or any nephews. Actually when Peter is here there isn't one – & here he is now he says for good. Oh dear this makes my Colonial life very difficult as the Col refuses to meet him. (Anyway it means I shall always have to go to *his* house which is so much less nice than having him here.) Never mind.

He brought Malraux[4] to luncheon to meet the vieille folle, Malraux never stops talking, a flow of sparkling intelligence, a most wonderful treat, & this was all directed at *me*, which I thought annoyed Raymond rather. You would love Malraux, he is made for you. As they left the house he said to the Col 'et comment est la soeur?' 'C'est un autre genre.' So I said 'did he like me?' 'Oui, il a dit je suis pour.'[5] Apparently he also said Mortimer is a Jewish name. I'd no idea he was such a tremendous *charmer*, I said this to the Col – perhaps too much – & the Col replied 'il se marie jeudi prochain.'[6] Typical! I slightly see why he has been kept from me all this time!

I simply shrieked at your letter about the old parachute & suit made out of Kit's. It *is* such a shame.[7]

Silence de glace from Jonathan[8] – I suppose he is almost on his way home by now though. You will so enjoy all his stories.

I've got 2 new hats of a beauty indescribable – one is a cloud of roses & pink tulle, the other a seagull with a bunch of violets in its mouth –

Can't find an afternoon dress that I like, but I'm going to Piguet to have a look, having *heard* of one there –!

I must stop this dull letter.

V. best love
        NR

[1] 'Hideous shepherdess', Jean Cocteau's nickname for Raymond Mortimer. 'It was he, years ago who said to Raymond Mortimer, who was making eyes at C's boyfriend, "allez-vous-en, affreuse bergère."' (NM to Violet Hammersley, 9 March 1955)

[2] A Mitford name for weekend guests who by Saturday afternoon had already outstayed their welcome.

[3] Do away with.

[4] André Malraux (1901–76). Novelist and essayist, whose largely autobiographical novels are set against the background of 20th-century world revolutions. Appointed by de Gaulle as Minister of Information 1945–6 and Minister for Cultural Affairs 1959–69. Towards the end of his life he lived with Louise de Vilmorin.

[5] 'And what's her sister like?' 'She's a different sort.' So I said 'did he like me?' 'Yes, he said he was all for.'

[6] 'He is getting married next Thursday.' Malraux married Madeleine Lioux, his brother's widow, in 1948; he was previously married to the writer Clara Goldschmidt.

[7] 'I have got a sewing lady at Crowood, she has made me 3 night gowns & 2 sets of underclothes from that old parachute – purest white silk.' (Diana Mosley to NM, 5 March 1948)

[8] Jonathan Guinness was learning German in Strasbourg.

To Evelyn Waugh   7 rue Monsieur, VII
13 March 1948

Darling Evelyn

I am sad to think of *you* reading Proust in English – there is *not one joke* in all the 16 of S. Moncrieff's volumes. In French one laughs from the stomach, as when reading you. I don't remember what you say about time,[1] I am an inattentive reader I fear. The later books are more enjoyable, & I began on Albertine, but you must have read the earlier ones to get the best out of them. But I see you are against.

Proust's mother was a Jewess – Proust I believe to be a French name. Hass (the original of Swann) is supposed to have been the only

Jew really to have been accepted into French society – member of the Société d'Encouragement & so forth. Proust himself knew a few aristocrats, as you suggest, Prince E[dmond] de Polignac, Robert de Montesquiou of course (Charlus) & such. (Pss de P. told me he wanted to dedicate his book to the memory of her husband but, at the mere idea, 'la moutarde m'est montée au nez'[2] & she got her solicitor to warn him not to.) But I don't think he was generally accepted in society. I'll ask the Colonel. The haute bourgeoisie would have been easier as his father was a very well known clever doctor.

I went today to luncheon with my one really Faubourg friend, a saint called Mme Costa de Beauregard.[3] Seven courses and three Dukes. Not like Fabrice. She said 'how is Gaston?' I said 'he wants you to ask him to meet *bishops*.' She said 'I will ask him to meet the modern St François Xavier.' Not at all the same I fear.

Oh do arrange yourself as the frogs say to read French. I thought you *did*, anyway.

Politics. I agree with every word you say,[4] only I humbly submit that communism is a high human ideal. I shall never formulate another political opinion, I am not clever enough.

I saw Diana [Cooper] all & every day for a week – now Lulu is back, silence de glace. Such a bore, I so love her company. Also 2 dinners I was invited to I have been put off in favour of Lulu, the hosts saying sadly that they know I will understand they can't make an enemy of Lulu she is too dangerous. I wish I were dangerous. *Do* come, I so long for you to see my blissful flat. But I know you won't. Instead I get Helen Dashwood.

I should think Miss Fry[5] & Henry very well suited both so sexy. Are you for?

My book is stuck for ever. The Russians the Spring the hats the clothes & a succession of English friends & above all the telephone – I can't, I give up.

Much love
   NR

---

[1] Evelyn Waugh had complained that Proust had no sense of time. 'In the same summer as Gilberte gives him a marble & Françoise takes him to the public lavatory in the Champs Elysées, Bloch takes him to a brothel.' *Letters*, p. 274.

[2] I lost my temper.

[3] The elderly and devout Countess Carl Costa de Beauregard was supposedly a half-sister of Violet Hammersley, Violet being the illegitimate daughter of Mme Costa's father, Pierre Aubry-Vitet. Her country house, Fontaines-les-Nonnes, was to become a haven to which Nancy could escape from Paris to write.

[4] Waugh had berated Nancy for what he regarded as her Communist sympathies.

[5] Jennifer Fry (1916–). Married to Robert Heber-Percy 1942–7 and to Alan Ross, editor of *The London Magazine*, 1949–85. Waugh had written that she was having an affair with the writer Henry Yorke.

To Evelyn Waugh   7 rue Monsieur, VII
24 April 1948

Darling Evelyn,

The great excitement of the week has been the death of Pierre Colle,[1] aged 38, of overeating. He *literally* burst. I leave it to you to do what you think best about telling Smarty. Well, when the horrid details became known which of course they did in a moment (oh the telephoning) all Paris went on to a diet of oranges & Vichy & the restaurants were in such a fit about it that the manager of the Méditerranée actually offered me a cocktail free, which of course I refused. Then somebody – the restaurateurs perhaps, had the bright idea of putting it about that it *wasn't only eating*, that he'd had a child at the age of 15 & furthermore that he'd been *too much in aeroplanes lately* – So with sighs of relief we've all fallen upon our food again –! I gather even Whispering Glades wouldn't have made much of a job of him & in fact they hurried him underground the very next day.

Not much news à part cela[2] – I haven't seen Diana [Cooper] since Sutro's party & now she's gone back for the King's – she came this morning at 9.30 with armfuls of tulips (my & Louis XIV's favourite flowers) but dashed off to the station, no time to chat. The heroine of my book[3] gets more like her every page, I suppose it is unavoidable. The book is going very slowly but not badly. I see *Vile Bodies* in French in all the bookshops.

Your shopping[4] sounds just like the Colonel – perhaps it's a thing which overtakes a chap like the change for us. ('I've got a little touch of the change' a charwoman once said to me.) Anyway last week he bought a marble statue of an Austrian Archduke which it took 8 men to carry upstairs & a huge screen, so that one can hardly get into his room now. He then got a picture said to be by the brother of Hubert Robert & another which may have come from the studio of Poussin. Though he stands by all this junk when teased I think, like you, he is faintly puzzled & not *quite* sure –

Momo [Marriott] has been here, spreading alarm & despondency which she learnt in America ('darling an unknown force of armed men is moving in Italy' she said last night on the telephone. 'Momo –!

moving in which direction?' but she was rather vague after that) but very affectionate. I love her she is one of my post-war loves.

Do come over oh do.

My Diana simply adored her luncheon with you, it is a treat to her to see old chums – & surely a treat for them.

I hear Gerald has left it in his will that he is to be stuffed & kept in the hall at Faringdon. I think *The Loved One* will have done a great deal of harm in these little ways.

Best love, I *expect* you to come.
          NR

[1] A Parisian art dealer, agent for Christian Bérard and several Surrealist painters.
[2] Apart from that.
[3] Although Lady Diana Cooper inspired some aspects of Polly's character in *Love in a Cold Climate* it is as Lady Leone, the difficult ex-Ambassadress in *The Blessing*, that she is unmistakable.
[4] 'I go out shopping after luncheon a bit tight & buy such peculiar things – 3 tie pins, a ½ ton marble 2nd Empire Clock, a solid silver 1830 candelabrum as tall as myself, a pearl grey bowler, six pounds of church candles . . .' Waugh, *Letters*, p. 276.

TO LADY REDESDALE   7 rue Monsieur, VII
3 MAY 1948

Darling Muv

Thank goodness you're back[1] & all right I was fearfully worried when I heard how sick you'd been, such a strain on the heart. Of course I always think about sleeping pills it's no good at all taking them when you can't relax they do more harm than good. Anyhow it seems to have been a most successful outing I'm very glad you went.

Not much news here. We've got a hen – Marie[2] brought her from Normandie to eat, but she is such a comic we couldn't bring ourselves to kill her so she lives in the garden & sleeps under the kitchen table & lays an egg *every every* day – 20 eggs in 3 weeks. Isn't this rather remarkable? Of course she gets an extra meal in the kitchen while Marie is washing up the dinner things! Diana Cooper says 'there you are – she kept her head' & I must say it really was that as the dinner party had been arranged round her & in the end we bought another one for it!

Peter went to Rome for the elections & his mother turned up & gave a cocktail party for Orlando[3] aged 90! The Vatican poster said 'In the polling booth Stalin can't see you but God can.'

Adelaide [Lubbock] has been here. I'm horrified by her account of Venetia [Montagu], literally eaten with cancer, she has had it removed twice & now has it in her leg. They say she can't live very long which is a comfort. Poor Venetia how terribly sad. Diana Cooper says everyone at home is having strokes & wherever you look you see crooked faces. She made me die with her descriptions of the Court ball, she says the young women put bolsters under their dresses to give the New Look. I suppose English clothes always have looked funny compared with Paris ones, it can't be quite new, though I dare-say the change is greater now.

I saw Paulette the other day, she lunched here with Clive Bell[4] who of course was fascinated by her being Helleu's daughter.

I suppose you go to the island this week so I'll send this there.

. . .

The greatest home breaker in Paris, Pat de Bendern, has bought a house there, the girls will have to look out! She is simply lovely & perfectly wicked, a very bad combination. I like her, but she has never crossed my path.

Do write again soon – did Bowd get a scarf?

Much love
   NR

Your description of USA simply fascinating – but *how* odd to prefer motor cars to servants – at least I find it so.

[1] Lady Redesdale had been to America to visit Jessica.
[2] Marie Renard; Nancy's devoted cook and housekeeper from 1947 until her retirement in 1969.
[3] Vittorio Orlando (1860–1952). Ex-Premier of Italy.
[4] Clive Bell (1881–1964). Art critic and author of *Civilization* (1928) which had so influenced Nancy when she was young.

To DIANA MOSLEY   7 rue Monsieur, VII
10 May 1948

Darling

You may imagine that O is talked of here but Princess E's visit & the utter ghastly drear & horror of the arrangements made for her by the Harveys. The French binges on the other hand are sure to be fun. I was getting desperate because Marie & the concierge of course expect me to go to everything & will regard me as utterly déclassée if I *don't* & the Harveys cut me on the double grounds of being mixed up with Gaullists & an habituée of Diana's embassy. However the angelic Eric Duncannon[1] has asked me to his cocktail party for nobody over 30!!! on condition I don't tell a soul I'm going, & the Colonel has got me asked to the exhibition she is opening, so that's all not too bad. The Eric party will be the most fun to go to of everything because he's only asking the *very* young & *very* smart French people so that she can see the clothes is the idea. The *dear* Harveys haven't asked the Coopers to anything at all, after sending their housekeeper to borrow all Diana's flower vases. I spent yesterday at Chantilly & you can imagine the chat. Eric says Ld Sherwood went in one evening to call on them (Harveys) & there was a real *row* about it just as there would have been with Farve, & the Ambassador shouting 'who let Lord Sherwood in?' as if he was some kind of savage animal! However it's no loss, those who have been there to meals say the food is revolting & not enough to go round – also, which the French mind rather, the placement is utterly mad.

Oh the fascination. Farve writes that Margaret[2] is coming in June & will I get her a room & give her all the money she wants. Yes & no. Money, as I explained, is utterly out of the question, I am very short myself.

Clarissa[3] is here, just back from America which she loathed – she says New York is hideous & she has never seen such hideous people & they all talk to you all the time (taxi drivers & so on) & say things like 'Well I think people ought to stand on their own feet.'

Not a word from Jonathan, how is he?

V. best love
    NR

Did I tell you I met the lover of Rosamond F.[4] – the one she lived with for ages here I can't remember his name. I was simply fascinated you can imagine. Dolly says she never saw 2 people so much in love & then suddenly one day R said to him 'Tu sais, c'est fini'. She must be a strange girl. He was heartbroken.

Had the great treat of going over all the shut up parts of Versailles with the curator on Sat. You *can't* imagine the beauty.

[1] Viscount Duncannon (1913–). Succeeded as 10th Earl of Bessborough in 1956. First Secretary at British Embassy in Paris 1948–9.
[2] Margaret Wright; parlourmaid and then housekeeper at 26 Rutland Gate. She was a trained nurse and looked after Lord Redesdale at the end of his life.
[3] Clarissa Spencer-Churchill (1920–). Niece of Winston Churchill; married Anthony Eden in 1952.

Rosamond Gladstone; daughter of Daisy Fellowes. Her lover was Raymond Carr (1919–), fox-hunting Warden of St Antony's College, Oxford, 1968–87.

To Evelyn Waugh   7 rue Monsieur, VII
21 May 1948

Darling Evelyn

Excellent about it arriving on her birthday which I have never known & never *can* remember birthdays – how does one unless a birthday book. *Masturbation.*[1] I used to masturbate whenever I thought about Lady Jane Grey, so of course I thought about her continually & even executed a fine water colour of her on the scaffold, which my mother still has, framed, & in which Lady Jane & her ladies in waiting all wear watches hanging from enamel bows as my mother did at the time. This sublimation of sex might be recommended to Harriet, except that I don't think it changed anything & I still get quite excited when I think of Lady Jane (less & less often though as the years roll on).

Diana has invited me to go & finish my book at Chantilly. I shan't hurry it at all – Jamie Hamilton has lost all his paper in the Bristol fire, & Winston I hear has taken 60 miles of cloth binding for his mémoires, so it can't matter when it appears, & now I have got a story[2] for once in my life I don't want to skimp it.

Your friend Baroness Blixen[3] is here, too much sunk in Nordic gloom for me. (So typical that my one Danish friend here should be called Moans [Mogens].) I really can't stand people who never giggle at all. (Moans doesn't either but he loves me.)

The Hell of the Harveys & their awful behaviour to the Duffs is such that in my book when (what Debo calls) the Utter Ghastly Drear, Boy Dougdale, marries the blissful heroine it is 'I, Oliver Harvey, take thee Leopoldina.'

Do come, Evelyn. S. Boots is coming, & he has a double here, so much so that when a friend of mine said 'You are Cyril Connolly aren't you?' he replied 'No, his double.' So I'm giving a party for them – think you should be there. (Or do you think it will hurt their feelings if I do?)

Much love
NR

Evelyn Waugh's letter to Nancy which provoked this discussion has not survived.
Nancy had difficulty with plots for her novels; only *The Pursuit of Love*, which was

so closely autobiographical, came easily. Waugh pointed out the basic problem: 'I foresee great professional difficulties for you. You have used your two great plots – Farve and Fabrice.' *Letters*, p. 236.
[3] Karen Blixen (1885–1962). Danish author, who wrote mainly in English under the pseudonym Isak Dinesen. Best-known for *Seven Gothic Tales* (1934) and *Out of Africa* (1937).

To DIANA MOSLEY   7 rue Monsieur, VII
25 May 1948

Darling

At last your miserable son has written, I thought he must be dead. I long for him to come & see Paris in leaf which he never has, & also for the moment we have a car, so we could go for expeditions etc.

He describes the cream in Switzerland saying he's never before had enough cream but you know it isn't only now, I well remember in the old days of plenty one *never* had enough, it was always in a silly little silver jug. Why?

Peter is back for good I gather, it is a tiny bit of a worry because he has nothing to do from morning to night & is already hankering for London. So I say then what about a divorce so that we could each live where we like & he says the treasury would never let me live here. I think they would, but the fact is for some reason he is absolutely determined not to have a divorce & I can't make out why, I really can't believe he's so very fond of me as I am completely beastly to him all day & trying to be nicer really wears me out, & I have awful remorse & then begin again. Well you *know*. I honestly do think marriage is the most dreadful trap & that human beings must have been mad to invent such a relationship though I suppose what makes it worse in my case is having had a 9 year break & then having to begin again.

Nobody except a husband can make one *cry* with rage, or make me cry at all, & now my hankies are *wet all day*. Oh dear. Still there must be many many worse husbands in the world.

The Colonel is being too awful to me about Palestine & Glubb Pasha & pretends that all the Arabs are really wicked English en travestie, so now when he teases I call it Glubbing – Colonel you're *not* to Glubb.

The Beits are here – Clementine too lovely & Alf his dear old self, it is bliss having them. I got very matey with them in the war you know & don't share the family view that Clementine is silly. You never saw anything like her jewels, but S Africa must be a heavy price to pay.[1]

Yes *moves*. On the hottest day of last year 2 men brought some huge marble topped tables to 20 rue Bonaparte & at the end Frederika[2] & I had to go to bed, but we never knew why as we had only sat & watched – with radiant *smiles*, & occasionally administered a glass of wine.

I am on a committee for driving French people to the Edinburgh Festival, how unkind. I hear Muv is going but as she loathes music can't conceive why!!!

Did you ever read anything so dull as David Cecil's last book?[3]

I had 60 lbs of sugar (about 4 stone I suppose) last year from America, I must tell you every *ounce* has vanished. It doesn't seem to make the faintest difference how much one has!!!

I couldn't read the China part of Harold,[4] had to skip. Of course I agree with every word of Raymond's review,[5] it makes me *cross* that H. doesn't do better & so naughty all that slip shod writing, really inexcusable. Still I did love the book for all that & so did Raymond. What weekly can one take in, better than the Cissy [*New Statesman & Nation*]? I'm getting fed up with it (except for Raymond whom I think really good).

All love
    NR

[1] Sir Alfred and Lady Beit spent part of the year in Cape Town.
[2] Frederika Davis; an English friend of Nancy, and owner, with Betty Chetwynd, of the flat in rue Bonaparte where Nancy stayed after her arrival in Paris.
[3] Lord David Cecil (1902–86). *Two Quiet Lives* (1948) was a study of Dorothy Osborne, wife of the 17th-century statesman Sir William Temple, and of the poet Thomas Gray.
[4] Harold Acton, *Memoirs of an Aesthete* (1948), a first volume of autobiography.
[5] 'Well off, precocious, cosmopolitan, devoted to the arts . . . Mr Acton cannot hope to be forgiven by the enemies of promise . . . His memoirs are disfigured by pimples of malice hard to excuse in one who has been so fortunate . . . Perhaps so wholehearted an aesthete cannot face the drudgery of writing as a professional . . . he skates over experiences instead of plumbing them.' Raymond Mortimer, *New Statesman & Nation*, 22 May 1948.

TO EDWARD SACKVILLE-WEST   7 rue Monsieur, VII
23 June 1948

Dearest Eddy

Many thanks indeed for writing – I am *very* sad,[1] I was so fond of her as you know & it seems such a dreadful waste of the charming beautiful & odd creature that she used to be. A victim of these terrible times & yet another case of somebody torn away from an environment which, whatever it really was, certainly suited *her*. The passage of the bullet became inflamed, it seems the doctors always knew it might do so & never said for fear of frightening my mother – there was nothing whatever to be done. Isn't it odd, just when her general health was so much improved.

Oh do oh do go to Diana [Cooper] – I shall be there most of July I think writing my book. As Davey again figures largely it would be most useful to have him around for a bit –! I used to be paralysed by Duff, & all the French are, but of course I'm so used to him now, & I really love him.

I've just been to a luncheon party so pompous, so full of Bourbon Parmes & d'Arenbergs, that the placement took 3 weeks to work out & resulted in nearly all the men sitting together. Isn't it *typical*!

Hoping very much to see you.

With love
        Nancy

[1] Unity Mitford died of meningitis on 28 May.

To Diana Mosley   7 rue Monsieur, VII
29 June 1948

Darling
    Daisy [Fellowes]'s party. Margaret [Wright]'s visit.
    Party first. Very brilliant & great fun – everyone you can imagine – Duffs, M-Laure [de Noailles], M-Louise [Bousquet], Dolly R., Bergeries, daughter Isabelle [de Broglie], son in law Castéja,[1] Hugh S[herwood], Aga & lovely new Begum. Twenty-four in all. The Aga is extraordinary just as one had always heard – 'Mrs Rodd? But your grandfather was a great friend of mine.' Can you beat it. He says grandfather was such a brilliant man ('I expect you know he just fell between 2 stools – it doesn't do for brilliant people to be snobs or for snobs to be brilliant'). It was the day of his 3rd Derby so he must have been in a specially good mood.
    Daisy's dining room the prettiest modern room you ever saw, like a pink & white sugar sweet. Wonderful toilets & jewels, specially *oh* the Begum's you can't imagine. I *do* mind not having one single jewel I must say. If – when – you see Daisy do say how much I adored it,

no good writing as she has vanished away. *So so* kind of her to ask me.

The visit. Heralded by a *flood* of reply paid telegrams from Farve. Went to meet them. The poor friend is an old lady of 100 who runs the Grosvenor – of course when they saw their bedrooms they were rather cast down – real little left bank hotel rooms, but when they heard the price they were forced to admit. Third floor & no lift, I guess the old Grosvenor lady will leave her bones among us. Margaret greeted me with the news that Mitford of Mitford[2] has died (shrieks).

However they are wildly enthusiastic & you know how that always wins my heart & as you know I really *like* Margaret.

The night of Daisy's party Prod & Ed [Stanley] went out & returned at *1 p.m.* the following day. Of course I thought they must be in prison – it is always my nightmare that we shall have our identity cards taken away – but it was just that they were on such a bat that they thought it was only breakfast time. Really at their age!!!

I never never see the Colonel it is too depressing I am reduced to writing. Sent him your Windsor letter which he adored of course. I keep suggesting that Prod might like to: join the war in Palestine (either side); go to Africa & look for a unicorn; go spying behind the Iron Curtain; go & run a Butlin camp; but he seems quite disinclined for any of these outings. I really *love* having him here, if only it didn't stop me from seeing the Col, but of course it does. When I go round to the Colonel's flat it is like some dreadful spy film & I end by being shut up in a cupboard or hiding on the escalier de service & being found by the concierge – so undignified I nearly die of it – apart from the fact that the whole of the time is taken up by these antics & I get about 5 restless minutes of his company!

Splendid about Tito isn't it – out of a window now d'you think? (I can't but love Tito rather all the same.) The Col says it's all nonsense, he's never been anything but a Russian general & they're just giving him a new job, but I think there's more to it but that may be wishing.[3]

Boring guests – finish later.

The Colonel says the Aga does the most dreadful things to the Begum – I said 'Oh & she looks *so* dignified.' He shrieked. You note by the way, that tout simplement délicieuse[4] wasn't there, at Daisy's.

I'm giving a grand luncheon party on Friday, dead with terror – I've got Mme de Chabrillan who is the sort of Lady Derby[5] of France (& I *don't* mean Ldy Isabel Mills Slade) & a grand old pederast the Marquis de Lasteyrie, a descendant of Lafayette & who lives in his beautiful house, & Mme Costa & my snobbish Sergeant [Preston].

Now to collect enough food for the regulation 8 courses. Pray Prod
will be in from the night clubs in time –

Margaret & friend are going round the night clubs in a Cook's tour,
I dread what they will see –

Best love
NR

[1] Count Alexandre de Castéja (1907–83). Married Princess Emmeline de Broglie in
1932.
[2] A distant Northumbrian cousin.
[3] Marshal Tito (1892–1980) had been accused by the Russians of straying from the
Party line. They called on him to repent or be ousted.
[4] Daisy Fellowes's teasing nickname for Lady Harvey.
[5] The grand and imposing wife of 17th Earl of Derby, whose grandson (18th Earl)
married Lady Isabel Milles-Lade.

To Violet Hammersley   7 rue Monsieur, VII
6 July 1948

Darling
    Everybody has left or is leaving Paris this week & I am off to the
Coopers to work, so you may not hear again for sometime. There
has been a wild spate of entertaining, parties costing between 6 & 12
million francs, dinners off gold plates, fountains of champagne, clothes
such as you never saw – all great fun. *How* rich the French are. I
never can get over it – living in their huge houses with huge gardens
in the very centre of the town, with between 20 & 30 servants – now
I'm getting to know more real French people, not the cosmopolitan
ones, I am *staggered* by the luxe in which they exist. The Costa
household is a cottage in comparison, & yet in London it would seem
the comble of luxury. Then they all keep huge country houses going
at the same time & *sometimes two*. I think the English are infected
with a cottage complex don't you, they can't really be so much poorer
as all that.
    I have made a sally into the high gratin & I must say it is heaven
– I very much hope to write a Paris novel next, with several chapters
on placement which is my favourite subject. 'Relations' one young
man said to me 'are always put at the bout de table – Dolly you see
is at the bout de table but that's not to say she's liking it –!'
    Yes Evelyn gave me his review of the Greene book[1] to read also
the book itself, & talked a great deal about it. I couldn't read it – too
sad & sordid for me. Evelyn much shocked by this admission –! I

said to E. that I could *never* understand the RC religion, *far* too arid & intellectual, & he laughed a great deal at that. Not the charge that is generally levelled.

How typical Huxleys & Harveys[2] – yes yes of course. Do you remember when Mme Costa said I was a snob because I don't like the Huxleys – well I'm getting more of a snob every day. Old Hore Belisha[3] came to see me & said he went to write his name at the Embassy & the old porter said 'Not much good doing that, sir, nobody ever gets asked to anything now.' All the French complain dreadfully, especially the grand dull ones who got asked to nothing by the Coopers & thought they would have an innings now –!

Bébé Bérard *is* Bérard –! Did you see him & did he kneel before you? I'm sure he would. I didn't think he really wanted to paint Debo much & can't think why she had the idea – so unlike her to pick on a good artist – (do you remember 'my fingers *itch* for an india rubber').[4]

Don't you think Diana's house is bliss? Such pretty objects & such a dear little house. She is certainly very happy.

I saw Rosamond L[ehmann] on a station in England, running, hadn't the energy to run after her. *Oh* the dowdiness of English women – has it always been the same or are they worse now – I can't remember. It is so fundamental that I suspect the former. The London New Look made me die of laughing – literal chintz crinolines. Apparently Dior went over 'et lorsqu'il a réfléchi que c'est lui qui a lancé tout ça il était prêt à se suicider.'[5]

M. de Lasteyrie said to me 'voici 40 ans que je suis membre du Jockey – et jamais je n'y ai entendu prononcer le nom d'un couturier jusqu'à cette année – maintenant on ne parle que de Dior.'[6] Isn't it queer?

Much love – if you write here they will forward.
     NR

---

[1] Waugh's review of *The Heart of the Matter* appeared in *Commonweal* on 16 July.

[2] 'Juliette [Huxley] seems hand-in-glove with Lady Harvey. She would be you would say!' (Violet Hammersley to NM, 4 July 1948)

[3] Leslie Hore-Belisha (1893–1957). National Liberal MP. Introduced pedestrian crossings lit by Belisha beacons.

[4] A remark Nancy alleged to have been made by Deborah while looking through Old Master drawings at Chatsworth.

[5] 'And when he realized that it was he who had started it all, he was ready to commit suicide.'

[6] 'I have been a member of the Jockey Club for 40 years and I have never heard the name of a couturier being spoken there until this year – now they talk of nothing but Dior.'

To Diana Mosley   7 rue Monsieur, VII
26 July 1948

Darling

Don't know when you'll get this but mustn't break the continuity –
also I'm here without book so it's a chance to write. Duff lent Chantilly
to the Derbys for their moon, there has been a running fight about it
between him & Diana since the engagement was announced, she
doesn't know Lady D & didn't want to clear out. Duff won, as he
always does, they've gone to England, I've come here (dust sheets
& my own delicious Nes-café, you know!) & as the car was in the
drive waiting to take us the D's rang up & said they'd rather stay at
the Ritz –!!!!

So I'm creeping back to work tomorrow & they (Duffs) return on
Tues: they are saying good bye to poor Venetia.

Oh dear, such a to-do. Peter is here & Golly's boys,[1] & last night
we went to dine at a restaurant I always go to with the Col, & there
was the Col with a girl called Margot de Gramont, a nice fat sad girl
who was a Resistance heroine & who has been for ages in love with
the Colonel. Well I could hardly bear that, then we went to see the
statues lit up at the Louvre & I saw the Col looking fearfully happy
walking round hand in hand with M. de G. I was sidérée [flabber-
gasted]. I quite made up my mind he had just, at last, proposed to
her – they looked to me exactly like that. So when I got back I got
out Prod's so called poison pills. Then I thought better just make sure
so I rang up the poor Colonel & he couldn't understand what it was
all about, but, though woken up, was absolutely angelic. I kept saying
but you looked so *happy* 'no no I'm not happy I'm very unhappy.' So
dreadful to prefer the loved one to be unhappy – I ought to want him
to marry, I know. He did say 'but *you* are married, after all' & I know
he really longs to be, & I feel a villainess to make all this fuss. So
this morning when he rang up I said 'Oh Colonel I'm ashamed of
myself' & he replied 'The rights of passion have been proclaimed by
the French Revolution.'

The fact is I *couldn't* live through it if he married & what is so
dreadful is I know I can stop him – or at least I think so – & that
condemns him to the great domestic discomfort in which he lives, to
loneliness & having no children. Perhaps I really ought to leave Paris
for good. I must say this has all plunged me into a turmoil – oh the
horror of love.

Later

I've just been to see him – told about the pills which I see to have been a great mistake, he's simply *delighted* at the idea 'oh you must you must, what a coup for me.' He says I take a novelist's view of marriage, that if he marries it will only be to have children & will make no difference at all – & that anyway there is no question of it with Margot as he likes her very much but doesn't find her at all attractive physically. All true no doubt as she has adored him for years – but I often feel in the end she'll make it –!

Oh I would have *loved* the boat[2] you know, so long as no sea going, it is just my book – I must finish it while it is going on well, before the war begins & before the Colonel marries.

Bliss about Decca being the only one to harm a Jew.[3] I said to Mrs Kliot after she had wailed all day 'but is money the *only* thing that matters in America?' & she said yes because otherwise, if you haven't any, you never get to know rich people!

The Tour de France has kept us all very busy. Bobet, the favourite & a *hero* to his public, after surviving the supplice des montagnes & a folle étape dans le mistral succumbed to terrible furoncles (ONE can guess where), then, 'Bobet, découragé, s'effondre.'[4] After which he wrote a very unsporting article blaming it all on his trainer Archambault. We've just been to see the finish, *very* dull with a horrid Wop winning it.

The Elwes boys not at all in the Jonathan-John Julius class – deadly – or perhaps like Edinburgh, young for their age. They certainly don't see the point of ONE. John Julius does like mad & nearly died when I told him about Isn't it *bliss* to be ONE.[5]

Best love darling
NR

[1] Peter Rodd's nephews, Peter and Dominick Elwes.
[2] The Mosleys had invited Nancy to tour the Channel Islands on their boat *Dedantre*.
[3] Nancy had written to Diana that Jessica's mother-in-law, Aranka Kliot, had complained that her son's marriage had ruined his chances in life. Diana replied: 'Kit [Oswald Mosley] says after all the talk & trouble only *one* Mitford has ever done any harm to a Jud – Decca!' (21 July 1948).
[4] 'Bobet . . . after surviving the torture of the mountains and a wild day in the mistral, succumbs to terrible boils . . . then, discouraged, collapses.'
[5] While in Holloway, Diana had said that in spite of the horrors of prison, 'It was still lovely to wake up in the morning and feel one was lovely ONE.' Oswald Mosley, *My Life* (Nelson, 1968), p. 410.

To Billa Harrod   7 rue Monsieur, VII
16 August 1948

Darling Billa,
  My book is now finished except for the minor detail that I am going
to re write it! But all the horrid hard work of inventing situations is
over. So the Waynflete Prof: of Moral Theology is incorporated in it
& I thought I'd better just ask you if I can use those very words –
magic to me – or had you some real Waynflete in mind – if so do
invent some other heavenly chair. Also what would he put on his
visiting card – Mr or Prof: nobody here can tell me. His name is
Cozens & his wife née Boreley – I hope no Cozenses or Boreleys
among dons?
  I was 3 weeks at Chantilly with the Coopers working hard & am
now shut up here without Marie & not answering the telephone –
result I wrote 12 000 words in one week. The telephone I am glad to
say *peals* away, if it didn't one would feel like hiding at sardines &
nobody coming to look. One person went up to 40 rings – I always
count, that was the best so far.
  Chantilly was heaven. I wrote all day in the stables & at meal times
emerged into a blaze of society, never knowing who there would be
made it so interesting. We had the Derbys (dreary) for part of their
honeymoon, the Cranbornes,[1] . . . Lady National Bagnold Jones[2] hell
but rather fascinating in an awful way, Ronnie Trees[3] old fat Ronnie
re-married to an earnest American beauty, heavenly heavenly Pam
Berry, easily my favourite, Cecil Beaton, runner up, & the Hof-
mannsthals & I suppose some I've forgotten. Then about 8 down from
Paris for every meal. Oh I know, there was a blissful girl called Lady
Lambton,[4] who came out of & returned into the blue & we all long
to know more about her – do you?
  Wonderful boiling weather & nobody else here (in the immeuble I
mean) so I sit in the cour (veranda) all day & don't a bit regret the
South. All my aunts write that the crops are ruined at home how
awful except doesn't it happen regularly every year?
  There is much more about Fanny in this book & I can see that very
soon she'll be leaving Alfred & her 4 children, & adopting one of
Linda's, & skipping off to a fast life in Paris! Oh I do so hope it's good
it is an utter fog to me now.

    Best love do write
        Nancy

One little detail rather worries me. Quite a lot of the scenes take place in Fanny's house & there is never an undergraduate there (I have a horror of unnecessary characters) but is this awfully odd & unnatural? If so I could drag in 1 or 2 I suppose. What d'you think?

[1] Viscount Cranborne (1916–). Succeeded as 6th Marquess of Salisbury in 1972. Married Marjorie Wyndham-Quin in 1945.
[2] Enid Bagnold (1889–1981). Author of *National Velvet* (1935). Married Sir Roderick Jones in 1920.
[3] Ronald Tree (1897–1976). Conservative MP. Married to Nancy Perkins in 1921 and to Marietta Peabody, daughter of the Episcopalian Bishop of New York State, in 1947. Owner of Ditchley Park in Oxfordshire where Winston Churchill went on moonlit nights to hold secret meetings during the war.
[4] Belinda Blew-Jones (1922–). Married Viscount Lambton in 1942. Their daughter Lucinda (1943–) married Billa Harrod's son, Henry, in 1965.

To Diana Mosley   7 rue Monsieur, VII
23 August 1948

Darling

My Colonel has just got back from his holiday thank goodness, looking much better. He was away a whole fortnight, Biarritz, & seems to have seen a lot of Lady Babar,[1] whom he is truly fond of. He says in the sleeper last night there was a terrible old wheezing man, totally bald, & this morning this ancient old grandfather said to him 'C'est bien Gaston Palewski? Tu te rappelles nous faisions notre science politique ensemble –!'[2] Colonel simply furious, can't get over it!

Don't pay the slightest attention to the silly little baby English papers if they say tube skirts. There is no change whatever. I went to Piguet, to cheer myself up (lonely) & I've heard all about Dior so I really know. What is very pretty this year are stoles (made of cloth & velvet if one can't afford a good fur) & fur lined boleros. And of course the *huge* fur hats are simply glam. Hat pins of dire danger. (Make a good deep waistband to your skirts – Empire trend.) . . .

Then I'll suggest the dédicace to Gerald.[3] I must say I think the book is good, now. I'm re writing the whole thing. The Col goes to London in Nov: for Chatham House,[4] but I think I'll come before that – anyhow we'll see how I get on. I must try & combine with Peter being here as it seems a waste to be away when he's away too, I can see so much more of the Col when here alone. Otherwise it's the horror of his flat, dodging his secretaries & so on – you know!

A letter from Peter saying he doesn't feel inclined to subscribe to getting the new flat as I make it only too clear that I only like having him for a fortnight in the year. As I hadn't asked him to subscribe, or expected it, & haven't had one single penny from him or his family since he joined up in 1939 & he has been here the *whole summer* this really is too much & the worm turned & I wrote & said it would be far better if we could be divorced. To which silence for a week & now a letter saying he is seeing about buying beds & so on for the flat.

I am really fond of Peter you know but the whole thing is complicated, & the person I live for is the Col & if he can't run in & out of my house at all times I know in the end he will feel lonely & his thoughts will turn to marriage. Also I *can't* see what poor Pete gets out of it as I'm not really very nice to him – surely he'd much better marry again & produce an heir to the lands & titles. What a worry – oh well, not really, but you know – I was rather cross –!

Lovely hot Turkish bath weather. There is a glass roof in the cour & I sit out, writing, all day even when it rains. It's a thing one always ought to have I think, *such* a boon, in the north anyway.

I've got Maugham's book[5] it looks very dull. Rather short of reading matter & my wireless is bust. It's a bore as I can't write all day, every minute of it –!

Best love darling
    NR

I saw a *most lovely* dress the other day & when I asked who made it (thinking Dior certainly) Hardy Amies. Quite as good as anything here, grey flannel & simply beautifully made, I was so impressed.

---

[1] Lady Alexandra Curzon (1904–). A sister of Oswald Mosley's first wife Cynthia. Married Edward (Fruity) Metcalfe in 1925.
[2] 'Surely it's Gaston Palewski? Do you remember we were at Sciences Politiques together?'
[3] *Love in a Cold Climate* was dedicated to Lord Berners.
[4] Palewski made a speech at the Royal Institute of International Affairs on 7 December, entitled 'France, England and Europe'.
[5] *Catalina* (1948), Somerset Maugham's last novel.

To Evelyn Waugh   21 Chapel Street[1]
28 October 1948   London, SW1

Dearest Evelyn

You are *really kind* to have taken so much trouble. I agree with
nearly all you say[2] – I've always known that Boy was too sketchy, &
that the beginning is clumsy. I have re-written the *whole thing* once
already you know. What I wonder is whether I can (am capable of)
doing better. You speak of Henry James but he was a *man* of intellect,
you must remember that I am an *uneducated woman* (viz punctuation)
& that I have done my best & worked hard already. What you say
about the minor characters I don't agree with. Your complaint is that
they are not photographs of existing people, but one must be allowed
to invent people if one is a novelist. I took the trouble to write to a
don's wife about Norma & she said quite possible.

Oh dear. You see I'm afraid that what you really criticize are my
own inherent limitations. Luckily you also find something to admire,
that is one comfort. But I do feel quite sure that I am incapable of
writing the book you want me to – I can't do more really than skate
over surfaces, for one thing I am rather insensitive as you know, &
for another *not* very *clever*.

I will have a go at Cedric's talk & do some revising on the lines
that you suggest.

   In haste *much love*
        NR

[1] Nancy was staying with her sister Diana.
[2] Evelyn Waugh: 'The theme is original & promising. There is not a boring sentence
(except p. 274) [a description of Lady Patricia Dougdale's rather indifferent house].
But it isn't a book at all yet. No more 40 hour week. Blood, sweat & tears. That is
to say if you want to produce a work of art. There is a work of art ther , lurking in a
hole, occasionally visible by the tip of its whiskers.' *Letters*, p. 285.

To Diana Mosley   7 rue Monsieur, VII
22 November 1948

Darling

. . . I enclose the Gen's press conference in full, it might interest
you.

How exciting about your dress. Next time do go & *look* at Hardy
Amies. Still this one sounds ideal, I hope they won't take for ever,
making it.

Randolph & wife[1] have just been there – she is very pretty, wonderful blue eyes. He in a charming mood – it was all very nice. He says as soon as there is television nobody will *ever* read another book. 'Why do people read? To pass the time. Well if they can do that without reading of course they'd rather.'

It seems there's already a terrible slump in books in America – oh Lord – What about ONE's living? . . .

Next day

A long letter from Peter who is in London saying he is tired of being cocu [cuckolded] & we must be divorced. Good. He speaks however of divorcing me in the French courts which is not good at all, but I don't think he will. Truly I doubt if he can – it would all depend on concierge's evidence & even then rather tricky as I've never spent a night or gone for a journey with the Col. I don't know whether French law has that thing about condoning but if so he has most certainly condoned, & for years.

I've countered with his Italian motor tour with Adelaide. But I don't think there will be, or need be, any acrimony & he'll let me divorce him in London. The nuisance is I shall have to abandon my French domicile & pay full taxes on my earnings.

Anyway it's an *enormous* weight off my mind – I really think it's too dreadful, being boxed up with somebody you no longer love & have no interests in common with. Also I shall now know where I am as regards money.

What shall I do about telling Muv? Let it seep in gradually or tell her just before the case comes on, which won't I suppose be for ages. She can't seriously *mind*, can she?

All love
    NR

[1] Randolph Churchill and his second wife June Osborne, daughter of Colonel Rex Osborne, were married in June 1948.

To EVELYN WAUGH   7 rue Monsieur, VII
11 January 1949

Darling Evelyn

Don't be so cross & don't tease me about not having children, it was God's idea, not mine. Do you really think it's more wrong to live in one place than another or wrong to go to fancy dress parties? I don't live here for food wine & elegant clothes but because I love the people.[1] Like Napoleon I wish to be buried parmi ce peuple que j'ai si bien aimé,[2] & one of my Xmas presents this year was a grave in the Père Lachaise, so I shall be.

Don't be angry with me for being happy, you must know as well as I do that happiness doesn't depend on exterior or political events & that the findings of UNO or fresh demands for peace in Nanking are not enough to damp one's spirits for more than the 5 minutes it takes to read them of a morning. I live among good & happy people & my days are *unclouded* from morning to night. You ought to be pleased, you are supposed to be fond of me.

I too earn dollars for the old land, & send them home like a good child to its mother, though not as many as you or this great genius who writes so much better than me, Miss Mrs or Lady Fremantle.[3] (Alas it wouldn't be difficult to write better than me, but I don't like the tone in which it was said.)

Cedric is not being well received in your new country. *The Woman's Home Journal*[4] says he is revolting & that neither they nor any other American mag will touch him.

I'll try & get your book[5] but if out of print may not be possible, for there is no machinery here as in London for getting O.P. books, a fact which is the bane of my life. Does yr friend really live at Gethsemani, Kentucky? Well.

I am translating the *Princesse de Clèves*, have you ever read it? I do love translating, it is the pure pleasure of writing without the misery of inventing.

I am reading Pascal, *Les provinciales*. Very strict, isn't he. . . .

I suppose you think I'm a whore & my immortal soul is in danger. About once a week, for a few minutes it worries me that you should think so. That I can understand though, what seems so unlike you is this Harold Nicolson[6] attitude of disapproval because I live among the flesh pots. (Did you see his article '*we* prefer our *nice little ration books*'.)

I must go out into the brilliant sunshine.

Love from
    Nancy

I went to the ball in black tights & a black beard hoping at last to have a success with the chaps. But they thought I was Edward James & *fled.*

Dolly Radziwill and Nancy at the
fancy-dress ball, by Mogens Tvede

1 Nancy had written: 'I am having a lovely life – only sad that heavenly 1948 is over.'
Waugh replied: 'What an odd idea of heaven. Of course in my country we cannot enjoy
the elegant clothes & meals & masquerades which fill your days . . . Laura is well but
hard-driven by the cares of farm & nursery.' *Letters*, p. 294.
2 Amongst this people I have loved so well.
3 Anne Huth Jackson (1909–). Journalist and author. An Englishwoman who had converted to Catholicism and moved to America. Married Christopher Fremantle in 1930.
Waugh had written to Nancy: 'She too gave her youth to the socialist cause and at
once left the sinking ship when her ends were accomplished. But her literary skill is
not as gravely impaired by the change . . .' *Letters*, p. 294.
4 *The Ladies Home Journal*, Philadelphia.
5 'If you can find Père A. Gardeil's *La Structure de l'âme et l'expérience mystique* it
would be a *great* kindness to send a copy to Thomas Merton, Gethsemani, Kentucky,
USA.' Waugh, *Letters*, p. 294.
6 Harold Nicolson (1886–1968). Journalist, biographer, politician and diarist. Married
Vita Sackville-West in 1913. Knighted in 1952. Nicolson and Nancy met occasionally
but were never friends; he wrote in his diary: 'She is essentially not an intellectual and
there is a sort of Roedean hoydenishness about her which I dislike.' James Lees-Milne,
Harold Nicolson, 1930–1968 (Chatto & Windus, 1981), p. 293.

To Billa Harrod   7 rue Monsieur, VII
20 January 1949

Darling Billa

I was so pleased to hear from you – Diana [Cooper] said she had seen you & that Roy's book[1] sounds *heaven* but would I as well as Dr Schumpeter[2] understand it?

I do hope you'll like mine, I *feel* you will though Evelyn & Chris [Sykes] downed it dreadfully, thought it bad beyond words & Evelyn said all the Oxford part was quite unreal. So I shall be fascinated to hear what you think. It's the Prof's wife who goes hunting that he objects to. On the other hand Heywood likes her one of the best & he, Gerald & Muv like the book.

America is taking exception to Cedric the *sweet* pansy. It seems in America you can have pederasts in books so long as they are fearfully gloomy & end by committing suicide. A cheerful one who goes from strength to strength like Cedric horrifies them. They say 'Cedric is too revolting for any enjoyment of the book.' So I write back 'how can you hate Cedric when he is such a *love?*'

Wynne,[3] launched on Mr Street [rue Monsieur] by you was launched on Paris by me. Then his shares slumped because not only dirty but smelt. So we leagued together & told him & now his shares fluctuate, but they are down at the moment as he lied to Diana about pyjamas under his trousers. But he is a dear old thing really & we all love him – & I *hear*, very talented for music.

Come & stay as soon as it is warm enough not to mind an unheated bedroom. Or, stay actually in a pub & live here. I long to see you.

But probably you can't leave the boys with Roy away. It's so warm now that I don't light my stove until evening, but it can't last. A *great* mercy while it does. . . .

My great new friend is Noel Coward, do you know him? Bliss. But he has gone away again now. He shakes like a jelly at one's jokes, I *adore* that.

Evelyn very cross because I happened to say in a letter that I was happy. Volumes of abuse resulted, taking the line that I only live here because of beef steak. So he has joined the goody-goodies.

Write sometimes

Best love
   NR

I fear Helen [Dashwood] is in very low water poor her.

[1] Roy Harrod, *Towards a Dynamic Economics* (1948).
[2] Joseph A. Schumpeter (1883–1950). American economist.
[3] Hon. Wynne Godley (1926–). Oboist, economist and pupil of Roy Harrod. He was studying at the Conservatoire de Musique.

To Violet Hammersley   7 rue Monsieur, VII
29 January 1949

Darling

Evelyn's letter *pure wickedness*, not fun at all. I wrote & said you are supposed to be fond of me, you should be glad that I am happy. He replied I am fond of you, very, & that is why I am not glad. Diana Cooper says he is like the negative of a photograph all the black white & white black.

I hope Leslie won't tell Osbert,[1] I had really forgotten they are such friends, I don't want to make trouble. But I'm sure he won't & anyway expect Evelyn has let Osbert know exactly what he thinks already. He says he has given Edith a thing called the beaux alarm which goes off like an air raid warning if somebody tries to kiss you. *She* lets it off when people ask about symbolism.

To go back to Evelyn's beastliness it all comes from being an amateur & not a professional Catholic. You & Mme Costa aren't like that or do you smilingly conceal from one that you see hell fire licking one's toes? (Perhaps smilingly is not the word for *you* my darling.) He has been too terrible about my book but the publishers are preparing for it to be another best seller & I must confess that for me is what matters, so that I can go on living here – all I care about. Evelyn said it could have been a work of art – yes but I'm afraid it's here & now & the Colonel I care for. I long for you to read it & then we will pick it over together.

Diana [Cooper] rang up just now & I read her a bit of your letter 'who is Mrs Hammersley?' 'my greatest friend.' So are you pleased? I die for you to meet her. When do you plan to come? I'll ask at Hotel de Suède next time I pass – those sort of hotels are 750 (16/-) a day as a rule, about a pound with breakfast – possibly a bob or two less. Do you bring Mrs Hook?[2] . . .

I am translating the *Psse de Clèves* it looks easy & is not. But at least one knows what it all means, which can't be said of modern writers.

Much love
    NR

[1] Waugh had written to Nancy, 'No sane man could envy Sir Osbert [Sitwell] his ostentatious progress through USA. Nor do the Americans respect him for it.' *Letters*, p. 294. Nancy forwarded the letter to Violet Hammersley who was staying with the writer L. P. Hartley.
[2] Violet Hammersley's housekeeper.

To DIANA MOSLEY   7 rue Monsieur, VII
17 February 1949

Darling

I thought my good nature with regard to Widdershin was inépuis-able [inexhaustible] but *this* is the *end*. The old brute in human form sent me a *whole letter of instructions* which I lugged down to the shop & handed them, receiving in return a little packet already sealed up. Now as you see I am blamed for the loss of her youth & beauty[1] – I shan't reply. If you see her you might say I am mortally offended, I am, too.

The funeral of Bébé [Bérard] was dreadfully sad & got me down. The huge beautiful church (St Sulpice) so full one could hardly get in & with everybody I know in Paris, from Jean Cocteau[2] to the little girl who makes my hats. In the cortège all the famous people of France as well as the sweet man who runs the bistro he always went to & such like. I think France is more truly democratic than we are in such ways you know.

Boris [Kochno], whom I have never cared for, with an expression of misery on his face that I shall never forget. Then such a weeny coffin, like a child's.

I was with all buddies, Jean-Louis Lucinge,[3] Cora,[4] Tony [Gandarillas], Dolly & so on. I'm sure the French love their friends more than we do, I've never in London been to a *sad* service as this was. I must say the cross we all gave, shocked as I was at the price (£60) was extraordinary – a huge thing 6 foot high at least, of nothing but Parma violets.

All these sudden deaths have depressed me – I think of the Col & feel terrified. Oh for the happy old days when nobody ever died so that it didn't enter into one's calculations at all.

Do ring up poor little Tony he is in great despair – his 3 best friends in one year or less & Carmen's fiancé,[5] I never heard such a run of bad luck. From what you say I fear for Gerald too, had hoped he was so much better. I can't but mistrust [Dr] Lancel.

I'm gloating over Duff's life of Haig[6] – the bliss of that war, one

might as well be reading about Waterloo – morne plaine. He (Haig)
so funny about politicians for whom he only has one epithet, cunning.
The only Frenchman he rather liked was Lyautey,[7] when I told the
Col this he replied 'Ah tiens – Haig était un enculé?'[8] Shrieks! He
does keep saying 'I do so enjoy my tête à têtes with Lyautey –'!! . . .

   Love
      NR

Apparently Decca is upon us – *goodness*! Col says I must have a party
for Thorez[9] & ask him (he dotes on Thorez).

[1] Violet Hammersley had asked Nancy to send her some face cream and wrote: '*You
sent me the wrong colour*. I know I originally asked for "abricot" which also was on the
pot you kept. Oh! Why did you get that awful shade. It exists in four shades. Now I
have nothing, and can't get it here. I am so vexed, and it's so unlike you to do that.'
(14 February 1949)
[2] Jean Cocteau (1889–1963). Poet (*Plein-Chant*, 1923), novelist (*Thomas l'Imposteur*,
1923), playwright (*Les Parents terribles*, 1938) and film director (*La Belle et la Bête*,
1945).
[3] Prince Jean-Louis de Faucigny-Lucinge (1904–92). A cosmopolitan aristocrat of great
charm who was equally at ease amongst the *gratin* and the world of artists and writers.
Married to Liliane (Baba) d'Erlanger 1923–45 and to Sylvia Régis de Oliviera in 1949.
[4] Cora Antinori (1896–1974). A Florentine who worked for Schiaparelli and later at
the famous interior decorating shop, Jansen. Married Prince Michelangelo Caetani in
1920. 'I went to the midnight Mass with Col & Cora Caetani & never have I seen
anything as beautiful as she looked, in a black satin long dress sweeping up & down
the aisle, curtseying, dipping into H. water, crossing herself & all. She is like a wonderful
classic statue that has been dripped on for hundreds of years.' (NM to Evelyn Waugh,
31 December 1947)
[5] Carmen Gandarillas's fiancé, Lord Derwent, had died suddenly at the age of fifty.
[6] Duff Cooper, *Haig* (2 vols, 1935, 1936).
[7] Marshal Lyautey (1854–1935). Popular and successful Governor of Morocco.
Palewski's first job was as his Political Attaché, 1924–5.
[8] 'Oh – was Haig a bugger?' General de Gaulle is supposed to have said of Lyautey,
'C'est notre seul Maréchal qui ait des couilles au cul. Dommage que ce ne soient pas
toujours les siennes.' ('He is our only Marshal with any balls on him. What a pity they
are not always his own.')
[9] Maurice Thorez (1900–64). Leader of the French Communist Party.

To Lady Redesdale   7 rue Monsieur, VII
13 April 1949

Darling Muv
   I am in such a whirl I hardly have time for anything, the town is
full of English people all expecting to have their lives arranged for
them. Nigel [Birch] comes next week, Cecil B is here, Sibyl Colefax

& the Sitwells, Momo Marriott, Jim [Lees-Milne] & countless others either here or coming. Then the French have all gone to their terres for the hols so one can only offer the English each other which is not at all what they hope for!

The prospects for getting the flat are good but all goes slowly & the lawyer eats money. I wish it could be settled once for all & I could get my things over.

Paulette [Helleu] came to luncheon. I had a party for Kenneth Clark, but she scarcely uttered. She put forward a theory that a lot of black marks on the drawing of her mother started off white & that the chalk has gone bad. K. said I bet you 5000 francs they were never white which she took until he explained how one can know it (with peroxide) when she hastily retracted. K. said he always makes his children bet as otherwise statements become too wild altogether! After this she never uttered again.

Debo is going to Diana for the Grand Prix, what fun. And I hope Woman may come to me.

Much love from
    NR

To Lady Pamela Berry   7 rue Monsieur, VII
20 May 1949

Darling Pam

I never knew such a one sided correspondence. I have been thirsting for all sorts of bits of news, but in vain. Randolph, Evelyn, Susan Mary,[1] Ava [Anderson] – soon, I say to myself, I shall hear this or that about them from Pam. Ha ha.

Well I've been able to study Evelyn from 1st hand the last few days & I saw him at every meal the whole of his visit, except one he had with M. Claudel,[2] & most of the time he was sweet, twice he was bloody & all the time funny. About all one can expect. He had a terrible terrible quarrel with Diana at Chantilly this morning & I was ground between the upper & nether millstones of their two strong passionate & violent characters so now I am feeling weak.

The aim of this letter, apart from the rather hopeless hope of getting one back from you, is to state that I leave this town for an indefinite period on 1st July & is there anything I can do for you before I go? It would be dreadful if you were to turn up counting on finding me & there I wasn't, & you were then obliged to send for all your retainers

& offspring & give them the treat of an afternoon on the beach at
Dover. Do come before July then I should see you. . . .

All v. best love
    NR

Supplement
I've just now received your omnibus letter – *that*'s better.
Well my plans. I go to Dolly Radziwill near Marseilles & there am to
be picked up by the Mosleys in a yacht & taken for what the papers
call a pleasure-cruise. (No pleasure to me as I vomit in a harbour on
a fine day.) Then, rather chastened, I shall return to Dolly. . . .

[1] Susan Mary Jay (1918–). Married 1939–60 to William Patten, Attaché at the American
Embassy. The Pattens were posted to Paris in 1944 and were intimate friends of the
Coopers. In 1961 she married the political columnist Joseph Alsop.
[2] Paul Claudel (1868–1955). An ardent convert to Roman Catholicism, writer and
diplomat. During their meeting Waugh 'thought Claudel was speaking some sort of
dialect but afterwards discovered it had been English all the time'. (NM to Violet
Hammersley, 28 May 1949) Waugh recorded the meeting in his diary: 'Every now and
then the old man's lips were seen to move and there would be a cry "Papa is speaking!"
and a hush broken only by unintelligible animal noises. Some of these were addressed
to me and I thought he said: "How would you put into English *'potage de midi*'?" I
replied: "Soup at luncheon." It transpired that he was the author of a work named
Partage de Midi.' *The Diaries of Evelyn Waugh* (Weidenfeld & Nicolson, 1976), p. 778.

To LADY PAMELA BERRY   7 rue Monsieur, VII
25 May 1949

Darling Pam
    I suppose our letters crossed – also can't make out if yours about
Evelyn was written since he got back from here? Oh dear he was funny.
Yes he says I am very bad for you, it's *all that happiness* he says. . . .
    Evelyn's visit. I saw him every day of it, but didn't dare invite anybody
to meet him except a famous priest called Le Père Couturier[1] with
whom dear little Evelyn quarrelled violently all through luncheon. He
also quarrelled to the death with Diana though I couldn't quite make out
why. Both say they can never forgive. Perhaps I told you all this.
    There's to be a party given for Diana by all Duff's mistresses 24
June, why not come over for it? I am the only non-mistress on the
committee which is Susan Mary, Alvilde, Maxine,[2] Ghislaine de Polignac,[3] Barbey[4] etc. I said what about Lulu [de Vilmorin] & they said
no she would boss everything & I said but wouldn't that save a lot of
trouble & they said they like the trouble. I so *love* being bossed on

account of my weak & indolent nature. So then I handed them a list of the 30 most hated people in Paris who I said must be asked because they are Diana's beloveds, which is true, & left & no more committee meetings will be attended by *me*. The Anglo Saxon women here are all right separately but when they get together words cannot describe (or perhaps I, in a future book, can).

Oh the telephone it hasn't paused for 20 minutes, how can one write anything connected – I shall have to go & live in the South I plainly see, for one thing I'm too cold it *can't* be good for one to freeze the whole of every summer.

I've got a Beauty of 18 coming tomorrow which is a lovely treat, she came with her mother to buy a ball dress, which she has duly done, & I've persuaded the mother to leave her with me for a few days. She is called Venetia Murray, daughter of my dear old drunken cousin the late Basil M & she is an old fashioned Beauty, that is to say rather large & in a perpetual state of puppy like ecstasy which I find very attractive – like a puppy which wags itself rather than its tail. I see I'm boring you.

Well now try & write again before another 6 months & do consider the mistress party without, dear, telling everybody that is what I call it.

> Much love
> NR

P.S. . . . Do you know all about Pat de B suing Diana for £100? It would be funny really if she hadn't written D such a filthy housemaid's letter that one's blood boils to think of it.

[1] A worldly Dominican priest with whom Waugh had disagreed over Picasso.
[2] Maxine Birley; top photographic model in the 1940s. Daughter of the painter Sir Oswald Birley. Married to Count Alain de la Falaise and then to John McKendry.
[3] Ghislaine Brinquant (1918–). Married to Prince Edmond de Polignac (1914–). A key member of the Paris smart set.
[4] Barbara Lutyens (1898–1981). Daughter of Sir Edwin Lutyens. Married to Euan Wallace 1920–40 and to Herbert Agar 1945–80.

To LADY PAMELA BERRY   7 rue Monsieur, VII
3 June 1949

Darling Pam

The *relief* of your letters at a time when every post comes with one or two about my book saying how hopeless I am about business which is indeed only too true. I seem to have given powers to deal with film rights to several different people & they are all cross – oh dear.

The mistresses' ball is a welter of horror as you might guess. Falaise wants us each to spend 40 000 francs on a ballet in which she is to caper round dressed as what she calls a licorne but you or I an unicorn. However I think clever little Lulu has fixed the whole thing by inviting the Duffs, & everybody smart in Paris, to Verrières that night, & as the party was whimsically kept a secret from Diana she of course accepted. As I look round at the mistresses at the so called committee meetings (minutes are kept!!!) I quite see why Duff has taken to drink of late. Give me old Lulu any day. I long to take my name off it & retire but feel that would be waste of a *good deal of copy*.

Princess Margaret just had the Duffs & me at Chantilly, wasn't it bliss for her? She seems quite all there, what there is of her. . . .

Well Diana once borrowed £100 from Pat's father in law (currency trouble) & now Pat is reclaiming it & writing these bloody letters 'I am not quarrelling with you, Diana, but unfortunately I need this money. I only wish I were rich enough to give it you as a present but I'm afraid I'm not so if you don't cough it up by return I'm afraid I shall have to tell Duff about your dishonest behaviour etc etc.' I don't think Diana has a leg to stand on, but it's not the way to write to her all the same.

The Colonel, I'm so furious with him. He went to a fortune teller & showed me on his hand: 'she says that's Emardine' (a gloomy old bitch he used to be in love with), pointing to a sort of pit-like line. 'Oh. And where am I?' 'I don't know – here perhaps' showing a weeny almost invisible thread. So I made a fearful scene & parted in dudgeon, I do think chaps are awful. I said 'Look at me I've given up everything – my family my friends my country –' & he simply roared with laughter & then of course so did I.

Dolly Radziwill is in love with Prince Kinsky & they waltz together until 4 every morning & when they must have a breather they pore over albums of the castles they used to own behind the Iron Curtain. It is like something in a play. Vive l'amour.

Neither the Harveys nor Sammy Hood[1] asked Diana to their parties for the Princess, don't you call it hateful? And so odd when you think how Diana makes a party go. New name for Lady H: Morgue Harvey.

Doubt if I shall be here 5th Aug *how* disappointing. Do you never come again except then? I'll do what you say about parcels.

Much love
     NR

[1] 6th Viscount Hood (1910–81). Diplomat. Counsellor in Paris 1948–51.

To Evelyn Waugh   7 rue Monsieur, VII
5 June 1949

Darling Evelyn

I am horrified by Sir Alf's action[1] but I doubt if it is on account of your alleged inhumanity to Honks [Cooper] as he has been giggling away about it for many a long moon. . . . He said to me as we drove down the other day for the Princess Margaret Reception that you had written Honks a most terribly nice letter & I laid it on again about how it was all a misunderstanding.

The worst of the Coopers is they don't count sight seeing as a factor of human life, their genuine amazement when one comes in having been to the musée at Chantilly is proof of that. With some of the world's greatest treasures under their nose they have been there exactly once – I greatly doubt if they have ever been to the Louvre & they don't even know the names of the lesser museums here.

Desmond Guinness is here. The lives of the very young are a caricature of *Vile Bodies* I think you have much to answer for. He has been living with the daughter of a Roman Catholic Yorkshire writer called A. G. Brown (the Col knows about his books, so typical – they are of the Rambler school). But 'she wants to marry a millionaire so she is engaged to an Indian.' I said to Desmond what are your plans for the future? 'Well I would *like* to be a great lover of famous women, but if I can't I will be an interior decorator.' I think I can tell him straight away which it will have to be.[2] Bryan now has 8 repeat 8 children did you realize?[3]

Two of Duff's mistresses are now living with 2 of Diana's nephews & the rest are clubbing together to give a party for Diana 'to whom we owe so much'. It is all rather odd I must say.

Tell what happens about White's please.

Of course as you know I think it very *naughty and silly* of you to take this line about Peter Q, but if it is really a revenge for what you

are supposed to have done at Chantilly I *can't* say it's quite right of
Fred. . . .

　　Love & to your Man Sykes[4]
　　　　NR

And thank your Man for his sweet nice letter.
I didn't steam open yours to Fr Dressmaker[5] which is proof of my
wonderful nature, Freddy & Honks were dying to.

[1] Duff Cooper had proposed Peter Quennell, whom Waugh disliked, for membership
of White's.
[2] In 1958 Desmond Guinness founded the Irish Georgian Society, which has saved
many of Ireland's fine 18th-century houses. He is also the author of several books on
architecture.
[3] Lord Moyne eventually had eleven children.
[4] Christopher Sykes had been unable to afford to accompany Waugh to Paris in May,
so Waugh took him as his secretary and paid his expenses.
[5] Père Couturier.

To Anthony Powell[1]　　　　　　　　　　　　　　ss *Alianora*
27 July 1949

Dear Tony
　　Thank you so much for your letter. I *am* pleased you like the book
– I've had a terrible drubbing in America 'no message & no meaning'
'adds up to nothing' etc, I've had to stop reading them so bad for my
inferiority feeling. Oh eloquent is dreadful I do agree I'll cope with it
when I get back. Clichés pour from my pen & I do try to suppress
them by degrees, but never get rid of them all!
　　Cannes is very odd, full of workers (English) in Rolls Royces &
luxury yachts – the black marketeers I suppose. But real working
class accents, not RAF or spiv.
　　I'm having a most wonderful holiday (holiday from what? as my
Nanny used to say) have had a month near Marseilles & go back there
tomorrow. Back in Paris in Sept do come & see me if you pass through
ever won't you, 7 rue Monsieur Suffren 7665.
　　Thank you *so much* for writing, it has cheered me up.

　　Yrs ever
　　　　Nancy

P.S. Diana met a Spaniard, great R.C., who said 'do you know Evelyn
Waugh?'
　　'Oh yes very well. *He*'s a Roman Catholic you know.'

'Just for a joke I suppose?'
We screamed with laughter –

[1] Anthony Powell (1905–). Novelist. Married Lady Violet Pakenham in 1934. Publications include *Afternoon Men* (1931), *From a View to a Death* (1933) and *What's Become of Waring* (1936). *A Question of Upbringing*, the first in his twelve-volume series 'A Dance to the Music of Time', was published in 1951.

To GASTON PALEWSKI   Château de Montredon[1]
4 August 1949   Pointe Rouge
                                  Marseille

Not very faithful – & I am waiting for news of you to decide my plans. Do you come here? Shall you be in Paris, or at Louveciennes? Marie must be back at the rue Mr by now so I can return any day if you like you dearest.

Diana Cooper writes that she may pass by here, why not take a lift off her & come & we could travel back together by day? Oh Colonel *do* – Dolly longs for you. . . .

Our little tranquil life, too quiet for you I fear ('very dull') rolls on. I feel better than I have ever since the war, but melancholy without you & always in constant terror now of losing you. But, like Tolstoy at the time of Lenin's funeral,[2] I am too indolent to move – not too indolent if I thought you were in Paris however, it's just I don't want to go back & find the rue Bonaparte empty & Colonel less (though full of Natoires & watches). There is nothing sadder than the tick tick of a hundred watches in an empty flat.

All the papers are full of the dicta of Gen de G's right hand man – clever Colonel. But now a little rest – I worry about your health.

[1] Nancy was staying with Dolly Radziwill at a cottage in the park of Montredon.
[2] Nancy's reference is not clear.

To GASTON PALEWSKI   [Château de Montredon]
[August 1949]

Colonel I see now that I am *nothing* to you – because to be nothing in comparison with Cannes & Charlie Beistegui must indeed be le néant – so goodbye.[1]

[1] Palewski arrived at Montredon, would not allow his luggage to be taken out of the car, and drove on after lunch.

To Lady Redesdale   Redesdale Cottage
10 September 1949   Otterburn

Darling Muv

Just a scribble – I'm off again tomorrow & then crossing over with Aunts Iris & Dorothy by motor on Tuesday.

Farve has become a good time boy – nothing but cocktail parties. One was given for me here last night – 10 neighbours – can you beat it. More in character:

'I was showing a blasted woman over the garden' – pause – 'I thought it was Lady Northbourne' – long pause – 'Well it was Lady Northbourne. She rang about twenty times & at last I went to see what it was & I said oh I thought you were a van.'

However she didn't come to the party. Doffie[1] did looking raving mad, with a hideous child & son in law. I do think the country is awful – the *people* – I could never live in it –

Saw a mass of friends in London besides Korda.[2] I said to Farve Korda has bought all those houses in Piccadilly where the Yorks lived & he said What Jack Cawdor has? Korda (un Jack) wants me to write a film for the little boy Henrey[3] so I said yes, so you must tell me anything you can about little boys, anything, I don't feel I know a thing. I ought to have come & stayed with you for copy if I'd known.

Much love
        NR

Bitter & pouring of course. Left Paris in the 90s.

[1] Hon. Dorothea James; sister of Lord Northbourne. Married 2nd Baron Bicester in 1922.
[2] Alexander Korda (1893–1956). (Not Earl Cawdor.) Film director. He had asked Nancy to produce a film treatment around the story of a child of divorced parents whose only idea is to keep them apart.
[3] The boy actor Bobby Henrey.

To Evelyn Waugh   7 rue Monsieur, VII
21 September 1949

Darling Evelyn

Having been brought up to believe (not by Uncle Matthew) that qui n'a pas l'esprit de son age en a tous les défauts[1] I am appalled to find that in this week's *Horizon* there is not one single article I can understand. It's not a question of 'I don't quite see what you're getting at' I simply *do not understand it*, it's like a foreign language. (Except for one fragment which is too sad to read – yes & why is everything always sad fragments now? You might say of modern books sadly fragmented instead of well documented.) What does it mean – ought I to commit suicide? I don't dare ask Cyril he is so touchy & he might think I imply a reproach.[2]

I've just done my preface to the *Princesse de Clèves*, 5000 words, long for me & am engaged on the bibliography & notes.

Haven't answered the telephone or seen anybody except Col since I got back – all very well & *I love* it only it's dull for the poor Colonel who complains I never have any news to tell him. If you wrote to me I could read it out to him – he is reading all your early works lent by Prince Bibesco.[3]

    Yours etc
        Worried

[1] He who is out of tune with the spirit of his age acquires all its defects.
[2] Articles in the September 1949 issue of *Horizon* included: 'The Literature of Extreme Situations' by Albert Votaw, 'A Fragment of Life Story' by Denton Welsh, 'On the Analysis of Moral Judgements' by A. J. Ayer and 'San Sebastian' by Ryunosuke Akatugawa.
[3] Prince Antoine Bibesco (1878–1951). Shrewd Romanian diplomat and close friend of Proust. Married Elizabeth Asquith, daughter of the Prime Minister, Herbert Asquith, in 1919.

To Evelyn Waugh   7 rue Monsieur, VII
6 November 1949

Darling Evelyn

All my friends have forgotten me & the only letters I get now are from chubb fuddlers saying that you can't fuddle chubb in Feb (long since pointed out with cold fury by Uncle Matthew himself) & one from a Mr Chubb asking to be put in touch with a fuddler.[1] Also one from Mr Berenson[2] asking where I have seen The Gamesters by Caravaggio, a picture he says he has long wanted to trace. Answer: I invented it (!) But you, Pam [Berry] etc never write now, it is so sad for me. I saw your man Sykes & he held out great hopes of an approaching visit oh *do*, I promise you needn't see Fr Dressmaker.

In spite of the badness of Laffont's translations you are regarded by many people here as the greatest (after Malraux or level with Malraux) living novelist, do be gratified.

Do tell what you think of Mr Fitzroy Maclean's book,[3] I have been living in it (lent by Momo).

I have translated a lovely play called *La Petite Hutte*[4] did I tell you.
I so adored doing it & now think only of writing a play but I suppose
ONE never could alas.

There are some lovely new rooms open in the Louvre, also I've
found a bearded lecturer who manages to get inside the houses of
lucky beggars (literally) who inhabit the great mouldering palaces of
the Marais. It is a mixed treat to see unrestored Louis XIV ceilings
partially hidden by washing & so on, but I go on going & when I am
rich I shall live in one.

My American publisher has invited me to go there, everything paid.
I said I am too old – true.

Hateful Evelyn do write, I live for the blue envelopes.

Love
    NR

[1] In *Love in a Cold Climate*, Uncle Matthew's greatest treat of the year was to spend
an afternoon chubb-fuddling in the river near his house.
[2] Bernard Berenson (1865–1959). Lithuanian-born American art historian; leading
authority on Renaissance painting.
[3] Sir Fitzroy Maclean, *Eastern Approaches* (1949).
[4] André Roussin's *The Little Hut* ran successfully in Paris for three years before moving
to England. 'It's a terribly funny play about husband, lover & wife on a desert island
– lover gets very low all alone in the hut while the husband & wife sleep in the big
one, insists on taking turns. Husband not absolutely keen but sees the logic, that they
have shared her for 6 years & might as well go on doing so. Then a handsome young
negro appears, ties up husband & lover by a trick & indicates that he will only let them
go if Susan will go into the hut with him, which she's only too pleased to do as he is
very good looking. "Disgusting I hear you say."' (NM to Lady Redesdale, 1 February
1950)

TO LADY PAMELA BERRY   7 rue Monsieur, VII
14 November 1949

Darling Pam
    I seem to be quite all right again. The thing about a visit to London
now is I *can't* really because of the Colonel & because of my film I
am trying to write – if I abandon it now I am done for. The Col is in
low water as his mother is ill, & when he is anxious about her I always
think he rather depends on me being there as he won't go out & see
people. He is just back from a political tour, & I had a letter from
Evelyn about a lecture tour – their experiences are really so typical
of the 2 countries. The Col overtired it is true, but stuffed with foie
gras & fine wines by his supporters & elated by having seen 2 Goyas &

one Christian-Greek Madonna in a tiny museum miles from anywhere. Evelyn cold, starved, overtired & utterly got down in every way. He seems very low too about the death of Peter Beatty,[1] so *odd* somehow that they shld have been friends. . . .

The French are beginning to regard Evelyn as one of the greatest living novelists, they call him Wugg & eat up any crumbs of information about him that I deign to let fall. They all *long* to meet him in spite of earnest warnings from me that it would be better not – I am talking now of my middle class French intellectual friends of whom I have an ever increasing number & love them madly. It is terribly annoying to me that they so long for Wugg when they have got lovely me who loves them in their midst. . . .

Fancy, tomorrow I dine at the Embassy. They seem to have garnered up all the déclassé English headed by les Windsors – why? I dread it beyond words – Gaston made me go saying it wld look silly & uppish to refuse & I saw he was right.

I didn't really mean French papers[2] though next time on this earth I make for a French womb, straight, & no nonsense. Had a long lecture from Col today about the amount of pig *IR*ON in the USSR, & how naught can stop their coming, in the middle of which I got up to aller m'inscrire au parti communiste. Seems only sensible. He is off to your favourite town la Baule on Fri – he says it's really a working class suburb & not at all a luxury resort.

There was a lecture about England on the frog wireless last night saying il est rigoureusement défendu d'avoir (in English) a drorp of cream een yoo*rr*e tea, ce qui veut dire une goutte de crème etc & the man went on for ½ an hour about this goutte de crème, it was *very* funny. It really does all seem a little bit mad. Will the Conservatives allow cream if they come in? Are you sure I shall be allowed to have things typed in England & sent over here, by *them*? It doesn't make a pin of difference as, thank heavens, I haven't got a vote.

Much love – are you in good with Evelyn, or at least vice versa, again? Oh I *do* hope so

    NR

[1] Hon. Peter Beatty (1910–49). Son of Admiral of the Fleet Earl Beatty. Unable to face the onset of blindness, he had committed suicide.
[2] Naturalisation papers.

To Evelyn Waugh   7 rue Monsieur, VII
20 November 1949

Darling Evelyn

The boulevardier[1] is well aware of his luck & goes round boasting of it & we are all gell-gell [jealous]. I haven't read the book yet but how I long for it I shall borrow boulevardier's copy.

Prod is here & has upset me very much by saying (A) Korda has no intention of using my script & (B) Ian Fleming only asked me to write a Paris letter for *ST*[2] as a joke & has no intention of using that either. It is very discouraging. I do so hate writing as you know & really have worked hard on the film & it really will be good, but I now feel quite disinclined to go on with it.

I wonder if I told you of my long talk with the D of Windsor – the thing is I've been away for 5 days & don't remember if I wrote to you before going. I went to Tanis [Guinness] who has a Surrey stockbroker's house in Normandy, pretty in its way, & we played bridge with gramophone full blast all day till 2 every morning. I won 16 000 francs so it suited me, also it reminded me of what life in England is like, which I had almost forgotten.

I don't correspond regularly with Ed [Sackville-West] – I wrote when he became a Catholic saying it must be like having a lovely new love affair & he didn't answer, perhaps he thought it an unsuitable simile but it's what I imagine it would be like & I can't think of anything nicer. . . .

I've got 400 000 [francs] advance for my 2 books from the respectable old house of Stock, so am very delighted. Laffont wanted them but I wouldn't as they have behaved so badly to various acquaintances & I so hated the translation of *The Loved One*.

I expect you love St Helena because you know nobody else will, like me & *La Princesse de Clèves*. Are you dying for the Gide[3]–Claudel letters – they are very outspoken, the ones I have read.

Been reading a short life of Lady Dilke by Sir Chas[4] – don't love her quite as much as when I thought she was more like ONE. Alas, a reformer & a suffragette. I thought she hated Marie-Antoinette as I do for bringing all that German taste here but no it is on brioche grounds I fear. But what is remarkable, she was the friend, correspondent & admirer, pupil really, of Ruskin – I think it extraordinary that she should have become the supreme authority on 18 Cent French decoration, don't you?

I am in correspondence with her niece aged 83 who is thrilled that

I should be such a fan. Lady D died the month I was born. Hundreds of her letters are in the Bibliothèque Nationale, perfect French, & yet she never seems to have lived here for long. How annoying!

> Much love
> NR

[1] 'Tell that flower of the boulevardes Sir A. D. Cooper that in the latest P. G. Wodehouse book when Gussie Fink-Nottle is arrested for bathing in the fountain in Trafalgar Square he gives the name "Alfred Duff Cooper".' Waugh, *Letters*, p. 313.
[2] Ian Fleming's suggestion that Nancy write for the *Sunday Times* was a serious one. Her first article, 'The Pursuit of Paris', appeared on 11 December 1949. A selection of Nancy's journalism was published in *The Water Beetle* (1962), edited by Nancy Mitford, and *A Talent to Annoy* (1986), edited by Charlotte Mosley.
[3] André Gide (1869–1951). Protestant writer, winner of the Nobel Prize for Literature in 1947. A homosexual whose marriage to his first cousin Madeleine Rondeaux in 1895 was unconsummated. His books include *Les Nourritures terrestres* (1897), *Les Caves du Vatican* (1914) and *Les Faux-Monnayeurs* (1925). Gide's correspondence with Claudel, 1899–1926 (published in 1949), throws an interesting light on two very different men.
[4] Memoir of Emilia Frances Strong (1840–1904), the Victorian expert on French art, by her widower Sir Charles Wentworth Dilke.

To EVELYN WAUGH   7 rue Monsieur, VII
7 December 1949

Darling Evelyn

You are horrid. You know quite well *I* didn't say I was the m b of the y ws[1] – I was appalled by the whole thing, specially as the article is deadly beyond belief (Prod says unreadable) & I'd hoped to creep in on the woman's page unnoticed. Never mind I've found a lovely picture for it as I know you will admit – I have to provide my own ill*eo*stration what Cecil calls, it is part of the horror. Now don't let's hear any more about it please. I *must* earn money when I can – I shall never inherit any as far as I know, haven't got any except what I make, & extreme old age looms all too near. Then I shall so want a little fire & perhaps a pair of steel-rimmed specs & a molar or 2 do admit. I think of O else. It (the article) won't do anybody any harm, it can't be worse or more boring than the existing woman's page (which is all about welfare in Scandinavia if you want to know, ask Laura if it's not true) & if unreadable nobody is obliged to read it.

Do come & get some specs oh do. Prod gets his here chez les frères Lissac. Prod is a worry to me. If I were an ordinary wife I should be wheeling him up & down the Invalides in a bath chair with a white stick to show he is blind. He can hardly totter now, or see anything & he has a duodenal ulcer. He sits all day editing his poems & waiting for the end & making me cry with the récit of my sins towards him. He speaks so low now that the other evening I was twice obliged to ask whether we had just had a long speech or a long silence. I have to wear my frownies[2] all day I'm so put out by the whole thing. Last night he went round the brothels with Duff I am thankful to say, hope it cheered him up.

Fancy the Canadian reviews of *LCC* are coming in now & they are thrilled about Cedric being Canadian they can't get over the bliss of it. I'm so surprised, thought they'd be X.

Mr Binkie Beaumont[3] is said to be pleased with my adaptation of *La Petite Hutte* so you may yet see that funniest of all plays in London. Prod on the other hand read my *Princesse de Clèves* & said it is the most gruesome sort of translationese he has ever seen. This has cast me into despair because I thought it so good & so much in a way like the original. Too much, evidently. Oh alas. I see that translating is one of the most difficult of all literary exercises, I mean translating a classic. The *Hutte* was lovely because I put my own words to Roussin's heavenly situations.

Who are these Berry boys you threaten me with?[4] Don't tell me the Kemsleys have children?

Diana [Cooper] said 'can't do it, I've got to take Graham Greene's mistress to the station' or words to that effect. Has he one? Did you know? I was riveted.[5]

I've sold my books here to Stock, an old-fashioned firm, very nice people, £400. Not bad? And got it what's more. Now we are having terrible trouble with translators oh the difficulty. Luckily I am allowed to supervise.

I wonder if Prod would be happier if he were a Catholic, do have a go at him Evelyn be like Claudel with Gide.

Best love don't tease me any more & don't read the *S Times* (useless request).

NR

[1] 'I was delighted to read that "the most brilliant of the younger writers" has joined the staff of the *Sunday Times*.' Waugh, *Letters*, p. 315.

[2] Strips of tape worn on the forehead to prevent wrinkling.

[3] Hughes Griffiths Beaumont (1908–73). Theatre manager, and director of H. M. Tennent Ltd. He dominated the West End theatre for forty years.

[4] Lionel and Denis Berry were sons of Viscount Kemsley, owner of the *Sunday Times*. Waugh had written: 'Well I suppose you will have to make a Paris home for the Berry boys (Kemsley) and that will be worse than anything.' (Evelyn Waugh to NM, 5 December 1949)

[5] Graham Greene was having an affair with Catherine Crompton (1916–78), wife of Henry Walston (knighted 1961). Waugh does not answer Nancy's question. He had, however, been to stay with the Walstons the previous year and described the visit in a letter to her without mentioning the name of his hosts. (See *Letters*, pp. 283–4.)

To Evelyn Waugh   7 rue Monsieur, VII
22 December 1949

Darling Evelyn

Happy Xmas – mine will be at Chantilly where a huge party will foregather on Xmas day itself I rather dread it. The Colonel's mother is dying & he is in great despair, I don't feel very cheerful.

I dined with the Windsors. She has an erotic picture by Boucher in her bedroom of 2 Lesbians at work. I said 'oh what's that' wondering what she would say. 'Well it seems there was some old god called Neptune who could change himself into anything he liked – once he was a swan you know – & this woman liked other women so he changed himself into one.' I did love the idea of Neptune clanking out of the sea covered with coquillages – maddening for Jupiter. I do hate that Duchess – but I love him. He said 'Did you read the life of my father by John Gore?[1] It was terribly dull.'

N: 'Well why did they give it to him?'

'Shall I tell you why? Because he's CHEAP. My family always do everything on the CHEAP you know.'

He's rather like Alf Beit, knows hundreds of facts. Somebody mentioned the duc de Berry. 'Murdered in 1824'[2] he said at once.

'Not very nice what that boy wrote about my grandfather & Xopher Sykes[3] – who are these Sykeses, do you know them?'

'Well,' I said, 'there was Sir Tatton –'

'Tatton. Yorkshire name. Shall I tell you how I know that? I was in the Navy with Commander Bower & his second name is Tatton. That was in 1909. I've worn the King's uniform for 40 years off & on.'

I don't know why I arranged the *S Times* articles without Peters[4] I was mesmerized by handsome Mr Fleming. Anyway as I haven't a contract or been paid anything it may not be too late & I've written to ask. Oh Prod. I feel in despair about him, he's got such expensive tastes.

V best love
    NR

[1] John Gore, *King George V. A Personal Memoir* (1941).
[2] In fact, assassinated in 1820.
[3] In *Four Studies in Loyalty* Christopher Sykes describes how his great-uncle's financial ruin was brought about by lavish entertaining of the Prince of Wales (Edward VII).
[4] Augustus Detlof Peters (1892–1973). Literary agent. Nancy took him on in June 1949 and his agency continues to handle her estate today. Peters negotiated energetically on Nancy's behalf and, being unbusinesslike, she was delighted to have his help; but they never became close friends, unlike Waugh whose agent he was also.

1950–1954

FRENCH LADY WRITER

> The day one sets foot in France, you can take it from me, PURE happiness begins . . . Of course I know it's partly that dear dear Colonel, but I don't see him all the time by any means & every minute of the day here is bliss & when I wake up in the morning I feel as excited as if it were my birthday.
>
> NM to Evelyn Waugh, 16 January 1952

DURING THE 1950s Nancy was at the height of her success. *The Blessing* was published to mixed reviews but was admired by her two literary advisers: Evelyn Waugh, to whom it was dedicated, and Raymond Mortimer. Praise for it came from such diverse sources as Arthur Koestler and Edward Sackville-West. Her adaptation of *The Little Hut* gave her great amusement and considerably increased her income. For Nancy's literary career, *Madame de Pompadour* was her most important book of the decade. In turning to history she found a new outlet for her talents. Plots had always been her greatest difficulty and the French eighteenth-century court provided a limitless cast of characters with whom she could readily identify, against a background she looked upon as the peak of human civilisation. Her four historical biographies are eminently readable since she had the gift of being able to assimilate a mass of indigestible historical facts and serve them up as a frothy, appetising and palatable dish. When historians accused her of writing books that read like 'further adventures of the Mitford family', she retorted: 'Very true, all history is subjective and these pompous historians describe their own families and that's how they manage to make them so dull.' Although she often complained of a

Pension Maintenon rue du p. Lebrun   Versailles   S&O

(7 Rue Monsieur VII)
(Suffren 7655)   27 Avril 53

Darling   How about the poor Doctor's wife?

If I don't write at once I never will so here goes
I really am working – 2 or 3 hours in the library here
& until midnight in my bed, & most of the day –
7 or 8 hours. Evelyn (who came to see me) says
its too much, one shouldn't do more than 4, but
it suits me. Everybody has their own system. The
library is bliss, they have of course everything & all
by round ONE, very different from B.M. or Nationale
I wish now I had it jacked out & to go to join L.L.
induced by Raymond. (Do tell Tashe is if you hear again)

I've got a letter from Binkie Beaumont saying I
must go to N york, everything paid, with the Hut. Goodness!
He says speaks as if it would make all the difference
if I went – how green – as I said Shakespeare & O
Wilde don't go & yet their plays run. I don't think I
can ginger myself up to it, really, all alone like that
What do you advise? Its not till Oct.

To Violet Hammersley, 27 April 1953

lack of method (her mother's fault, again), she was painstaking in her research and cannot be faulted on grounds of accuracy.

Nancy's passion for Paris remained one of her most positive pleasures. In a foreign city, her inclination to disregard anything that did not conform to her ideal was easier to sustain, and the refined veneer of sophistication in the smart, intellectual, brittle Parisian society in which she moved was one that suited her well. Of the French she wrote to Evelyn Waugh: 'They *seem*, which is all that matters, to love one so much.' The frustration of her relationship with the Colonel was eased by her literary success, by her popularity, and by her many friends. Like an eighteenth-century chatelaine in the days of the Grand Tour, she made her flat an obligatory staging-post for visitors from England.

The obverse of Nancy's passion for France was her growing distance from England. It was as though she could not combine loyalties to two such different countries and had to decide in favour of one or the other. In Lady Pamela Berry, who was at the centre of political and literary London, she found a perfect recipient for her teasing and exaggerated attacks on England.

In the early 1950s Nancy's sister Diana settled in Orsay, twenty miles from Paris. Since they spoke every morning on the telephone, their letters became less frequent. Nancy disliked all her brothers-in-law ('Why will one's sisters marry these sewers?') and Sir Oswald Mosley, or Sir Ogre as she called him, was no exception. None of her brothers-in-law liked Nancy any better than she liked them, but Nancy could not do without Diana's company and she was a regular guest at the Mosleys' house.

Nancy's best and funniest letters during this period were to Evelyn Waugh. He was never in love with her but held her in deep affection and, despite his sometimes acerbic criticisms, admired her books. In many ways a correspondence suited their friendship better than actually seeing one another. When they did meet, Nancy found Waugh's discontent and rudeness difficult to deal with, while he was irritated by her determination to see everything French through rose-coloured spectacles. Though their meetings often ended on the brink of a quarrel, an exchange of letters introduced an insulating layer between these two prickly characters and inspired some of their best writing. Waugh's greater intellect and the anchor of his Catholic faith restrained Nancy's frivolity, while her teasing and enthusiasm leavened his tendency to misanthropic bitterness. Their correspondence is among the most amusing in twentieth-century letters. Nancy considered Waugh

a great letter-writer, 'in the class of Voltaire'. More than half her
three hundred letters to him were written during the 1950s; the
selection has had to be limited owing to the number of Waugh's letters
that would need to be quoted in full for Nancy's to be adequately
explained.

To Evelyn Waugh   7 rue Monsieur, VII
7 January 1950

Darling Evelyn

Well I drew a veil over Xmas at Chantilly, having blotted my copy book by inviting my really impossible friend M. de Polnay[1] for the day. There was a huge party, 26 for luncheon 26 after (& whisky flowing) & I wrongly thought he would be intimidated by all these *excellences* & high class writers & Dukes & things but no. He got drunker than anything I ever saw & Duff was X though is it for Duff to be X about drunkenness? (I enclose a photograph[2] & you are not to say you have seen it as it's really very disloyal of me to send it – loyal to you however.) Well then I was intensely embarrassed so retired to my bedroom with 3 others & played bridge. Honks [Cooper] was X, everybody was X, & I don't think they've forgiven me & indeed I see the point. When I scolded M. de P. after, all he said was 'I didn't break a *thing*' in tones of genuine surprise.

Thank you for your letter about Smith I agree with every word. Mr Hardy[3] reminds me in one way so much of Prod, that is, whereas in human disagreements & quarrels it is fair to assume that it's 6 of one & ½ doz of the other, he & Prod both always insist that they were 100% in the right. Prod now lays *all* his failure in life like an enormous baby at my door, & though I must obviously have some responsibility for it, I refuse to admit the whole. Smith certainly succeeded in teaching G.H. to write – to his own undoing poor old man.

Now you must read Queensberry's *Wilde & Douglas*[4] – another stunning account of a relationship & curiously enough the best of all the many books on Wilde *I* think. After prison he reminds me so much of poor Bobo when she got back from Germany – in so many little ways. Oh dear how sad. And Q. *so much* like my father. I was riveted by it.

Lovely party last night for the fête des rois, a ball at Marie-Laure de Noailles' at which all the guests wore crowns. It was too pretty – in her beautiful house like a museum. The 3rd party in a week, too much for me.

I have translated (adapted really) a very funny play called *La Petite Hutte* for Mr Binkie Beaumont & he is pleased. I'm so excited, wouldn't it be fun to have a play put on. The author who is a great love doesn't know any English at all so I've got away with all my own jokes & dialogue & just kept his situations which are heaven. I now long to write a play myself.

Dull letter I fear – do write, I live for yours.

All love & to Laura
      NR

[1] Peter de Polnay (1906–84). Hungarian-born author of some sixty works of fiction and non-fiction, few of which met with any great commercial success. Nancy was a faithful friend to him and his wife and helped them financially to educate their son. 'My exuberant friend I sometimes hate & sometimes love.' (NM to Violet Hammersley, 9 November 1949)
[2] Of Duff Cooper.
[3] Waugh had reviewed *Logan Pearsall Smith: The Story of a Friendship* (1949) by Robert Gathorne-Hardy, and found it 'full of unconscious and conscious dishonesties'. Gathorne-Hardy was Pearsall Smith's secretary and presumed heir, but under the terms of his will he received only some books and pictures while the residue was left to the art critic John Russell.
[4] Francis A. K. Douglas, Marquess of Queensberry, *Oscar Wilde and the Black Douglas* (1949).

To DIANA MOSLEY   7 rue Monsieur, VII
11 January 1950

Darling

. . . Prod is making my life hell. Our money can be transferred only through his bank, & we get it in Nov: so I had carefully budgeted till then – darling he still hasn't sent me any though I've given him £600. What I suppose is that it has gone down the drain of his overdraft. He doesn't answer letters or show any sign of life. It is really impossible to go on like this. I've now written to our solicitor but don't really see what he can do about it – I'm in an utter cleft stick – meanwhile fearfully low in funds – though I have some gold as you know & can sell that if in straits. If only he would allow us to be divorced, but I can see he never will & when I did raise the question a year ago talked of divorcing me which of course I can't have. I don't think he is méchant [ill-intentioned] you know but he lives in a cloud of unreality. I've said over & over again I'll pay the overdraft if only he'll send some money here, he simply doesn't answer. Now he talks of standing for Parliament which of course would fix me for ever vis-à-vis income tax. I feel very low altogether I must say, it is dreadful being in the power of such an enfant terrible & I am in his power financially in spite of the money having been earned by me. As he is always in England (though by way of hating it) I think there's but little chance of me being considered a foreign resident & it looks as if I shall have to pay full taxes on what I have earned. Alas I don't earn much in

America, & that little is halved, 15% agent & 30% tax. I've got about £1000 there now, net.

What a wail, but really you know I can't sleep for worrying, & look at it how one may there doesn't seem to be any possible way out. . . .

    All love
       NR

To Evelyn Waugh   7 rue Monsieur, VII
13 January 1950

Darling Evelyn

Well the Lesbians.[1] Not yours. No *robe* anywhere in sight, just a lovely huge fair fat lady lying on top of another & various cupids hovering about. Much more like Fragonard than Boucher I thought. Very beautiful, I was gell-gell.

No I am not a Nazi & don't believe in doing away with unhappy people – in fact now that I am happy myself I don't believe in suicide any more. Oh dear, Prod. Yes all you say is true, but can it be my fault?[2] I feel it must be partly, though last time he was here he said that for the last 12 years he has considered himself as married to Adelaide [Lubbock] which seemed to let me out & was a great relief to me.

I think you ought to read the correspondence of Claudel & Gide. It is easy, classical French & full of things that would interest you & is an account really of Claudel's 24 years' struggle for the soul of Gide. They haven't spared their punches, either of them.

How awful about the overdraft. I expect you are having the sort of financial crisis Farve used to have periodically which generally resulted in giving up one Sunday paper & bronco instead of bromo. But to arrive at that the grown ups used to be closeted for hours with & without hommes d'affaires. If it's any consolation to you it never made a pin of difference, though the worry seemed to be appalling at the time & went on being appalling for months.

About the French words in my article – I'm glad you approve. What you say was just what I'd figured out.[3] My fan mail very funny. 18 people have sent labels to show that Philippe R[othschild] has labelled his bottles like that for 20 years, one writes to ask which year Mary Russell Mitford was born & another 'sweet of you to say the parties break up for the Mass – in my hotel I was kept awake *all night* without any break at all'. Must I answer them? I *can't*.

Can't you import wine through Berry Bros? How do people lay down cellars nowadays? I think one is allowed 12 bottles in one's luggage (tho' I don't know why I think it) but they make you pay on every drop. I sometimes bring brandy for Handy.[4]

Here is the catalogue in case you'd like to have it – I've got two copies. The stuff does seem cheap to me.

The weather here is like a gentle March, heavenly I think, but you know how much I hate the cold.

All love
        NR

P.S. M. Dior is going to Rome to see the Pope. Holy Year is thus brought home to us all.

[1] Waugh had asked for further details about the Duchess of Windsor's painting by Boucher.

[2] Waugh had seen Peter Rodd and wrote to Nancy: 'Nothing you told me prepared me for the truth. He had locomotor ataxia and a waistcoat made of an old rug . . . If it were not for his socialism I should have great compassion for him. I thought people like you & he believed in putting the decrepit into gas chambers.' *Letters*, pp. 318–19.

[3] Waugh commented on Nancy's article, 'Paris Windfall' (*Sunday Times*, 8 January 1950): 'An excellent feature of your articles is the French. What the English like are phrases of which they easily understand the literal meaning, if possible with words that look just like English words, and have quaintness & drollness.' *Letters*, p. 319.

[4] Handasyde Buchanan (d. 1984). Joined Heywood Hill in 1945, became a partner in 1953, and retired in 1974. Married Mollie Friese-Greene in 1949. 'I always think Handy is like a villain in a Dickens novel, his heart is obviously *ink* under a certain sinister veneer of charm. I love the old creature but one has to see human beings as they are.' (NM to Heywood Hill, 2 December 1964)

To Lady Redesdale   7 rue Monsieur, VII
14 January 1950

Darling Muv

Could you without too much trouble order me some of the printed paper you speak of, & postcards? And tell them to send the bill? It would be a *great* kindness. For fan mail etc ideal. . . .

About O Wilde. The fairy stories are delightful & *Earnest* is a classic & terribly funny on the stage, I've never read it. A part cela, his genius certainly went into his life, conversation & so on & that is what gives him an aura which is hard to analyse. Just as with Dolly Wilde, & just the reverse of the case of Proust, *his* genius all went into his oeuvre & his letters are deadly dull & so, I feel, was his presence. I thought, reading between the lines in Q's book, that he really *hates* A Douglas for having, as he explains, ruined his family. But the Douglases are pourriture, all except Cathleen's daughter who is, it seems, a saint & has married a clergyman! My old father in law, a terrible prig, knew Wilde well (& pretended that he knew nothing of les moeurs which I don't believe) but said nobody has ever been so brilliant in the world. Of course that was it. Of course another thing is, nearly all clever men are pederasts & they all hang together & regard Wilde as a sort of martyr for the cause! . . .

All love
    NR

To Evelyn Waugh   7 rue Monsieur, VII
19 January 1950

Darling Evelyn

You are *not* repeat *not* to show the photograph of Sir Alf[1] to anybody at all – it was most disloyal of me to send it & I've regretted doing so ever since.

Do try & be noble, like Claudel. Oh the letters, I've lived in them – I think you could read them all right, it is a simple, classical French, & it seems to me that for a Roman Catholic they are indispensable. The day when Claudel, from one short passage in *Les Caves du Vatican*, realizes that Gide is a pederast he writes a letter which made my blood run cold, I can't think how Gide could have read it. Instead of cher ami he starts 'au nom du ciel, Gide –'

Before this the correspondence was loving & they were wonderful to each other, such admiration of the other's works & such mutual help (Gide correcting Claudel's proofs when he was in Japan etc). Claudel of course wanted to convert Gide & very nearly succeeded & his letters on the duty of Catholics are tremendous – he says it is *everybody's plain* duty to be a saint. He is so great that he dwarfs the fascinating Gide I must say completely, though there is nothing petty about Gide, no taking offence (even when C. writes behind his back to his wife). When the storm has broken Claudel begs Gide to see a charming priest who lives at Clichy – Francis Jammes[2] begs him to see another at Passy (do try my dentist) & Gide does so, but notes in his journal 'it will take more than these priests to turn me into a père de famille'.

Poor Mme Gide. He says he loves her more than life itself but can't go to bed with her. But she is no Jane Carlyle – they are all so *noble* in this story. Can you tell me what Claudel was converted from? Gide says Claudel overpowers me – he has more money more health more genius more faith & more children than I –

Claudel says: 'Il y a une police nécessaire contre les empoisonneurs.' They haven't met since 1926.

Did you see Honks Cooper's advert for a lady gardener? Well, after a hundred letters, one saying I turned an Indian jungle into a glorious English garden with sweet peas, she has chosen one. I can't but feel it will end in tears, but we shall see.

The *Sunday Times* like my piece & would like it more often, but I've refused. It wouldn't be so good & would stop me writing anything else. I've told the publishers to send you my *Princesse de Clèves*, it is supposed to be out next month – I'd be very glad to know what you feel about it. Prod says it's the most awful translationese he ever read – very hard to avoid in a classic where every meaning *must* be reproduced. After that I've been thinking a great deal about language & came upon a Penguin Conrad. Well in a way he writes in translationese – it's not like the writing of an English person is it & that's what gives it such freshness & colour I believe. I've begged the 2 people who are translating my books to re-write whenever they feel like it, specially the dialogue, & you can do that when the author is alive & consenting, but *I* can't do it to poor Mme de Lafayette, clearly. Claudel has some very interesting things to say about translating English & French but I didn't understand it all because I don't know the terms of grammar – I literally don't know what subjunctive for instance means. Is it too late to learn? If not is there some easy book that would tell me? Oh *can* I be bothered? The horror of not having been educated when young.

Please excuse this long letter. Korda is still sitting on my story (to the consternation of Mr Peters, I seem to have committed an arch folly in sending it) so I've no work at present. Claudel–Gide make everything else seem such small beer that I can't settle down to a nice book –!

All love
    Nancy

[1] Waugh had threatened to take the photograph Nancy had sent of Duff Cooper to White's, 'when I next visit that nest of vipers'. He eventually sent it to Cyril Connolly.
[2] Francis Jammes (1868–1938). Catholic poet. Author of *Les Géorgiques chrétiennes* (1912) and *Le Livre de saint Joseph* (1933).

To Diana Mosley   7 rue Monsieur, VII
10 February 1950

Darling
   . . . I don't really think of becoming a Catholic.[1] I believe in God
& always feel I'm on very good terms with him & when people say
'yes my son has entered la Trappe & in a few years he will be talking
with God as I am talking with you' I always think, though don't say,
well I continually talk with God without going into la Trappe. I suppose
Evelyn would say I shall burn for thousands of years for such presump-
tion – we shall see. What I do feel is, if you are a Catholic then you
must be a whole hogger like Claudel & Evelyn & not half & half like
Jim Lees-Milne, for instance. . . .
   I believe Farve will be in London, too lucky. Do make Muv give a
dinner for me on Monday 20th or Tues 21st or both. I've definitely
taken a room at the Hyde Park.
   I thought the *Old Room*[2] awfully good. I even thought all the bits
about Polnay helped to make a picture of the whole FitzGerald set up
that one won't forget, though I agree that individual passages are
maddening.
   Off to lunch with Dolly for the Warrenders[3] (forget his new name)
I can hardly bear it, she made me. . . .

   All love
      NR

Must return here 27th –

[1] Nancy had mentioned the Gide–Claudel correspondence in a *Sunday Times* article,
which prompted Diana to write: 'Your article on Sunday so good . . . Are you going
to become a Catholic? I have a sort of Ahnung [presentiment] about it but perhaps I
am wrong.' (7 February 1950)
[2] Peter de Polnay, *Into an Old Room: The Paradox of Edward FitzGerald* (1950).
[3] Sir Victor Warrender (1899–1993). Created 1st Baron Bruntisfield in 1942. Married
to Dorothy Rawson 1920–45 and to Tania Kolin in 1948.

To Gaston Palewski   Hyde Park Hotel
21 February 1950   London, SW1

Dear dearest
   Oh the French pictures[1] are such a mimic [*sic*] oh you should come
over. And what I loved even more, being me, 4 Louis XIV busts of
him, Henri II, Turenne & the Grand Condé, in bronze with armour

in bronze doré, on Boulle pedestals, belonging to Wellington (loot of course). 'Ah – h – h.'

The pictures are chiefly the Claude, Poussin, H Robert & one or 2 Watteau & Fragonard. The others aren't the very best of their kind, but the Claudes I've never seen surpassed.

Momo is a lady[2] & they had a cocktail party of generals to celebrate. Well these gens were all the young men I used to dance with at 18 & chucked for aesthetes at 19, & haven't seen since, so of course they were thrilled to see me so famous & wicked. . . .

Korda doesn't like the film he says it's too sophisticated. Far from being a blow this is a great relief to me, now I can settle down & make it into a novel[3] & not always be thinking of the camera. And novels make far more money.

The *Hutte* has been announced as a forthcoming production & Mr Beaumont aux petits soins, great bouquets of flowers, his secretary ringing up to ask if there was any play I'd like seats for & so on, very nice.

Pam [Berry]'s party consists of 2000 people. I'm dining first with the Rothermeres & they have a party the next day, for the last of the results.

I've got you a nice little case – oh I do hope you'll like it. You wouldn't like glass (18 cent. Waterford) candlesticks? *'No.'*

Goodnight dearest
    NR

[1] 'Landscape in French Art 1550–1900' at the Royal Academy.
[2] Major-General John Marriott had been awarded the K C V O.
[3] Nancy reworked her film treatment into *The Blessing* (1951). A film was later made of her novel.

To Violet Hammersley   7 rue Monsieur, VII
2 March 1950

Darling

I am terribly sorry – truly, wicked though I may be – over all your troubles which are all REAL. When I am wicked is when you make a burden of owning large & beautiful houses in Chelsea which others would be glad of, etc! . . .

I'm busier than I can say, writing over the play against time. Mr Peter Brook,[1] the intensely brilliant young (25) producer came here & we went over it together in detail for 3 days. He has gone to Spain

& it must be all ready & typed for him on his return 1 May, after which I gather they hope soon to go into rehearsal & it is supposed to come on in June. Then they want me to go on tour with it – all great fun I think as it will only go to Edinburgh & Brighton both of which are fairly comfortable.

I love Mr Brook, he is strongly reminiscent of John Sutro, & is one of the cleverest people I've ever met also knows perfect French which is a great help in this. . . .

I sent Gide–Claudel to Muv, or rather Heywood did, by mistake really. However she has read it carefully & pronounced herself entirely on Gide's side – 'That *awful* Claudel, going on like that.' Isn't she drôle.

Not much news. I have been absorbed in these theatrical friends, the powerful Mr Beaumont came over to see me & also Noel C. I must say it all amuses me & they are all so very nice & very buttering up about what I've done. The salon is a bower of lovely blooms.

Best love & don't be cross if I don't write again at once I am truly very busy.

NR

. . .

[1] Peter Brook (1925–). Theatre and film director. Director of Productions at Covent Garden Opera House 1947–50. Producer and co-director of Royal Shakespeare Company, Stratford-upon-Avon. Settled in Paris in the early 1970s to work with a cast of actors from all over the world. Inaugurated his theatre, the Bouffes du Nord, in 1974. 'Peter Brook is an angel & a human being & saves my life.' (NM to Heywood Hill, 20 July 1950)

TO LADY REDESDALE   7 rue Monsieur, VII
28 March 1950

Darling Muv

To say I screamed at your letter would put it mildly, I must admit the idea of you being entirely on Gide's side is the funniest thing I ever heard in a long life. Well I have no moral feelings, specially, about all that, but *I* couldn't help being on Claudel's side for his strength, single mindedness & the beautiful French he writes.

I've been rather unfaithful I fear about letters but am so busy. The flood of English arrivals has begun, all expecting ONE to get them rooms which is more impossible than ever – this morning I trailed round to 6 hotels with no results & the Ritz is said to be full till October. Good trade for the French, but a bore for me.

Yes the Barons Redé[1] & Redesdale have but little in common. Redé is suspected of being R*ae*der in truth, though he *says* he is Baltic, & has been called in *Samedi Soir* La Pompadour de nos jours. He lives but for luxury, beauty & social life – a less lively Cedric. He looks like a tie pin, thin, stiff & correct with a weeny immovable head on a long stiff neck. Not bad, though I prefer his patron, a fat jolly Chilean called Lopez[2] whom I can't but love on account of his collection of Louis XIV silver.

A Lt Colonel writes asking if I know what sewer really means to which I reply that as the daughter of a tea planter I *do*.[3]

Next Sunday's article is partly about Farve & Pierre Loti as you will see if they don't cut it.

I positively dread the arrival of Decca as I'm sure she has turned into one of those puritanical Communists & if so I can't bear it, remembering what *bliss* she was. Will they ever be allowed back into America d'you think?

I saw the Duke of Rutland, off to Debo yesterday, I felt quite envious. But here it is like May, I sit out all day, not the time of year to exchange for the Irish climate I feel.

I've bought a beautiful table de salon from which 6 can eat, a thing I've been looking for for months. Terribly pleased with it.

No news as you observe. My 2 books have been translated into French & *Pursuit* comes out in June – a great success is predicted for it.

All love
    NR

[1] Baron Alexis de Redé (1922–). Son of Oscar Adolf Rosenberg, an Austrian Jewish banker ennobled by the Emperor Francis Joseph in 1916. Described by Chips Channon as 'the Eugène Rastignac of modern Paris'. He lived in the Hôtel Lambert on the tip of the Ile St Louis, one of the most beautiful houses in Paris.
[2] Arturo Lopez-Willshaw (1900–62). Conspicuous member of the *tout-Paris* who entertained on a grand scale at his house in Neuilly. Famous for his collection of furniture and precious objects. Preferred men, but married his cousin Patricia Lopez de Huici.
[3] Uncle Matthew's favourite term of abuse was 'damned sewer'. It had nothing to do with drains; 'suar' means 'pig' in Hindustani and was a word learned by Lord Redesdale in Ceylon, where he worked as a tea planter after leaving school.

To Raymond Mortimer   7 rue Monsieur, VII
5 May 1950

Dearest Raymond

Thank you so much for your letter, you are not nearly as 'terrible pour moi' as Evelyn.[1] The thing about semi colons etc is I can't burden busy writers like you & Evelyn with horrid old typescripts & however much you both angelically say do I *couldn't*. So I must find some; expert whom I could pay to do it for me. It won't arise again for ages however. Oh I am so overdone, it's trying to combine work & clothes & going out & English visitors & I quite see why it is that elderly writers get bad tempered – yesterday I really longed for the H bomb so terrible became my hatred of the human race. However a *very* smart dinner party in one of the most beautiful of all the houses here (Anne di Amodio née la Rochefoucauld) put me back in a fairly good temper again – such objets de musée on every hand, such food & such Dior dresses on such pretty silly ladies.

Now about the VISIT. I think of O else, but must just wait & see when the *Petite Hutte* goes into rehearsal because they seem to say I must be there & you know how I can't leave Paris for too long ever for fear it should melt away while my back is turned. I would love to come early in June if that suited all of you, but will know for certain next week when Peter Brook has seen powerful Binkie.

Oh *Kon Tiki*,[2] how I lived in it, got it on the strength of your review.

    Much love to all
       NR

I never told you – Vi [Trefusis] said 'you know Raymond was once rather in love with me' to which I replied 'Oh I *know*, FEARFULLY, he's OFTEN said so to me.' Whereupon she nearly fell off her chair with surprise & amazement & excitement & thrilling new ideas. So it's my new technique with her.

[1] Waugh: 'The punctuation is pitiable but it never becomes unintelligible so I just shouldn't try. It is clearly not your subject – like theology.' *Letters*, p. 286.
[2] Thor Heyerdahl, *The Kon-Tiki Expedition. By Raft Across the South Seas* (1950).

To Lady Redesdale   7 rue Monsieur, VII
8 May 1950

Darling Muv

Millions of happy returns – fancy 70. You are so lucky, not one
grey hair. I saw a lady wrote to the papers who was married in
1880 & what a terrible snow storm there was, did you see? I was
impressed.

So glad you'll be in London, more jolly really for such an anniversary
though I don't regard 70 as such a landmark as, for instance 30. The
Marquise d'Harcourt was 100 this month. She said to her daughter
'what *are* pederasts?' 'Oh mother I really can't tell you.' 'If you can't
tell me when I'm 100 when can you tell me?' She was ordering a
dress for the birthday party & said to the dressmaker 'I expect *my*
clothes to last quite 10 years.'

. . . Do go to Heywood & take 3 or 4 books, as a birthday present,
for island reading – please do, otherwise I can't give you anything for
such an age.

I've been awful about writing but so busy you know & I have such
thousands of boring letters to answer daily – Johnny Drury-Lowe
saying he will be in Paris, you know the sort of thing, as well as fan
letters still, often 2 or 3 a day.

If people *knew*. However I suppose it's better than being the kind
of writer who has none!

   Much love & kisses
        NR

Summer at last here.

To Lady Pamela Berry   7 rue Monsieur, VII
17 May 1950

Darling Pam

. . . I do *die* for the christening. My plans entirely depend on Mr
Binkie & the play which may come on June or July. As soon as it is
launched I plan to go to Taormina where Fulco[1] has invited me – he
is my great new friend – & to my darling Dolly R at Marseilles, &
get a little bit boiled up.

I love the picture of you in bed reading about bulls. Seeing nobody
of course. Do you know Peter Brook? He was terribly funny about
Spain, said everything is so badly produced & they ought to hire him

for a year or 2. Everybody I know here has been in Spain this year, Spain & Rome.

So I had Evelyn from Friday morning to Monday & still love him though at one point I felt obliged to ask how he reconciles being so horrible with being a Christian. He replied rather sadly that were he not a Christian he would be even more horrible (difficult) & anyway would have committed suicide years ago. I took him to see Marie-Laure [de Noailles] & he said afterwards 'While I was looking at that lady's pictures I found a Picasso so I've hidden it. They won't find it again for months I hope.' He really *is* a leetle beet mad isn't he. What's so dreadful about Evelyn is his snobbishness. He met my publisher, a charming middle class Frenchman, & was so dreadful to him I had to apologise, to the publisher. Then he met Prince Paul of Yugoslavia who is *exactly* the same *kind* of person, rather wet, full of culture, & oh the difference 'twas to me so to speak. Not quite right, is it? I said 'do you never think to yourself "here is another human soul struggling, as I am, to the light?"' But he didn't seem to say he did. Never mind.

I must get up. I've found a wonderful birthday pres for the Col, a clock signed by Thomire for nearly nothing so am off to see about it. He sends you his love by the way.

Fond love
    NR

. . .

[1] Fulco Santostefano della Cerda, Duke of Verdura (1898–1978). Jeweller. Trained with Chanel before setting up his own business in New York in 1939. Author of an autobiography, *The Happy Summer Days: A Sicilian Childhood* (1976).

To EVELYN WAUGH   7 rue Monsieur, VII
22 May 1950

Darling Evelyn

I enjoyed your visit terrifically though of course the responsibility harrowed me & so did the fact that for some reason Xopher [Sykes] got a very much better lunchyon (as Col calls it) here than you did & of course shovelled it in without noticing what loovely stoof it was. The food here is really outside my control on account of Marie being a saint.

A letter from my Dad, to whom I write saying if you don't hear from me as often as you ought to it's because I have such a mass of writing. He says yes *don't* people write a lot of meaningless letters I can't think how they can afford it I can only imagine they must steal stamps from their servants. Quite a new idea to me.

I see why mediatized is grand. It is far grander to come down in the world than to go up (nouveau riche, nouvelle noblesse etc) isn't it.

Who is Emily Post[1] please? The *NS & N* says I am the modern she.

Are you *loving Nothing*?[2] I am. But R Macaulay[3] is miserably bad.

I didn't tell you – when I apologized to Dolly R for my country clothes she said 'mais chérie, il n'y a qu'une chose détestable, c'est une demie-toilette' (meaning a quick change without a bath) 'et on peut être décoiffée, mais pas mal coiffée.' Isn't she bliss. So all was well.

I shan't be able to write for an age which is why I seize my pen at once. Tomorrow 40 intellectuals here to meet the H[amish] Hamiltons – then Peter Brook & Robert Morley[4] to talk about the play, then Debo & Mr Peters together, oh my *life*.

Are you noticing the perfect style & syntax of this letter?

I had a long talk with Col, who *loves* you by the way, about the people you hate. He says you only like first class people. Well it's not enough, that's all, though possibly flattering to ONE to think it.

I have been asked, with several Cedrics, to a dinner for Sumner Welles.[5] Momo & Susan Mary Patten can *hardly* bear it – so *unsuitable* they keep wailing & echoes of the wails have come back to me, greatly to my delight. I do love doing serious ladies in the eye.

Well dearest goodbye.

Love to Laura – hope she's better, do say.

Love
   NR

[1] 'Emily Post is not a very gratifying comparison. She was the great American authority on etiquette and a very bad authority too.' Waugh, *Letters*, p. 326.

[2] Henry Green, *Nothing* (1950).

[3] Rose Macaulay, *The World My Wilderness* (1950). A novel.

[4] Robert Morley (1908–92). 'He's the only actor I've ever met who is a human being.' (NM to Jessica Treuhaft, 10 September 1965)

[5] Sumner Welles (1892–1961). American diplomat and politician. Under-Secretary of State 1937–43.

To Lady Redesdale   7 rue Monsieur, VII
24 May 1950

Darling Muv

Oh dear I've been doing my twice yearly accounts how you would laugh or perhaps cry. It consists of writing down sums, compiled from memory, or my engagement book, on bits of paper I pick up as I go along (cocktail invitations & so on) & then adding them up – even I can see it's generally wrong – or subtracting them. Yesterday I got £800 on the back of Hoytie Wiborg[1] & at the end had forgotten if it was coming or going so to speak, & indeed what it meant at all! The inescapable fact seems to be that for 5 years I've been spending £2000 a year & all my savings have gone. I haven't yet paid any tax, if I have to I am more or less done for. Anyway I can't count on making £2000 a year, no writer can, so I must cut down but HOW? If I knew where the money *went*, that's what I can't find out & the little sums I write down don't add up to anything like that so where *does* it go? Anyway it's gone. Anyway I've got no debts, unless to Inland Revenue, which is one comfort.

Now all depends on the *Hut*. I'm told everybody to do with it in London is borrowing money on its success which is thought to be certain, but plays never are certain of course.

How *can* one live more cheaply than in 2 rooms with one servant, no motor, never travelling, & entertaining most moderately (though continually, I have had more than 100 people for meals since 1st Jan). Isn't it a worry – I had a fainting fit at the end of the morning from the worry. I do know I have spent over 500 a year on clothes, & that I *am* being drastic about, so much that I've no evening dress at all & have refused every evening invitation this summer on that account – not that I mind, specially. It must be remembered that when I came here after the war I had to get every single thing new after 5 years of buying nothing at all & now I've a lot of fat to live on.

Pursuit did better because I sold it 3500 to films, 1000 reprint society & 1200 serial rights. *LCC* has actually sold much more in the time, but didn't get these extras.

Well this *is* a deadly letter, but who can I wail to if not you?

I had a lovely party yesterday for French publishers to meet H. Hamilton – 40 of them. He couldn't get over it – said if anybody got 40 English publishers in one room there would be a pitched battle. On the contrary this went with a swing & they stayed from 6 till ¼ to 9!! . . .

V. best love
    NR

When does Wid go to you?
No need for worry actually this minute unless In: Rev: want thousands
as I have about 6000 in hand (Farve gave me 5 as you know) but I
must take a pull, but how??? I've just seen P de Polnay who said
'Hamilton is terribly worried about you.' My heart went into my boots.
'Yes, he's afraid you'll make so much over this play that you'll never
write another novel.' If it's only that!!

   What I need is some really good homme d'affaires to control me
but where to find him unless I marry some bore with that end in
view!! I believe that's what Colette did.
P.S. Your local Duke[2] has just eloped with old Margaret Sweeny, can
you beat it?

[1] Mary Hoyt Wiborg (d.1964). Expatriate daughter of Cincinnati ink baron Frank B.
Wiborg. Lived in Quai Conti in Paris where she gave many parties. Well-known for
her social aspirations and her preference for women.
[2] The 11th Duke of Argyll married Margaret Sweeny on 22 March 1951; they were
divorced in 1963.

To BERNARD MINORET[1]   Redesdale Cottage
9 August 1950   Otterburn

Dear Bernard (if I may call you that)
   I loved getting your letter which I ought to have answered ages
ago but you don't know how busy I have been.
   I'm in the middle of a tour of the great industrial towns, with Roussin's play & have taken a few days off to stay with my father before
going on to Newcastle. . . .
   Touring with a play is new to me & very fascinating. I re-write
large chunks of it in the morning, see them rehearsed every afternoon
& then watch how the audience takes it as compared with the old
version. Then there are the actors to cope with – terrible. Any good
line they have to say is 'my good line' – anything rather poor is 'that's
a very flat line of yours, darling' (to me!) I never knew such people
– *very* friendly & nice however. We open in London in a fortnight –
Roussin joins us at Leeds. I'm a tiny bit nervous of what he will say
to all the many alterations but I guess so long as it goes well & makes
money he won't mind. I never think people's artistic consciences
extend to translations!

I envy you the Midi, terribly, & long for some sun. Don't know when I shall be back in Paris. Do write again if you have the time to 10 Curzon Street W.1., they forward my mail from there.

Yrs ever
    Nancy

---

[1] Bernard Minoret (1928–). French playwright, novelist and wit. Co-author, with Philippe Jullian, of *Les Morot-Chandonneur*, the saga of a grand French family, in which each chapter parodies the style of a famous author.

To EVELYN WAUGH   Redesdale Cottage
9 August 1950   Otterburn

Darling Evelyn
    I'm in bed with no writing paper so you must lump this.
    Here with my dad, in a tiny cottage stuffed with old masters between which hang oil paintings by a local lesbian of my dad's Staffordshire terriers. It's on a beautiful moor, the cottage, an oasis from these huge industrial towns whose station hotels are now my home. I leave for Newcastle this afternoon alas. Well you know what it's like from your lectures, but I shall have had a solid month of it, except for 3 days here. I am letting off steam in a *Sunday Times* article on *Britain*.[1] . . .
    Shall I see you in London? I'll be there from 20th–about 1st Sept, staying with Mark O.G. at Kew. 10 Curzon are supposed to be forwarding my letters, though I *never* get any.
    Travelling as Mitford not Rodd I find I am quite famous – people even come to hotel bedrooms for signatures & bring my books to the stage door (greatly to the rage of the actors).
    The leading lady[2] who is a beauty not unlike Camilla [Sykes] keeps a husband, the image of Smartyboots, in her bedroom. They have breakfast at 12.30 & luncheon at 4, in bed, in duffel coats, every window sealed. I had to go & see her so I know.
    I feel very dépaysée, & my wireless talks English not French which I should have foreseen but hadn't – Haven't seen a single French sporting paper so I've missed the end of the Tour & don't even know who won. They want me to go to America with the play in Oct: but once bitten twice shy – Rex Harrison, of whom they speak in bated breath, comes to see it on Sat with a view to acting in it over there.

Best love, do write
     NR

The pictures in the Edin: & Glasgow galleries can only be described as *smashing* – have you seen them?

[1] 'So now I know what it must feel like to be a foreigner in Britain. My impression is that the hotels are good, that the art galleries are full of treasures, and furthermore run with great taste, energy and discrimination, and that the food, though not good, is not as bad as people suppose. The railways are truly terrible, however, and so is the climate. During the whole month of August I have worn nothing but last winter's clothes, and I think there has hardly been a sunny day.' 'Britain Revisited', *Sunday Times*, 27 August 1950.

[2] Joan Tetzel, an American actress, played the wife, Robert Morley was the cuckolded husband and David Tomlinson the disgruntled lover. The sets were by Oliver Messel.

To GASTON PALEWSKI   The Queens Hotel
15 August 1950   Leeds

Oh dear darling this silence! I tried to ring you up but no reply so I HOPE you are on holiday somewhere but I mind terribly not knowing. Do just send a post card won't you saying

                    I AM ALIVE AND WELL

so that I can read it.

I'm bound to say I'm rather enjoying all this & wouldn't have missed it for a good deal, it's intensely amusing to see all these stage people at their tricks. The temperament, unbridled by one ray of intelligence, of actors, has come as a revelation to me. The most spoilt of pretty rich women – Momo herself – simply cannot compete.

Also it's amused me to see all these great towns which ordinarily one just passes in the train.

I've bought a beautiful silver coffee pot which adorns the various hotel bedrooms I occupy.

London next week.

Fond love you *dear dear* HATEFUL Colonel.
     NR

To LADY DIANA COOPER   On my way home
6 September 1950

Darling

I must describe a visit to the Joneses[1] – the angelic Enid has just seen me onto the boat – while fresh in my memory. I did so think of you all the time.

First meal, a letter from a woman who had been assaulted by one of those vast dogs was read out. The dog, she said, appeared to be in the charge of an amiable lunatic. On hearing these words the said A.L. burst into tears which streamed down his face mingled with blood, I don't know what from. Enid mopped it all up, but not often enough. Pandora[2] screamed from time to time & gave me expressive looks. The baby[3] screamed throughout & kicked its chair & rattled a spoon.

I was then taken to the drawing room & shown a dying dog which had been fearfully bitten by the other dogs. Buckets of blood everywhere. Sir Roderick, outside, was scrubbing sick (don't know whose) off a cushion.

Next meal was taken up with a discussion as to whether an operation (unspecified) could be afforded for Timothy, who sat sadly listening. £3 for the anaesthetist, £2 for the theatre, £2 a day for the room etc etc. Finally they decided to be daredevils & Timothy was told to 'go in' at 5.30 on Sunday evening.

At the 2 other meals I had there the Birleys[4] & Sonia Cubitt[5] formed a barrier between the Jones family & the crudest facts of nature & I was able to eat the delicious food with the attention it deserved.

Pandora's baby screams & bangs all all day. Enid said on the way to the boat that she is offering the electrician's wife £1 a week to look after it. She says it's a regular regular Clifford but anybody else could tell her that it's a regular regular Jones – the image of Laurien[6] in fact.

Is this disloyal of me when they've been so kind? I can't resist it. Peter Brook said R. Morley's great fault is he is so disloyal & I replied well I'm very disloyal myself so it's not a thing I ever mind at all. He said he'd never heard anybody own to it before – awfully surprised.

I'm so fearfully happy to be on my way home after all these terrible (rather terrible) weeks, you can imagine. I shall never get mixed up in another play if I can help it though there were great compensations in the way of funniness & the niceness of all concerned. But *oh* England! I thought I was so wonderful about it in my monthly – which I enclose in case you didn't see it – but I have received a rain of anonymous letters: 'go back to the Paris brothels where you belong, always an ENGLISHMAN' etc etc. 'Who are you, anyway?' one began. So hard to answer really!

When do you return? I shall be working probably, with telephone cut off – that is my noble intention anyhow.

Fondest love
    NR

[1] Sir Roderick Jones and his wife, the author Enid Bagnold. They lived in Rottingdean, Sussex. Their daughter-in-law Pandora's sister, Anne Clifford, married John Julius Cooper in 1952.
[2] Pandora Clifford (1930–87). Married to Sir Roderick's son Timothy 1948–60 and to Hon. Michael Astor 1961–8.
[3] Annabel Jones (1948–). Beauchamp Place jeweller. Married 4th Viscount Astor in 1976.
[4] Sir Oswald Birley (1880–1952). Extraordinarily prolific portrait painter. Married Rhoda Pike in 1921.
[5] Sonia Keppel (1900–86). Sister of Violet Trefusis. Married to Hon. Roland Cubitt 1920–47.
[6] Laurien Jones (1921–). Daughter of Sir Roderick Jones. Married to Hon. Rowland Winn 1952–5 and to Count Anne-Pierre d'Harcourt in 1955.

To Mark Ogilvie-Grant   7 rue Monsieur, VII
19 September 1950

Dear OG

I *can't* remember whether, in the hurly burly of London, I wrote you a proper b & b. Anyway I do thank you terrifically for my visit which was bliss in every way.

The play is a success luckily so all the slight attendant horrors have been worth while & I am rich. The returns, which I get every week, go up by hundreds & make lovely reading as you may suppose.[1]

Here everybody is back more or less, full of the usual interesting holiday news, how hot it was in Venice & so on & one is supposed to listen with bated breath. They aren't a bit impressed when I tell how cold it was in Leeds, I note.

But Diana [Mosley] says the two naked furry Americans next to them on the Lido were reading *Love in a CC* out loud to each other & she kept hearing 'brains said Uncle Matthew' in terrific American accents!! Isn't it a yell. Tim Bailey[2] says he always asks them *why* they like my books & they reply 'Kinda cute'.

I must go to sleep.

Fond love & *many* thanks
    NR

[1] *The Little Hut* ran in England for 1,261 performances and netted £1029 in the first two months in royalties for Nancy.
[2] Nancy's first cousin.

To Evelyn Waugh   7 rue Monsieur, VII
25 September 1950

Darling Evelyn

It's an age since I heard from you. The *Sunday Times* asked me to do a 'short but astringent' caption to your photograph in Portrait Gallery however I said no. I wonder who they'll get 'must be somebody who knows him well'.

Would you like to hear about Smartyboots only keep it a secret please. Well the smart old creature sent his mistress[1] off to join Farouk & lived for quite a while in affluence here on what she managed to put up her knickers at the casino & remit. Then he got £40 out of the *Daily Mail*, saying he must have a manicure & so on & then would see Farouk with a view to identifying the unidentified blonde. When he arrived at Biarritz however Farouk refused an interview but lent him the blonde for his birthday. Meanwhile blonde, as well as her gambling money, was given £100 a day but only on condition she spent it during the day, so she bought bales of stuff, crates of sugar & so on which have all been sent in the Egyptian bag to Sussex Place.[2] Now this all excited Boots to a frenzy & he rushed her off to the consul (on his birthday) to marry her, but the consul didn't believe him when he said he was a widower, why? & wouldn't marry them. Then Farouk gave her a jewel said to be worth £1000 & sent them both packing. Oh & I forgot to say he would have interviewed Boots if B had consented to be flown to Cairo to see the Prime Minister first, but Boots seeing himself probably hamstrung in the Bosphorus, very wisely refused.

This is the main outline of this interesting tale, there are countless little details as you may imagine which my aching arm refuses to write. But you'll get it out of Boots if you try, he loves telling. I had it all like a lovely serial story day by day like Rip Kirby oh *did* I enjoy it. . . .

Tomorrow I dine with the Windsors & on Tues I go & stay with an old Catholic Royalist super gratin friend in her lovely lovely house so after all that I'll write again only you must reply. Perhaps a letter from you was amongst those abstracted & lost by Prod when he passed through Paris & I was away. He does more harm than a bomb.

Best love
    NR

[1] Barbara Skelton; married to Cyril Connolly 1950–54, to Connolly's publisher George

Weidenfeld 1956–61, and to Derek Jackson 1966–7. In her autobiography, *Tears Before Bedtime* (1987), she gives her account of this episode.
[2] Cyril Connolly's house in London.

TO EVELYN WAUGH   7 rue Monsieur, VII
30 September 1950

Darling Evelyn

I call them the insect-women[1] oh aren't they horrible & so mal-élevées. I mean Cyril brought Miss S[kelton] to a v. small cocktail party I had & she sat & read a book! Mauvais genre they call it here. Then my brother in law Jackson has turned up with Mrs Bluefeet,[2] whom I haven't seen since we met her together, with Mrs Orwell in tow as a sort of dame de compagnie. All in corduroys & sandals. I *can't* bear them. Cyril said to me the trouble with you Nancy is one can't imagine you sitting on one's lap – have you ever sat on anybody's lap?

No I said, with some vehemence, nor have I ever allowed anybody to kiss me (almost true).

Sibyl's death was announced as 'Sibyl, mother of M. Colefax' – so somehow unsuitable.

I've been staying with my dear old Mme Costa de Beauregard in a house in which nothing has changed for 100 years. In the drawing room sit 4 old ladies, who have stayed there all of every summer since they were born & M. le Curé aged 87, who has been M. le Curé there since he was 27. Last all saints' day he asked Mme Costa, as he always does, for her list (people to pray for) & she gave him by mistake her private list, so he read out Louis XIV, Thérèse (old cook), Landru,[3] le duc d'Aumale, Marie-Ange (old gardener) etc etc. We asked her why Landru & she said she heard he had no family to pray for him so she always does every day. The house is like that in *Les Malheurs de Sophie*, extremely elegant in front & backing onto a basse-cour with vast manure heap covered with hens. The farmer, a handsome young man, has 18 children & to Mme Costa's sorrow none of them intend to take orders. But the youngest is only 4. The eldest daughter brought her fiancé to see Mme C. while I was there, a ravishing young man who had been in the Congo & SEEN PIGMIES. It is all like another world, the world you love but which would bore me, though I like to see it in progress. I fear it will end with her death (the daughter in law is an Englishwoman,[4] a beauty, with service flat tastes) but at present everything is kept up as it should be, there is no feeling of decay.

This letter is meant to say bon-voyage & *do* come here later on. I'll protect you from the middle classes I promise.

Farouk has now got somebody called Honey child (her Xian name) & has given her a better jewel than he gave Miss S. Cyril went to see a flat here belonging to somebody I know, with a view to renting it. The concierge said 'you can't let it to him.' 'Why not?' 'Well he had a beard & high heeled shoes & looked like an assassin.'

So my friend won't. It's like the old Turk who saw Napoleon isn't it –[5]

    Best love
       NR

Don't know what you mean about England – champagne seemed to me to *pour*.
Thank you for *Helena*.[6] I'll write when I've read it. Have you heard the name of Duff's novel *Operation Heartbreak*.

[1] Waugh had complained to Nancy about his friends' choice of wives.
[2] Janetta Woolley (1922–). Owner, with the Connollys, of the house in Sussex Place. Married first to Kenneth Sinclair-Loutit and known as 'Bluefeet' because Waugh had once, on a visit to Connolly, seen her going barefoot through the house. Subsequently married to Robert Kee 1948–50, to Derek Jackson 1951–6, and to Jaime Parladé.
[3] Henri-Désiré Landru (1869–1922). French murderer accused of killing ten women and a young boy whose bodies he burned in his kitchen stove.
[4] Elizabeth (Doodie) Millar (1908–). Married Count Amedée Costa de Beauregard in 1940. 'Doodie, sometimes so really funny, describes the meat at her mother in law's as looking like a dead spaniel on the dish.' (NM to Diana Mosley, 13 December 1950)
[5] At the beginning of the century an old Russian who claimed to have seen Napoleon was asked what he looked like: 'He had a long white beard.'
[6] Evelyn Waugh, *Helena* (1950). Novel about the mother of Constantine the Great.

To Evelyn Waugh   7 rue Monsieur, VII
9 October 1950

Darling Evelyn

You've made it only too plain that you don't care 2 hoots what I think about *Helena*[1] so this is merely to thank you for a handsome volume which (I don't mean the contents) made me gasp & stretch my eyes. Lady Honks [Cooper] was kept awake all night by it (contents).

So thank you very much.

Love from
    NR

I shall never be able to have a Turkish bath again.[2]

[1] 'Don't puzzle your pretty head with it. It will be all Greek – or worse still English – to you. But put it on a shelf & look at its back now & then & think kindly of me.' *Letters*, p. 336.
[2] In *Helena*, Waugh gives a graphic description of the murder of the Empress Fausta, who is steamed to death behind the locked doors of a Turkish bath.

To Lady Redesdale   7 rue Monsieur, VII
20 October 1950

Darling Muv
   . . . Robert Morley, who is excessively cautious & pessimistic, writes 'we can now safely say that the *Hut* is a smash hit', & told Peter that in his view it will run for 2 years. But with the stage you never really can tell, it is *so* tricky.

I've got a beautiful Dior dress, day, which is worn over a crinoline, I feel like a Victorian lady for purposes of loo – very inconvenient! It's so plain however that I can wear it in the street & I see by the looks I get that, like the *Hut*, it is a smash hit. 'Tu ne te prives de rien'[1] a French friend remarked.

Colonel dined with Fulco de la V[erdura] last night – the King of Italy kept them waiting ½ an hour & when he came the Duchess of W said to him 'My King went of his own accord but you were kicked out & I don't think you ought to make us wait for you' which set the tone for a merry evening.

Dolly whom I went to see had just come from the death bed of Mme Sert.[2] Mlle Chanel was there doing up the corpse 'alors, Coco était en train de faire ses ongles – j'ai trouvé ça très bien de Coco – seulement je dirais – elle l'avait un rien trop maquillée.'[3] Literal *Loved One.* . . .

   Best love
    NR

A letter forwarded *S Times* saying 'Are you the Nancy Mitford I used to know, one of 3 daughters of Captain Mitford? Does my name strike memory's chord?' I feel rather sorry for this other NM don't you?!!!

[1] You certainly spoil yourself.

[2] Misia Godebska (1872–1950). Leading figure in Parisian artistic and social circles. Married the wealthy painter José-Maria Sert as her third husband. 'She was Diaghilev's great friend, always sat, glittering with jewels, in his box at the ballet, and had a salon of real importance for dancers, musicians and painters. Mme Sert helped to win the Battle of the Marne. "Send the troops up in taxi-cabs," she said, half as a joke, to General Gallieni, thus solving a problem which had baffled the entire general staff.' NM, *Sunday Times*, 3 December 1950.

[3] 'Well, Coco was doing her nails – I thought it was kind of her – but I must say, she had slightly overdone the make-up.'

To EVELYN WAUGH   7 rue Monsieur, VII
10 November 1950

Darling Evelyn

All right (I was in a bait).[1] Well *of course* I loved *Helena* – you are a master of narrative & I read it solidly in a day how I do when I enjoy something. I particularly enjoyed the detective work in Jerusalem – of course the beginning – & of course the Roman part. After she left England it became a little foggy to me & some of the life went out of it until Rome. I think from the non-Catholic reader's point of view it's a pity you don't tell about the conversion & I think Constantius might have been a shade more of a person (I was going to say attractive). He is too much like Oliver Harvey – could Oliver Harvey have held down the Roman Empire for a record length of time?

Anyway it's completely absorbing & fascinating, every page. Stock are more than pleased with it & also with your translator – what made you choose her?

Next Wednesday I cut off telephone etc & begin. Yes I shall dedicate it to you if it's good enough.[2] I am very nervous over it but once I've begun I expect it will seem easier. Since I started this letter I've been rung up 4 times – you see how one's poor brain isn't given a chance to bite on anything. Were it not for the Col I should retire to an orange grove to await the end (as my father always says). . . .

Don't you think *Operation Heartbreak* is the most awful name you ever heard? I call it Op: Sickmake – now you're *not* to repeat, Duff would kill me.

Col just back from Djibouti where his presence won an election for the Gaullists. He said 'we had a terrible list, headed by the Armenian in *Black Mischief*.'[3] I haven't seen him yet & must now trot round all the neighbouring churches with candles for his safe return – I was in a fit of terror – aeroplanes.

You know Gladwyn Jebb is the love of my life – wonderful for me that he has made good.[4] He is a very very nice person let me tell you. Duff loathes him so I rub in how famous he is with Duff's adored Americans. By the way do the Americans you meet start the chat with Tell me about yourself? I've had it twice lately.

Best love
    NR

[1] Waugh's reply to Nancy's previous letter had been mollifying: 'Goose. Of course I value your opinion above all others about most things. But well no not about religion . . . And I genuinely didn't want you to try because I knew it would be a bore to you. It was love that prompted me to ward you off it. Don't even open it or cut a page, I implore.' *Letters*, p. 338.
[2] *The Blessing* was indeed dedicated to Evelyn Waugh.
[3] Evelyn Waugh, *Black Mischief* (1932).
[4] Lord Gladwyn had been made UK representative to the UN, a post he held until 1954 when he became Ambassador to France.

To Violet Hammersley   7 rue Monsieur, VII
21 November 1950

Darling
    Never cut off from you. No it is the telephoners I must eliminate, & have done so. Col lunches most days & I read him what I have done & he says, as he always does, But will the general public be amused by this? The funny thing is, they always are.
    No it's not your friends except quite superficially (i.e. English wife, French husband & old French grandmother – conversation piece with Mme Rodel, M. le Curé etc). The characters are utterly unlike: Grace = me-&-my-sisters, Charles-Edouard = Col, Mme de Valhubert = Dolly Radziwill, M. de la Bourlie (her lover) = any old duc. In Paris, some of the gens du monde are unmistakable, but they won't mind. The child's nanny is stealing the picture so far – asking for floury potatoes on arrival in Provence etc, she is really funny I think. I do wish you were here to help. Perhaps I'll go to the I of W Ritz if there is one later on & read it to you. Col is a great help on the practical plane of course.
    I'm so glad you're going for Xmas, nice for Muv. I think she's sad really about Tello.[1] She writes much more depressed than usual.

Best love, keep in touch
    NR

[1] Rita Shell, Lady Redesdale's old governess, had died.

To JAMIE HAMILTON   7 rue Monsieur, VII
13 December 1950

My dear Jamie

You are kind – I've been longing for the Fr novelists & thought I couldn't afford it – I've got into a fit about my old age just as I remember my father used to, & walk everywhere to save taking buses. Also I'm terrified of not being able to deliver the goods any more like Noel Coward. The novel I'm writing now is very dull, of course I know people like that at least I guess they must when I try & read best sellers, but still it's rather a worry. However, I peg away sadly at it, I've done ½ the first draft so think the whole thing will be finished April or May. It's far the best constructed of them all, a deadly virtue I admit. Perhaps it's not as bad as I think, I always get cold feet in the middle.

I hope Yvonne is all right again, do give her my love.

Love from
    NR

I've sent *Hut* to Peters to send you, he gets so easily cross I have to mind my step.

To GASTON PALEWSKI   Wilmington
26 January 1951   Totland Bay
                                                     Isle of Wight

Dear darling

So I've arrived off the little toy boat & feel very dépaysée but I think it's *good* & will be perfect for working. But the cold is like cold water, no vers à soie!

Dined with Pam [Berry]. All the talk is of Bev*an*[1] being kicked (physically) out of White's by John Fox[2] & how now he'll hate the upper classes more than ever, & how Hartley Shawcross[3] never leaves the tape machine because he thinks he will succeed Bev*in*[4] who may die. I saw Nigel [Birch] who says all you say exactly & the Conservatives seem to on the whole but he says they should never have gone in to Korea because we 'haven't got enough policemen to look after the jewels'.

Bookshop full of Evelyn saying to an American bore 'I'm going to your country'. 'USA?' 'No, Jewry.' I think I told you. They were very cross with him – well *really*.

The *luxury* of staying with Momo & her kindness I can't describe.
Malcolm[5] says 'I hear you're roughing it with the Marriotts – I suppose
you'll go back & say England is quite all right – now I stayed with a
retired general & his little wife & they really have everything they
want.' Well, they do!

Oh I hope you're all right & surrounded by les femmes du monde.
Pam says I said 'I asked all the pretty ones to meet Evelyn – Marie-
Laure [de Noailles], Elizabeth,[6] Momo, Cora [Caetani] –'

Dearest Col goodbye – I'll write every day.

NR

Rather wonderful not to be bullied all the time with 'et à part cela?'
Oh no, *not* wonderful really I'd give anything anything to hear it.
All Jacobean news, please.
I'm so TERRIBLY COLD.

[1] Aneurin Bevan (1897–1960). Labour MP. Minister of Health 1945–51.

[2] Hon. John Fox-Strangways (1908–61). Second son of 6th Earl of Ilchester. He really
did kick Bevan on the steps at White's.

[3] Hartley Shawcross (1902–). QC and Labour MP. Attorney-General 1945–51.
Created a life peer in 1959.

[4] Ernest Bevin (1881–1951). Labour politician. Secretary of State for Foreign Affairs
1945 until his death in 1951. He was succeeded by Herbert Morrison.

[5] Malcolm Bullock (1890–1966). Conservative MP 1923–50. Knighted 1954. A friend
whom Nancy valued for his sense of humour and sharpness.

[6] Elizabeth Ridgway (1904–62). Married, as her second husband, the pianist Prince
George Chavchavadze. She was very overweight and, like the other women Nancy is
supposed to have arranged for Evelyn to meet, was no longer in her first youth.

To Diana Mosley   [Wilmington
6 February 1951   Totland Bay]

Darling

Forgive paper – in bed away from block! Must write before my
daily work & *awful* writer's cramp begins.

A lovely post this mg. including one from Col who is off to Morocco
so that is an utter weight off my mind, I really can't tell you how much
of one, I was in despair at leaving him to gloom alone not very well.

Well the book I hope & think is good. I read it to Wid but all she
says is 'delightful' & hardly laughs, but I think doesn't hear it in spite
of aid. No help at all as Gerald used to be & I *had* rather hoped. Of
course it's not really funny like the Uncle M. ones (tho' Hector Dexter
the American is a good laugh) but I think it runs along & makes a

picture. It's certainly better than old Enid-bagses.[1] I know the reviewers are going to say snobbish, oh dear.

In other ways Wid is wonderful I shriek from morn to night. *What* the Totlandites must think. As she is almost stone deaf the conversations in the street are like consequences. 'Lovely day isn't it?' 'Oh I'm *so* glad she's not worse.' 'We're all just off to London.' 'Very well then I'll look in tomorrow.'

Yesterday she said 'The wind is very disagreeable on one's neck' & then seeing a bore approach, 'We have to go home – our *necks*, you understand, our *necks!*'

At first I felt dreadfully cold but am getting used to it & the room where I work is boiling, it's bathroom bedroom etc that are literal fridges.

I've told her she ought to get in 12 tons of wood – well, don't you agree, the way things are going. She nearly had a stroke, but the idea has an awful fascination for her, & she constantly reverts to it.

. . . I adore Isle of Wright & Col sends to I of Writhe – why does it get here? . . .

I've done about ¼ of the book, must try & get to London before Muv goes to isle & then, if it suited you, might go a few days to finish at Crow[ood]. . . .

The Wid's *Sévigné*[2] is génial terribly terribly good I wish you were going to do it[3] not old screw Lehmann.

Much love darling
Do forgive scribble
    NR

So *delighted* by Nicky's wonderful reviews, a first novel[4] can seldom have had such good ones.

[1] Enid Bagnold, *The Loved and Envied* (1951). A novel.
[2] *Letters from Madame de Sévigné*, translated by Violet Hammersley, was published by Secker & Warburg in 1956.
[3] The Mosleys ran a small publishing imprint during the 1950s, Euphorion Books, which brought out Nancy's translation of *La Princesse de Clèves* (1950).
[4] *Spaces of the Dark* by Nicholas Mosley, Diana's stepson.

To GASTON PALEWSKI   Wilmington
9 February 1951   Totland Bay

Colonel your writing on an envelope – I thought I would faint. And I was able to read every word. It must be the accident like when deaf children can suddenly speak after a bomb. But you are fixed for the future now I know you CAN.

So I see you're better you dear darling, but now be good & have a good rest in that lovely place. *How* lucky about the PICTURES.[1]

The book gets on. Not quite as quick as I would like, I'm so longing to get back to you but I see it will be another month before I can. Charles-Edouard is *wonderful*, Mrs Hammersley laughs the whole time when he is on the stage (I read it out every other day). It's a more living portrait than the romantic Sauveterre now buried for ever at the Père Lachaise & I'm glad I killed him off.

Ch ED is you to the life. ('Et les jolies femmes?') . . .

Very favourable article in *D Telegraph* saying the Gen opened resistance to the Communists by refusing them those ministries & had it not been for him France wld now be a Czechoslovakia.

I went all across the island to an antiquaire said to be hopeful, but there was nothing but native craftsmanship (Battersea enamel etc).

Nothing here but natural beauty of rather a Victorian turn – Tennyson lived here & we go for his walk on a Sunday & lunch in his house, now a Southern Railway Rest House (sold, furniture, books, photographs & all by his grandson who always refers to him as the Bloody Bard).

Well you darling be good be good. I must to my work.

Love
          Connaught Hotel

[1] Palewski was staying at the Villa Taylor in Marrakesh which belonged to his friend Charles de Breteuil. He had written to Nancy that there was a fine 18th-century painting in the house and old portraits of the family.

To ANTHONY POWELL   Wilmington, Totland Bay
24 February 1951   As from: 7 rue Monsieur, VII

My dear Tony

I would love to see you, but as usual am only stopping in London 2 days on my way back, in March. But surely you come to Paris sometimes? I'm always there, at the above address.

I've sent the book to Jacques Brousse,[1] a great friend who sometimes reads for Stock, so when I get back I'll ask what he advises. I should have thought best to begin, after all it's a thing in itself.

You want to be very careful with French publishers, some are so dishonest & English authors sometimes never see a penny they have earned. Stock, Plon & NRF & Albin Michel quite all right, naturally. Stock gave me an advance of £400 on my two books, on receipt of the MS, which seems to me very good. And has done them beautifully.

Isn't it agony thinking of things for *them* to do, how I agree. So unfair too the way Dickens & Co could use opening graveyards, long lost wanderers, & illegitimacy & so on, all closed to us! The one I'm on now, being about Paris mostly, hasn't been so bad in that respect though terrible in others. Out in Sept: I hope.

Do come to Paris, & come & see me.

Yrs
     Nancy

[1] Jacques Brousse translated into French *Don't Tell Alfred*, *The Water Beetle*, *Voltaire in Love*, *Madame de Pompadour* and *The Sun King*.

To Evelyn Waugh   7 rue Monsieur, VII
12 March 1951

Darling Evelyn

. . . My book is being typed. Shall I have an uncorrected copy sent straight to you? Only dearest dear no use telling me to put it in a drawer & re write it in a year's time. I haven't the force of character to do so though I will make any minor alterations you may be good enough to propose. You must remember the copy will anyhow require a good deal of correcting – I didn't have quite enough time for that with the MS & had to leave it as I can't bring myself to post them ever! I do so long to know what you think of it. I think the best so far, but of course one always does with the last effort.

I am so happy to be back it's like being in heaven. But I loved the I of W & the extraordinary *Cranford* life there. The doctor & his wife, who are sweet, were raving about *Helena*. *I* always like to hear of that sort of public, I expect you rather despise it. The post master *himself* arrived with your telegram saying 'Mr Evelyn Waugh is in Paris' – Mrs Hammersley was so furious (at him having read it I suppose or because it was cheek?) but I roared. She took me to the local bridge club & I heard '& of course when in London I went to Nancy Mitford's naughty thing' – wasn't it lovely for me.

I got free specs from the health scheme in 3 days so was glad to see how well that works – blond tortoiseshell.

Oh I am happy to be back though!

Much love
     NR

I'll have it sent unless you say no but oh dear I rather dread your comments, sure to be a douche of cold water.[1]

[1] Waugh replied: '*The Blessing* is admirable, deliciously funny, consistent & complete; by far the best of your writings; I do congratulate you with all my heart & thank you for the dedication.' *Letters*, p. 346.

To Evelyn Waugh   7 rue Monsieur, VII
2 April 1951

Darling Evelyn

I *don't know why* you have this idea of the Captain.[1] He is flabby to the core. What about the guilty sun bath while the matinée is on, & leaving everything to the Crew, who choose *and* produce the plays *and* see to the financial side *and* run his house (he can't even get his own breakfast when they go). He is described as a charming lazy intellectual & doesn't seem to me to belie that in any way. His inability to make love to Grace is another form of flabbiness. Why do you say breezy & pushful? Truly I think you are wrong. The thing is I entirely agree with you about what he ought to be like, but it seems to me he *is* like it – ?

Debo could drive a car at 9, I well remember her doing so. Somebody had to work the clutch for her. I have re done Fauntleroy & it's ever so much better – also the telephone conversation, which isn't vital to the story. How awful about Sigi being 25, I had so congratulated myself on his development between a backward 6 & a forward 9. Of course French children are different – somebody once said to me a French boy of 14 has a heavy moustache, 2 mistresses & a hoop!

Heywood writes that Boots' wife marks him for tidiness, lovingness etc & if less than 6/10 she turns him into Shepherd Market where he spends the night. He says isn't it like the *Blue Angel* –!!

Please don't think I've taken no trouble over revising – there are corrections on every page of the typescript & I had done the original MS over & over again – I re-wrote the whole thing twice. People always think I dash off my books with no real work, but it is not so, I very honestly do my *best*. I've *pored* over the Capt ever since your letter, but truly, except for his appearance, I don't see what you mean or that he is ever brisk or executive in the least.

Dexter is really taken from Hiss[2] & many of the things he says I copied straight word for word out of the trial. After all Dexter is born in America & is an American communist, not a Russian dressed up, which would be utterly false. As it is it seems to me to hold water.

I have to defend myself against the Col too. He says no father would leave his child up on that horse. I say the child is in *no* danger, since children have no fear of height, & it is far more amusing if he is there on his own. Col also doubtful about the heartless treatment of the children at the ball. But he admits (with guilty giggle) that Ch-Ed is to the life.

Dearest Evelyn now *please* don't be too governessy & say I take no trouble because it hurts my feelings.

Love from
     NR

Letters here are 4d now & understamped ones get delayed which is why I mention it, not only meanness –

[1] Ed Spain, the Captain in *The Blessing*, was based on Cyril Connolly. Waugh had complained that the character did not ring true: 'The harem is oriental and can only be maintained by flabby, dependent men. Not brisk men of action.' *Letters*, p. 346.
[2] In January 1950 Alger Hiss was found guilty of perjury in concealing his membership of the Communist Party.

To LADY PAMELA BERRY   7 rue Monsieur, VII
9 April 1951

Darling Pam

I *am* so glad you like the book, as I can see you really do & it was heaven getting your telegram & long letter to reassure me. When I'd finished it I wondered if it wasn't a bit dull, & horrid old Col, the first to read it, kept saying it was too slow & had such dreadful longueurs at the start, & that Nanny must come out as she was so dull etc etc & I even wondered if H. Hamilton would want it. However he is enthusiastic, & Evelyn too (who always tells the truth) & now you, so I feel it must be all right. I *bet* you the French will lap it up, they only like books in which they come out badly & the great criticism of *P of Love* was 'je ne marche pas avec Sauveterre –' & how no French-man would have thrown away her mink coat to give her a better one –

I wish I'd been less merciful to the Americans, but Gaston kept begging me to tone it down & not tease them too much. He dined last week with some real horrors there are here called Bolum or something & Mrs B's mother said 'do you know Marly' (where Gen: Eisenhower is living) & Col said 'oh yes my mother lives there in a little farmhouse.' 'Then I hope she makes a good profit selling eggs & butter to the General, tell her not to mind what she asks, they are terribly rich.' Of course Col simply screamed, but think how cross some people would have been. Aren't they brutes. My publisher said to me yesterday 'The Americans don't realize that what the French live for is literature.' But how could they realize it when they themselves can hardly read? They (the Americans) think of nothing but money it seems to me, anyway they talk of nothing else. This new occupation is getting us all down here & dear old Heck would be unrecognizable if I were to re-write the book now!

Yes Sir Conrad is school of Duff, but he won't mind do you think? I thought it flattering. I thought I'd tell Duff it's meant to be Malcolm [Bullock] & vice versa.

Yes isn't it a worry about Evelyn – boredom is a really terrible complaint, I know because I've suffered so much from it in my life. One of the reasons for liking to live here, I am *never* bored. . . .

I went to the Comédie Française twice yesterday, afternoon & evening. There *are* some lovely plays, do come soon.

Momo is here & I am in full hero worship. I see her as the heroine in white satin & myself as the confidante in white linen – a sort of poor man's Momo.

Did you see that Loelia[1] was on the list of the 10 worst dressed women, with Princess Elizabeth, Princess Rita[2] & Co? I did so shriek (*Samedi Soir*).

I do hope you haven't been too much pestered about the MS. Nancy Spain,[3] who edits some trade booksellers' paper wanted it, & Peters my agent, & I told them you had a copy because from here I couldn't really organize it. I expect it has all sorted itself out by now.

Best love darling & *thank* you for all you say
    NR

What news of Ava [Anderson]?
The Koestler book[4] fascinated me – like mine it's about Paris now, but the Paris of bars & nightclubs & poor people's flats, you can see the difference (!) *Terribly terribly* good.

[1] Hon. Loelia Ponsonby (1902–). Married to 2nd Duke of Westminster 1930–47. 'How awful about Loelia *minding*. Everybody here has been saying, one thing, she won't mind a bit, she doesn't care what she puts on.' (NM to Lady Pamela Berry, 16 April 1951)
[2] Rita Hayworth (1918–87). Film star. Married to Prince Aly Khan in 1949.
[3] Nancy Spain (1917–64). Journalist. Literary critic for the *Daily Express*. 'Nancy Spain is a rough north-country peasant on the make & anybody who knows her at all knows

she is not conversant with upper class manners. Ceci dit, she's not a bad girl at all.'
(NM to James Lees-Milne, 17 July 1955)
[4] Arthur Koestler, *The Age of Longing* (1951).

To Evelyn Waugh   7 rue Monsieur, VII
11 May 1951

Darling Evelyn

I would *love* to go with you as far as a day train could take me back, it would be a terrific treat. Beautiful France in June is something I've never seen. But all depends very much on the Col – he's engulfed in his election (standing against Duclos, the Communist leader in the reddest part of Paris) & depends on me for a little home life, or at least I think he does. So perhaps we could leave it open. Anyway I'll find out a good gastronomic itinerary for you. Honks [Cooper] is dying for you to settle at Chantilly, I think she has written.

I was riveted by Spender.[1] Funnier than anything even you have written – I had to put it down & *scream* time & time again. Pink as I may be (synthetic cochineal Diana calls it) I can't but see the hysterical funniness of my fellow pinks.

Isn't it dreadful about the poverty. But need *girls* go to school – I thought only boys, & that the girls could learn Greek from a local priest & les soins de beauté from their mother. Perhaps this is a romantic dream. I was dragged up with none of it, worse luck, hence the grammar. It would be far cheaper – face cream costs less than gym shoes you know, & a sprig of rosemary in rain water, the foundation of a good complexion, nothing at all. (You ought to read *Gigi*.[2]) You would be richer if you lived here, but perhaps not happier – though I don't know why not.

Diana M, just back from Ireland, tells of going to mass (Aly, her son, is very religious) in the R.C. church at Lismore. It was *crammed* with people, all crying so that their tears splashed on the stone floor, & sobbing out loud, & when she asked why they said 'It is Connolly day.'

How horrid, 100 best authors, so invidious. Typical Festival idea – all right for you & Henry. How can one get the list, I long for it – I *love* H. being Pooter at the volunteers' ball.[3]

Jonathan is engaged so we are all excited. Lovely Miss Wyndham.[4] Diana says he must marry at once, he'll never find such another beauty, & *so nice*.

Later. A letter from Mrs Hammersley 'If Stephen S had any guts, which he hasn't, he would kill Evelyn Waugh'. Why? Beastly review I guess.

> Fondest love
> NR

[1] Waugh had written a scathing review of Stephen Spender's autobiography *World Within World* in *The Tablet*, 5 May 1951.

[2] By Colette (1944).

[3] As part of the Festival of Britain, the National Book League arranged an exhibition around 'The 100 Best Books' by contemporary writers; Waugh's *Decline and Fall* was selected. Waugh wrote to Nancy: 'Oh I must tell you I went to the 100 Best Books with Bright Young Yorkes. Mrs Yorke senior came all the way from Forthampton for the event and a loutish son who shakes hands with a clenched fist. Well it was a private view with a bar and Henry started handing us all glasses of sherry. "That'll be twenty bob" said the bar maid. It was just like Mr Pooter at the volunteers' ball. Henry was so upset he walked straight out to the Ritz Hotel opposite and bought & paid for bottles & bottles of champagne.' (8 May 1951)

[4] Ingrid Wyndham (1931–). Married to Jonathan Guinness 1951–63 and to Paul Channon, son of Chips Channon, in 1963.

To Lady Pamela Berry   7 rue Monsieur, VII
11 June 1951

Darling

Thrilled by your letter because of course we eat & drink & breathe Burgess[1] & nobody thinks of anything else. The frog papers are quite sure it is sex & so really am I, because ONE's mind always flies to love. Sergeant [Preston] who is here says B is the most disreputable human being alive today but I expect being American he is biased. Col will love your letter too next time he comes up to breathe (6 meetings a day now). The papers here say he is the best of all the election speakers. I went to the big meeting on Fri – very good except they are all so tired they looked green including the Gen. Malraux was smashing – Col greatly hampered by the microphone breaking down, it was such a disappointment, his excellent speech hardly heard. Quite well reported though.

A French paper (just received some cuttings) says *The Princesse de Clèves* has appeared in America under the title *Love in a Cold Climate*. . . .

Just had a long talk with Diana M about diplomats. Sir O's theory is exactly yours, only he thinks Burgess was probably always communisant & Maclean horrified by the trend towards war, & both together thought out some Hess-like mission & (what Debo calls) buggered off. I suppose if they were just bouncing about on some double bed they would have been found by now. *Oh* the fascination.

My telephone is now being tapped, it's never happened before. Do you think they are doing it with all English people or what?

I must get up. Do write anything you know, we pant for inside inf:!

Love
 NR

[1] Guy Burgess and Donald Maclean had disappeared on 25 May and their whereabouts was still unknown.

To Gaston Palewski   St-Pierre du Château
12 July 1951   Hyères
              Var

Dear darling
 The place is a nest of singing antiquaires – 2 in Hyères (& huge I've seen the frontage, shutters down as it was late) one on the way to Toulon, 3 in Toulon, one very expensive, etc. So hold on for the guéridon I beg & let me see what there is here.

Korda is to give me seven million 500 000 francs[1] so dear dear Colonel I can give you a nice present ('No').

I think you are the most good & charming man in the world ('How true that is'). And my life is a desert without you ('I know I know'). But I really need a holiday & specially the sea – I forget from year to year how well it makes me feel. And the effect is instantaneous, like magic. Could you not take a night train & come only for 2 or 3 days – you are very much invited. Tony [Gandarillas] speaks of it continually. Do you know Hyères? It is a beautiful old town & we look down on the old red roofs while behind the house there is a romantic landscape of endless wooded mountains ('Nature I hate'). Twice a day we go to the sea by motor, very comfortable with bathing cabins. Tony is a charming host, as anybody could guess. It is all more civilized than Montredon but I miss dear Dolly.

Goodbye you dearest. Keep me informed of your plans if any.
 NR

[1] For the film rights of *The Blessing*. Released as *Count Your Blessings* (1959), it was directed by Jean Negulesco and starred Maurice Chevalier.

To Gaston Palewski   St-Pierre du Château
[July 1951]   Hyères

Dear dearest

I am so passionately sad & lonely without you that I think I will
come back to Paris, unless there is any hope of you coming here? I
long for that, not only for selfish reasons but because it would be *so*
good for you. It's such a healthy life here, & not boring, not a bit
like Montredon. Tony is always all for an outing & there are lots of
neighbours. I suppose what Evelyn calls poor Louis'[1] party will be
assembling soon. 'Who is this poor Louis Diana [Cooper] talks about
all the time?'

I enclose a balloon for *The Blessing*.

Jean Hugo[2] & the sinister Frosca[3] are here having a holiday from
J-H's wife. I can see that Tony & everybody are hopefully expecting
me to be bowled over by his charm, but so far I've only seen him in
a bathing dress & it hasn't operated.

I think the Frosca lady too awful (don't know her name – perhaps
she hasn't got one).

Now dearest Col I could get Marie back next week if you'd like,
so just say. I long for you more than sea & sun & mountains, much
as I love all these.

    NR

[1] Paul-Louis Weiller (1893–1993). Rich and powerful industrialist. A long-standing and
generous admirer of Lady Diana Cooper who was much criticised for accepting, in
1951, the gift of a mink coat worth £4,500, which she christened 'the coat of shame'.
His summer retreat, the Villa Reine Jeanne at Bormes-les-Mimosas, was not far from
Tony Gandarillas's house.
[2] Jean Hugo (1894–1984). Painter and formidable womaniser. Great-grandson of
Victor Hugo. Married to the painter Valentine Gross 1919–32, and to Lauretta Hope-
Nicholson in 1947.
[3] Frosca Munster (d.1963). Russian-born friend of Christian Bérard and Jean Cocteau.

To Gaston Palewski   St-Pierre du Château
20 July 1951   Hyères

The Viscountess[1] has just been to see me. She complains that she is
dishonoured for ever because the young pederast[2] won't go to bed
with her.

N   But Marie-Laure he hates women, clearly.
ML   That has never stopped me yet.

N   And is obviously a virgin.
ML   I specialize in them. What can I do?
N   Try marrying him. Americans like marriage lines – they get them
     going.
ML   (Screams & goes away)

I see wicked words about the over-subtle English. However there
is no Eng: colony here so I can survive it, this time.

I feel so well. In just over a week I feel well instead of half ill as I
have for so long. That's why I say *come* even for a few days. Surely
they can form their old government without you, or do you have to
stay in order to prevent them doing so? Let them form it & then go
back & bring it down. Oh Collikins *do*.

I'll get your news from Tony I hope, he promised to ring you up.
He returns on Monday.

   Best love you dear dear Colonel
        NR

[1] Marie-Laure de Noailles. She lived near by at the Château St-Bernard.
[2] Ned Rorem (1923–). American composer. A pupil of Nadia Boulanger, influenced by
French music and French society. Author of several volumes of diaries.

To EVELYN WAUGH   7 rue Monsieur, VII
29 August 1951

Darling Evelyn
   Our Mr [A. D.] Peters has just put on such an odd act. He telephoned this morning saying he was de passage & we arranged for
him to come here at 3. As the clocks were striking I saw him come
into the cour [courtyard] – I had a heavy vase of flowers in my hands,
went into my bedroom, put it down, fidgeted with the flowers a minute
& went to open the door. No sign of Mr P. It is now ¼ to 5. Do
admit. He is rather a fantaisiste I believe, I've noticed it in him before.
But it is terribly annoying as there are a hundred things I wanted to
ask which seem too trivial or (specially) too rapacious to write. Money.
I long for it. But huge sums appear on paper & none in the bank
except the London bank which is no more good to me than – ha, at
this point the telephone rings & a breathy female voice says in English
that Mr Peters has had a puncture & will be along in ½ an hour. What
can it all mean? More anon.
   Well he came. Nothing was said as to why he was late & I didn't
mention having seen him 2 hours before. VERY ODD.

Oh dear your poverty. It's like the little door in Alice – so much in life is like that. Even I rather suffer though I don't need money as you do. But people say – 'oh Book of Month in America, of course 5 years ago that *was* something but now it's very small beer.' By the way I wrote to my agent over there who is utterly ½ witted AND calls me Nancy though a complete stranger & said I must have your article on me[1] when it appears & she sent pages back saying of course she'd get it for me if she could but I must explain more about it etc. So I've given up. She also asks for my telephone number which is on *every* letter I have *ever* written to her –

A long letter from a Hungarian pen pal who has been deported saying it's not too bad, plenty to eat, but no nail varnish or hair dye but I can send them to her butler who goes out to see her every week.

Aren't other people's reviews a bore. I get many clippings of the books of Lady Somebody Something & even smaller fry who are said to be school of me. Perhaps I ought to refund you the threepences.

The Colonel is making his mark in the Chambre. But he complains bitterly of lack of air & lack of eloquence. Où sont les Lavals d'antan?

I met Miss Anita Loos[2] at luncheon. But they are all the same & she is not even well dressed. I then went & ordered the plainest little wool dress you ever saw from Dior £168. It's the last time. I humbly asked if they wouldn't take off the 8 but no they cried you are very *lucky*, all the prices are going up next week. They made me feel I'd been too clever for words. But after I felt guilty – all the poor people in the world & so on. It's terrible to love clothes as much as I do, & perfectly inexplicable because I'm not at all vain & Col who is the only person I care for doesn't know sackcloth from ashes.

I've got a small egg[3] of yours in an old nest – did you know? I feel guilty as you might have wanted to boil it while here – only saw it after you'd gone.

Jonathan [Guinness] is a bad boy. I sent an expensive present & loving letter – deep silence. I hope it means that he is happy. I thought John Julius & his fiancée[4] looked silly & I don't believe they sleep together either.

Here comes the Deputy [Palewski] in his usual wild hurry.

Much love
   NR

---

[1] Waugh wrote a profile of Nancy for *The Book-of-the-Month Magazine*: 'Nancy received no education at all except in horsemanship and French. Liverish critics may sometimes

detect traces of this defect in her work. But she wrote and read continually and has in the end achieved a patchy but bright culture and a way of writing so light and personal that it can almost be called a "style" . . . Nancy, who, having voted socialist and so done her best to make England uninhabitable, broke from her chrysalis, took wing and settled lightly in the heart of Paris where we find her today. Her present, glittering book [*The Blessing*] gives a picture of what she finds there.'

[2] Anita Loos (1893–1981). Author of *Gentlemen Prefer Blondes* (1925).
[3] Waugh entrusted Nancy with some of the fees from his French translation rights. She kept these 'nest eggs' for him to spend on his visits to Paris.
[4] Anne Clifford; married to John Julius Cooper 1952–85.

To GLADWYN JEBB   7 rue Monsieur, VII
Beistegui Ball Day[1]
[3 September 1951]

My dear Gladwyn

I was awfully pleased to get your letter. I've missed you both very much all this time, though grattified (can't spell it) by the news of your *enormous* fame.

So glad you are coming here. A horrid little shed is being run up by the Musée de l'Homme (my favourite exhibit is Squelette Anglaise) & I wish you could hear the comments of the burghers who like to walk there with their children of an afternoon. The chauffage, we learn, is by rayonnage – not very reassuring when you think what a Paris winter can be like. But I expect the Shirley Morgans[2] of this world will shiver there while *you* sit on a great gold throne somewhere else.

My *Blessing* has had the most awful reviews you ever saw,[3] but Evelyn Waugh & Somerset Maugham have praised it & the public is forking out. As one can't have everything I'd rather it was that way round. I've ordered a copy for you, to be sent to F.O.

Please ring up the very minute you arrive, I die for you.

With love
        Nancy

The dear Colonel, now a dear Deputy, sends his love.

[1] Charlie Beistegui's ball at the Palazzo Labia in Venice was the highlight of the season. 'I suppose it's rather dotty not to go to the Ball. But a dress of the mingiest description would have been £200 – the whole thing would have cost £300 I guess, *hardly* worth it. I feel as if I have already lived through that ball a hundred times.' (NM to Lady Pamela Berry, 25 August 1951)
[2] Shirley Morgan; married 7th Marquess of Anglesey in 1948. She was the daughter of the British novelist Charles Morgan, author of *The Fountain* (1925), a Francophile whose books had a greater success in France than in England.
[3] George Thomson in the *Evening Standard* complained, 'Gone are the outrageous

fun, the wealth of richly comic personages. In their place we are offered a gentle picture of French high society painted by a well-disposed foreigner. It is not what Miss Mitford's readers have been brought up to expect.' 24 July 1951. Lionel Hale in the *Observer* wrote, 'I am not very much amused. In a music-hall, there is the curious sensation of watching a comedian trying too hard. Miss Mitford is as far removed, artistically and spiritually, from a red nose and baggy checks as the Golden Arrow could carry her. Yet somehow she generated in me the same reaction.' 22 July 1951.

To JAMIE HAMILTON   7 rue Monsieur, VII
14 September 1951

My dear Jamie

. . . I know why people (many at least) don't like *The Blessing*. They think all the French characters are stock figures of literature. The trouble is that stock figures of literature (e.g. the dirty old German professor) exist like anything in real life too. Here's a letter, don't return it, from Xandra Haig[1] who has been living in the same world as I do here – just to show you that really it *is* all true. Also I had a terribly nice letter from Mr Maugham, quite unsolicited as I didn't send the book. He thinks it is my best – & he has always lived in France.

It's a bore because, as I can only write what I know, I shall never be able to get away from the damned frogs now. But I shan't write another novel for many a long long year.

I would rather like to do the book on Paris, though can't quite see what form it would take. But I can't begin on anything at all until I have settled the housing problem & I can't settle that until I've got a few million francs in my pocket. It seems I don't become a resident here till Jan: so all my pounds are useless to me until after that date. And the dollars haven't begun yet.

Do try & get the *Book of Month Magazine* (U.S.A.) Evelyn has written an eulogy of me for it.

I do hope you're not worried about having printed so many *Blessings*. What a bore, I'm *so* sorry.

    Love from
        Nancy

[1] Lady Alexandra Haig (1907–). Daughter of Earl Haig. Married to Rear Admiral Clarence Howard-Johnston 1941–54 and to Hugh Trevor-Roper, later Lord Dacre of Glanton, in 1954. She had written: 'Your descriptions of the Ferté dinner party are quite wonderful – not even exaggerated. Is M. de Tournon by any chance Fred de Cabrol? If so you have not exaggerated him! . . . That dinner party is like any party at Amodio's.'

To Lady Pamela Berry   7 rue Monsieur, VII
19 November 1951

Darling Pam

You *have been an angel*, struggling with my wireless & hair dye & so on. A very funny thing about my hair is quite suddenly it has become hardly grey at all. But it will go back no doubt & then I've got my little bottle. The wireless is a different one, I know because I wrote the French wavelengths into mine –!

I've been awful about writing, but somehow busy from morning to night & the days never long enough. And this weekend I've been correcting *Pigeon Pie*, a book I wrote during the phoney war & which I now see is all about you. A heroine called Sophia, with 2 friends in the Cabinet. I must say it amused me, it takes one back to those days with hundreds of little details I had quite forgotten. It came out 6 May 1940 so you can imagine if it sank like a stone. Jamie wanted to republish all my early books but this is the only one I can allow, & it is very badly written I fear. Not surprising as I wrote it in a 1st aid post with the wireless on all day. But I must say it's rather funny.

I hear your Govt has stopped Noel from singing 'Don't let's be beastly to the Germans'. As far as I can see it's their only constructive step so far.

Very disloyal of you not telling about the great Duff row at the Dorch: However I have other sources of information, luckily. I can't help feeling rather glad I live in polite Paris. A French journalist came to see me yesterday to find out why I live here – I said because of laughing. Yes, he said 'on ne rigole en effet pas à Londres.'[1] It always rather fixes me when they ask that as I can't say 'ask the concierge at 1 rue Bonaparte why I live here', can I very well?

I've let myself in for a dinner for the great ball.[2] Goodness the boredom. All these things eat up one's time & I long more than ever to live in the country.

Much love write write
     NR

I'm going to Rome before Xmas – are you coming back here, if so when?

[1] 'You don't laugh much in London.'
[2] In aid of the Hertford Hospital and attended by Princess Margaret.

To Lady Pamela Berry   7 rue Monsieur, VII
[December 1951]

Darling Pam

Of course I know what wild joking times you have with your Cabinet friends, how you roll on the carpet at Rab Butler's[1] jokes & choke nearly to death whenever Buck Delaware[2] opens his mouth, so that often & often I wish I lived in London to share in these hilarities (I'm told Mr Eden's poem on Tom Driberg's wedding must be heard to be believed[3]). And of course *we never* get a bit of fun. So I must make a small boast, & tell you what I had at luncheon today.

F.M. Earl Montgomery of Alamein,[4] whom I sat next to at luncheon got a napkin & twisting it round his shoulders imitated the mannequins at Dior. It was quite something. He had been there this morning & had the whole show put on for him alone, don't you love him for it? I said aren't they pretty? meaning the dresses, he replied only one, meaning the mannequins. I'm IN LOVE, *and* he knows *The Blessing* by heart & says blissikins & everything, can you beat it? He said to Gladwyn (yes oh the luck, Gladders was on my other side) I didn't expect she'd be like that & Glad said why? & he said 'I mean so *nice*.' Oh do be impressed – I am, fearfully.

I want the TRUTH about Lady M Grosvenor – not Buck's & Rab's jokes & the maiden speech etc but just *is it or not true*?[5] Loelia must know. I say too, what price Loelia's father's book[6] – beats *The Blessing* in my view, *how* I loved it.

I saw Mrs Rab & I said is your husband very depressed & she said very briskly not a bit, he just doesn't think people ought to have everything they want. So unlike ONE who thinks everybody should have everything & all forms of bliss – the difference between HERE & THERE, really. Do you roll on the floor with her too?

Then I saw Randolph who was nice at a really lovely Chantilly luncheon of only 7 – Lulu [de Vilmorin] & lover, & Bill Elliot.[7] And this evening was the Windsor party which I enjoyed because I love French literary teas & had several admirateurs including I must confess one or two Dexters.

Now darling I'm off to Via Giulia 167 Rome & will require a letter or two because it is exile to me & I passionately mind leaving my dear dear Col & Paris & everything even only for 10 days.

Do you know the F.M.? Momo never said he was *like that*.

Best love WRITE
    NR

[1] R. A. Butler (1902–82). Conservative MP. Chancellor of the Exchequer 1951–5. Created Baron Butler of Saffron Walden in 1971.
[2] 9th Earl De La Warr (1900–76). Postmaster-General 1951–5.
[3] Tom Driberg, a confirmed homosexual, married Ena Binfield on 30 June 1951. This is possibly a reference to Osbert Lancaster's 'Ode on the Wedding of Thomas Driberg, Esq., MP'. Quoted in Francis Wheen, *Tom Driberg* (1990).
[4] Field Marshal Viscount Montgomery of Alamein (1887–1976). In March 1951 he was made Deputy Supreme Commander to Eisenhower, commanding the Allied Forces of NATO in Europe. Nancy and Montgomery kept in touch through Christmas cards. She particularly treasured his, which were usually photographs of himself in incongruous settings such as on a visit to the porpoises at a sea aquarium in Miami.
[5] There was an unfounded rumour that Lady Mary Grosvenor, daughter of 2nd Duke of Westminster, was turning into a man, in which unlikely event she would have been heir to the dukedom.
[6] Frederick Ponsonby, *Recollections of Three Reigns* (1951). An autobiography by the Private Secretary to Queen Victoria and Edward VII and Equerry to George V.
[7] Air Chief Marshal Sir William Elliot (1896–1971). Chief Staff Officer to Minister of Defence and Deputy Secretary to the Cabinet 1949–51.

To GASTON PALEWSKI   [Rome]
Saturday [December 1951]

My own dear dear darling

I can hardly bear life without you, but you can't imagine with what adulation I have been received here. Old professors dash at me & say I am greater than Katherine Mansfield, that nobody has ever understood the Latin temperament as I have (Polish really but still). Parties for me every day & the pourriture beside itself with excitement. Rather nice you must say. Of course I am in a fog, know nobody's name & said to a very grand Italian, thinking he was English 'I suppose you know a lot of Italians?' which went down very badly. You would scold & 'what are the news' would bring but poor results. 'Who is Charles-Edouard?' they all say. 'Every Frenchman' I reply, falsely.

I read the *Figaro* & see that everything is rather embêtant. Chuck it Colonel, & come away for a little holiday after Xmas.

I worry about you. Back on Wednesday at midnight. I feel as if I'd been away a year.

Be faithful
NR

To Lady Pamela Berry   7 rue Monsieur, VII
4 January 1952

Darling Pam

. . . The Cabrols[1] & Co have asked me to write a little sketch for
them to act so it is to be an old French Duke & his wife sitting in
their tourist-infected château while their only child explains to them
that she is now a man. Everything she says is echoed by what the
tourists are saying, you can imagine how it might be funny. They are
having a revue this year to replace the usual ball – Charlie [Beistegui]
is supposed to have killed balls for ever.

Well Rome was a fantasy. I had 6 parties given for me & generally
the first person I saw was Edda.[2] (Prod wouldn't set foot in any of
the houses but I felt as I don't live there I might as well see what is
on.) They adore my books there & I was literally lionized which is
far from unpleasant. Whereas the English look upon me, quite rightly,
as an inferior PG Wodehouse, the poor Wops speak of my wonderful
psychological insight & how I am greater than Katherine Mansfield &
am the new Thackeray, & of course it went to my head like wine.

The chef de cabinet of Gasperi[3] gave a big luncheon for me & rather
startled me by saying never again will he or any of his friends vote
for Xian Democrats who have thrown away their huge majority &
great opportunities & done exactly nothing. He had a huge photograph
of Humbert[4] on his piano & spoke bitterly of the way in which *we*
(according to him) hurried him from the country.

I found out after that this man Camerini (nice & clever) is only chef
de cabinet et en ce qui concerne les affaires étrangères – he is a
diplomat – which is why he could speak so plainly. The political situation is clearly very bad & the whole country is running down – hardly
any schools open, no social services, hospitals an absolute racket &
run on bribery & so on. The Conservatives at home who object to
paying for these things might be rather more reconciled if they could
see the misery in a country where they do not exist. But of course
somebody like Diana Coo is all for it *and* unemployment *and* every
hardship for the poor, she thinks it makes them more amenable.

Roman society is much worse than Parisian because though the
rich, as here, are utterly selfish & thoughtless, unlike here they have
exactly nothing in the upper storey & are quite ½ witted. Their houses
beautiful as they are, are very badly arranged, hideous furniture, cold
& comfortless. Except for the apartment of Langheim,[5] a Jewish pansy
uncle of Grace Radziwill,[6] who has extraordinary things. Borromeo[7]

has some lovely French furniture but in a hideous modern flat.

I met all the vieux meubles such as Dss of Sermoneta who sent for me to go & see her, Mario Praz[8] & so on, & re found old buddies notably D'Arcy Osborne[9] who was very faithful & on the doorstep every morning to take me out sightseeing. He is in love with the Queen & the Pope & has tinted life-size photographs of both in his room. The women are quite astonishingly dowdy, just like English women, in short tight skirts, violently over dressed from 6 pm onwards & awful tweeds in the morning.

Did you get the *Atlantic Monthly* I sent you with my article on Chic.[10] Oh yes of course your mag rather went for me over it saying it didn't help the export trade.

There is an American couple quiet & cultured called Roberts[11] who *are* the Pattens except he doesn't wheeze. Not bad though. They gave a dinner party for me.

If anyone wants to be buttered up & made to feel good Rome is the place – they go *quite mad* at the sight of a new person poor things, like in a prison.

Gaston has given me such a beautiful Louis XVI bronze, I can't wait for you to see it. . . .

Best love
NR

[1] Baron Frédéric de Cabrol (1909–). Married to Marguerite (Daisy) d'Harcourt in 1937. A fashionable couple in Paris who organised an annual event for charity.
[2] Edda Mussolini, eldest daughter of Il Duce. Married in 1930 to Count Nobile Ciano (1903–44), Mussolini's foreign minister.
[3] Alcide de Gasperi (1881–1954). Italian head of state 1946–53.
[4] King Umberto.
[5] Baron Paolo Langheim; a banker of Yugoslav origin who lived in the Piazza Navona where he gave lavish parties, often for men only.
[6] Grace Kolin (1923–). Married to Prince Stanislas Radziwill; became the third wife of 3rd Earl of Dudley in 1961.
[7] Count Manolo Borromeo; one of the best-looking Italian men of his generation.
[8] Mario Praz (1896–1982). Author of *The Romantic Agony* (1930) and *An Illustrated History of Interior Decoration* (1964).
[9] Sir D'Arcy Godolphin Osborne (1884–1964). Envoy Extraordinary and Minister Plenipotentiary to the Holy See 1936–47. Succeeded his cousin as 12th Duke of Leeds in 1963.
[10] 'What is Chic?', *Atlantic Monthly*, October 1951. 'Elegance in England is of such different stuff from that in any other country that it is not easy to make foreigners believe in it at all . . . It is based upon a contempt of the current mode and a limitless self-assurance . . . the women are elegant until they are ten years old and perfect on grand occasions.'
[11] Mr and Mrs Laurance Roberts; he was head of the American Academy in Rome.

To Evelyn Waugh   7 rue Monsieur, VII
5 January 1952

Darling Evelyn

How deeply boring, your letter never came. But probably will be
forwarded when the Taffys[1] return from winter sports.

People aren't ladies any more (didn't you know that) in England.
Here there is the great dividing line of *bien* – Rosie [Rodd] is not *bien*
I admit, but I thought her beautiful nice & funny which is quite a
lot. . . .

There's a great row (open letters) going on between Mauriac[2] &
Cocteau – the same old Gide–Claudel row on more spiteful lines 'Tu
dis que les pierres ne parleront pas – une pierre a parlé: Toi. Je
t'accuse d'inculture' (the worst thing a Frenchman can say to another).

Of course old Mauriac wins really but not in such a steam rollerish
way as Claudel did over Gide. One rather nasty touch was when he
said to Cocteau 'do remember you are now 66 & very soon you will
have to meet your God'. Poor Cocteau (like me) sees himself as an
eternal 28 & won't care for this at all.

I only ask the '50s to be as heavenly as the '40s – for me. I suppose
you will blow up. But everybody must see the world out of his own
little window & *I* enjoyed every moment of the 1940s. What is so
nice & *so* unexpected about life is the way it improves as it goes
along. I think you should impress this fact on your children because
I think young people have an awful feeling that life is slipping past
them & they must do something – catch something – they don't quite
know what, whereas they've only got to wait & it *all comes*.

I've got a nice present for Hattie & the next traveller can take it.
Thank her for her very well written letter.

You won't make a quick dash over here to see your MS in the
Galerie Mazarine? I believe you would be fascinated by the exhibition[3]
– which has been prolonged another fortnight such a huge success is
it.

I'm dreadfully bored by the lone captain[4] are you?

Fondest love, Happy N.Y.
        Nancy

No foreigner, not even I if I were Lord R, can get into *the* Academy.
Don't cite [Charles] Morgan, he is a member of one of the 5 Académies
housed in the Institut de France but *not* the Académie Française.

[1] Gustaf (Taffy) Rodd, married to Rosemary Dove 1948–66.

[2] François Mauriac (1885–1970). Fervent Roman Catholic novelist whose books explore the conflict between religion and sensuality. Winner of the Nobel Prize for Literature in 1952. He walked out of Cocteau's play *Bacchus* and wrote an open letter to the *Figaro littéraire*, accusing Cocteau of writing profanities. Cocteau riposted with venom: 'You say that stones cannot speak – a stone has spoken: you . . . I accuse you of a lack of culture.'
[3] The manuscript of *Brideshead Revisited* was on display in an exhibition of British books. 'I saw *Brideshead* & was impressed – so clean. My MSS have telephone numbers etc. scribbled all over them – I love the Col & things like that.' (NM to Evelyn Waugh, 25 November 1951)
[4] Captain Kurt Carlsen, master of an American freighter, had spent six days alone aboard his crippled ship. He was towed to safety by a British tug.

To Harold Acton   7 rue Monsieur, VII
27 January 1952

Dearest Harold

I've told Heywood to send you 2 books as an Xmas card rather belated – the Montherlant & *Les Mémoires d'Hadrien*[1] which many people think a masterpiece. Not me, though I enjoyed it, but I shall like to hear your views.

Mme de Beaumont (Edith)[2] has died. She lay in her ballroom in white lace & everybody popped in here after. 'Pour moi c'était le dernier des bals' said one, & another 'white lace, such a good way of using it up, I never know what to do with old lace.'

I can't like Gavin [Henderson], even for old sake's sake, I frankly think he is a Beast.

Just fancy, 200 American ladies gave a luncheon for me last week. Rather what the French call 'good sport' since they are all the wives of Dexters! I was introduced as one of the 6 daughters of Doctor Redesdale.

I hear the dear Romans are very cross about my letter on Rome in *Sunday Times*[3] & the Dss of S-[ermonet]a burnt it in public. How touching – I only said Rome is a village centred round the vicarage – surely it would have been much more insulting to say Rome is a provincial town!

Unlettered D'Arcy however delighted by what I said about his harem of 1000 boys.[4]

The Sutros are in Uruguay I miss them. John gets even more heavenly every year, don't you agree, & Gillian is greatly improved of late, I truly love them both. Besides she is a decoration with her pretty clothes & tiny waist.

Les gens du monde are going to do a revue for charity & one of the scenes is to be a tableau vivant of Le sacre de Napoléon with Arturo Lopez as Boney.

On this pleasing note I leave you dearest Harold.

Love from
      Nancy

I might go to Violet [Trefusis] for Easter would you be there?

[1] Marguerite Yourcenar, *Mémoires d'Hadrien* (1951).
[2] Edith de Taisne de Raymonval; married in 1907 to Count Etienne de Beaumont. Between the wars they gave legendary fancy-dress balls where the decors would be by Picasso or Derain; the costumes, run up by Chanel, would be designed by Christian Bérard or Jean Hugo and Jean Cocteau would write the opening speeches.
[3] 'Rome is a capital city only in name; in fact at heart it is a village, with its single post office, single railway station and life centred round the vicarage.' *Sunday Times*, 6 January 1952.
[4] Sir D'Arcy Osborne was Governor of the Borgo di Ragazzi, the 'boys' suburb', where a school for homeless orphans was set up by priests after the war.

TO LADY PAMELA BERRY   7 rue Monsieur, VII
19 February 1952

Darling Pam

Yes I fear the whole thing has turned us into a laughing stock, so thoroughly overdone.[1] 'A country of Queens indeed' as somebody said. It seems to have turned YOU into Lady Waverley. I had to look twice at the signature to make certain the letter did not proceed from her. In fact, from *your* account of *her* at the funeral I can't help wondering if *Vice Versa* has not occurred.

I saw in some paper that Buckingham P is now going to be turned into a clinic & the young couple will be living somewhere more suited to the modern age. Lord North Street perhaps? You & Dot[2] will have to keep the razor gangs within bounds if so.

And now, with a loud hurrah, we wake up to Susan-Mary-Week.[3] But why wasn't she creeping round the bier with all the rest of you on those flat heeled shoes? Asking architectural questions in a reverent but audible whisper? So unlike her to miss a treat. I should like every word of the visit but only if your present mood of mellow, ripeness-is-all Jingo-ism has given way to a more normal outlook.

A military gentleman of my little group, I may tell you, was *rather shocked* at the slovenliness of the procession to Paddington & I hear that your Prime Minister made a wireless pronouncement in very doubtful taste, but I expect you were sobbing so loud you couldn't hear it. (Every time *I* tuned in to London I got an earful of Elgar.) Have you been to Windsor to have a peep at the dead flowers? I hope your friend arranged them himself, he sounds a regular Mr Spry.

Diana Coo is back, quietly crying it off at Chantilly. Violet has plunged into a deuil [mourning] d'Andromaque, but then she is one of the family.[4]

Best love
    NR

[1] The funeral of George VI had taken place at St George's Chapel, Windsor, on 15 February.
[2] Lady Dorothea (Dot) Ashley-Cooper (1907–87). Married Antony Head in 1935. He was Secretary of State for War 1945–56 and was created 1st Viscount Head in 1960. They lived in Cowley Street just round the corner from Lady Pamela in Barton Street, adjacent to Lord North Street.
[3] Susan Mary and Bill Patten were on a visit to London to see his doctor.
[4] Violet Trefusis's mother, Mrs Keppel, had been a mistress of Edward VII, and one of Violet's wilder fantasies was that she was the King's daughter.

To Lady Pamela Berry   7 rue Monsieur, VII
20 February 1952

Darling Pam
    Perhaps I rather overdid it in my letter of yesterday & if so I am sorry. You know with me, partly I am by nature mischievous & partly I hate hypocrisy & rather hate Kings though I see that with the Empire etc they are perhaps necessary.

I feel if we are to have one how *much* nicer to have a young queen than that very dull man. But you know I *love* England & only live here because of Col, it would never have occurred to me otherwise, & it's a more respectable reason than tax dodging which isn't at all in my line. If I love France too I suppose there's no harm in that. But what I haven't got & never could have is what you might call the *Cavalcade* outlook.

Anyway don't be cross – your letter was *very* provocative too!

Love
    NR

To Lady Pamela Berry   7 rue Monsieur, VII
22 February 1952

Darling Pam

Oh good oh good. Well I rang up Momo & said I've written to Pam
to say the whole thing was thoroughly overdone & Momo said in an
awed voice 'overdone? nobody in London will ever speak to you again'
& rang quickly off & hasn't rung up since. So my nerve (even my
IRON nerve) was shaken because after all one doesn't want to wound
people's sacred feelings.

(1) I don't belong to the Windsor court[1] & though I *love* him (not
her) I regard him as totally unsuitable to be a King – indeed with his
extraordinary rapacity he would be a second King John & pull out the
teeth of Victor Rothschild & John Sutro until they gave him gold. If
we *must* have a Chieftain I prefer Queen E whom I regard as entirely
perfect in every way.

(2) I don't live here in order to win the Gratitude of the French but
because I like it. I don't consider it a sacrifice – I think I am the
debtor, on the contrary. All these fascinating Englishmen look too
much like old bombed houses for my liking, it is no deprivation to me
not to see them.[2]

(3) *Daily Express*.[3] Well I never know whether one should or should
not see these journalists but as after all they are earning their living
just as I am, I always do so & usually it is quite all right (*Evening
News* was).[4] I think the rule should be all except Beaverbrooks. This
pretty & apparently nice woman sat & chatted for an hour & just as
she was going she said 'why do you like living here?' & I said 'well I
am surrounded by people I love.' (I think she said don't you miss your
friends.) 'Who for instance?' Floundering in this deep water I said
'Marie'. The rest was of course invented by me.

I wonder if you could tell me in what way except their talent for
arranging flowers this govt differs from the last? Foreigners are always
asking me & I don't feel I know.

Such a *darling* gorilla ambled in last night, accompanied by wife in
red trousers & gold earrings. He is called Douglas Glass, a photographer. Do you know him? Very preferable to another totally strange
pair called Sir Lionel & Lady Smith-Gordon[5] whom I loathed.
Tomorrow Ld & Lady Beveridge,[6] also strangers. Isn't it odd. I suppose it's the £25,[7] they hope for a free glass of water.

Fondest love
   NR

Oh I long for you to read *Pigeon Pie*, of which you are the heroine. Shows what a genius I must be, to have written it before I even knew you & long before you were grown up.

[1] Lady Pamela had written: 'Oh dear how tactless I have been, of course I shouldn't have mentioned the Royal family (though it was rather difficult not to last week) as I remember now you are dedicated to a tabouret at The Windsor Court.' [February 1952]

[2] Lady Pamela: 'Malcolm [Bullock] is very worried about you giving up England in exchange for only becoming a Displaced Person – he says – because France he feels is the last country to give you any gratitude for it and in the long run will only react like a man to whom one has just said "but *look* what I've given up for you".' [February 1952]

[3] Lady Pamela: 'By the way what was that nonsense you gave the *Daily Xpress* the other day about men not mattering as much to you as a maid. Count yourself lucky I didn't ring them up and give them the truth.' [February 1952]

[4] 'I've Changed My Mind About Authors', an interview with NM by Gwen Robyns, *Evening News*, 12 February 1952.

[5] Sir Lionel Eldred Pottinger Smith-Gordon (1889–1976). Chairman of Broome Rubber Plantations and Arusha Plantations Ltd. Married to Eileen Adams-Connor in 1933.

[6] 1st Baron Beveridge (1879–1963). Responsible for the Beveridge Report which laid the foundations of the Welfare State. Married to Jessy Philip in 1942.

[7] Exchange control limited the sum of money each traveller could take abroad to £25.

To Gaston Palewski   Lismore Castle[1]
10 April 1952   Co Waterford
                                       Eire

My dear dearest Colonial

You will say, one way or another, won't you? The programme is, if you do come, here until 21st then Rosses[2] then I must go to my sister Pam. . . . Anyway I know you wouldn't stick more than 9 days or so. ('How well you know me.')

Lovely pictures in Dublin – a wonderful Hogarth & an Hubert Robert, untouched by the hand of Mlle Cécile Robert, of J. J. [Rousseau]'s apotheosis at Ermenonville. A beautiful huge Boudin & several horrid little Chardins, very middle class & depressing. A Greco (du vrai) a Velasquez (not so sure), etc etc. Big collection.

If you go to Dublin I'd like you to take a look at 20 Sèvres plates chez David Wine.[3] 1766. I think they are excessively beautiful & perhaps not expensive, £100.

I've bought a sugar bowl by Matthew West ('Ah! Matthew West!') so now my coffee arrangements will be NOT BAD.

I don't know whether to hope you will come or not – I'm always so terrified of the bored-&-hungry noise. It would do you good that's certain & amuse you I *think*. The party will be small – Lloyds,[4] Heads, Trees.[5] Aly Khan for one night – but he will have gone I think. Many chateaux to visit.

May I give you a little kiss? 'NO.'
          N

---

[1] Nancy was staying with the Devonshires.
[2] The Earl and Countess of Rosse lived at Birr Castle in Co Offaly.
[3] A prominent antique dealer.
[4] 2nd Baron Lloyd (1912–85). Married Lady Jean Ogilvy in 1942.
[5] Michael Tree (1921–). Married Lady Anne Cavendish, sister of the 11th Duke of Devonshire, in 1949.

TO GASTON PALEWSKI   Lismore Castle
[April 1952]   Co Waterford

Dearest

Oh I'm so terribly sad it's made me feel ill all day. I get so worked up about you, much too much, you ought to be pleased at being the *centre* of somebody's life (but poor me, really). But I was right to stop you coming just for a week end. But what will you do to have a rest? Please please write to me. I worry & worry about you, & this would have been so perfect, it is terribly bad luck.

Then you know I get so sad without you & without the telephoning in the morning. I think I'll never go away again. But back next week – & then perhaps you'll have gone, & I do hope so. Perhaps to Rome?

Colonel I feel in a black cloud of depression, everything seems to be going wrong just now, my flat so unsatisfactory, no idea for a book in my head & now this bitter disappointment.

Never mind. But please do write to me.

          N

TO EVELYN WAUGH   7 rue Monsieur, VII
26 April 1952

Darling Evelyn

Total to me is the mystery why you don't live in Ireland. I should have thought the round peg would have happily dropped into that round hole years ago. Never have I seen a country so much made for somebody as *it* is for *you*. The terribly silly politeness of lower classes so miserable that they long for any sort of menial task at £1 a week, the emptiness, the uncompromising Roman Catholicness, the pretty houses of the date you like best, the agricultural country for Laura, the neighbours all lowbrow & armigerous & all 100 miles away, the cold wetness, the small income tax, really I could go on for ever. (*So* cross about my article,[1] they cut out every joke – they generally do I must admit but this time I thought they went too far. Having wired to me 'masterly performance' & thus raised my hopes. Never mind.)

Do explain, at length. I remember you went to look at a Castle, so what happened? Perhaps you saw an elemental & fled incontinent? But any priest can fix an elemental, surely.

I enjoyed it really & it certainly did me good. But those islands have a lowering effect on my spirits which quite alarms me because what would happen if I had to go back & live in them? Gaston I had to put off, it was too disappointing he'd actually taken his ticket. But when he could get away Debo was house full, & full of rather dull old aunts etc, & none of the other visits fitted for dates. But I see he would enjoy it & next year he must come.

My flat is painted & I'm buying furniture like mad – it looks so pretty I long for you to see it. The heaven of being back, summer is here too.

The bright young Yorkes[2] are at Lismore. Debo has never seen them, she invited their *son*[3] who it seems is a genius, an all round masterpiece of nature, but he couldn't go & she got them instead. I've seen very varied reviews of *Doting*,[4] have sent for it – bet I shall enjoy it.

Much love – write –
        N

[1] 'Over to Ireland', *Sunday Times*, 27 April 1952. 'The Irish, whose qualities of mind and heart were so cruelly misused for centuries, are now applying all their energy to becoming a nation. They have made up a language and are busy trying to learn it, without much success, judging by the fact that they still have to print an English crib under all notices and forms which are written out in Irish.'
[2] So-called because in about 1930 Waugh was puzzling as to who all his 'Bright Young' friends could be, and jokingly mentioned two of his most serious contemporaries: 'I suppose bright young Roy Harrod and the bright young Yorkes.' (Diana Mosley to the editor.)
[3] Sebastian Yorke (1934–).
[4] Henry Green, *Doting* (1952).

To Lady Pamela Berry   7 rue Monsieur, VII
22 May 1952

Darling Pam

Well I dyed (sic) my hair with that boot-blacking, spread rotten egg
over face *and neck*, got myself up to kill in a new dress from Schiap
(given away, she has become the little woman we have all found in
the Place Vendôme) & received 120 critics booksellers & chums in
my garden.[1]

This was yesterday, 6–8. At ¼ to 9, Marie-Laure arrived in a ball
dress. Never have I been so tired but, much as I loathe cocktail
parties it *was* fun.

I think a mixture is so much more amusing than only les gens du
monde don't you? Prominent & unmistakable in the crowd were the
old bombed houses – Harold [Acton], Claud Russell,[2] Tom Dupre &
Tony Rumbold[3] – they stood like wonderful landmarks of my past.
Cyril who is here wouldn't come – it seems we are brouillés à mort
because of the Captain,[4] & flustered American hostesses keep ringing
me up & saying their dinner for Glenway Wescott[5] is now put off to
next week, & I'm not taken in for a moment. I note that *I'm* the one
to be scrapped, not Smartyboots – I note it without bitterness.

There is a new problem for the hostess here do you have it? which
is this. Chaps ring up & say can they bring their homosexual wives.
'You know Hans, you met him at so-&-sos' or 'Roberto who is staying
with me' or one just said 'my partner' like a deb dance. Then these
fearful gorillas appear. They have no conversation & are not even
pretty or not to ONE anyway. Schiaparelli is quite firm & says no –
what do you do in London? Now dear don't tell me that in London
men are men because I know all about it even if I don't actually live
there, & I know it consists of a few bombed houses impotent since
years & the others. There was a letter in the *D. Mail* (continental)
saying life for an English woman alone in France is one long silent
suffering so I wrote & said 'I live alone in France & have the whizz
of a time' & they published it. Do admit.

Terrible troubles, no doubt to have been anticipated over the
Revue. To begin with nobody would act in my sketch because word
went round they would never be asked out in London again if they
did (on acc/ of D of W). So I had to fall back on 2nd choices who are
all terribly – the producer says hopelessly – bad. Then the compère
of the whole thing on whom I *utterly* depended to do the commentary
has fallen out. I'm seriously thinking of withdrawing, because, funny

though it is, I can see it will be a full time struggle for a month, worse than Huttikins, & no pay & probable total failure in the end.

What price Arturo [Lopez] going to London in his yacht? You know the last remaining worker in bronze doré in France has been working on the saloon day & night for 8 months. I guess she will sink like a stone when she gets into the Channel – all that metal on board. . . .

I've chucked the idea of going home in July – too much struggle, too nice here & too dirty in English trains. Also I hear not a room to be had in London until November.

Momo has got a new friend called General Pug[6] – at least this is what it sounds like. I hear her saying things like General Pug is looking for a flat. I don't know if he's a bombed house or a Dexter.

Evelyn says the upper classes have left London except you & Dot [Head].

Much love do write
   N

[1] To launch the French edition of *The Blessing*.

[2] Sir Claud Russell (1871–1959). 'A diplomatist of the old school . . . Tall, dark, slim, with a slightly etiolated air of well-bred indolence, and fine aristocratic features . . . But against these assets was set a complete failure to practise the art of pleasing.' Obituary in *The Times*, 19 December 1959. Married Athenais Atchley in 1920.

[3] Sir Anthony Rumbold (1911–83). Diplomat. Counsellor in Paris 1951–4. 'He is most extremely clever, elegant, agreeable and nice. By far our most shining light at the F.O.' (NM to Prince Clary, 15 September 1961)

[4] Cyril Connolly eventually forgave Nancy: 'When I was in London I made up my quarrel with Cyril. He was at a dinner party, sitting across the table from me – never said hullo, looked freezing, & I was desperate for an opening. Bobbie Helpman, next to me, said "Do you know who I miss most in the world? Constant [Lambert]". I could see that Cyril was listening, & I said to him "Do you know who I miss most in the world? You." And he melted.' (NM to Evelyn Waugh, 10 December 1953)

[5] Glenway Wescott (1901–87). American novelist and poet; his publications include *Apartment in Athens* (1945) and *The Grandmothers* (1952).

[6] General Lord Ismay (1887–1965). Chief of Staff to Churchill 1940–46. Secretary-General of NATO 1952–7. 'He was universally known as Pug, for he looked like one and when he was pleased one could almost imagine he was wagging his tail.' John Colville, *The Fringes of Power* (Hodder & Stoughton, 1985), p. 752.

TO LADY PAMELA BERRY   7 rue Monsieur, VII
29 May 1952

Darling Pam
  Mises au point.
French trains are perfectly clean because electrified. When I have

been in England I always have to spend pounds on having *all* my clothes cleaned, even after a few days, it is one of the miseries.

Bombed Houses. Not impressed by the elderly Don Juans whom you produce as examples of unbeatable glamour. You may get away with them with Susan Mary, but I have seen them, lavishing their powers of seduction, since school room days – from a distance I admit. No pansies in London? Indeed! Here, I must say, most of the normal men *are* married, it is thought to be normal for them to be so, because normal Frenchmen, unlike the Bombed Houses, like to DO IT every day, not just once a fortnight perhaps.

I dined last night with a lot of earnest & important Americans (not chez Patten) & they played a game – each person had to say 'what is THE STONE OF INSULT?' One said it marks the division between 2 tribes – another it's the stone where the women of the village wash their clothes, another it's the stone in the Bible whoever shall cast it first etc. They said oh how interesting & symbolical you are all being – Mrs Rodd what are *your* thoughts about this stone? I said 'I see it as a very small diamond offered for ONE's virtue.' They all rose to their feet & said it was time to go home & they hurried into their huge sick coloured motors & left one to be taken home by the only Frenchman present who was doubled up with giggles I must say. Do admit. They were called John Huston[1] (*The African Queen* said the hostess, what could she have meant?) & Glenway Wescott don't they have lovely names & 2 others unknown regular Hecks though & they talked for *one hour* about a Japanese film[2] & I got in bad from the start by saying I only like historical films with Sacha Guitry dressed up as every king of France in turn.

Oh American highbrows!

Later

I'm utterly done for after rehearsing my sketch for 2½ hours. But *my* it's going to be funny. I've altered it a lot & written a lovely ending – I do think you'll have to come over for it.

The seats are only £8 now, by the way. . . .

Have you seen *Billy Budd*? It's just like luncheon at Chantilly 'Don't like the French, the damned Mounseers.' The French didn't like *it* either & walked out in shoals & *Figaro* critic said 'I hope my article won't be as long & boring as the opera was.'

As our only contribution to the Festival it seems rather a pity. Never mind, the English have other talents no doubt.

Love from
    N

[1] John Huston (1906–87). Film director. *The African Queen* had just been released.
[2] *Rashomon* (1951). Directed by Akira Kurosawa.

To Evelyn Waugh   7 rue Monsieur, VII
16 June 1952

Darling Evelyn

I talked to an old trout younger than me I expect with girl of 12 about Teresa[1] & she said the difficulty would be lessons as no day school would take a child who couldn't speak French. Then she said do beg him to consider the convent school at Morfontaine, a beautiful château (she said) & absolute perfection in every way.

I mention it because she & another lady were so insistent, & because I think it will be difficult to find the family you are looking for. If you did think of it I would get you further particulars.

I long for your book.[2] I'm reading Tony's[3] but the sad thing is I seem to be going blind – can't read all day as I used to & even writing an article gives me a headache. I told this to a French critic who said it's a very good thing for a novelist not to be able to read – yes but what about the hours of boredom? I shall start going to balls again – in fact I now see why it is middle aged people who like balls so much.

One Fr paper said *Blessing* was un roman d'une élégance rare, so I was pleased.

About Tony – I don't think his novels have enough story, in every other way they are perfection. I do think Catholic writers have that advantage, the story is always there to hand, will he won't he will he won't he will he save his soul? Now don't be cross.

Peter de Polnay's travel book[4] is very amusing, I laughed out loud several times. Good print too, so I read it all yesterday. I hope *Men at Arms* has good print. You see I've given up going to balls in order to read more & it is very disappointing to find I can't. Spectacles by the way are no help. I got a pair from your health service in the I of Wight & they give me a *far* worse headache than none, though I have recourse to them when desperate i.e. when reading your letters.

A friend of mine came over from England for one of the balls & said to his dinner partner 'who is that over there who looks so nice?'

'There is nobody nice here' was the reply.

Fond love do write
        N

[1] Waugh had asked Nancy to find a school in France for his daughter Teresa.

[2] *Men at Arms* (1952). The first volume of Waugh's 'Sword of Honour' trilogy.
[3] Anthony Powell, *A Buyer's Market* (1952).
[4] *An Unfinished Journey to South-Western France and Auvergne* (1952).

To Lady Redesdale   St-Pierre du Château
6 September 1952   Hyères

Darling Muv

. . . *Pigeon Pie* has had better notices in America than any of my books isn't it unaccountable. It's selling madly. When I *think* how poor I was when it came out, almost starving (literally really – I used to lunch at Sibyl [Colefax]'s awful canteen for 1/- & I can still remember the pain I used to have after it) I feel quite cross, though it's nice at all times to have a little extra money.

About doctors – I heard a woman in the Ritz saying 'On lui a fait des soins si terribles qu'il en est mort dans la nuit.'[1] I've just read a life of Louis XIII who was literally killed by doctors at the age of 42. Several times he seemed on his death bed & they gave up their 'soins' upon which he always rallied. This was put down to the prayers of the Paris convents – nobody put 2 & 2 together. Richelieu who *adored* him urged the doctors to more & more terrible soins & stood over him to see that he did all they said. You know he was married for 23 years before Louis XIV was born. At the beginning A of A had several miscarriages – then they became very much estranged. Finally the courtiers got them into the same bed by a trick & alerted all the convents within reach – the nuns prayed all night & Louis XIV was the result! Isn't it an odd story.

I went to Monte Carlo for a few days – I always rather love it. Johnny Lucinge gave a ball – very pretty, on a beach in full moon.

I love the way you say Ali & Max [Mosley] arrived with no clothes but of course you can lend. Why of course? I could only oblige with my Diors were it me! I hear the collections are prettier than ever this year oh how fatal!

After a tremendous heat wave I fear the weather has broken up. I begin rather to long for Paris, but don't exactly know when I shall leave here. I've been asked to Venice & might go for a few days.

Best love from
        NR

Love to Jonnican & Ingrid & Catherine[2] (a name I cannot like though I don't mind Kate).

To Gaston Palewski   St-Pierre du Château
13 September 1952   Hyères

Dearest

I am worried by your letter.[1] I suppose the answer must be that like the curé you must go through the motions of belief until it returns. But will it & can it return? The Gen: is not God, & the Bible says put not your trust in Princes (by which it does not mean Johnny Lucinge).

I wonder when you leave for Yugoslavia – Monday I believe. I shall be at the Grand Hotel Venice from Mon: night for 6 days or so. Next year perhaps I'll take a flat in Venice & perhaps you would come & stay – I get low & sad when weeks go by without seeing you.

We have had an intensive social life here with various new faces such as Denise Bourdet[2] also an English household of unutterable dreariness picked up by the Don on the beach.

Peter Rodd, living now entirely in his little yacht, was requested by an American Admiral to leave his moorings to make way for an American warship. He politely declined, signing his letter Yours colonially, & the whole of Golfe Juan is now watching the fray, very much on Prod's side. He has hoisted a signal 'No women on board' I must say Prod does make one laugh – do you remember when he & Gerry Wellesley,[3] governing 2 districts in Sicily, had a fearful row & Prod closed the frontier?

I think you will enjoy Yugoslavia & the complete change. I go home from Venice I think end of next week. I long for the rue Monsieur & I *long* for you.

N

. . .

[1] Palewski had written that he was depressed by the political situation and that his faith in de Gaulle being returned to power was dwindling.
[2] Denise Rémon (1892–1967). Married to the playwright Edouard Bourdet. Parisian figure in literary and café-society circles, and author of several works of biography including *Edouard Bourdet et ses amis* (1945).
[3] Gerald Wellesley (1885–1972). Became 7th Duke of Wellington in 1943. Nancy and he had been friends since the 1930s, meeting occasionally. They corresponded regularly and he kept her letters, which have not been made available to the editor. 'He was the last of the chaps, just not old enough to be my father, who were with the Rodds

in Rome . . . & who had a special kind of way of looking at life, highly civilised & funny.' (NM to Duchess of Devonshire, 16 January 1972)

To Evelyn Waugh   7 rue Monsieur, VII
27 September 1952

Darling Evelyn

Goodness it's good.[1] Apart from the shrieks (loudest of all when Corporal Hill shot himself) the things I thought *génial* were the relationship of the father with the other people in the hotel & the way in which you take yourself off in the act of administering snubs. I *love* de Souza, & of course the Brigadier. Neither the wife nor the sister seem real to me but I can't say why. You see women through a glass darkly don't you.

I love the way English Roman Catholics are exactly as snobbish as middle European princes, I never knew it was so, but it has the ring of truth when you tell about it. Was it wise to kill off Apthorpe?

I only saw Connolly's review[2] well really I suppose, considering the box & also your dédicace[3] with which all Venice rang, it could have been worse. I really don't feel impelled to read the great master work about a fish.[4]

I shall be in London 14th–24th Oct – any hope of seeing you?

I did love Venice. If *Hut* succeeds in N.Y. I intend to take a flat there & a gondolier next summer & do it all slap up. But it's a big IF & in my view it will run for 2 nights.[5]

I've just paid income tax here for the first time. On a sum over £2000 they take, including super tax, just under ⅓. Seems reasonable compared with ours doesn't it. But of course the indirect taxes are far larger than at home. Income tax is 18% super up to 40% but you are let off ⅓ of everything tax free if you are in the category of artist.

I've seen nobody but Momo – have been doing a Venetian article & Aug: Hare[6] & answering millions of letters. But last night I permitted myself to read you.

Much love & thank you for sending it
   N

[1] *Men at Arms*. Waugh had inscribed Nancy's copy: 'Well here it is, darling. Laugh if you can where you can.'
[2] A lukewarm critique in the *Sunday Times*: '. . . for the first time I found myself bored by the central section of a Waugh novel. . . . One raises the silver loving cup expecting champagne and receives a wallop of ale.' 7 September 1952.
[3] Alluding to Connolly's wartime occupation of editing *Horizon* and fire-fighting, Waugh

had inscribed his copy 'To Cyril, who kept the home fires burning'. Quoted in Martin Stannard, *Evelyn Waugh. No Abiding City* (J. M. Dent, 1992), p. 307.

[4] Ernest Hemingway's *The Old Man and the Sea* was reviewed by Connolly in the same article.

[5] The play opened on Broadway in October and ran for 29 performances. *Theatre Arts* described it as 'a mild diversion that never quite comes up to expectation'. December 1953.

[6] 'Odd Mr Hare', a review of Augustus Hare, *The Years with Mother*, edited by Malcolm Barnes. *Sunday Times*, 9 October 1952.

To Evelyn Waugh   7 rue Monsieur, VII
27 October 1952

Darling Evelyn

I never understand publishers' statements – I have tried with this one but truly can't. But if something is wrong would Mrs Bradley[1] not know about it?

The Burberry flat was like a fortune teller's & I got very nervous but Bertrand Russell did appear after a longish wait & fascinated me. He is so exactly like members of my family long since dead, inflection of voice & so on. Very much puzzled by the modern world I thought. I'm sure that when he was a socialist all those years ago he thought that cottagers would be better off *in their cottages* but hadn't envisaged Crittall windows & ice-cream. (Do you notice that nobody speaks of ices any more, always ice-cream.) He said to me 'are you happy?' 'Perfectly happy from morning to night.' 'Good gracious you're the first person I've ever heard say that.'

Oh dear why are people so sad, I wish I knew.

Come soon.

Love
   N

[1] Agent for both Nancy and Evelyn Waugh in Paris.

To Heywood Hill   7 rue Monsieur, VII
28 October 1952

Dear Heywood

I was sad to leave, though it is nice to be back. I would like to have at least two lives wouldn't you.

Bertrand Russell was fascinating – he said I go regularly to *The Little Hut*. I have always wondered who it is that goes regularly &

now we know – Old Philosophers. He is, in other ways, exactly as I had supposed. . . .

Keep in touch & love
     N

To Heywood Hill   7 rue Monsieur, VII
12 November 1952

My dear Heywood

I am to do a life of Mme de Pompadour – what are your feelings? H. Hamilton very enthusiastic.[1]

My difficulty is going to be bibliography & above all getting the books. I'll go & see Bloch[2] later today, meanwhile bear me in mind from that point of view. I must try & do as little Bibliothèque Nationale as possible because my poor old brain doesn't function much in such places.

I bought a flat yesterday for Marie's niece to live in (poor little thing has been engaged for 3 years & no hope of getting married because nowhere to live). The agent said 'there is another one but I don't recommend it, so full of chinoiseries.' 'But I *adore* chinoiseries,' I began in full Mitford voice. Of course he meant jiggery-pokery!

I know you are Xmas rushing, but don't forget Pompadour & after the rush we might do a bit of Cliquing.[3]

There was a short sketch of her I seem to remember a year or 2 ago – any good? Might that give a bibliography? I'm really starting from scratch & would welcome any suggestions. I know much more about Louis XIV than Louis XV. Francis W.[4] may be able to help me. I shall call on him.

Love from
     N

Put me down for Haig's diaries[5] (Eyre & S) I *die* for them!
R Gary *Les Couleurs du Jour*, Gallimard, is absolutely 1st class I think.

---

[1] The idea had come from Lady Pamela Berry. 'When will you realise you must write a book about Pompadour? Heywood says there isn't a thing – not a thing about her. Do get down to it – I so ache for it.' (Lady Pamela Berry to NM [February 1952])
[2] Camille Bloch's bookshop in the rue St Honoré.
[3] 'The bookseller will put an advertisement in his trade paper *The Clique* . . . He will be snowed under with copies at about a shilling each, and will then proudly inform his

customer that he has "managed to find what you want", implying hours of careful search on barrows, dirt cheap, at 30s. the three.' *Love in a Cold Climate*, p. 9.
[4] Francis Watson (1907–92). Assistant Keeper of the Wallace Collection 1938–63, then director from 1963–74. Surveyor of the Queen's Works of Art 1963–7. Knighted in 1973. 'Francis Watson came yesterday he has become the greatest snob on earth. I wonder why fine furniture & snobbery so often go together? I love him so don't repeat these disobliging thoughts.' (NM to Alvilde Lees-Milne, 2 April 1970)
[5] *The Private Papers of Douglas Haig 1914–19* (1952), edited by Robert Blake.

To Mark Ogilvie-Grant   7 rue Monsieur, VII
15 January 1953

Dear Gentle

I really shouldn't write letters since unlike you I am working hard.

You might like to hear a letter I received this morning & I *swear* it's true.

'My grandmother, born Mitford, married a farm labourer called Potts. In spite of the opprobrium attaching to the name I persist in calling myself Mitford-Potts. I live alone in a bungalow & shall almost certainly be murdered by one of the many people who think all Mitfords better dead.

Yrs sincerely Mavis (I swear) Mitford Potts.

P.S. Don't think I admire your idiotic books.'

Not bad? There were pages more, too.

Do tell about female novelists. Poor things, it's rather a harmless way to earn a living I suppose.

I should love to come to Greece though perhaps not with Alvilde who, fond as I am of her, lowers my spirits. I would like to go ALONE with YOU, like George Sand & Musset. But I can never leave Paris really. . . .

Fond love
         N

Do be careful, I'm always hearing of people being HAD UP. Coronation Year cleansing scheme.[1]

[1] Homosexuality was still illegal.

To Harold Acton   7 rue Monsieur, VII
16 January 1953

Dearest Harold

You are having a hateful time, I'm *so* sorry. Old age & death, what a prospect for us all – & we have no sons to soften them for us when our turn comes. Gaston laughs at me because I save up for my old age – but even so I see an institution looming: 'morte dans la misère'.

I lent Vi's book[1] to a very snobbish Frenchman; he said 'I looked at the family tree & I could see that it was nice' just like in your poem. Can you tell me why it had what I believe are called 'rave notices'???

Louis XV's doctor (this is parc aux cerfs days) told him he mustn't make love so much. 'But you said I could, so long as I didn't use aphrodisiacs.' 'Ah Sire, change is the strongest aphrodisiac of all.' When he was 15, on his wedding night, he performed 7 times & one of the Marshals said not a cadet at St Cyr could have done better. Really the Bourbons. But the Marquise never enjoyed it though she *worshipped* him. It is a very odd story.

Yes I do miss John [Sutro] terribly – I rather need a *crony* here. Old Lasteyrie is one in a way. The English (embassy etc) are really terrible except for the actual Ambassador & Minister who are of course too busy to be cronies.

Best love from
Nancy

[1] Violet Trefusis, *Don't Look Round* (1952), a book of reminiscences. When Violet asked Nancy for a title, Nancy suggested 'Here Lies Mme Trefusis'.

To Evelyn Waugh   7 rue Monsieur, VII
19 February 1953

Darling Evelyn
You *are* faithful & clever. I'm sending for all those books – & Ste Beuve's *Port-Royal* has been republished here. I've always known I must read that. The *Encyc. Britannica* which I've got, is a help in a small way & I do more or less grasp the functions of the parlements but not how they are constituted. They seem to represent the King rather than the people. Nobody here knows, it *is so* ODD. Colonel hastens to change the subject – I asked my lawyer who *fled*.

Are you busy? If not, one word of advice. Who am I writing for? Hamish Ham wants me to do it as a novel & that I won't (can't really). But I feel it's no good doing it as though for, say you & G M Young because though you may read it in order to be able to tease for the next 20 years, G M Young won't bother to read it at all. As for my public such as it is they won't give a damn for parlements or Jansenism.

The question really is how much politics should one put in? She was intimately concerned with them for about 5 years, only the beginning of the 7 years war. Wars are simple, even that one, compared with the internal stuff. I wish you wld just put on a P.C. the name of a typical reader – he whom I should be out to entertain without irritating. Oh it's no good asking you, you are such a tease & anyhow it will be the same in the end.[1] One does what one can in life. As you were.

You wld hardly believe that anybody who had after all spent one year in a convent could know so little about the R.C. religion as Mme de P. She was incapable of grasping what it was all about, though so clever in many other ways.

I would love to see you – are you coming over at all?

Best love and THANKS
    N

So many things I want to ask as I plod along. References: a bibliography at the end? *Not* footnotes I think.

[1] Waugh replied: '. . . to be enjoyed by Honks [Cooper] & Pam Berry . . . Write for the sort of reader who knows Louis XV furniture when she sees it but thinks Louis XV was son of XIV and had his head cut off.' *Letters*, p. 393.

To Evelyn Waugh   7 rue Monsieur, VII
24 February 1953

Darling Evelyn
Thank you very very much. I did read Taine before starting, but had to give it back, & at that time, knowing so little, much must have gone over my head. Tocqueville is clearly the boy. What you say has clarified my ideas, & as for needing to *know* oneself, curiosity pushes one to that I find.

I wanted to ride my anti feminist hobby horse & say that Mme de P though prettier & better educated was quite as hopeless as the female deputies today. But I'm not sure. The modern view is that *all* came from the King & that she acted as a private secretary to that intensely shy & inarticulate man. But the policy was his (renversement des alliances etc).

The defeats of '59 were the direct result of Closter Seven which was Richelieu's fault & Richelieu was her enemy of always. After that, lack of good generals which takes us back to the system. (Nobody not noble could have a high command.) Oh how one *longs* & *longs* for Maurice de Saxe.[1]

I'm fed up with French historians – no index & never a date. It must be child's play to write books on the Brownings or Carlyles compared with this. Still I am carried on by the jokes which are truly heavenly.

I saw Pomp more as Daisy Fellowes, but now you mention it she must have had something of Phyllis.[2] Always at home in her comfortable pretty room like that. But did Phyllis fall in love (except Hubert [Duggan] I know she was with him). Pomp literally worshipped the King, he was God to her, & never from the age of 9 thought of anybody else. Very cold, physically, which makes it perhaps understandable, her great faithfulness, no physical temptations.

I went to the Chambre the other day. There is an earnest Communist lady called Rose Guérin, a deadly bore, & when she gets up to speak the deputies begin to hum a tune the words of which are 'Ne parle pas Rose, je t'en supplie'.[3] How *can* women be so idiotic as to go butting in to male assemblies?

Have you followed the case of the Finaly children[4] it is intensely fascinating & nobody here talks of anything else.

Much love & thank you again
    N

I suppose we belong to the last generation which will be able to understand the mentality of a man like Louis XV. He was not so different from – say – my father or Eddy Devonshire, in outlook & prejudices, but the type will soon have died out I imagine.

Oh you mean Quebec '59? I think she *can't* be blamed for that, it was due to the decay of the navy since before her time. She gave a million of her own money for the defence of Canada.

[1] Comte de Saxe (1696–1750). Created Marshal of France in 1746. Led the French army during a period of victories.
[2] Waugh: 'I imagine Mme de P. as Phyllis de Janzé. Phyllis did too I think.' *Letters*, p. 394.
[3] 'Don't speak, Rose, I beg of you.'
[4] Robert and Gerald Finaly were two French orphans whose parents died in Nazi concentration camps. They were brought up in a Roman Catholic children's home until an aunt in Israel applied for them to live with her. The head of the home refused and the children were hidden; their aunt was eventually awarded custody after a two-year legal battle.

To Billa Harrod   7 rue Monsieur, VII
23 [May] 1953   [Pension Maintenon
                                         Versailles[1]]

Darling Billa

No only disappointed. In a way it's a good thing if you come later, I'm working so hard in fact I begin to think I've never worked before, & am deplorable company as a result, know no gossip etc. My system is pathetic, I don't know how to take notes, no French book has an index. I have no memory, so I have to read all of every source before writing each sentence. However the result seems rather good, to *me* (!)

I want to get over the worst before I start hay fever as it's difficult to write when streaming. However this weather in May is sure to mean a cold June so perhaps I shan't have it badly.

My flat begins to look A DREAM & the garden is very nice now, or will be when the rhododendrons put in to please Marie are over.

I do love Versailles I would like to live here & will when old I mean old*er*. . . .

   Much love
     N

I've got to go to England in July I think to correct typescript of the book etc where will you be? I'm told Venice this year is off, too many tourists expected.

[1] Nancy was researching *Madame de Pompadour* (1954).

To Evelyn Waugh   7 rue Monsieur, VII
17 July 1953

Darling Evelyn

H Hamilton came over to fetch the Marquise & took her to his hotel yesterday afternoon, to read before dinner. I was to meet him at dinner & nearly *died* on the way, thinking he might say he was sure some other publisher would like it & so on. However, radiant smiles & (verbal) caresses, so the dear girl will see the light of day. Oh the comfort 'tis to me.

John [Sutro], who is here, says he will take me down to see you in his motor. Would that smile on you? I shall have to find out what *work* I'm supposed to do, I seem to be getting a lot of social engagements. I must try & get my eyes fixed up – can't read at all now. Also do you think there would exist in London a teacher of punctuation? I did so try, with this book, but from what Jamie says ('can't get on very fast, I'm too busy putting in commas') I can see I've not succeeded – & as for paragraphs –!! I did buy a book on the subject but it fogged me worse than ever. I would like to become a good writer, & it should be possible because I see I have the exact temperament required, as well as some talent. Not enough intellect, no education & no technique. C'est embêtant.

The Coopers asked Rosamond Lehmann to stay for 10 days & left, themselves, after 3. I don't know if they sent her the poisoned jug as well. It's quite a technique they've got, isn't it,[1] a lowering treatment. She was very weepy about it. Then they made her, as a sop to their own consciences no doubt, ring up a French person she hardly knows & suggest herself for a few days. She didn't want to a bit, but Diana forced her. The lady was delighted & just as R was ringing off she said '& what is so specially wonderful, I've got Lucian Freud[2] here' whom R *detests*. Do admit it's funny! But not for poor Rosamond, whom, for the first time, in her adversity, I rather liked. Oh do look at those commas – they came quite naturally.

I had a nice chat with a Prof Ross.[3] He is off to North Norway where he expects to find some Danish dialect hitherto lost. He wanted to see me about note paper & so on. He has written a paper about all that for some Finnish university – I told him he should publish it in London, under the title of Are you a Hon? He would make his fortune. He blenched.

Much love I do long for you
    N

[1] During a visit to Chantilly in April, Waugh and Duff Cooper (now Lord Norwich) had quarrelled even more venomously than usual. The precise cause of the row is not recorded but Lord Norwich accused Waugh of 'sponging' and offered to teach him how to hold his wine. (See *Mr Wu & Mrs Stitch*, edited by Artemis Cooper [Hodder & Stoughton, 1991], p. 180.) On his return to England, Waugh, who was beginning to suffer from the hallucinatory symptoms described in *The Ordeal of Gilbert Pinfold*, spread the story that Lord Norwich had attempted to poison him.
[2] Lucian Freud (1922–). Painter. Grandson of Sigmund Freud. Married to Kathleen Epstein, daughter of Sir Jacob Epstein, 1948–52, and to Lady Caroline Blackwood 1953–7.
[3] Alan S. C. Ross (1907–'80). Philologist. Professor of Linguistics, University of Birmingham 1951–74. Originator of the term U and Non-U. In his article in *Neuphilologische Mitteilungen* (1954), he drew on *The Pursuit of Love* as a source of upper-class speech.

To Evelyn Waugh   10 Warwick Avenue[1]
22 August 1953   London, W2

Darling Evelyn

I'm so glad you liked the extract & thank you for the remarks about punctuation which I shall study.

Raymond [Mortimer] most kindly read the MS. He says the book is extremely unorthodox & reads as if 'an enchantingly clever woman were telling the story over the telephone', that many people will dislike it extremely but that as far as he is concerned I have got away with murder. He says perhaps I should have left out wars & Jansenism which read as they might if written by Fragonard.

I was rather taken aback – I had seen the book as Miss Mitford's sober & scholarly work – but then I saw him & he had obviously enjoyed it though he says the whole enterprise is questionable & many will find it very shocking. He says don't re write, it won't be any better if I do, but he has made a lot of suggestions (in the text)[2] & I'll take it back to Paris & work on them.

A D Peters read it. He thinks many of the anecdotes should come out but Raymond says not. I can't take everybody's advice anyhow. I think it must be very uneven in the writing, & I must look at that again. I've told H.H. to wait another month.

The history expert Dr Cobban[3] was forced to admit that he had enjoyed it, & made surprisingly few observations.

So –

I think Randolph is *too* disgusting.[4] Whatever one may think of your letter, & I think you went too far really, it was quite indefensible to show it. In France that is the *one* rule, never make trouble. Nobody would ever speak to him again if he lived there. People who do that sort of thing undermine all civilized intercourse & make society impossible. But I have never liked Randolph since the evening when he hectored the Colonel at the top of his voice in a restaurant. He exemplifies a sort of brutal island rudeness which is one [of] the things I have fled from, & which you never never meet with in France.

The play, after glittering rehearsals with Peter Brook & me saying never has it been so good, has not come up to our expectations. Unfortunately an enormous, enthusiastic audience at Brighton is spoiling the actors dreadfully. I don't think for a single moment that it will do in New York & I'm thankful not to be going.

I return to Paris on Friday & only live for that – I feel quite different with the ticket in my bag. Everybody here so kind & I've enjoyed it all in a way but I don't feel very well & I long very much for the Colonel.

Back to Brighton this afternoon. I shall be in London Monday & Tuesday, Brighton Wednesday – it is all rather tiring.

Much love
    Nancy

¹ Nancy was staying at Heywood Hill's house while attending rehearsals of *The Little Hut* before it went to America.
² 'Someone said to Raymond M, "I hear you took a lot of slang out of Nancy's book." "Not really. I suggested that she might not say Louis XV was perfect heaven 3 times on one page." ' (NM to Evelyn Waugh, 15 December 1953)
³ Alfred Cobban (1901–68). Professor of French History, University of London. Author of *A History of Modern France* (3 vols, 1962–5).
⁴ Randolph Churchill had shown Lord Norwich a letter from Waugh cancelling a weekend invitation: 'I have just learned the alarming news that Norwich is to be of your party next Sunday. Please believe that it is not only fear of infection that makes me ask you to excuse me. I find him so impolite that I really can't sit at table with him.' *Letters*, p. 406.

To Evelyn Waugh   St-Pierre du Château
15 September 1953   Hyères

Darling Evelyn

I really think that, next to starting a book, the worst thing in the world is finishing one – having finished it I mean. I have lost the poor Marquise, as the Dauphine said when she died (we she said really) & I miss her fearfully, my constant companion for nearly a year. Also I feel doubtful about her reception – the photographer royal¹ may be very representative of MY PUBLIC, whatever that means. However as I don't need money for the moment I shall be very contented if a few, such as yourself, approve of her.

I came away from England with a deep contempt for the theatre public – & a resolution never to work for it again as long as I live. Any finer points there may be in the play pass entirely unobserved – the name of Dr Kinsey² is introduced & they laugh for 5 minutes. Peter Brook, one of the cleverest people I have ever met, has been entirely corrupted in the 3 years since I first did the play with him. Well, I suppose it is the same public that reads one's books & if so all I can say is to hell with it. A great eye-opener to me. But at least with a book you don't have to sit listening to their asinine guffaws.

I did think London too awful. I suppose no town can ever have changed so much in 7 short years. If I had to live in England again I think I would go to the Isle of Wight – at least it smells good.

Here I am en plein dans la pourriture.[3] My dear old host cooks up his drugs in the kitchen, Marie-Laure de Noailles next door has a Spanish lover who knocks her about & sleeps with her butler, & in the local pub Jean Hugo & Frosca Munster, both over 60, are having an illicit honeymoon. The joke is they all spend their time trying to keep these facts from *me*. I am supposed to be very prim, a sort of English governess who must not on any account be shocked. But I do nothing but sleep – all night, 12 hours & most of the day. I was quite done in when I arrived.

What a bore, your quarrel with Duff. Now you'll never come to Paris again.

Much love
        N

[1] Cecil Beaton had read *Madame de Pompadour* and was very discouraging about it. He agreed, however, to illustrate the cover.
[2] Dr A. C. Kinsey's report, *Sexual Behaviour in the Human Male*, was published in 1948, and *Sexual Behaviour in the Human Female* in 1953.
[3] Surrounded by decadence.

To EVELYN WAUGH   St-Pierre du Château
25 September 1953   Hyères

Darling Evelyn

I have been to Belgium. Very ugly, very nasty people, wonderful food, wonderful pictures. You might enjoy it, as the whole human race seems uniformly nasty to you.

No, Louis XIV & the cardinals never went near the sun, but died of gangrene in the *most unlucky* parts of their bodies (at least he did & so did Cardinal Dubois). So you can take your choice. I never do sprawl in it now, I remember too well when I was young seeing old ladies of 48 with their skins, mahogany, one mass of well oiled cracks. I made a resolution that never would I get like that & nor I have. But it does me good to run about the mountain here & bathe & have bright sunlight filtering through my clothes. If you could see me you would understand. I go home on Monday.

A usually reliable source informs me that your quarrel with Duff has taken a *new* & *nasty* turn.[1] Operation Mincemeat seems rather a come down – pity they didn't call it Sickmake all the same.

Are you fascinated by the great Culme-Seymour Jackson scandal?[2] I can't remember if we've talked about it.

How much money a year do you need to live on? It interests me to know. I can do on £200[3] a month, & I've saved up enough to bring me £100, then the *Sunday Times* is £30. So if I could save up a little more I should be home. But oh the *Hut* is shut, & that lovely steady hot water bottle of £300 a month has been taken out of my bed. I feel very chilly. I'm sure it won't succeed in America. What of John's play[4] – have you seen it?

F-M the Viscount M. of A., K.G. has asked me to luncheon. I'm very curious to see the set up. When I met him I thought he was *bliss* do you know him? So pretty.

Much love
          N

3 Aunts & Stephen Tennant arrive in Paris next week, do admit.

[1] Waugh: 'I can't think what you mean by my "quarrel with Duff". I am on terms of tender intimacy with him.' *Letters*, p. 409. This particular row had indeed come to an end; after a heated exchange of letters Waugh had offered his excuses to Lord Norwich who accepted them and apologised in turn.
[2] Derek Jackson had eloped with his wife's half-sister Angela Culme-Seymour. He lived with her for three years but they were never married.
[3] Approximately £2,500 today.
[4] John Sutro had discovered, admired and invested in a production of *The Devil's General* by the German playwright Carl Zückmayer.

To LADY REDESDALE   7 rue Monsieur, VII
15 October 1953

Darling Muv

Oh the Wid. Came for one night, stayed for 3 & wore me out. She is a truly awful guest – all the classic things, borrowing clothes, making one pay the cab & so on but far the worst part is the energy. Talk about over 70. She can do 8 times more than I can & reduces me to a pudding of exhaustion.

She never once wore her own shoes, but all of mine in turn (just took them from the cupboard) & of course has stretched them terribly, apart from the fact that I particularly hate the idea. The bathroom stinks of TCP, a smell I've *never* been able to stand, & in the morning it makes me feel sick. Aïe –! Ceci posé she is rather bliss I must say – though I have to refuse to go into shops with her. She turns the whole place out, with no intention of buying, *or*, if she does make a tiny purchase, she accuses the assistant of cheating her over the change. Her purse is full of pre French revolution coins which the oldest living man has never seen, & which she proffers – outraged when they are refused.

I went to Monty[1] yesterday – kept her out of the car with difficulty. She wanted to be dropped in Fontainebleau at the house of a *friend*! . . .

Clementine [Beit] lunches here today & I'm to take her to a collection. Wid still here of course so I couldn't ask Dolly as I'd promised, all very difficult! Never mind, I do love her.

Farve wants me to go for Xmas but I don't think I *can* face it. That awful journey just when I've got back here. I'd rather go to London when *Pompadour* appears in Feb & then perhaps go on up to Redesdale.

Much love
        N

[1] Field Marshal Montgomery and his staff were living at Courances, a château near Fontainebleau belonging to the Ganay family.

To EVELYN WAUGH   7 rue Monsieur, VII
19 October 1953

Darling Evelyn

Charmerende of vittig som Oscar Wilde, funklende som Evelyn Waugh.[1] These magic words occur on *L in a C Climate* in Danish. Written by a member of *your* public darling I suppose.[2] (*Our* public really.) How was the trip? You were evidently preoccupied with ART.

Well I had my luncheon with Monty. He is terribly like my Dad – watch in hand when I arrived (the first, luckily) only drinks water, has to have the 9 o'clock news & be in bed by 10, washes his own shirts, rice pudding his favourite food. All my books by his bed & when he gets to a daring passage he washes it down with Deuteronomy. But oh the glamour! He sat me next him although there were a French marquise & an English peeress at the bout de la table. I do hope I did well – not absolutely sure though. He took me to see an awful little English garden with maples turning red, & I was obliged to say that I couldn't look – too ugly. He *was* surprised. His ADC told me he said to a French general 'I know what you're like – I've read *The Blessing*' & the Frog replied 'Yes well *I've* read *Love in a C.C.*'

What thick rich paper Danes print their books on don't they.

What are you up to? Settling down for the winter? Oh how I dread it.

What is happening in the French church, I can't make out. Do be a duck & send me the address of *The Tablet*, I want to take it in (& I am not fishing to be given a subscription). Or do you advise the other one more. Does the English church ever make a stand against Rome? Is the French church doing so now? What do you feel about the prêtres ouvriers [worker priests]?

Monty says his French ADC cheats over taxes & then goes to Church as if it wasn't a sin to do so. He also says he (the ADC) thinks the poor will be in a sort of servants' hall in heaven. Well so do you.

I'm finishing *Enthusiasm*,[3] it is lovely.

Monty loves Tito & is all for him. Do you love Monty – did you ever go over the top with him? That's what I should enjoy. La Gloire.

Momo has been here – she is very pro German which I think, for a Jewess, is low.

Much love
     N

What can funklende be? It sounds most improper.

[1] As charming and witty as Oscar Wilde, as sparkling as Evelyn Waugh.
[2] Evelyn Waugh had sent Nancy a postcard from Brussels entitled 'The Romance Reader' which showed a large naked lady, lying languidly on a bed, reading a novel. On the back Waugh had written '*Your* public, darling?'
[3] *Enthusiasm* by Monsignor Ronald Knox (1888–1957). Catholic chaplain at Oxford University 1926–39. Waugh wrote his biography in 1959.

To Evelyn Waugh   7 rue Monsieur, VII
30 October 1953

Darling Evelyn

Many thanks for your letter & address of *Tablet* (how odd, somehow, Sloane St).

I've been most exceedingly busy doing nothing – not a moment to myself & yet seeing nobody. I don't quite understand it. Now I've cleared the decks for the proofs of *Pomp* & here they aren't, very tiresome. Yes I *utterly dread* her appearance & keep holding up poor H Hamilton on various excuses. For one thing I now believe it (the book) to be very bad & badly written. I am more at sea than ever about punctuation. I think I had better give up writing altogether, it is too difficult for me. One faint ray of encouragement is that Peter Q[uennell] has taken another chapter for *History Today*.

I am surprised at what you say about Monty.[1] I had always supposed that Alexander was an amiable nincompoop, like Eisenhower. The courtship however was of short duration – I did myself in by saying that English gardens are so hideous I can't look at them.

Why is FOG now called SMOG? I am getting out of touch I fear. When we were little we used to enjoy a good pea souper.

I say have you read *The Go-Between*?[2] Lovely stuff. Yes Operation Embarrassment[3] is very hard to laugh off. (It reads much better in French by the way.)

Prod lives on a small yacht, usually tied up at Golfe Juan. He is a perfectly happy human being & the idol of the local population there. He looks exactly like some ancient pirate – bone thin, pitch black, white hair & beard & dressed in literal rags. He wears steel rimmed spectacles. He has a villainous Spaniard who does the chores – when, on one occasion this fellow displeased Prod he ran up a signal 'Mutiny on board'. However nobody in the modern world, except Prod, can read these signals any more so nobody came to the rescue. Last time he went to England he was shown that list of dutiable goods at the customs. He asked for paper & pencil & wrote down everything that is on it: 'perfume handbags ladies underwear etc etc'. It took ages & they had to keep the train. Then they asked him to open his suitcase & it was empty. So they said they would have him up, but Prod said 'you can't have me up for declaring what I haven't got, only for not declaring what I have got.' Do say he's lovely. If you want a bit more Basil Seal you would be well repaid for a visit to Golfe Juan. I might come with you. Just at the moment I am on cool terms with the old boy because a form which he must sign in 2 places so that I can recover about £3000 in tax rebate, has just come back after *18 months* signed in *one place*. It's almost too much to bear. He has had it since April 1952. In a covering letter he states that he is off to Italy, no address, & will I pay a bill for him at the Travellers. No, I won't. Mutiny in the rue Monsieur.

That's Prod – as you asked.

I've been staying with my holy friend Mme Costa de Beauregard. She is now 85. She spends always 8 & sometimes 10 hours a day on her knees in a totally unheated chapel. Her maid goes & leads her out at meal times otherwise I think she would never move. After dinner she keeps up a flow of wickedly malicious conversation until 1 A.M. I shall miss her dreadfully when she dies.

Much love
    N

[1] Waugh: 'I have always heard the worst accounts of him. I suppose that his charm for you is the contempt of the Americans. We thought him a whipper snapper who did down good Lord Alexander by sucking up to journalists & politicians.' *Letters*, p. 411.
[2] L. P. Hartley, *The Go-Between* (1953).
[3] Lord Norwich's memoirs, *Old Men Forget*, had just been published. Waugh described them as 'all an enemy could ask'. *Letters*, p. 412.

To GASTON PALEWSKI   4 Chesterfield Street[1]
21 November 1953   London, W1

My dear dear Duck
    Nobody here talks about anything *at all* except buggery it's too extraordinary. Half the public wants it officially recognized & sanctioned & the other half wants burning alive quartering etc etc to be restored as the normal penalty. Meanwhile most of our friends are looking very fidgety. Evelyn was holding forth on the subject when Cecil [Beaton] appeared – Evelyn said Ah now *Cecil* will be able to tell us all about buggery. There was an awful row & Cecil left the house.
    Evelyn is in one of his moods. He said to me that he is in love with his daughter aged 11 'very convenient, I don't need to keep a mistress. I have to keep Margaret anyhow'.
    He was thrown out of a party & pushed into a taxi in which lay the somnolent forms of Randolph & Ed Stanley. They woke up & said to the cabman 'go somewhere amusing' so he took them to a brothel (bordel) where the p....ns [tarts] were all discussing the influence of Bernanos[2] on Mauriac. They stayed until 10 the next day.
    So now you see the atmosphere into which I am plunged.

Good Colonel I love you
    N

[1] The Devonshires' London house.
[2] Georges Bernanos (1888–1948). Ardent Catholic author of *Sous le soleil de Satan* (1926) and *Journal d'un curé de campagne* (1936).

To Gaston Palewski   4 Chesterfield Street, W1
27 November 1953

Dear darling

I miss you. I'll be back late on Friday next, so ring up on Saturday morning. I've got you a present, but it is no pleasure to contemplate it, between the enormous sums it cost & the enormous fury with which it will no doubt be received. I shall give it to Pauline[1] to give you so that she will essuyer the worst of the storm.

People here are furious with you. I had to threaten to get up & go from a dinner last night, to stop Aly [Forbes] who was saying more than I could stand. I keep off politics as you know I always do, but the English employ a frontal attack which I have become unused to. (There is a rumour that I am only going to Winston's party in order to make your speech to him.)

The line is that you and you alone are preventing the recovery of France by bringing down every government in turn. You see how insidious this is. As for their bloody old army,[2] I don't understand & never have understood the issue, & really cannot reply. Not that I wish to – I have no desire to be one of those female meddlers who make a laughing stock of the person they are trying to boost.

[. . . incomplete]

[1] Palewski's housekeeper: 'Proust's Françoise to the life'.
[2] The European Defence Community, proposed by the French in 1950, had been the object of controversy for three years. The project was eventually abandoned in 1954 following France's unwillingness to make concessions.

To Raymond Mortimer   7 rue Monsieur, VII
5 January 1954

Darling Raymond

Greatly relieved to get your cheerful letter – I was a little bit worried as week after week went by & no article. We've been very much cut off here by the postal strike – however it's an ill wind & I've taken advantage of it not to send a single card. A less agreeable consequence was that I had 12 hours (at night) in which to correct my proofs. As I found hundreds of mistakes & I am an awful proof reader, specially at 7 A.M., I should think there are still thousands left.

Jamie in the usual idiotic hurry – well, not quite his fault – it is B-o-M for March & he must begin printing.

Oh the election![1] Never has anything been so hysterically funny. I went every day with the heavenly Evangeline[2] (a great comfort owing to the Ambassadorial motor) & we sat there bursting (with laughter!) Also it became very exciting & towards the end we were in agonies lest we should miss the final session. However, all was well & we were at our post! Now I've lost my job on the *S. Times* because Coty is not a Protestant at all – the boredom of it.[3] Everybody said he was, Gaston said of course he is – & of course he's NOT. Poor Miss M has got her facts wrong as usual.

New book. The trouble is my imagination won't switch off all of THEM at Versailles – I haven't got them out of my system. Perhaps when *Pomp* appears, & I get the reviews & so on, I shall lose interest but at present my mind is full of nothing else. It's a bore, because I can't see where it can lead – I really can't be the modern Le Nôtre & anyway no point as we have the dear fellow himself.

Duff.[4] I minded dreadfully. He was like a very nice uncle to me & very much part of my life here. I do so wonder what Diana will do. What a comfort he saw his book into print all right. Gaston says the General has written a beautiful letter to Diana. Oh that General! Colonel is today Commander of the Légion d'Honneur. I'm so pleased. I put out an enormous hint about how much I should like the humble stitch (after all, *Violet*)[5] to which he merely replied over my dead body. Do admit it's a shame – I chiefly want it to impress the concierge I must say.

Give my love to all Brontës – keep in touch. I think of going to Daisy at Cap Martin, about the end of Jan – when might you go South?

All love
N

A wail from Wid – oh dear oh dear what now?

[1] René Coty (1882–1962) was elected President of France on 23 December 1953.
[2] Evangeline Bruce, wife of David Bruce (1898–1977), US Ambassador to France 1949–52.
[3] Nancy was not sacked from the *Sunday Times*; she gave up her regular column because she was finding it increasingly difficult to come up with ideas. 'The fact is perhaps I am getting stale & had better give up – what do you think? I don't mind one way or the other, a bit. It's quite a sweat doing it, in fact I regard it as a sort of mental discipline more than anything else.' (NM to Heywood Hill, 26 June 1952)
[4] Lord Norwich died of a brain haemorrhage in the early hours of New Year's Day. He and Lady Diana were on board ship en route to the Caribbean.
[5] Violet Trefusis was awarded the Légion d'Honneur in 1950.

To Lady Redesdale   7 rue Monsieur, VII
8 January 1954

Darling Muv,
    I've only just got this, because of the strike I suppose. Half one's
letters arrived & half didn't, it was very muddling. . . .
    I went to Duff's service – C of E at its most uncompromising. Our
Bishop is so low church that he thinks singing hymns is idolatry so
we sat while one was *played*. The French were amazed by the whole
thing! It was bleak, I must say. His death a great blow to me – he
was like a very kind uncle or brother & I depended on them both
more, I think, than I ever realized. Now I believe she will live in
England. His death was nothing to do with the journey thank goodness. She had taken blood for a transfusion with her, in case of another
haemorrhage, & everything was done. He said to the ship's doctor
'Am I dying?' & the doctor said 'oh *no* I've seen people far worse
than you who have been quite all right.' But he suddenly collapsed. I
wonder if really it was cancer & they never told him. If so it was a
merciful death. Poor Diana. . . .

    Much love
        N

To Heywood Hill   7 rue Monsieur, VII
4 March 1954

My dear Heywood
    You *have* cheered me up about *Pomp*. The worst of living alone (a
state which I personally prefer) is that there is nobody to say 'oh well,
not so bad – this & this is rather nice' when one begins to see things
en noir [gloomily]. I quite see it wouldn't do at all for a pessimistic
character – as you know life generally appears to me in a rosy light.
    A wildly tiresome thing has happened. Galignani,[1] against all the
rules & to whom do I say it, displayed *Pomp* 5 days before [W. H.]
Smith got their copies – but the worst, for me, is that no chums have
had theirs. You know how here people expect to have read the book
before it comes out. I'm rung up all day by furious friends saying
where is my copy? & although I've spent nearly £50 on these wretched
copies I shall get no credit whatever for it. Nobody realizes the author
has to pay – they regard free copies as their due & the only credit
one gets is for sending them before the shops have them. The worst

is Momo who rings up after every post saying it hasn't come – really
I feel like saying why not trip round to Galignani & buy one.

On the 19th I am to sign the book chez Smith. There is already a
banner *all across* their window saying so – I can't walk up Rivoli it
embarrasses me so much! Do come over for it. I would literally be
dying of horror except that Mr Ward of Smith's is such a duck &
keeps saying 'Oh no, it will be very nice.' So perhaps it really will be,
but I shall never forget doing it in the Bon Marché & nobody coming
near me except one old lady who asked the way to les jarretières
[suspender belts]. . . .

Give my love to Tudor Hal.[2]

Love from
        N

[1] A bookshop in the rue de Rivoli selling English titles.
[2] Betty Batten; a mutual friend.

To Lady Pamela Berry   7 rue Monsieur, VII
9 March 1954

Darling

I did enjoy our conversation & I'm very much pleased you like the
book as it was really written because you said you wanted to read a
life of her. I would have dedicated it to you, only felt I must make a
gesture to Dolly whose niceness to me since I've lived here has been
unimaginable.

I told the Col you asked what I thanked him for – he shrieked with
laughter & said really Pam is dreadful.

I'm having an enormous row with van der Kemp[1] over the horrors
he has erected in the park at Versailles. I do wish you would organize
a lot of titled folks to tease him about it whenever he goes to London.
Intellectuals are no good. Like me, according to Cyril bags, he only
cares for blue blood. When he says it's not his fault & he hates it all
as much as we do, don't listen for a minute. If nobody asked him to
dinner until the reflectors were all removed, they would be taken
down tomorrow. Do join the society to tease v.d.K. (I quite like the
old boy, but he has the brains of a child of 2.)

I wrote to Cyril 'why do you say I think sudden death funny? I hate
the idea of it (true) – it was the one thing I didn't like about the air
raids.' Oh I did love his review.[2] But I'm rather surprised that both
he & Harold take the 19th century view of Louis XV, the high moral

tone & sanctimonious note, which modern historians have completely dropped. I thought Harold's[3] review dull & unfair to tell you the truth, but I terribly enjoyed Cyril's. But your Prof Gooch[4] is easily my favourite – do I dare write & thank him? Do you know him? I long for Freddie [Birkenhead]'s.

All love
    N

[1] Gerald van der Kemp (1912–). Chief Curator at Versailles.

[2] Connolly: 'Miss Mitford's outlook on life resembles that of a worldly schoolgirl. She admires money and birth and romantic love . . . good food, fine clothes, "telling jokes", courage and loyalty and has no use for intellectual problems or the lingering horrors of life. Death, however, if sudden, is vastly amusing.' 'Love at Versailles', *Sunday Times*, 7 March 1954.

[3] 'It is a wonderful story, and Miss Mitford has told it with her own lightness and skill. It is the sort of book that the Book Society love choosing, since it will be enjoyed by educated and uneducated alike. But it is not history.' Harold Nicolson, *Observer*, 7 March 1954.

[4] G. P. Gooch (1873–1968). 'This is history – authentic history – without tears.' *Daily Telegraph*, 4 March 1954.

To HEYWOOD HILL   7 rue Monsieur, VII
13 March 1954

My dear Heywood

I've got a letter from Dr Cobban saying he'll bet my reviewers have never read an original 18th century document, or any secondary stuff since Carlyle. Wouldn't they be furious at this news! But far the most beastly doesn't come under this category, it is A J P Taylor in the *Manchester Guardian*.[1] In a way I think his review holds more water than Harold & Cyril's – he doesn't object to the history – or indeed deign to mention it at all – but to the fact that somebody like me should poach on the sacred preserves. He obviously couldn't bear the book. I don't know much about him, do you? Gooch is easily my favourite so far, though I did love Cyril's for being so funny. . . .

I thought Toynbee[2] most awfully good – oh what a picture of them all it makes. I almost hope Decca won't read it, it is so living a likeness of Esmond, too poignant.

Oh my fan letters, the boredom. (Would it be more boring not to have any?)

I've just had Lord Kemsley[3] on at me, as Nanny would say, to write only for him & once a week. He said 'you'd find your column much easier to write.' I said 'perhaps, but it would be impossible to read.'

W. H. Smith have surpassed themselves. Their huge window is filled with *Pomp*, pictures of her in the nude, & a very dirty old velvet hat with a trailing feather. I mean a real one.

A few more reviews. *Don't* say I said this, but the fact is none of them know their subject, & that is why they seem so confused & contradictory. Freddy Birkenhead quotes *Tocqueville* who is considered a joke here, & *Lecky*! I think Cobban has hit the nail on the head.

Love from
        Nancy

A gun battle with burglars in the next street – I dashed round but arrived just too late. It did sound lovely.

---

[1] 'All those who admired *The Pursuit of Love* will be delighted to hear that its characters have appeared again, this time in fancy dress. They now claim to be leading figures in French history . . . In reality they still belong to that wonderful never-never land of Miss Mitford's invention, which can be called Versailles as easily as it used to be called Alconleigh . . . Certainly no historian could write a novel half as good as Miss Mitford's work of history. Of course he might not try.' A. J. P. Taylor, *Manchester Guardian*, 12 March 1954.

[2] Philip Toynbee, *Friends Apart: A Memoir of Esmond Romilly and Jasper Ridley in the Thirties* (1954).

[3] 1st Viscount Kemsley (1883–1968). Chairman of Kemsley Newspapers 1937–59 and editor-in-chief of the *Sunday Times*.

To A. D. PETERS   7 rue Monsieur, VII
2 April 1954

My dear Peter

I'm only too glad to leave the matter entirely in your hands – I've really felt very undecided about it.[1] All I hope is that Mr Klopfer won't ring me up or – much worse – COME over. He threatened to do that once. Could you mention that I've gone for a long holiday to Siberia?

I suppose we couldn't simply leave it for the moment & sign a contract when I've got a new book in mind? Wouldn't that be more sensible? I won't waver if you don't because, as you know, I am entirely in your hands in these matters.

I've chucked the *Sunday Times*. I was getting too stale & had begun waking up in the night in a panic about what to say – instead of waking up with some good ideas which had to be written down at once. Journalism isn't my talent, & even the pay, once the tax has come off, not so very alluring (I pay, in tax, ⅓ of what I make). But it isn't *that*, it's simply that I can't any more.

Yrs
　　Nancy

Will you tell Mr Montgomery that I'm *delighted* about all these contracts.

[1] Nancy was unhappy with her American publisher, Random House, where she dealt with Mr Klopfer, and was planning to move to Harper & Brothers.

To Cecil Beaton　　　　　　　　　　7 rue Monsieur, VII
14 April 1954

Dearest Kek
　You are a dear duck to write. I hope you noticed that I followed your advice in almost every respect, except that I didn't sit down & do it all over again which, I still feel, would have been useless.
　I'm off to Moscow[1] – 23 May, for the season – the Opera, the races, & a *big ball* on 10th June. You don't know how excited I am – I feel like Carmen 'where are the officers?' As, it seems, there are to be Russian buyers here next autumn, the big houses are falling over each other to lend me dresses. Perhaps I shall stay there for ever, in a pretty white wooden house with a lime avenue & droshkies, what d'you think? My American acquaintances here are too angry to speak.
　I love the cover of *Pomp* & so does everybody – except those who are constitutionally against covers at all. I think it was such a witty idea having her dressed & naked like that.
　My great boast is that I hear the F-M [Montgomery] talks of O else (but *Pomp*) & has told his new ADC that he must have read it before coming to join up. Do admit.

Much love – do come over soon
　N

[1] Nancy's friend, Sir William Hayter (1906–), Ambassador to USSR 1953–6, had invited her for a two-week visit.

To Heywood Hill   7 rue Monsieur, VII
1 May 1954

My dear Heywood

My crazy friend Prof: Ross has written such a lovely pamphlet for
la société néo-philologique de Helsinki, printed in Finland but written
in English, on upper class usage in England. Entitled 'Linguistic class-
indicators in present day English'. It has sentences like 'The ideal
U-address (U stands for upper class) is P.Q.R. where P is a place
name, Q a describer (manor, court, house etc) & R the name of a
county . . . . but today few gentlemen can maintain this standard &
they often live in houses with non U names such as Fairfields or El
Nido.' (What will the Finns make of it?)

Anyway it seems to me a natural for the Xmas market, illustrated
by O. Lancaster & entitled Are you U? I've suggested this to the
Prof (who may of course think it dreadfully infra dig) & I've told him,
if the idea appeals to him to send you a copy & you would perhaps
advise about a publisher.

It is dreadfully funny throughout because written in a serious scientific style. I'm glad to say *P of L* is one of the source books. He is a
great new character in my life & a card if ever there was one – U
himself, & in my expert opinion he has got everything right but ONE.

I still haven't got my visa – Iris Hayter thinks they are busy reading
my books, but one of the secretaries here says it all depends on
Burgess!! They've had my passport for an absolute age.

I'm dealing with Spiers[1] & don't think he'll like what I say very
much. Malcolm [Bullock] promises me that he appears as that in the
1914 army list – can I *utterly rely* on his word??

Some journalist wrote that I am short of a plot & the result is plots
pour in by every post. Many letters begin 'I am in a clinic & the
doctor tells me that somebody ought to write the story of my life . . .'
doesn't it conjure up a picture! They (the plots) are all non U &
therefore no good to ONE.

Love from
    N

[1] Sir Edward Spears (1886–1974). Altered the spelling of his name in 1918. Extraordinarily successful liaison officer between the British and French during the First World
War. In 1940, he was responsible for bringing General de Gaulle to England, but later
quarrelled with him. Nancy's review of his book *Assignment to Catastrophe*, in the *Daily
Mail*, was 'strong meat'. She described it as 'truly poisonous', probably because of the
cruel portrait it included of Palewski. An unkind description of his physique ended:
'Oddly enough M. Palewski considered himself something of a ladies' man.'

To HEYWOOD HILL   7 rue Monsieur, VII
23 May 1954

My dear Heywood
    . . . Well I'm off. The Soviets went to ground with my passport &
the Embassy (ours) said 'there's only one card left for us to play, you
must go yourself & try & get it out of them. But take a book, &
make no plans for the rest of the day, they will keep you there for
hours.' So off I went – gave my name – was immediately ushered into
a huge room, full of pictures of Stalin, whose occupant rose to his
feet crying 'je vous attend depuis des semaines.'[1] It was quite sinister
– come into my parlour. I was out in the street again, with visa, in 2
minutes! Then I went to Cook & said 'can you send me to Moscow?'
thinking perhaps there would be more difficulties. The man simply
looked through a heap of brochures 'come to sunny Monte Carlo' &
so on, until he got one saying 'come to lovely Russia' & sold me the
ticket there & then. So I leave here on Friday & arrive Moscow Sat
9 p.m. having spent the night in Stockholm. Isn't it thrilling.
    There is a very good book called (rather ambitiously) *France*,[2] by
a Cambridge don by name of Charvet. I was sent a proof to read. It
is much the best & clearest book I have read in English on the French
constitution, empire & so on.
    Prof Ross most indignant at the idea that his Finnish pamphlet on
U speakers might be turned into an Xmas best seller. Oh what a pity.
    Voilà – that's all my news.

    Love from
        Nancy

[1] 'I have been expecting you for weeks.'
[2] Patrice Edouard Charvet, *France* (1954).

To GASTON PALEWSKI   British Embassy
Letter begun 30 May 1954   Moscow

Dear dear Colonel
    I had such a fascinating journey. When I got to Helsinki the plane
for Moscow was waiting only for me. (Very different from the packed
Scandinavian lines I'd been on until then.) There were a Host &
Hostess, & it was a pretty little plane rather like a cottage all blue &
white, with plush curtains. No nonsense about fasten your safety belt
– & no safety belt either. At Leningrad I got a huge form to fill in
(any wormwood roots or stags' antlers?) & then they said now you

would like to rest, & I was taken to a lovely drawing room with a real
sofa which I lay on while the Host chatted happily away about Joy in
Work. It was all very soothing. A sweet man said should he telephone
to the Embassy & tell them I was on my way? Personal attention
(what Pam calls petits soins, so different from what one gets on BOA
or Air France).

The huge plain, hour after hour, very impressive I thought.

This morning, imagine the luck, a parade in Red Square for the 300
anniversary of the Ukraine belonging to Russia. I've never been in
anything so exciting since the Air Raids. From very early morning
dear dear workers, looking rather like dear dear Gaullists, streamed
past my window dancing & singing & laden with flowers. The parade
itself was worth coming here for alone. One knows what such things
must be like, but knowing is not seeing. The massed bands, punctuated by guns not drums, the endless clockwork marching, the glorious
toughness of Bulganin[1] whizzing round in a huge motor, the Migs
almost hitting the onion domes as they go over, all enacted for 5 or
6 dreary little business men in ill fitting suits. This performance is
succeeded by the workers & their flowers which fill the huge square
& make it look like a morning garden. I truly never saw anything so
beautiful.

In the afternoon we went to Yussopoff's country house. A fearful
give away I thought of the upper classes here. The house itself, poor
architecturally, is just saved by being painted yellow & white & by
its beautiful situation looking over the huge blue river. Inside not one
even reasonably good object meuble or picture. A few what they call
here Gubert Roberts, but I should say by GR's mistress more likely
– everything else 'school of' to the last degree. The lustres, the
parquet & so on really shoddy. In the garden an obelisk with obsequi-
ous wording was erected every time the Czar came to dinner. Shades
of Kinsky abounded: 'my old coachman Hans' in person was lolling
in a deck chair by the theatre which he sternly refused to open
for us.

Then a dinner chez Joxe[2] for 40 people at which I sat on the host's
right. He was very agreeable & afterwards became very jolly. He has
a mistress in candy stripes – it is of course the only love affair going
on among the diplomats & is watched with an awful fascination by the
others. Dancing after dinner – home very late & very tired.

Alas William [Hayter] doesn't want me to write – as I had feared.
Would you, dear Colonel, keep this letter, I'll write a diary when I
get back just for myself – & I forget things so quickly.[3] . . .

3 June

Last night the ballet. The story: Mlle Pototska (sic) ravished away from Lançut by Mongol hordes. The tartar King madly in love with her – his favourite wife murders her – he grieves & puts up a fountain to her. I kept thinking of Dolly's 'Alfred' & shrieking. It is very thrilling when the hordes arrive in the middle of a garden party at Lançut.

So much to tell, but this must go now & I shan't have another chance of sending one.

The rest of my visit very cut & dried. I leave here Tues: & spend 3 nights in Leningrad, pure sight seeing. Friday night at Copenhagen – *not* Stockholm. I'm so sorry if you've written already – I would have written a word to the Ambassador but didn't do so in case you had *not* & it would have looked rather odd.

I couldn't *bear* Stockholm, it lowered my spirits – the hotel is horrible.

Home Sat afternoon 12 June – come & dine tell Marie if so. If I don't turn up make a little fuss – I shall be quite alone from Tuesday onwards.

Love, you dear dear duck
        N

[1] Nikolai Bulganin (1895–1975). USSR Premier 1955–8.
[2] Louis Joxe (1901–91). French Ambassador to Moscow 1952–5.
[3] Nancy eventually published an account of her visit to Russia in *The Water Beetle*.

To Evelyn Waugh   7 rue Monsieur, VII
20 June 1954

Darling Evelyn

Oh Russia *was* fascinating. So much more beautiful than I'd expected for one thing. I was 11 days in Moscow & 3 days quite alone in Leningrad (Hotel Astoria). I wonder if you got my postcard.

I can't write about it for publication. William would rather not & I feel I couldn't anyhow – the Russians were so nice to me & it would be a poor return to mock at them. Many American women do this, & exhibit their pathetic clothes in smart New York shops, I don't think it is decent human behaviour. But I am writing every detail for chums & will send.

I must tell you – I asked to see Soviet writers. But I was told that on 29th of May they had all gone to the country, to write. But I saw a lady from the State publishing house. I said to her 'how many copies would a best-selling novel sell?' She replied 150 million. 'Goodness' I said 'I can't wait to come & live here.' She said as they often do, it is a stock phrase 'This has its good side & its bad.' 'Well I can't see what the bad side can be for the writer. What is the name of a novel which has sold 150 millions?' 'Well there is The Testing of the Steel – &, of course, Cement.' By this time I was distinctly giggly. They are just like Americans just as I knew they would be. The *Pravda*, reviewing a novel while I was there (one gets the *Pravda* in English, it is a joy) said: 'The Seasons is well written & well observed. This is quite so. But this novel does not summon to anything nor struggle with anything –' Just what the Americans always say about ONE's books. *Pomp* by the way *very* badly received there – they say it seems to have been written by Daisy Ashford.[1]

We are all very much pleased about the new government,[2] though I wish Col could have had a job. But he could only accept War or Foreign Affairs & Koenig was the obvious choice for War. Better than a minor ministry – remain as he is, just Vice President.

How fascinating about Cecil's book.[3] I was invited to a Foyle luncheon for it. No I shan't come to England – I've had enough of hideous clothes & uneatable food to last me for many a moon, in Russia.

I feel rather worried about your great new goodness, I hope it's all right.

I didn't know about Chatsworth.[4] I must say I can't feel as desperately sorry for D & A as I would if they cared for the objects.

Oh my happy life. It came over me in waves, when I was away, how lucky I am, & when I woke up & realized I was back in my own bed an enormous smile spread over my face. But I'm more than glad I went. I brought buckets of caviar & asked all the greediest people I know. They sat in a holy circle & never spoke to me once, except to say, in loud asides, that the others were making pigs of themselves.

I'm trying to find out what it would cost to get my essay on Russia printed – if too much (I am utterly ruined) I will send you the typescript first, before it is in ribbons.

Fond love
   N

[1] Daisy Ashford (1881–1972). Child author of the inimitable *The Young Visiters* (1919).
[2] Formed by Pierre Mendès-France, leader of the Radical Party.
[3] Cecil Beaton, *The Glass of Fashion* (1954). Although Waugh found the book 'curiously incompetent', he refused to review it. 'It shows how I have softened since my lunacy . . . Ten years ago I should have romped into it.' *Letters*, p. 425.
[4] After the death of 10th Duke of Devonshire, important works of art were taken by the Government in lieu of death duties. They included the *Liber Veritatis* of Claude,

Rembrandt's *The Philosopher*, Holbein's cartoons of Henry VII and VIII, the Van Dyck sketchbook, Rubens's *The Holy Family* and a Memling triptych.

To Jacques Brousse[1]   7 rue Monsieur, VII
[1954]
[postcard]

I quite forgot to tell you – *Pompadour* is banned in Ireland. This always happens because one or 2 sentences are objected to, & sometimes one cuts them out in another edition. So I eagerly asked what were the operative paragraphs & was told it was banned because of the title. Are you shrieking?

[1] Nancy's friend and French translator.

To Hugh Thomas[1]   7 rue Monsieur, VII
11 July 1954

My dear Hugh

. . . I was looking through a little book my sister used to keep called What are you like? & in which people had to answer a sort of questionnaire, & one of her friends (aged 17) answered 'what is your greatest ambition?' with 'to be a diplomat', & it was Donald Maclean. So his wish came true all right. Tony Rumbold also wished that.

You couldn't write me 5 or 6 lines from Ivan the Terrible's famous song from the famous opera of that name? The hero of the play[2] I'm doing has written this opera & I'm in trouble over the song. The sort of thing I used to be able to do on my head AT YOUR AGE. But I daresay you have other things to think of.

I must go now & see if a Russian visa will stop me getting a Spanish one.

Yrs ever
Nancy

[1] Hugh Thomas (1931–). Historian. Author of *The Spanish Civil War* (1961). Created Baron Thomas of Swynnerton in 1981. Married Hon. Vanessa Jebb, daughter of Lord Gladwyn, in 1961. He and Nancy met in 1953 at the Cambridge Union; when he came to Paris in 1954 he helped research *Madame de Pompadour*.
[2] Nancy had been asked by the American impresario Gilbert Miller to work on the English version of *l'Heure éblouissante*, a play by Anna Boracci, which had been a success in Paris the previous year.

To Lady Pamela Berry   7 rue Monsieur, VII
13 July 1954

Darling Pam

Fréjus must be quite near Tony – but I think I'm going to chuck Hyères. The Colonel's mother is dying & he is dreadfully sad & low & I don't like to leave him alone in Paris, at a time when there are no little duchesses to amuse him even. I'm going for 10 days on *Sister Anne*,[1] to the Balearics & then I think I'll fly back here from Barcelona.

Col has been very low of course about everything, but not so much since Mendès F took over. As you know he has always maintained that all that is needed is an able & energetic man – as the man of genius who does exist *won't* play – & Mendès F is that & honest & Col agrees with all his ideas. So he feels far more hopeful than a month ago.

Didn't you think Russia is far more like England than any other foreign country? The awful clothes, the awful food, no wine, the deeply ingrained Calvinism, the gloom, the indifference to sex. On the day when they all danced in the streets the sexes danced together, just as they do at home at the Women's Institute dances. All that tea, too, & the smokiness of Leningrad, the sun never getting at your skin, though glowing hotly overhead.

Mr Bohlen[2] told Momo I couldn't have wandered about Leningrad alone, I must be lying if I say so. In fact, I asked for a guide or interpreter twice & never got one, & was *entirely* alone the whole time. But it's not a difficult town to find your way in, & I expect I was better off without the gramophone record which you describe.

The Colonel proudly shows your card (11 Downing) to all his English friends NONE of whom have been invited. I think you had it printed specially for him. Dreadful if he calls your bluff & *goes* & finds you alone with Gen: Spiers.

Yes how does the Almighty account for the continued existence of Ld Beaverbrook?

Then I'll see you end of Sept that will be lovely. . . .

Much love
      N

[1] Daisy Fellowes's yacht.
[2] Charles E. Bohlen (1904–74). US Ambassador to USSR 1953–7 and to France 1962–7. Married Avis Thayer in 1935.

To Gaston Palewski   St-Pierre du Château
10 September 1954   Hyères

Dear dearest

I am never really blessée [wounded] by you – I tell myself that you are an oddity of nature, not like other men, but I love you. But I was fed up with not knowing anything – though I admit it's my own fault for going away.

Colonel a week *isn't* enough. You wouldn't think of a little séjour in Venice later on. Naturally not – though you wouldn't hesitate if I offered you some disgusting picture of a maggoty fox by Courbet, costing twice as much.

I've been offered 6000 (six thousand) dollars a *week* to go to Hollywood.[1] I wonder if I'd better do it, as I have no book in view.

The Duc de Morny has turned out very different from you – a new type to which I am rapidly turning. ('Then I'm afraid you won't succeed' G.P.)

Oh dearest I worry about you.

I shall be back in Paris today week.

A little love & affection would be very welcome though quite unexpected.

     N

Stay away as long as you possibly can – every day helps.

[1] To work for MGM on the final script of the film *Mary Anne*, taken from Daphne du Maurier's novel.

To Gaston Palewski   St-Pierre du Château
11 September 1954   Hyères

Dearest

I've been thrown into a turmoil by your letter[1] & the idea of all these dollars, all coming together. But if you are sad, as I can see you are, & if your prospects are no better I can't go away for months & leave you alone. Or am I no good to you? Oh how I wish I could open you like a book & see what is there. Nobody has ever been such a riddle to me.

At the same time do I want to go? Do I want more money? Le côté interessé de tout ça[2] says yes, but when I reflect a moment what do I find? One life, not very long, no heirs – then why do what one doesn't want to, simply for money. Would I consider it, apart from the money? Of course not. Then I think, dollars for France – perhaps it's my duty. They say 6000 dollars a week for up to 6 months – 48 million francs, if it were six months. 48 million francs, & come back to find the Colonel married to Mme Abrami.[3]

Do you really see why I am in a turmoil?

N

[1] Palewski had written that he was feeling depressed and exhausted.
[2] The self-seeking side of me.
[3] Renée Haim de Hobeken; widow of Pierre Abrami, a doctor. She was not a girlfriend of Palewski, but he would have known her since she was a champion of the MRP party. She died in the dining room of the Hotel Royal Monceau in Paris and a wit was heard to say: 'Madame Abrami was so *mondaine* she even invited Death to luncheon.'

To GASTON PALEWSKI   St-Pierre du Château
[September 1954]   Hyères
Monday

Dearest

So I decided against Hollywood, after 2 days of slight hysteria. I realized that it's not a question of whether you need me or not – the point is I can't live without you. I should be too miserable & it can't be right to make oneself miserable for dollars.

You know Colonel you have let yourself get too depressed, & if you go on you will be ill. You've stayed too long in Paris & life has got out of perspective. I beg of you dearest to stay away as long as you can & to lead a very healthy life – no motor car, walks (especially up & down hill) & bathing. I worry about you day & night it's dreadful being able to do nothing, except worry – that's the worst of this sort of relationship, one is really so helpless. But do listen to me for once & look after yourself. The body & the mind react on each other you know & there is *nothing* worse for a constitution like yours than lack of exercise, because that is what calms the nerves.

Oh dear Col
     N

. . . Nora [Auric], Marie-Laure & Co *can't* get *over* me refusing all that cash – it makes them quite furious!!!

To A. D. PETERS   St-Pierre du Château
Sunday, 12 or 13 September 1954   Hyères

My dear Peter

I can't (just as you knew). A sort of black misery descended on me at the idea of staying among those people I despise, & doing work I despise, for money which I don't absolutely need.

What's nice about you is that you never mind one saying no – Mrs Sanders[1] would have had a stroke!

I go home next Saturday.

Yrs
    Nancy

[1] Marjorie Sanders of Sydney A. Sanders & Co., Nancy's American agent.

7 RUE MONSIEUR VII.
SUFFREN 7665.

6 Sept 55/

Dear Handy,

Can I have the book on the
Kremlin please?

Could you possibly get a few
more copies of enclosed & send to
enclosed list for me - charging me
of course 4/- a copy or whatever
retail price would be. (Made for
you, this mag:)

Such a wonderful Encounter
mail - furious baronets, furious
Scotchmen, furious friends saying
how vulgar I am, furious Frenchmen
saying they are not like a chicken

To Violet Hammersley, 10 July 1962

1955–1957

A TALENT TO ANNOY

> The fact is with me, my love of shrieking is
> greater than my amour propre. My skin is
> thick. And, great protection, I can never take
> myself seriously as a femme de lettres. So I
> suffer less than most people.
> NM to Evelyn Waugh, 11 October 1955

In January 1955, with de Gaulle's blessing, Gaston accepted a minis-
terial post in Edgar Faure's government, one of the many revolving-
door administrations of the Fourth Republic. This was in addition to his
work as a Deputy and as Vice-President of the Assembly. Increased
responsibilities meant that Gaston had even less time for Nancy than
before, so she allowed herself to leave Paris for longer periods,
especially during the summer months. In 1956, she went to the island
of Torcello in the Venetian Lagoon to work on her second historical
biography, *Voltaire in Love*. She found Venice an ideal place to combine
work with pleasure; she would write in the mornings, bathe at the
Lido in the afternoons and spend her evenings with friends in the
cafés lining the Piazza San Marco or dining in palazzos or restaurants.
For the next fifteen years she made annual visits to Venice, and her
enjoyment of these summer months helped a great deal to compensate
for Gaston's absence.

When Stephen Spender – then editor of *Encounter* – asked Nancy
for an article on the English aristocracy she seized upon it as a wonderful opportunity for a large-scale tease, relishing the chance to poke
fun at the upper classes and to mock those who tried to imitate them.
Deliberately hoping to provoke, Nancy quoted from an article

on upper-class usage by Professor Alan Ross, who had coined the terms 'U' and 'Non-U'. Not even she realised what a sensitive nerve she would be touching. The September 1955 issue of *Encounter* was an immediate sell-out, the press took up the issue, and U and Non-U passed into the language. One of the funnier aspects of the affair was the serious debate it provoked on both sides of the Atlantic, bringing Nancy a not altogether welcome notoriety. The following year, Hamish Hamilton republished the article in *Noblesse Oblige: An Enquiry into the Identifiable Characteristics of the English Aristocracy*, which Nancy edited and which included contributions from Evelyn Waugh, John Betjeman, Christopher Sykes and Peter Fleming. The book was a best-seller and generated a huge amount of publicity, but it ended up by boring even Nancy.

To GASTON PALEWSKI   Long Crichel House[1]
1 January 1955   Wimborne
                                           Dorset

You dear good Colonel how I wonder what happened – why you withdrew the Palewski amendment etc.[2] I shall never know because when I inquire de vive voix on my return I shall get 'enough, woman.'

Are you married yet? The wedding took place privately between Pamela, daughter of Lord & Lady Digby & Colonel Palewski The Scots Guards (ret). Better very private or somebody you know might make a fuss at the altar. It's lucky she's so very Catholic I mean in case you ever wanted to join the MRP.

Everybody at Chatsworth very sad you didn't come. But I couldn't help wondering what we should have done to amuse you all day. At luncheon they sit down one side of the table so as to watch the races on television. Here on the contrary, everything is arranged for every minute & I believe you would have enjoyed a visit here. Such a lot to see, in this neighbourhood.

Dear darling try & be good. If you want to get in touch with me, 4 Chesterfield St W1 is my headquarters.

   With love & a kiss dear Colonel
      N

Happy New Year.

[1] Nancy was staying with Raymond Mortimer and Eddy Sackville-West.
[2] In January 1955, faced with the impossibility of reforming the regime, de Gaulle withdrew from the political arena and dissolved the Rassemblement du Peuple Français (RPF).

To CASS CANFIELD[1]   7 rue Monsieur, VII
11 February 1955

Dear Mr Canfield

Thank you *so* much for *The Day Lincoln Was Shot*.[2] I've had my nose in it all of this day, the sort of book I absolutely love. Oh what dreadful people – all dreadful if one loathes Lincoln himself, &, as you may guess, *I do*. Though I admit that the others were even worse. I've read nothing lately but books about brutes – Gladstone, Victor Hugo, Ruskin & now Abraham, but of course this one is perfect because one knows for certain that the brute is FOR IT, in a very short time, whereas the others went on & on until you could scream.

I would have liked a much more detailed account of the end of Booth – the only fault I can find with this lovely book.

Thank you again very much.

Yours sincerely
    Nancy Rodd

[1] Director of the American publishing company Harper & Brothers. 'I said is Cass
short for Cassowary but no, Cass is his name. Really Americans!' (NM to Jessica
Treuhaft, 28 August 1957)
[2] By James Bishop (1955). ' "Abraham Lincoln. I detest Abraham Lincoln. When I read
the book *The Day Lincoln Was Shot* I was so afraid he would go to the wrong theater.
What was the name of that beautiful man that shot him?" ' 'She Doesn't Like Us', Art
Buchwald on NM, *New York Herald Tribune*, 9 April 1957.

To Violet Hammersley   7 rue Monsieur, VII
13 February 1955

Fiend & Kidnapper of Twins
    Enclosed is for your armoury against Mme Costa.
    There was a lovely huge dinner at the Embassy last week & I sat
next Jean Cocteau. He told me he has a godson & at Xmas he felt
rather guilty about this child to whom he had never sent a present,
so he went off & bought a beautiful big pink mechanical rabbit. He
received a very cold letter – il paraît que mon filleul est colonel.[1]
    Last night I dined with Gladwyn & we went to Leeveeng Roooom,[2]
which, in French, is an excellent play. During dinner Col telephoned
to say he had been offered a portefeuille & should he accept? He has,
however, refused, which is really what I hoped he would do. He is
very fond of Pflimlin[3] who is a great friend, but the MRP sticks in the
gullet I must own. . . .
    My Swedish publisher writes that the 1st edition of *Pomp* is sold
out – 6500 copies – not bad he says for a country of 7 million people.
He begs me now to write about some other lady – but who? *You*
perhaps, beginning with Philip IV[4] & ending with Leslie [Hartley].
    I saw Doodie[5] yesterday. Like all the idiots here she was vaccinated
& of course her leg swelled up & she's been very ill.
    There was a tiny outbreak of smallpox in Brittany & oh the fuss
there has been. Nine hundred people died in Paris alone last month
of cancer & nobody turns a hair. Isn't it odd.
    I haven't seen Mme Costa but I know she is still dressed like a
widow or worse because I sat next M. Corbin & he said 'who has
Mme Costa lost?' & when I told him it's almost a year even he could
hardly believe me!
    Cocteau said Rosamond [Lehmann] is translating I forget what of

his & it turned out he thought she was a very old lady. I said well fairly old, about my age, & he couldn't get over it. Of course she started very young didn't she.

   Love (teaspoonful of)
      N

[1] Apparently my godson is a colonel.
[2] Graham Greene, *The Living Room* (1953).
[3] Pierre Pflimlin (1907–). MRP Deputy. Minister of Finance 1955–6.
[4] Somerset Maugham once jokingly described Violet Hammersley as resembling a cast-off mistress of Philip IV.
[5] Madame Costa's daughter-in-law Elizabeth. Her husband, Amedée, had died the previous year.

To Raymond Mortimer   7 rue Monsieur, VII
7 March 1955

Darling Raymond
   Much amused by your & Harold's articles yesterday[1] – the (1955) Devonshire House set won't like *his* much, the Duchess is revered by them. I'm about to embark on the book.
   Went to Groussay to see Charlie [Beistegui]'s theatre which really is something – about the size of a small Paris one, complete with luxurious dressing rooms etc. There were 2 ministers, Col & Bonnefous,[2] 2 ambassadors & a duke (Massigli, the Spanish, & Brissac) several princesses & a général – yours. Charlie's is a foreign house, so I got the Academician, Lacretelle[3] (& an ex minister, Cornu[4]) & we talked much of you. He is furious with Atticus, who, he says, upped Sacha Guitry & downed Claudel. He said 'if you see Lord K[emsley] do ask that French matters should be left to R.M.' I generally forget to read Atticus but I see this week he has been very fair about Cocteau – perhaps egged on by R.M.
   So strange about Cocteau – he is utterly furious, more than furious, ulcéré & courroucé, because he is not in Cecil's book!!! He told Denise B[ourdet] 'Cecil a dû bien se moquer de moi quand je me suis levé à l'Ambassade pour lui porter un toast.'[5] Can you beat it, Raymond? Marie-Blanche [de Polignac] wept on my shoulder because Mme Lanvin is not IN – well that is comprehensible, but for *Cocteau* to mind defeats me. I tell them all until I burst that Cecil has got everything wrong en ce qui concerne l'Angleterre, so hardly surprising if his French bit is incomplete. But somehow he has put it across

them that he is the great arbiter of elegance who will go down to posterity etc, & they MIND.

Port-Royal[6] much more riveting than I had expected & not stiff at all, as some say it is. The 2½ hours without entr'acte go like a flash. Only ONE is entirely on the side of Archbishop King & Pope. The fact is Montherlant hates women too much to make them sympathetic, & they come out as terrible earnest theological *bores*. Very likely they were, I can't help feeling. There's a wonderful moment at the end when a little nun sees something we don't – shudders, & flees, & then in comes Mrs Hammersley to the life (new order, taking over).

Mlle Jaloux (expert from Versailles) came rather doubting to see my screen which I thought had perhaps belonged to fat, hairless M[arie]-A[ntoinette]. She positively jumped when she saw it – said M de Nolhac had terribly wanted to buy it for the château but it had fetched 40 000 francs in those days & so on. I'm delighted of course. She says the embroidery was done by fat hairless herself!

    Best love
       Nancy

[1] Reviews of two books about the 5th Duke of Devonshire's wives: *Georgiana* edited by the Earl of Bessborough and *Dearest Bess* by Dorothy Margaret Stuart. Raymond Mortimer's article ended: 'To sympathise with these effusive creatures we must make an effort of historical imagination.' *Sunday Times*, 6 March 1955. Harold Nicolson wrote of Elizabeth: 'She creeps fox-like through the book: her sneaky racoon snout peeps out at us from every page . . . she was "a poor little creature" to whom life had been so very, very cruel. Yet she sponged on the Devonshires all their days.' *Observer*, 6 March 1955.
[2] Edouard Bonnefous (1907–). Minister of State 1953, Minister of Public Works 1957–8.
[3] Jacques de Lacretelle (1888–1985). Author of *Silbermann* (1922), famous account of the schooldays of a young Jewish boy.
[4] André Cornu (1892–1980). Minister for the Arts 1951–4.
[5] 'Cecil must have had a good laugh when I stood up at the Embassy to toast him.' In fact, Cocteau is mentioned four times in *The Glass of Fashion*, and there is even a drawing of him by Beaton.
[6] Henry de Montherlant, *Port-Royal* (1954).

To VIOLET HAMMERSLEY   7 rue Monsieur, VII
15 March 1955

Cystitis INdeed!
I heard of you, arriving at the island with a 20lb salmon in that black net which sometimes drapes the hats taken from my cupboard. *Salmon-itis*, you can tell Dr Broadbent, with my compliments.

Oh if I could draw, I would write an illustrated Life of You. The nets, the veils, the shawls, the scarves, the crêpe, the cape, the wildly waving weeds, the unvarying get-up of cliff & turf & cresson & rue de la Paix. Who could do justice to it?

I'm having a day in bed which I love more than anything on earth, & do about once a month. 'She's been in bed 17 years.' 'Oh Mrs Ham *how* lucky.'

I've been asked to write a hugely long article for *Encounter* on the English aristocracy.[1] Can't quite decide, but if I do it it will contain volleys of teases. It's a series – French German Italian & Spanish too by various experts. I rather wish I'd been allotted the French, really, only it might have killed darling Mme C[osta]. . . .

Massigli says the *M. Guardian* is the best paper in Europe & therefore the world, & I agree. I rarely see any other & when I do I can't get over the dullness – the *M.G.* has a giggle on every page.

Do help with the aristos – I need lots of ideas. Thought I'd say the vast majority belong to C of E, the few who believe in God are R.C.s, X Science & Ox Group. Also stress the fact that they would rather do anything – even wash up & cook – sooner than work for a living. If money doesn't fall from heaven they cheerfully (isn't Lady So & So wonderful) do without. One thing I'm asked is who are the eccentrics of this age? Who? . . . HELP.

. . . Salmon poisoning never lasts very long so I expect you're better by now.

Love from
Gerda

[1] 'The English Aristocracy' appeared in the September 1955 issue of *Encounter*. 'My article is very brilliant . . . I lovingly linger over it, adding telling phrases.' (NM to Mark Ogilvie-Grant, 14 March 1955)

To GASTON PALEWSKI   40A Hill Street[1]
2 April 1955   Berkeley Square, W1

You dear Colonel

Well, Winston's party was very enjoyable & everybody dressed in the most extraordinary robes, one has forgotten what London ladies look like in the mass. I remember you saying pauvres petites dans leurs affreuses robes, si gentilles[2] –

All are impressed by the grandeur of your new station[3] – I think you ought to come over & cash in.

The Chauvels[4] seem to be a great failure so far – do try & send somebody attractive to the Embassy here.

I got rather stuck with Mr Attlee at the party – he is no conversationalist I fear. Nobody knows a *thing* about whether Winston is or is not going & it makes them all very fidgety. They say Anthony [Eden] is dying for it. Meanwhile Winston has got a pet bird & thinks of nothing else, it sits drinking whiskey with him & makes messes all over the official documents.

You're a good Colonel. I love you. Back on Wed afternoon.

N

[1] Nancy was staying with Momo Marriott.
[2] Poor little things in their hideous dresses, so sweet –
[3] Palewski had been appointed Minister of Disarmament and Nuclear Development.
[4] Jean Chauvel (1897–1979). French Ambassador in London 1955–62.

To Lady Redesdale   7 rue Monsieur, VII
Easter Monday [11 April] 1955

Darling Muv

I'm dreadfully sorry to hear that you had such a miserable journey in one of those freezing trains *peculiar to Blighty*. (Can't resist a slight crow that you have at last seen for yourself what it's like, as it never fails with me – so much so that I find it hard to believe that any are heated.) Of course it's because the English are so *good* & never complain & their sad reward is to live in the most uncomfortable country in the world. I remember a Canadian saying to me 'if we were in Canada the passengers would get up & wreck this train'. And do you remember the lady to whom I said 'you ought to revolt' & she replied 'we *did* revolt against tinned beetroot.'

Oh dear, it's such a triste réveille, dressing in the freezing cold, I am truly sorry & hope you are quite recovered.

I've just finished *Dearest Bess* – oh what a bad editor this D Stuart, who is she I wonder? Of course one longs for the journal without her fatuous comments & inaccurate footnotes. Personally I prefer Bess to Georgiana by very far – at least she had something in the upper storey. . . .

I went to Orsay yesterday & asked D[iana Mosley] what she *could* have meant by saying the Fr aristocracy is starving but it seems she was telling you about the Sabrans, who are very poor (though I'm glad to say they have a tante à héritage who keeps up beautiful Ansouis). I did think it almost too odd, because the riches of the great families like Noailles, Polignac, Rohan, Gramont, La Rochefoucauld, Hinnisdaël, Ganay etc etc are literally fabulous by any standards, & unlike the rich English they keep up state in Paris *and* the country.

I'm buried in my article on the aristocracy. The French always say that the great proof that we don't work is no shooting on Sunday. If they didn't shoot on Sunday, they say, they never would be able to at all!

My young friend Hugh Thomas has just called, rather battered after a fight with a German last night. Oh dear I said must we begin all over again?

I suppose if I go to Greece I shall be stoned – better really to stay at home.

Much love
    N

To Sir Hugh Jackson[1]   7 rue Monsieur, VII
16 July 1955

Dear Sir Hugh

Just back from Greece & so delighted to get your letter & that you like *Pompadour*. Not being accustomed to historical (or any) research I didn't keep nearly enough notes, so don't know where I saw about the wounded being well treated after Fontenoy, but I put nothing in the book without verifying it by contemporary statements.

I do remember seeing that the bourgeoises of Lille, usually so frivolous, were exceedingly good on this occasion. But even so it can't have been much fun to be wounded in those days.

Yes the great excuse is that M-Antoinette came to a wretched husband & a profligate court at the age of 14. So did Catherine of Russia. Many women have wretched husbands, it's a thing they must be prepared for. People never make excuses for men because they have wretched wives, I notice. If Fersen was her lover, & I'm sure he was, it makes her really too despicable because the one thing they all believed in was le sang de St Louis etc etc.

How I wish *S Times* had printed your letter – so good of you to write.

Yours sincerely
    Nancy Mitford

[1] Sir Hugh Jackson (1881–1979). Amateur historian. Son of Sir Thomas Graham Jackson, the eminent architect. His letter about *Madame de Pompadour* sparked off a correspondence with Nancy which lasted until her death. They never met, but exchanged over 150 letters. In Sir Hugh, Nancy found someone with whom she could discuss her historical books, who would sympathise with her admiration for the past and who shared her increasing dislike of the modern age. They remained until the end on formal terms: he addressing her as 'Miss Mitford' and she always calling him 'Sir Hugh'.

To EVELYN WAUGH   7 rue Monsieur, VII
2 August 1955

Darling Evelyn

You must have been pleased at the note of high lunacy on which Ld N-Buxton[1] concluded the correspondence. May all your enemies perish thus – darling Rufus is evidently a candidate for the bin.

I was going to the Riviera this week but am now rather sadly obliged to stay here as Peters has picked up a very remunerative piece of work for me. I'm to write the English dialogue for a film on M-Antoinette (quite funny when you think of the fuss).[2] As I haven't earned a penny yet this year I feel I must accept, & much as I long to go back to the heat am bound to say that Paris is heavenly at present.

Everybody has gone – at least, 2 millions have – except le bon géant, as a paper described the Col.

My learned friend Mrs Arthur[3] places *Os & Gs*[4] among the great novels of the world – she held forth for half an hour on its merits. If you knew the extent of her knowledge learning & taste you would be gratified. (Normally her mind is engaged upon Mme Guyon & the Abbé Brémond.)

Poor widowed Smartyboots[5] – rather sad, isn't it, when he so loves to be the one that chucks.

Who wrote the *Observer* portrait?[6] Randolph's ghost? I thought it very very good.

 Much love
     Nancy

P.S. Decca arrives with her children end of the month. I'm half delighted & half terrified. Seventeen years –
What are Stinchcombe's[7] plans for welcoming F. M. Bulganin?

[1] Rufus Alexander, 2nd Baron Noel-Buxton (1917–80). He and Nancy Spain had arrived uninvited at Piers Court and were sent packing by Waugh: 'They attempted to effect

an entry into my house and wrangled until I dismissed them in terms intelligible even to them.' *Spectator*, 8 July 1955. Spain's version of the incident in the *Daily Express* provoked a sharp attack by Waugh in the *Spectator*. Lord Noel-Buxton tried to defend himself and denied that he had greeted Waugh with the words: 'I am not here on business. I am a member of the House of Lords.' Nancy sided with Waugh: '. . . it is no wonder if elderly writers become bad-tempered. Dogs which are constantly baited turn savage, and writers are supposed to be more highly strung than dogs. I am not as famous as Mr Waugh, but nobody would believe the extent to which I am teased and tortured by strangers.' *Spectator*, 22 July 1955.
[2] Nancy had infuriated many of her French friends with an article in the *Sunday Times* which described Marie-Antoinette as 'one of the most irritating characters in history . . . frivolous without being funny, extravagant without being elegant, her stupidity was monumental.' 'A Queen of France', 22 May 1955.
[3] Esther Murphy (1895–1962). American intellectual. Married to John Strachey, MP and journalist, 1929–33, then to Chester Alan Arthur, great-nephew of the US President. 'Esther was a large sandy person like a bedroom cupboard packed full of information, much of it useless, all of it accurate. I was truly fond of her.' (NM to Evelyn Waugh, 3 December 1962)
[4] Evelyn Waugh, *Officers and Gentlemen* (1955).
[5] Cyril Connolly's second wife, Barbara Skelton, had left him for George Weidenfeld.
[6] The unsigned profile described Waugh as 'a man of great if rather tigerish charm' and ended, 'Embittered romantic, over-deliberate squire and recluse, popular comedian, catholic father of a family, Evelyn Waugh is one of the oddest figures of our time.' *Observer*, 31 July 1955.
[7] Waugh lived near Stinchcombe in Gloucestershire.

To CHRISTOPHER SYKES   7 rue Monsieur, VII
6 September 1955

Darling Christopher

I loved your letter. I *love* Smok[1] if only for having had you – but I was brought up to love & revere him. My downness on Bts & Kts is because since living here I've become very conscious of *places à table* & I'm FED UP with having Momo placed miles above me, & Clementine Beit too & Hellbags.[2]

I didn't want to put in the Ross stuff at all but wily Spender[3] made me – good for sales I don't doubt. Evelyn says, & I wish I'd thought of it myself, that each family invents its own U-talk & thinks all other common. He agrees with me that U speakers can instantly be spotted, & asks why, since, as he truly says there is little in common between the voices of – say – Andrew D[evonshire] & the late Lord Curzon.

I longed to put U Scotch non U Scottish, but as one's publishers insist on changing it, my books are full of Scottish (though once, in *Pomp*, I got by with Scotch). In my ignorance I thought the Wakes were totally bogus. All that part was written for me by a young friend in the college of heralds as a matter of fact.

When Gaston read the article he merely said 'Who is this Scrope? He must be a bore.'

I should have made it more clear that poor Fortinbras sold all at the very moment when things were getting much better – typical of him.

Je m'ennuie de vous.[4] Won't you come over soon? I was thinking the other day how I never see you.

I went to Greece & thought so much of dear Bert [Robert Byron] – perhaps the dead person I miss the most.

Next year I plan to go to the Smok lands. All this is merely in search of warmth – I get colder & colder & only feel really happy when it's over 90.

I made great friends with Paddy Leigh Fermor[5] – do you know him? He is a shrieker & how rare they get.

> Fondest love
> Nancy

[1] Nickname for Christopher Sykes's father, Sir Mark Sykes (1879–1919). 'By the way you are down on Baronets. All part of your French drive against Smok.' (Christopher Sykes to NM, 2 September 1955)

[2] Helen Dashwood.

[3] Stephen Spender had persuaded Nancy to include excerpts from Professor Ross's article on upper-class usage in 'The English Aristocracy'.

[4] I miss you.

[5] Patrick Leigh Fermor (1915–). Travel writer and translator. Married Hon. Joan Eyres Monsell in 1968. Author of *The Violins of St Jacques* (1953), *Mani* (1958) and *A Time of Gifts* (1986).

To RAYMOND MORTIMER   7 rue Monsieur, VII
8 September 1955

Darling Raymond

She knows it would be perfectly deadly without me in heaven, & needs me to cheer up purgatory for *her*. That's why.[1] . . .

A letter from Willie M[augham] saying he can't be U as he says toilet paper. Ugh.

Heaven forbid that I should ever put you off coming here, but October *is* an awful month on account of that wretched motor-show. I was hoping to go away then & get a little fresh air & Indian summer – but all depends on this film. They are days behind their schedule.

If they want me in Oct: they have to pay £150 a week but equally I have to stay (contract). If you do come shall I give a cocktail party for you? I'd love to if you could bear it.

Then my Communist sister may be here – Eton crop, pince-nez & men's trousers. She is in London with husband & child. Child has been told that Debo's money comes from selling slaves. Debo says Goodness if we had any slaves we wouldn't *sell* them. I don't die for her as much as I pretend to when I write.

Aren't the Turks being lovely.[2] The French think of course that it's the Intelligence Service in turbans – I do hope so.

How are you? You sounded rather low when you last wrote.

Dear old Harold-bags, nearly as anti-French as you, has got Versailles all wrong.[3] What about the 250 bathrooms in the castle? I had to write & scold. Then wot's all this about unkindness? I think it's the English who are so direct & brutal & make one cry at meals – here all is honey & butter. No Frenchman goes on at one like Randolph or Ed Stanley – it simply could not be. Do admit.

If you get an extraordinary mag called the *Compleat Imbiber* it has a story[4] by me. I was paid with 25 bottles of whiskey.

Much love
    N

[1] Raymond Mortimer reported Violet Hammersley as having said: 'What a lot of Purgatory Nancy will get! We were taught not to hit a man when he's down.' He continued: 'That is the latest from Totland Bay. You're lucky, or she is polite, you are consigned to Purgatory and not to the everlasting bonfire.' (7 September 1955)
[2] There had been anti-Greek risings in Istanbul and Izmir.
[3] Harold Nicolson in *Good Behaviour* (1955) writes of 'Lounging courtiers, chattering rubbish . . . lolling in the foetid ante-rooms of Versailles'.
[4] 'A la Mode', *The Compleat Imbiber* (1956).

To Lady Redesdale   7 rue Monsieur, VII
14 September 1955

Darling Muv

After a tremendous day of it yesterday with Mr Gotfurt – from 10 AM to 8.30 & again after dinner – I've finished my adaptation & am now quite free. He seems very satisfied. The film will be wonderful[1] – they start today, what a rush, really! . . .

A flood of letters re *Encounter* – mostly fans, though some abuse 'I am circulating it in the monastery – the Prior much impressed by it'. 'My typist is so angry she refuses to type a letter to you' & so

on. It was wicked old Spender, eye on sales, who egged me on to do
the U stuff. I went to W.H.S. here yesterday – manager dashed at
me saying all sold out the first day. Heywood, who usually sells 20
had sold over 100 last week. I'm pleased, as they gave me 3 times
their usual rate, so I feel I've earned it.

    Best love
        Nancy

[1] *Marie-Antoinette* (1956). By Jean Delannoy, starring Michèle Morgan and Richard Todd.

To Gaston Palewski   Wilmington
[October 1955]   Totland Bay

Dearest
    Only a word to say do come to Debo next Wednesday 19th, she
very much hopes for you – Edensor, Bakewell, Derbyshire.
    If you don't come, I implore you to send me a word there to say
how you are. I worry & fuss & fidget about you. I haven't been at
all well, but am recovering here. I didn't much enjoy London, I felt
too anxious about you.
    Last night I dreamt I was engaged to Lord Darnley, & was wonder-
ing how you would take it when I woke up & remembered that he is
dead (to my relief I must add). . . .

    Dear good, I love you
        N

To Hugh Thomas·   7 rue Monsieur, VII
18 November 1955

My dear Hugh
    Oh well – if what you like in life is large new buildings large new
motor cars & cold new cocktails I see that America is just the place
for you. However don't despair. There is a terribly pretty new hotel
in Bond Street & I hear that very soon one won't be able to see
dowdy old St Paul's any more for the lovely steel & concrete cliffs
which are going to surround the dusty old bore. As for here, how you
would rejoice. The nice old hôtel de Rohan near me has been knocked
down & high time too, & a delightful edifice of 7 storeys is being run
up by Arabs (I only hope they are *underpaid* & *insuffisamment logés*,

with *aucun confort*). Great are MY sufferings, but I'm glad somebody is pleased.

Saint-Simon[1] has cost me rather more blood, sweat & tears than a novel would, but I think it's fairly all right. The whole thing is a prolonged tease on Harold [Nicolson], really. My good Mr Philips (yank) comes to type it out presently. He needs a lot of money to pay his psychoanalyst. I said to him 'what's wrong with you?' 'I can't seem to be able to work with people.' 'Well you work with me all right.' 'Everybody isn't like you, Mrs Rodd.' Rather true.

I hope your first post abroad will be Athens (unless of course you are lucky enough to go to UNO). They, the Greeks, have been most successful in hiding, destroying or spoiling anything old. Daphne is surrounded by huge nylon-clad legs outlined in Neon lights.

I really don't know if I *can* see you on your way to the South, but anyhow telephone & if I'm in a *very good mood* . . . .

Yours
      Nancy

. . .

[1] An article to mark the bicentenary of Saint-Simon's death. 'The English have not treated him well . . . Sir Harold Nicolson and Mr W. H. Lewis, both of whom quote largely from him in their *Good Behaviour* and *The Sunset of the Splendid Century*, seem to regard him respectively as a clever bore and a gifted liar. He does not really please Englishmen.' 'The Great Little Duke', *New Statesman & Nation*, 3 December 1955.

To Evelyn Waugh   7 rue Monsieur, VII
19 November 1955

Darling Evelyn

Are you alive? I have been buried for 3 weeks in an article on Saint-Simon, the most difficult thing I've ever done I think, & very brave to take it on! I hope it's more or less all right – I've got in one or two nice teases anyway, & got my own back on Harold N for saying that my *Pomp* was not history.

It all arose because I wrote to John Raymond[1] & told him what you said about his Belloc article. Of course he trod on air 'the Elder's approval has given a great lift to the spirits' & immediately asked me for an article! (*N.S. & N.*)

I do love you being the Elder, & the fact that all those young men would give pages from Raymond or Cyril for one line from you, you old crusty-pots.

Madame de Pange, descended from a lady in waiting of M[arie]-A[ntoinette], also beheaded, has asked me to her son's wedding.

M. de Mun, whose name speaks for itself, told me that the culte for M-A is something quite new. I think I am forgiven but I shall have to watch my step.

I had Decca here for a week – unchanged and so sweet. Also her Romilly daughter who is a beauty. I very much hope she'll send her here in a year or 2 to learn French & then I must find her a nice French husband (receipt for happiness).

I go a great deal to see them turning the film of which I did the English dialogue. It will be one of the very best historical films – & *so* pretty to look at. It's like a Turkish bath or a railway journey, being in the studio. Nobody can get at one – such bliss.

With love from
          Nancy

[1] John Raymond (1923–77). Literary critic and author. 'Mr John Raymond is nice & clever & likes me so of course I like him.' (NM to Evelyn Waugh, 19 July 1955)

To Gaston Palewski   7 rue Monsieur, VII
Sunday [January 1956]

Colonel

I see I have offended you & I am very sorry, I beg your pardon. I only understood in the middle of last night as I lay on my b of d thinking furiously that you had abandoned me because being ill bores you. Suddenly with a great jump I saw what it is.

It came from a silly desire to show Geoffrey[1] one can buy things at little shops which he never will do. Then I always regard those 2 things which I chose myself with another eye. (He knew about the inkstand already because of having the pair.)

I have never mentioned anything else to anybody except once to Diana which you know. I must say everybody knows that all the pretty things in my flat were given me by you & it would seem rather unnatural if I never gave you a present. I apologise. But I think it is a little thing to set against 15 years of faithful & unchanging love.

[1] Geoffrey Gilmour (d.1981). A mild-mannered English homosexual friend of Nancy whose apartment in the rue du Bac was full of fine objects and furniture.

To Duchess of Devonshire   7 rue Monsieur, VII
29 January 1956

Dear aged 9[1]

  I've just had a letter from my Dutch translator saying will the 'cave of the nobles' do for H*u*n's cupboard? I think you'd better write & explain that it is a hen house – that'll fox him.

  Tell Em [Cavendish] I loved her letter.

  I've had horrible flu – better today but it really floored me for 2 days, couldn't lift my head.

  Susan Mary [Patten]'s kid went to the Bois (equivalent of Park) & told her little friends that her father was dead & the worst of it was that S-M was pregnant & the governess had given notice. So enormous wreaths began to pour in at the Patten house. Don't you love it?

  Pam Berry is here, very funny & unrepentant about all her anti-Clarissa [Eden] activities.

  I'm off to Alvilde on the 13th, longing for it. Any hope you might be in the jungle?

  Wid is lovely. She doesn't a bit realize how lucky to have so many reviews & writes in a *rage* at every adverse sentence. Did you read mine? It was about her more than the book.[2]

    Much love
        NR

Have you seen Vicky in this week's *NS & N*?[3] It *tickled* me even when ill.

[1] Nancy used to pretend that her youngest sister had the mental age of a nine-year-old.
[2] Nancy's review of Violet Hammersley's translation of Madame de Sévigné's letters was published in the *New Statesman & Nation*, 14 January 1956. 'She has not so much translated the letters as rewritten them in English, and the result is a very odd, amusing book.'
[3] The cartoonist had drawn Eden standing at the helm of a storm-swept ship, flanked by Macmillan and Butler, with Beaverbrook striding the deck waving a paper headed 'Hands off Eden'. The caption quotes from Lewis Carroll's 'The Hunting of the Snark', about the Beaver that saved the ship from wreck 'though none of the sailors knew how'.

To Hugh Thomas   7 rue Monsieur, VII
26 February 1956

My dear Hugh

I've just got back from the Riviera – not the luckiest outing I ever
had – horrible weather & my pearl necklace, not insured, stolen in
the train bleu. This is in a way a double blow, I can hardly live without
the necklace & it means the train bleu has entirely lost its character
& is now a place like any other public conveyance where you have to
be careful. Ay di me.

Yes, can you BEAT the U-fuss?[1] People now round on me, saying
what a bore it all is, but really they've only got to leave off. However
if it stops the corruption of our language by Americanisms it will have
done some good, perhaps only snobbishness can stop it. We have no
Académie & my grandmother used to say 'Mothers are the guardians
of the English language'. (The fathers were supposed to be too much
inclined to bring home military or parliamentary slang & clichés.) . . .

Did you love the *Beggar's Opera* at the Pagode? I went twice. It is
a good faithful cinema for old adoreds.

I think & hope I'm here for good now – so hate moving about.

      Yrs ever
          Nancy

[1] Hamish Hamilton reprinted 'The English Aristocracy' in *Noblesse Oblige* (1956). 'Can
you get over them going *on* with U? I mean really we've had enough – even I have &
you know how one loves one's own jokes. As we are on the subject the best was: I'm
dancing with tears in my eyes 'cos the girl in my arms isn't U.' (NM to Evelyn
11 June 1956)

To Hugh Thomas   7 rue Monsieur, VII
15 March 1956

My dear Hugh

Oh good gracious no, I know my place I hope. Not a life of Voltaire,[1]
just a Kinsey report on his romps with Mme du Châtelet & her romps
with Saint-Lambert & his romps with Mme de Boufflers & her romps
with Panpan & his romps with Mme de Grafigny. I could go on for
pages. . . .

We are in full swing of the Q Mother's visit. I am amused to observe
the antics of the gens du monde here, anybody can see they have
never had a Court in living memory. Their manque de naturel is quite
stunning I think partly because they dope themselves with substitutes

like Prince Paul & the Comte de Paris, & when faced with the real thing they don't know how to cope. The Ministers & Marshals, who have a more highly developed sense of realities, are perfectly at their ease.

I would love to discuss all this with the lady in question, but of course one never could. She twinkles away, looks constantly entertained & is quite perfect. I'm off now, in a caramel toque of *great* beauty, to the Anglo-French thing for her – interested to see if Maurois[2] will be there. He wasn't last night to my joy. (Such a *bore* that he's become such a first class writer.)

What did you think of Prod – he's not nobody. I love old Humph [Hare].

Come for Low Week – Evelyn Waugh will be here. I don't dare let on I don't know when it is.

Please tell John Raymond the book on Versailles[3] is perfection, the very best thing on my sort of subject that I've read for ages. I can't get down to it though until all the junketings are over – Q Mother followed by Heywood Hill & I'm in the middle of spring clothes to boot. Keep in touch.

    Yrs ever
       Nancy

[1] Nancy had begun work on *Voltaire in Love* (1957). 'I'd rather do a novel, but not unless really inspired . . . I am quite pleased with my last 3 – no use writing dreary pot-boilers & lowering the level, do you agree?' (NM to Violet Hammersley, 29 February 1956)
[2] André Maurois (1885–1967). Anglophile novelist and historian. Author of *Les silences du Colonel Bramble* (1917), *Les discours du Docteur O'Grady* (1922) and *Disraeli* (1927). In spite of his Jewish origins, Maurois was pro-Vichy at the beginning of the war. Churchill supposedly said of Maurois that he had thought him a friend but discovered he was only a customer. Spent most of the war in USA and North Africa.
[3] Ian Dunlop, *Versailles* (1956). Favourably reviewed by Nancy in the *New Statesman & Nation*, 14 April 1956.

To Violet Hammersley   7 rue Monsieur, VII
16 March 1956

. . . I greatly enjoyed the doings for the Q Mother. After a very agreeable huge dinner chez les Carter we went to the Embassy where the Jebbs[1] really had assembled the very cream of the Tout Paris. It was intensely elegant & I think the Guest must have been rather fascinated. Jebbs very good at that sort of thing because not the least nervous. The Harveys would have died of it. The comic element supplied by Hoytie [Wiborg] who, as the Cake came into the room, flung herself like Sir Walter Raleigh in the Royal path. I said to Cynthia wasn't it lovely & Cynthia said yes but I wish you could have heard her, she was asking for a medal for her work in the Resistance!! (Terribly Pétainist in fact.)

My old white Dior dress perfectly lovely, one of the 3 or 4 best. These dresses *are* worth getting in spite of the awful price (£250) because you feel comfortable in them. My brooch, fixed on a pink bow round the neck was admired even by Rothschilds!!

I've been eating up Dumaine's wicked book, praying Muv will never see it 'Elle habite rue Monsieur, écrit des romans faciles et mène une vie qui l'est tout autant –' He says of Helen Dashwood 'conservée dans la frigidité et le snobisme' & of Lady Stanley 'elle n'avait, n'a, n'aura jamais de charme'.[2]

Yesterday I put on my caramel toque & went to the Interallié where the English colony was gathered in all its dowdiness. I saw Doodie looking hungry in the distance. The Queen had been having a cosy tea with Massiglis Colonel & Diana Coo, haven't seen Col yet to hear.

Love to Muv. Since she got her aid she has stopped writing I don't blame her. One day you will tell me why her aid is free & yours costs £40.

Love from
N

[1] Gladwyn Jebb was made Ambassador to France in 1954. 'The Jebbs are a success *beyond all hope*. I've never heard the French, the monde, the intellectuals, the politicians & the man in the street so united in praise of anybody . . . Cynthia has developed in an extraordinary way you know – she is so good & at the same time surprisingly worldly wise.' (NM to Violet Hammersley, 4 July 1954)

[2] Jacques Dumaine was head of protocol at the Quai d'Orsay after the war. In his diaries *Quai d'Orsay, 1945–51* (1955), he writes of Nancy: 'She lives in the rue Monsieur, writes light-weight novels and leads a life which is equally easy-going.' Nancy regretted that the law of libel in France prevented her from taking Dumaine to court for insinuating that her easy-going life implied loose morals. He describes Lady Stanley as 'never having had, nor ever going to have, any charm'.

To Lucy Norton[1]   7 rue Monsieur, VII
21 March 1956

Dear Miss Norton

Mr Brain of H H[2] gave me your translation to read which I did last night. I don't understand what the fuss is about. That IS Saint-Simon – if they don't like it they must publish something else. It seems to me perfection. The trouble is they know nothing. Mr Brain said there are too many obscure characters by which I suppose he means Cardinal Dubois. Good luck to him!

I shall tell them all this with great force – the reader must bring a little baggage or do they want Told to the Children?

They refused Mrs Hammersley's *Sévigné* you know, on much the same grounds. What about Raymond – have you been in touch with him?

Yrs sincerely
    Nancy Rodd

. . .

[1] Lucy Norton (1902–89). Translator of the memoirs of the Duke of Saint-Simon. Nancy wrote the preface to her *Saint-Simon at Versailles* (1958).
[2] Richard Brain; editor at Hamish Hamilton.

To Evelyn Waugh   7 rue Monsieur, VII
25 March 1956

Dear Evelyn

Colonel Bedford[1] is delighted with your praise – I've never heard such a shriek. Like us he greatly admires the book, & like you cared for it less after the arrival of Caroline. He says he is a conservative character & had got used to Melanie.

I am much less critical & all seemed perfect to me, I do hope those idiotic critics will do their bit. I think, to be fair, that terribly as they over praise 2nd class books, they do pounce with relief on good stuff when they see it. I spoke of *A Legacy* to John Raymond who is here & he said at once that he had heard of it from a colleague on *NS & N* who is going to praise it highly.

The real Mrs Bedford is a small, fair, intensely shy woman, about 40 I suppose, half German. There is something very *sweet* about her, but never would you suspect talent & when a mutual friend sent me the book I dreaded having to read enough to be able to comment. You know! Of course I was immobilized for days.

I've just telephoned to John Raymond who said 'it's only a quarter past you know' & then said 'oh I'm sorry, I thought you were somebody I'm going to Church with –' Is he a co religionist of yours? I do like him so much, & so would you.

Well I live for Low Week. If my telephone is cut off (I must begin to work) please send a word. I need you.

Love
  N

[1] Nancy had sent Evelyn Waugh *A Legacy* (1956), a novel by Sybille Bedford. In his letter of thanks he replied, 'I wondered for a time who this brilliant "Mrs Bedford" could be. A cosmopolitan military man, plainly, with a knowledge of parliamentary government and popular journalism, a dislike for Prussians, a liking for Jews, a belief that everyone speaks French in the home . . . Then, of course, it came to me. Good old Col.' *Letters*, p. 471.

To Raymond Mortimer   7 rue Monsieur, VII
6 April 1956

Darling Raymond

I'm in a very bad way – simply cannot work. What can it be, it's not like me. I've cleared the decks to any extent, refused all invitations (even Covent Garden for B & K[1]) warned everybody off the telephone etc & then I sit playing the wireless & gazing sadly at *La Jeunesse de Voltaire* & other tomes & simply can't get on. Of course I'm sure really in my heart that Voltaire is too unattractive – il manque ce côté poétique de Dear Good [Louis XV], & du Châtelet even worse. I can't say they bore me exactly but they don't inspire me. I don't know whether to go pegging on or chuck the whole thing?

I still worry about *A Legacy*. Heywood says he forces everybody to buy it but it doesn't 'sell itself' yet. John Davenport[2] spoke up – Evelyn will do it in *Spectator* & now I've swallowed my pride & written to Nancy Spain who has promised to read it. When you think of the pretentious rubbish that does go down with the public it seems a shame for something so superior to be neglected like this. Fancy you knowing her – I do because of my great new friend Madame [Esther] Arthur – I think there's something very *sweet* about her. Have often wondered about Mr Bedford!!? She's in London you know 5 Osten Mews SW7.

Luckily for the Jebbs, if unluckily for ONE's pen pals, the Royal Visit went like clockwork. Those who felt they should be asked (300 were) were all there & the rest were sour but not surprised. Odette [Massigli] had 6 people to tea Brissacs Gaston Diana Coo Charlie B[eistegui] which was too few to give offence I suppose. Colonel seems to have done most of the talking, a sort of ping pong with Diana.

I think you should read Mitford's *Garter Mission to Japan*.[3]
Col is in Morocco & writes rather optimistically.

Love
   N

[1] Bulganin and Khrushchev were on a visit to England.
[2] John Davenport (d.1966). Literary critic for the *Observer* and the *Spectator*.
[3] Bertram Mitford, *The Garter Mission to Japan* (1906). An account by Nancy's grandfather of his visit to Japan with Prince Arthur of Connaught, to bestow the Order of the Garter on the Emperor.

To Lady Redesdale	Torcello[1]
20 June 1956	Venice

Darling Muv

The mystery of the W.I. is extreme. Another huge batch of them today, mostly working class. WHY are they interested in Byzantine art? It is an intensely esoteric taste – I really didn't appreciate it until I went to Russia & goodness knows I am more sophisticated than they are. The books on it in English are few & very expensive. So why do they crowd onto an uncomfortable steamer & take an hour's journey to a tiny island where there is nothing else to see? Oh do explain. I simply long to ask them. The French who come are all of another class, the professorial I should say, that is quite understandable. The Americans come for the restaurant & don't go near the churches – & they come luxuriously in motor boats. The Germans come once a week with a lecturer with a megaphone. But the English, aching feet, come limping off the steamer & gape round & then ache back again, leaving a *litter* behind that makes me die of shame. (Player's Navy Cut wherever you look & flapping *Daily Mails*.)

What's the news of Phil [Prynne]?

Kind friends in Venice have discovered I'm here & keep asking me to meals, but I've been wonderfully firm. But tomorrow I go for the night to Eliz: Chavchavadze who has got Willie Maugham. I look forward to it. Victor Cunard comes out quite often & brings the gossip – it seems there's an old boy in Venice, a great friend of *my friend* Stephen Powys, who has wonderful Widow stories. *Should* I tip your porter? *Do* you think 2/- would be right? He's coming out to dine one evening to swop Widowiana.

I've been here 4 weeks today – can't believe it. The local papers are full of U, huge, rather learned articles.

Much love
     N

[1] Victor Cunard had recommended an hotel on the island of Torcello as a place where Nancy could work in peace.

To Diana Mosley   Torcello
25 June 1956

Dereling
It couldn't be colder than it is here. For about a week I've *suffered* – too idiotically I believed Victor who said it wld be unbearably hot & only brought summer clothes (thinking of Athens last year). I now find he's one of those who feels hot whatever the real temperature. At first it *was* lovely, but now it's real Ascot weather. I have to get into bed, to work! I seriously think of going home, where at least I can have a fire, & beginning again at Tony's in Aug: Only it wld mean dragging Marie back & I don't quite like to.

Voltaire is whizzing along. He *is* lovely, & she extraordinary. All the French books about them entirely overlook the fact that she was so learned that even modern physicists know about her work. She translated Newton – imagine it.

I spent the night with Elizabeth in the flat you chucked. She had Willie Maugham for dinner & we spent an intensely agreeable evening. I see Victor all the time. The Italians call him King Lear don't you love it. It must NEVER get back – I think he's suicidal already & it might knock him over the edge.

One of the waiters here aged 16 said May I ask you something? Was H. G. Wells an atheist. So I said I was going to see a great friend of H.G.W. & wld find out. Willie said certainly not – agnostic. So then a great hunt in the dictionary for agnostic, where it isn't, so I explained the meaning to an assembled group of Torcello ites who said Oh that's what we are – we would like to disembowel all priests. Willie was awfully pleased to think that H.G.W. is still read in the world. Not in England I fancy.

It seems the Biennale has hit a new low. Evelyn ought to come out & do a reportage.

When do you go to Spain? I suppose it *will* be hot there, but I've lost faith in the weather. P'raps I'll go & live in Noel C's island which does sound reliable.[1]

Love from
Nanceleeng

The society people here HATE each other don't they? They are all in despair because Charlie [Beistegui] is only coming for a month.

[1] Noel Coward had recently bought a house, Firefly, on the island of Jamaica.

To GASTON PALEWSKI   St-Pierre du Château
24 July 1956   Hyères

Respectful, &, one hopes, respectable friend
   Your letter was a *comfort*, & I could read it.[1]
   Tony [Gandarillas] arrived with a portfolio of poisons, including an imaginary conversation with yourself. Now all sit looking to see how I am taking it so that I have to wear a perpetual grin. It is very exhausting, & I long to be at home with Marie in a way, though rather dreading empty Paris in pouring rain. A sort of meridional torpor has descended upon me, as I see it has on you.
   Then Tony himself is in serious trouble, which I will tell you if I ever see you again, & I don't quite like to leave him alone. He is very nervy & weepy. Altogether my life seems too complicated for words.
   Respectfully
        C[onnaught] H[otel]

P.S. The word European, with which we are bored nowadays from morning to night, was so little known in 1740 that Voltaire had a long controversy with the Abbé de Saint-Pierre as to whether it should be European or Europain.
   In *my* philosophical dictionary I shall have: European: Pro-German, neo-Fascist, or Fascist qui n'ose pas dire son nom,[2] bore.

[1] Since Nancy's arrival in Venice at the end of May, she had had little news from Palewski and was missing him badly. She longed for him to join her, knowing full well that he would not, and at the same time dreaded his boredom if he did. Her unhappy letters are scattered with attempts to pin him down for the rest of the summer and allusions to the other women he might be seeing in her absence.
[2] Which dares not speak its name.

To Gaston Palewski   St-Pierre du Château
9 August 1956   Hyères

Dear Good

I've got such a funny piece of gossip, Odette M[assigli] is having
an affair with John Lehmann. He has never liked a woman before &
indeed has only one normal friend whom he bombards all day with
questions on *normal* procedure. Every conversation is said to end
with a deep sigh & 'all this sounds very tiring – bad for my work'.
Are you shrieking, Colonel?

I go home on the Mistral, Thursday 16th.

A post card from dear Champion[1] this morning but no jokes only
faithful thoughts.

The Ivoires[2] (Empire) rang up Alvilde & swooned with happiness
& said how wonderful you are. 'I know.'

So see you one of these days.

        N

[1] Palewski's secretary.
[2] Leonard and Norah Ivory were English expatriates who lived in the South of France
and bred Pekinese dogs. Palewski had met them during the war.

To Lady Redesdale   St-Pierre du Château
12 August 1956   Hyères
                                            home next Thursday

Darling Muv

Well I was sent a thing to fill in about myself for an encyclopaedia
of modern writers (American of course). They sent samples from
what other writers had put about themselves & they were all My
father was a poor trapper & I was born in his hut or My father was
an unemployed seaman & I was born in a tenement on Bowery, so I
thought to be à la page & put My father was the son of a peer & I
was born in a London slum. I didn't know the *D Mail* had got hold of
it. Really!

Cocteau said to me did you enjoy Torcello? Yes but how did you
know I was there? Oh they show your room before anything else.
. . .

I wrote & asked Aunt Iris how Unkel is, she replied so good of
you to take time off sunbathing to enquire. Very badly received, as
I've been literally slaving for months & hardly even go to the sea to
bathe – every other day if that. People think hot places must be for

holidays but I can work better in heat & a bright light – above all that.

How cross everybody is getting – Eden Nasser & co! I think it's all a lot of hot air don't you? *Manchester G* very calm.

Noblesse is out in USA & has already sold 10 000 in just over a week. How dotty. I haven't subscribed to cuttings but my publisher says he'll send a selection – if they are funny I'll send them on to you.

I go home on Thurs: rather dreading the cold & wet. I shall have to go to Geneva next – Besterman[1] says I can have a room at Les Délices – I think I told you all that. But not yet, when I'm further on.

Much love
N

Auntie seems to have adored the island.

[1] Theodore Besterman (1904–76). Voltaire scholar and editor of his collected letters.

To Ogden Nash[1]   7 rue Monsieur, VII
28 September 1956

I love you, Mr Ogden Nash

Nancy Mitford

[1] Ogden Nash (1902–71). American poet and author. Nancy wrote to him after reading his hilarious poem 'MS. Found Under a Serviette in a Lovely Home'. Addressed to 'Dear Cousin Nancy', it was inspired by *Noblesse Oblige*. One of the verses runs:

> Cousin Emmy Lou is pretty aristocratic herself; in
>   spite of her weakness for hog jowl and pot-
>   likker, she is noted for her highborn pale
>   and wan flesh,
> And where most people get gooseflesh she gets
>   swan flesh,
> And she said she thought you ought to know that
>   she had been over the royal roster
> And she had spotted at least one impostor.
> She noticed that the Wicked Queen said 'Mirror,
>   mirror on the wall' instead of 'Looking glass,
>   looking glass on the wall,' which is perfectly true,
> So the Wicked Queen exposed herself as not
>   only wicked but definitely non-U.
>   *New Yorker*, September 1956

To EVELYN WAUGH   Fontaines-les-Nonnes
19 October 1956   par Puisieux
                                   for a few more days

Darling Evelyn

In such a case how can one tell what really happened?[1] If however intention counts at all we can be sure he intended to die within the rules. He minded passionately about Xian burial & one of the greatest fusses of his whole life was made because Adrienne Lecouvreur was refused it. At Cirey he built the chapel next door to his bedroom so that he could hear the Mass when he was ill. He loved God, I promise you.

You know how good you are at thinking of titles for books oh could I wheedle you into thinking of one for me now? What it should be is Voltaire's love affair, but without that tiresome rhyme. The theme of the book is the behaviour of this oddest of human beings during a long love affair (a very testing relationship). Besterman has suggested Love & Genius but I don't quite like that & Heywood says for goodness sake call it what it is. Colonel Voltaire perhaps – really no they aren't very much alike & even I can't make them.[2] As for Emily heaven preserve ONE from being like her. (It's all right, heaven has.)

Our hostess, at luncheon, suddenly asked Where did William the Conqueror die? Old M. de Rohan-Chabot aged 90 came out of his dream & said 'Et qu'est ce qu'il faut étudier pour le dîner?[3] . . .

Tomorrow the Bishop of Meaux comes to luncheon always a tremendous occasion.

   Much love
      N

[1] Waugh had written to Nancy: 'I am interested in your statement that Voltaire was shriven. Has this now been proved? As you know there has been endless controversy on the subject for two centuries. About a year ago there was a correspondence in a popish journal – I think *The Tablet* – & I was left with the impression that the priest was called without his consent and only performed his office after V. was comatose. It will be most cheering if you have evidence to the contrary. I have always supposed him the vilest of men. It will be lovely to see him in the role of Col.' (14 October 1956)
[2] Waugh suggested: 'How about "Sense & Sentiment", "Brain & Heart", "The credulous sceptic", "Voltaire in Love", "Emily's thorny bed"?' *Letters*, p. 476.
[3] 'And what must we study for dinner?'

To Diana Mosley   7 rue Monsieur, VII
28 November 1956

Darling

Momo has arrived & is having rat week. She is said not to be
SOUND. When she telephoned to Daisy, Daisy rang off!!!! (When I
think of Daze in the war.) People go on about her just like me and
Marie-Antoinette. Dolly admits it's the same violence.

I said to Gladwyn surely the P.M. has done for himself by going on a
sunny holiday[1] & Gladwyn said not at all, subscriptions for his fare are
pouring in to No. 10. Can you beat it. It's what I always say, the favourite
line of the Englishman's favourite poem is *somebody blundered*.

A policeman came to see me, asked a hundred questions, knew the
answers before I spoke & made notes on my dossier (I so died to see
it). He said we are checking up on the English here for the Queen's visit
– do you know where Madame Trefusis is? I said Madame Trefusis is
much too snobbish to kill the Queen. I must say he roared. I suppose
they think I'm a dangerous regicide because of M-A.

I've just come from Alexandre.[2] Well, we complain of Denise. He said
come at 12 & you won't have to wait – I lunched here at 4. I must say
the whole circus is exceedingly drôle & there's never a dull moment.
My hair is now like Suzanne Lenglen[3] & only needs a bandeau.

The latest coup de Louise de V[ilmorin] is rather funny. She began
to smother Barbara Hutton[4] with *presents*, canchia trees, truffles,
valuable-looking bibelots, & so on, invited her to Verrières & made
her read out her (B.H.'s) poems. Nobody has ever thought of this
approach before & the net result is said to be 5 millions *so far*. La
Silvia[5] very nervous & Jean,[6] we hear, NOT PLEASED. Are you
shrieking?

I go to Mews on Sunday – ay di me I'm so happy in this jungle I
do hate to move.

   All love
      N

[1] Anthony Eden left London for Jamaica to recuperate from an operation.
[2] Fashionable hairdresser in the rue St Honoré.
[3] Suzanne Lenglen (1899–1938). French tennis champion.
[4] Barbara Hutton (1912–79). Generous and spendthrift heiress to the Woolworth
fortune. Inherited $26 million from her grandfather in 1919 and left $3500 in the bank
when she died. Produced two volumes of poems, *The Enchanted* (1934) and *Peking
Pictures* (1935).
[5] Silvia de Castellane (1909–). Childhood friend of Barbara Hutton who had benefited
from her generosity.

[6] Count Jean de Baglion (1909–93). Decorator and a friend of Diana and Nancy. He also received financial support from Barbara Hutton from time to time.

To GASTON PALEWSKI   Long Crichel House
6 December 1956   Wimborne

Dear Good

I'm enjoying myself. London is a battlefield. Randolph has been kicked down the steps of White's by Andrew [Devonshire] & is in the London Clinic, cries of traitor fly to & fro & most people aren't speaking to Pam [Berry]. I count as a foreigner. Susan Mary was kicked downstairs by Ld Salisbury & is said to have sat up in bed at the American Embassy writing memoranda.

I saw Ivone Kirkpatrick[1] who said what will the French feel when Nato packs up? I said I supposed they might feel rather unprotected like when your father, whom you detest, dies. But will it pack up? Almost certainly, next year. I said then they'll have to make a bomb; he said they can't, they've got nowhere to test it. What about St Pierre et Miquelon says I? Susan Mary should write a memorandum about this.

You dear little thing, I shall ring you up on Tuesday.

          N

Pam has got such a beautiful picture – all in tones of brown & said to be by Nattier ('She must give it to me')

[1] Sir Ivone Kirkpatrick (1897–1964). Diplomat. Permanent Under-Secretary of State at the Foreign Office 1953–7.

To DIANA MOSLEY   7 rue Monsieur, VII
24 December 1956

Dereling

I must say being alone is nice, I do wonder why people so long for company, marry old sticks for it & so on. I think travelling alone is so much more enjoyable than with somebody, for one thing one sees more when not distracted by chat. On the other hand I would always like a *courier*.

Oh I had such a time getting back, & would still be in the smog with no plans for meals etc (having said goodbye to everybody) had it not been for a fan in Air France. He penetrated the disguise of Mme Rodd, said he would do anything for me & got me onto one of

the only aeroplanes to come for days. Also he kept ringing up &
telling the position so that I didn't have to sit at Waterloo. It is night
in London – blazing sun at Orly & only grey *here* (sunny the moment
you get away from Paris).

Muv was lovely with the 800 cooks besieging the mews. She got
one, a jolly girl who cooked very well but left at the end of the week,
I suppose on discovering that she was expected to lead an entirely
vertical life, no chair either in the 'kitchen' or in her bedroom.

People at home very fed up with the Hungarian refugees who, they
say, are all Communists but then what did they expect? Sneering
aristocrats?

The P.M. seems firmly in the saddle, I think he must be cleverer
than one supposed.[1] . . .

I saw old Driberg, very nice & giggly. I said 'I hear you made £50
000 out of Burgess.'[2] 'Not a tenth of what *you* make with your books.'
'Yes Tom, a tenth.'

Happy Christmas, lucky NY & all love from
 Nancy

[1] Anthony Eden remained Prime Minister until January 1957, when ill-health forced
him to resign.
[2] Tom Driberg, *Guy Burgess: A Portrait with Background* (1956). The *Daily Mail* paid
£5000 for the serial rights.

To EVELYN WAUGH   7 rue Monsieur, VII
31 December 1956
2 January 1957

Darling Evelyn

Did Miss Harriet write that long, informative & well-composed
letter of her own accord or was it the result of torture? I am greatly
impressed by it, but I rather hate the idea that her whole Christmas
may have been ruined by 'have you written to Mrs Rodd, Harriet?'

I note that she has no French – nor, it seems has the Berry girl in
spite of Pam's French room & all.

I've written the first page of my book & feel better. Isn't starting
difficult! So I went out & bought a dress I couldn't afford & have now
downed tools until after les fêtes.

It was very nice to see you but I was rather shocked by your great
intimacy with those dull actors & wished we had been you & me &
Pam. I admit that the actors are both *very pretty* but prefer to see

them on the boards. Conversation in England *has* become dull hasn't it? Either pounding rudeness like that of Randolph, Ed (& yourself when fully sane) or else a sort of under water quality. I only mean in company. Has it always been so? I think the way they flog that old dead horse Suez is almost unbelievably dull. I seem to remember that it was the same when I was a child over free trade & protection (always comes back to *trade*, with les Anglais).

So, have a happy new year. I was sorry to see the end of 1956, which I greatly enjoyed.

Love from Nancy

To Diana Mosley   7 rue Monsieur, VII
10 March 1957

Dereling

I long for news of everybody's *health*?

Evelyn wrote about his case.[1] When it seemed to be going so badly he offered his parish priest 10% of what he made. The result was electrifying – Sir Hartley [Shawcross]'s mother in law had a nearly fatal motor accident & he had to give up in the middle & one could *see* the prayers working on the jury. (So unfair on poor N. Spain!) I've asked what percentage the priest would take for putting in a bit of time on *Voltaire*?

I'm very much torn at present between leaving in *lovely* details of Fred's[2] homosexual orgies or making it a book fit to be given (as *Pomp* was) for school prizes. I wonder which pays best? I shall end by falling between 2 stools, as even I can't write down some of the lovely stuff eet ees too moch.

The fabulous Britisher, as the NY papers call Momo, has just telephoned and Daisy and Bettine [Abingdon] and Diana [Cooper] – all the time-wasters in fact.

Besterman is as much of a tease as Voltaire, one can't say more, but unfortunately without the funniness. Can you imagine giving your life to Voltaire without having one ray of sense of humour? He is driving me mad.

Much love *do* write even a p.c.
        N

[1] A libel action brought against Nancy Spain for an article in the *Daily Express* saying that the sales of Waugh's books were poor.
[2] Frederick the Great of Prussia.

To Duchess of Devonshire　　　　　　　7 rue Monsieur, VII
25 March 1957

Dear 9
  Names
  Zaïre, Zoraïde, Aïda, would fox the women's institute. Philadelphia (Delphi for short), Lily, Ada, Zéphire, Colombine, Eglantine, Lilac, Privet, Aïssé, Bérénice, Giroflée, Cora, Daisy, Edmée, Mirabelle, Esmeralda, Una, Esther, Natalie, Nin, Momo, Virginia, Evangeline, Ursula, Hecuba, Morgana, Susanita, Foxglove, Foxhunter. I don't know any more. What does it look like?[1] It must suggest something (Elsa Maxwell[2] might be a nice name). What about Alice (Ali for short) or Morny? Or Douro?
  No news at all because of work.

  Much love
     N

Lucky it's over for Widoweek.

[1] Deborah's daughter, born on 18 March, was eventually christened Sophia Louise Sydney.
[2] Elsa Maxwell (1883–1963). Celebrated American hostess and gossip columnist, noted for her eccentric parties. Described by Cecil Beaton as a 'huge billowing rhinoceros mass'.

To Lady Redesdale　　　　　　　　　　Hotel du Rhône
15 April 1957　　　　　　　　　　　　　Geneva

Darling Muv
  . . . I came here on Thursday & almost immediately fell ill. Feel better today, but I had to spend nearly 2 days in bed which is a terrible bore as the hotel is v. expensive. However I've done the work I came for & can now get on & finish my book.
  The Queen's visit a huge success from this end, I do so wonder if she enjoyed it. I never saw anything so beautiful as the decorations both public & private. On the Ile St Louis somebody had made a bouquet as big as a tree entirely of real roses & lilac, & they had filled a lot of the trees with flowers & it was like fairyland. As I couldn't face going to the Embassy (4 hours on one's feet) I went to Priscilla Bibesco's[1] house on la pointe de l'île & saw the boats go by.

The jewels of Mme de Devonshire[2] provoked much comment & even the Queen's clothes were quite all right, so *they* had all made un petit effort, too, which was appreciated.

Besterman is a very odd creature. I've seldom disliked anybody so much, & yet he is NOBLE. In spite of the fact that he himself is to write a life of Voltaire he has let me see all the new letters which entirely change the story & which he could easily have kept dark until I'd finished & nobody would have been the wiser. It must have been a temptation – I don't know that I, in his place, would have behaved so well.

Mrs B talks about nothing but servants as people do in England. It is very dull. The pretty little Délices is turned by her into an English country house in the Aunt Dorothy taste.

I go home today thank goodness.

Love
   N

[1] Priscilla Bibesco; daughter of Prince Antoine Bibesco, married to Simon Hodgson.
[2] Lady Mary Gascoyne-Cecil (1895–1988). Married 10th Duke of Devonshire in 1917. Mistress of the Robes to the Queen 1953–66.

To Jessica Treuhaft   7 rue Monsieur, VII
8 May 1957

Darling Soo

Another thing about the non-U way[1] is each letter costs about £5. 4. 6½ & as *I* haven't been left a huge legacy by careless will-makers I prefer the old 30 franc way.

If Dinkie [Constancia] came over in June, she could spend the hols in England & come here for the rentrée des classes in Oct: I know Mme Michelon (not Vachon) gets very booked up so as soon as you know for sure I'll go & see her. I shan't hate Dinkie that's quite all right but no baby sister *please*. I'll talk French to Dinkie so then her language won't worry me. (It seems in America one's not allowed to say a fortnight, it has to be half-a-month – oh no Susan I'm too old, I *can't*.)

Yes my American publisher is mourning over Art's Article.[2] But the *Ladies Home Journal* – oh I told you all that.

A friend of mine was in New York & a shop assistant said goodbye for now, after selling him something & he stared sadly at her & said goodbye for *ever*. So, goodbye for the present.

    Much love Soo
        Nancy

[1] 'Any sign of undue haste, in fact, is apt to be Non-U, and I go so far as preferring, except for business letters, not to use airmail.' 'The English Aristocracy', *Encounter*.
[2] 'She Doesn't Like Us': ' "I don't like Americans or America. I'm getting old and only have a certain amount of time and I don't want to waste a day in a place where I would be miserable." "Is your dislike of Americans based on anything that happened in your childhood?" "How ridiculous. I didn't even know America existed before the war." "So you started hating them when the war came?" "Yes. I'll never forget what a bore it was when they joined the war. We were having a wonderful time and they came along and spoiled our finest hour." ' Art Buchwald, *New York Herald Tribune*, 21 April 1957.

To Lady Redesdale   7 rue Monsieur, VII
14 May 1957

Darling Muv

    Travail & labour both come from words meaning torture & I'm afraid it generally is. Certainly for me it is physical torture & I realized last night that I have had a perpetual headache for a whole year. This morning eyes un swollen & no more watering which when I'm working goes on all through breakfast. MS went off to London yesterday. . . .

    Big dinner at the Embassy to say goodbye to Ld Ismay. Of course he was in floods. The French think it so queer the way Englishmen cry such a lot, Winston & Monty & Pug & Duff all tremendous blubbers. Can you imagine [Marshal] Juin or Gen de Gaulle crying in public!

    I hope to go to Debo about 29th May & to Venice middle of June for a month or so. I leave here 23rd & go to Raymond Mortimer for a long weekend before Ireland. Oh PLANS how I loathe them.

    Much love
        N

To Lady Redesdale   7 rue Monsieur, VII
19 May 1957

Darling Muv

    How is your arm? I didn't know you'd had trouble with it but Diana told me. It does sound horrid.

I'm off to Ireland, Debo on Thursday, stopping off for a long week end with Raymond Mortimer who will have read my book. Hamish Hamilton sent me a long enthusiastic telegram ending what bliss to be your publisher, so that's all right –

Terribly funny Anglo French literary luncheon last week for young (sic) Fr & Eng writers to get to know each other. I sat between young Priestley[1] & young (80) Chamson.[2] The English women, who included Jacquetta Hawkes & Rebecca West, were all dressed pour le garden party (freezing day) in flowing chiffons & huge hats.

Priestley was furious because Graham Greene was at the grand table with Gladwyn & neither Priestleys were.

Then we had *Titus Andronicus* a more disgusting play I never saw, tortures, murders, mutilations in every scene, culminating in a woman eating her own children in a pie. The French, who of course didn't understand a word, received it with wild enthusiasm. Couldn't help thinking of Voltaire who said that Shakespeare was a great genius sans une étincelle de goût[3] & that no people love a hanging so much as the English therefore naturally they also love his plays.

I'm now off to lovely *Lakme*!!![4]

Do tell about your arm.

Much love
    N

[1] J. B. Priestley (1894–1984). In 1957 he published *Thoughts in the Wilderness*, *The Art of the Dramatist* and *The Glass Cage*. Married in 1953 to the writer and archaeologist Jacquetta Hawkes (1910–).
[2] André Chamson (1900–83). Author of *La Suite cévenole* (1948) and *Suite pathétique* (1969).
[3] Without a spark of taste.
[4] Opera by Léo Delibes (1883).

To GASTON PALEWSKI   Luna Hotel
28 June 1957   Venice

Dearest

I am enjoying myself. A little mild social life of the sort I like, a little beach life & a little sight-seeing. The Graham Sutherlands[1] are here, he is a charmer if ever there was one. You must meet him one day. Unfortunately she is a dreadful bore & won't let him talk so there's not much hope for another man. A woman can find herself beside him at a meal & get him going. . . .

Dr Tait (friend of the Massiglis, Malcolm etc) is here, he is interested in lunatics & went off to see the local asylum. The director of it annoyed him very much by taking him first to the chapel saying it is 18th century. Chacun son goût. The 18th century means nothing to Dr Tait but madmen are his hobby.

I lunched with Somerset Maugham, who is rather in love with Wendy.[2] I said I knew you would be Willie because you always like pretty young women. He was awfully pleased. Old Winston seems to be on his last legs, but perhaps old Willie exaggerates a bit.

Bassanos not open yet to the General Public.

With love, you good Col
     N

[1] Graham Sutherland (1903–80). Painter. Married Katharine Barry in 1927. He went every year to Venice for summer holidays. His ill-fated portrait of Churchill was completed in 1954 and destroyed a few years later.
[2] Wendy Reves; wife of Winston Churchill's pre-war literary agent. She lived at Roquebrune in the South of France.

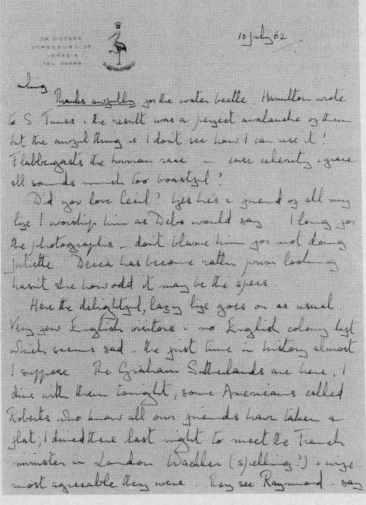

CA CICOGNA
DORSODURO, 23
VENEZIA
TEL. 20488

10 July 62

darling

Thanks awfully for the water beetle. Hamilton wrote to S. Times & the result was a perfect avalanche of them but the awful thing is I don't see how I can use it! Flabbergasts the human race — ease celerity, grace all sounds much too boastful?

Did you love Cecil? Yes he's a friend of all my life I worship him as Debo would say. I long for the photographs — don't blame him for not doing Juliette. Decca has become rather prim looking hasn't she how odd it may be the specs.

Here the delightful, lazy life goes on as usual. Very few English visitors & no English colony left which seems sad — the first time in history almost I suppose. The Graham Sutherlands are here, I dine with them tonight, some Americans called Roberts who know all our friends have taken a flat; I dined there last night to meet the French minister in London Wackler (spelling?) & wife most agreeable they were. Roy see Raymond — say

To Handasyde Buchanan, 6 September 1955

1957–1962

TRANSITION

She goes on saying that everything is going
swimmingly with the Colonel . . . but one
goes on hearing rumours that the whole thing
is breaking up which, from loyalty, one always
denies. But my theory is it really is all over
bar the shouting, that all her good spirits (or
at least most of them) are a bluff and that her
almost savage teasing of friends is a sort of
safety valve operation.

Victor Cunard to Billa Harrod,
17 August 1957

In July 1957 a letter from Gaston reached Nancy in Venice announcing his appointment as Ambassador in Rome. He had asked General de Gaulle's help to secure the post, and it was the only personal favour de Gaulle ever requested of the Government during his years in retirement. Gaston's main reasons for wanting to leave Paris were personal: he was inextricably involved in an affair with a married woman who lived just around the corner from rue Monsieur and his private life had become very complicated as a result.

Characteristically, Nancy's letters make hardly any mention of the Colonel's departure and to her friends she made light of it, yet it marked a real break in their relationship because he now made it clear that he could manage very well without her. Although she saw him only too rarely in Paris, she had believed that he relied on her companionship and they often spoke on the telephone. Besides, she could get news of him through mutual friends and could read of his activities in the newspapers. In Rome, however, he would be comparatively out of reach.

An ambassador's life was perfect for Gaston and he spent five happy years at the Farnese Palace, rearranging it to his taste and enjoying the social and artistic life of the city, soon earning himself the nickname 'M. l'Embrassadeur'. Nancy made brief, almost clandestine, visits to see him each summer, Gaston came occasionally to Paris, and they continued to correspond. Very few of the letters that Nancy wrote to him in Rome have survived; since he was without his discreet secretary, Madame Champion, he may have destroyed them. For the same reason Gaston's letters to Nancy were handwritten, rather than typed, in his almost illegible hand. They gave her news of his movements – such as an audience with the Pope with whom he got on 'admirably well' – but, like all his letters, they were detached and noncommittal. The only personal note was his signature: 'Regina Hotel' or 'Principe di Piedmont Hotel' now replaced 'Connaught Hotel', a private joke Nancy and he had shared since the war when she had been prevented from going up to his hotel bedroom.

Despite the gap left by the Colonel's absence Nancy's buoyancy of spirits and her will to be happy meant that the pattern of life in Paris went on much as before. She made annual visits abroad to friends: to Anna-Maria Cicogna in Venice, to Mark Ogilvie-Grant in Greece, to Edward Sackville-West in Ireland, to her mother in Scotland and Deborah in England. In 1957 Peter, whom Nancy had been trying for years to divorce, finally announced that he wanted to remarry, and agreed to Nancy divorcing him on the grounds of a breakdown of their marriage. In 1960 she published her eighth and last novel, *Don't Tell Alfred*; the reviews were unenthusiastic but the book sold very well. *The Water Beetle*, a collection of her essays published two years later, was a reminder of Nancy's fine talent as a journalist.

To Gaston Palewski   Venice
13 July 1957
[telegram]

O DESESPOIR. O RAGE. O FELICITATIONS.[1]
NANCY

[1] Palewski took up his post as Ambassador in Rome in October 1957 and stayed until August 1962.

To Violet Hammersley   7 rue Monsieur, VII
2 [August] 1957

Darling

The Colonel is off to the Palais Farnèse in the form of Ambassador to Rome. I thought I'd told you. He is very much pleased & I think he'll love it, really made for him. He goes in Oct after which I shall be as free as air & never out of the Temperance Hotel. . . .

Dined with Monty & the Jebbs, just the 4 of us, you know how he always rather fascinates me. We talked about generals having luck – he said I had luck when Gott was shot down.

N 'Perhaps it was lucky for us too.'

M 'Yes it was. Gott was very much above his ceiling – he would have lost Egypt.'

John Marriott says this is quite true & it was Providence who shot down Gott!

I've been sweating away at the collections; torture really in this weather but I can't resist. Nothing new, but all very wearable & lovely stuffs.

Lots of people here, still, as always. Cecil B is here for the month. He has done a lovely cover for *Voltaire*. I'm busy with the proofs, lists of illustrations & so on so must leave you.

   Much love
        N

. . .

To Osbert Lancaster   7 rue Monsieur, VII
19 November 1957

Dearest Osbert

The advantage of never seeing an English paper is that one comes fresh to Maudie. Oh she is lovely. She has become so elegant I long to copy all her clothes – and then of course she is always right about everything. Thank you very much for sending her – she shall circulate in Paris instead of Xmas cards. Deeply flattered to have been *twice* mentioned.[1]

I went on Friday to sign my book at Smith's & found lovely Art Buchwald (our local funny man who *is* funny) calmly signing his (uninvited).[2] I was expecting to be hit on the head either by Americans or French, or both, but it was quite peaceful & I sold 98 copies, mostly to Swedes.

A Swiss has just telephoned from Geneva to ask if I will translate his novel. Funnily enough I won't. When I said so he replied then I shall have to fall back on Miss Nancy Spain. Good luck to him.

> Much love
> Nancy

P.S. I shall be in London the whole of December.

[1] The 1957 collected cartoons of Osbert Lancaster contained two references to *Noblesse Oblige*. One shows Maudie Littlehampton eating off her knife, saying, 'Oh, to hell with Nancy Mitford! What I always say is – if it's ME it's U!' In the other, Maudie is reading *Towards Equality: A Socialist Party Manifesto*; she stops her daughter from playing a record, saying: 'No, darling! Not while mother's trying to read Mr Gaitskell's answer to Nancy Mitford!'
[2] Nancy was signing *Voltaire in Love*, and Art Buchwald his reminiscences, *I Chose Caviar*. Buchwald described the event in 'An Autographing Match': 'At six o'clock the tally was in: Miss Mitford had signed 96 books; we had signed 45. It was a fair fight and it wasn't the first time love had triumphed over caviar.' *International New York Herald Tribune*, 18 November 1957.

To VIOLET HAMMERSLEY   7 rue Monsieur, VII
14 January 1958

Darling

. . . I got back here to find a heap of presents & cards like a haystack & have been writing to thank ever since. Hence the silence. Dreadfully sorry about your back, what can it be?

My visits to the major novelists were very successful. The food of all 3 about equal (not good). Leslie[1] had the warmest house & warmest heart, Evelyn by far the coldest house & Tony Powell the coldest heart but the most fascinating chats and a pâté de foie gras. He raked up some old characters from my past; Henry Bath & new wife (a great improvement on Daphne) Billy Jolliffe, now Ld Hylton & Ld

Lieut:[2] That was all very interesting. Leslie had dear Sir Moley[3] & the David Cecils.

I find all these writers take themselves very seriously & Tony Powell speaks of *Punch*, of which he is literary editor, as though it were an important vehicle of intellectual opinion. . . .

The Duchess of Windsor has got those things on her skin like you[4] – which confirms my idea that only wicked people get them.

Marie-Laure [de Noailles]'s lover didn't turn up for the N-Y dinner so she sent Tony Gandarillas to fetch him & Tony found him in a four day old pool of blood having opened veins. So you may imagine that it has made 1958 for Tony. But I am sorry, I was fond of old Oscar.[5]

Went to see the little house at Versailles that I've been hatching for years. I think it's now definitely for sale & I shall soon have to decide. Oh goodness!

Much love
    N

[1] L. P. Hartley (1895–1972). Novelist. Author of *The Shrimp and the Anemone* (1944), *Eustace and Hilda* (1947) and *The Hireling* (1957).
[2] 4th Baron Hylton (1898–1967).
[3] Sir Orme Sargent (1884–1962). Diplomat.
[4] Liver spots.
[5] Oscar Dominguez (1907–57). Spanish painter, former Surrealist. His fixation with the greatness of Picasso's work drove him eventually to drink and suicide.

To Jessica Treuhaft   7 rue Monsieur, VII
3 April 1958

Darling Sooze

Not off writers, but frantically busy. About 100 Farve letters to answer[1] & three jobs hanging over me, including a long, serious (!) article for *Harper's* magazine on WHY I hate America.

No I don't take in clippings & love to see any thanks very much. My publisher sends a few (*Life, N. Yorker* etc) & so far they are favourable & I seem to be on the best sellers list whatever that is. Glad you liked it.[2] . . .

I've just got back from England. Three funeral services – such tear jerkers Susan with the old hymns (Holy Holy Holy) & the awful words, I was in *fountains each time*. Then the ashes were done up in the sort of parcel *he* used to bring back from London, rich thick brown paper & incredibly neat knots & Woman & I & Aunt Iris took it down to Burford & it was buried at Swinbrook. Alas one's life.

The will is almost too mad.[3]
I'll write again very soon.

Much love & to Dinkie
        N

---

[1] Lord Redesdale died on 17 March 1958. 'It is sad, but the odd, violent, attractive man he used to be had already gone except for an occasional flash.' (NM to Evelyn Waugh, 24 March 1958)

[2] *Voltaire in Love* was praised even by Nancy's most assiduous critics, such as Harold Nicolson. Amongst her friends only Mark Ogilvie-Grant demurred: 'I'm sorry to see that Voltaire sent you literally to sleep. Whether or not it generally has that effect it seems to be selling. Bertrand Russell likes it, but I don't imagine he ever sleeps.' (NM to Mark-Ogilvie-Grant, 13 November 1957)

[3] Lord Redesdale cut Jessica out of his will as he was concerned that she might give her inheritance to the Communist Party. Nancy felt this was unjust and presented her share of Inchkenneth to Jessica who subsequently bought out her other sisters. However, the island proved more trouble than it was worth and the Treuhafts sold Inchkenneth in the late 1960s.

TO MARK OGILVIE-GRANT   7 rue Monsieur, VII
16 April 1958

Dear Old
    Yes, your grave side gramme was much appreciated. Muv says when one's old one doesn't mind anything (mustn't it be lovely) & I think she's all right really.
    I went to the Wid. It was bitter weather & she mourned about not being in Greece with ye. 'If only the *Bank* hadn't *Failed* –!' Well *she* minds *everything* at 81. In the middle of the night she surged into my room saying 'Child I am dying – doctor! doctor!' With death rather in mind I was alarmed. Got her back to bed where she then felt better. Said she thought she had swallowed 100 china plates! (As a French friend remarked il n'y a qu'elle[1] –!) I said next day I couldn't help noticing she called for the doctor, not the priest. . . .
    What's your summer? I think I *must* go to Muv oh dear how I don't want to but you know – remorse –

Much love
    O.L.

---

[1] She is unique.

To Gaston Palewski   7 rue Monsieur, VII
19 May 1958

Oh Colonel I seem to be living all those old years over again today.
But what has so changed the French?[1] Or are they enclosed in their
own deepest feelings? I am. I can't speak to anybody except Marie –
such an old & whole hearted Gaullist. I ask her what is this apathy?
& she says people are tired of it all. Qu'ils se débrouillent[2] is the cry.
(Too rich? Too bourgeois?) . . .

I long for your voice so passionately. I can't imagine today without
you being there – I stayed in all yesterday expecting you to telephone.[3]

Ah Colonel, you see I am in one of my states. Write a little (lisible)
line if you don't come soon. I go to London & Scotland 5th June.
Don't abandon me. Perhaps you too have changed – too rich perhaps
& happy –? BOURGEOIS perhaps? Not a word one used to associate
with you!!!

[1] France was living through the tense weeks before the fall of the Fourth Republic.
The Algerian crisis was at its height after the army *coup* on 13 May and there was the
threat of a military takeover in France. De Gaulle was returned to power on 1 June.
[2] Let them get on with it.
[3] Palewski was on a brief visit to Paris.

To Gaston Palewski   7 rue Monsieur, VII
12 June 1958

Dearest
The reason for my resignation is that I'm no use to you. When
things go badly you don't need me, when they go well you turn to
other, prettier, ladies. So I seem to have no function – le portefeuille
est vide.

We are both trapped & frustrated in our different ways – I must
say we take it well, neither of us shows a sad face to the world nor
are we specially embittered.

En ce qui vous concerne I don't believe the General can do without
you. His path is much thornier than perhaps he realizes. . . .

I sat for 3 long days by the telephone & then heard that you had
had a talk with Hoytie [Wiborg] it was too much to bear.

To Diana Mosley   7 rue Monsieur, VII
27 December 1958

Dereling

Spanish Al[1] came to luncheon yesterday. He looks very well & of
course made me shriek with his accounts of Life in London. 'Now
Ingrid's rock'n roll – we call that the Mayfair rock –' I must say, it is
an underworld they live in & I was really shocked to hear that all the
girls have babies the whole time which go off to orphanages poor little
things. One did think contraception existed at least. Spanish A *very*
sweet.

Everybody here seems pleased at the idea of a *franc lourd*[2] except
me. It will take me at least a year to do the sum – I've never been
able to keep a bridge score without the noughts.

After my Xmas luncheon Walter Lees[3] took us all over Niarchos's[4]
house. Exploded for ever is the myth of Emilio's[5] good taste. *Darling!!*
I can't begin to tell & if I did you'd hardly believe me. Only wish I
could send a photograph of the electric light fittings as a start. John
Russell[6] who was with us said it's no surprise to him, he has seen
N's pictures & not one is of any interest whatever. The house reminds
me of Du Barry's at Louveciennes as done up by Coty in about 1920
I suppose – a form of bad taste one thought dead. I believe I'd rather
live in a Le Corbusier house, c'est tout dire.

Much love, Happy N.Y.
N

[1] Alexander Mosley was working as a courier, escorting English tourists to Spain
(cf. Basil in *Don't Tell Alfred*).
[2] On 1 January 1960, the nominal value of the French franc was divided by a hundred;
100 old francs thus equalled one new franc.
[3] Walter Lees was in charge of Stavros Niarchos's Paris office.
[4] Stavros Niarchos (1910–). Shipping tycoon. Perhaps an over-rich Christmas lunch
explains Nancy's reaction to his house. His collection included not only superb French
18th-century furniture and silver, but an important El Greco, a Matisse and a Picasso.
[5] Emilio Terry (1890–1969). Franco-Cuban interior decorator, who designed Charlie
Beistegui's theatre at Groussay.
[6] John Russell (1919–). Art historian and critic.

To Lady Redesdale   7 rue Monsieur, VII
19 March 1959

Darling Muv

It was very nice having Debo here. She & Diana (my goodness
they have become eccentric) rushed about Paris in huge long coats

& their heads tied up in white satin like two beauties distracted by tooth-ache. Woolworth bags bulging open & a hundred parcels dangling from their arms. The staring that went on, you can imagine! Debo bought, I thought, a lot of expensive rubbish, rather on the lines of the clothes Diana buys at Harrods – rather less nice in fact. Of course Paris isn't arranged for that sort of wild two-day shopping – it takes an age to buy properly here. However a good time was had by all, including me!

Did you read this morning about the Doctor whose most grisly nightmare (described with horror as possibly leading to suicide) was that he lived in a large country house with a drive? Typical of the times, dear.

Deep silence from Wid so I suppose she is busy with housework – Mme du Deffand into Mrs Dale.

When do you go to your eternal snows?

Fancy I sent some fruit from the Midi to Phil & Aunt Iris & in each case it arrived *on* their birthdays. Do admit how queer – naturally I'd no *idea* when the birthdays were.

Dark & cold here, oh bother.

Much love
    N

To Lady Redesdale   7 rue Monsieur, VII
28 April 1959

Darling Muv

I didn't write as not sure where you are but I see it's still London. On Friday I go to Brussels (our Embassy) for 2 or 3 days – greatly look forward to it as I love Rachel Labouchere.[1] She is a sort of Kitty Nairne,[2] that kind of person.

The dinner was great fun. I only go out once every 2 years & when I do I love it. So amusing to see the dresses & jewels. Dinner was at 8.30 & *at* 8.30 P. Margaret's hairdresser arrived so we waited for hours while he concocted a ghastly coiffure. She looked like a huge ball of fur on two well-developed legs. Shortest dress I ever saw – a Frenchman said it begins so low & ends so soon. In fact the whole appearance was excessively common.

The Q, covered with barbed wire, looked SWEET & as cheerful as the other was cross. I suppose she [Princess Margaret] had had a good time in Rome with a lot of international bad hats & didn't care about a rather pompous dinner party. The Ganays not pleased when she suddenly chucked their luncheon. Altogether she has not left a good impression & *France-Soir* mentioned the word *maussade* [sullen].

I dined with the Massiglis for the Edens – he doesn't look so ill but she dreadfully strained I thought. She had been up at 7 judging at the Floralies so it may have been that.

Much love – I'll write from Brussels to Isle.
      N

[1] Rachel Labouchere; married to Sir George Labouchere, Ambassador to Belgium 1955–60.
[2] Lady Katherine Fitzmaurice (1912–). Succeeded as Baroness Nairne in 1944. Married 3rd Viscount Mersey in 1933. A great friend of Nancy, Diana and Debo, who appreciated her charm and quiet wit.

To Lady Redesdale   7 rue Monsieur, VII
30 May 1959

Darling Muv

Decca has gone I see, you will miss her. I do hope all your ill people are better & that you've got a cook otherwise I know you live on jugs of cream which must finally affect *even your* liver. I've told Decca I will give her my share of the island & what I hope is that the others will do the same. It seems to me the very least, after the way Farve treated her. What does she want it for? She doesn't say. Atom base I suppose – you'll probably see Khrushchev arriving any day, to be greeted with jugs of cream by the simple islanders. Murdo[1] will have to look sharp with the mail.

What other visitors (apart from Kru) have you coming?

Not much news. I go out rather more than usual & am writing a long article on Fr salons,[2] very dull, for which I've been offered 500 dollars so felt I had to. I hate writing articles they seem to me almost as much trouble as a book. A journalist said the other day 'it's known in Fleet St that you & Evelyn W are the two most difficult people to get anything from'.

Much love
      N

[1] The boatman at Inchkenneth.
[2] 'Some Rooms for Improvement', American *Horizon*, November 1961.

To Jessica Treuhaft   S. Vio 373
4 August 1959   Fondamenta Zorzi
                                       Venice

Darling Soo

Oh dear I do wish I could have seen you once more. But when you are châtelaine of the island will you not come more often?

There's an American here called Wrightsman[1] who talks exactly like Hector Dexter in my book. We get marks for the sentences we can make him say with the words 'over a million dollars' but it's an easy game. He says Getty is hardly rich at all, not a penny more than 800 million dollars. Come & live in Yurrup Susan, come on, you'll never make 800 million dollars however long you stay there & Benjy[2] will learn nothing as you very well know.

I've kept this flat on until the 12th, I do so love it here, then I go home & hope not to move for ages.

I wonder if you'll see Muv again, I do hope so. I worry about her, she must be so miserable without José.[3] Oh dear, exactly what happened to Farve, his dog he so adored died. And that silly Christine,[4] lolling on the operating table. (Operations are for rich people, yes Susan.)

On this note I close, with fondest love, keep in touch, WEIGH.[5]

     Susan

[1] Charles Wrightsman (1896–1986). Oil magnate, philanthropist and art collector. 'Old Chourlie is the 7th richest man & about the 4th nastiest but I love him, he makes me scream with laughter. Yesterday he announced sadly that the Ritz is an undeveloped area. He is always rather sad. Weighs himself twice a day.' (NM to Evelyn Waugh, 21 June 1961) Nancy described his wife Jayne as 'Head girl of N.Y. charm school, not bad at all', which was high praise for an American.
[2] Jessica's son, Benjamin Treuhaft (1947–). He became an expert piano tuner.
[3] Lady Redesdale's dachshund had died.
[4] The cook at Inchkenneth. She had been operated on for appendicitis.
[5] 'Yes the weighing weighs. You see when I write to my other friends I put the letter in an envelope & off it goes. But with you one has to wander about looking for a weighing machine.' (NM to Jessica Treuhaft [1957])

To Lady Redesdale   Fontaines-les-Nonnes
12 October 1959   par Puisieux

Darling Muv

I know I'm awful about letters but I'm trying to work. Hope you received *Encounter* with my piece?[1]

At last election results – I see Sir O got about $^1/_{10}$ of the votes which I suppose is rather good with no party backing?[2] Pleased it's over as it must have been tiring for her.

Wid is being tremendous. Today the whole house in a fandango as it's the big annual luncheon for the Bishop. At the busiest moment, just as all the servants were slaving to make everything nice, at about midday, she said she would DIE if she couldn't have a lavement [enema]. Nobody here can do it – they sent to the village – no luck. By this time all were concentrating on her. Then she said she *might* live if she could have a suppository so the house was searched from top to toe & at last one was found. Result: luncheon ½ an hour late. Do admit. (The suppository worked when we were out for a walk of course.) The Bishop is a duck – he was here all day from 9 A. M. There were 4 other priests & a few neighbours & luncheon went on until 3.30 I was *dead*.

Have you read *The Prof*?[3] You'd love it. Can you get it from a library or should I send?

Xopher [Sykes]'s wife has had a stroke so there were floods, but the floods became a sea of tears when she didn't die & every time a letter arrives to say she's a bit better it casts a gloom. What I love is no attempt at dissimulation!

When do you come South? Fearful drought here, really worrying but one can't help enjoying the sunshine.

Much love
    N

[1] 'The Tourist', *Encounter*, October 1959. ' "Foreigner, differing from speaker in language and customs, outside the Roman Empire; rude, wild, or uncultured person." The Barbarian of yesterday is the Tourist of today and he still preys on the rich old cities where our civilization began.'
[2] Oswald Mosley stood as Union Movement candidate for North Kensington in the general election and received eight per cent of the vote. He had launched the party in 1948 to promote the wider union of Europe.
[3] Roy Harrod, *The Prof: A Personal Memoir of Lord Cherwell* (1959).

To Lady Redesdale   7 rue Monsieur, VII
16 December 1959

Darling Muv
    I didn't like *Xmas Pud* very much. It's too slight for broadcasting, such jokes as there are were thrown away & the production was

somehow vulgar I thought.[1] However I'm very glad you were less critical – . . .

Oh Christmas cards. I get about 4 every day from people who sign John or James & haven't faintest notion who they can be – the rest look so expensive one longs for the cash instead. Then all one's humble French friends (painters, Marie's nieces, Colonel's secretary & so on) send visiting cards which one is supposed to return. A perfect *bore*.

Better to have a sensible man doctor I really do think. But then I am a wild anti-feminist.

I fly DV to Manchester today week. Probably I've told you this already. Then Crichel till 7 or 8 of Jan: & then Alvilde can almost certainly have me. If not an hotel can't be too difficult then.

Alvilde gives a ghastly tale of the horrors which are being perpetrated in London, really unbearable.

I hear you have written a snorter to Hastie[2] oh good – keep it up.

At this juncture parcels arrive – a GHASTLY ash tray from the *Sunday Express* & a book the size of a Baskerville Bible from my American publisher. Again I long for the cash as I plunge both into the W.P.B.

Diana gives a terrible account of your cat, such a wrecker? Alas old animals are so much nicer I love my cat now, but it took about 8 years.

Much love
N

Perhaps you ought to be a *little* more in the hands of doctors –![3]

[1] A dramatised version of *Christmas Pudding* had been broadcast by the BBC.
[2] The family solicitor.
[3] Lady Redesdale's views on doctors were close to those of a Christian Scientist. 'My mother, whose views on health were rudimentary, who had never heard of hygiene and did not really believe in illness, had one medical superstition which nothing could shake. Pig, she thought, was unclean.' *The Water Beetle*, pp. 12–13.

TO HEYWOOD HILL   7 rue Monsieur, VII
9 March 1960
[postcard]

No I haven't had it[1] – do send as soon as you can. The bit in *The Queen* was funny in one way – she has quite unconsciously copied from my book instead of from real life & various modifications of the truth demanded by novel form are now taken as true. Passionately interested to read it all. I believe her husband has re written it or helped a good deal as it is *his* voice, if you know them both. My mother stood by her through thick & thin. I rather expect to be in London a few days end of March. . . .

[1] The first volume of Jessica's autobiography, *Hons and Rebels*, had just been published.

TO JESSICA TREUHAFT   7 rue Monsieur, VII
11 March 1960

Darling Soo

Many thanks for sending your book which I have read with great attention. I think it's *awfully good* – easy to read & very funny in parts. A slightly cold wind to the heart perhaps – you don't seem very fond of anybody, but I suppose the purpose is to make the Swinbrook world seem horrible, to explain why you ran away from it.

I loved the idea of shooting Hitler – a Hon: did shoot at old Musso who thought it exceedingly funny – had there been two, foreigners would indeed steer clear of the denomination!

I've no intention of having a go at Kru next week. I rather long for the circus – a million cudums [Communists] are being brought from all over France (the local cleaner will probably appear in *your shirt*, yes Susan).

I long for the reviews & shall no doubt receive them as my press cutting people always send references to Mary Russell Mitford as well as to Lord Milford Haven. Heywood Hill, who always knows, says it will sell thousands.

Awful dust wrapper – silly old Gol[lancz] had much better have stuck to that Left Book Club cover (do you remember how ghastly it was the way books were *left* & piled up month after month?)

No news – I'm shut up, writing one myself. [1]

Esmond [Romilly] was the original Teddy boy wasn't he, a pioneer of the modern trend & much more terrific than his followers. When does it come out in America?

    Much love
        from Susan

[1] *Don't Tell Alfred* (1960). Nancy had been working on her final novel since the previous autumn.

To Heywood Hill   7 rue Monsieur, VII
16 March 1960

My dear Heywood

Will you tell Miss Moll [Buchanan] I have got myself low in actual
pounds & will pay her in May & promise not to forget (as I seem to
have done with her last bill). Hope the frail little barque won't founder
on this rock.

Decca's book. My sisters I can see mind more than I do (I've got
it by the way so don't send). It is rather dishonest for an autobiography
because she alters facts to suit herself in a way that I suppose is
allowed in a novel. (But as I have taken full advantage of that I can
hardly blame her I suppose!) She is beastly about aunts & people who
were always more than kind to us & very far from rich used to give
us huge tips & presents & treats. Diana is outraged for my mother
– I had expected worse, to tell the truth – & of course minds being
portrayed as a dumb society beauty!!

Altogether there is a coldness about it which I find unattractive,
but of course made up for by the *great* funniness –

I'm coming over Ap: 4th for 2 or 3 days. It wouldn't be possible to
see Cliff's[1] the Boy for Me? You wouldn't be a sport & take me, in
the interests of art?

I feel until one's actually seen him using his mike like a gun rolling
on it like a savage puma one can't know what it's all about. If you
feigns (fain?) it what about Miss Liz[2] as an escort?

    Love
        Nancy

[1] Cliff Richard, the pop singer.
[2] Elizabeth Forbes, who had worked at Heywood Hill's bookshop since 1946.

To Lady Redesdale   7 rue Monsieur, VII
17 March 1960

Darling Muv

It seems you haven't received *the book* which is almost too odd
unless it went to the island. I long to know what you think. Diana
minds it more than I do – I suppose because I have said my say (in
novels) & she hasn't had a chance to! It is very funny & runs along
well, but there is a chill undertone one doesn't quite like. I suppose
Decca is one of those women who can only feel affection for husband
& children. It's not an honest book & doesn't even bear reading

carefully – too much contradiction. Of course Esmond is the original
Teddy-boy or juvenile delinquent & would be considered quite ordinary now. I do wonder when the book will appear in the shops.

I'm coming over, to say goodbye before you fly to the Pole, on 4th
April. Will stay at Debo's – I'm bringing over her clothes which are
lovely. . . .

Momo who had a cancer in the food pipe, inoperable, has been
cured by rays. It's a sort of miracle as everybody thought she would
die. She comes here next week.

I shall be looking for beach clothes in London (they are too expensive here) so do note if you hear of any lovely ones by chance.

Much love
    N

I really think Decca is too horrid about our aunts & uncles who were
always so nice to us when young.

To Jessica Treuhaft   7 rue Monsieur, VII
30 March 1960

Darling Soo
It wasn't quite my fault about the non-weighed letter (too long to
explain). Shan't occur again.[1]

My translator Jacques Brousse rang up just now & said 'Stock
(publisher) are reading *Diana's novel.*' I put him right & he then said
with a sort of scream – he is very hysterical – 'oh I *told* them she is
far too beautiful to write a novel.' If they do it I advise you to let him
translate it as he's used to Mitfordiana.

Muggeridge was horribly funny I thought in *N.S. & N.*[2] but the
review very good. I agree, I like the [*Tele*]*graph*[3] best, but all have
been spiffing, not one adverse note. Clever thing, you'll make pots.
Reactions
Muv is pleased & amused. Diana not pleased at being presented as
a dumb society beauty & is really down on the book, picking too much
on details & inaccuracies. We are all sorry you were horrid about
Uncle Tommy, always kind to us & really such a comic, original & in
his way clever person. Debo really I think likes it but she had only
read half when I saw her. Kept saying how sad – how sad – one didn't
realize – & so on.

The Widow is to be Arbiter of All on account of knowing us from such early days, but she is gadding in London at present. I'll pass on the Arbitration.[4]

I suppose on account of you & the Hon: Violet Gibson who shot off Mussolini's ear, I was ordered by the police here to report twice a day during Kru's visit. However I made the embassy tell them not to be so silly & all was rescinded.

I saw the old fellow 4 times by chance quite near & waved, from you. All the cleaners were keenly there.

I sent the book to Sigrid (my maid when I first married) & she simply loved it – I sent her letter to Muv who will perhaps pass it on. I'm always pleased when simple people like one's books, it's a good sign.

Constantia Fenwick[5] says when she used to stay with us she had no idea so many pots were on the boil, everything seemed quite ordinary.

Love to see your friends but I shall be away (working) the whole of May I *think*. Please tell them to ring up in case I don't go after all or have returned –

Much love
    N

Versailles has fallen through – I am very sorry.[6]

[1] Nancy's letter of 11 March, sent by surface mail, had taken a long time to reach Jessica.

[2] In the 'London Diary' column Muggeridge wrote: 'To survive in the new climate of ostensible egalitarianism, the upper class (and the monarchy) had to become a soap opera. The Mitfords have made a considerable contribution towards showing how this can be done.' *New Statesman*, 26 March 1960.

[3] *Hons and Rebels* was reviewed by the Earl of Birkenhead in the *Daily Telegraph*, 25 March 1962.

[4] Violet Hammersley took exception to the portrayal of Jessica's parents: 'One would conclude from the book, I think (if one was an outsider) that Muv was a good-natured queer fool, and Farve, of course, a madman. But I think it is a sad book, and leaves a reader wondering why this country home and large family of children, and much of the "good things of life" should have been so intolerable.' (Violet Hammersley to NM, 30 March 1960) She wrote to Jessica that she was 'surprised' the book was so well written, but that she found it 'entertaining', 'interesting' and 'well constructed'. (8 April 1960) Her main grievance, however, was that she herself was never once mentioned.

[5] A childhood friend of Nancy.

[6] The house in Versailles which Nancy had been hoping for some time to buy.

To Evelyn Waugh   Lismore Castle
24 May 1960   Co Waterford

Darling Evelyn

No I didn't review it. When I wrote to her I said I thought there
was a chill wind & she was rather hurt. We are on the best of terms
& always have been. What I feel is this. In some respects she has
seen the family, quite without knowing it herself, through the eyes
of my books – that is, if she hadn't read them hers would have been
different. She is absolutely unperceptive of my uncles & aunts, Nanny,
Dr Cheatle[1] & the characters whom I didn't describe & who all could
have been brought to life but simply were not. I haven't said this to
anybody but you as it sounds so conceited. Esmond was the most
horrible human being I have ever met. I did say in my letter to her
'you have presented him as the original Teddy-boy' but none of the
reviewers made that point.

Clever of you to see the two voices. I am quite certain much of it
was written by Treuhaft who is a sharp little lawyer & who certainly
made her write it in the first place. The words cash in are never off
his lips. (I quite like him but *oh* Americans.) The Romilly daughter
[Constancia] is (was, 2 years ago) a stunning beauty.

I've just written the last words of my book. It's not good. I am
truly very much handicapped now by my eyes being so poorly – can't
read it over & over as I used & therefore I fear it reads jerkily.

I've been here the whole month & go home on Friday. Most of the
time with Eddy West about 13 miles from here. I'm stunned by the
beauty, emptiness & *pure* pre-new-world atmosphere of Ireland –
can't imagine why you don't live here. Some v. nice neighbours, too.
Marvellous butchers, one had forgotten what meat can taste like.

I think that's all. Debo has carried off your letter – she *terribly* hates
& minds the book.

    Much love
        Nancy

I think they are secret Communists now – call themselves Liberals.
But when in Paris their bedroom is always knee deep in *l'Humanité*[2]
I note.

---

[1] Dr Cheatle was the GP at Burford when the Mitfords lived at Asthall.
[2] Organ of the French Communist Party.

To Duchess of Devonshire   7 rue Monsieur, VII
23 June 1960

Dear Miss

I love this Emma – she is serious & good & clever & punctual & reliable & very fascinating to look at – & shrieks to boot.[1] If asked for a character I will supply a good one. A treasure. Now she is going home to cultivate her garden & feed Doris's[2] bantams, or so she says. I shall miss her v. much, but of course I am off myself.

Hamilton likes the book[3] – I waited to hear & then went a bust at Lanvin. Coral tunicked eveninger & a v. pretty short black affair avec bows (white satin) all over one's shoulders. Quels horribles prix, but that one knew. I had to sneak in when Bettina [Bergery] wasn't about as she tries to impose her taste, but I must say she turned up trumps over lending to Em.

So I shall be better dressed at Venice I've always had slight dregs there up to now. I go 4th July – S. Vio 373 is the address.

Tante Brigitte[4] made me give a luncheon for the Edens – now they can't come & I am *left with her*. (All our friends are mad & Nancy Cunard certified.) Never mind – my own fault for leaving it to her but I was v. busy correcting masterpiece. Don't repeat. . . .

Did you see Evelyn's interview.[5] I'd have given anything. He naturally loathed it – says he was driven by poverty. It will whizz up his Penguins – mine did.

I LOVE ROSES. It's gladioli & hydrangeas & lupins & dahlias I so loathe. Nobody understands about me & flowers; one day I will make a statement. Wild roses touch me to the heart like nothing else in the world.

Keep in touch, pray.

Love
   N

Reading & adoring *Q. Eliz* by Jenkins.[6]

[1] Emma Cavendish, Deborah's seventeen-year-old daughter, was in Paris for a few weeks learning French.
[2] Deborah's younger daughter Sophia was nicknamed Doris. 'She is all the Mitfords rolled into one & I see rocks ahead.' (NM to Gaston Palewski, 13 December 1962)
[3] 'I've finished *Don't Tell Alfred* oh what a relief. It seems awful twaddle to me, now, but Gladwyn who has read it thinks it's all right. How difficult it is to say what one wants. I find writing becomes far more difficult, not less.' (NM to Evelyn Waugh, 18 June 1960)
[4] Lady Bridget Parsons was a sister of 6th Earl of Rosse, whose wife was the former

Anne Armstrong-Jones, mother of Lord Snowdon. The French newspapers used, therefore, to refer to her as Princess Margaret's 'aunt'.
[5] Waugh had appeared on the television programme *Face to Face*, interviewed by John
Freeman.
[6] Elizabeth Jenkins, *Elizabeth the Great* (1958).

TO A. D. PETERS   7 rue Monsieur, VII
29 June 1960

Dear Peter

Oh good I am so glad you like it. I entirely leave it to you about
serialization of course. I only say I hope for as much money as possible
(old age). Perhaps *Ladies H.J.* but it may be too anti American for
them.

We are a bit worried about Sam White[1] (Mockbar) & possible libel
– I daresay Jamie told you. He, Mockbar, sends me threatening
messages by emissaries – I won't see him any more. He is a vile liar
– two statements I can remember on which his whole page was built,
with a wealth of detail, were *totally untrue* & practically every week
he has to retract something.

I don't believe any jury would uphold him. Still we don't want the
book to be suppressed. All of you know more about these things than
I do. Here there is no law of libel & one forgets how strict the English
are.

About the date of the story – it must be left a bit nebulous, between
56 and 58. I think the best will be for me to be more vague about
Uncle M's age. I must try & have galley proofs I think – when would
that be? I shan't be back here until mid-August & it's jolly difficult
with Italian incompetence to receive a parcel there. I go on Monday
S. Vio 373 – Fondamenta Zorzi Venice.

I think that's all.

Yrs
      Nancy

Don't let anything be printed except from the top copy will you.

[1] Sam White (1911–88). Paris correspondent for the *Evening Standard* and the *Daily
Express*. The portrayal of him as Amyas Mockbar was Nancy's revenge for a piece
White had written in the *Standard* in 1958. He reported Nancy as having said that
Maurice Chevalier, who played Charles-Edouard in the film *Count Your Blessings*, was
the most vulgar man she had ever met. Chevalier threatened to walk off the set and
Nancy demanded a retraction from the *Standard* which was refused as she had spoken
before witnesses. 'Talk about dire, Sam White whom I nurtured as people nurture a

young lion (he wouldn't eat *me*) has eaten me.' (NM to Mark Ogilvie-Grant, 7 May 1958)

To Raymond Mortimer   7 rue Monsieur, VII
30 June 1960

Darling Raymond

Of course, naturally, I'd give anything to have an opinion from you. Only I hate the idea of you reading it in the corrected & re corrected typescript which must be like an unmade bed by now. Page proofs? It would be an enormous kindness.

I miss Monty who comes the day I leave – a dire disappointment as one can't see too much of that old bird. I always say some clever attractive chap ought to go & live near him & take down his table talk. It would be well worth it. Nelson blew his trumpet & so did all the Elizabethans. I suppose it was Dr Arnold who stopped that sort of rot, Sir.

I gave a huge luncheon for the [Anthony] Edens, huge for me at least, 12. When the selle d'agneau appeared Marie began to say it wouldn't go round. The maître d'hôtel, however, said 'Ne vous en faites pas – ILS (speaking as though of lions at the zoo) mangent très peu en ce moment, ILS sont tellement invités.'[1]

Don't you love it. Indeed there was masses left over. It went off very well & the frogs, mostly young, were most polite & bowed as though to royalty. I think they were pleased to be invited. His prestige here is enormous – I even found Marie cleaning the chandelier saying 'pour M. Eden'.

Do come to Venice it would be so nice.

Janet[2] read me your letter about Nancy Cunard, whom I have never known. How dreadful. Rather strange that she & the Duchess of Atholl are now both off their poor heads (Spain). Women should never take up causes, that's what it is. Janet sweetly waded through my book & likes it.

Violet [Trefusis] asked me to dinner last night. I accepted – then discovered that all Paris was going, a buffet dinner. So I rang up & said you know I can't bear crowds, do let me off. She swore I'd got it all wrong & it was a dinner of 12. When I arrived there must have been 60 people. I turned tail – she pursued & *cried*.

Not to make a silly fuss I stayed & made a corner with Bourbon-Bussets & the George of Denmarks who had *all* been through the same motions of telephoning to put off & been lied to!! My reward, when leaving, on the stairs, a loud scream & a feeling of being knocked over by a wave – Tante Brigitte falling on me. I was really frightened but got off with a slightly sprained hand. She not hurt at all. But isn't Violet the limit!

Love
   N

[1] 'Don't worry – THEY hardly eat anything at the moment, THEY have so many invitations.'
[2] Janet Flanner (1892–1978). Paris correspondent for the *New Yorker* 1925–75.

TO VIOLET HAMMERSLEY   S. Vio 373
24 July 1960   Venice
                         I leave for Paris 12 Aug:

Darling
    What Victor [Cunard] has got. This is what I was instructed to tell his brother: myocardial fatigue, weakness of coronaries, cardiac weakness, no thrombosis as yet. I don't know what it means, you may. He looks perfectly terrible, will be in bed at least another 6 weeks, perks up when he sees one but the doctor says he falls into black despair as soon as one has gone. I go up there every other day, missing the beach, 3 hours altogether in broiler-buses. Never mind – the thing is I feel he is dying though I may be wrong. Now the Lees-Milnes have taken the house & he has got to be brought back here in two ambulances (land & water) it's all a fearful worry. I think it was partly brought on by the madness of N. Cunard – I mean by her going mad. She went to an hotel at 3 A.M. & when the night porter aged 90 showed her her room she ordered him to sleep with her. She then set fire to a policeman. She is now in a bin whence she writes heartrending letters to poor Vic. Do write to the old boy – Casa Freia, Asolo, Treviso.
    A part ça I am having my usual heavenly time. How I love it here. The hospitality of the Venetians is extraordinary – in nearly 3 weeks I have only had two meals here. In a way it's a waste as Oliva the maid is a smashing cook. If I ask people here they force me to go to them instead.
    The shoes have tiny little low heels. I'll see what I can get – what size do you technically take?
    I adore Ann Fleming[1] & she's not méchante the least little bit; clever, good natured, lively as you saw & was once very pretty. Not

nice to her husbands, but that is special – I suppose Mr Right never quite turned up.

Did you see the *Cornhill* account of a visit to Evelyn?[2] Masterly.

. . . I came upon William Hayter's daughter[3] & young man, so I whizzed them round in a gondola, which the young can never afford (£3 for 2 hours) & elicited from them that they were camping out at Mestre in one small tent. Didn't dare ask anything so old fashioned as are you engaged? She looked tirée aux 4 épingles[4] I must say. ISN'T it odd?

Love from
    N

[1] Ann Charteris (1913–81). Married to 3rd Baron O'Neill 1932–44, to 2nd Viscount Rothermere 1945–52 and in 1952 to Ian Fleming, creator of James Bond. 'A great & life long friend I love her – in fact she's almost the only person to whom I've left something in my will. Jealous?' (NM to Violet Hammersley, 12 November 1964)
[2] By Edward Sheehan, *Cornhill Magazine*, Summer 1960.
[3] Teresa Hayter.
[4] As if she had stepped out of a bandbox.

To Violet Hammersley   7 rue Monsieur, VII
22 August 1960

Darling

Oh dear they *don't make* the pricked shoes any more. All I can do is to give you my old pair which are too big for you. We'll see. When do you go to Fontaines?

I do love Cheese leaving without permission.[1] It's like something in *Uncle Tom's Cabin* – is she leaping from ice-floe to ice-floe over the Solent? Have you sent Mrs Hook[2] to the Totland slave market to buy another? To be quite honest, wicked as I know you to be, do you regret the days when all this was possible?

Can't remember when I last wrote. Did I tell about the Tynans? (In Venice) I don't want to repeat myself.[3]

I went down to Diana – there were Max & the Daughter[4] who is now worshipped by all. D & Sir O are going to *stay* with the Loredans[5] in Venice – L is secretary of the neo-Fascist movement & no decent Venetian will speak to him. Meanwhile Diana says Sir O has never been so busy – it makes my flesh creep. No doubt we shall all be in camps very soon. I've ordered a camping suit from Lanvin – the price is so terrible that even I feel guilty & won't dare confess it. But I tell

myself old age looms as well as what *you* call the millennium, & a new
suit is *so* cheering.

Lettice Ashley Cooper.[6] Yes she's a dear. A cherished neighbour
of the Lads. What on earth is Pim? (what they drank.) I see I'm quite
out of it in spite of all the prep: I did on young people for my book.
Oh bother – what are jeans? Did you enjoy the party?

I saw a picture of David S.[7] sponsoring an object, apparently for hatching out or perhaps I mean brooding over young chickens, which, said
the caption, is a model for Liverpool Cathedral. Ay di me. A broiler
cathedral, just the thing for nowadays. Pray read him this paragraph.

   Fond love
      N

[1] Violet Hammersley's maid had given notice.
[2] The housekeeper.
[3] Kenneth Tynan (1927–80). Writer and theatre director. Drama critic for the *New
Yorker* 1958–60. Married to Elaine Brimberg 1951–64 and to Kathleen Halton in 1967.
'They arrived with letters for us all in Venice, but nobody much liked them. Rudely
late for everything, badly dressed & uppish.' (NM to Duchess of Devonshire, 14 August
1960)
[4] Max Mosley married Jean Taylor on 9 July 1960.
[5] Count Alvise Loredan and his wife Bianca.
[6] Lady Lettice Ashley-Cooper (1911–90). A Dorset neighbour of Raymond Mortimer
and Eddy Sackville-West.
[7] David Stokes; Violet Hammersley's son-in-law, an architect.

To Raymond Mortimer   7 rue Monsieur, VII
1 September 1960

Darling Raymond

The kindness of you! I'm greatly reassured that you like it because
the only other non-book trade reader, Gladwyn, made thousands of
excellent corrections on the typescript, & went over it with me for
an hour at least & made NO observation which rather shook my nerve!
Entresol shatters me & the odd thing is neither he nor Gaston spotted
it (Gaston read it by the way & was also very non-committal). You
see like all awful spellers I go out of my way to make difficulties for
myself. I had it so firmly in my mind that entr'sol was correct I didn't
even bother to look it up. Curse curse as Lidi Clary[1] would say.
Perhaps Jamie will correct it but he was groaning at the idea.

Protagonist *I always* thought meant chief actor – then while I was
writing Mrs Ham wrote to me using it as supporter – I looked in the
dictionary & it seemed to allow that use. Oh curse curse again. An

igame is a super super Préfet, a word constantly in the papers & on the wireless. When Gen de G is in doubt (I'm sorry to have to say this) the igames are more often consulted than the deputies!

Yes, just what I felt about italics – it flows on so much better like that.

The stupidity of the hurry. I did the proofs in 2 days with the result I had such a *frightening* headache I could neither read nor write a word for two more. I sat in the dark & mourned over Victor whose death I am minding passionately. The only thing to cheer me up at all was the arrival of a Martian from the Elysée with a Cinderella-like invitation to dine there for the Jebb send-off. Luckily I've got a brand-new ball dress from Lanvin eating its head off in my cupboard.

That old Daisy has written a nouvelle[2] which isn't bad at all in a sort of Firbank way.

Cristiana Brandolini[3] whom I'm in love with has bought the rest of Violet T's house here. I foresee interesting fur-flying. (Xiana is Northey,[4] except for the bits which are Debo.)

Fond love & renewed thanks
Nancy

Have I thanked enough? It's from the bottom of my heart.
The dictionary says first actor etc, *champion of cause*.

[1] Gräfin Ludwine (Lidi) zu Eltz (1894–1984). Married to Prince Clary-Aldringen in 1916.

[2] Daisy Fellowes, *Sundays, A Fantasy* . . . (1960). Originally published in French as *Les dimanches de la comtesse de Narbonne* (1935).

[3] Cristiana Agnelli (1928–). Married Count Brando Brandolini d'Adda in 1947. 'She is a clown, most funny, very naughty, mischievous (not spiteful a bit) & in many ways like all of us – one of 7 adoring brothers & sisters. They are both angelic to me.' (NM to Duchess of Devonshire, 11 August 1959)

[4] The heroine of *Don't Tell Alfred*. 'She was like a small exquisite figure in enamelled glass, with hair the colour of a guinea; her eyes the liveliest and most expressive I ever saw; not very large, brilliantly blue . . . there was something indescribably lovable about her, she radiated affection, happiness, goodwill towards men.' (pp. 61–2)

To Prince Clary[1]   Fontaines-les-Nonnes
30 September 1960   par Puisieux

My dear Alphy
    . . . I was staying with Dolly & Marie de M[2] when the Belgian engagement[3] was announced & there were high cries of if only Alphy were here to tell us who these Moras de Aragon can be! Now I'm

with my dear & holy Mme Costa de Beauregard who pronounced 'Il paraît que, point de vue naissance ce n'est guère plus brillant qu'Armstrong, mais M. le Curé a des renseignements très rassurants sur son âme.'[4] Certainly she, la Fabiola, is very plain, but that is thought, here, to be just as well.

Mme Costa, at 86, is painting an altarpiece 3 metres high depicting St Roch. We all have to pose in turns – a certain Baron de Ruben is St Roch – I am une pénitente in a white veil. One of the figures (very gratin, low forehead & hideous jutting chin) is said by me to be Mme de St Roch – but this has not been well received.

What a horrible summer! It seems to have become hot for just long enough to kill Victor & then relapsed into gloom. I had a pathetic letter from John Marriott. Momo is kept quite under drugs – only conscious a few minutes every day. They talk of operating again, but as he says what for?

Then dear little Ostrorog[5] came & spent a day here & dropped down dead on arriving back in Paris. Cast a fearful gloom!

I'm going to England for my book (which you will receive early in Nov:) & to stay about the place with various friends unless I suppose one is paralysed by a railway strike.

Cristiana is *sure to be in love* – at her age voyons! We must only hope she won't lose her head!

Love to you both from
    Nancy

[1] Alfons (Alphy) Fürst Clary-Aldringen (1887–1978). Known to English friends as Prince Clary. In 1945 he and his wife Lidi fled their estates in Bohemia and settled in Venice. From the late 1950s until her death, Nancy wrote more than 260 letters to the Prince. They exchanged gossip about friends in Venice and England and when she embarked on her historical biographies, his wide understanding of Europe was invaluable. A year before his death he published an autobiography, *A European Past* (1977); Diana Mosley devoted a chapter to him in *Loved Ones*.

[2] Marie de La Rochefoucauld Doudeauville (1901–83). The dutiful wife of 8th Duke of Mouchy whom she married in 1920. Her mother was a Radziwill.

[3] King Baudouin of Belgium was engaged to Doña Fabiola de Mora y Aragòn.

[4] 'Apparently, insofar as birth is concerned, she's no better than Armstrong, but M. le Curé has some very reassuring information about her soul.' (Princess Margaret had married Antony Armstrong-Jones in May that year.)

[5] A neighbour of Nancy in Paris.

To EVELYN WAUGH   Fontaines-les-Nonnes
17 January 1961   par Puisieux

Darling Evelyn

Yes one has to make one's own decisions.[1] First of all though, *never*
Mme La Princesse unless the person is royal. Non-royal Princes get
their titles from Savoy or the Empire, it is not a French title. Also
never Mme la Comtesse (except on envelopes), it wld be like saying
Her Grace the Duchess, old fashioned, no longer the usage.

As one writes for the English eye I put the Comtesse with a capital
C. A comtesse is not comparable to an Eng: countess – she may be
infinitely less (the wife of the great great grandson of the second son
of a count, marquis or duke) or infinitely more, like the Comtesse de
Paris. What I do in books as in life is to introduce the character as
the Comtesse de X & refer to her afterwards as Mme de X. In the
case of a duchesse I refer to her as the duchess (in English). It seems
to run more smoothly. You still say Mme la Duchesse when speaking
to one but only servants say Mme la Comtesse. Only the King says
Comtesse.

The head of a family is Comte de X; all the rest are Comte Jean
de X, the same with princely families (though the head is generally a
duke). Jacqueline is Psse Jean de CC (La Psse on an envelope).

Wouldn't Kingsley Amis enjoy this letter.[2]

Love from
N

Example of my own method:

All eyes now turned to the door through which the Duchesse de
Dreux-Brézé slowly advanced on the arm of M. Furet. This duchess,
whose private life was, to say the least of it, tumultuous & whose
piety was only equalled by her immeasurable greed, was one of the
greatest beauties of our own or any other age . . . .

There was a low murmur from the dowagers' bench when the
Marquise de Q took the floor with her husband's cousin, Comte Jean
de Q. A little while later, at the supper table, I heard Mme de Q
asking, in her small reedy voice, for a glass of ginger pop. There
seemed to be no available footman (I learnt afterwards that those who
were not already lying, drunk & insensible, on the back stairs, had
rushed to the hall in the hopes of handing his coat to the Swedish
ambassador well known to every lacquey in Paris for his ridiculous
habit of dealing out colossal tips), so M. de Q got up & went himself

to the sideboard. As soon as his place became vacant it was occupied by the Marquis de Q who addressed himself to his wife. Although what he said was inaudible everybody knew that he was supplicating her, for the sake of their sixteen children, to respect her own position in society. Trembling with rage Mme de Q rose to her feet & told M. Furet that she would be requiring her carriage at once. The unfortunate host, seeing that this ball which had cost the aspirations of a lifetime as well as etc. etc.

My pen seems to have run away with me.

¹ Waugh edited and wrote the preface for *The Life and Times of Madame Veuve Clicquot-Ponsardin* by Princess Jacqueline de Caraman-Chimay (1961); he had asked Nancy for advice on French usage.
² Kingsley Amis (1922–). Writer, whose eponymous hero in *Lucky Jim* (1954) was then a symbol of anti-Establishment revolt. 'I liked *Lucky Jim* for its funniness, but it made me sad, as do all evidences of declining civilisation.' NM, *The Times*, 20 November 1961. Knighted in 1991.

To EVELYN WAUGH   7 rue Monsieur, VII
7 June 1961

Darling Evelyn

If you're not busy (& if you are, *when* you're not) will you explain something to me?

You know *death* – (my brother Tom aged 3 said once Grandfather, you know *adultery* –)

Well, one dies, is buried & rises again & is judged. What happens then between death & the end of the world? Are we what the French call en liberté provisoire? Do we sleep? But I'm always hearing people say he's in a better place *now* or he knows *now* this that or the other. Do elucidate. I asked Mme Costa but she is too deaf, I couldn't get through what I meant; she merely said she prays for me, not, I thought, very hopefully. My dear Bishop of Meaux I was so fond of has died. M. le Curé hates me, I wouldn't ask him anything. One or two friends (Catholic) were quite as much puzzled as I am, when I put it to them, & said they wld be glad to know what I find out on the subject.

I've been in Ireland & enjoyed it in a quiet way, as I always do. At the end of this month I go to Venice, back here in Aug:

Death again. It seems there is in Rome a saintly child who died, recovered, & when asked what it had been like said perfectly heavenly so they let him die again. Well that's not sleep, but at the same time

he can't have had the court martial so how can it have been heavenly?
. . . If we go to heaven first, then have the resurrection of the body
(like finding your motor after a party) & then have the court martial
& then go to hell that seems awfully disappointing?

Oh DO TELL[1]

Love
N

[1] Waugh's reply was comprehensive: 'At the moment of death each individual soul is
judged and sent to its appropriate place – the saints straight to heaven, unrepentant
sinners to Hell, most (one hopes) to Purgatory where in extreme discomfort but
confident hope we shall be prepared for the presence of God.' *Letters*, p. 567.

To Violet Hammersley   7 rue Monsieur, VII
23 June 1961   23 Dorsoduro, Venice[1]
                after Monday

You really do reduce everything to its most sordid. Well yes, cheap
if you like, but so was the little flat I used to take. But it will certainly
be nicer for me; with dear old Vic not there I should have felt a bit
lonely.

I've put Evelyn's masterly exposé into the archives. Briefly it is
this. We die & are judged at once. Saints (?) go straight to Heaven.
Sinners straight to Hell. The rest of us get varying sentences in
Purgatory. At the Last Trump those still remaining on earth are
judged. Those who are serving their sentences have to join up with
their bodies (like finding one's coat after a party I hope the arrangements are efficient). The only bodies who rose again at once are Our
Lord's & Your Lady's. The body (the good) is US because we do not,
like the Mahomedans, believe that body & spirit are two separate
things. I wrote & asked Evelyn why, if the body is us, we are not
told to take care of it but on the contrary encouraged to tease it. He
said that Cyril Connolly's idea that the body ought to be fed on foie
gras & covered with kisses is not regular – the body must be mortified.
Oh yes – the end of the world is also the end of time. Isn't it interesting! I can hardly wait.[2]

The Wrightsmans came to luncheon. He bought a picture from the
Duke of Leeds[3] – the Duke pocketed the cash but poor Charlie is not
allowed by our government to have the picture. Did you ever hear
anything so dishonest. So the poor old boy is £140 000 out of pocket

(a mere flea-bite however). I love old Charlie he is so funny. He says the Ritz here is an under-developed area.

The British Isles in *summer* are insupportable. Nobody lights anything, I nearly died in Ireland though it's comfortable at Eddy's, very.

Hurrying off to do a hundred last minute chores.

Love
   N

[1] Nancy had been invited to stay with a Venetian friend, Contessa Anna-Maria Cicogna, daughter of Count Volpi. 'She is almost perfect I think – calm, punctual, affectionate, clever & sometimes very funny.' (NM to Violet Hammersley, 2 July 1957) Violet Hammersley had teased Nancy by pointing out how much cheaper it was going to be to stay with the Countess than renting a flat.
[2] Violet Hammersley replied cuttingly: 'Evelyn Waugh's exposé is only what we have all read many times in the Bible.' (26 June 1961)
[3] The portrait of the Duke of Wellington by Goya. It was eventually bought from Charles Wrightsman by the National Gallery for the price which he had originally paid.

To Duchess of Devonshire   23 Dorsoduro
3 July 1961   Venice

Dear Miss

They say on the beach that if the First Lord[1] doesn't . . . . . . every day he has a headache.

I said What about the First Lady? Oh Jackie doesn't like it that often. I think First Lord (my own unaided joke) is very brilliant. . . .

I've sold *Alf* for a film – English so not much money, still £5000 & royalties. I never thought it could make a film so this is a windfall. No good investing with everything so high (my Printemps shares went up £1000 in ONE DAY last week) so I'll keep it to see me through the war perhaps. When does it break out – do ask the First Lord.

The Duchess of Bedford[2] (Mme Millionaire) has got Nicole de Bedford on her luggage or N de B. So Mark tells me. D de D would be a bit too much perhaps?

Marina Luling[3] has got the most wonderful shawl I ever saw from Cyril Connolly[4] in Dublin. I *must* have one but how? Does one pay duty or could it be posted to you to keep for me (on your honour not to wear it of course).

Much love, write
   N

. . .

[1] President J. F. Kennedy (1917–63). 'Andrew [Devonshire] says Kennedy is doing for sex what Eisenhower did for golf.' (NM to Jessica Treuhaft, 18 December 1961)
[2] Nicole Milinaire became the third wife of 13th Duke of Bedford in 1960.
[3] Countess Marina Luling; sister of Anna-Maria Cicogna, who lived at the Palladian villa at Maser.
[4] Sybil Connolly, a Dublin dress shop.

TO EDWARD SACKVILLE-WEST   23 Dorsoduro
4 July 1961   Venice

Darling Eddy

I wonder if you are at Edville – anyway I'll try it.

It's almost unbearable here without Vic, kind sweet & angelic as all the friends are. Like in a dreadful dream I went to the old man who loved horlogerie [clocks] to take him my 1820 repeater which he always got on its feet. But the shop window was full of plastic clocks & inside a potato faced youth shooed me away saying old rubbish can't be mended. Then I went on to Victor's rooms to see Maria but I cried so much I had to beat a retreat. I felt a hundred years had gone by, not 10 months. Edward Cunard[1] is here & rings up in Victor's voice which also upsets me. He's fallen very ill here, having come *so nicely* to see himself that Maria is all right & has now been 6 weeks in a fearfully horrible clinic with not a single friend of his own here. I feel terribly sorry for him. But he's no substitute for old Vic, as almost any of my sisters would be for me. I never knew him before. Pour comble, Alphy [Clary] is away for another week.

You know how much I love the Italians but half the fun used to be discussing their exotic lives & intricate personalities with Victor. Well, one can with Alphy. So it was a blow to hear that he is with 'my friends in the Midlands' i.e. the Portlands.[2]

Really dreadful of me to complain, I'm so petted & spoilt here, a bedroom looking through trees to S. Giorgio M, a charming maid who seems to do nothing but iron my clothes & all the friends busy seeing that I'm never left alone to mope. Boiling, baking weather which I love – hotter in the water than out.

Last night we dined in a villa near Padua with the Ity Amb to India who told me he was at a conference & the Polish delegate said 'Is the English delegate (Andrew [Devonshire]) a Communist?' 'Oh I don't think so.' 'Well he picks his nose just as we do.'

I'm to do a piece for *The Times* on what I like reading.[3] What a surprise they'll have when it's Scotty-potty & Michelet. The fact is I like so little & can't get through what I don't like.

Eliz: of Yugoslavia[4] is here with the man she eloped with, an American to END ALL. Oh I feel sorry for Prince Paul whose adored she is. He (the husband) came to dinner last night in a pink coat.

Much love & to all Irish eyes
    Nancy

---

[1] Sir Edward Cunard (1890–1962). He was in Venice clearing up his brother's flat. 'Meeting Nancy at luncheon, he said: "Oh, hullo, I've just spent the whole morning burning your letters to Victor." There was a moment's silence, and then somebody said: "In that case you've burnt a fortune."' Diana Mosley, *Loved Ones*, p. 147. The loss of the letters was a great blow to Nancy who planned to write her memoirs: 'as I've never kept a diary & they would have been so useful'. (NM to Violet Hammersley, 13 August 1961)

[2] 7th Duke of Portland (1893–1977). Married to Ivy Gordon-Lennox in 1915.

[3] 'A Taste of Honey', *The Times*, 20 November 1961.

[4] Princess Elizabeth of Yugoslavia (1936–). Married to Howard Oxenberg 1960–66 and to Neil Balfour 1969–78.

TO DUCHESS OF DEVONSHIRE   The Warden's Lodgings[1]
26 November 1961   New College, Oxford

Dear Miss

Thank you so much for ALL – I did have a lovely time.

The dinner for Muv was delightful, no hogs, just Mr Niarchos[2] & Kensington.[3] Muv, whom I've seen such a lot this time, is sad about Honks. She said, so truly, Diana has had a disappointing life & what makes it worse in a way she can't say so or talk about it. However Hayter says the boys here & at Cambridge can't have enough of Sir O. – they don't agree with him but he fascinates them. She has given Max the car – I knew she would.[4]

Mr Crossman[5] is a charmer, one of those jolly ones. Sly no doubt. I enjoyed the dinner. They wld have asked Em [Cavendish] but said no hope on a Saturday night. You'd think it was a mining village! She's coming tomorrow but I shall have gone. You must get to know the Hayters I know you would love them.

Freezing chez [Osbert] Lancaster – thought oi would doi. The John Hopes[6] for dinner. I was pleased to see Liza & quite liked him – couldn't quite see what all the hatred is about . . .

There was a sociologist at dinner here. She said while professionally we deplore them, your books are admitted to be a very useful sidelight on the upper classes. What *can* sociology be? I must look it up in the dictionary. There were 12 people, the clothes ranged from beehive to deadly.

I must get up.

Love
    N

[1] Nancy was staying with Sir William Hayter, Warden of New College 1958–76.
[2] John Stuart (1925–90). Nicknamed 'Stavros Niarchos' as his colouring was more Mediterranean than Scotch.
[3] Hon. Kensington Davison (1914–). Opera administrator and critic. Younger son of 1st Baron Broughshane, Mayor of Kensington 1913–19.
[4] Max Mosley had been lent his parents' car.
[5] Richard Crossman (1907–74). Journalist, diarist and politician.
[6] Lord John Hope (1912–). Created Baron Glendevon in 1964. Married Elizabeth Maugham in 1948.

To Prince Clary   7 rue Monsieur, VII
3 January 1962

My dear Alphy

Would you pop the enclosed into a post box next time you pass one – it is one of my sordid economies to do this with prepaid letters.

I went to the two most awful réveillons in history. Pre-Christmas to Babs Wright.[1] She offered a buffet dinner, Place de la Concorde, which she overlooks, lit by real torches, & carols. As Maurice Bowra was coming to spend Xmas with me & I was giving a huge luncheon for him on Xmas Day, I thought I would save his pocket from taking me out to dinner & told Babs I would bring him. The dinner was: cold TINNED ham & cold hard mince pies. Then we sang carols which was rather fun I'm bound to say. Bring me flesh & *bring me wine*. Poor Maurice's tenor boomed in vain – not a drop. Really this Babs is a menace. She rang up a friend of mine & said You haven't answered Mrs Hooper's invitation to her cocktail party – as though one ever did answer, in Paris (cocktail pties I mean).

The New Year's Eve was *much* worse chez Daisy Fellowes. The reason I accepted was I've got a very expensive & beautiful *dress* eating its head off in my cupboard. So far, as I've only worn it twice, it seems to have cost about £150 an outing so I thought, take it out again & it will go down to only £100.

Well of course on N Y Eve no hope of a vehicle so I wrapped up & started to walk when I fell upon a miracle-cab. Only, then I was ½ an hour too early. So I made him go to the Hotel d'Orsay, next door

to Daisy & sat in the hall until 8.45. The employés of course thought
I'd been posé un lapin [stood up]. On the dot (as Windsors were
expected) I walked across the street – found the whole party already
assembled & having already run out of conversation. When the
Windsors arrived Daisy greeted them: Thank God you're here –
these people have all been here since 7. Imagine how pleased they
all were! I thought the evening would never end. I sat next the Duke,
whom I like very much but he seems to have had a coup de vieux –
the wonderful memory gone & he is decidedly deaf. Hard work. The
Duchess very well dressed as usual with a diamond ring as big as the
Sancy, no wonder they are always broke! Daisy said to me in this
house one curtseys to the Duchess, which I mutinously did. Every
bore in Paris was there. However I did get a lift home.

Last night I went to an Anglophile play in which the characters
drank endless cups of tea & constantly played God Save the King on
a gramophone & then stood to attention. The curtain went up to
Tipperary on bagpipes. I became perfectly hysterical – the people
next me saying ça c'est bien les Anglais.[2]

I'm *too sorry* about the sad time you are having – oh dear – I do
feel for you.[3]

Hope you are not too cold.

Love to both
    Nancy

I see there's a postal strike so you may never get this.

What of Portugal?!
Have you read *Fox in the Attic*?[4] If not I'll send it – or go to Heywood
Hill's bookshop 10 Curzon St & tell them it's your Xmas present from
me. Quicker like that.

[1] Beatrice Clough; Conservative MP 1941–45. Married, in 1942, Paul Wright (knighted
1975), who was Councillor to the UK delegation to NATO in Paris 1961–4.
[2] That's the English all over.
[3] Prince Clary's sister had been unwell.
[4] Richard Hughes, *A Fox in the Attic* (1961).

To Jessica Treuhaft   7 rue Monsieur, VII
11 January 1962

Darling Soo
    Very faithful to get *Horizon*[1] – I'm glad you thought it all right. Yes
Paris still harbours many an old mistress of Miss [Dolly] Wilde – most
Lesbians seem to live for ever – oh why did she have to go?

How much do you want Borniol's[2] catalogue? The thing is I pass their shop every day (china wreath over the somewhat chilly observation: 'Regrets') & can't bring myself to go in. Pure superstition – it's like a nervous horse & the knacker's yard. If your book is giving trouble that's the surest sign it will be good.

Am I to understand that Dinkie[3] has Run Away?

Why is Aranka's shop folding? Oh poor old thing what a bore for her.

Do you think there can be a paper called *Esquire*? They wrote (practical joke?) & asked me to answer a questionnaire.

Q If you had your life all over again what wld you do?

A Moon about on a perfectly huge unearned income.

Q What makes you boil? (American for angry I imagine.)

A The United Nations.[4]

And so on. (I've got up a little fund for comforts for mercenaries by the way.) They have such a hard time that quite small amounts of money (or balls of silver paper) make a great difference. Also they feel they are loved & so on – you know, just like Nanny's lepers. If *Esquire* turns out to be real I'll put a little ad: I think. The Americans are *so* rich & generous. I'm told if you advertise please send a dollar they always do & some people have yachts & things on the proceeds. How lovely & mad they must be.

When Ld Stanley of Alderley,[5] who had become a Moslem to tease, was buried, his brother Lyulph, as the body was lowered, took off his hat & their brother Algernon said not your hat you fool, your practical burial footwear.

Keep in touch – love from
    Sooze

One farthing buys a hot drink for a mercenary. (The only trouble is the darlings don't really *care* for *hot* drinks.) Now if you save up your old string – oh but I feel you won't so what's the good –

[1] Nancy's article 'Some Rooms for Improvement' had appeared in American *Horizon*.
[2] Henri de Borniol, undertaker's. Jessica was researching *The American Way of Death* (1963).
[3] Constancia Romilly.
[4] Other questions and answers included: '*Chinks in the armour*. No memory and very small powers of concentration', '*Persisting superstition*: Superiority of the white races', '*Secret satisfaction*: Pleasing the English public in spite of the fact that it is prejudiced against me.' *Esquire*, August 1962.
[5] 3rd Baron Stanley of Alderley (1827–1903).

To Evelyn Waugh   7 rue Monsieur, VII
10 April 1962

Darling Evelyn

Do try & get it into your head that whatever else you may be you
are *not a bore*. I think you are wasted on people like Buchan-Hepburn[1]
with whom one would sooner have been seen dead than dancing, in
my recollection of old ballroom days. Funny of you to eschew civilization as you do. Voltaire used to say one has to choose between
countries where you sweat & countries where you think. Life is short
& it is better to stay in the latter. Specially YOU who don't even like
sweating. Another thing. This news about you boring the bores seems
to come from Clarissa, with whom you are not on good terms? Not
quite convincing.

Isherwood. Well I agree with every word in that long letter to *TLS*[2]
this week. I'm not sure I'll ever be able to speak to another pederast.
(But oh the brilliance of the beginning. Later the blanketing dullness
of America descends.)

I've written a long description of Captain Scott's last months for
my book.[3] (It made me cry twice.) I do wonder *why* I have! The book
I call *The Water Beetle*, hoping to disarm.

I'm going to Ireland 27th Ap for 3 weeks. Perhaps I've told you
this already. Will be here for the whole of June. Come. What are your
plans?

Rain rain GO TO SPAIN. It pours, all & every day.

Much love
N

---

[1] Waugh had been to stay in Trinidad with Patrick Buchan-Hepburn (created Baron
Hailes in 1957), Governor-General of the West Indies 1957–62. Clarissa Avon reported
back to Ann Fleming that the Haileses had found Waugh boring; Ann Fleming lost no
time in passing this on to Waugh.
[2] A letter from J. W. Quinton criticised a review of Christopher Isherwood's novel
Down There on a Visit for failing to draw attention to the book's 'amoral sentiments':
'it is fashionable for critics to attack Waugh for the special brand of socio-religious
exclusiveness that is apt to falsify his scale of values in this way, while Mr Isherwood's
far more questionable (and more easily imitated) standards are apparently accepted
with admiration.' *The Times Literary Supplement*, 6 April 1962.
[3] 'Aspley Cherry Garrard has said that "polar exploration is at once the cleanest and
most isolated way of having a bad time that has yet been devised". Nobody could deny
that he and the twenty-four other members of Captain Scott's expedition to the South
Pole had a bad time; in fact, all other bad times, embarked on by men of their own
free will, pale before it.' 'A Bad Time', *The Water Beetle*, p. 15.

To Gaston Palewski   7 rue Monsieur, VII
1 June 1962

Colonel. The Argus de la Presse[1] still haven't sent me the article[2] so I don't know what I am supposed to have said or to whom. I must say I am completely innocent. Since I got back from Ireland I've seen few people & nobody within miles of a journalist – no éditeurs for instance or literary hangers on of any kind. I am most careful never to speak of you. If people say what does Gaston think I say he never talks politics with me & I hardly see him (too true).

If I understood rightly what you said it is *terribly humiliating* for me if I'm supposed to go about pretending to be au mieux[3] with you. After all, Colonel, I am all the same a respectable person. I always thought you would stand by me whatever happened. You seem only to blame me – it's wrong of you. If I'm supposed to have given an interview I think it should be denied, but I am paralysed by not knowing exactly & by your silence.

I think you don't quite realize that I am here alone, nervous & unhappy & worried & don't like to talk about it (with whom could I?) If you weren't involved I would go straight to Maître Richard but I can't do anything until you give a sign of life.

[1] Press cutting agency.
[2] Palewski had returned to France in April, when he was appointed Minister for Scientific Research by Georges Pompidou. It has not been possible to trace the article in question.
[3] On good terms.

To Lady Redesdale   7 rue Monsieur, VII
10 June 1962

Darling Muv
    Here she is, *with many thanks*. The piece[1] comes out soon – don't know when – I've done the proofs. I'll let you know. Yes I've given up the *S Times* it is insupportable (literally). What do you take in now? I like *Sunday Tel*.
    I'm buried in *August 1914*.[2] It is marvellously well done & *so* entertaining as well as fascinating. One laughs out loud. The photographs are v curious, everybody so FAT. It shows what skeletons we have all become. Even the Kaiser who one thinks of as quite thin (besides E VII I suppose) is solid like a tree. Only the German uniforms are

smart – King George & the Tsar look like Debo out shooting. Oh I am loving it & it is immensely long.

Paulette came yesterday to borrow one of my Helleus for an exhibition at Dieppe. She says she went to Versailles, that fountain where he used to paint, & scrapings from his palette are still on the trees!!! She spends her time denouncing bad contemporary drawings which are sold as being by him & his work is whizzing up in value. Her husband the Admiral [Howard-Johnston] came – so funny to see the difference – in Xandra's time he was so disagreeable, now he is a dear.

Diana has read me out bits from her mémoires they are too lovely. She remembers everything, how I envy that. I could no more write mémoires than fly. But there is said to be a drug which brings things back & she thinks it is in what she takes for migraine. Perhaps.

Much love
   Nancy

[1] 'Mothering the Mitfords', a portrait of Laura Dicks, the Mitfords' nanny, published in the *Sunday Times*, 26 August 1962, and in the chapter 'Blor' of *The Water Beetle*.
[2] Barbara Tuchman, *August 1914* (1962).

To Lady Redesdale   7 rue Monsieur, VII
13 June 1962

Darling Muv

I'm so sorry to hear from Woman that you had a choke – how too horrid, I can't imagine anything worse – except perhaps what happened to Denise Bourdet at Salisbury station. She had gone there (first time in England since the war) to stay with Cecil Beaton. Got out of the train, saw Cecil, very smart & handsome & as she went to meet him *her skirt fell off*. You know Frenchwomen never wear slips or petticoats, so there she was in a navy blue jacket & short little white knickers!! Imagine! She had done up the zip & forgotten the hook & as the skirt was lined with taffeta it was down without warning once the zip had slipped! However she seems to have been simply delighted – she says Cecil's face was wonderful to behold!

The book called *August 1914* is a feast – I'm buried in it. You must get it.

Now *don't* choke again.

Much love
   N

To Evelyn Waugh   23 Dorsoduro
10 July 1962   Venice
                                                   Here until Aug then Paris

Darling Evelyn

I must tell you that I don't love Pam as I used to. She is spoilt &
I think it's Michael's fault, also I suppose the newspaper world is
completely corrupting – anyway her faults are getting worse & she
doesn't mellow. I think what she did to you is unpardonable. (Droll
idea, to invite you with that man-eater I must say.)[1]

Well hundreds of water beetles appeared[2] – some accompanied by
other poems saying Nancy of course never got beyond the letter U,
what a lot of spare time people seem to have. But I can't use it.
Flabbergasts the human race by gliding on the water's face with *ease
celerity and grace*. Won't do – what a bore.[3]

I expect Diana [Cooper] will come after I've left. I imagine she'll
hate being here – even I find it too full of ghosts. I see Victor getting
off every steamer (I used to sit & wait for him on the steps of the
Salute every morning to go to the Lido) & I miss him so much I
almost wonder if I wasn't in love with him. It's the jokes of course.
The receipt for being missed is to live in a small society of which one
is the life & soul & not to die too old. I love my Italian friends but
there are many jokes they wouldn't see. For instance I heard 'there
are 4 Amurrican worships in Venice' & was vaguely imagining people
like Cass Canfield & wondering who when I realized it was WARships.
Nobody to tell it to.

I didn't feel I could face Wilde.[4] I greatly enjoyed a book called
Crash 1929,[5] which depicts American worships in full discomfiture,
also *Aug: 1914*. Short of a book I bought the *Code of the Woosters*[6] &
have been shrieking but the selection of Penguins is deplorable, in all
the shops they are the same: *The Day of the Triffids*[7] what can that
be & *Ldy C-y*,[8] in literal hundreds. Someone has blundered. None of
yours or mine, I can always fall back on either at a pinch.

The boys on the beach all have tiny wirelesses tucked away with
their private parts so that hands are free to fondle. These little objects
give out an indescribable din. Isn't science wonderful, really the world
is becoming so vile that one won't mind dying half as much as somebody like Mazarin did.[9]

Much love
    N

Sister Diana is writing her mémoires, they are dazzling and scream-
ingly funny.

[1] Waugh: 'Ten days ago Pam Berry asked me to stay for the night. I found her in an ugly mood railing against all her social superiors. To stop the flow of vilification I led her to politics, said I thought U Thant an enemy and added: "The government must be pretty hard up to get people to meet him. They even asked Laura and me." ' *Letters*, p. 587. Following this interchange, a piece appeared in the *Sunday Telegraph* alleging that Waugh claimed to be on intimate terms with the British Prime Minister. 'In our youth there was much talk of "sneak guests", "sneak hostesses" are something quite new.' (Evelyn Waugh to NM, 4 July 1962)

[2] Hamish Hamilton had appealed in the *Sunday Times* for identification of the rhyme which gave its title to Nancy's collection of essays:

> The WATERBEETLE here shall teach
> A sermon far beyond your reach:
> He flabbergasts the Human Race
> By gliding on the water's face
> With ease, celerity, and grace;
> *But if he ever stopped to think*
> *Of how he did it, he would sink.*
>
> Hilaire Belloc, *A Moral Alphabet*

[3] Nancy adapted Belloc's rhyme, replacing 'sermon' with 'lesson', 'flabbergasts' with 'aggravates' and, at Waugh's suggestion, altered the fifth line to 'Assigning each to each its place'.

[4] *The Letters of Oscar Wilde* (1962), edited by Rupert Hart-Davis.

[5] J. K. Galbraith, *The Great Crash, 1929* (1955).

[6] P. G. Wodehouse, *The Code of the Woosters* (1938).

[7] John Wyndham, *The Day of the Triffids* (1951).

[8] D. H. Lawrence, *Lady Chatterley's Lover*. Printed privately in 1928, the unexpurgated version was eventually published by Penguin Books in 1960. Penguin was prosecuted for obscenity and acquitted after a celebrated trial.

[9] Jules Mazarin (1602–61). Governed France during the minority of Louis XIV. Created Cardinal in 1641. He amassed a colossal fortune and a collection of priceless works of art. His last words were: 'Et dire qu'il va falloir quitter tout cela.' ('And to think I will have to leave all this behind.')

To Gaston Palewski   23 Dorsoduro
25 July 1962   Venice

Dear Colonel

I don't understand your policy. I saw your marriage in the *Daily American* & my whole life seemed to collapse[1] – now I have reconciled myself to it, so reasonable, such a solution to all your problems. But you always said you would tell me – I quite understand *not* telling because almost too difficult & I know when I once left somebody who minded I did it in that way, anything else seemed impossible. (The question is, too, what have I ever been in your life – about like Gaby or Marella or something different – I've never understood.)

All the same I find it odd of you, after a month's silence, to write comme si de rien n'était[2] & ask how I am. I am very sad & also don't know what to do with myself. I can't live in Paris where I miss you more than anywhere, especially it would be too painful with your arranging an hôtel particulier just round the corner so that I would see you from time to time. (Or Avenue Foch – Monsieur est trop bon.) So I feel perplexed I must say. Perhaps I could settle here but then I would miss the French, & what about old Marie? So – you see –

Dolly writes to say you look very tired – oh dear I hope at least you are happy.

Love
        N

I return on 4th Aug:

[1] A gossip item in the *Daily American* had reported that the French Ambassador to Italy was about to get married. It was a false alarm, but Nancy had been dreading such an announcement for many years.
[2] As if nothing had happened.

To GASTON PALEWSKI   7 rue Monsieur, VII
13 August 1962

Dear Col

. . . Our new Ambassador to Moscow Sir Humphrey Trevelyan is here in a Russian family for 3 months learning the language. Is that not energetic! But he's a brilliant man. Tony [Rumbold] said to him if you met Donald in the street (Maclean) what would you do? Ask him in for a drink of course![1]

Lovely weather so I hope you can sunbathe & swim.

No other news.

Love
        N

[1] When Sir Humphrey Trevelyan (1905–85), Ambassador to USSR 1962–5, found himself sitting in front of Donald Maclean during a performance at the Moscow opera, he was very relieved when Maclean ignored him. (Lady Trevelyan to the editor.)

To LADY REDESDALE   7 rue Monsieur, VII
22 August 1962

Darling Muv

Oh *goodness* I thought it would make you *laugh*.[1] I always feel one's young self is like a completely different person one can view quite objectively & laugh at – in my case at least this is true. Of course one can't very well write about a Nanny & leave out the mother & for the modern reader one must explain the complete difference of the relationship between mothers & children in those far off days from now. If I did a portrait of you (which I won't) you would come out quite different from the oblique view seen, as it were, across Nanny. In any case everybody knows you are Aunt Sadie who is a character in the round & is you in middle life exactly as you were. Now I'm in a fit of worry about the dust cover which is a very funny caricature of that photograph of me as a baby with you & Farve. I *suppose* you won't mind it as nobody ever seems to mind caricatures & you are very beautiful in it – but then I never thought you would mind the other. It's one's eccentricities people love one for – I couldn't have presented you as a sort of Violet Mason[2] could I?

All I can say is you must forgive & I'm very very sorry if you are annoyed, because I can't stop it now unless I stop the whole book which would cost thousands of pounds. Oh dear, it has cast a cloud.

Lovely having Decca here. We went to get her a dress & found a terribly pretty one which can be made in time for her to take on Tuesday.

Dinkie has gone to Ohio. Terribly funny if she runs away with Ali[3] – when I say this both mothers look pensive.

Much much love & I grovel – I am really terribly distressed & disappointed as I'd imagined you simply shrieking over it.

          N

[1] Lady Redesdale was upset by her portrayal in 'Blor'. Nancy describes her as 'living in a dream world of her own' and goes on to say: 'So what did my mother do all day? She says now, when cross-examined, that she lived for us. Perhaps she did, but nobody could say that she lived with us.' Lady Redesdale wrote to Nancy: 'I wish only one thing, that you would exclude me from your books, I don't mind what you write about me when I am dead, but I do dislike to see my mad portrait while I am still alive.' (18 August 1962)

[2] Violet Mason, a neighbour at Swinbrook, head of the Girl Guides.

[3] Alexander Mosley was studying philosophy at Ohio State University.

TO DUCHESS OF DEVONSHIRE   7 rue Monsieur, VII
23 August 1962

Dear Miss

    . . . Colonel & Jayne Wrightsman lunched here with the T[reuhaft]s. Col says Bob is very clever & very nice. Jayne rather said if they don't care for the Ritz why not try the Lancaster, but she was sweet really & they all swopped addresses & she said she would show Bob the N.Y. museums. He said afterwards I didn't tell her I'd lived in N.Y. for 25 years.

Widow is the limit. She writes to say she has been rushed to Barts & given a blood transfusion. Silence for 5 days so I ring up Monica [Stokes] (a struggle to get London just now) to be told she's quite all right & receiving vast crowds. She wasn't rushed at all, it had been arranged for weeks. Admit.

I'll go to Woman, with Muv, end of Sept (20th I think) so if you were at C-worth early Oct all would fit in like clockwork.

Muv fairly shirty about 'Blor' but Honks thinks she'll calm down. Fact is, I gather she had the usual slight bust up with Decca about education & very likely it (the article) seems another reminder of that vexed subject. I've written & grovelled. The fact is I can't help seeing my childhood (& the whole of my life) as a hilarious joke, whereas I think Muv feels a tiny bit sentimental about early days.

Did you hear how Decca told 'Grace Darling'[1] to a NY entertainer who now sings it to a raving audience having changed it to 'Grace had a Jewish heart'?!!!

Oh the General, what a worry.[2] Col telephoned after the shooting having spent the afternoon with him. He says he seemed so very sad when they said goodbye.

Much love
N

. . .

[1] Grace Darling (1815–42). The daughter of a lighthouse-keeper on the Farne Islands who, in 1838, rowed nine shipwrecked men to safety, thus making her a national heroine. As children, the Mitfords used to sing a song about her, the chorus of which went: 'But Grace had an English heart / And the raging storm she brav'd / She pull'd away, mid the dashing spray, / And the crew she saved.' Jessica wrote a life of Grace Darling in 1988.
[2] De Gaulle had escaped an assassination attempt on 22 August when the car in which he was travelling was sprayed with bullets.

To Lady Redesdale   7 rue Monsieur, VII
2 September 1962

Darling Muv
Of course I am now tortured with feelings of guilt. It was mad of me not to send the typescript – out of sheer meanness I only had one

because more than one makes the typing much more expensive & one never seems to use the copies.

I must say in self defence every word in that article (every word about you & Farve I mean) appeared almost word for word in the early chapters of *P of Love*. Of course the book goes on long enough for you to come out of your ivory tower. But you never made any observations on the early part.

Anything which *now* seems odd or unfortunate in my childhood wasn't your fault it was that of the age we lived in. Children were not considered then – or at least girls weren't.[1]

The Duc Decazes & my neighbour Bagneux (French equivalents of Farve) *loathe* Paris. They both live here, groaning, in order to educate their children. This *could not have happened* in the England of your (& my) young days. To state that it did not happen is not to reproach you but the whole social structure. I carefully said in the essay that the relationship of parents & children is quite different now.

But the person who appears completely vile is *me*!!

Just tell me which day you go to Woman – she has vanished into Middle Europe & I can't remember if she said 20 or 22 Sept. The idea is that I should amuse you while Wondairfool [Pamela] cooks. I hope there'll be enough to eat (joke).

Much love
    N

No more efforts at autobiography I've learnt my lesson.

[1] Lady Redesdale had written: 'It seemed when I read it that everything I had ever done for any of you had turned out wrong and badly, a terrible thought, and can't be remedied now.' (29 August 1962)

To Gaston Palewski   Fontaines-les-Nonnes
31 October 1962   par Puisieux

*Un*faithful not to have telephoned.

I lunched at Brosio's & there was your current fiancée. Curiously hard to tell one from another of these excellent blonde ladies – whatever made you pick on me I wonder?

The Bishop of Monaco is here. What a BRUTE. I've heard a lot of poison about the Gen but never such a stream of *ordure* – I couldn't sleep I was so angry. Mme Costa very nearly lost her temper, it seems she did quite with the Curé for the same reason, & they parted trembling with rage – no blessing.

Jean de Gaigneron: 'I am very deceived & annoyed.[1] He puts everybody against him etc etc' – can't you hear it! He is *treu* however the good soul!

The boy[2] here has had a microphone in the drawing room & has heard a lot of home truths to which he makes allusions désagréables à table. It was discovered by Mme Rodel who heard Mme Costa & the Curé talking in an attic at midnight. She went to investigate & found this naughty child playing a recording to himself. Oh how I laughed when I heard but everybody else is deceived *and* annoyed.

Good Colonel goodbye
          N

[1] *Faux amis* for 'disappointed' and 'upset'.
[2] Jean Costa de Beauregard; Madame Costa's grandson.

To Evelyn Waugh   7 rue Monsieur, VII
23 December 1962

Darling Evelyn
    Happy Christmas.

I'm *so wondering* what you will make of Sybille Bedford's new novel called (v. bad title I think) *A Favourite of the Gods*. It has been tremendously advertised by the Lesbian World here as better than *A Legacy* which it is certainly *not*. There are of course excellent things & one reads on, but to me there is a certain naïveté, underlying a sophisticated story, which pulls one up from time to time & then the characters are of wood. Wooden figures after Henry James. The strange thing is that this tough little person & ferocious Lesbian, always dressed as a motor racer, should choose to write about an age of elegance, beautiful Princess, unfaithful (but fond at heart) Prince & so on. A sort of *Golden Bowl* upside-down. Oh do say what you think, I'm so curious to know. Make Collins send it if they haven't already. The beginning – the first quarter – is excellent & one thinks it is the prelude to an unfolding which doesn't happen – in fact the flower dies in the bud. Hardly one joke.

What about Nassau?[1] I think the *rudeness is so disgusting*. How I loathe Americans more & more.

I enjoyed myself in England by dint of only going to London in a thick fog. I was 10 days at C-[hats]worth – two monster shooting parties of 14 people all old friends of long ago, white where they used to be black & much less fierce. Friendly in fact. Your adorer General Laycock[2] was there with a v. governessy wife I thought, well she was a governess so that's in order.

Arriving at Orly I ran into Cecil [Beaton] & Raymond [Mortimer] off to Madagascar & was *so* glad not to be going. It is delightful here – a million people have left Paris & the result is one can move about by day & sleep by night. Marie & I are alone in this courtyard. The Sutros & Harold will partake of my turkey.

> Much love – bonne fête
>   Nancy

[1] President Kennedy and Harold Macmillan met in Nassau on 18 December and agreed that instead of developing the British-made Skybolt missile, the US should provide Britain with Polaris missiles. General de Gaulle was neither invited to the meeting nor consulted.
[2] Robert Laycock (1907–68). Chief of Combined Operations 1943–7. Married Angela Dudley Ward in 1946. Knighted in 1954. He had been Waugh's patron during the war and his commanding officer.

1963–1966

MOURNING

Now I've hardly any correspondents left,
except family, it makes one's breakfast very
dull. (Though Debo's letters make up for all.)
NM to Cecil Beaton, 15 April 1966

The death of Nancy's mother in 1963 was the first of many deaths
that cast a long shadow over the last decade of Nancy's life. Losing
her mother affected her more deeply than she had expected and
her sadness was heightened by the coolness that had always existed
between them. The following year Violet Hammersley died, robbing
Nancy of one of her oldest friends. With the death of Madame Costa
de Beauregard, Nancy lost both a friend and a second home. Nor was
her own generation spared; the death of Victor Cunard at the age of
sixty-two had been a fearful shock to her and in the space of a few
more years she lost Edward Sackville-West, Evelyn Waugh, Dolly
Radziwill and Mark Ogilvie-Grant. In her last letter to Mark
(26 November 1968) she wrote: 'I had a dream. Robert [Byron] rang
up from Paris & said he was alive & coming down by the next train
with Mark. It was *so vivid* that when I woke up I thought it was true.'

In 1968 Peter Rodd died; he was exactly Nancy's age. 'I feel very
sad about Prod & of course remorse. But I couldn't live with him, I
don't believe a saint could have without going mad.' Whenever she
lost a friend Nancy would strike out their name in her address book
and put a cross next to it with the date of their death. During the
1960s crosses appeared next to the names of Esther Arthur, Malcolm
Bullock, Denise Bourdet, Alfred Cobban, Betty Chetwynd, Daisy
Fellowes, Roger Hinks, Momo Marriott, Frosca Munster, Phyllis

Woman comes,
on business.  Orsay
27 Feb 66

Dear Miss
I was greeted by the dreadful, though
not unexpected news of Mme Costa's death.
This leaves me without almost my
greatest friend here & a second
home — I am in despair. When
Dolly goes I don't know what I shall
do — most unwise to have these
much older friends, though I must
say they have survived dozens of
my contemporaries.
At Chippenham the ticket collector

To Duchess of Devonshire, 27 February 1966

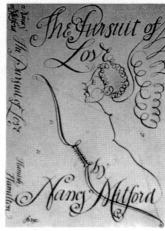

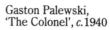
ABOVE LEFT: Nancy in the drawing room at rue Monsieur, *c*.1948.
RIGHT: Cover of *The Pursuit of Love* (1945)

Gaston Palewski, 'The Colonel', *c*.1940

The garden of rue Monsieur: Nancy's flat was on the ground floor

ABOVE LEFT: Lady Pamela Berry and Lady Diana Cooper. RIGHT: Billa Harrod, 1945

Fontaines-les-Nonnes, Countess Costa de Beauregard's house, where Nancy was a frequent guest

Raymond Mortimer in Florence where he was staying with Violet Trefusis, late 1950s. ABOVE RIGHT: Eddy Sackville-West painted by Graham Sutherland in 1954

Cyril Connolly, early 1950s. BELOW RIGHT: Nancy on the steps of rue Monsieur, 1952

Gaston Palewski
as Ambassador
in Rome, painted
by Claude
Samson in 1958

Nancy and
Deborah in
Venice, 1960

Cecil Beaton by
Augustus John,
1952

Osbert Lancaster's cover for *The Water Beetle* (1962), taken from a photograph of Nancy with her parents in 1906

BELOW: Nancy, early 1960s. RIGHT: Deborah and Andrew Devonshire with their children Emma and Peregrine, at the christening of their daughter Sophia, 1957

Left to right, Cecil Beaton, Nancy, Deborah, Pamela, Diana, Andrew Devonshire, at Peregrine Hartington's wedding to Amanda Heywood-Lonsdale, 1967

BELOW LEFT: Jessica with Violet Hammersley, early 1960s. RIGHT: Nancy's Christmas card for 1966, showing her at rue Monsieur just before she moved to Versailles

Jessica and Bob
Treuhaft, early 1960s

Evelyn Waugh
painted by Feliks
Topolski, 1962

Gaston Palewski and
his wife Violette in
front of the Château
du Marais

Nancy in her garden at rue d'Artois, Versailles, 1971

Left to right, Diana, Pamela, Deborah at Nancy's funeral, Swinbrook, 7 July 1973

The library at rue d'Artois

Prynne, Osbert Sitwell and Nina Seafield. She minded passionately about their deaths; much of the energy that others put into their families Nancy put into her friendships and, although she was not yet sixty, her friends' deaths were a shadowy foreboding of her own.

It was not in Nancy's nature to brood. Letter-writing had always provided a distraction from unhappiness and she continued to write letters prolifically. Nobody could replace Evelyn Waugh, but she tried to fill the void by writing more frequently than ever to her sister Deborah, to Raymond Mortimer, Heywood Hill, Prince Clary and Sir Hugh Jackson. She started on a new book, a life of Louis XIV at Versailles which was published as *The Sun King* in 1966. A worldwide best-seller, it made Nancy very comfortably off and in a characteristic act of generosity she eventually left her money to a trust to be administered after her death by Deborah for the benefit of any of her family or needy friends: 'You see they have such ups & downs, such sudden changes of fortune.'

Mr Cass Canfield 49 E 33 St, NY 16

+1960

Victor Cunard, ~~Poutenhall, Bedford~~
Kimbolten 270 ...
Venice ...

+1958

Dr Alfred Coblam, 11 Westbourne
Park Road, W2. Bay 2392
+

~~Randolph Churchill ...~~

David Cecil 7 Linton Road Oxford
tel. Ox: 59783

Noel Coward, Spithead Lodge
Warwick Bermuda Jamaica

Curtis Brown 347 Madison Av:
N.Y. 17

+20 Feb 1966

Comtesse Carl Costa de Beauregard, 9 rue
Barbet de Jouy, Ségur 27-17 ...
Doodie Ségur 8987 ...
Chateau de Fontaines les Nonnes, par
Pusieux (9) S.M (dial 11)
Doodie Villa Natamis Cap d'Ail
AM

+1961

Miss Chetwynd, 26 r Bonaparte, Danton 550

Princesse Jean de Caraman-Chimay
26 Cours Albert I Bal 36.25 (9)
Ste Preuve ... les Pierrepont / Aisne
(C2 ND de Liesse)

Prince Marc de Caraman Chimay
21 rue du Montdévulle 16e

Lady Diana Cooper ... 8687
~~Chantilly 93~~ ...
Vicomtesse de Contades Aut 8398

A page from Nancy's address book

LETTER BETWEEN DUCHESS OF DEVONSHIRE
AND NANCY MITFORD
18 January 1963

Chatsworth
Bakewell

[Deaths, wills and tombs were the subject of continual jokes between Nancy and her sisters. This letter, and the one that follows it, were prompted by Nancy having asked Deborah if she would make arrangements for her funeral and the design of her tomb. The Duchess of Devonshire's questions are printed in italics.]

This Way to the Tomb.
To the French lady.
Is it true that you have left money in your will for a tomb and that I am to see about it?
True.
Where do you want to be buried?
Near to wherever I drop off the perch.
If you die miles away from there do you want to be buried there all the same?

Whatever seems the easiest for all dear ones. I don't want a gangster's funeral, only a TOMB. *No cremation.*
Have you got any thoughts on the Tomb?
Large & showy, with angels & a long inscription saying how lovely I was & greatly missed.
Do you realise that I can't speak French, and have you allowed for an interpreter in your Will? (I mean if you want to be buried in France.)
Marie tells me you speak perfect French. Colonel can assist or Mogens. N.B. The Will is a proper *French* one. It will be much easier for everybody, & entail smaller duties, if the will is proved here. I noted that, at the death of Miss Chetwynd. If there's an English will it takes about 6 months before anything can happen at all & is an endless trouble to the Embassy & so on. It is in my safe – the combination of said safe 7. 7. 8. is at Hastie's also so you needn't remember it (for odd sixpences). My French lawyer is Maître Richard 13 rue des Saints Pères – I think Hastie's know that too. A duck, if ever there was one.

LETTER BETWEEN DUCHESS OF DEVONSHIRE   Chatsworth
AND NANCY MITFORD   Bakewell
24 January 1963

Tomb's Way
To Fr L
I forgot – a Memorial Service? Where
No – funeral where I happen to die.
Is the Tomb to be where you're buried, I mean say you die in Timbuctoo, then *where do you want the Tomb?*
Yes, Timbuctoo. Then it will be something for *visitors* to *visit.*
Lots of clergymen and other fussy people are livid at the idea of angels, but I suppose I'll be able to impose my will. (Naturally I'm all for them.)
Yes, please impose.
Would something like this do? Here Lies The Remains of The Distinguished French Lady Writer. This Tomb was erected in her memory by her sorrowing 9 yr old sister paid for by odd sixpences saved by same writer.
Yes all right if you want to pretend you paid for it.* Sorrowing is the stuff! Could I have a bit more on those lines?
* oh I thought you meant odd 6ds stolen by you.
Any special coffin?
No. Make sure I'm dead though. By the way if I die here I believe

* oh I thought you meant odd ods stolen by you,

Tomb's Way

From THE DUCHESS OF DEVONSHIRE.

To

Fr L

NOTES:

I forgot — a Memorial Service?
Where?

Is the Tomb to be where
you're buried, I mean say
you die in Timbuctoo, Then
where do you want The Tomb?

Lots of clergymen — other
fussy people are livid at the
idea of angels, but I suppose
I'll be able to impose my will.
(Naturally in all of them)

Would something like This do?
Here lies The Remains of The
Distinguished French Lady Writer
This Tomb was erected in Her mem-
ory by her sorrowing
Date 24 Jan 1963 ...... sisten
paid for by 99 yr old ...... sister

REPLY:

No — funeral
Where I happen
to die

Yes, Timbuctoo
Then it will be
something for
visitors to visit

Yes, please improve

Yes all right if
you want to put
you paid for it *
Sorrowing is
the stuff! P.T.O
Date ......
...... by same sister

Letter between Duchess of Devonshire and Nancy Mitford, 24 January 1963 one is buried at Chantilly with the lads (French for stable boy). Naivair moind though I wld prefer the Père La Chaise's dump if it could be managed.

Irrelevant weather news: I've got out the 1947 weatherbook and in the famous Feb of that year there were 268° of frost – This Jan there have already been 278° – There are 8 more nights to go. Last night there were 37° of frost at Rowsley (2 miles away) 34° at Edensor and a mere 32° here – positively stuffy.

Golly!

Do you put marge for tits and nuthatches? (No jokes about Nutnatch.)[1]

[1] 'Aunt Natch' was the nickname given to Nancy by Deborah's children.

To VALENTINE LAWFORD[1]   7 rue Monsieur, VII
1 February 1963

My dear Nicholas

Before the showers nay the waterfalls of praise begin to engulf you I must get in my drop. Oh how I am enjoying your book[2] – I don't know how long it is since I had such a treat. I am obliged to ration myself for fear of finishing too soon & you don't know how unusual that is – I generally finish off a book by turning 3 pages at a time & into the poubelle [waste bin] (whence these wretched time-wasters are retrieved by a young student who lives chez Monseigneur à côté & who gives my concierge a box of chocs at Christmas in return). Yours will go straight into the book case I need hardly add.

But what I can't understand is how a real European like yourself can go & live with savages? Oh do explain. It's so terribly unnatural. I've only got as far as Wigs – perhaps you do explain later on.

What I love about your book is that from the first page one trusts you to tell the truth; that one shrieks with laughter; & that it is written in *English* (I've only found one Americanism & can't remember what it was). So. Shall I ever see you again?

Yrs ever
    Nancy Rodd

[1] Valentine Lawford (1911–91). Known as Nicholas by some friends. Diplomat and writer. Retired in 1950 to live in America with the photographer Horst P. Horst. 'Yes Lawford is a great friend . . . he was always with Emerald & Sibyl in olden times. Quite unchanged.' (NM to Violet Hammersley, 9 April 1963)
[2] Nancy had been sent a pre-publication copy of Lawford's book, *Bound For Diplomacy* (1963).

To Violet Hammersley   7 rue Monsieur, VII
9 April 1963

Darling
  Yes there will be some testing moments at the final judgement
when we are all asked our thoughts during Lent 1963.
Mme Costa: 100% holy.
Mees:[1] A curious mixture of good & evil.
NR: 'I'm obliged to say that in Lent 1963 I thought of *literally nothing*
but clothes.'
Judge: 'How old were you then?'
NR: 'Fifty-eight your Holiness.'
Judge writes in longhand: Mme Costa goes straight to heaven – Mees
has a spell in a hot spot – NR goes back to the cells for further
questioning. . . .

    Must stop – love
        N

[1] The name given to Violet Hammersley by the servants at Fontaines.

To Violet Hammersley   7 rue Monsieur, VII
19 April 1963

Darling
  . . . A piece of interesting gossip. Your godson[1] never got a knight-
hood for writing Queen M's life & do you know why? Because he
couldn't resist *telling all London* about a party at which the D of
Edinburgh's (Prince Alfred I mean) favourite ADC was found dead
wearing a lovely tea-gown! Jamesie found hilarious letters on the
subject in the Windsor archives!! Are you shrieking?
  So glad you've got Rosamond [Lehmann], that will be company.
  I've just done a review for *Sunday Tel* of Mrs Wyndham's life of
Mrs Leverson.[2] The book is very bad & my review very unkind so I
imagine I shall be in trouble. I never read her life of Mme de Genlis,
did you? From this book I can't imagine anything she did would be
much good.
  My wedding get up is too lovely.[3] It will be something to live in for
many a year & I'm glad now that I was forced to buy it. Never would
have but for the wedding.
  Roger Hinks[4] retires in Sept I shall miss him. He's not as wicked
as they all make out by any means.

I've got my usual extinction de voix – Marie has just produced some pastilles compounded of cocaine, opium, belladonna, iris de Florence, aconite. If that doesn't cure me what will? I am keenly sucking away.

Total silence from all the Fontaines coterie. I thought once Christ was Risen there might have been a sign, but no.

Much love
      N

[1] James Pope-Hennessy (1916–74). His biography *Queen Mary* was published in 1959.
[2] Violet Wyndham, *The Sphinx and her Circle. A Biographical Sketch of Ada Leverson 1862–1933* (1963). Nancy's review ends: 'Rather suddenly the Sphinx dies. "What was her secret?" asks Mrs Wyndham. Perhaps it was that, although she was very much of her age, she managed to avoid the worst of its silly superficiality. We cannot say the same of her daughter's book.' (28 April 1963)
[3] Nancy accompanied her mother to the wedding of her distant cousin, Angus Ogilvy, to Princess Alexandra. 'I was delightfully elegant in black & white & large yellow felt cartwheel, later sold to Debo for Bazaar Work with a reduction.' (NM to Mark Ogilvie-Grant, 6 May 1963)
[4] Roger Hinks (1903–63). Art historian who worked for the British Council in Stockholm during the war, and then in Rome, Holland, Greece and Paris. Nancy called him 'the Turkish Lady', as he used to sit on a balcony in Athens, like a Turkish lady, watching the world go by.

To Violet Hammersley   Lismore Castle
28 April 1963   Co Waterford

Darling
      The wedding was splendid & I greatly enjoyed it but *oh* the get ups I never saw worse. I'm *sure* English women are dowdier than when I was young. The hats were nearly all as though made by somebody who had once heard about flowers but never seen one – huge muffs of horror. In front of me a green satin top hat with pink carnation dangling. The dresses & coats not only didn't fit but had not been ironed. The colours of the year are pale green & pale brown, very often mixed. Joan Aly Khan,[1] next to me, had a paisley satin coat green & brown, a green net & bow on unbrushed hair & blue satin shoes & she was quite one of the best. Muv, in black velvet, lace & diamonds, was marvellous she looked so pretty. The angelic police let her car stay outside so that she got away before anybody.

The bride is a *true beauty*. Q of Spain rather splendid – the Queen excellent, though in washy green which I do hate – Pss M unspeakable, like a hedgehog all in primroses – Pss Anne quite lovely, the Foreign Royals very pop-eyed – . . .

In London I dined with Gerry Wellington & the Jebbs. Can't thank you enough for [Hotel] Adria which I like better each time, I had such a delightful room at the very top.

Paddy [Leigh Fermor] is here, Stoker[2] & friend. I suppose I go to Eddy on about Wednesday – home on the 10th I've got my ticket. That's all I think.

Much love
    N

Debo was dressing for the ball when I arrived in London, she was a rock of diamonds & looked wonderful.

[1] Hon. Joan Yarde-Buller (1908–). Married to Loel Guinness 1927–36, to Prince Aly Khan 1936–49 and to 2nd Viscount Camrose in 1986.
[2] Peregrine Hartington, Deborah's son, was nicknamed 'Stoker' after Adrian Stokes, a family friend.

To Mark Ogilvie-Grant   Inchkenneth
14 May 1963   Gribun
                                     Isle of Mull

Dear O.G.

Muv is failing – we are all here – it is very poignant. She feels so ill; keeps saying how I should be loving it if I were well. We've got two adorable nurses & take the nights by two hours each, lucky there are so many of us!

Two days ago she seemed to be going – she said perhaps, who knows, Tom & Bobo & said goodbye to everybody & said if there are things in my will you don't like do alter it. I said but we should go to prison! & she laughed. (She laughs as she always has.) Then she rallied & here she still is – we long for her to go in her sleep quietly.

Of course *we* are half the time in tears & the other half shrieking, as you may imagine.

For two days we were storm bound & in the middle, in a short moment of calm, wonderful Mr Ogilvie-*Forbes*[1] (wish it were Grant) came over, settled into the bothy & will stay. Did you ever hear such kindness!

Fond love
    N

[1] A neighbour on Mull.

To GASTON PALEWSKI   Inchkenneth
21 May 1963   Gribun

Thank you dear Colonel for your kind letter. Things here have been better the last two days as my mother is now unconscious. Before that it was dreadful. Now she is slipping away & feels nothing.

Fancy, we never thought we would get here in time – now it is nearly a fortnight. I've been off the island once for half an hour. It is wonderfully beautiful, the house truly comfortable & marvellous food so really one can't complain. As for the sadness, it comes & goes in waves. I have a feeling nothing really *nice* will ever happen again in my life, things will just go from bad to worse, leading to old age & death.

I expect you'll be in America when I get back – I shall come as soon as the funeral is over.[1]

    Love, good Col
       Nancy

[1] Lady Redesdale died on 25 May, soon after her eighty-third birthday.

To EVELYN WAUGH   4 Chesterfield Street, W1
29 May 1963

Darling Evelyn

Your letter arrived at a very good moment for me, just as we were leaving the island, & cheered me up considerably during our journey South of 12 hours.

We took my mother over the water to Mull on a marvellous evening, 8 pm, with the bagpipes wailing away, it was very beautiful. All the men of the neighbourhood came, all talking Gaelic to each other (since you ask).

During a great storm, when we were cut off for 2 days from Mull, at the start of her illness, an intrepid neighbour called Ogilvie-Forbes rolled over in a sort of rubber ball, moved quietly into the bothy & never left us again. He is a co religionist of yours. Well he held a service over her coffin which was too perfect in every way & greatly appreciated by us & by the dear fellows who did all things one has to.

It seemed all *real*, not like when one dies at the London Clinic. Also the good Scotch doctor didn't insist on cruel things to keep her

alive a few more days – the nurses said in a hospital it would have
been very different.

We are all pretty tired. The funeral is tomorrow.

Much love & thank-you dearest Evelyn.

    Nancy

And for 2nd kind letter which has just arrived.

To Violet Hammersley   7 rue Monsieur, VII
19 June 1963

Darling

I know you think I take a frivolous view of the Profumo affair[1] –
though I suppose even you must have occasionally allowed a wan
smile to play over your features – but I really can't understand the
English attitude to *her*. They hound a poor man almost to death for
going to bed with her & then turn her into a millionairess, with rewards
of every kind & now are going to make a film of her life story. How
do you explain that? Dr Ward's[2] face is enough for me, I would believe
anything of him. Who will be your new leader? I'm in love with Mr
Wigg[3] but I loathe horrid Mr Wilson.[4] Tell all.

There was a ball in this street last Sat – I went to sleep with music
floating over me, opened an eye at 6 AM, it was still going on & when
Marie went to Church at 7 she found about a hundred pretty young
people in evening dress. After that I could hear them having breakfast
& playing tennis! The energy! I'm told they all do this – go to Church
after the ball. It's quite new I'm sure. . . .

I hope to see Mme Costa & will write when I have.

    Love
      N

Freezing cold here.

[1] On 4 June, the MP John Profumo admitted in the House of Commons that he had
lied about his relationship with Christine Keeler.
[2] Stephen Ward was accused of living on the immoral earnings of Christine Keeler and
others.
[3] George Wigg (1900–83). Labour MP for Dudley 1945–67. Created a life peer in
1967.
[4] Harold Wilson (1916–). Elected Leader of the Labour Party in February 1963; led
his party to victory in October 1964.

To Cecil Beaton   7 rue Monsieur, VII
25 August 1963

Darling Kek,

Thanks for the jolly P.C. I've also got my sister's book about Ameri-can body-snatchers[1] it is exceedingly awful & funny. . . .

My summer was heavenly & the barbarism of Greece an amusing interlude in the heavily over-civilized life of Venice.

I saw Margot[2] & her company perform three times. *She's a marvel*; the Russian jumps about very energetically; the others are like house-maids (male & female) & the clothes (none by you, why?) far more dreary than those of the Bolshoi. But Margot makes up for all. Nureyev told a Greek friend of Mark's who had him on his yacht that the English only cheer when he leaps & know nothing about ballet – he gave the impression that he may well go home again. Lifar,[3] whom I saw in Venice, says he's a lazy boy & won't work. I suppose you've seen him in London? Rather handsome, like Mark Sykes.[4]

Now I'm off to England for dear little Emma's[5] wedding – a nursery wedding, they both seem to be about 14. Dread time of year for knowing what to wear – in the country too! Poor Debo got a coat at Dior's – came over specially at great inconvenience – & they've let her down as per. So she's got to borrow one from Kitty Mersey – don't shriek like that it's very unkind. I've got a perfectly beautiful *hat* in thick green satin stripes & black velvet lines, like a mediaeval hat or one of those worn by African women, it's a smashing object but God knows what to wear it *with* & of course no time to get anything. Still I feel I've made un petit effort.

Oh poor Frosca [Munster] – I fear there is no hope. She has had a sad life or I suppose so; how can one ever tell? I think she was probably rather wicked in her young days. Talking of wicked, Graham S[utherland] showed me a coloured photograph of his picture of Daisy [Fellowes] – stunning, that's all. Her terrible cleverness comes out because she insisted on almost no face & nothing but chic get-up so no chance to make his usual map of lines!

Much love
   N

When do you come out of prison?[6]

[1] Jessica Mitford, *The American Way of Death* (1963).
[2] Margot Fonteyn (1919–91). Prima ballerina. Her celebrated partnership with Rudolf Nureyev (1939–93), who defected from the USSR in 1961, was launched with a performance of *Giselle* with the Royal Ballet in 1962.

[3] Serge Lifar (1905–86). Dancer, choreographer and biographer of Serge Diaghilev.
[4] Son of Christopher Sykes.
[5] Emma Cavendish, aged twenty, married Hon. Toby Tennant, aged twenty-two, on 3 September 1963.
[6] Cecil Beaton had been in America since the beginning of the year working on the film *My Fair Lady*.

To Viscountess Mersey   Chatsworth
3 October 1963   Bakewell

Darling Wife[1]

I hear that vile [Diana] Mosley, wishing your situation[2] for herself no doubt, has given me a poor character & dared to say I can't cook. Now any fin gourmet will tell you that the test of a cook is how she boils an egg. My boiled eggs are FANTASTIC, FABULOUS. Sometimes as hard as a 100 carat diamond, or again soft as a feather bed, or running like a cooling stream, they can also burst like fireworks from their shells & take on the look & rubbery texture of a baby octopus. Never a dull egg, with me. C'est tout dire.

Now *Mosley*'s cooking consists in going to the *charcuterie* for some horrible concoction which she places in an oven & too often forgets the match. An hour or two later a stone-cold dish is reverently removed with the oven-glove and placed upon a fire-proof table mat. Disappointment is noticed on every face when jelly can be seen where gravy ought to be. Then she is extremely unpunctual – will EB[3] really enjoy Spanish hours in Sussex? When she wants a cosy day in bed with the wireless she feigns headache.

No dear, take the hint & send for Rodd.

Stoveling. Oh yes, never a dull moment until the day when the chimney catches fire & flames lick the cornice. Twice I've found 6 or 7 *sweet* pompiers [firemen] in my bedroom. But if it burns peat that is less likely to occur I must say.

Marie's nephew's letter to his mother from Chatsworth (where he has gone to learn English & do odd jobs) is worth guineas. Like at Tante Marie's he says there is far too much to eat. He's adoring it & says (after 2 days) he feels as if he had lived in England all his life, 'The weather is grey but the air is pure'. That's the stuff – it'll get purer & purer I can tell him!

So may I hope for a favourable reply?

Love from
      Nancy

. . .

1 Mitford nickname for a great friend of either sex.
2 Lady Mersey had advertised for a cook.
3 Edward Bigham, 3rd Viscount Mersey (1906–79).

To SIR HUGH JACKSON   Fontaines-les-Nonnes
11 October 1963   par Puisieux

Dear Sir Hugh

Thank you very much for your letter – how murky everything
seems to be. When I was in Venice I thought that perhaps masked
naked men, orgies & unlimited spying are an accompaniment of mari-
time powers in decline. Certainly the whole Ward affair comes straight
out of *Casanova* – except that Keeler would have been a nun & Ward
the Abbé de Bernis. I went to Samos from Athens when poor Ward
was in a coma – no papers on Samos – at last I made a friend go to
the police station to find out what had happened: 'Dr Ward is dead.
You have lost a fine man –'!!

Samian wine, by the way, is delicious!

Yes I had a cloudless six weeks & felt quite guilty about friends at
home. A slight bore in Greece is that one is discouraged from swimming from a boat as there are sharks. This is quite new & said to be
Nasser's fault, he is supposed to beckon them through the canal to
eat us all up. I don't greatly fear death but it would be too ridiculous
– even one's greatest friends would laugh if one were eaten I feel!

I am writing a little pot-boiler on Versailles,[1] to be illustrated. One
of those boring books millionaires give each other for Christmas.
The publisher asked for it & I've nothing else on hand so I said all
right.

I hope you are well. I'm here on my annual visit I always love.

Yrs ever
        Nancy Mitford

. . .

1 *The Sun King* (1966). 'No more readable book has ever been written in my view!!!!!'
(NM to Duchess of Devonshire, 23 January 1965)

To EVELYN WAUGH   Fontaines-les-Nonnes
26 October 1963   par Puisieux

Darling Evelyn

Thank you very much for your lovely book.[1] I read it again & again of
course couldn't stop until the end. But it gives rise to certain reflections.

I'm afraid that, in literature at any rate, middle aged people become dull. Take *War & Peace*. As soon as all those charming, funny, touching adorable Rostovs are married, settled in life, they are so different & so stodgy that we are quite glad when the book comes to an end. I find the same with you – except that with you one longs for it to go on – I'm not sure but I see the difficulties. I loved the two young ones, the little one saw of them. Now Evelyn seriously, do you think being brother & sister would really have stopped them marrying? I call this rather naïf. Lord & Lady Dunmore, my father's great friends, were brother & sister so one always heard. They had a very happy marriage, I don't believe young people today would care a fig & NOR WOULD BASIL SEAL – but the trouble is Prod has turned into you & this falsifies everything. It is a great mistake in fact because never the twain could meet & it's wrong to try & make them. I do agree that naughty people are often reformed when they become rich but I don't believe however rich *Seal* was that he would have become that sort of good citizen, or broken his daughter's heart over such a silly quibble. Or was he meant to be jealous? If so we are in deep waters indeed. Perhaps it's all too short – I don't know, but I'm not convinced. Were you, really?

Abbé Girard, the nicest of the priests who come here, asked for *Voltaire Amoureux*. I said to Mme Costa what should I put as a dédicace? She said perhaps nothing – I'm afraid if you do it will be very compromising for him after his death; you are (in English) such a beautiful young (sic) lady, it's not as if you were Mme de Pange! In the end she made me put avec mes sentiments respectueux. I shall be interested to know what he makes of it.

Decca is lecturing all over America on dead bodies. It now appears that Bob has got a sort of self-service firm so they stand to make millions apart from the royalties. It wanted thinking of as Gladys my maid used to say.

Love – *thanks*.
    N

[1] *Basil Seal Rides Again* (1963). Waugh's last work of comic fiction.

To Theodore Besterman   7 rue Monsieur, VII
12 December 1963

My dear Theodore
    Your essay gave me a great deal of pleasure – I read it twice – you are a marvellous essayist, such a rare talent. I only disagree with one

thing in it – I don't think idiots are ever happy. I've known many, all wretched, & a loony doctor friend of mine says it is one of the dreadful things about madness, mad people are so so unhappy. He even says it doesn't much matter how they are treated, you can't make them sadder, they are already in the depths. (The happy idiot is rather like the noble savage in fact.)

A bookseller came to see my Voltaire[1] yesterday – I wish you could have heard his exclamations at the beauty of the production & supremeness of the editing. Oh la-la –!

Love from
    Nancy

[1] The standard collection of Voltaire's letters, edited by Besterman, eventually in 107 volumes.

TO VIOLET HAMMERSLEY   7 rue Monsieur, VII
12 January 1964

Darling

. . . Diana & I went to a masterly lecture by somebody called Sir Anthony Blunt.[1] It was at the Louvre in *completely perfect and fluent French*. Who is this Sir? I am in love. I shall leave him something in my will. Jealous?

The tapissière who is doing up Muv's sofa says it's the most beautiful one she has ever had in her shop. By the way there's a Signac exhibition on at the Louvre.

So warm here it's like Spring & smells good after the snow which thank God has all gone. It lay for one day looking divinely beautiful.

That's all.

Love
    N

[1] Anthony Blunt (1907–83). Surveyor of the Queen's Pictures, 1952–72. His knighthood, bestowed in 1956, was revoked in 1979 following his exposure as a spy for the Soviet Union during the war.

TO DUCHESS OF DEVONSHIRE   7 rue Monsieur, VII
30 January 1964

Dear Miss

. . . Thought Raymond's piece was perfect, didn't you?[1] I've now seen the pathetic last post card saying please tell Nancy I am very ill indeed & can't write. Of course we've had such like before, one must admit. Still she ought not to have been alone at night if she was sick all the time – the p.c. was two days before she died. Never mind, over now, & as you say she was spared an awful long death bed which is a mercy because for one thing she was afraid of death. I expect Mme Costa will go the same way very soon, I mean her heart will just stop. It's in a bad state. She says her clever little country dr: told her Wid was much more ill than she knew, this summer, & had gone down very much since last year. She is sad but not terribly so, I think she feels they'll meet again soon. She doesn't mind dying. . . .

   Love
     N

[1] Violet Hammersley had died after a short illness. Raymond Mortimer wrote in her obituary: 'In her eighty-seventh year she retained more completely than anyone else I have known her feminine charm and beauty, a beauty that reminded me of El Greco's daughter . . . Right to the end she brimmed with humour and wit in her talk and letters. Never have I met anyone more individual and fascinating.' *The Times*, 30 January 1964.

To Gaston Palewski   Chatsworth
24 February 1964   Bakewell

Dearest Col
   . . . We shall arrive back after luncheon on Monday 2nd so do ring up if you have time in the evening.
   Alvilde is here & a huge party of relations.
   Raymond wrote very sadly saying we shall all soon be dead. I said but think how lovely it will be to see Lord Byron & Louis XV. He replied you are lucky to believe in heaven & a heaven peopled by those usually supposed to be in hell.

   Love from
     Nancy

To Heywood Hill   Saniet Volpi[1]
28 May 1964   Tripoli

My dear Heywood
   I've sneaked off to bed from a vast dinner party – the only benefit (being able to do so) of having had 7 days of fever from having been vaccinated – terrible waste of one's hol. I thought I'd never be well again & Pierre Cardin[2] ante'd up with the news that *he* has been ill

for 2 years after vaccination. He looks like death & I was deeply depressed but this morning I woke up well, only tired.

All Venice friends here & adorable Jeanne Moreau[3] & no problems exc: some Mostyn-Owens[4] a left wing London pair clearly known to you because they've got all the shop jargon about how splendidly Handybags [Handasyde] describes battles & so on. Do enlarge. Debo only knew that he has relations who breed goats – when I asked he gleamed & said Oh yes, Mostyn Majesty. These Mostyns went to the bazaar & had a long, cosy, left wing get-together with Arabs who told about how lovely Nasser is & then said You once had a great man, Mussolini. That floored them – though it was rather nice of them to tell, I thought. Brando calls them the Apple & the Caterpillar. . . .

What it's like here. Well the house & huge park, or garden, are Paradise, I've never seen in my life such a beautiful place. Outside it's Eire. Yes you can go for walks & Anna-Maria makes the It: Amb: take her bicycling on his cook's borrowed bike. The bazaar is rather fun but sad to see the acres of nylon, plastic baskets & so on. Full of Anglo Saxons as there are huge bases here still. The Italian farms have all fallen into total decay; the desert has crept back where it had been made to flower & the inhabitants sit about waiting for Oxfam all day – every wall propped up by a few able-bodied chaps, as in Eire. Donkeys & goats everywhere, shops selling cheap luggage, all notices in 2 languages, ascendancy architecture spat upon (Leptis Magna) – I've told Eddy to rechristen Cooleville Warmville & transport it bodily here; except for the climate it's the *same place*. The muezzin no longer bothers to climb the minaret, he just puts on a gramophone record which is amplified & sounds like the Beatles IN one's bedroom.

On 2 June I go to Istanbul to stay with Count Ostrorog[5] who is said to have the last beautiful old Turkish house on the Bosphorus. Shades of dear Roger [Hinks]. (Debo rather doubtful of this venture specially on hearing that it's the Asiatic side.) He also lives in the rue Mr & I know him fairly well & he always invites me so I thought I would. The address is c/o him – Kandilly, Istanbul – there a week, then to Mark at Athens & home middle of June for good to enjoy those quiet months in Paris when I'm alone in my house.

Well Marie. I interviewed a treasure – 30 years with the same people, marvellous cook, perfect lady's maid dying to come. So Marie decided to stay another year. That's life I guess – anyway thank goodness.

The Ball! I shall keenly unfold my paper next day. Did I tell you my landlord's daughter went to a ball at Donnington & said the girls were all en Saint Germain des Prés d'il y a huit ans[6] & the mothers in *long woollen skirts*. Informal I suppose. She couldn't get over it. . . .

> Love from
>   Nancy

[1] Nancy was staying with Countess Cicogna in the villa acquired by her father when he was Governor of Libya.
[2] Pierre Cardin (1922–). The couturier. His company was launched in 1950.
[3] Jeanne Moreau (1928–). Actress. Starred in François Truffaut's *Jules et Jim* (1961).
[4] William Mostyn-Owen; art historian and auctioneer, and his wife Gaia (Servadio).
[5] A brother of Count Ostrorog whose death Nancy mentions in her letter of 30 September 1960.
[6] Dressed in a style fashionable in St-Germain-des-Prés eight years ago.

TO DUCHESS OF DEVONSHIRE   Kandilly
4 June 1964   Istanbul

Dear Miss

Without any disloyalty I must tell in your private ear that this part of my holiday beats all. In fact, except for Fontaines, I don't know where I've ever felt so comfortable staying away. The truth is, however much one may love the very rich there is always a barrier – the eye of the needle I think lurks in the background – well no, nothing to do with actual cash because look at you & Honks & Sonny [Portland], it must be that vile café society which stamps them. All becomes unreal. (Not Brando.)

Yesterday we walked about the town from 3 to 9 & I feel until one has seen this place one hasn't lived but how can anybody see it unless lucky enough to be shown it by my host? We never ran into a single tourist (haven't yet done Ste Sophie & the sérail) & he says they never go to any of the churches & mosques we saw – the Turks discourage them from the popular quarters. Even more fascinating than the mosques are the old wooden houses in kitchen gardens, miles & miles of them, the darling little streets, the *bears* oh don't, horses – recs[1] everywhere. Hardly any plastic objects to be seen – all receptacles are copper & earthenware. Then the people so friendly. The mosques shut at 5 but somebody always volunteers to go & get the guardian. We stopped at a crowded café for coffee & a glass of water – immediately two people gave their chairs & one of them paid for us.

Very different from the atmosphere at Tripoli. Did I tell you those wretched photographers were kept in a cell for hours at King Fizz airport – missed their plane of course, searched, questioned, not allowed to telephone & only got off the next day more dead than alive!

I've got a letter from an American woman I met once saying her husband is suffering from brain damage from a drug he took in N York (whose fault is that?) & she is stranded in Mexico City, why go there then? & will I send some money immediately. I WON'T. Then one from a Swede asking if I can send her some old *Tatlers*. No.

Nothing from you. Thanks.

The water life is so nice. You always leave the house in a boat. Just down the beach is Flo Nightingale's old hospital at Scutari – nothing changed since her day, to look at.

Please note my address next week will be c/o Old Gent 27 Odos Aristonikou Athens 407.

Love
    N

I feel *really well* now for the first time but I'm so thin. (Interesting.)

¹ A Mitford word for chickens.

To Evelyn Waugh   Fontaines-les-Nonnes
20 October 1964   par Puisieux

Darling Evelyn

Of course I loved your book – such a picture of one's youth – all the visual part of it so brilliant – & the characterization of chums. I didn't know 'old Baz' [Murray] had been a friend of yours how odd that I didn't. He has got a saintly daughter you would love called Ann & a beauty called Venetia not saintly at all.

When I first grew up, if there was an evening with nothing on I used to get onto the top of a bus & drive through the suburbs – I always thought they would be the place to live in (any of them in those days) with their pretty little houses buried in lilac & often a paddock or stables like the real country. I hated the real country (boredom) but always longed for fresh air & trees.

Too heavenly here as usual, perfect for work, esp as Mme Costa has given up bridge as a sacrifice to get her 20 yr old grandson back onto the straight & narrow.

My book has come to a pause & I'm off to Paris for 10 days.

We had the Bishop of Monaco (just the 3 of us) he took off his X

& ring & thumped Chopin waltzes on the piano with many a wrong note. He says the Pope is longing to get rid of the Bishops. Mme Costa evidently disapproves of the Council – she won't hear about it, saying they bake the bread & I must eat it but I don't want to look on.

Have you read *Les Mots*?[1] I think you would love it. I too read Marlborough[2] – there's something not quite right isn't there, but it's useful for the clear exposé of the battles. My book is going to have hundreds of pictures, 40 in colour. I put up a good deal of resistance at first but have come round to the idea. To begin with it's so good to be able to show everybody's face – then the mode of life becomes more clear in the mind – finally one can have as many maps & genealogies as one wants. It will be a Penguin after a year or 2. Mr Rainbird[3] what a sinister name, who is assembling it *claims*, as the *Daily Telegraph* wld say (I write to them once a week about their awful use of claim, to no avail of course) well he claims that he got orders for 100 000 copies at Frankfurt book fair wh, at 3 gns, seems more than promising.[4] Peters is all for it.

Decca went to Forest Lawn & they seem to have told her yes this rich English lord was here & when his wife died & she was buried here & he got the bill he was so furious he wrote *The Loved One*.

Voilà.

Much love
     Nancy

[1] Jean-Paul Sartre, *Les Mots* (1964). An autobiographical essay about childhood.

[2] Winston Churchill, *Marlborough: His Life and Times* (4 vols, 1933–8).

[3] George Rainbird (1905–86). Publisher, and inventor of the coffee-table book.

[4] *The Sun King* was published to enthusiastic reviews and sold a quarter of a million copies within two years. Even more important to Nancy was that General de Gaulle read the book and recommended his *cabinet* to read it.

To CHRISTOPHER SYKES   As from:
8 December 1964   7 rue Monsieur, VII

Darling Chris

I'm struggling with a book on the high heeled periwigged Monster. My favourite chapter is on Ld Portland's embassy to same. I wrote to adorable Sonny [Portland] not that I call him that, also the adorable's ex librarian now with Gerry [Wellington] – neither of them could answer my query, indeed the adorable I think had never heard of the 1st Earl. Now I've remembered that he must be an ancestor of yours

& as you are slightly more lettered than the adorable you may know the answer.

My grandmother had a story about Portland going in a coach with L XIV – the King indicating that he shld get in, P obeying without any façons of after you Sire & the K saying yes I always heard you were the most polite man in Europe.

Now, I can't find this in any mémoires, even *Dangeau* who writes down every ½ hour of Louis' day, nor in that lovely diary of the embassy (Portland's) at the London Library. So I thought I'd dreamt it until some old ambassadress trotted it out the other day. I long to tell it as it illustrates so beautifully my theory that Portland was chosen because he knew how to behave.[1] 'What British bulldog,' says I, 'would have known about the Hand, the Fauteuil, the Door & the Carosse? Or that HBM Ambassador must not shake hands with the Président du Parlement? Portland knew.' I love this Earl – why don't you write his life?

How are you? It's an age since I saw you. I'm going to Debo on the 19th, home 1st Jan & thereafter I don't move. The adorable is coming to shoot on Boxing Day I believe – I want to work on him for the Mignard portrait I believe exists, for my book.

Much love from
    Nancy

I say wot's all this about Boney being poisoned? Do you believe it?[2]

[1] Christopher Sykes replied: 'I suppose the story may just be "oral tradition" like Alfred and the Cakes but for Heaven's sake put it in your great book. Winston put the cakes in his.' (12 December 1964)
[2] The recurrent conspiracy theory that Napoleon died from arsenic poisoning on St Helena.

To Duchess of Devonshire   7 rue Monsieur, VII
1 February 1965

Dear Miss
    I think it was more sensible not to go,[1] but oh how television diminishes everything. I went to Dolly's & saw it all. As the commentary (excellent) was in French we were spared Eisenhower who I gather did the English one. Interesting how all the American leaders have such heavy colds they can't go for ½ an hour to St Paul's! They ought to have dogs' throats grafted or sheeps' tonsils, you never

heard of a dog with a cold. (Oh sheep do cough rather I must say.)
They might have rabbits' brains while they are about it too.

I thought Wilson & Uncle H[2] quite perfect – heard them on the
wireless. Sir Alec[3] all right & Mr Grimond[4] as per. You know what I
think of HIM. Tries too hard.

I'd like to see Potty[5] under shock – perhaps it's what he needs you
know & now he'll be the *cleverest and lead us*.

No news I'm on a last spurt with L which goes to be typed
tomorrow. No it won't be one of those huge books – quite all right
for reading – but will have hundreds of pictures which I love because
you can prove your point with them – viz, the Dauphin's wonderful
rooms, all destroyed, you can show what they were like, also everybody's FACE, so important. I think it will be really fascinating. Then
it comes out in a Penguin. I read every word of the Tutankhamen
book,[6] companion vol: – good big print too. . . .

I heard something on the wireless which made me *crave* for Mrs
Ham[mersley] – a man saying when somebody has committed a murder he feels very ill & ought to be most carefully treated for a long
time. Screams!

It poured here non stop for 3 days including the funeral day – very
hot & sopping. So I think they were lucky to have it dry though cold.
Today is June in Jan too heavenly.

The dresses sound exactly what I like which is always so fatal!
When do you come? . . .

Much love
N

[1] Winston Churchill's state funeral had taken place on 30 January.
[2] Harold Macmillan (1894–1986). Prime Minister 1957–63. Married to Andrew Devonshire's aunt, Lady Dorothy Cavendish, in 1920.
[3] Sir Alec Douglas-Home (1903–). Prime Minister 1963–4.
[4] Jo Grimond (1913–). Leader of the Liberal Party 1956–67.
[5] The Duke of Gloucester (1900–74). Returning from Churchill's funeral, the Duke
overturned the Rolls-Royce he was driving. His wife was badly injured in the accident;
he was thrown clear into some brambles and nettles and was merely shocked.
[6] Christiane Desroches Noblecourt, *Tutankhamen* (1963). Sold over 1½ million copies.

TO JESSICA TREUHAFT   7 rue Monsieur, VII
5 February 1965

Darling Soo

I shall be here in March as I've promised to work on a film[1] (for
MGM) with a Belgian friend – a funny film about cannibals, yes Susan

I'm afraid they *eat* the dear fellow sent by UNO. We went to the Musée de l'Homme to see a real film on the subject – the audience except for us was nothing but ancient anthropologists SCREAMING with laughter. I'm engaged by MGM mid March for 6 weeks & then hope to go to Lismore. Dying for you.

I dined with Randolph full of tales of the funeral. The Duke of Norfolk who ran it was too wonderful, thought of everything – borrowed 40 umbrellas from the Lost Property Office in case it should rain at Bladon. Two days before, the Chief Constable of Oxford telephoned to say *Time & Life* had got an operations centre in the village school how could he get rid of them? (Clemmie[2] had begged no journalists there.) The Duke said well you'll be wanting an operations centre yourself, Chief Constable, so at 12 o'clock on the day of the funeral you must requisition the school. The whole thing was too marvellously organised as one saw on T.V. & Woodrow Wyatt[3] said to Randolph *Thank God* the Duke isn't chairman of the Conservative party! No Americans turned up because Rusk[4] had got a little cold & couldn't go for ½ an hour to St Paul's & Eisenhower had been offered 100 000 dollars to do a broadcast so his chair was empty too & he was busy broadcasting in the crypt.

We dined in a restaurant & of course everybody recognized Randolph & of course we were shrieking with laughter. I hope they put it down to hysteria.

Then Andrew [Devonshire] turned up yesterday so I've had a lot of English news & views.

I'd adore to see that interview. The woman who did it looked like a sort of sad dog dressed up in French clothes – she told a friend of mine she hadn't dared send it to me, so I knew it must be the worst. I never mind for America as I don't really really believe it exists you know – won't give interviews any more in England, except for one journalist I trust. They always invent.

Honks is in South Africa hugging Verwoerd & lucky thing lying in hot sun. How we do all spread over the globe. Woomon is in Switzerland still.

Louis XIV has gone to be typed I miss him.

Much love
    N

[1] This has not been possible to trace.
[2] Clementine Hozier (1885–1977). Married Winston Churchill in 1908. Created Baroness Spencer-Churchill of Chartwell in 1965. Nancy's father and Clementine were first

cousins; there was also a rumour that she was the natural daughter of 1st Lord Redesdale.
[3] Woodrow Wyatt (1918–). Labour MP for Bosworth 1959–70. Journalist and joint founder of the television documentary series *Panorama*. Created a (Conservative) life peer in 1987.
[4] Dean Rusk (1909–). US Secretary of State 1961–9.

TO SIR HUGH JACKSON　　　　　　　　Fontaines-les-Nonnes
18 February 1965　　　　　　　　　　　　par Puisieux

Dear Sir Hugh

Your letter has made my joy. Really the *placement* at St Paul's! Of course I can see that Randolph's wives would rank the same – except that Pamela, née Digby, is a Hon – but Ly Blandford *must* have been put next Osiris[1] as a tease. Do you suppose she had Blandford the other side then? Odd isn't in it.

Interesting what you say about June [Churchill]. I always liked her. Anyway the child[2] will be *the* beauty of her generation, I never saw such a face. *Pamela Randolph.* He thought he was going to be killed in the war & proposed to every girl in London in about four days (wanting a son). She was a red headed bouncing little thing, regarded as a joke by her contemporaries; had never had the slightest success & flew to the altar with him. To do her justice she couldn't have put up with the treatment he metes out to his wives – even his friends, who didn't much like her, admitted that. . . . I really cannot write more, having a certain native prudence, but she lived in Paris for about 10 years & I could tell you some tales. Then, again to the general amazement, she married an infinitely dreary American with whom she seems to have settled down. There is *nothing* to be said for Randolph but, Clementine C being my cousin, we were brought up together & I really love him & have never experienced, though often witnessed, the rough side. He was my brother Tom's greatest friend. We don't usually gossip about the 20th century do we!

I've got, by the same post, a telegram from my publisher of the most fulsome praise of my book, so that's all right as he is a well-educated middle brow & certainly knows what will sell.

Have you read Ly Longford's *Victoria*?[3] I've been plunged in it for days. It's not a work of art, & *far* too long, still, highly enjoyable. Lytton S[4] will never be bettered I think, but there is room for a more detailed account. . . .

　　Yrs ever
　　NM

¹ Lady Blandford was formerly Mrs Aristotle Onassis.
² Arabella Churchill (1949–). Daughter of Randolph and June Churchill.
³ Elizabeth Longford, *Victoria R.I.* (1964).
⁴ Lytton Strachey, *Queen Victoria* (1921).

To Elizabeth Longford[1]   As from:
19 February 1965   7 rue Monsieur, VII

My dear Elizabeth

I've come up to breathe from writing a book about Louis XIV &
the first thing I did was to read *Q.V. Oh it is so good* – I've been
screaming with laughter for several days on end.

I always thought there was a good deal of resemblance between
the two Monarchs but I now see that, such as there is, it's very
superficial. The length of their reigns, their views on the Lord's
Anointed & their preference for servants over aristocrats are about
the extent of the likeness – oh & the asides of the entourage, but
that exists in all Courts. I don't know where or how but I got it into
my head that Q. Vic. studied Saint-Simon for rulings on etiquette –
from your book this is clearly not true & she didn't care for etiquette
in the least. Louis XIV used it as a means of keeping an inflated Court
of several thousand people in order – she didn't need to do that.

It's amazing how she managed to remain exactly as naïve at 80 as
at 18, considering that she was always surrounded by cynical men of
the world. I think she was almost *too* stupid – didn't it get you down
rather? But I can see you are fond of her.

I know that this is stating the obvious, but one is struck by how little
difference there is between 17th cent & 19th cent in all essentials. I
must say, dentists or no dentists, I would have vastly preferred not
to live now. Don't dream of answering – I know how the heart sinks!
Wish I ever saw you – if you come to Paris at all, here I sit – in the
telephone book.

Love from
        Nancy

¹ Elizabeth Harman (1906–). Married 7th Earl of Longford in 1931. Her many books
include a two-volume life of Wellington: *Years of the Sword* (1969) and *Pillar of State*
(1972), and *The Royal House of Windsor* (1974).

To Heywood Hill   7 rue Monsieur, VII
11 March 1965

My dear Heywood
Thanks so much for your letter – all rather *sad* but never mind.[1] I
had one from Molho [Buchanan] saying tell all friends everything will
still be nice in the shop.

Disillusioning about Jebb cuisine[2] – I always thought C was supposed
to be a good maîtresse de maison. Broilers are a menace – we got
one by mistake – Marie said its insides were like soup, its gizzard
(meant to be hard) a sponge & there were other horrid symptoms
I've forgotten. You can tell, to avoid buying, by the claws being long
like an American lady's nails, from not scratching in the earth, its
comb not being quite quite & its eyes *sunk*. We've never had another
but one is told never to eat chicken in a restaurant now. (It was
uneatable by the way.)

I've finished the book but have engaged to write dialogue for a
lovely film, for MGM (to make a nice lot of money & amuse myself,
excellent combination) so from tomorrow I shall be busy again – v.
difficult to explain to idle friends who all say but I thought you'd
finished! . . .

Mrs Law[3] makes my joy & recounts such extraordinary things about
the Old Land – people seem to be out of their minds. Debo says not
quite true.

    Love & to Anne
       N

Water Beetle had 'rave' notices here chiefly owing to Hysterico
[Jacques Brousse]'s brilliant translation – it's called *Snobismes et
Voyages*. I think Snob is a magic word.

[1] The bookshop had been sold to Henry Vyner. Heywood Hill continued to work
part-time until 1966.
[2] Heywood Hill had written to say that at dinner with the Jebbs he had been given bad
chicken.
[3] Joy Law was editorial director of George Rainbird and author of *The Kings and
Queens of France* (1976) and *Dordogne* (1981). She undertook the picture research for
The Sun King, Frederick the Great and for the illustrated version of *Madame de Pompadour*. Nancy soon found her indispensable and fully appreciated her contribution to the
success of the books.

To Duchess of Devonshire   Leixlip Castle[1]
18 May 1965   Co Kildare
                                        Eire

Dear Miss˙

I say how glad I am not to know that toothy rudderless family[2] &
only to be blinded by the flashing whiteness of their molars through
the medium of photography (when I keenly look in another direction).
Sewers. I saw Pam Berry has given a bust of L[oved]O[ne], in a
topless evening dress, so I suppose you have softened towards her?
No more for fear of needless needling.

I'm adoring it here for the great prettiness, the champagne welcome
(Desmond said he couldn't sleep for excitement) the fire in one's room
& general niceness. The Alice in Wonderland-ery is total which for
only 2 days is funny. Viz – yesterday afternoon an American family
arrived Pa Ma & daughter. Teeth. Mariga said You are the friends
of Mr Macklehenny.[3] No – no – we're not his friends.

Me (hopefully) His enemies perhaps? Oh no we're sure he's
dourling.

Mariga (looking out of the window) Here comes your enemy Mr
Macklehenny.

Americans (fearfully agitated) But we're *not* his enemies we're sure
he's a lovely person.

Mariga May I introduce Mr M.henny, Mr & Mrs Marikovsky?

Americans (reproachfully) O'Leary.

So it went on. Nobody ever knew why they had come. *Vast* car.

Tomorrow sale of Castletown[4] wh Desmond is bidding for against
Muv's friend Butlin & in the evening Opera in Italian Ambassador's box.
I am dazzled by all this high society to which I am so unaccustomed.

The rain goes on. There is a drought. I said to Mr Ed [Sackville-
West] I don't want to hurt your feelings but surely a pipe from the
gutters would be the thing? Oh but there's never any *rain* here. Oi
geev up.

Irish paper has just been brought in (you see how kind – all this v.
different from what Mr Ed gave me to suppose during an anti Mitford
broadcast) & I read: the future of a million sea trout is not very bright.

I must get up. Oh by the way when Mariga told the housemaid,
her aunt (me) was coming she said I hope she'll be able to manage
the stairs.

    Love
        N

[1] Nancy was staying with her nephew, Desmond Guinness, and his wife Mariga.
[2] The Kennedys.
[3] Henry P. McIlhenny (d. 1986). President of the Philadelphia Museum of Art, connoisseur, collector and scholar. Lived at Glenveagh in Donegal.
[4] A magnificent 18th-century house saved from demolition by Desmond Guinness and bought by him as the headquarters for the Irish Georgian Society.

To HEYWOOD HILL   7 rue Monsieur, VII
21 May 1965
[postcard]

Please send Desmond Guinness Leixlip Castle Co Kildare an *Ox: Classical Dict:* say Love from Auntie.

One of Oonagh's sons[1] loomed he *is* Struwwelpeter. Struwwelpeter there he stands with his filthy hair & hands etc I longed to get up & recite. He was accompanied by a black-a-moor too. Perhaps those nursery books are at the root of the trouble, plus Bond for train wrecking. More peaceful here. Yes the mice *admit* to taking £850 to pay us £108, I quite agree, but what can one do? Nibble nibble. I think I'll leave all to Stoker, the only person I know who can afford an inheritance!

Love
     N

[1] Hon. Garech Browne (1939–). Son of 4th Baron Oranmore and Browne, who was married to Oonagh Guinness 1936–50.

To HAROLD ACTON   7 rue Monsieur, VII
24 May 1965

Dearest Harold
September *is* a better idea, as I shall be weighed down with bathing apparatus on my way to & from Venice. I simply long for it – such an age since I saw you.

Yes it's wonderful how the insects of a single week, as Voltaire used to call them,[1] have no influence whatever on the public – any more than they had in his day. The fact is I don't believe anybody reads their effusions. It has always amazed me that true writers like the Sitwells (& old Voltaire himself) should mind what they say – my policy is that of the ostrich: I've long ago given up press cuttings. What's the point of being upset, even for half an hour? It's not as though they helped one to do better – they are purely destructive & when they praise it's for the wrong reasons.

Ireland was delightful. Not one gleam of sunshine, but I'm used to that now & hardly mind it. I stayed with Eddy, Debo & Desmond all very jolly. Bryan Moyne's eldest daughter[2] is engaged to an Honest Injun said by Bryan to be 'a *general favourite*'. She is reported to be already, in a sari & jewelled forehead, bowing the knee to idols.

Irish gardens beat *all* for horror. With 19 gardeners, Lord Talbot of Malahide has produced an affair exactly like a suburban golf course. It was invaded, when I saw it, by Philadelphia Mothers oh-ing and ah-ing. You'd think people would have the sense to let the landscape alone, encouraging cow parsley, buttercups, lilac & old fruit trees if they must have flowers. Eddy Sackville goes in for vicarage flowerbeds & Debo I'm sorry to say for Glorious Technicolour cherries from Old Japan.

Have you read *l'Etat sauvage*[3] (prix Goncourt)? There's a good, funny & *short* novel for you.

Like you I worry about Evelyn. He never writes unless one insists & then sounds sad & unwell. I believe the present Pope has broken his heart.

Much love – I'm already excited for Sept:
Nancy

[1] Critics; Harold Acton had just published *Old Lamps for New*, a collection of short stories, which received poor reviews.
[2] Hon. Rosaleen Guinness married Sudhir Mulji on 12 June 1965.
[3] Georges Conchon, *l'Etat sauvage* (1964).

TO SIR HUGH JACKSON   7 rue Monsieur, VII
9 June 1965

Dear Sir Hugh

I must tell you of a strange encounter. I was lunching, as I often do on Sunday, at the local bistro when a *lower-class* Englishman came & sat by me. He didn't know French – however I forbore to explain that beefsteak is beefsteak etc, & let him muddle it out, thinking that's half the fun, abroad. But then he turned to me very politely & said I see you are English (I was reading the paper) may I ask something – could you direct me to Notre-Dame-des-Victoires? I'm very anxious to go there. Well, I wrote it all down & gave him bus tickets. But I was dying to ask why he wanted to go there? Was it to put up

a votive offering? He'd never been in Paris before & was leaving at
once.

At dinner that night I told this story & a view was put forward that
he might be a keen Bonapartist (comme tous les Anglais, d'ailleurs[1])
& wanted to see the church where Josephine secretly placed the first
flags sent home by N. Well, I'm a fairly keen Bonapartist but I didn't
know that & can hardly believe he did! He launched into a virulent
attack on present day England saying the Eng: deserve everything,
for their general hopelessness. A man of about 35 I suppose. Wasn't
it odd!

The *D. Tel:* is quite wild about France I can't think where they get
their ideas – their correspondents here seem sane & well informed.
I didn't see the article about the Cte de Paris. If the General really
favoured him surely he'd be getting some publicity? He is given a
modified V.I.P. treatment & the Gen: always comes up with a wedding
present for those hideous daughters – apart from that one never hears
of him. The nobility doesn't like him (& most of them pretend to think
he is a Bernis) & *le peuple* ignores him. I remember he once said to
my great friend Louis de Lasteyrie Je hais la noblesse française & L
replied Elle vous le rend bien, Mgr!![2] Time will show if the *D.T.* is
right – I would love to be offered a bet! As you say, Egalité is not an
ancestor de tout repos.

I've been re-reading Sieburg's wonderful Napoleon[3] (100 days) but
couldn't do Waterloo, it is too sad. Poor Ney. All that mud, too – oh
the gloom.

Never knew about L XIV and the shaving! Poor duchesses – they
had to kiss him EVERY day!

Yrs

    Nancy Mitford

[1] Indeed, like all the English.
[2] I hate the French nobility & L replied They hate you back, Monseigneur.
[3] Friedrich Sieburg, *Napoléon* (1956).

To Sir Hugh Jackson   7 rue Monsieur, VII
16 June 1965

Dear Sir Hugh

Thanks awfully for the enclosed.[1] Of course one never can guess
what our good General may do next – I don't believe the French
would stand for a restoration but I may be wrong. Paris is said to be

a clever man but 'Madame', as they call her, is a tremendous goose & adores café society. (So, no doubt, would Marie-Antoinette have!) The children have all, I think, married Germans & that is not popular. . . .

I ought to have asked the 'lower class man' what he wanted from N-D des V – but I am a tremendous non-asker of questions & no doubt miss a lot of interesting facts thereby. Rather odd for a novelist I must say. The church is the north side of the Place & is filled with votive offerings so I feel quite sure he had some heartfelt wish he thought would be *exaucé* by a visit to it. I said to him you will find the church in the middle of one of the oldest & most historic parts of Paris but he seemed uninterested – simply said oh –!!!

Paris again. Yes his father was Duc de Guise. One of *his* gentlemen was M. Aubry-Vitet, the father of the old lady I half live with at Fontaines-les-Nonnes. Another gentleman was the Comte de Bernis of whom Paris, youngest of a large family of girls, is the literal double. I've seen many photographs of Bernis & they have got the same very odd face. So tongues have wagged. Very indiscreet to write all this but I feel you will not betray me!

I go to Greece for a week 28th – & then for a month to Dorsoduro 23, Venice.

I'm paralysed with hay fever as always in June.

Yrs ever
    Nancy Mitford

P.S. I'm so cross with Raymond Mortimer. He kindly read my L XIV for mistakes – in last Sunday's review of Péguy he has cribbed a whole sentence from me – 'If the French are divided into Gauls & Franks . . . . Colbert was the quintessence of the Frank', says I, repeated word for word by R.M. about Péguy. Do admit it's rather *much*!

[1] An article on the Comte de Paris in the *Daily Telegraph* colour supplement.

To Gaston Palewski   23 Dorsoduro
7 July 1965   Venice

Dearest Col

You'll have to come & see the Guardis so come this month oh *do*. They are wonderful, tho' the very prettiest belong to that friend of yours I so deplore, Thyssen.[1] (I suppose he fits in to Palewski the Play Boy side of your nature – speaking of which I note that one of your fellow roughs met the usual end in the Bois de Boulogne.)

I never saw the light so pretty here & the weather is perfect, rather cool with a hot sun & cloudless sky.

Raymond comes tomorrow – the Sutherlands (Graham not Duke) are here & of course Clarys & all the usuals who aren't dead. I had a long sad talk with our banino, Vittorio, which consisted of him reciting the names of dead people & me crying & saying Oh Vittorio. It ended with e Beistegui – finito. Too true.

So do come

Love
   N

There was a great storm which just missed Venice, otherwise they say the whole town would have been destroyed. It was the day before I came.

[1] Baron Hans Heinrich von Thyssen (1921–). Industrialist and art collector.

To Duchess of Devonshire   23 Dorsoduro
9 July 1965   Venice

Dear Miss

Eddy! I'm *shattered*.[1] Had no idea, on acc of never bothering to look at the paper I suppose – I mean I do look but often not at the deaths. Graham Sutherland said what a pretty shawl you've got on – I said Eddy gave it to me – he said Eddy who's dead? DEAD? I nearly fainted.

Yesterday Raymond loomed from France. I said to A-M [Cicogna] he can't know – what are we to do about breaking it to him? But in accordance with this strange modern way of ignoring the forms he did know & had come all the same. Poor Raymond I think he is in despair. Not only were they like brothers but it means the end of Long Crichel which I guess Eddy paid for mostly. We still don't know why or how he died – do you?

O dear, I *mind*. Monsewer.[2]

Much love – do tell if you hear anything
   N

[1] Eddy Sackville-West, aged sixty-three, had collapsed with acute asthma cardiac failure and died at his house in Ireland on 4 July.
[2] After a musical-hall comedian known as Monsewer Eddy Gray.

To George D. Painter[1]   23 Dorsoduro
2 August 1965   Venice
[postcard]

I won't bother you with a letter. Have been living, like everybody
else, in your book & am struck by the extraordinary resemblance of
M.P. to Voltaire. Same goodness & nobility beneath an apparent
spitefulness. Both always ill – obsessed by les gens du monde whose
attitude to them both was identical – obsessed by the idea of Italy,
where Voltaire never went at all – lovers of painting. The young
secretaries so similar (only Voltaire was quite normal). Origins about
the same, I mean social position of the parents. I think this can't have
struck you, as there is no mention of Voltaire, & that it might amuse
you.

     Nancy Mitford

All the démêlés [quarrels] with publishers identical; the re writing &
disinterest in money as both were rich.

[1] George D. Painter (1914–). Biographer and incunabulist. The second volume of his
biography of Marcel Proust had just been published.

To George D. Painter   7 rue Monsieur, VII
17 August 1965

Dear Mr Painter

I am considerably elated by your letter – there is nobody in the
world I would sooner be praised by.[1] What you say about Fédéric so
true – those sort of people can't bear the idea of a woman in the offing
& no doubt the trouble between him & Voltaire really came first from
Emilie & then Mme Denis. How I long to write a life of Fédéric but
the gigantic Carlyle overhangs him & I fear there's nothing to be
done.

I was laughing in the street the other day – ran into somebody I
know – felt a fool & began to explain that I was thinking how Carlyle
calls Frederick 'the Princikin'. The *person* didn't understand a word
of what I was saying & looked extremely puzzled!

My copy of your book is 'out', I mean *lent* (dread word to an author
I know) so I can't look up page 334 – I'm a fearfully careless reader
& see I must have overlooked something.[2] While I was reading I kept
thinking but whom does he remind me of? And only when I came to

the to-do with the publisher it struck me in a flash – then I saw the whole extraordinary resemblance.

How I wish *you* would now do the definitive life of Voltaire. It is possible, as Besterman's work is done. Poor soul, he wanted to write it & sent me the first chapter. Unfortunately he had forgotten Voltaire's saying if you want to bore the public tell them everything. It was completely hopeless – even I could hardly read it & God knows it's a subject that fascinates me. Do you think Besterman is an Indian? Roger Hinks met him here & put forward the idea & I *know* he was right. Have you ever looked Best: up in *Who's Who?* He is a very curious person[3] – has been so very good to me.

To go back to your book. I do love the way you write about people only just dead, or sometimes still alive, as if they were ancient Romans.

Antoine B[ibesco] I knew very well – he was fascinating, funny & sly – SLY (not shy). My sister, & I by the way, think Marthe[4] must have written the page about her herself. Goodness she must be thrilled with it! Poor Princess Dolly Radziwill, widow of Loche, charmed Peyrefitte into leaving Pr Constantin out of his Capri book.[5] But I doubt if she'll see yours unless some kind person puts it under her nose. Of course the La Rochefoucaulds, Mouchys & so on all descend from him – but they are non readers. *I* rather minded your attitude to the Helleu family – have known them all my life. Helleu was such a charmer. But on the whole you have completely hit off your ancient Romans.

I mustn't bore you any longer. If ever you come here DO come and see me.

> Yrs sincerely
> Nancy Mitford

[1] 'Among the books I had in mind all the years I was writing, as a sort of unapproachable ideal, were your *Madame de Pompadour* and *Voltaire in Love*. They are the only great biographies in English literature since Lytton Strachey.' (George D. Painter to NM, 4 August 1965)

[2] In a letter to NM, Painter had pointed out: 'I was indeed conscious of the extraordinary resemblance in character and innermost essence between Proust and Voltaire, and even planted a sort of code reference to it, as I did with various matters which didn't seem quite to "come into" the book in more extended form, on p. 334.' (4 August 1965) The page in question reads: 'Proust sat benign, holding court; and Fernand Gregh's daughter Geneviève, noticing the band of maidens and men round his throne, was reminded of the aged Voltaire revisiting Paris on the eve of his death.' *Marcel Proust*, vol. II (Chatto & Windus, 1965).

[3] Theodore Besterman was Investigation Officer of the Society for Psychical Research

1927–35; his publications include *Crystal-Gazing: A Study in the History of Scrying* (1924), *Some Modern Mediums* (1928) and *Mrs Annie Besant: A Modern Prophet* (1934).
[4] Marthe Lahovary (1888–1973). Author of numerous novels, essays and memoirs. Married her cousin Prince Georges Bibesco in 1905. Before the First World War she was close to the Crown Prince, and in the 1920s she was the mistress of Lord Thomas of Cardington, Secretary of State for Air. Painter wrote of her: 'In Paris this astonishingly young tree-nymph from Romania, with her violet-green eyes and talent budding into power, was received as a reigning beauty and a genius; truly, for she was both.' *Marcel Proust*, vol. II, p. 169.
[5] Roger Peyrefitte, *l'Exilé de Capri* (1959). Novel based on a famous French homosexual scandal. Painter had written that Prince Constantin Radziwill, Dolly's father-in-law, was the original of Proust's Prince de Guermantes in his later aspects as a homosexual.

To Evelyn Waugh   7 rue Monsieur, VII
10 September 1965

Darling Evelyn

You mustn't bother about a film.[1] As Voltaire said of critics, it is the insect of a single week. *The Blessing* I know was murdered – I never saw it & now it is forgotten. But a book goes on for ever.

Mr Slade[2] came with the *P of Love*. The songs very pretty – the dialogue terrible. I tremblingly asked if I might re-write it – he allowed me to, then was kind enough or clever enough to say that it was far better – as indeed it was! Funny how few people can write dialogue – I shall never in future sell any rights without stipulating that I must do it myself.

I feel for you over the Church.[3] Even I *mind terribly* the thought of immemorial beauty being cast away in a few months. How lucky I am to believe in God without any religious instincts or needs. I hate this Pope – to hell with the Pope is a sentiment with which I cordially concur.

Do you know, my eyes are cured. I've no idea why – I thought they would get worse and worse, & now they are as good as when I was young & I can read all night if I want to. What a strange machine the body is! Oh dear how hateful, not tasting food – but I think it's a temporary condition?

I'm so sorry you are low in spirits. Why don't you come here to have a change? Of course *I* always think one can't be very low in Paris but that depends on liking the French & I'm not sure you *do*! (Do you remember Père Couturier?)

I expect I shall like La Pietra[4] – I always like grand houses. People find the Malcontenta depressing but I think to wake up there in the morning is a positive happiness. I'm off to Harold, on Sunday.

Much love & to Laura
    Nancy

[1] 'The film of *Loved One* is a great annoyance to me – one of the few occasions when Peters has let me down. He sold it years ago to a mad Mexican for a paltry sum with the assurance that it would never be produced . . . The next thing I heard was that an American company had bought the rights from the Mexican and were producing an elaborate travesty.' Waugh, *Letters*, p. 633.
[2] Julian Slade (1930–). Author and composer of *Salad Days* (1954). He adapted *The Pursuit of Love* as a musical.
[3] The Vatican Council's approval of vernacular liturgies had upset Waugh. 'The buggering up of the Church is a deep sorrow to me and to all I know. We write letters to the paper. A fat lot of good that does.' Waugh, *Letters*, p. 633.
[4] Harold Acton's villa in Florence.

To Jessica Treuhaft   Fontaines-les-Nonnes
15 November 1965   par Puisieux

Darling Soo

Elle est comme ça[1]

I note that I've been vile. My excuse is that the French, curious as cats, always want to SEE one. Take publishers – mine have amalgamated with Hachette & as soon as this happened I got a message saying would I call at Hachette's & see my new publisher. Answer, I would *not*. Why *see*? Can't he read? It's all the most fearful waste of effort, in my view.

However, 4800 francs is worth an afternoon as I fully realize & as soon as I get home (next Tues:) I'll cope. It's more the principle than anything else as I've got nothing whatever to do at present.

A human touch, let's face it, how I screamed.

I've got such pretty new writing paper but it is thick & rich & demands the scales so you won't get the treat as you are always in such a hurry.

Diana wears a baroque brooch given her by you & says it is her treasure. I hope your hard heart is touched. Sisters, Susan, oh S*oo*!?!

Mossiker,[2] of course. I long to see how she copes with that amazing tale. I've got a whole chapter on it in my book so am fairly well qualified to review hers. I greatly admired the necklace book.

If I were a young man & not an old lady I would join up with Mr Smith,[3] though more for the fun of it than the principle. I believe he may keep going for a while, like the Jews in Palestine, but it can't be permanent – or unlikely to be. But I can't help loving lost causes.

Meanwhile the English wireless on which I depend, down here, for Eng: news, has become a great bore, harping.

Mademoiselle Marie, the housekeeper, has offered me one of the housemaids when my Marie retires – the said h.maid would rather be in Paris. I think she has also mentioned it to her so whenever we come face to face we give each other looks like a young couple whose parents have arranged a marriage for them. She is quite enormous, about twice as tall as me, but I must say a nice kind face.

Gen de Gaulle has given all the 5 opposition candidates 4 hours on télé (each) at *peak listening time*. It's so clever – they'll bore everybody's pants off. He himself is going to speak once, for 5 minutes. Do admit it's rather drôle.

The electricity strike (engineered by you Soo?) must have been quite something. A friend of mine once went to a cktl pty in NY & found the hall of the building full of well dressed people waiting for the lift to be mended. He said what floor do the Xs live on? The second floor. But nobody except him could face the stairs.

Fond love from
    N

[1] That's the way she is.
[2] Frances Mossiker; author of *The Queen's Necklace* (1961) and *Napoleon and Josephine* (1965).
[3] Ian Smith had declared unilateral independence for Rhodesia on 11 November.

To Jessica Treuhaft   7 rue Monsieur, VII
27 November 1965

Darling Soo
    . . . I suppose that black out was rather like air raids, than which there was no greater fun on earth. Only I wouldn't like to be caught in a lift with Americans who always want to go to the loo non stop.

No Susan, I'm against the war in Viet Nam. I think it wrong to pour Napalm on little yellow people simply to keep Wall St on its legs. There's more to be said for the Rhodesians – at least they live in the place. Also the Americans are such ghastly Tartuffes, pretending to hate colonialism when anybody else benefits from it & then look at them! Human nature all over –

A man wrote to me from Leeds saying in my piece on tourists I declare that none come to this part of Paris. 'A few months ago I was in the rue Mr & I saw a guide pointing out to a crowd of blue-rinsed matrons the home of Miss Nan Mitford the famous American lady writer.' I suppose Jessica & Nancy rolled into one equals Nan. Oh how I screamed!

About Benjy & Virgin Isles, Susan just think back. Between Xmas with Muv & Farve or glam: new friends in S of France which wld ONE have chosen?

Love
    Soo

Why does he think I'm against Mrs M[ossiker]? On the contrary I am FOR & I long for the book because one always loves reading about what one knows already, for some reason!

To JOY LAW   7 rue Monsieur, VII
29 November 1965

Dear Joy,

As one always likes to blame others for one's own shortcomings I blame on my parents, for not educating me, my utter inability to keep notes. I work in a welter of books on the floor all round me, write, generally in English, straight into the MS. & then of course can't always find the source. In self defence I must add that my eyes are already strained to their full extent & if I had to make notes, as well as look up *and* write, it might finish them.

I *can't* write in moderation, have to plunge on at full gallop you see. (Parents again, NO DISCIPLINE.)

C'est comme ça.

Why *was* she called Anne of Austria? I've never discovered. Does Miss Clephane[1] know? Simply because she was of the house of Austria via Philip II I suppose, but Marie-Thérèse was never called that. I see that Erlanger in his long & excellent *Louis XIV*[2] (just appeared) doesn't explain.

Why historical figures are called this or that is often a puzzle. For instance *why* the Empress Frederick? You never hear of the Empress Franz-Joseph or the Emp: Leopold.

Love
    N

[1] Irene Clephane; writer, translator and expert indexer.
[2] Philippe Erlanger, *Louis XIV* (1965).

To Raymond Mortimer   7 rue Monsieur, VII
21 January 1966

Darling Raymond,

The Group.[1] Some think the funniness is unintentional & I would love to, since I really loathe Mary Mc & am jealous. But I fear not. For instance she explains how Americans don't house-train their children so that their drawing room sofas are generally sopping (often covered with sopping fur). One character takes her baby to visit a much richer grander friend – baby left with the servants – noises are heard off – friend goes out of the room & comes back saying 'Stephen shat'. It's full of such gems & a description of the sexual act which makes you gasp for breath with laughing. It seems if a man intends to go on with an affair (he loves me he loves me not) *the great sign* is that he allows you to leave your douche in his bathroom. Oh it's too lovely.

Yes *our* Moors Scandal[2] (only black-a-moors, not fells) is enthralling. I've just met at luncheon, at last, a human member of our embassy, a great charmer, press attaché – must find out his name. He said one can't follow the affaire under 2½ hours a day – I said it gets them from me. Briefly, it's the whole story of secret services in the full horror of their idiocy. Gaston says at one time he used to get their reports every morning on his desk & nobody would believe the dottiness of their goings-on. Ever since the events of North Africa, French & Moorish police have been hand in glove & scratching each other's backs – what an odd mix: of mets: – as, Mr Press Attaché says, ours are hand in glove with the police of our ex Arab protectorates.

Luckily Ben Barka was no doubt a frightful villain himself so one can enjoy the whole thing without minding about the victim. But I fear it may be a great bore for our friends who have still got estates in Morocco. Jokes abound as you may imagine. What a pity you're not here.

Now it seems the British teams in the Monte Carlo Rally have been cheating like hell. Honestly – first our bridge experts & now our drivers – only, just as the bridge experts were Hungarians so the drivers are Finns. Ay di me – how typical of the times.

That poor little boy (Rodd)[3] I knew nothing until your letter – then Press Attaché told me (he is half Italian & knows the Rodds) & then I saw that super crook (for whom I have a slight weakness) Dominick Elwes in the street & he told me. He says that Saul was driven mad by people wanting him to have a job – no doubt this would drive D. himself mad! Anyway I didn't know him so I'm not upset except for the horror of it. He hanged himself. OH! Must quickly write to Peter.

I think that's all your queries. Keep me informed of progress. Dolly, as well as bed, was given *calcium*.[4]

Much love
    N

Dolly is living in Troyat's *Tolstoy* & will lend –

[1] Mary McCarthy, *The Group* (1963).
[2] The French 'Moors Scandal' involved the kidnapping in October 1965 of Ben Barka, leader of the Moroccan opposition; his body was never found and the responsibility for his disappearance never clearly established. In England, Ian Brady and Myra Hindley had been accused of murdering three children, whose bodies were found buried on the West Yorkshire moors.
[3] Saul Rodd (1933–66). Son of Gustaf and Yvonne Rodd, and Peter's nephew.
[4] Raymond Mortimer was suffering from sciatica.

To Duchess of Devonshire   7 rue Monsieur, VII
4 March 1966

Dear Miss
    . . . A letter from Gerry [Wellington] which made me scream aloud. It's a sort of poem on the passing of Bromo & now of an Army & Navy substitute for it. The wicker basket containing the strong supple sheets, held in place by a paper weight engraved at the Pontifical Mosaic Factory with the family arms, has been, according to him, superseded by the Roll. 'My grandson Charles tells me they even have the Roll at Chatsworth, though it reposes in the mahogany box & there is not yet the final degradation of the wall fitting.' Oh dear me, yes, I hate it too. Here one can still buy sheets *but they are pale blue*. I was able to tell him that in my bathroom at C-worth there is still paper as well as roll but probably this comes from some ancient store.

I wish you had cart horses instead of those dwarfs.[1] Here the last Dobbins who used to pull the ice carts are condemned to death unless somebody rescues them. As it's in all the papers I guess somebody will. Their *faces* oh well, we know. All the stable hands in floods – even the tough journalists shaken with sobs.

Just heard, by mistake, an English lesson on French wireless. Attention please. Teacher *has* a little dog (not has got). The little dog is eating his soup. How unlikely. *Attention please* – what can it mean? Shall I write up? Utterly useless. Ay di me.

I see this letter is nothing but complaints how boring. There's really no news. So long.

Love
    N

---

[1] Deborah had a stud of Shetland ponies.

To Sir Hugh Jackson   7 rue Monsieur, VII
4 April 1966

Dear Sir Hugh

It's an age since we wrote. They are still printing my wretched book & have been for months & now I see another one on the same subject is coming out in April – it's all too boring, that will make three with Erlanger's deplorable effort which has been hailed here as one of the twenty *greatest books on history*. I really think the French have gone mad, but of course I can't say so except to you or they'll think it's sour grapes. . . .

I think the world is getting horrider more & more quickly. I intend to buy a house in Versailles when I find one & lead the life of an ostrich there. My dear Mme Costa has died aged 92 so no more Fontaines alas – & I can't always live in a town, not even Paris. At Versailles one can stump about the park – even go riding there – & get a little fresh air. They've done up all the rooms in the château now & it's like a very expensive hotel. Can't say that to anybody but you either! Give me that great crumbling fairy palace I used to love so much! Anyway they can't spoil the outside.

I spent a night in London the other day, first for two years, & nearly died of it. I only went in order to get a Briggs umbrella – well that has already come to pieces. £10. No comment.

How are you?

Yrs
    Nancy Mitford

To Laura Waugh   7 rue Monsieur, VII
11 April 1966

Oh Laura I am so miserable.[1] I loved Evelyn I really think the best
of all my friends, & then such an old friend, such a part of my life.
As for you, what *can* one say? If I feel like that about him what must
his loss mean to you?

And then the public loss is so great – he was far the best living
writer of English without a doubt.

For him, one can only say he did hate the modern world, which
does not become more liveable every day. (It is always my consolation
for the death of my brother Tom, how much he would have hated it.)

I *absolutely forbid* you to answer – I know you don't like writing
letters & you will receive millions – but I had to send you a word.

   Much love from
      Nancy

[1] Evelyn Waugh died on 10 April.

To Duchess of Devonshire   7 rue Monsieur, VII
12 April 1966

Dear Miss

I'm most fearfully upset about Evelyn. I heard it on the Fr: wireless
in the night (which I'd turned on for the Joanna which of course I'm
loving every minute of) went to sleep, was half asleep anyway, &
woke up thinking I'd had a horrid dream that E was dead. Oh alas. I
believe of all my friends I really loved him most. *The Times* was
completely perfect, wasn't it.[1] I wonder who'll *do* me (always back to
no: 1).[2] Victor was in the middle of it when he died, I guess E's was
Anthony Powell. . . .

A funny old friend of mine called Lucy Norton lives with an old maid
at Oakwood Court where they had, in the flat below, the same as
Honks Coo.[3] So I urged her to put a chain on her door which she has
done, saying at any rate it will keep out the Nuns who push their
way in & ask for money – I always refuse *on religious grounds* (my
underlining) & when at last I've got rid of them they go down in the
lift *smugly praying for my soul*.

Evelyn. In his last letter he said 'Honks Cooper thinks I'm dying.'
I must ask her why – was he supposed to be very unwell? But he
seems to have gone to Church.

I shall take Colonel & Mogens to see the house & unless they are really too discouraging oi boi – unless I've dropped dead before, pace Emma (who will expect it more than ever now). . . .

Much love
        N

[1] Christopher Sykes's long obituary began: 'Waugh was essentially an artist in prose. In an age where care for the exact word, for the form of a sentence and for good grammar are all too rare, Waugh set himself from the first a high standard of writing.' It concluded: 'Though continually complaining of boredom and disliking any crush of acquaintances he remained deeply devoted to a select circle of friends, to whom he was always the most generous and amusing of hosts.' *The Times*, 11 April 1966.
[2] Raymond Mortimer was to write the obituary of Nancy in *The Times*.
[3] Lady Diana Cooper's London house had been broken into by masked men who tied her up and stole her valuables.

To Jessica Treuhaft   Lismore Castle
4 May 1966   Co Waterford

Darling Sooze

Yes I'm in despair about Evelyn – he was such a close friend & I suppose knew more about me than anybody. I think he was v. miserable in the modern world. It killed Théophile Gautier in 1871[1] (& may well end by killing me). I'm burying my head in the sand & have bought a house at Versailles in which to moulder until I fall down dead as Debo's children confidently expect me to at any minute. I said to Emma why did Clare (Toby's aunt) die? Well, Aunt Natch, she was 60.

Is the District Attorney the man who puts the rope round your neck while puffing a huge cigar? Well done Susan.[2]

I don't know when we shall see Louis-Louis – it's being printed now. But as soon as there are copies you'll get one. . . . The book seems to be second or alternative B of the Month in America for Sept, which pleases the publisher and probably facilitates distribution. . . .

A fan (sort of, not very enthusiastic) letter from America ends: How many Mitfords are still writing? They must be getting along in years now. Too true.

Love
        Susan

Rudkin's[3] father has died so he's gone off to put him (one hopes) in a Mitford. Do you get 10%? That's the on dit in Paris.

¹ In fact he died in 1872.
² Robert Treuhaft was running for election as District Attorney.
³ Mark Rudkin, an American who occupied a small apartment above Nancy in the rue
Monsieur. When she moved to Versailles he took over her flat.

To ANTHONY POWELL   7 rue Monsiéur, VII
28 May 1966

Dearest Tony

French publishers! I give up. Poor old Mr Rainbird my owner can't
make them take my next with pictures (part of its point – not coffee
table but profusely illustrated) though they will take it as a book with
no pictures at almost the same selling price. Hardly to be credited.
The booksellers shrug their shoulders in despair. I only mention this
to show the general dottiness. In your case I think you only need wait
& see – with your prestige somebody is bound to play sooner or later.
The more I see of translations the more I wonder whether such
writers as you ought to allow them at all – they are practically total
betrayal in my view – the palest shadow of the original emerges.

I mind passionately about Evelyn. I see that he is one of the people
I have most loved in my life – perhaps one only realizes that when
death intervenes. I shall always miss him. All these blows make one's
own end more supportable, there is that to be said.

Do be in Venice in July. I arrive there the 2nd & stay about 5
weeks. Telephone 20498 – chez Contessa Cicogna.

I've bought a small house at Versailles & hope to move there before
Christmas with any luck.

    Love to you both
        Nancy

To DUCHESS OF DEVONSHIRE   7 rue Monsieur, VII
1 June 1966

Dear Miss

The Embassy. I don't know if you ever saw it in Cynthia's time?
She had decorated it too beautifully, with the people from the Louvre,
found which bits of furniture went where in the days of Pauline
[Borghese], etc. Now, modern airport furniture, modern pictures, of
dripping entrails, yards & yards of them, covering those huge walls.
The charming room where Wid was born has dark *red* & *black* wallpaper, paintwork black & green. Child! I dined there, Reillys¹ away,

with Cynthia who naughtily showed all. It's as though Chatsworth had been re decorated by a dentist from New York. There was a dinner party (Cynthia told me) for the Gladwyns – everybody very smart & jolly & the menu was the following: tinned soup, BAD chicken, definitely the poisonous sort nourished with fish meal, I forget the pudding but it was awful & when somebody asked for sugar the butler said O.K. The dinner I had there was what you would expect at an English vicarage really but the meat was quite good. Tinned soup with macaroni letters you know A Z Q R D floating in it & tinned peas. MISS.

May I have Emma's address? Her sweet little friends lunched here & Arabella Churchill, Charles de Bagneux, John MacDermot,[2] son of the Minister & gt nephew of Frank's & John Raymond who arrived sober but *scarred* oh dear as Honks says that's what they come here for! It was awfully jolly. Arabella has got the EYES, thus *proving* that Clemmie is the daughter of Grandfather but she is a bit of a pin head & in my view not a real beauty. Awfully giggly & nice. The whole thing went pretty well, but the English & foreigners *are* oil & water & I think one shouldn't try to mix them really. MacDermot is very nice indeed & clever I think – he & Arabella chatted throughout while I struggled to make John Raymond talk French which Emma's friends prefer.

I was so tired after it I was fixed for the rest of the day – hardly able even to read a book.

Tomorrow is Colonel's party. I'm going with Xiana [Brandolini] & Mogens & possibly Derek [Jackson] though one is told he has gone to Geneva to be married. I do hope Woman won't mind. Much agony & ex: about what to wear – I'm all right if it's fine & done for if not.

Must flee now.

Love

O[ld] F[rench] L[ady] W[riter]

[1] Sir Patrick Reilly (1909–). Ambassador in Paris 1965–8. Married to Rachel Sykes in 1938.
[2] John MacDermot (1947–). Son of Niall MacDermot, Labour MP and Financial Secretary to the Treasury 1964–7.

To Duchess of Devonshire   23 Dorsoduro
23 July 1966   Venice

Dear Miss

Oh dear I'm afraid it's cool in the North & that always spoils the fun by making one feel guilty.

The Wrightsmans are here on the biggest yacht I ever saw, with a bar & such rubbish. Old Chourlie began taunting about the Bri-ish & I said yes & I'm very sorry to see that Wall St is decidedly shaky & he said he sold *all* his shares exactly when I did which makes me feel less of an idiot than Rich Ron thinks I am. Interesting. Charlie says we treated our poor people too badly for too long – I was rather furious but afterwards I thought of Asthall where there was water & electric light in the stables but not the cottages – servants' bedrooms in London houses & so on & wondered if there's something in what he says, though I don't see why that should stop them working now, quite. A French person said the other day it's more comfortable living in a country which has had its revolution.

Funny about Charlie. He is universally loathed & he is the only Yank I *rather like*. In his mail he found a letter from his French chef what he calls 'resigning' because he wants to educate his kids in France. He is completely stunned by this – why, the kids could have become American! He, the cook, used to be the head chef at the Elysée & the General sent him away & had nothing but army cooks as an economy. Charlie said I would fall off my chair if I knew what he pays him but I dare say I wouldn't you know, my nerves are rather strong.

He was on about doctors being so wonderful & I said funny thing one can't help noticing how all one's friends keep dying & he said I was telling him. . . .

That's all – an interim report on Chourlie.

Love
    N

A letter from Prof: Ross. He says the middle classes now think it is rude for one man to call another by his surname.

To DUCHESS OF DEVONSHIRE   23 Dorsoduro
28 July 1966   Venice

Dear Miss

Could Andrew bring my ill fated umbrella? T'would be the action of a saint. . . .

I spent yester shopping & bought at Roberta the same dress in navy blue as last year's in red. For some reason I liked that dress better than any I've had for years – so soft & comfortable. £40 with cardigan, not bad!

Mme Stehlin,[1] the ladylike French woman, hates me. Hatred breathes from her. Brando went down to the flat below, where she is staying with Guido's tenant, on some pretext & said what do you think of Mrs Rodd? Elle n'est pas commode[2] was the answer – on further probing it seems she fears I will put her in a book. 'Ow pretentious says Brando, I said I'm never afraid of that, I'm not interesting enough!

Much talk of the deep freeze duchesses baying for their tiaras in 50 years' time.[3] So to amuse Alf [Clary] on a wet day I told him (think of his voice please) 'It's not possible.' 'Why?' 'No. It's not possible because you see there's the SOUL.' 'Might it not come back?' 'No. You know if you weigh a person just before he dies & again just after, he is much lighter.' 'Do you mean the soul is heavy?' 'Yes. It is very *heavy.*'

Tell heirling[4] he ought to come for the Max Ernst exhibition. Even I think it marvellous. The wet days led to much sight seeing so were not wasted.

I sat next to Charlie Wrightsman 4 meals running. Now they have gone. I asked him what changed him from a polo playing tycoon into an art collector & it was seeing a Louis XV commode. He said I've spent 8 million dollars on objects of art.

To the beach – hurray.

N

[1] Anne-Marie Schob; married to General Paul Stehlin (1907–75). Head of the French delegation to NATO 1960–63.
[2] She's not easy.
[3] The newspapers were full of talk about cryogenics, the theory that it might one day be possible to preserve people in a state of suspended animation at a very low temperature.
[4] 'I always think what a mercy not to have children but now I see Sto [Peregrine Hartington] I'm not so sure . . . Perhaps I will leave him *everything.* He's the only one (nephew) I feel like this about.' (NM to Duchess of Devonshire, 10 September 1964)

To Sir Hugh Jackson   23 Dorsoduro
4 August 1966   Venice

Dear Sir Hugh

I'm still here for another week, my enjoyment distinctly modified by a total extinction de voix. Having struggled away for several days of huge luncheon & dinner parties I have now collapsed into my bed – a bore for everybody. The funny thing is, however chatty people

are by nature, if you can't put in a word here & there they dry up.
The town is full of amusing people – a French general called Stehlin
who was intimate with Goering before the war & sent home accounts
of the full extent of Nazi rearmament which of course nobody read –
Mary McCarthy – Isaiah Berlin[1] – John Sparrow[2] as well as all my
delightful Italian friends, it's really annoying to miss it all. The doctor
thinks he will get me vocal again in a day or two – let's hope!

I'm reading a life of Goethe, roughly translated from German into
American. I see that after Tolstoy he was the nastiest living person
– I wonder why geniuses have to be so horrible. I expect the writer
of this very poor book misses a good deal of the point – one could
make Voltaire unrelievedly horrible I suppose by not really understanding him. As I don't know German I daresay I shall never get
under the skin of Goethe & must take his genius for granted.

Fifty-two years now from the outbreak of war which I well remember. I really think the world of today is worse not better? & getting
worse all the time? If on top of all, there is to be black ruin the outlook
is poor. A Frenchman said to me there is much to be said for living
in a country which has had its revolution. Yes but we are always told
we have had ours, bloodlessly & painlessly – perhaps in fact the
tumbrils are ahead! Certainly Mr Wilson seems more powerful every
day in England & more slavish in America. C'est à ne rien comprendre.
I shall bury my head like an ostrich at Versailles.

I hope you will receive the book very soon now. It is full of misprints
which are not my fault & of mistakes which are, so that I quite dread
what the critics will say. You must be truthful. Don't write before the
20th Aug: as I shall be on the move & letters get lost when two
million people are displaced! After that, rue Mr.

Yrs
     Nancy Mitford

[1] Isaiah Berlin (1909–). Philosopher and author, Fellow of All Souls College, and President of Wolfson College, Oxford 1966–75. Knighted in 1957.
[2] John Sparrow (1906–92). Warden of All Souls College, Oxford, 1952–77.

To Sir William Hayter   7 rue Monsieur, VII
19 September 1966

My dear William
    Your letter! I know I've had good reviews, can't complain, but there
is always the odd young man who says what's the point of telling all

this rubbish we know by heart anyway, sowing DOUBT in my mind. Such praise, from you, dispels it at once. Mr Silvers, who edits that excellent *NY Review of Books*, has very kindly written to warn me he is obliged to print a savage attack by one Behrens,[1] a historian from Cambridge. I shall now read Mr Behrens with your letter in the other hand like a talisman.

As for your book,[2] I long for it. I thought of you when I got a letter from Russia (only from an English pal) with a *fox terrier* on the stamp – one of those old fashioned dogs which look as if they are made of pipe cleaners. So beautifully unsuitable but somehow typical.

I'm very busy indeed setting up a little house I have bought at Versailles. Hope to be in before Christmas – but I can't really go away until after the move. It's a house without any interesting features, but old, sunny, full of light & dead quiet, big garden & I think, by the time I've practically rebuilt it, will be very pretty. The rents in Paris are going up to more than I can afford & only millionaires now can have houses here with gardens. I think Versailles is a good solution for me.

Once I have moved I shall leave Marie to find her feet there & go to England. I'll warn you in good time.

Thank you again for writing – love to both
  Nancy

Ava [Waverley]: Can I dine with you on Tuesday, Nancy & can I pay you in pounds? What an odd suggestion! I haven't heard its like since we used to leave 3/6 on Sibyl's mantelpiece.[3]

[1] Catherine 'Betty' Abigail Behrens (1905–89). Fellow of Newnham College, Cambridge.
[2] *The Kremlin and the Embassy* (1966).
[3] At Sibyl Colefax's 'Ordinaries', guests were invited but paid for themselves. 'I hear Ldy Colefax has people to dinner every Tuesday & charges 3/6 or 6/6 with wine. How very disagreeable that must be – do you suppose the butler hands a plate like in Church (a bag would be fatal in *our* set) . . . Saw Gladwyn. He says the Colefax guests leave their money on the mantelpiece having filled in a card to say how many liqueurs etc they have had. The squalor!' (NM to Violet Hammersley, 29 November 1939)

TO SIR HUGH JACKSON   7 rue Monsieur, VII
29 October 1966

Dear Sir Hugh

I love: poverty is a never-ceasing little plague. It must be far worse when one has been enormously rich like the Clarys, but they never mention it & take things like standing for an hour in a bus with a lot of steaming peasants (as we did once on some outing from Venice in pouring rain) absolutely as a matter of course. The French workman turned up with the diamonds[1] (which no doubt they sold as badly as possible) but an American ambassador *literally stole* a dinner service given to Clary's ancestor by Marie-Antoinette – an awful story. They had entrusted it to him.

Talking of words. Don't you hate 'he ordered him shot'. I continually see that. Also the current use of *this. This* I believe instead of I think so, etc. There is a dreadful middle European infiltration now which no doubt comes from American Jews. The wireless does nothing for the English language &, like poverty, is a never-ceasing little plague. We were strictly brought up not to say very pleased – very interested. I see it everywhere. Le style est l'homme. The fact is that if people can be bothered to talk & write properly they get their reward *not from the critics* but from the public. I'm sure a well written book lives longer than a badly written one of the same interest. Certainly everybody listens to Gen de Gaulle, even if they loathe his policy, for the sake of the marvellous French – & the English language was Winston's great weapon no doubt.

Oh yes & don't you hate we don't have any, instead of we haven't got any. I hear it everywhere. As for pronunciation n'en parlons pas. Even Prince Philip sometimes offends. One of my bugbears is lornch for launch[2] & unfortunately it's a word continually used by the little plague with reference to those silly Americans & their method of wasting money.

Yes my house at Versailles is half-way (about 7 minutes walk) between the two stations to St Lazare & les Invalides. I haven't got a motor (I don't have a car) & will go up & down in the train which is now much quicker & far more peaceful. Fancy you having been at the same family as Winston! At that time various English boys went to a Mme Passy at the Désert de Retz. I wrote about the Désert once & received quite a lot of letters from retired generals & judges who had been there. . . .

Yrs ever
    Nancy Mitford

[1] Before escaping from Czechoslovakia in 1945, Princess Clary put her jewels in a brown paper parcel and gave them to her Belgian valet. Against all odds, he managed to deliver them safely to Prince Clary's sister in Brussels. They were not sold.
[2] Like many of her generation Nancy pronounced the word 'larnch', just as she pronounced laundry 'larndry'.

To Mark Ogilvie-Grant   7 rue Monsieur, VII
28 November 1966
my birthday – one more step
towards THE END

Gentle

If I sounded a little bit put out it was because I wasn't expecting ye – at least I thought there would be a warning bell – & was appalled to think not only was no fatted calf choking out its little life but that I actually had to lunch with my Italian friends & leave ye – *so so* much unlike the treatment I receive at Athens.

You were thought very faithful to come to Versailles. Funny you shld say 10 times Kew Green – I always think that is about the increase in everything. Prod & I lived quite comfortably with always one & sometimes two servants on £500 a year which went down to £300 in the war. We had a car, a biggish house, went abroad & so on. When we had P.G.s one year in Naples we made them pay £2 a week & on that we got a first class cook, two or three maids & took Sigrid with us from England! Wine galore, I well remember. I wonder why ye were not there – Robert & Poor Sweet were. . . .

I hear a stork is nesting at Covent Garden to the general amazement. *What can this portend?*

Harold [Acton], writing about *Sun King*, takes exception to the word Sodomite which, he says, reminds him of Mr Odom & the Bishop of Sodor & Man. I asked what I ought to call the adherents of that cult & he says metallists. All right – so long as one knows. . . .

Much love
    O.L.

. . .

To Jessica Treuhaft   7 rue Monsieur, VII
28 November 1966

Susan

This *lovely* weighing-in paper. You are a saint to send *N. Yorker* wh I had not seen. Old Mr Canfield sends from mags called Illinois Mass. & things like that which none but the Illinois masses have ever heard of I should think & which cheatingly copy the observations of the Pasadena Chronicle or the Massachusetts Illustrated. He writes occasionally, gloating over the fact that he has sold half the number of copies printed in Sweden. Id[1] wouldn't care for *him* as a publisher.

Well the book cases left the Isle about a month ago – Mrs McF wrote to say so & I sent her a small present which she duly cashed I note in my bank statement but did not thank for. Since then, silence de glace. As a matter of fact the longer they take the better it suits me as the house is a total mess for the moment. I went down unannounced yesterday (Sunday) & the men were all there working. I said you are wonderful – they said we are a bit behind, thought we'd better catch up. You wouldn't find English workmen doing that I fancy. They think I'll be in next month however – indeed only the painting now remains to be done. Exciting.

Somebody said you were caught bugging (what *is* bugging? I didn't like to ask) the students of an American university. Susan – think of poor MUV. I said, oh she's capable of anything. Too true.

I've made friends with Mary McCarthy at least my hate has turned to love but her hate may not have but I am wooing her. Not with a view to *actual bugging* though.

Fond love
   Soo

[1] Ann Farrer, Nancy's first cousin, had just published an account of her struggle with mental illness, *If Hopes Were Dupes*, under the pseudonym Catherine York.

1967–1968

VERSAILLES

Have you been to Versailles yet, it is my
spiritual home & at this time of the year is the
most divinely melancholy place in the world.
NM to Thomas Mitford, 16 October 1928

For some years Nancy had been anxious to buy a house of her own. The lease of the flat in rue Monsieur had become precarious and her rent was rising steadily. Moreover, even though she liked to scorn country life, her desire to move out of Paris runs like a leitmotif through her letters, and as early as 1949 she was complaining to Evelyn Waugh, 'I long & long to live quietly in Provence & not always feel over-done', but 'it's the Colonel who stops me'. Now that the Colonel was only an occasional visitor or a voice at the end of the telephone Nancy saw no reason to remain in Paris. Many of her friends, however, worried that a move to Versailles would cut her off from the way of life that suited her so well. Friends in Paris would be less eager to lunch or dine with her if they had to drive for forty minutes there and back, her English friends passing through would be unlikely to drop in, and she would see even less of the Colonel than she did already. But like all Nancy's decisions, once her mind was made up she never questioned her resolve and insisted that her life would go on much as before.

The house she chose was small and unremarkable, but for Nancy its charm was the sunlight that flooded through it at all times of day, and the garden. She transformed its suburban neatness into a wilderness of cottage flowers and derived enormous pleasure from watching poppies and cornflowers struggle up between the weeds.

4, RUE D'ARTOIS
78. VERSAILLES
T 950-59-16
MONTREUIL

30 Ap 68

Dear Sir Hugh

Your poem! I laughed so much that I upset the coffee — then I read it over the telephone to my sister who said between gasps of laughter does he realize he could go to prison for that? What a lovely trial; you would be the hero of the British race & nation.

I love Frederick he is everything I like, brave, funny, no nonsense, marvellous taste, common sense, interested in everything. He had a sad life because by the time he was 50 all the people he loved had died & also he knew quite well that his nephew was no good. Have you heard

To Sir Hugh Jackson, 30 April 1968

Her social life slowed down only marginally; she continued to give successful lunch and dinner parties and to have English friends to stay. From time to time she took the train up to Paris to see the Colonel and he came to visit her. For two years she was very contented.

In the summer of 1968 she started to work on her last biography, a life of the Prussian king, Frederick the Great, whose mocking and cynical nature naturally appealed to her: 'He is everything I like, brave, funny, no nonsense, marvellous taste, common sense, interested in everything.'

To Christopher Sykes   4 rue d'Artois
[January 1967]   78 Versailles

Darling Chris

I knew Evelyn first (before Diana) & that was *after Decline & Fall*.
I was the greatest friend of Evelyn Gardner & when they married I
stayed with them at Canonbury Square. Then E went away to write
Vile Bodies & I stayed to keep her company, then she ran away &
then he sort of fell in love with Diana who was pregnant – all described
I think in *Work Suspended* (which I haven't got here).[1]

Yes he always helped with my books & invented the title of *P of
Love*.

I'm very *bad* at reading out something I've written – my voice falls
away & I become bored and boring. The best for me is to answer
questions, not too much prepared. Perhaps if that can't be arranged
you could say NM tells me – something like that?

Diana is in South Africa – her address: Coppers, 55 Bath Avenue,
Rosebank, Johannesburg.

There. I'm at your entire disposition. If you could see me now your
heart would bleed – je suis dans un désordre indescriptible.[2] BUT not
one single object lost or even scratched during the so-much-dreaded
move. I can hardly believe it. They load everything onto a sort of
platform which then rises to the level of one's windows through which
the objects gently float! No more lugging on the staircase. You don't
even have to empty the drawers & cupboards.

    Much love
       Nancy

[1] Christopher Sykes was preparing a broadcast on Waugh in which both Nancy and
Diana took part.
[2] I'm in an indescribable muddle.

To Sir Hugh Jackson   4 rue d'Artois
29 January 1967   Versailles

Dear Sir Hugh

Yes the Fr movers are extraordinary. They even kept the little
heap of pennies under my big clock, to balance it, & put them back
in the same place & started it again. The system is, *everything* is
wrapped up, however small, & every book separately & all the furniture from top to toe. Then they load the things at street level onto a
platform which rises to the level of the rooms & the things float in

through the windows – none of that wrestling on the stairs. It took three whole days & I haven't got so very much furniture. They even make your beds & would probably cook your dinner if you asked them. They were so adorable – we parted in silence & tears & ENORMOUS tips. The high spot was when old Marie said, must I give my valise to the men? Well, Marie, I'm giving mine. Frantic whisper: there's a thousand pounds in it. So we took a taxi. Isn't that France all over! I said I suppose it's in a stocking? & she said yes it is. I wish you could see this vast heiress! . . .

We have had the treat here of Mrs Kennedy's effusions to an American journalist. Can't quite see our Queen carrying on like that – she seems to be the one absolutely perfect element in England now.

I wonder if you ever read the letters of the Stanley of Alderley family which I edited before the war. Hamilton is going to republish them so I've been reading them – goodness they are amusing – I'd quite forgotten. Such a picture of a naughty Victorian husband & his neglected huge family (12 children, 8 survivors). As so often seems to happen, I believe there is now only one male heir. My grandfather Redesdale had 5 sons & there is no heir at all.[1] I must get a new peerage but oh! the price!

I seem to have rambled on rather boringly – will try & do better next time.

Mr Brown[2] said to our ambassadress[3] you've got neither the looks nor the personality to represent England in Paris. And he's *quite right*, for once.

Yrs
    Nancy Mitford

[1] In fact Nancy's grandfather's fifth son produced a son, Clement, who became 5th Baron Redesdale. His son, born on 18 July 1967, inherited the title on the death of his father in 1991.
[2] George Brown (1914–85). Labour MP for Belper. Secretary of State for Foreign Affairs 1966–8.
[3] Lady Reilly. Brown's wounding remarks found their way into the British press.

To Sir Hugh Jackson   4 rue d'Artois
19 March 1967   Versailles

Dear Sir Hugh
    Of course I screamed with laughter at what you sent me. But doesn't it seem mad, with the example of America before our eyes,

to import all these poor blacks & create a racialism which has never existed in England! . . .

Have you ever read E F Benson's Lucia books? They used to make my joy – now Heinemann's are reprinting them & they are funnier than ever. I'm doing an article on them for the *Sunday Times*.

I lunched with van der Kemp, the curator of Versailles. He has got Colbert's splendid flat in the palace; a rich American wife has done it up & they entertain le tout Paris very well & amusingly. What's more important to me, he sent me workmen to hang my pictures which they did too beautifully (counting prints I've got about 60 & could never have done it myself) & now they come on their free day to dig in the garden – a service which is impossible to get in Paris. Indeed life here is far easier than there, in every way & half the price. I'm thankful to have moved – never did a more sensible thing.

Those dreadful Gauls tried to unseat our good General. I've got a television now, really in order to see the politicians & I can tell you Mitterrand,[1] who is a brilliant demagogue, makes one's flesh creep. When I first lived here he was regarded as a slightly sinister joke but now I think he's worse than that. I saw Edelman[2] who had been with him & who gathered that he too would oppose our entry into the CM. Hope Edelman will publish that. I don't believe any French people want us, that's the awful truth.

I must get back to Lucia.

Yrs ever
    Nancy Mitford

[1] François Mitterrand (1916–). President of the Federation of Democratic and Socialist Left 1965–8. Elected President of France in 1981.
[2] Maurice Edelman (1911–75). Author and journalist. Labour MP for Coventry North 1950–74. A committed Francophile and well-known figure in Continental politics.

To Duchess of Devonshire   Adria Hotel
21 April 1967   London, SW7

Oh Miss. Two nights here & off in 10 minutes & I've filled a life time. Aunt Ween & Emma, as well as rewriting *P of Love*.[1] Item: Enter Uncle Matthew (drawing room) carrying a gun, six stoats & a dog fox. Really rather a shame to alter it! I took out 3 large wheel barrow loads of references to Lords, Debrett & ladies & generally cleaned it up & it may not be too bad but I have misgivings. I asked about the actors. Fabrice is a mature Continental type, can't wait to tell the

Col. (A journalist said to me who is G. Palewski & why did you dedicate your book to him? I said a Frenchman I knew in the war who gave me a hand with street names & so on.) . . .

Love
N

[1] The musical version played to Bristol audiences in May 1967, but a cool reception from the critics meant that the money could not be raised to take it to London.

To Gaston Palewski   23 Dorsoduro
20 July 1967   Venice

Dear Good

Are you all right? I think the post is a bit odd, but no letter at all. Do take up the rusty pin.

Same as usual here, only hotter which suits me. I begin to live when the Italians go on about *Infernale*. The Wrightsmans have come & gone & with them a lady who owns & edits *Newsweek* & *Washington Post*.[1] She said French public opinion is solid against the Gen. I said how do you know? She said for one thing 5 ministers went to the 4 July party at the Bohlens. I said when ministers are against a policy they show it by resigning not by going to cocktail parties. Ghastly fool I nearly added. She's now gone off to see Tito who will presumably trot out the usual dope.

I've been reading *The Ring & the Book*.[2] I suppose you have – wonderful. Also a book (not Eckerman) of conversations with Goethe.

The Brandos & Fulco [Verdura] come next week.

Marina [Luling] has been here she looks ill & sad & I worry about her. Anna Maria does I'm sure though she says nothing – she is also very miserable about her Tripoli house which she regards as gone.[3] All are bellicose & Jewish – Marina wears the star in diamonds made by Fulco! How strange; one always hears nobody wants war any more & yet the moment there is a smell of one everybody wants it ex: the General who is conspué [decried] by all for wanting to stop it. I keep out of the conversations or might get angry.

Do manifest
N

I return 14 August.

[1] Katharine Graham (1917–). President of the Washington Post Co.
[2] By Robert Browning (1868).
[3] As a result of the six-day Arab-Israeli war in June 1967.

To Viscountess Mersey   4 rue d'Artois
7 October 1967   Versailles

Darling Wife

I hear you are far from well & *under* (such a curious usage) some
great doctor. Oh I'm so sorry & hope that the old quack will soon
have you on your feet again.

My sisters tell me you are not a practical gardener – I mean it's
no good asking you to advise on when to put in aconites. It seems
that your forte is to stand on a hillock & direct about fifty men, skilled,
to sow things in acres or to cover forests with white morning glory.
What I need is a deep talk with Link[1] about rose disease how disgusting.

I've just heard on the wireless that there's no point in writing books
any more because the electric brain can do it better. I'm all for it so
long as I don't have to read the Brain's effusions, don't feel they are
made for me. Also last night on télé we had a day in the life of a
Soviet writer oh dear v. different from a day in the life of a French
Lady Writer. A Soviet writer is allowed two rooms *as well as* a kitchen
but he seems to spend his whole time either on the telephone or
running to publishers' offices, one never saw a sign of a pen. He's
allowed a fortnight's holiday every year – holiday from phoning I suppose. Oh yes the ghastly thing is, all the S.W.s live in the same block
of flats.

Well, as I'm not a S.W. I must get back to work.

Much love & do tell your progress with a chart if possible I love
charts.

        O F L W

[1] Bert Link was head gardener at Chatsworth 1939–78.

To Gaston Palewski   4 rue d'Artois
8 October 1967   Versailles

Oh dear Col do telephone – I'm really frantic for news & Pauline
doesn't seem to know very much except that you've got a torticolis
[stiff neck] which is such a beastly thing.

No news here – I see nobody at all on acc/ of Frederick[1] whom I
love more & more. I plainly understand why he has such a bad press
– it's the English at their tricks again. George II & his ministers
loathed him – the cause of the House of Austria is presented as the

Cause of Freedom!! & so on. The English are marvellous propagandists, we see that now! Still Fred was a twisty customer no doubt.

A letter from Raymond who has read Chips [Channon]'s diaries. He says they are terrible, so stupid & snobbish – he wonders that Paul Channon, who doesn't need the cash (to put it mildly) could have allowed them to be published. But Paul Channon whom I saw the other day thinks they are S-Simon un point c'est tout.[2]

Hoping for a favourable reply I remain your Excellency's humble & obedient servant.

[1] Nancy had started work on her last book, *Frederick the Great* (1970). 'The best book I've ever written & next to *King Solomon's Mines*, ever read.' (NM to Raymond Mortimer, 18 August 1969)
[2] And that's that.

To GASTON PALEWSKI   Bramfield Hall
18 November 1967   Halesworth
         Suffolk

Good Colonel

It was so nice to hear your voice yesterday – I worry about you. Ava is going to send you some anti anti-biotic medicine. Everybody sends love & sympathy. *'I know.'*

This is the Gladwyns' pretty house – no party so it's very restful, which I needed.

Stoker rang up for your address naughty boy to thank for your lovely present, which he adores but you know what children are like when faced with writing letters; I think it reminds them of lessons. I said so how are you, dear one? I'm having that well-known thing called conjugal bliss. So Mrs Yes-no Poultry's god daughter[1] seems to be turning up trumps, oh good.

Everybody is on about Chips's diary – you can't think how vile & spiteful & *silly* it is. I'm thankful only to be mentioned as having sat next him at dinner – you are in the index as J-P Palewski & when one turns to the page there you aren't. It's edited, by a moron, like that. Horrible about the Gen: 'crossed the road so as not to shake hands with him; everybody loathes de Gaulle'. One always thought Chips was rather a dear, but he was *black* inside how sinister! Of course Diana Coo upholds the book. 'If it's so bad why are you all talking about it?' I suppose the answer is anything sooner than talk about the £.

All love, dear Good
   N

¹ Amanda Heywood-Lonsdale married the Marquess of Hartington on 28 June 1967. Her French godmother was called Madame Esnault-Pelterie.

To Duchess of Devonshire   4 rue d'Artois
4 February 1968   Versailles

Dear Miss

Mrs Green, of the *Observer*, telephones. Will I write an article on Love? No. Can Mrs Green of the *Ob:* come & interview me about Love? All right. Mrs Green came yesterday, apparently aged 14, with short crumpled skirt, fat white knees & when she sat, short, fat, white thighs. Incredibly sweet. Well it seems all the young people in England are *in despair* about Love & Mrs Green described this despair so vividly with such a wealth of realism & detail that I soon saw she too was in despair. She says they all talk non stop about WHAT WENT WRONG? For hours & hours about W W W? I said but how do they have time – I thought they all had jobs? It seems jobs don't take ones mind off it, W W W, one scrap. She said when you're old do you stop falling in love? I said certainly *not* & pointed to Emerald, Princesse Mathilde, Mme du Deffand, all rising 90 & suffering martyrdoms. At this she literally welled. Oh dear. She was so nice. I don't believe French people go in for all this weltering emotion but I may be wrong. Mme du D never fell in love at all until over 60 & blind – Psse Mathilde certainly had a steady most of her life but the fuss began when she was past 70. We talked for hours – what will the result be! Luckily it is to appear in *Ob:* coloured sup: which nobody sees.¹ I asked her if she knew Emma – I always think those people with thighs must all know each other but evidently not. I greatly recommend Mrs Green though I fear suicide may claim her before one's friendship can ripen.

May you come, when others are in Positano. Yes what *will* they do of an evening? Honks holds out faint hopes that you may. Come with Alvee in a car – I've told her she must bring one or it will be W W W with a vengeance.

Do you know it costs 1/9 every time I write – 2/3 if on this paper. What *would* Mrs Ham have said! But I had to unburden about Mrs Green.

There is an insect horse in the town, selling lavender. A literal & valuable looking insect. Come.

Love
    N

Sitting in bed in boiling sun oh the bliss. When do I expect Honks?

[1] The interview with Maureen Green appeared in the *Observer* colour supplement, 28 April 1968. Nancy is quoted as saying: 'To fall in love you have to be in the state of mind for it to take, like a disease. You have to be very much wanting it, expecting it. Then if you see anyone and he is at all attractive you are ready to start all the strange imaginings, ready to run around indulging all his most selfish whims. You imagine he has such extraordinary qualities and at the same time you do know partly that he can't be quite like that in reality. There are always these two feelings together . . . Your emotional life is in an arid state; there is a vacuum which must be filled, willy nilly. It is delightful and very painful. Delightful at the beginning, less so later on . . . Romantic love, after all, is totally unrealistic; it's a dream, wholly subjective. People fall in love with the most extraordinary people.'

To Valentine Lawford   4 rue d'Artois
23 February 1968   Versailles

My dear Nicholas

May I *really* sometimes consult you about Frederick? You see I took him on, without knowing German, because practically all the sources are in French – nevertheless it is a handicap. The definitive Life, by Koser, doesn't seem to have been translated – however there are several French books, by honest 19th cent: historians, which owe everything, & say so, to Koser. So one has the facts at one's disposition – for his nature one has his letters & works, Voltaire's letters & so on. The great puzzle is the homosexuality which simply is not mentioned by such as Lavisse – skimmed over with groans by Carlyle & probably who knows bowdlerized out of F's letters by the editors. (I sent for Algarotti's letters to Ld Hervey – they are all about TRADE very odd & interesting but surely some tender passages must have been removed?) Of course Voltaire roundly says that F was a sodomite but V always had it in for him really after the final quarrel. The fact that there were no women at all at his court means nothing. Perhaps he was a eunuch, as has also been suggested; nobody ever saw him naked. One wld like some proof & there really as far as I can see isn't any, either way.

I've got such an interesting pamphlet, issued by the Royal Medical Society called *Porphyria, A Royal Malady*.[1] It seems that Mary Q of Scots had it & many of her descendants including Fred: & Frederick-William &, of course, Geo III. It's really our old friend *veiners* – the symptom is fearful irritability caused by unbearable pain which, since it can't be explained, has hitherto been regarded as imaginary or hysterical. Perhaps Voltaire suffered from it too.

You are kind about Katte's burial place[2] – yes I would like to know

if really not a trouble & esp: if there is some sort of monument
one could photograph. I'm going to Germany on 24 Aug: to look for
illustrations & see the sites – incl: of course Bayreuth & Dresden.

I shall divide the book like this: Frederick-William, Voltaire (to
include all the artistic side of F), Maria-Theresa & Old Age – four
parts into which his life falls quite naturally as it happens – they hardly
over-lap at all.

I think if I could bring off this book & if it had the same enormous
public as *The Sun King*, it might do a little good from a European
point of view. English people regard F the G as a sort of Hitler I
believe.

The Thirty Years War – I shall call you Father Courage, it's the
bravest thing I ever heard.[3]

Oh dear the *NY Review* has become unreadable so now where does
one turn for literary criticism?

Yrs
    Nancy

[1] Porphyria, a hereditary disease, was diagnosed by Dr Ida McAlpine and Dr Richard
Hunter. In sufferers the body manufactures too many porphyrins, the pigments responsible for the red colour of blood.
[2] Valentine Lawford had offered to ask the descendants of Hans Hermann von Katte,
Frederick the Great's friend who was executed on the King's orders in 1730, for any
documents they might have.
[3] Lawford's lifelong (unfulfilled) ambition was to write a history of the Thirty Years
War.

To Valentine Lawford   4 rue d'Artois
2 March 1968   Versailles

My dear Nicholas

I say *you are a saint*! I feel I've been as tiresome as a pen pusher
who wrote last week to ask me if I would tell him all I know about
sanitation under L XV – & if not by return of post, to his secretary,
as he will be away – for a book on Casanova! Honestly! Nothing like
making others do one's work. But it is lovely for me to be able to
chat on the subject.

Personally I don't believe much of what Wilhelmina[1] says – though
one must admit that some of her tallest tales are corroborated by
honest Guy Dickens & Sauveterre the Fr amb. For instance I'm sure
she fancied Katte herself.

The death of Katte, recounted by eye witnesses, never comes out the same twice. Did Frederick actually see it? I think not. Everybody at Küstrin was on his side & did what they could to make it less horrible. I think poor Katte was quite convinced that it was all play acting & he wld get off at the last moment (like in *Tosca*).

I know everything has to come back to complexes but I don't think F loved his mother or hated his father enough for him to have had an Oedipus. Of course everything to do with homosexuality was deeply buried away in the 19th cent (did you read the book about J. A. Symonds?[2] It's *so* funny) & I've got an awful feeling that as soon as my book has appeared, burning love-letters, like those of Voltaire to his niece – which I got only just in time – will come to light & down all my theories. I feel that question A is not in his case truly interesting because I don't think he ever *loved* anybody and that whether or not he fondled pretty young officers after breakfast is really immaterial. He was gai comme un pinson[3] only 6 weeks after the death of Katte. 'Erotic undertones' (Wilhelmina) may well be a literary convention. They adored each other as children, much less when first grown up & again towards the end of her life. Frau von Wreech appeared after a gloomy year of no civilized contacts & he tried out his poetic talents on her – another literary affair I think. Barberini seems to have been sheer play-acting. (I have to write on this vile paper because the P.O. is shut for two days & everything else has to be weighed.)

Fredersdorf certainly seems the most interesting relationship one knows of. When I've got a bit further forward I'd be too grateful for translations of one or two letters you regard as telling – & the originals for the German edition. I haven't begun yet on the correspondence & am aimlessly ambling about in byways such as a huge life of Milord Maréchal (Keith). I suppose he was the greatest friend of F's maturity – no nonsense there you'd think – but he never had a woman in his life exc: one of those vague Turkish ladies, more like a daughter (or a paravent [screen]?)

Goodness F must have been funny – that's why I love him so much. The jokes are perfect.

What you say about Horst is very interesting.[4] The illustrations or rather the question of a photographer is theoretically out of my hands but in fact they do listen to me. It would be so marvellous to have somebody who understands what it's all about. They sent me a dotty little Italian for *The Sun King* who did things like parking his car in front of the Bernini statue before snapping 'to give scale'. Honestly. We could hardly use any of his work in the end & I think it taught them a lesson. If you are in London in the Spring & Horst had time

he might go & see my picture lady the géniale Mrs Law. Oh how I
hope for you here.

I've just taken time off to read Lytton S.[5] Rather wonderful &
terrible how *all* can now be said.

With many more thanks for your notes, carefully filed away.

Yrs
     Nancy

I've got until July '69, hope it will come out the next year, '70 (autumn).

[1] Wilhelmina of Prussia (1709–58). Frederick's sister.
[2] Phyllis Grosskurth, *John Addington Symonds* (1964). 'Couldn't put it down. Things
like "if I come & stay I must bring an old peasant without whom I find it difficult to
travel" – the old peasant being a dazzling gondolier of 30 called Angelo.' (NM to Mark
Ogilvie-Grant, 19 January 1968)
[3] Happy as a lark.
[4] Lawford had told Nancy that his companion, the photographer Horst who still owned
a family home in East Germany, had offered to help with illustrations for her book.
[5] Michael Holroyd, *Lytton Strachey* (2 vols, 1967–8).

To Jessica Treuhaft   4 rue d'Artois
8 March 1968   Versailles

Darling Sooze
    Alas, I must get on with Fritz or how I would have loved Mexico.
He is a vast subject because he lived to be so old & what to leave
out is a worry. Your bolshie friend in Berlin, if one could persuade
him to take an interest, might be a real life-line.

    Soo you would have screamed. It seems I signed a thing in *The
Times* saying I would help any American who is anti the war. So Dot
Head, who also signed, wrote & said would I help an American
deserter called Wagner. Well of course I'd forgotten about signing (if
indeed I ever did) & said certainly not I hate deserters worse than
death. So now everybody is *furious* exc: yr. Hen [Deborah] who is
in fits of giggles over it. I think it may be some time before I'm invited
to sign anything else – oh good.

    Re the Change. I never had it. One fine day when I was a young
thing of 56 I had that boring & utterly pointless curse for the last time
& have never ceased being thankful. You know REST is everything
but I'm sure you don't put that into practice. If you're having a horrid
time it may well stop you from wanting to work – but I think the
desire comes *from working*. I mean I've been pegging away now for
months & only in the last week or two have begun to see a glimmer

& it's always like that with me. Makes it so hard because one is without real enthusiasm to carry one over the most difficult part. What subject have you got in mind?

Love to the piano tuner [Benjamin] & black Dinkie if you ever see them & also to the Hungarian Communist [Robert Treuhaft].

Sooze

To Duchess of Devonshire   4 rue d'Artois
9 April 1968   Versailles

Oh saintly 9, I'd forgotten that awful *personal*.[1] Roughly my song is this: the BBC ought to be for England what the Académie is for Fr, a guardian of the lingo. Now I must go at it with slightly kid gloves on acc/ of silly old U & non U. I say on the whole the *announcers* are good & when you turn on you know at once you are in England, not the U of America. I then go for the *guest* speakers (are they called that?) I say I don't think pronunciation matters much, it changes every 50 years or so, but I do mention the changes I have *noticed* (without saying they make me sick) & so far I've got INcrease, WestMINster, cabinut, Ufrica, countree. Host*ess* goes in, thanks; any more?

Then I absolutely go for the talkers – how they begin elaborate sentences wh they can't finish & flounder about with ums & ers; but I say the chief horror is over-emphasis. Instead of saying '*people aren't very nice about him*' he has to be '*undergoing character assassination*'. *This* is always used to emphasize: 'I think so' or even 'mm' becomes '*This I believe to be true*'. People don't *say*, they *claim*. *Nowadays* is *this day and age*. They don't *meet* or *think*, they *meet up* & *think up*. G. M. Young used to say let the English language take care of itself – meaning don't fuss – & that's what they won't do.

Then I tell how when writing a film script I used the word ineluctable – was told nobody wld know what it meant but, I said, I thought people now are educated – if they don't know it they can go home & look it up. Pitying smiles were all I got. That's why I want you to tell one or two examples from the new Bible if at your finger tips. Then I shall say nobody except experts on the 16th cent: understands every word of Shakespeare & yet people flock to his plays. Oh yes – glad to note that Sir A. D[ouglas]-H[ome] says Asiatic, & end by saying Mr Alvarly Dell[2] still pronounces English as I'm accustomed to hearing it. V careful not to say right or wrong but just what old Rip van Winkle used to hear.

That vile tree is about to perform I note (pink plastic). You can't think how marvellous my weeds in the grass are going to be – daisies galore, huge thistles, poppies already quite big & cornflowers ditto, wall flowers & the little children's dower & forget me nots passim; while we live on dandelion salad. This garden is so satisfactory, when you sow a seed you reap like mad.

A friend of Wife's wrote (signed Ursula Wyndham[3]) & I had to spend a valuable ¼ hour looking *up* to see whether Miss Mrs or the Hon (oh the work people give one) to ask a historical question. Why not go to the London Library & find out, I don't write to experts every time I want to know some detail. Then I was quite cross & only answered for the sake of Saint Mersey. Will you tell her I've found out that she is descended from Colbert now that is quite something & I wish I was.

Best love
    N

Also going to say (*Listener*) how hopeless women are in public life – the only two anybody has ever heard of are those hereditary rulers the Queen & Mme Gandhi.

[1] Nancy was writing an article on what she thought about modern-day English language. It was published in the *Listener*, 16 May 1968.
[2] Alvar Liddell; wartime newscaster. The stress fell on the last syllable of his surname, hence Nancy's transcription.
[3] Hon. Ursula Wyndham (1913–). Author of two volumes of autobiography, *Astride the Wall* (1988) and *Laughter and the Love of Friends* (1989).

To Heywood Hill   4 rue d'Artois
10 April 1968   Versailles

My dear Heywood

I knew of Lady Cranbrook's[1] death too late, I thought, to write. Also I think those letters (except from those who have been intimate with the dead person, which are often very welcome) are the greatest bore on earth. Give my love to Anne. You will miss Lady C, I know.

I'm awfully excited for your visit. I work non stop, hardly go to Paris & see nobody exc: the regulars so I shall welcome a spot of English gossip. Frederick amuses me to death he is so clever, funny & wicked.

Violet Tre: telephoned could she come to tea? No I shan't be here I said, very politely – Could she come tomorrow? Then I saw red &

said Violet what is all this about? It's now two years since you wrote saying I was vile & how right Rose Macaulay had been to loathe me & we haven't spoken since. Why do you suddenly want to come to tea? V., rather confused: I'm sorry if I have given offence. N. You haven't given offence you have given me an excuse. Goodbye. She is *so awful* about me according to all my friends, even the moderate Cohen,[2] that I don't feel guilty but it was temper that took over. It's years since I've really lost it, I'd forgotten the feeling. But over *jam* I easily might owing to my great passion for Frank Cooper's lovely product. . . .

I'm writing an article for the *Listener* on the change in the Eng language since Rip van W came to live here. I'm being very careful only to say change without implying for the worse. . . . Can you think of any horrors, if so do put them on a P.C. I know I shall have dreadful esprit d'escalier when the copy has gone in. There is also what I call the basic mentality of reducing everything for the uneducated to understand, but why since people now are educated? Do send a thought or two. They're giving me lots of time.

Best love
   Nancy

Oh Lytton. We must have a long gander on that (this).

[1] Heywood Hill's mother-in-law.
[2] Geoffrey Gilmour. 'You know about Geoffrey being Cohen, I suppose it comes from Jefferson. If he ever finds out we are going to say it's short for Kohnor, don't know how to spell, you know the gem.' (NM to Mark Ogilvie-Grant, 25 April 1966)

To Duchess of Devonshire   4 rue d'Artois
17 May 1968   Versailles

Dear Miss
   Of course one always lives on a volcano here[1] it's part of the charm. Then one can't help seeing the point of these poor little things – the dullness & ugliness of daily life. One of their cries is down with concrete – hear hear, but do they also mean down with Chatsworth? I daresay this civilization is breaking up & no great loss either – though no doubt ONE will be most uncomfortable. . . .
   I suppose there is going to be general paralysis here – Marie heard the postman saying Tout va changer & already he comes about an hour late with all the neighbours' letters instead of mine. Ay di me. However keep on writing in the hope. So far I think they've all arrived

including more boring fans than ever; very soon I shall have to stop answering.

Sir Hugh [Jackson] says our gaols are stuffed with murderers & robbers having a lovely time & *he* would like to see them at the tread mill, a gaoler with a whip to keep them lively. Honks says he must be a relation of another Jackson we know.[2]

The wireless is going on strike so we shan't know what's happening until the Jacquerie arrive. I wonder if Honks can get back. Can't help slightly enjoying the excitement though I know it's wrong.

Love
   N

[1] France was in the grip of a students' uprising and the threat of a general strike.
[2] Derek Jackson attended a meeting of important scientific advisers during the war, at a time when a strike was threatened in the aircraft industry. Jackson asked what the country's position was with regard to lead supplies. The puzzled answer was 'Very good, why?' 'Well,' said Jackson, 'put it in the whips to whip the workers.'

To Sir Hugh Jackson   4 rue d'Artois
26 June 1968   Versailles

Dear Sir Hugh
    Letters are whizzing again now.
    I wrote a day to day diary of the *évènements* which came out in the *Spectator*[1] – they still haven't sent me copies – if they ever do I will try & let you have them. As I telephoned the copy to them (it took 1½ hrs each time & nearly killed me) I know it will be full of boring misprints, also I had to leave the punctuation to the editor; all the same I think it gives an idea of what life was like down here. I would have loved to have seen the riots but couldn't move from here as all transport was at a standstill & I haven't got a motor. There seems to have been much more shouting than fighting & the police were simply wonderful, so patient & good. Luckily we have got a first class préfet de police.
    I can tell you, it's very alarming to live through an attempted Communist take-over. The workers were terrorized by faceless unknown Communist agents. THEY. The whole thing had been organized down to the smallest detail & when THEY decreed the strike, the workers, who knew that whereas, if they obeyed, the General would do nothing to them if he won, THEY, if they did not obey, would have some horrid revenge, felt they had no choice. 'Some man from St Cyr came

& told me I must stop work.' The General's timing was perfect; he had the courage to let the thing go from bad to worse until everybody could see for themselves the truth of the situation & then, at exactly the right moment he put a stop to it. If he had acted sooner we should have been told there never was any plot, all invented by him. Now I think everything will be all right except that the economy has had a nasty jolt. They say it will take 18 months to recover but I've often noticed that French economy is resilient.

Yes why is everybody Harold nowadays? Such a horrid name.

I'm off for my summer travels – Greece, Venice & Potsdam. It seems that the Germans were much better informed than our police here & had sent two warnings to the Govt which they simply did not believe.

Address in Venice 23 Dorsoduro. I'll be there on 16 July.

Yrs ever
    Nancy Mitford

[1] 'France, May 1968: A Revolution Diary', 31 May 1968, and 'A French Revolution Diary', 7 June 1968.

To Gaston Palewski   23 Dorsoduro
19 August 1968   Venice

Dearest

I leave here 25th – home 5 September & no address really in between.

There's a lot to criticize in *Pompadour*[1] but on the whole I'm satisfied with it. The print of the text is so good for one thing & there are hardly any misprints in that. Nothing perfect my Uncle Tommy used to say – so true. I hope to have a nice lot of *devises* [foreign currency] to lay at the feet of the General.

Have you begun *The Eustace Diamonds*?[2] I see Anne Rosse as Lizzie to the life – Hinchinbroke[3] as Lord Fawn & many another resemblance – I'm sure you will be reminded of old colonial days in London. . . .

I've read Harold N's vol III[4] now. It is dreadful when he becomes old, so poignantly sad, & he does so very soon. When only my age he begins to feel a weakening of mental power & physical stamina. Ld Salisbury was here & said Harold was such a good back-bencher but when he got into the Govt he was in a permanent state of terror & quite hopeless.

People come & go here it is an amusing procession – often people I've known well & never see now. Philip Hardwicke[5] was here & amazed them all by his Col Blimp exterior, clever talk & the fact that he knows Andy Robilant.[6]

Later

I've just seen l'Allouette[7] the ambassador to Prague & he invites me to stay. Very kind indeed & perhaps I will. It's so kind I can't get over it & as a matter of fact I've got a letter from some Czech professor saying I must go there – I'm sure it's true & I've always wanted to see Prague anyway. What a kind man – he says write & tell me when you are coming.

I do hope you've got good weather at Trouville.

Letters take an age – I'll send this to Paris.

Love
    N

[1] *Madame de Pompadour* had been reissued with illustrations as a companion volume to *The Sun King*.

[2] By Anthony Trollope (1873).

[3] Viscount Hinchingbrooke (1906–). Eldest son of 9th Earl of Sandwich, he disclaimed the titles for life in 1964. Conservative MP 1941–62.

[4] *Diaries and Letters of Harold Nicolson* (1968), edited by Nigel Nicolson.

[5] 9th Earl of Hardwicke (1906–74).

[6] Count Andrea Nicolis di Robilant (1899–1977). Married Gabriella di Bosdari in 1920 and Alice Allen in 1937.

[7] Roger Lalouette; French Ambassador in Prague in the mid-sixties.

To Duchess of Devonshire   4 rue d'Artois
28 September 1968   Versailles

Dear Miss

. . . Well I dined at the Embassy,[1] their first dinner. Mary telephoned & I greeted her invitation with a volley of oaths saying no no, on no account & then suddenly thought it's too beastly so I went. I predict TOTAL SUCCESS. The effort is huge, she is so nice to everybody & as for him he cuts himself in 4 as the French say to be agreeable. Millions of footmen – though I did hear one say can I tempt you to a little sherry it's a fault on the right side because for 10 years now nobody has been tempted to anything there. They treated me like a precious bibelot & he said whenever you dine here in future you must stay the night. I explained that I do really prefer lunch &

indeed dinner parties kill me now. A daughter on the pretty side only with no nose AT ALL. The ghastly food lift is at least hidden behind a screen but Mary is in despair about it. Cynthia [Gladwyn] who was there said but we did quite well without one to wh Mary replied you should hear Gravitt (C's butler) on the subject! The company was Joxes, oh what are they called – the last Amb: in London & Raymond Aron[2] 12 in all. Good but not smashing food. The thing was the great friendliness. Mary looked very pretty in a rather matronly way. They have bought a weighing machine for him. She's only been to Patou so far, they'll be pleased. Cynthia is staying there & giving a hand I think.

Rather a sad letter from yr Hen [Jessica], talking of gloom. Oh dear is it Benjy? One doesn't like to enquire. She may come after Xmas. Anyway she has met Dot [Head] & of course they are twin souls, succouring deserters & the like. Dot complained of me & they had a nice disloyal talk about me.

So – really to report Embassy.

Much love
N

[1] Christopher Soames (1920–87) was the newly-appointed British Ambassador to France. Married in 1947 to Hon. Mary Spencer-Churchill, Winston Churchill's youngest daughter and a cousin of Nancy.
[2] Raymond Aron (1905–83). Author of *l'Opium des intellectuels* (1957) and *La Lutte des classes* (1964). Fellow student of Sartre at the Ecole Normale, he was the principal opponent of Marxist ideology after the war.

To Heywood Hill   4 rue d'Artois
24 October 1968   Versailles

My dear Heywood
    Terribly pleased with the photographs.
    I went to see Cohen yesterday back from some evidently *wild* London swinging – black eye – the works. He said it came from an operation: Opération Balançoire I guess. He & the Head Swinger were poisoned almost to death at the Dorchester – altogether he *has* been living dangerously. Of course one ought to note all his thoughts they are so lovely. . . .
    Handy's hairs. I turned on the Home Service the other day – you know how one has to translate what they say as one goes along – in plain English, an interviewer said why don't you like your art school? to which the young lady replied (now I am quoting): Because they

don't allow me to put REAL pubic hairs on my statues. Another day
I turned the knob & heard '. . . sores on the penis . . .' Heywood!
It would have killed my father who loved the wireless so much.

I went to sign *Le Roi-Soleil* at Gallimard's yesterday. Outside somebody had written à bas les éditeurs bourgeois so I told M. Gallimard
who said calmly I expect that's my son. They said the Eng: reviews
of the *Anti Mémoires*[1] have been *terrible* owing to political bias –
Hamilton is so upset he has gone to America. I never see Eng: papers
– were they so bad? I said how does Malraux take it? He laughs.

The great family excitement is the Apotheosis of Sir Os.[2] Did you
see *Panorama*? I long to know what it was like.

I'm really buried in work (Fred) have had to take an extra year so
it will come out in '71. On 4th Nov I go to Prague to stay with the
Fr: ambassador there, in aid of the book. I'll go to East Germany in
the Spring, with Pam & her car.

I'm so glad Cyprus was such a success – perhaps you'll do it every
year?

>   Love & to Anne
>   Nancy

. . .

[1] André Malraux, *Antimémoires* (1967). The memoirs of an ardent Gaullist, published
by Hamish Hamilton in 1968.
[2] Oswald Mosley had been interviewed on *Panorama* by James Mossman about his
autobiography, *My Life* (1968). The programme attracted 8½ million viewers, a record
for that time.

To Duchess of Devonshire   Palais Buquoy
6 November 1968   Prague

Dear Miss

I'm terribly glad I came. You never saw such a marvellous town –
I put it after Paris & Venice & only after Paris because I happen to
prefer French architecture. Miles before Leningrad. There are acres
& acres of marvels & every now & then you turn a corner & there
is a forest, a real one, not a public park.

The Russians are pathetic & vile. Dreadful stupid looking very
young dwarfs. The shop windows which would be a joke if not so sad
– tasteful displays of paper clips or plastic waste paper baskets –
simply fascinate the Conquerors, they stand glued. It seems they are
told 'see how these Czechs live, on YOUR money – Russia has been

subsidizing them for 20 years'. As nobody can speak Russian, or would speak to them if they could, everything is believed.

I've seen an incredible lot of people as well as things. Went to call on a Professor in Alphy's mother's house (Kinsky) 'I've got all the Clary archives in that cupboard.' 'Oh indeed!' All the foreigners here love the Czechs at least the ones I've seen do. Our Eng: amb: is a nice clever man who speaks Czech[1] so of course he is being replaced at Xmas by one who doesn't.

The general level of drabness tells the tale of 20 years of socialism, I suppose Mr Wilson hopes to make England like that, how strange. Everywhere Liberté (in French) is painted on the walls & photographs of Dubcek[2] among the paper clips. The embassies all have little lorries which go to a German market town for food – here there is nothing but red cabbages like in my garden. Smashing food in this house of course. The amb: goes out shooting a lot which it seems is marvellous – black with pheasants – & is an invisible export. You can shoot a bear for 4000 dollars. My plane was full of people with guns. Coming? With Lord Sefton? . . .

Love
    N

Everybody here so KIND. .

[1] Sir William Barker (1909–). Ambassador to Czechoslovakia 1966–8. He was replaced by Howard F. T. Smith.
[2] Alexander Dubček (1921–92). Popular President of Czechoslovakia who led the Prague Spring uprising against Soviet hegemony.

To Jessica Treuhaft   4 rue d'Artois
15 November 1968   Versailles

Darling Sooze

Prague fascinated me. It is too beautiful for words to describe & the Fr embassy, where I stayed, one of the prettiest houses I ever saw. I was shown everything of interest by a Prof: told off to lug me round. But oh dear it is sad. Russians everywhere, gazing into the shop windows, which are about on a level with Moreton in Marsh during the first war, as if they were in the rue de la Paix. Poor things, they are very small, very young & look as if they had never had a proper meal in their lives. Nobody can speak to them & my Prof, who is a Cudum [Communist], says their officers tell them that the

Czechs are lazy dogs who have been subsidized by USSR for 20 years 'Everything here belongs to you really'.

I'm exhausted, having had a young lady from *Sunday Ex:* for 3 solid hours interviewing me & I'm also nervous as I can't remember what I said. Interviews are the devil. I only accepted because I want to broadcast that I'm on Frederick, hoping to deter others. If it's funny I'll send but I expect it will only be shaming. She was an awfully nice young lady but unconscious I guess of what might embarrass ONE. The great thing they always ask is why do you live in France? You'd think they would see why, for themselves.[1] She's pregnant. I said is it your first baby? And she said the first successful one. I longed to probe but am too polite!

Have you noted all the carry-on about Sir Os? He says he was never anti semitic. Good Gracious! I quite love the old soul now but really –! Also I'm very cross with him for saying Tud [Tom Mitford] was a fascist which is untrue though of course Tud was a fearful old twister & probably was a fascist when with Diana. When with me he used to mock to any extent & he hated Sir Os no doubt about that. If Randolph had been alive he would have sprung to his defence. I miss Randolph.

That's all for now – to work.

Much love
    Soo

[1] 'What does she think of England now? "I don't like the rudeness, which is very, very strong now and which didn't exist before . . . I feel a hostility from people in England I hardly know, because they think I sound frightfully superior. Working class people there don't like my sort. They are very rude and very offensive. I prefer French gallantry."' Jillian Page, 'I can't write novels, now, says Nancy Mitford', *Sunday Express*, 24 November 1968.

TO PETER QUENNELL   4 rue d'Artois
30 December 1968   Versailles

My dear Peter
    I don't want to bore you but there is nobody here who takes the faintest interest in Fritz's sex life. It is such a puzzle to me. The story of the young officer after breakfast comes from Voltaire after the quarrel when nothing was bad enough for F, so it may or may not be true. But when you remember that homosexuality in those days was considered such a sin that it was punishable by the stake (in France)

it seems unlikely that someone so careful as F would have put himself in the power of any pretty young officer? I don't mean that he could have been had up but public opinion –

Katte, I suppose, was pretty certainly a love, but they were public school age so that means nothing (Katte's great nephew I probably told you has written to beg me not to perpetuate this monstrous libel).

Keyserling was his great & greatest friend for years – they used to be shut up together for hours on end & K not allowed to go near the window for fear of being seen. Yet, at the height of what you'd think was an affair, it was K who wrote to Algarotti saying come as quickly as you can (when F's father died). When Keyserling fell in love with a woman & married her F wrote 'he is not the first person who has had his head turned by love' – he gave fêtes & parties for the wedding & liked the lady very much. When K died two years later F was utterly heartbroken & cast down for months; did all he could to help the widow & orphan. I may be naïve but none of this seems to add up.

Algarotti lasted a very short time as a love, if he ever was one, though F liked his company & conversation. He had nothing to do with him for 5 years after A had written a cheeky letter – quite at the beginning of their friendship. This hardly looks like passion.

No women at the Court. But pederasts love women as a rule. I think it was because he couldn't stick the Queen & if there had been women it would have been too rude not to include her. At Rheinsberg, where there were women, he used to say that there could be no good conversation without them.

I think perhaps I fail to understand the nature of homosexuality – I am excessively normal myself & have never had the slightest leanings in that direction even as a child. My own feeling about F is that he was almost or quite sexless. I suppose Monty is – Napoleon was as sexless as a Corsican could be – these people are interested in power.

The thing is, shall I weigh the pros & cons as I see them or simply tell the story & let the reader deduce what he likes from it?

(Alphy [Clary] was on about you again in his last letter perhaps he's in love.)

The interest of a love affair lies in the changing nature of the relationship & if there is no evidence available how can one describe it? Allez-oop with young officers is really very dull.

Don't bother to answer. Dr Halsband[1] says he'll know more about Algarotti presently & impart.

Thanks for lovely card –

Happy 1969
N

---

[1] Robert Halsband, historian, author of *The Life of Lady Mary Wortley Montagu* (1958).

1969–1973

THE LAST YEARS

On 15th I've got an appointment with a
London dr & if he doesn't cure me I think I
will mettre fin a mes jours . . . because I can't
see the point – if it's a punishment I think
I've been punished enough.
NM to Raymond Mortimer, 1 October 1970

During the autumn of 1968 Nancy suffered from increasingly severe
pains in her back and legs. The doctors initially diagnosed sciatica but
when several weeks in bed failed to alleviate the pain they thought it
might be a spinal injury. In early March 1969 her general practitioner,
Dr Dumas, felt a lump in the region of her liver and insisted that she
undergo tests. Soon after Dumas's visit Gaston came to see Nancy
and she greeted him with a teasing: 'Colonel, I've got cancer.' The
Colonel felt unable to tell her the real reason for his visit: he had
intended to break the news of his forthcoming marriage. The next
day, however, he returned to tell her that he was engaged to Violette
de Talleyrand-Périgord with whom he had been in love for many
years. It cannot have been unexpected news for Nancy but it was no
doubt a cruel blow to her pride. Gaston had long indicated that he
could never marry her because she was divorced and a Protestant.
Yet so, too, was Violette. Nancy spoke of the marriage as though it
were of no importance, certainly not to her and not even really to the
Colonel, and on the surface little did change between them.

Nancy was operated on in April and the tumour in her liver was
found to be malignant. The surgeon told Diana and Deborah that
Nancy had three months to live and advised them not to tell her as

4 RUE D'ARTOIS
78000 VERSAILLES
950 59 16

29 March 73

Darling Clem

I've been meaning & meaning to write
now probably too late for Africa; I've been
desperately ill; they sent me back with steadily
worsening thrombosis saying it was nothing - I've been
in tortures (Louis XVIII but they laughed, horrid jokes, at
him) superimposed on the usual pain - imagine!
I live on pain killer. Now I've got a very nice
lady specialist since 3 days & feel rather more
hopeful - I'm obliged to have a nurse whom I
loathe - can't put foot to ground. I am was here -
simply angelic & did the dire things; it half killed me
that she had to but nurses aren't easy to find even at the
ghastly price they take   I once got out of bed -
skeleton that I am - Mme Guimont could hardly
get me in again I was really frightened its an
awful feeling (My bed is rather high) And oh the
pain!   The nurse I've got now is OK but an

To Lady Beit, 29 March 1973

it could only aggravate her condition. After the operation the pain disappeared but soon returned with a vengeance. Despite the doctor's prognosis, Nancy lived for another four years, most of the time in tormenting pain. The cause was a rare form of Hodgkin's disease, a cancer of the lymph cells, which in her case was rooted in the spine. The correct diagnosis was not made until 1973, by which time Nancy had suffered countless agonising tests and treatments both in Paris and in London. At the beginning of each new treatment her optimism and hopes were rekindled and sometimes there was a temporary amelioration. Despite constant pain and the debilitating effects of analgesics she managed to finish *Frederick the Great*, which under the circumstances was a triumph of will.

The burden of caring for Nancy fell to her sisters. As Diana lived near by she took charge, but Deborah was a regular visitor and Jessica came over from America. The sister whose presence Nancy most welcomed, however, was Pamela. Though they had never been very close – they corresponded infrequently and their interests rarely overlapped – in her illness Nancy treasured Pamela's unhurried nature, gentle humour and Zen-like tranquillity.

By 1970 she was no longer strong enough to write a book, and found distraction and relief in reading and in her correspondence. Over the last four years of her life she sent more than a thousand letters to her sisters and friends, in increasingly faint and shaky handwriting. Most are poignant accounts of the progress of her illness and make harrowing reading, yet they are remarkable for their coherence and lucidity and, above all, for the irrepressible humour and tenacious love of life which resurface whenever the pain subsides a little. A lifetime's refusal to yield to sadness gave her a fortitude which can only be described as noble.

To Sir Hugh Jackson   4 rue d'Artois
28 February 1969   Versailles

Dear Sir Hugh

I'm in bed with degradation of the spine whatever that is – falling
down like an old house I suppose. It is excessively painful but I am
stuffed with drugs & am able to work which is the main thing. Thought
I would write & ask what you feel about Soames[1] etc; (I listen a great
deal to the B.B.C. & heard that people love *The Forsyte Saga*[2] so
much now that Soames to most Eng: people only means S. Forsyte.
Oh can I really have heard it or is it my over-heated imagination?)

Of course one can't help rather loving it, the quarrel I mean, for
the entertainment value but it seems to me shameful &, far worse,
stupid. The English seen from over here have become so odd. For
instance I heard a Fellow of the Royal Society saying that the RS
hopes that very soon there will be a law by which, at a certain age,
people will count as legally dead, have all their money taken away &
be treated, quite kindly (he only said *quite*) as children. Also babies
must only be legally born 2 days after they leave the womb so that
during those days the dr can decide if they are worth keeping or
should be knocked on the head. Nice for the mothers! All this in a
loud, upper class for once, cheerful voice. He said the world will never
be a far better place until Christian ethics are forgotten. I think the
world was a *far* better place 40 years ago but I suppose I've got the
wrong end of the stick. Then the *words* they use on the wireless now
– I mean words one wouldn't mention to one's sister – are shouted
out, it's too disgusting. However all this keeps my spirits up & a
letter from you would send them soaring. So far I've resisted hospital
which the drs are on about & am in my own pretty room.

Yrs

    N.M.

[1] Christopher Soames had been accused by the French of leaking to *The Times* a
distorted account of a confidential meeting with de Gaulle in which he had outlined his
proposals for Britain and the Common Market.
[2] John Galsworthy's novels had been made into a popular television serial.

To Duchess of Devonshire   4 rue d'Artois
29 March 1969   Versailles

Dear Miss

    . . . Colonel (married)[1] has just been. He makes that face – 'it's all
too silly'. He's to go on living rue Bonaparte but oh Pauline has left &

that's too awful for him. I found him a nice soul & think & hope he is kind to her but of course I pity them both. He rushed to see Pauline's new home in Savoy with her granddaughter who has got a large village grocery, it sounds divine. No doubt she will *rule* as she always does.

Well I did the tests, it was like a horror-comic. No meal, but much worse, a large jug full of liquid was injected taking 10 minutes. The instruments looked as if they had been bought 2nd hand from Dr Cheatle's father. Then they kept on leaving me naked in pitch darkness which at first I thought was to reduce me to obedience but after a while I realized they were developing the photographs in a kitchen sink next door like children with a Brownie. Everybody completely *sweet* I need hardly say. The snaps have just arrived & lumpling is terrifying simply huge. I wonder if it's my twin brother (it has happened I believe) little old Lord Redesdale shrieking away. He might be an addition to rue d'Artois & Diana's dinner parties. I see him like Mr Ed [Sackville-West] with a white beard & a beret – hope he can cook.

The result of being pulled about rather is I felt awful today but better already. Honks came for the outing, wondair.

Love
    N

[1] Gaston Palewski married Violette de Talleyrand-Périgord (1915–) on 20 March, his sixty-eighth birthday, thus fulfilling his maxim: 'le mariage est une terre promise vers laquelle on se hâte lentement'. Recently divorced from Count James de Pourtalès, whom she had married in 1937, Violette had been a friend of Palewski and a rival of Nancy for many years. Through her mother Anna Gould, daughter of the American railway magnate Jason D. J. Gould, she was heiress to the magnificent 18th-century Château du Marais and to a large fortune; from her father she inherited the Prussian title of Duchess of Sagan.

To Alvilde Lees-Milne   4 rue d'Artois
1 April 1969   Versailles

Darling Alvee

Well the Col – I didn't tell you in my last letter as it was still a secret. It's an awfully odd story which I will recount sometime à vive voix. She's a sort of dead person, an anti-person, always very amiable but with no apparent reason for being on this earth. He's to go on living in the rue Bonaparte & the Marais at weekends.

My health drags on the same. I did all the tests & am now waiting to hear what is thought of them. If I can't go to Germany,[1] where Pam & I & Joy Law are to be the guests of the Communist government!!!

(screams, as all will be so furious) I shall die of disappointment that's all. It's now 5 weeks I've been in bed being a nuisance to everybody – though apart from that fact, none could mind less than I do. It's the pain I object to. The doctors never loom, they are far too busy injecting blood into the lunatics who kill & maim thousands every day on the roads. I said to Marie this morning how nice it was in old days when doctors used to look in to see how you were & she says even in her village where things were far from perfect the dr wld come along in his gig & see what was up. Oh gig oh isn't the world vile. Now you telephone & some horrid secretary says she will faire la commission. No doubt they think at one's age it's hardly worth bothering – but then they ought to finish you off. I'm told they do in England. I'm *so* sorry about yr servants, that is perhaps the worst. Kitty Mersey in same case has found a proper English couple – a real butler. Let's hope.

Much love
    N

[1] To visit Frederick the Great's palaces and battlefields.

TO VISCOUNTESS MERSEY   Clinique Georges Bizet
23 April 1969   29 rue de Chaillot
                                    Paris 16

Darling Wife

I'm in the most heavenly clinic with 3 star meals & nuns. Operation tomorrow, Marie plans to be in Church – admit the sweetness, also I feel like a King of olden times being prayed for by one's subjects.

Woman was wonderful. Somebody told me I ought to have a companion for my tortoise so she went out & got one: 'The excitement is intense – the tortoises are hand in glove –' She is *too perfect* when one isn't well, so quiet & then does all the things one wants without asking. She says she will come back when I leave here. As for Elle [Deborah] one can't help noticing that she only comes when there are wills in the wind – when I see that large black plastic bag & large, welling with croc tears, blue eyes I shall know I've had it. Saint [Diana] says she will be here throughout which is too good & holy. In short my sisters are perfect not that I doubted it.

So that's it.

Much love
    Lady

. . .

To Raymond Mortimer   4 rue d'Artois
6 May 1969   Versailles

Darling Raymond

I've just got home & found your letter. What I had was very odd – insupportable pain low down in back & leg – much time wasted on X rays of same – then my Paris doctor came down & made straight for my tummy where, in the region of the *waist*, he found a huge lump. More time had to go by with tests & X rays & I was in such fearful pain I once cried for 6 hours. I don't think the drs here like one to be in pain – they say it's very bad & tiring, but this was so terrific I suppose nothing but injections wld have stopped it. Anyway I was finally sawed (or sawn) in half like I forget which martyr & that pain went for ever & I hardly felt the operation's results, isn't it extraordinary that they can chop you up & you *feel nothing*. I didn't even know I had a tube until the surgeon came & took it out! The only vile thing was the goutte à goutte [drip] but I only had it once. I was in the most heavenly clinic with nuns, sun all day, 3 star food. The kindness of everybody. So in the end I really enjoyed myself though glad to be at home & in a SOFT bed.

I knew the Gen wld be beaten[1] (I always know by the neighbours) & I know why. There is a tax called Valeur ajoutée [VAT] which drives people literally mad – not paying it but doing the sum. (I hear you're going to have it in England – good luck to you.) Ever since this vile tax was invented people have been in vile tempers &, I wld like to say to the finance minister, so would you be if you had to spend every evening doing this incomprehensible *sum*. The carry-on of *la gauche* is as good as a play, over the nominations one often laughs out loud at the wireless. How ridiculous democracy is, I fear.

I was going to Potsdam next week as the guest of Herr Ulbricht – rather hoping for a grace & favour house at Sans Souci. Then Henri Lubomirski[2] (l'Abbé-Prince) was to take me to see the battlefields. Very hard to bear putting it off.

I took the Lundis[3] to the hospital. Of course I think Ste Beuve is a genius because he agrees with all I feel about Fred – indeed on several occasions he makes the same observations as me. Viz: that Fred: is a great French writer & historian; & a most extraordinarily good man. Besides so funny. We should have loved him.

Gaston's marriage is for those of riper years. Viz, no nonsense about living in the same house in Paris, he goes on rue Bonaparte. Nothing changed whatever in other words.

Mary (Soames) says of Coz: Clementine [Churchill] she is drearily struggling up the slope. I think that's so sad when one would really like to be off.

See you in July – oh good.

Love
       Nancy

The latest in Violet's running fight with the Brandos: she got a detective to find out if their title deeds are in order (of course not) & reported them to the gérant [manager]. They are stunned by her wickedness.[4]

[1] General de Gaulle resigned on 28 April after a referendum on regionalisation went against him.
[2] L'Abbé-Prince Henri Lubomirski (1905–86). A Jesuit priest and old friend of Nancy who lived at Kalisz in Poland.
[3] Charles-Augustin Sainte-Beuve, *Causeries du lundi*. Articles by the most famous 19th-century literary critic.
[4] Violet Trefusis occupied a wing of a house in the rue du Cherche-Midi where the Brandolinis lived.

To Cecil Beaton   4 rue d'Artois
14 May 1969   Versailles

Darling Kek

Thanks so much for writing. Oh the Reaper. I minded passionately about Mark[1] – I suppose he was my oldest intimate friend; he really knew all about me. The reason, so odd, is that he was the only young man my father liked & therefore one could invite him without the risk of his being shaken like a rat. I remember my father shaking Mervyn Clive[2] & saying: I'd sooner take a housemaid out shooting than you, *Lord Clive*.

Anna-Maria says so truly that it would be perfect if we could all go together, it's the piecemeal reaping that is so painful. I fear that we should, in that case, be obliged to leave with Poppy[3] – oh well, why not?

Much love
       Nancy

[1] Mark Ogilvie-Grant died on 13 February, after an operation for cancer of the oesophagus.
[2] Viscount Clive (1904–43). Eldest son of 4th Earl of Powis. A childhood friend of the Mitfords who was killed in the war.

³ Poppy Baring; married Peter Thursby in 1928. A smart lady often photographed in *The Tatler*.

To Theodore Besterman   4 rue d'Artois
6 July 1969   Versailles

My dear Theodore

Well I gulped it down in two days.¹ It is masterly & so fascinating. All this summer I've been reading the letters so really I knew the facts but even so I couldn't stop until I'd finished the book.

You are very unfair to Frederick but of course I knew you would be from the footnotes to the letters. Voltaire behaved *outrageously* in Berlin. But my view of the whole relationship is: it's a pity these two great men ever met. Their correspondence is beautiful but the physical propinquity brought out the very worst in them. My only criticism of your book is that you never see the scamp there was in Voltaire or perhaps you do see it & are too much afraid, if you allowed it to appear, of what the old wretch would say to you when you meet in the Elysian Fields? That's it Theodore – admit!

My love for him is more comprehensive than yours; I love the fiendish side & love much less all his *New Statesman*like nonsense (I don't mean Calas² & so on – I honour him for that).

You don't explain, what I've never understood, why was he suddenly allowed to go to Paris? Or, if never exiled at all, why did he suddenly think he could safely do so?

Very elegant of you to quote me in the text & I am deeply gratified.

How *could* you say that Fédéric is like Hitler? Honestly! Dishonestly – as you know very well.

Love from
    Nancy

. . . And millions of thanks for sending me the book.

¹ Theodore Besterman had sent Nancy his biography of Voltaire.
² Voltaire campaigned for the rehabilitation of Jean Calas, a Protestant merchant from Toulouse who was wrongfully accused, tortured and broken on the wheel for the murder of his eldest son. Three years after Calas's execution Voltaire succeeded in getting the verdict quashed.

To Peter Quennell   4 rue d'Artois
7 July 1969   Versailles

Dearest Peter

Thank you for your lovely letter. I think I'm on the mend at last but ever since Christmas I've been in bed in more or less degrees of anguish. Unable to work, but Fritz has been my constant companion. I've read most of what he wrote & the 100 volumes of Voltaire's letters which mercifully I bought (Besterman). I suppose F & V are the two most amusing people who ever lived & I really do know them. Like you, I love the 18th century more & more – practically everything has declined since then – & I loathe romanticism almost as much as Frederick did. Except, as you say, for darling Lord Byron, your new clientèle are a sad lot.

Now I've got Besterman's huge book on Voltaire. It is written with Voltaire himself considered as the only reliable source & without a scrap of fun. The old boy, if he reads it in the Elysian Fields, must be surprised at the way all his wickedness is not only justified but positively sanctified. It's odd how no writer (biographer) on Voltaire ever has a sense of humour – one can't understand such worship of the old villain by those whom the jokes pass by. Of course B has got his relationship with Frederick all wrong – he is absurdly unfair to F & compares him to Hitler. He is very chic with me & quotes me in the text. I wonder if you will review the book – Longmans. In spite of all I've said it is very fascinating.

It's going to be a great bore if the real historians discover the Secret of the Lady Writer[1] – viz: a special relationship with God. I envisage Sir George [Weidenfeld]'s annual or bi annual visit to the Wailing Wall armed with his Spring & Autumn lists, while Jamie [Hamilton] counters in the Kirk. Up to now, in my case, an occasional reminder to the Almighty has done the trick but of course if the whole thing becomes a business one will be out distanced. Candles are an awful price now. I wonder if Eliz: Longford employs a saint or if she formulates a direct demand. Ceci dit, I greatly enjoyed Antonia's book.

How I would love a nice long chat with you.

Love from
    Nancy

---

[1] Peter Quennell to NM: 'As you know, Antonia Fraser has brought off the greatest literary coup of the last few years; &, when I compare the sales of *Mary Queen of Scots* with those of *Alexander Pope*, I don't feel quite as glad as, no doubt, I should. But I was relieved to learn from her mother that the Longford family attribute their

success largely to the *Power of Prayer*! They were on their knees, whenever they could spare a moment, for several weeks before the book came out.' (2 July 1969)

To Brian Pearce[1]   4 rue d'Artois
17 September 1969   Versailles

Dear Mr Pearce

Thank you so much for your letter, post card & *Washington Sq.* When I have a bad day & can't work I long for reading matter as I'm a terribly quick reader. Yesterday *W. Sq.* saw me through. I love your preface. I suppose I'd read it before as I knew the story but of course it entranced me. My view about marrying for money is that people must have a reason for falling in love & that is often money, but doesn't prevent a marriage from being as happy as when founded on other reasons: sex, power & so on! I would like to have had a word with the doctor! But I think he was one of those fathers unable to bear the idea of his daughter marrying at all.

Misprints. I was thinking, while reading for Frederick, how old books never have them, they are among the wonders of progress. Partisan for artisan is rich. The worst is that the reader NEVER twigs.

    Yrs
        Nancy Mitford

Your eyes? Sometime do let me know how they are.

[1] Brian Pearce; author and translator. He had sent Nancy a copy of Henry James's *Washington Square*, for which he had written an introduction.

To Duchess of Devonshire   Savoy Hotel[1]
24 October 1969   Berlin

Dear Miss

Back in the West! This Berlin situation is so strange – East so quiet & poor, West so noisy & rich you feel a thousand miles away but when we looked on the map we are perhaps ¼ hour walk from the hotel we've left. I know I'd rather live in the East part, except of course for the terror. We loved all the people we saw but they were mostly museum folk, buried in their work & probably quite happy, but there is that sinister feeling always in iron curtain countries. People don't tell the truth, quite. Then an Englishman who has chosen the East, friend of Decca's, came to see me; I felt very sorry for him he looked *desperate*. When I said do you like it here he replied that he was fed up with his work & wld give anything to *travel*!!

You know, how *can* Decca go on believing in it all. I shall tell her, it's all right being a commy in our countries but wait until you are nabbed by the real thing! For 10 days we haven't moved without a policeman. I must say it suited me because I love being looked after & all plans made & the said policemen were so very friendly & jolly. Still it's a funny feeling. I thought we got pretty dirty looks, in our huge Russian cars, from the population. Anyway we had a perfectly wonderful time, no trouble was too much for our looker afterers & we got really fond of them. But how will they ever snap out of it? God knows. Checkpoint Charlie is *gruesome*.

Home on Sunday.

Love
    N

Haven't got Decca's address.

[1] Nancy was feeling well enough to make the postponed visit to Germany to collect material for *Frederick the Great*. She was accompanied by her sister Pamela, and Joy Law and her husband.

To Valentine Lawford   4 rue d'Artois
8 December 1969   Versailles

My dear Nicholas

Thank you very much for Fredersdorf. I have sent it to Mrs Law who does the illustrating & she will return it to you.

I'm not really on terms with [Alexis de] Redé so I think the snuff box will have to go, it's very sad as we are short of them. I can't remember why but we don't like each other & I feel unable to write. . . .

Redé had a ball on Friday & the next day the Brandolinis & Loewensteins[1] lunched here to tell. Four feet of snow came down in the morning & they arrived at 3.30. Anyway the ball. If Redé lived in England he would be in prison for race relations. The open courtyard was lined with naked niggers, bearing torches, who had to remain there all night. (One was seen putting on a cardigan but the slave driver had that off him in a jiffy!) Also there were naked black children on elephants. The slaves had their telephone numbers in luminous paint on the soles of their feet. It all sounds very old world – estimated cost, £30 000. Well worth it no doubt.

That's all the news. Have a Happy Christmas.

Love
  Nancy

[1] Prince Rupert Loewenstein (1933–). Merchant banker and financial adviser. Married Josephine Lowry-Corry in 1957.

To Raymond Mortimer   4 rue d'Artois
17 December 1969   Versailles

Darling Raymond

How can I ever thank? It's so so good of you. I obey blindly, though Prince Henry sounds so odd that even Carlyle, who calls Fred: Friedrich, calls him Prince Henri. Alas those know-alls at Rainbirds will crow – I said, we leave it to Mr Mortimer & that's that.[1]

I correct all day, over & over again & never fail to find some bévue [mistake], isn't writing difficult. So poss: some of your finds are already coped with.

Do you think Frederick so German? I see him as a purely 18th cent: character & in some ways so modern. It seems to me his reign, after FW's, is into a Watteau out of a Rembrandt. *Battles*. It is the sorrow of my life never to have been in one – I suppose a cavalry charge must be the nearest thing to heaven on this earth. When I was little I was so jealous of my gt. uncle for being killed in one (against the Boers – so wicked when I was a child & so wicked again now).

V. hard on my poor old dad that he died too soon – if murder had been allowed when he was in his prime our home would have been like the last act of *Othello* almost daily – it's a shame. Various characters, like Lloyd George, would soon have been dealt with, at least one of my aunts & innumerable neighbours. It *is* unfair.

I long for the 24th.

Much love
  N

[1] Raymond Mortimer had advised Nancy to anglicise French and German proper names.

To Duchess of Devonshire   4 rue d'Artois
8 January 1970   Versailles

Dear Miss

Pain killers. If one has a perpetual pain this is what happens. They
kill it. They also give you a headache, make you stupid & stop you
going to the loo. Then after about 4 hours the pain comes back & as
well you have got a headache & can't go to the loo & feel like death
as well as having the pain. What they are good for is something like
migraine which, when it's over is over. Do you see?

If I weren't afraid of it not working & permanently ruining my brain
what there is of it I would have tried to take an overdose of something
ages ago because I would much much sooner be dead than have this
awful pain all the time. However when I am stronger I will go to the
doctor who cured Vincent Labouret.[1] At present I am as weak as a
kitten & yesterday fainted & had to have brandy – I can't go to Paris
like that. . . .

By the way thank you for your kind & sympathetic letter. I should
add to this loud moan that I don't have the pain *all the time* but when
I've got it which I have now I think I do. Compris? The morning is
awful.

Tomorrow comes dear Mrs Law.

Woman has been so bad – like me she could only go to the bathroom
on all fours & unlike me has to go down a ladder to it. Oh misery.

Best love
    N

[1] A neighbour in Paris.

To Raymond Mortimer   4 rue d'Artois
16 February 1970   Versailles

Darling Raymond

This is only to unburden myself & requires no answer as I know
you are sur le départ.

Well, Hadfield[1] has flattened Monsieur's wig all right (you remember Mr would never wear a hat for fear of flattening his wig?) Anything
in my book the least bit idiosyncratic has been turned into High School
English, often involving hideous repetitions (in one case the words F
the Great appear 4 times in a single sentence). This is on the galleys
& I am enjoined to alter nothing. I am in a furious rage, I have put

back *all* & written to my agent & a snorter to Hadfield & a letter to *Les Isvestias* [*sic*] to warn Russian authors to think twice before choosing 'freedom'. Among many other horrors they have substituted Scottish for Scotch. My two Scotch grandmothers, Ld Macaulay & Carlyle never said anything but Scotch & I WON'T HAVE IT. I've asked A D Peters what I can do if they ignore my corrections – I suppose they will since I had already sternly said Top Copy (with *all* your corrections incorporated) was NOT to be touched. I'm in such a fantigue [*sic*] about it that all my aches & pains have come back – I said to Joy Law they are killing the *goose* that lays the golden egg. They can hardly deny that I do that!!

Oh *Wellington*[2] is wonderful. Unfortunately I've finished it, having read Waterloo four times. Of course can't help being on the side of Boney but oh what a lovely battle! And Boney was done for I suppose even if he had won it.

I've greatly cheered up having thought of a subject – Clemenceau.[3] What would you say to that? He's everything I like – a man of action + intellectual + joker & plenty of documentation (oh yes indeed!)

Much love – do admit about Hadfield – ghastly middle brow FOOL.

N

My sister Pam came into my room the other day saying our funny old cousin has died meaning B Russell!!!!

[1] John Hadfield; editorial director at George Rainbird. 'Hadders the Horrible . . . That vile middle brow ex High School Hadders.' (NM to Joy Law, 19 February 1970)
[2] Elizabeth Longford, *Years of the Sword* (1969).
[3] Georges Clemenceau (1841–1929). Founder of the Radical Socialist Party. French President 1909–11 and 1917–20. Nancy changed her mind: 'I don't think I can manage Clemenceau. It's the ponderousness of the 19th cent.' (NM to Raymond Mortimer, 8 April 1970) In any case she was too ill to contemplate beginning work on another book.

To VISCOUNTESS MERSEY   4 rue d'Artois
16 March 1970   Versailles

Darling Wife

A WONDER post this mg – all the loved ones – you, Alphy, Decca, Woman & Heywood Hill (whose letters you know, beat all for funniness) except the Ugly Duchess [Deborah] who has given one up. I'm reading Clemenceau's last effusions to his last love (he is 85) & he has got two old sisters he is fed up with about the age of me & Honks viz about 90: I suppose the U.D. writes about us to that horsey lady in the same terms: My sisters of whom I am tenderly fond, one dying of arthritis & the other dying of I forget what etc etc but one can't help noticing he never goes near them.

I would love to have my face ironed. Cecil B pointed out last time I saw him that it is a mass of wrinkles too true & I would love to say to Mme Guimont[1] just give un petit coup de fer à mon visage.[2] . . .

Cristiana Brandolini came in her new Dior it's a shriek I mean it *is* the dressing up box. Rust which used to be one's least favourite for the Spring when navy blue with touches of white used to be the note. Long charlady skirt, low boat shaped neck, not filled in with all the pearls of the east but a little brown silk bow round the bare neck. On the navel a hideous gem. I felt most fearfully dowdy, old Mlle Clemenceau to the last. The skirt is split, up to we know where of course. Boots.

On Sunday which is Hassan's[3] day off the gracious living of rue d'A collapses. The butter stays in silver paper for fear of dirtying a plate – I had cheese & brioche for lunch & was to make porridge for dinner shown by Woo. But I bought some milk in a sort of celluloid container *which I couldn't open* so I drove a nail into it upon which two great jets of milk burst forth like Moses smiting the rock, was it Moses? one into my eye the other on the floor neither in the jug. So when H appeared this morning with my brekker he got a warm welcome I can tell you. Hitherto on these dire Sabbaths I've had Woman exercising her genius you see. I think the note must be in future to forget about food & wait for Monday.

Do come soon.

Much love
　　N

No *I'm* not on 'Woman's Ar', it's the lady who came to put me on a record for the Blind just another affliction for them poor souls. I'm afraid the Women would think *me* very vieux jeu quite ignorant of V.D. etc.

[1] Nancy's cleaning lady.
[2] Just give my face a little iron.
[3] A young Moroccan cook who replaced Marie after her retirement in 1969.

To Raymond Mortimer   4 rue d'Artois
18 April 1970   Versailles

Darling Raymond

You mustn't blame the Fr: doctors *anent* (as Sir Hugh Jackson always says) pain killers. For months they have begged & implored me, sometimes in tears, to take them. My philosophy is this. (A) If we are sent a pain in the leg it must be for some reason unknown to us – if we dodge it the result might be bad in other ways. (B) I have got a little spot of grey matter & I don't want to spoil it with drugs or drink or anything else. My horror of drugs is the greatest of all my many prejudices.

The last week at the hosp. (I came back yesterday in an ambulance) was the most devilish I have ever known. I was cast on my back, no pillow, unable to write & almost unable to read, with, as fellow, the wife of a vigneron from Champagne.* She refused a chink of window & indeed had to have heavy linoleum curtains drawn over it & DID, all night, into a pot between our beds never emptied or covered! Oh Raymond! Then all the things they did to me, wheeling me on a stretcher to a torture chamber dans le sous-sol, hurt fearfully. Colonel came unexpectedly & found them wheeling me back & was so appalled that he told Diana she must get me out. As she had always been quite against me going in & it was he who forced me to, this seemed rather unfair!

Anyway they seem now to think they can do something for me & meanwhile I have collapsed as regards pain killers in spite of my brave words above.

As I lay there I held over my head whenever I could Mauriac's *Vie Intérieure*. *Never* again will a group of intellectuals have so much fun as he, Jammes, du Bos, Maritain, Bernanos & the others had over Gide, Mme Gide & God. Say what you like, God is really more interesting than human beings are, & Mauriac more interesting than Robbe-Grillet.[1]

My garden is paradise. Having been mocked about long grass & weeds I am now praised by professional gardeners for the prettiness. Then Hassan has repainted practically the whole house while I was away – he *is* a good boy, the best thing that has happened for ages. How lucky I am how I long for you to come & see for yourself.

V. much love
     Nancy

* and I don't mean Odette Pol-Roger!

[1] Alain Robbe-Grillet (1922–). *Nouveau roman* author who tried to demonstrate the perception of persons, objects and situations freed from any psychological interpretation. He put his theories into practice in a novel, *La jalousie* (1957), and on the screen with *l'Année dernière à Marienbad* (1961).

To Raymond Mortimer   4 rue d'Artois
25 April 1970   Versailles

Yes, but then what are my pains a warning of, which have no cause? Now that the doctors have completely failed to find one I am inundated with offers of quacks. I think, you know, that if I had taken pain killers all this time my general health would have been destroyed by now – but I'm beginning to fall back on them on the worst days.

Do listen to my maunderings on BBC, Bank Holiday 25 May, at 10.30 a.m.

How can you say we know literally nothing of somebody among whose works we live? And certainly he is & always has been an interesting TOPIC – you can't deny that, Raymond. Do you know Fulco's story – St Peter to the assembled throng: 'You are about to see God & there are one or two things I want to tell you – in the first place she's black.'

Oh the jazzy Mass I saw on the télé! The Catholics here say the true religion will come back to us from the East.

I think your friends whose sufferings were attenuated by those of others in a ward must be very hard hearted. I minded passionately the screams of the poor Romanian lady, & felt better, though *much* more uncomfortable, with my next neighbour the apparently hale & hearty vigneronne. But Mme Suchard my great friend here, the chemist's wife (whose goodness to me has never failed & nor has that of M. Suchard) tells me that the doctors are more & more against public wards & that the new hospitals are all being built on the principle of private rooms however small.

You ought to have been a *god*father. It's so nice to have famous ones. My uncle Tommy [Mitford] had Thos: Carlyle. I think Cyril[1] is quite lucky, he will see the little treasure at the charming early stages & be comfortably below ground by the time he is a long haired sewer.

Mary Rennell[2] came – she was in a train the other day which the sewers completely tore to pieces – she is a calm soul but she was *shaken*. My old French gov: said to me I have always loved young people so much but now they frighten me (she lives in London). I think here, since the riots, the police really have got the upper hand.

Perhaps, like religion, law & order will come back from the East. They have no trouble with students in the GDR!!!

My garden, in the most jejune possible way, musical comedy 1918, is simply a dream of beauty.

Much love
    N

. . .

[1] Cyril Connolly had had a son, Matthew.
[2] Nancy's sister-in-law.

TO HAROLD ACTON   4 rue d'Artois
28 April 1970   Versailles

Dearest Harold

I have just spent two delightful days in your company. With Osbert [Sitwell]'s, I rate your mémoires[1] the highest among our contemporaries because they combine entertainment value with truth & because your own personality, which we all think unique, comes out so strongly. I can't tell you how good I think them. Emerald at last has justice. Tell him to say something memorable – I can hear her. You've got the funniest of all stories about Brian H[oward], which I'd never heard – Gillian Sutro – I'm thinking at random – Evelyn – our French friends – all so perfect that whenever I want to remember them I shall read about them again in your book.

I spit upon the reviews that I saw, except that of Nigel Dennis. As I said to Diana, one of them complained of too many names in the index but these names are Caravaggio, Vitruvius, Mme Geoffrin & so on whom the clever young critic seems to take for American hostesses – good luck to him! I must disagree with you about two of your heroines but I suspect that they are woman haters who don't show their best side to me & I suspect that you *may* be right as you always are except, in my view, as regards them.

I shall have first hand news of you from Gaston who is flying like Armand to the bedside of Violetta in a few days.

How I loved your account of Diana's visit[2] – the Colonel dies for his cheque for £100 & a few jewels. £100 is such a funny sum & I can't think of anything you can buy for it nowadays. My grandfather Bowles founded *Vanity Fair* with a capital of £100 which I suppose is = to £10 000 now.

My health is not very good. I had a fortnight in the Hôpital

Rothschild – no private rooms & my mates had not been trained by the English nanny. It was in order to undergo tests which alas produced no results at all & the doctors are yours sincerely puzzled.

I think & hope that *Frederick* may amuse you – he is being printed now & will lie on your coffee table & I hope on your lectern in October.

Much love & thanks for an enormous treat.
        Nancy

I disagree too about [Roger] Hinks but of course he was very strong meat.

[1] Harold Acton's second volume of autobiography, *More Memoirs of an Aesthete*, had just been published.
[2] Lady Diana Cooper had been to see Violet Trefusis in Florence. Believing herself to be dying, Violet gave Diana a cheque for £100 and asked her to choose an eventual bequest from amongst her jewels.

TO SIR HUGH JACKSON   4 rue d'Artois
30 April 1970   Versailles

Dear Sir Hugh

Thank you for another fascinating Waterloo letter. I can't remember Eliz L[ongford]'s nom de jeune fille [maiden name]: she was that rare bird when I was young, an undergraduate at Oxford (now one would say student I suppose). She was as beautiful & merry as she was brilliant – everybody courted her & lucky Frank Pakenham got her. (I was frantically jealous of her.) They had 8 children, now mostly grown up, & became Roman Catholics. We never meet but the friendship endures – I love Pakenhams anyway. Frank is a goose but a great dear. He worries about the dull lives of those people who tortured little girls to death on moors – I can't say I do but it shows a Christian nature.

Thank you for the stamps. The glue is so poor that I had to buy a tube to stick them on – I won't charge you for it. They ought to give back all one's stamps. Letters from a sister of mine who lives in a small Swiss village arrive in a day – from London anything up to nine days. . . .

I've asked for two lots of page proofs – I'm so anxious for your verdict. I only pray the printers will have attended to the work I did on the galleys. Isn't the misprinting horrible nowadays? The papers often read like a joke – nobody cares a bit. You never see a misprint in old books & we know Balzac wrote his novels on the proofs. Now they charge you pounds for the tiniest alteration *and* telephone from London begging you to think again on account of their wretched time-table! Oh how I hope I shall go to a different kind of world next time – I would like to be a pretty young General & gallop over Europe with Frederick the Great & never have another ache or pain. All very well, Frederick himself was never without one & Maréchal de Belle-Isle had to give up soldiering because of his sciatica. One can't escape I suppose in any century.

Yrs ever
    Nancy Mitford

TO RAYMOND MORTIMER   4 rue d'Artois
31 May 1970   Versailles

Darling Raymond
   Venice from 10 July about –? Come on. You'd like my company – I AM an old fashioned Liberal & I strongly feel that if blacks want to play cricket (strikes me as odd but let that pass) they ought to be allowed to. But if people must demonstrate I suppose it's cheaper, & nicer for the police, to stop the 'ole thing. Since living – well not actually *living*, co-existing – with Hassan, now known as the Beamish Boy, my view of le tiers monde [the Third World] is greatly modified. He is a dear soul but the thought of giving him a vote makes me shriek. My considered opinion is that the world has been wretched ever since the abolition of slavery. A bas [down with] Wilberforce. Beamish *is* a slave (he knelt to his former owner to thank for being given to me) & look how happy we both are. *Look* I mean come & look. . . .
   Keep in touch

   Fondest love
    N

I keenly listen to the election speeches though – like Hassan – I am voteless. Heath[1] is considerably more horrible than Wilson in my view.

----

[1] Edward Heath (1916–). Conservative Prime Minister 1970–74. Knighted 1992.

To Raymond Mortimer   4 rue d'Artois
10 October 1970   Versailles

Darling Raymond

English doctors have killed ¾ of my friends & the joke is the remaining ¼ go on recommending them, so odd is human nature. We have seen the same thing with Louis XIV & Fagon.[1] You may say I long for death well yes, but I long even more to be cured. Dr Selmes hasn't killed anybody known to me & has cured 3 so I don't mind trying him. If he doesn't do, Grace Dudley will take me to Munich – then Monica Stirling will take me to Lausanne. My good doctor here says il faut frapper à toutes les portes.[2] I shall get to know Europe. I haven't been to England for three years & had hoped never to go again.

I will telephone if I can, but Josephine [Loewenstein] is putting me in the little boy's room where there is surely no telephone. The Dr will only know when he sees me – but I understand he may do something & send me home for a month, or put me in a nursing home at Guildford, where he lives, or keep me in London for treatment for a week or two. I'm so *lucky* to have those angelic Loewensteins to go to they are prepared for anything they say.

The pain is worse than any I have had which is saying a good deal & I wonder how I can endure the journey but I'll have Debo thank goodness.

I've always felt the great importance of getting into the right set at once on arrival in Heaven. I used to think the Holland House lot would suit me – now I'm not sure. One would get some good belly laughs no doubt, but Sans Souci might provide more nourishment. The Paris salons are all under the thumb of tiresome, jealous ladies – I can't see myself in the rôle of the Dsse de Choiseul quite. The thing is, one must be careful in a new place not to get into uncongenial company. Let's make for the same objective – what do you think? I wonder what Louise[3] is doing about it.

Your journey sounds heavenly I would love to do it one day. I know so little of France exc: Paris & that awful old *coat* as the English call it. (The *coat* & the *eel* always make me shriek.)

There I've bored you for long enough.

Much love et j'espère à bientôt.

    N

---

[1] Guy Crescent Fagon (1638–1718). Louis XIV's doctor, whom Nancy described as a 'killer of Princes' in *Madame de Pompadour*.

[2] One should knock on every door.
[3] Louise de Vilmorin had died in December of the previous year.

To Theodore Besterman   11 Holland Villas Road
19 October 1970   London W14

My dear Theodore

How awful they are, only just to have sent you *Frederick* I'm so furious. Thank you very much for your kind & praising letter – I feared you would think I had been too much on F's side in the great quarrel. You know my love for Voltaire is not as unquestioning as yours, though very real, & I can't help thinking that he used Frederick too much & loved him not enough. It was really that the physical contact didn't do.

About teasing.[1] I am a tease & I know all about it. There's always surely an element of cruelty – for instance teasing an animal is cruel. Haven't got the dictionary here. Frederick teased often unkindly & sometimes cruelly but he didn't hang draw & quarter, or rack, or break on the wheel like others of his day. I'd much rather be teased!

I'm here to see a doctor – I've got a broken back & am in pretty good rack-like torments. If he cures me I will ring up & see if we could meet but at present I can't make plans.

Yrs ever
    Nancy

[1] Theodore Besterman to NM: 'No word occurs more often in your book than "teasing" (I should say about a hundred times) but what you call teasing I call cruelty (and so I'm sure do you in your heart). Frederick was in fact so cruel and so dishonest intellectually that these things outweigh everything else.' (11 October 1970)

To Gaston Palewski   11 Holland Villas Road, W14
23 October 1970

Dearest Col

I am having a very horrid time, no doubt. The treatment has plunged me into an extremity of pain which nothing can relieve. If in the end it cures me all will be forgotten, one can but hope so.

My host & specially my hostess are completely angelic – I don't know if I could have endured it all alone but I lie in bed with my door open & everybody comes in & out & it is all so cheerful & all are so young I am kept going. Also he has got a perfect library so there's masses to read. *Talleyrand* gets better as it goes on but it is surprisingly dry I think.

I rang up Ava [Waverley] & with her usual surenchère [one-upmanship] discovered that she has got what I have but MUCH WORSE. So like her. I was supposed to dine with Cecil [Beaton] last night but I literally could not move, oh dear I'm afraid he must be angry with me. I didn't put him off sooner because I thought it would amuse me so much to go. It was a dinner of 8 being televised for his Life on Television so of course all London was dying to be asked. I'm bound to say I didn't know all this until later.

Ma chère Colonel –

I bought, in waves of pain, a long black (sham) sealskin coat like Proust's, it is very funny but also very pretty.

I return, come what may, on the 3rd. If I'm not cured by then it means he can't cure me.

Ma chère etc.
I am etc.
　　Connaught Hotel

Very low

To Jessica Treuhaft   4 rue d'Artois
13 November 1970   Versailles

Darling Soo

How kind you are to bother about me & even to PHONE I did think it so angelic. This cure hasn't worked so far & I am in the usual horrid state, very bad at this moment.

I might have enjoyed London but was most of the time in raging pain; I doped myself up for a party the Loewensteins gave to put me in the picture. They had, as well as the fancy dress contingent, the Governor of Pentonville, a handsome humorous man called Miller[1] – he said, looking at the gilded youth, I don't suppose this is the last time I shall see some of them. He had got a lot of Maoists from some riot, the day before. He said to them: This is chairman Miller's little black book & I'd be obliged if you would learn the rules. They laughed. He says the place is not too bad but badly organized – he's just arrived there, to put it in order.

Hassan was too perfect in my absence – painted my bedroom & the staircase & all is dazzlingly clean. He is a good boy, I'm too lucky to have him – imagine coming back to Mlle & her complaints or some slut. I see people in London really miserable with bad mad or incompetent servants. The high spot there was a sight of Stoker's baby William.[2] He knocks all the babies I know off their perches – a powerful personality aged 9 months. Stoker & Al [Mosley] who now work together were most kind & attentive to old ill Aunt. I think young people, who have got such a bad name, are simply angelic at least all the ones I see both here & in London. They look a bit odd I admit. Stoker reminds me so much of Tom – he moves in exactly the same way. But William is only like himself, I couldn't see a glimmer of anybody.

Much love Susan I'll keep you informed of my health but seem to be heading for the Home of Incurables as fast as I can.

N

[1] Alastair Miller; Governor of Pentonville 1970–72.
[2] Nancy's great-nephew, the Earl of Burlington, was born on 6 June 1969.

To Viscountess Mersey   4 rue d'Artois
15 November 1970   Versailles

Darling Wife

I'm having a correspondence with Wellingstein [Wellington] which is fast turning nasty. He wrote complaining that his 'librarian' really nurse, companion, saint & martyr (incidentally quite illiterate) Francis Needham, drives him mad at meals by what Gerry calls 'thanking for the potatoes', a middle class habit deriving no doubt from the necessity of sucking up to the servants. He adds that Mr Needham, being the son of a parson, *is therefore* middle class. I think this carries Duke's Disease too far so I wrote & said *I* was brought up to thank for the potatoes & I think, like many such habits, it is old fashioned rather than middle class & certainly nothing to do with pandering to the servants because when I was little one didn't need to. A very snooty reply to the effect that it's certainly not old fashioned, 'my father, born in 1849, would not have dreamt of doing such a thing'.

I'd never given the usage a thought until now but have become rather interested in it – have you got any views?

I loved seeing you & described your get up in great detail to Honks – it was completely perfect. Clever Wifey. It has the required element of fancy dress with a certain sober restraint marking the gentlewoman.

I rose from my bed of pain last night to watch *La Famille Forsyte* on télé – was deeply disappointed. But they've already got to Fleur

– I expect the fascinating part was Irene & Soames, as in the book.

Honky is so funny about télé. She is glued much more than I am but according to Catherine[1] all passes, on her screen, in a rain storm – of course Honks finds that it tires her eyes very much. As the lowest peasant of the Danube now owns a perfect set one can't really sympathize very much!

Have you read Barrie?[2] It's a rare feast. I'm fearfully short of a book – as I read two a day & they cost £4 each this is chronic with me – I shall have to write one soon for something to do. But what about??

    Much love
        Lady

[1] Catherine Guinness, whose nickname for her great-aunt was 'Octopus Untruth' from a character in *The Kitten Pilgrims*, a Victorian children's book.
[2] Janet Dunbar, *J. M. Barrie: The Man Behind the Image* (1970).

TO JESSICA TREUHAFT   Fitzroy Nuffield Hospital[1]
7 April 1971   London W1

Soozy Woo

I couldn't write esp not on this thin paper as I've been upside down in a strait jacket. Very much better, cured by an Honest Injun after nameless useless horrors had been perpetrated by the Faculty here. I had: a lumbar puncture AGONY, a major operation AGONY, deep rays SICK & FAINT for a fortnight *pain getting steadily worse*. The whole thing will have cost £3000 then in comes the Orient & I'm off home on Fri taking a lady doctor for the voyage. Never be ill where you don't live. Yes but I was in such torments I had to try everything. Anyway it's heavenly here & the Sister is called Sue making me feel at home. A saint.

Woman has been staunch, staying here week after week to be with me. This morning she took me to have irrigation for a lump I had in the colon. Figs, the gift of Woman. Good God said the nurse here comes a *whole* fig. Your fault I said to Woo – picture the screams! She said my fault for not chewing. Anyway I feel much better.

So that's it. Hey for Hassan & the rue d'Artois!

    Fond love
        Sue

[1] Nancy had undergone an operation to relieve a fused vertebra; it weakened her and left her in as much pain as before.

To Raymond Mortimer   4 rue d'Artois
Monday   Versailles
[postmarked 24 May 1971]

Darling Raymond

My news is horrible. I'm in pain (I don't think agony is too strong) all & every day now without a let up. I'm quite crippled, can't go downstairs or leave my room though I do sit in a chair & dress. They give me something so strong 'you can perform a minor operation with it' (only the Frogs would think of such a thing!) but it has very little effect & only lasts 7 hours & I'm not allowed another. Then I take a mixture of cocaine & morphine so you may imagine what all that does to the grey matter. I see nobody but Gaston, it's too depressing for people I won't let them come. My good Moor & saintly femme de ménage are towers of strength. I feel in great despair – what have I got? Nobody can find out it seems. Of course London was the knock out, leaving me so completely weak & the Dr here thinks the greatly increased pain is due to the cobalt rays. They took hard on £3000 – the G.P. alone was £600. Now they write suggesting cortisone but Dr Dumas is wildly against so what is one to think? Half of Blaikie's[1] letter is complaining because I don't call him Stephen – I wrote & said if I called Dumas *Bernard* I think he would have me certified on the spot.

So I read & read as you may imagine. At present a life of Eliz Garrett Anderson[2] not my subject but very well done. Her two grandsons, looking exactly like her, used to go out hunting & people fell in love with them. (Not me.) Then *The First Circle*[3] in which I *lived*. Somebody sent it so I swallowed my hatred of Nobel Prize winners & embarked. Then a masterly book by a Dutchman called *Napoleon For & Against*[4] (Penguin). Then I re read Osbert's memoirs which I confidently think are a great English classic & the only memoirs of our day which deserve immortality. How dreadful it is that Sachie should have turned against Osbert in his misfortunes – if Georgia's fault she must be a Devil. When I'm at my worst it is Sherlock Holmes & Lucia. Any suggestions are welcome – I've got London Library and Harrods.

Oh Raymond what is to become of me? Colonel says Cécile de R[5] pique une dépression nerveuse.[6] I say give her a pain in her leg for a week & she'll soon snap out of that. Never has the world seemed more beautiful & agreeable to me than it does now.

The B.B.C. rang up & asked what I think of Mr Heath's French accent? I longed to say it's his *English* accent which is so fearful but thought I'd be in trouble again so pleaded illness & cried off.

My neighbours have just sent 2 fresh eggs from their hens & a Meissen egg-cup. People say the French are so mean.

There. What a wail!

Much love
   N

Chateaubriand is so hateful that I can't even enjoy the writing. I believe I would feel the same about d'Annunzio if I could read Italian. Did you see Philippe's book?[7] In its denigrating modern way very good & in parts even very very funny.

[1] Stephen Blaikie; one of Nancy's doctors at the Nuffield Hospital.
[2] J. G. Manton, *Elizabeth Garrett Anderson* (1965). A biography of the pioneer woman doctor (1836–1917).
[3] Alexander Solzhenitsyn, *The First Circle* (1968).
[4] By Pieter Geyl (1949).
[5] Cécile de Rothschild (1913–). Well-known for her flair for collecting paintings, for her Spartan elegance and for her friendship with Greta Garbo.
[6] Is having a nervous breakdown.
[7] Philippe Jullian, *D'Annunzio* (1971). It was dedicated to Nancy.

To Heywood Hill   4 rue d'Artois
2 August 1971   Versailles

My dear Heywood

Cynthia [Gladwyn] is the limit – though all is *so* kindly meant. First she ordered me to drive to the other side of Paris, an hour at least each way, to see a faith healer. As the smallest movement hurts you may imagine what this would have done to me. I wriggled out of that whereupon I get a perfectly raving letter from an R.C. priest[1] in London (medal enclosed) saying that C had begged him to do what he could for me so he said a mass & advised me to get in touch with Mme Costa on high who might do a spot of interceding. Meanwhile the Almighty, thinking no doubt that all this was going too far, decided to give me a booster & I had some appalling days. Then Cynthia begged me to take to Xian Science. I'm afraid I wrote rather sarcastically both to her & her Abbé pointing out that if prayers could do the trick I should have been cured long ago since the only saint I ever met, old Marie, never lets up with hers. The implication that the pain is a figment of my imagination maddens me as you may understand.

As for Mme Costa, she was by no means such a saint as they all make out & may be having difficulties of her own up there.

I tried Nicky Mosley's book.[2] How can people read such stuff? I love the way he sort of stands back, breathes deeply, & inserts some dirty thought, too obviously in order to be with it. One simply longs for a plot & when it becomes obvious there won't be one the book (by the way, jokeless) drops out of the hand which reaches for a tune on the wireless. Faithful Joy Law arrived with 20 books she had wormed out of various publishers so I'm all right for a bit though I plainly see I shall only be able to read a ¼ of them – viz: there are two by L. P. Hartley! . . .

What do you feel about illustrated books? Now that I am used to them I feel the need for pictures & really hate reading (as in a new life of Rudolph II) about agate vases which I can't see. Also I do love to know what people looked like. I think the ideal is my *Pomp*: in pocket sized well printed paperback?

Much love
N

---

[1] Fr Jean Charles-Roux. His letter could not have been calculated to annoy Nancy more; he enclosed a scapular of the type Marie-Antoinette wore at her trial and wrote, 'What a great and not only charming woman she was! Yet still so misjudged!'
[2] Nicholas Mosley, *Natalie Natalia* (1971).

To Jessica Treuhaft   4 rue d'Artois
24 September 1971   Versailles

Darling Sue

Yes quite true about B. Cerf[1] & *L in a CC*. Marvellous title, to which I owe much. Same applies to *P of Love* (Evelyn Waugh). After that I thought of them on my own. *Voltaire in Love* is poor but it's v. difficult.[2] When I was in the bookshop I learnt that a book must be called what it is & not something like the Divine Emissary which lasts as long as people can remember the reviews. That's why *Amer: Way of D* is so splendid.

I go on being better & putting on weight. I was down to 39 kilos which I think, not sure, is about 6 stone[3] & I'm now 45. This time last year, on A. Maria's scales, I was 49 & even so could hardly bear to undress on the beach I looked so sinister.

I've learnt a lot about human nature during these horrible years, mostly good. One thing, both in France & in England, people to do with illness – ambulance, servants in clinics, X ray photographers, you know, all the hangers on, are very very kind. So they ought to be but one wasn't sure they would be.

Then, very natural, this, one's friends come & say *'anything, anything on earth* I can do & I will.' You say some quite small thing – you know me, I hate being a bother, & it happens to be the only thing on earth which, for a lengthily explained reason, they can't do. It simply never fails & nowadays I always say 'nothing whatever you are too kind' upon which a look of great relief crosses their faces. Now, everybody thinks *they* have cured me with faith & so on. One sends water from Lourdes (by post!!) another a little tin medal. Tom Driberg had a mass said for me, v. exp:, & was worried lest God shouldn't twig who it was for as I was called Pansy Dodd. Great relief that G turned out to be so clever. I tell everybody 'It's YOU who have cured me *you* YOU YOU'. In fact it is two little green pills far away without a city wall.

> Much love dear Soo
>   Suzy

[1] Bennett Cerf (1898–1971). Founder President of Random House 1927–65; US publisher of *Love in a Cold Climate*, he had suggested the book's title.
[2] Nancy had forgotten that this, too, was Evelyn Waugh's suggestion.
[3] Approximately 85 lbs.

To Tom Driberg   4 rue d'Artois
26 September 1971   Versailles

Dearest Tom

I am so truly grateful to you, & if the *mieux* doesn't quite coincide in its dates I feel that a sort of collective will must have helped. The actual day when I knew I was better was the day after you came here – I'd taken the pill for two days before, without much result. The improvement goes on & slowly my weight goes up. You can't ever know what I have suffered & for so long, I wouldn't wish such pain on anybody, even on the late lamented Adolf. Do go on praying – I will let you know what happens. If I fell back into my old state it would be too cruel.

It's very sad for me, I used to believe so unshakeably in God but I can't any more – or at least as, manifestly there must be some force, I feel, like Frederick the Great, that He takes no notice of individuals. My old retired servant Marie is a saint, a true Christian, poor, meek, generous, forgiving, clever & funny – she lived in Church on my behalf with no result whatever. So much for prayer I felt.

I'm not *cured* now. I wake up with or am woken up by the pain which rages until the pill has taken over in about an hour. The relief is total. So do peg on. I don't want to live on drugs, I need my wits & they certainly stupefy one.

With love & gratitude
(known to God as)
    Pansy Dodd

To Jessica Treuhaft   4 rue d'Artois
[October 1971]   Versailles

Darling Soo

Thanks for your letter you needn't answer this but you might like to know that I go on having prac: no pain & it still feels heavenly because I have enough to remind me what it was like. The only drawback is great giddiness – I am talking to an old ambassador (here, I can't go out) when hey presto there I am on all fours as if about to kiss his toe. I'm, naturally, weak, I weigh now less than 6½ stone (the putting on stopped but I've not lost it again) & I'm giddy, so shopping which I so long for is out of the question. I can't begin my memoirs but I think about them. I've got the advantage over you of the drelders[1] being dead.

I shall say about Muv: I had the greatest possible respect for her; I liked her company; but I never loved her, for the evident reason that she never loved me. I was never hugged & kissed by her as a small child – indeed I saw very little of her . . . I don't believe this really applies to you & Debo? Certainly Debo loved her & Diana did in old age but not when we first grew up. She was very cold & sarky with me. I don't reproach her for it, people have a perfect right to dislike their children but it is a fact I think I must mention. If you write memoirs at all they must throw some light on the personality of the writer, if, as in my case, nothing ever happens. They only begin when I am 40 & came here but of course there will be flash backs.

Did you read Mary Mc's book?[2] (Susan do write one like that about the Americans! I said to Honks oh why doesn't she? & Honks said because she is a Crusader.) Did you scream at it? It had awful reviews here & I believe in America too – the reviewers are honestly too dim nowadays. Then she got on the wireless to explain a bit & the interviewer had never read the book so they never spoke of it at all. I daresay the public will be faithful, but it wants a bit of a lead, at first.

We shall know in three weeks whether the TV will do the Mitford saga & then I'll put them in touch with you if they do it. The trouble is me having sold *P of L* to films for a pittance 100 years ago. The owner is making trouble. Unfortunately *P of L* is the key book.

Lovely autumn weather, a great help to me. I'm out of doors all day.

> Much love Soosie
>   N

¹ 'Dread elders'. When Jessica wrote *Hons and Rebels* her mother was still alive.
² Mary McCarthy, *Birds of America* (1971).

To HAROLD ACTON   4 rue d'Artois
16 October 1971   Versailles

Dearest Harold

Violet rang up & said could she come & see me. I said no Violet – let us be pen pals. When can I come down? Never. Upon that there was a long witches' incantation of which I didn't hear one word (witches' language probably) & she rang off. As a student of human nature don't you find it strange to hate somebody as violently as, de tout évidence, she hates me & to want to see them? My one idea is to keep the few people I really dislike at bay.

My pain is very much better but that is owing to much stronger drugs than any French dr would allow. The result is I am pretty dotty, I remember nothing – also, after all I have been through I'm fearfully weak. Fortunately none of that matters very much – when I feel tired I go to bed. But you know all that by experience.

Cora [Caetani] comes to see me with two huge doggies who make messes all over my garden. I weigh much less than she does, didn't think it possible. I love her for the funniness. The Hugh Thomases came, they revere you – children so sweet, esp: my godson who says of Napoleon I love him – when can I see him? I've sent a record of 'The Two Grenadiers'. I too have worshipped Napoleon so I know quite a lot of such things – makes it easy to give presents to a godchild! In the 2 Grenadiers it is so lovely Napoleon being the Kaiser which always evokes those handlebar moustaches. I've never quite understood how William II came to be THE Kaiser as though rating far above Charles V & so on.

I simply loved the enclosed. The Duchess of Beaufort, nervous about her dinner partner at some B[uckingham] P[alace] banquet said to Debo it's all right, I've got Lord Longford – I hear he's so nice – interested in photography.[1]

Best love
    Nancy

[1] Lord Longford was a crusader against pornography.

TO JESSICA TREUHAFT   4 rue d'Artois
18 October 1971   Versailles

Darling Soo

Your letter is too wonderful. I don't mind picking your brains because I shall put in a foreword that our childhood has been *done* in *Hons & Rebels* which, one hopes, will give it a boost. My book will start with the journey from London–Paris (2½ days I think) 7 Sept 45 & the Paris one found. But of course Muv, Bowd & Co are still prominent & will come into it with enough flash backing to make them credible, if they ever could be!!

I think I was telling lies if I said Muv wanted to marry me off.[1] The suitors at that time would have been Nigel Birch & Roger Hesketh.[2] I think I was probably in a blind temper about something else & talked wildly. One of the reasons for my respect is that she never did urge marriage without inclination & I hardly think she knew who was rich & who was not. Both of them were. I would have liked to marry Robert Byron but he was a total pederast – his mother, not knowing it I imagine, wrote after his death he always loved you the best. This wretched pederasty falsifies all feelings & yet one is supposed to revere it!

I think I shall do a chapter on Mr Phelps[3] (how surprised he would be) & how I imagined all Americans to be like him & how *he* wouldn't have left a pretty young lady to drown[4] while consulting his lawyer & how *he* would not have seen Lt Calley[5] as a national hero. Mr Phelps was decent.

It's a bore, my health. These drugs are much stronger than any Fr doctor would allow – they make me stupid, tired & muzzy. I couldn't possibly start a book, write it down & send it in, in this condition. I tried not taking them – Mme Guimont found me gasping & rolling &

quite unable even to find the life-giving packet. In other words this wonderful painlessness is utterly due to them. But the drs are beginning to fuss. My frog doctor – a charming new one I got by accident & who lives down here – says they would only be allowed here for 6 days! He is my 24th. He is all for the drugs. I'm not, really, except that the pain now is unendurable.

The good & excellent Hassan is back again – Zara[6] comes every Sunday. Fancy, this scrappy lot of servants costs me £3000 a year. I suppose would be considered cheap in America.

> Best love dear & dearest Soo
> Soo

I shall give the MS to all sisters to read & will take out anything that might annoy.

[1] Jessica to NM: 'Another thing I remember – but perhaps you've forgotten, or perhaps I dreamed it: when you were about 29, we were going for one of those long, wet Swinbrook walks when the rain seemed like one's inner tears of bitterness because of boredom & general futility of that life. You told me how Muv had just given you a terrific dressing down for not being married, having just turned down yet another proposal for marriage, & that you would be an old maid if you pursued this hopeless route.' (13 October 1971)

[2] Roger Fleetwood Hesketh (1902–87). Talented amateur architect and Lancashire landowner. Married Lady Mary Lumley in 1952. Their son Robert married Nancy's great-niece Catherine Guinness in 1990.

[3] An American banker who rented Mill Cottage at Swinbrook before the war. Nancy used to spend many afternoons playing bridge with him and his wife.

[4] In 1969, Senator Edward Kennedy waited ten hours before reporting a car accident at Chappaquiddick Island in which his passenger, Mary Jo Kopechne, was drowned.

[5] Lt William Calley was sentenced to life imprisonment after the massacre of five hundred Vietnamese villagers at My Lai in 1968.

[6] A Portuguese girl who helped in the house.

TO DUCHESS OF DEVONSHIRE   4 rue d'Artois
29 October 1971   Versailles

Dear Miss

I see I'm on the verge of being scolded (holier than thou is beginning to raise its hackles). I repeat & can't repeat too often that all sisters will receive copies of the book & will have the right of veto. If one writes an autobiography it's not enough as so many people seem to suppose to tell how many housemaids one's father employed – one must UNMASK oneself. Roughly speaking I shall say what an unsatisfactory relationship I had with Muv, to explain my love for old ladies:

Aunt Vi [Stuart-Wortley] (Peter's), Mrs H[ammersley], Mme Costa, & others. I would like vaguely to try & find out if this relationship, shared with Decca & Honks, but not with you & Tom, was one's fault or hers. The others loved her in old age: I deeply respected her & liked her company & jokes but never loved her. Owing to your *right of veto* I shan't mind asking questions & shan't leave things out for fear of annoying, which might not annoy at all. That was Decca's great mistake in my view. I might make each of you write a review of Decca's book. Incidentally my book will begin in 1945 when I came here with flash backs at the death of Bowd Muv & Farve. I won't bore the public again with our childhood to the extent of more than a few pages. Never thought of Muv as bossy far too vague.

Thanks very very much for the spencer – tell how much. If I'm a bore remember I haven't been to a shop for 3 years. Could I also have the dressing gown you speak of, it's one of the things I asked Honky to look out for. They have divine ones here at Franck but when she goes to Paris she never gets further than the Louvre[1] so I don't ask – but I *terribly* need a dressing gown. Could you tell Harrods to send it (my acc/ in name of Mitford) to me c/o Honks in Chelsea for bringage. . . .

Now pack up your Church Army uniform & keep in close touch.

Fond love
     N

Wooms is here but for such a short time but it's *so* dull I can't urge her to stay a few days.
Do you realize that *envelopes* are soon to be very valuable you should keep a few as a dowry for Celina.[2]

[1] The Magasins du Louvre, a now defunct department store. Franck et Fils, in the rue de Passy, still exists.
[2] Lady Celina Cavendish, Deborah's granddaughter, was born on 4 October 1971.

TO JESSICA TREUHAFT   4 rue d'Artois
28 November 1971   Versailles

Darling Sooze
     Thanks so much for ye robe. I must keep it preciously as my illness makes me so cold that even in heat waves I have to wear woollen robes in bed. It is so divinely pretty I die for the day of wearing – it's exactly like a rose I've got here.
     Rather splendid the way all is blowing for you in gaols.[1] I only

hope you won't get into trouble, I have vaguely horrid ideas about interrogation: 'Did a young lady call on you last week?' 'Nobody did *ow*! Don't do that again please, yes yes a pretty young lady came.' 'To write a book about prisons?' 'Not at all, about the psychological effects of Love. *Aow* I never felt anything so horrid I shall write up about you *aow aow* stop it, now this minute, yes to write a book about prisons' (*Thinks*: after all it's going to be published it can't be a secret) '& I may say my dear you are *not* the hero of this book by a long chalk *aow* oh *do* stop it it's past a joke.' 'I'm off now to have a little chat with Mrs Treuhaft – see you later.'

The height of the vogue, clever little Miss.

How kind you are to say you will look out some letters – such a boring task. Later I'll surely be grateful. I'm not well enough to start work as yet & in any case my scheme is to write down what I remember & then pad out or fill in from letters – or correct the most violent errors (unless they are funnier than the truth oh *I hope* I shall be honest). The idea is to put what the others think of your book into mine, me as umpire. Yes disapproving is right, bossy wrong: Honky says the 10 years dividing us brought many a change for the worse. Tom & his clever friends, I & my pretty ones were dispersed, there was no longer a library where one could sit quite alone & read away from the revereds, one sat under the nose of the male revered. Perhaps you weren't allowed to have people to stay? Our friends were certainly a great help specially all the Oxford ones.

What *could* Xerox be? A sort of anti-senility?

Oh dear I think people get nicer with age – I hope I have. But perhaps they need a stiff dose of Xerox. Must stop or weighage must take place such a bore for poor old Beamish [Hassan].

Fond love
N

[1] Jessica was researching a book on the American prison system, *Kind and Usual Punishment* (1974).

To RAYMOND MORTIMER   4 rue d'Artois
19 December 1971   Versailles

Darling Raymond

Only to say Happy Xmas & 1972 & that at last the doctors have ante'd up a pain killer which kills pain so that I no longer roll about gasping with it. Of course, nothing perfect as my sailor uncle used to say & the drugs render me stupid & incapable of concentration but most people are that so who cares! I don't quite know how I'm expected to earn my living but for the moment I am kept, like many another lady, by *The Sun King* (350 000 copies CAN you tell me why?)

I trusted your word & sent for *Napoleon*[1] & was quite right to do so, I am loving it. Next I'll read James on Trollope[2] which I long for & I hope he tells, among other mysteries, why Trollope had so much usage du monde & even of the intricacies of the peerage – things like peeresses signing with an initial only: S. Redesdale. How could he have known? I suppose like Proust, by asking, I suppose he found some sort of Eddy in the bogs.

If I can overcome my disabilities I will write souvenirs, beginning in 1945 so that I need not repeat Uncle Matthew & Decca's book & my own novels. What is the best book of souvenirs you ever read? Some say Mme de Rémusat. I know you don't like Osbert's as much as I do, you complain of the style. Perhaps all style in the end gets on one's nerves – in the end I had to give up my staple diet of Trollope & H. James because of it.

I'm going to G. Gilmour for the fêtes as of course Hassan has to live up the birth of Christ like any Christian. So I shan't be alone here. What are you up to? Pauline?[3] Do send yr news.

Love
   N

[1] Vincent Cronin, *Napoleon* (1971).
[2] James Pope-Hennessy, *Anthony Trollope* (1971).
[3] Pauline Potter (1908–76). Married to Baron Philippe de Rothschild. Raymond Mortimer often spent Christmas holidays at Mouton, the Rothschilds' château near Pauillac.

TO RAYMOND MORTIMER   4 rue d'Artois
27 March 1972   Versailles

Darling Raymond

Delighted to see your writing & to know you are in my clutches again. I must complain – I'm so fearfully bad. The strong & according to French dr dangerous drug I take seems to have no effect any more & yet I don't dare leave it off. As I'm not one of those heroes (do they really exist?) who can be in agony without letting anybody see it, I've had to stop people from coming here it's too depressing. So it's books & more books. How glad I am not to be one of those kids who can't learn to read. But often I'm too bad even for that oh do be sorry for me. I think every day I *must do* something but what? It seems such a pity to skip on to the next world while basically I'm enjoying this one so much & then so difficult. Even if I knew some sure & certain method I can't help thinking how horrible for my nice servants who I think love me, sisters & so on. But I depress them all fearfully I'm afraid.

Having got that off my chest as to a father confessor, I grieve about your horrible & no doubt expensive journey. It's dreadful to see beautiful places now one has known in the past. I've never been anti semitic in my life but I am now when people tell me what Mme Golda[1] has done is doing & will do to our holy places. How could we have delivered them to the *Jews* of all people – madness! The Arch Touche-à-Tout[2] as my father used to call him did make some mild protest which THEY managed to suppress. I have become Mrs Ronnie Greville. The longer I live the more Christian I become – Christian civilization with all its faults has been by very far the best in historical times – do admit.

Now the treat of Teresa Hayter's book[3] – a better written more educated less funny *Hons & Rebels*. It seems one of the teases is to call people like us bourgeois so the book is *H of the Bourgeoisie* a swipe at Iris & William [Hayter]. Of course all she tells is horrifying but surely World Revolution, which she advocates, would be far worse? I'm reading *The Miserables*[4] – you can't compare the lot of poor people then & now – in another 150 years everything might well be all right without the horrors of World Rev:? I said to my char: this morning I'm tortured by the thought of Bangladesh, some woman in quite as much pain as I am & no bidet. She said crossly they're used to it, whether the pain or the bidetlessness I couldn't make out. I'm not going to torture you with another sheet but have you read the book about killing the Gen:?[5] It's riveting.

Much love
        N

[1] Golda Meir (1898–1978). Prime Minister of Israel 1969–74.
[2] Archbishop.
[3] *Hayter of the Bourgeoisie* (1971).
[4] Victor Hugo, *Les Misérables* (1862).
[5] Frederick Forsyth, *The Day of the Jackal* (1971).

To James Lees-Milne   4 rue d'Artois
20 April 1972   Versailles

Darling Jim

Many thanks for your kind congrats – you may imagine that I am delighted to have been given the only honour I ever coveted.[1]

The spoiling of the world is dreadful though to me it is compensated for by the prosperity & happiness of its occupants. Sad that apparently you can't have one without the other. But if you read as I do long sad Victorian novels (*Les Misérables* for instance) you do realize the enormous progress that human beings have made since those days which are not at all remote.

One hates everything new, at our age. I often wonder what refined elderly Venetians must have felt when all those coarse marble out of scale churches were suddenly dumped all over the town. You would have written to *The Times* I bet.

The doctors have at last admitted that what I've got is one of the two or three most painful things one can have – the very worst is something on your face called tic douloureux. Bags not having that as well –! I'm frantically bad at present. The English doctor who sounds so clever is coming to stay here & the idea is to try & find some sort of pain killer. I think I am very stupid about drugs – none seem strong enough. Alvee wants me to sleep with a nun, I should think that would cure one of anything, what a good idea. Luckily *on the whole* I sleep well & that saves my bacon no doubt. I wake at 6 & then it all begins – I try & dope enough to read my book till brekker but the morning is horrible.

Much love to both
N

[1] Nancy was made Chevalier of the Légion d'Honneur on 8 April.

To Viscountess Mersey   4 rue d'Artois
31 May 1972   Versailles
                                                      78000. This is new please note.

Darling Wife

I hasten to write before being submerged (not sure if I wish to be or not!) about C.B.E.[1] which it seems makes its dazzling appearance tomorrow. First *and last* it seems, because a book I've got called *Titles* – which I have faulted over the Queen on an envelope but never when it comes to the humble station to which I belong – says never on an envelope & of course never never on a card. In other words ONE knows & nobody else. Oh yes, I sit at dinner above a knight's widow, I shall simply have to find one but all the knights I know are unmarried for a certain reason. *Wanted* knight's widow – £100 offered to any who will come to dinner & sit below Mrs Rodd.

Colonel went to see the Duke's body[2] & came away very low – for one thing he loved him, & he says the Duke looks so worried. I've never seen a dead person but I know they generally look peaceful. It's such a *mercy* he died before the Duch, what would have happened to him? They seem to have had no intimate friends at all – *she* has got *nobody* Diana keeps saying. Oh dearest dear we *have* all got each other haven't we? (How one always thinks of oneself.) And I shall have the knight's widow as a stop gap, you can share her if you like but for you she won't have the primary use of showing how grand you are. But she may be a cosy soul & a bridge player I bet.

How I *love* silly English army or F.O. or school jokes. Gladwyn's book,[3] very fascinating but stiff, only politics, has got a few such jokes of a supreme silliness which I adored but *what* are the frogs & huns & wops going to make of them? Or indeed, in 50 years, English people? I love him for them.

Fondest love dearest dear do start finding the Home & don't forget an attic for the knight's widow.

N

[1] Shortly after receiving the Légion d'Honneur, Nancy was awarded the CBE.
[2] The Duke of Windsor died in Paris on 28 May 1972.
[3] *Memoirs of Lord Gladwyn* (1970).

TO ANTHONY POWELL   4 rue d'Artois
13 June 1972   Versailles

My dear Tony

At last a letter I can enjoy answering; I'd never heard of C.B.E. only O.[B.E.] & feeling rather suspicious I asked who else has got it. When I heard: you, Raymond & Rose M[acaulay] my doubts were dispelled & I eagerly accepted.

The luncheon with Cyril was like a farce I wonder if he told you. He did that thing which (& I'm sure Violet would agree) I simply hate, of *bringing food*. After all, one has ordered the luncheon for good or for bad & I think it extremely rude to provide the entrée. However

I concealed my feelings (by the way it was plovers' eggs) & we each took one. They were raw & went all over everything.[1] Then, greatly subdued, me boiling more than ever, we went down to the diner where I had provided a bottle of Château Lafite for Cyril – the other male guest being Gaston who never drinks anything but a sip of white wine. Cyril refused the wine which really threw me into a fantigue as this lovely stuff had to be consumed by me & the moon-faced wife. The truth is Cyril is not sortable & I shall never ask him here again. Evelyn was quite right about the Bog. I must add that now that wine is £10 a bottle one's French friends say beforehand if they are off the booze, Raymond says that Cyril's little dodge for making himself loved is to fill his glass & then not touch it. He never mentioned being in trade which would have fascinated me & I know nothing about that.[2]

> Best love to you both
> Nancy

[1] 'Cyril wanted to take her something special . . . so we got quails eggs at Hédiard or somewhere grand – they did not say they sold them uncooked, & as they were always sold cooked in London – hard boiled – & they were beautifully packed, we assumed, & indeed so did Nancy when we produced them, that they were cooked.' (Deirdre Levi to the editor.)
[2] Cyril Connolly was gathering famous modern first editions with a view to profitable resale.

To Cyril Connolly   4 rue d'Artois
7 July 1972   Versailles

Dearest Cyril
    Your postcard of a month ago went to rue d'Artois in Paris,* I suppose it lay in the concierge's box whence rescued by somebody who seems to know me – can't read the name!
    I was much pleased to be the Companion of you & Harold A. as well as of the ghostly Empire. I'd never heard of C.B.E. but I'm told it's a good sort & Christopher S[ykes] advised me to accept. I wish I could go with you & collect it. My odious malady has suddenly taken a turn for the worse.
    I think it's simply awful about the *Ob* & Evelyn's diary.[1] Not that I care, I quickly & not very sincerely say in advance, about the dreadful surprises ONE is sure to have, but on general grounds it ought to be properly edited. I do wonder who?
    A diary can be made into anything & is dynamite I always feel. EVELYN'S doesn't bear thinking of!

Yes it could not have been Audrey Parr who always had the most glamorous lovers, the duc d'Aoste & so on.

Gaston has got the Grande Croix of our Legion – yesterday. That IS a good sort indeed.

The doctor loomed at that point & said he was glad to see me working! People think that writing books is so easy one can do it in raging pain. I'm afraid that I can't, I have to be on top of the world & even then find it fearfully difficult. This doctor is a gentleman, very unusual here, & a kind of saint. His grandfather was the friend of Henri de Mun so you see the milieu – his father the youngest X de Guerre there has ever been – 17, Verdun.

I hope you'll come again.

Love from
    Nancy

* You did put Paris as well as Versailles – you mustn't.
P.S. I got a letter of congrats from Peter de Polnay saying he always feels that success in literature is due to luck more than to talent! I'm bound to say he has had particularly bad luck poor old soul.

[1] From 1 April to 13 May 1973, the *Observer* serialised 'The Private Diaries of Evelyn Waugh', edited by Michael Davie. The extracts chosen were inclined to be the most disobliging. Raymond Mortimer to NM: 'Evelyn's diaries have included remarks supposedly made by me that I believe to be the product of his novelist's imagination – and they make me seem even sillier as a young man than I was . . . However, he is far more unjust to himself in these diaries than to anyone else; and his old friends like John Sutro and Osbert Lancaster are horrified.' 23 April 1973. *The Diaries of Evelyn Waugh* was published in 1976.

To Jessica Treuhaft   4 rue d'Artois
3 August 1972   Versailles

Darling Soo

I remember once, long after you had abandoned us, somebody said to Farve whom would you like best to see coming round the door & he said Decca. I feel the same & in Sept I shall – oh *good*. Since I wrote I've had a horrible thing – a pain like the end of the world (contraction of a group of muscles set off by my bad nerve). Most luckily I was in my room & fell upon my bed – the dr came very soon & gave me a knock out injection but I couldn't move for 24 hours & lay in my dress. No nurse to be had here or in England but Mme Guimont was heroic & slept here. Now I can get out of bed & wash etc but the pain, the usual, is horrible & I am really low. Everybody is away incl: the dr who said in a cheerful holiday voice if you are ill ring up the pompiers [fire brigade]. Woman who always said she would come if I was in need can't because of on rushing guests from abroad. But Alvilde will – what a saintly friend. You see I'm all alone with *good* Hassan, quite all right while Mme Guimont was here, might be embarrassing if I were taken ill like that again. I hope NOT it was a nightmare.

Various jokes keep one going mainly the antics of Mr Govern[1] & what the Fr papers call the Colistier.[2] Poor colistier – I can't see what it's all about as he was cured & he looks so nice. George III was never cured but he rates as one of our best kings for his brilliant policy of decolonization, ahead of his time.

How sad Hassan won't be here when you come I would have liked you to see him. Also I fear the holiday lady can't cook at all – cleaning is her strong point. Never mind. I do hope I'll be better – if somebody could ante up a better pain killer I would be.

V. much love
   N

. . .

[1] George McGovern (1922–). Democratic presidential candidate in the US elections.
[2] 'Fellow candidate'. Thomas Eagleton (1929–) ran for Democratic Vice-President; he resigned after admitting to having had electroconvulsive treatment for depression.

To GASTON PALEWSKI   Fitzroy Nuffield Hospital, W1
27 October 1972

I worry about you & doctors.

An old grey beard like Varré (who killed Duff by letting him go on that journey) has been doing the same thing for 50 years, is quite out of touch with the new school of medicine. Oh how I wish you could come to the Westminster hospital here whose brilliant young équipe [team] is looking after me & I'm sure curing me (though I do suffer still). These boys alone diagnosed what I have got. It was I myself who chucked out those old beasts who messed me up so terribly last time & I who said I must have young ones. Surely in Paris there must be a young school or are they too busy contesting? (They are right to contest but it takes time.) I have discovered that protocol can be blown away & everybody has the right to choose their own doctor – I did it in 24 hours to the fury of the old wretches. I'm *quite quite* sure now they will cure me & you know how sceptical I had become.

How I wish you had a clever entourage – only poor Léa[1] is clever &
she can't speak.
   Do think of what I say.

   Love from
      N

This time last week I couldn't write a letter (except about the chaud-
ière – crevée bien entendu –[2])
Don't abandon me: telephone.
Above ALL don't let yourself be taken to America. My boys say the
treatment there for cancer, known as the Heroic! is brutal beyond
words & they say never cures, just prolongs an invalidish life which
you & I could never endure. Oh please please keep me informed.

[1] Palewski's dog.
[2] The boiler – broken of course.

To Dr Powell-Brett   4 rue d'Artois
2 April 1973   Versailles

My dear Dr Powell-Brett
   The great & awful may take a few days because they love to make
difficulties – for instance they may say the drugs must be on another
sheet – I hope not. In the end they give way.
   From a medical point of view I must point out that I've been twice
to London now in the hopes of being cured of a vile pain which for 4½
years has made my life unbearable. It still does. The thrombosis is
simply an added misery – THE pain is still there. It comes down
suddenly as it always has & makes me howl. The pain killers are
better than the ones I had at first, thank goodness. That is why I ask
if in your view & that of Dr Hanham I've got it for life? I've never
been so bad or at least never worse. Nothing to do with the leg which
is better. She has just given me an injection, because even Pethadine
was no good, & that has worked as you see I can write.

   Yrs ever
      Nancy Rodd

If the blood is good why is the pain so awful?

To Duchess of Devonshire   4 rue d'Artois
18 April 1973   Versailles

Dear Miss

. . . Probably Honks has told you that greatly to everybody's relief
I've decided to keep my old Gamp. She is zero as a nurse – much
worse with the bed pan than Woman is – can't give an injection without
agonies of pain & the thing coming to pieces & having to start again
& so on but on the human plane I like her. She & Hassan hit it off,
she never wants a day out & she doesn't come into my room & bore
me.

Powell-Brett came kindly bringing pain killers but no suggestions
for a cure. I suppose I'm on my way out really I wish it was over.
You will see that my servants Hassan & Gillie get enough money &
I mean enough by today's enormous standards. Violet [Trefusis] made
proper wills resulting in *total* muddle, it hardly seems worth the
fatigue. Poor Lesley Blanch,[1] in desperate need, books don't sell
much, was left enough to make her easy – from an empty account in
America & after a few weeks of blissful anticipation found she would
get nothing at all. All my cash, about £70 000, is at Paris Morgan's in
French shares exc: for about £10 000 floating about loose in my current acc/ but which may mostly have gone on nurses etc by then.
When? How I would love to know & be able to tick off on my dahry.

My legs (both now) are no better & hurt horribly – I've no strength
at all, can't sit up in bed because if I do it brings on the awful pain. I
take the line of least resistance & lie here flat on my back drinking
pain killers. Can't see what is to cure me, the good body hasn't got
a chance, but can't see what is to kill me either. In fact it's all the
Good Body's fault for playing up like this!

Your grandchildren sound like studies, but William's the boy for
me. *Born* to be P.M. or as I urge on Stoker, Archbish: of Cantuar.
I do wonder about Sto's new job[2] incidentally with gravest doubts.
Helping young writers Honkie says but who are they, where are they
& *where are the young readers*? I daresay the dear boy knows best?
He has been in the book trade for long enough. They say here nobody
looks at télé any more so that seems to be their chance. Hassan &
the aged nurse are glued to télé, I think mostly old films.

Here's my lunch in.

Love
    N

[1] Lesley Blanch (1907–). Author of *The Wilder Shores of Love* (1954) and *The Sabres*

of Paradise (1960). 'She is the most difficult person on earth, never never satisfied or
pleased with anything. At the same time she is full of charm & a very good friend.'
(NM to James Lees-Milne, 26 September 1970)
[2] Peregrine Hartington had gone into partnership with Alan Ross in London Magazine
Publications.

To Raymond Mortimer   4 rue d'Artois
28 April 1973   Versailles

Darling Raymond

Silly old Evil not worth a thought. When he, or the ignorant ill-
intentioned editor (who?) praise, they cover all with a slime of vulgarity. I expect I really did say that about Hamish who is probably not
enchanted.[1]

I am delivered to the French peasantry. My perfect femme de
ménage, *good* Hassan & an infirmière of the lowest class. I feel like
a refined Prussian officer who has been picked up on the battle field.
Men & women come in & out of my room whatever is happening I
can't stop it. So I let myself swim. The infirmière washes you like
the kitchen floor when she remembers to – if you ask her to brush
your hair you get a sharp blow with the hair brush. BUT when she
arrived she said it was inadmissible that anybody should be allowed
to suffer so much & she stood up to the doctor with gros mots & got
morphine injections for me which nobody ever has & she told Diana
she used to go to her room & cry after seeing me. (She calls me *ma
mie*.) Of course she doesn't know how to give them & the pain is
intense! It all suits me perfectly & is far better than having an
infirmière de luxe at £20 a day – the old brute is £10 a day, thought
very cheap here. I see nobody except Diana & Gaston & them rather
seldom. I read & read. Last night was murder – I had discovered that
I'd never read *Framley Parsonage* one of the very best & it carried
me on. I had got rather tired of Trollope but at his peak he is a great
help. I can't move at all which is painful in itself – absolutely no
strength.

I like those books about villages. I read Isherwood on his parents[2]
vastly preferring the normal parents to the ab or super normal son,
fascinating picture I thought of pre-1914 gentlefolk. Harold fished me
out a truly awful but readable novel called *Jane our Stranger*[3] & the
funny *Vestal Fire*.[4] It's practically a book a night when I'm wretched.
Gibbon fills the gaps.

I can't see what is either to kill or to cure me, so lie expensively here. I've made an enormous, or it seemed so, killing on the Bourse, sheer profit of about £30 000 of which I have milked off 8. But with nurses at £10 a day & living what it is, up & up, it no longer seems bottomless though helpful. What a situation to be in. I'm not exactly bored but rather sad & the pain though greatly attenuated now can still be dreadful.

So that's the news – with fondest love

Nancy

[1] *'Wednesday 18 June 1930* . . . I had tea with Nancy Mitford at the Ritz. She was worried because Hamish had told her on Sunday evening that he didn't think he would ever feel up to sleeping with a woman.' *The Diaries of Evelyn Waugh*, pp. 315–16.
[2] Christopher Isherwood, *Kathleen and Frank* (1971).
[3] Mary Borden, *Jane Our Stranger* (1923). By the American-born wife of Sir Edward Spears.
[4] Compton Mackenzie, *Vestal Fire* (1927).

To James Lees-Milne   4 rue d'Artois
24 May 1973   Versailles

Dear Jim,

It's very curious, dying, & would have many a drôle amusing & charming side were it not for the pain wh the drs try in vain to control. Debo was here for some days – the PRESENCE is so delightful. We had screams over the Will & the Dame [Alvilde]'s share 'But she'll be furious if she only gets *that*'. I've got a horrid old Gamp who gangs up with the forces of darkness or so it seems in the night when I long for Blor[1] or Marie. Hassan is a *saint* – he charges about into bed pans & so on & is far less embarrassed about all that than I am. Gamp, known as Beastly, *will* not shut the door & Colonel minds. I am hoping to get a more refined sort presently, it's not part of their training here.

Thanks so much for the books – I'm now down to the local *Tatler* called *Chronique des Altesses* – photographs of Paul Louis Weiller mostly, but I shall gladly try the Trollope. How disappointing the Life of him was.

The doctors will not give one a date, it is so inconvenient they merely say have everything you want (morphia).

Much love
Nance

. . .

[1] Her nanny.

To GASTON PALEWSKI   4 rue d'Artois
8 June 1973   Versailles

Dearest

I'm truly very ill, ça ne va pas comme vous vous apercevez par mon écriture. Je souffre comme je n'avais pas imaginé, la morphine fait très peu d'effet et fait très mal en rentrant; l'horrible infirmière que vous avez dû voir ici disait toujours dans son accent Marseillais ça pique quant ça rentre – je peux vous dire qu'elle avait raison. Je peux vous l'affirmer. J'étais livrée à cette personne que je haïssais, surtout la nuit pour deux mois; Debo est venue à mon secours (on ne trouve point d'infirmières ici paraît-il) avec une charmante personne anglaise.

Je pense et j'espère mourir, mais le docteur ne croit pas ou pas encore – s'en est trop la torture. Vous ne savez pas.[1]

I'm very weak & would love to see you now the *Beast* has gone one day but I can't move. My telephone doesn't seem to work or else you don't hear & that upsets me so I hate being telephoned to. The pain *is so bad* I can't think of organizing things & can hardly write at all & if you don't hear the telephone it makes things so difficult.

Love
    Nancy[2]

Hassan has been too wonderful.

[1] I'm truly very ill, I'm very bad as you can see from my writing. I suffer as I never imagined possible, the morphine has very little effect and hurts very much as it goes in; the horrible nurse, whom you must have seen here, always used to say in her Marseilles accent 'it pricks as it goes in' – and believe me she was right. I can assure you. For two months, particularly during the nights, I was at the mercy of this person I hated; Debo came to my rescue (apparently you can't find any nurses here) with a charming English person.

I hope and believe I am dying, but the doctor doesn't think so, anyway not yet, the torture is too great. You cannot imagine.

[2] This was Nancy's last letter; she died on 30 June. Palewski was the last person to see her alive; he visited her in the morning and although she appeared to be unconscious, she smiled as he took her hand. Perhaps she recognised the bark of his dog as it ran up the stairs.

BIOGRAPHICAL NOTES

BOWLES, Sydney (1880–1963). 'Muv'. Eldest daughter of the MP Thomas Gibson Bowles. Her mother died when she was seven and Sydney took over the running of her father's household. She described her early life in an unpublished memoir, *Five Houses*. When, in 1904, she married David Mitford it was said of them that they were 'so beautiful they were like gods walking on the earth'. A serene, equable and down-to-earth disposition enabled her to weather her children's stormy careers. Nancy caricatured her as Aunt Sadie, whose distinguishing qualities are eccentricity and an almost callous reserve, a characterisation regarded as exaggerated by her other children. Nancy and she were never close but corresponded with unfailing regularity.

HAMMERSLEY, Violet (1877–1964) née Williams-Freeman. 'Widow', 'Wid', 'Mrs Ham'. Born in Paris, where her father was a diplomat and where she spent her early years. Somerset Maugham, whose father was then the British Embassy solicitor, was a childhood friend. Married Arthur Hammersley, a rich widower twice her age, in 1902. He died in 1912, leaving her with three small children. In 1923 she lost most of her money in the failure of Cox's Bank, confirming her in her innate pessimism. One of Nancy's most successful teases was to call her 'lucky'; she considered herself deeply unlucky and always rose to the bait. Her letters to Nancy are often headed 'Horror-Child'. She was a talented pianist and the friend of many writers. Her own literary output was small: *Thackeray's Daughter* (1951), a life of Lady Ritchie, written in collaboration with Lady Ritchie's daughter, and a translation of Mme de Sévigné's letters (1956). Her health was poor and she was something of a hypochondriac. Osbert Sitwell wrote a short story about her, '. . . That Flesh is Heir To', in which he paints her as a carrier of every disease that flesh is heir to, with a bag stuffed full of germs.

MITFORD, David (1878–1958). 'Farve'. Second son of 1st Lord Redesdale. His elder brother was killed in 1915 and he inherited the title on his father's death in 1916. Until 1914 he worked in London as office manager at *The Lady*. After the war he moved to the country to look after his estate. Memorably depicted as the irascible, idiosyncratic Uncle Matthew in Nancy's novels.

MITFORD, Deborah (1920–). 'Debo', 'Miss', 'Nine', 'Henderson', 'Hen'. Sixteen years younger than Nancy. Married Lord Andrew Cavendish, younger son of 10th Duke of Devonshire, in 1941. The Duke's eldest son was killed in 1944 and Andrew inherited the title on the death of his father in 1950 when Deborah found herself chatelaine of Chatsworth, one of England's greatest country houses. She has dedicated herself to its rehabilitation and is the author of *The House* (1982), *The Estate* (1990), *Farm Animals* (1991) and *Treasures of Chatsworth* (1991).

MITFORD, Diana (1910–). 'Bodley', 'Honks', 'Nard'. By common consent, the beauty of the family. Married 1929–34 to Bryan Guinness and in 1936 to Sir Oswald Mosley, leader of the British Union of Fascists. An admirer of Hitler, she and Mosley were imprisoned 1940–43 under Regulation 18B that suspended habeas corpus. In 1951 the Mosleys settled in France. Author of an autobiography, *A Life of Contrasts* (1977), *The Duchess of Windsor* (1980) and *Loved Ones* (1985).

MITFORD, Jessica (1917–). 'Decca', 'Susan', 'Soo'. Ran away from home to join her cousin Esmond Romilly, who was fighting in the Spanish Civil War, and whom she married in 1937. They moved to America, where Jessica remained after Esmond's death in 1941. In 1943 she married Robert Treuhaft. She joined the Communist Party and has devoted herself for many years to campaigning for civil rights and left-wing causes. Publications include two volumes of autobiography, *Hons and Rebels* (1960) and *A Fine Old Conflict* (1977), *The American Way of Death* (1963) and *The American Way of Birth* (1992).

MITFORD, Pamela (1907–94). 'Pam', 'Woman'. Described by John Betjeman as 'the most truly rural' of the Mitfords. An acknowledged expert on poultry. Suffered a bad attack of polio at the age of three. Married to the distinguished physicist Professor Derek Jackson 1936–51. Her interests were very different to Nancy's, and they corresponded infrequently. During her last illness, however, Nancy longed for Pamela's 'heavenly presence' above all others.

MITFORD, Tom (1909–45). 'Tud'. Educated at Eton, then studied for the Bar. He and Deborah were the only members of the family who were always on speaking terms with all the others. His sisters tried to enlist him in their different causes, thus he was a paid-up member of Mosley's Fascist party yet remained on good terms with Jessica and her husband Esmond Romilly. His interests were intellectual and diametrically opposed to his father's: he loved music, philosophy, literature and the law. To some extent, as they grew older, his sisters transferred their feelings about ideal manhood, focused on Farve during their childhood, to Tom. Very good-looking and attractive to women, he never married and was killed in Burma on 30 March, shortly before the end of the war.

MITFORD, Unity (1914–48). 'Bobo', 'Bowd', 'Song'. Romantic, unruly and a natural rebel, she took pleasure in shocking people. In 1933 she visited Germany with Diana and attended a Nazi Party Congress at Nuremberg; captivated by what she saw, she returned to Munich in 1934 to learn German.

In 1935 she met Hitler, fell under his spell and until the outbreak of war spent most of her time in Germany. When Britain declared war she tried to commit suicide. The bullet she shot into her head failed to kill her but remained lodged in her brain. She lived as an invalid until the wound became inflamed and she died of meningitis.

OGILVIE-GRANT, Mark (1905–69). 'Old Gentleman'. Talented caricaturist and fine amateur botanist. A discreet homosexual who, before the war, was keen on his cousin Nina Seafield; her family considered him unworthy. Shared Robert Byron's admiration for Victoriana and for Dame Clara Butt, the massive contralto. Since he was always ready to burst into heartfelt renderings of his favourite Scottish ballads, Byron called him 'a waft of artificial heather'. In 1930 he was Attaché to Sir Percy Loraine, High Commissioner in Cairo. Joined the Scots Guards in 1940, was captured in Greece and spent most of the war in prison camps. Settled in Athens after the war where he worked for the oil company BP. His talents for friendship, party-giving and cooking made his house a centre for Athenian–English life.

PALEWSKI, Gaston (1901–84). 'Colonel', 'Col'. Descended from a Polish family who settled in France in the eighteenth century. Educated at the Sorbonne and Ecole des Sciences Politiques. In 1924 he joined the staff of Marshal Lyautey, and was adviser to Paul Reynaud 1928–40. In August 1940 he joined de Gaulle in London and became his principal political adviser. After a short period in East Africa where he was in charge of the Free French Forces, Palewski was appointed head of de Gaulle's *cabinet* and held that post in London, Algiers and Paris, resigning with de Gaulle in 1946. In 1947 he played an active role in founding and running the Rassemblement du Peuple Français. Elected a Deputy in 1951. When de Gaulle withdrew from politics in 1955 Palewski joined Edgar Faure's government, but resigned later that year. Ambassador to Rome 1957–62. President of the Constitutional Council 1965. Married Violette de Talleyrand-Périgord in 1969. Author of an uninspired posthumous autobiography, *Mémoires d'action* (1988).

WAUGH, Evelyn (1903–66). Novelist. Married to Hon. Evelyn Gardner 1928–9 and to Laura Herbert in 1937. Considered one of the greatest stylists of twentieth-century English literature. Nancy relied on him for advice on her books which he imparted generously although he was often severe in his reactions to her work. Became a regular and important correspondent of Nancy's after her move to Paris. Publications include: *A Handful of Dust* (1934), *Scoop* (1938), *Brideshead Revisited* (1945), *The Loved One* (1948), the 'Sword of Honour' trilogy (1952–61), *The Ordeal of Gilbert Pinfold* (1957) and an autobiography, *A Little Learning* (1964).

INDEX

Numbers in *italics* indicate letters to the correspondents concerned